ANALYTIC JURISPRUDENCE ANTHOLOGY

Edited By
ANTHONY D'AMATO
Leighton Professor of Law
Northwestern University

LexisNexis™
Matthew Bender®

ISBN#: 0820570699

Editorial Offices
744 Broad Street, Newark, NJ 07102 (973) 820-2000
201 Mission St., San Francisco, CA 94105-1831 (415) 908-3200
701 East Water Street, Charlottesville, VA 22902-7587 (434) 972-7600
www.lexis.com

(Pub.3575)

CONTENTS

Editor's Preface

This Anthology may serve as a supplementary reader for undergraduate, graduate, and law-school courses in Jurisprudence, Legal Philosophy, and Introduction to Law. Or it may serve as the textbook for a jurisprudence course. Alternatively, it may be dipped into by anyone interested in the fascinating issues of legal philosophy.

The book addresses Analytic Jurisprudence (as contrasted with Social Jurisprudence).

Analytic Jurisprudence concerns the internalities of law—what law is and how we determine what it is, whether it is consistent and by what standards we measure consistency, how law works and how we determine how it works. These and cognate questions, which go to the heart of the formal enterprise of law, are of primary significance to the practicing attorney. In one form or another they implicate and help structure every question in dispute in every single case and negotiation.

In contrast, Social Jurisprudence, which is not covered here, deals with what we might call the externalities of law—how law connects to, is informed by, or derives from, social values, policies and norms. These matters are of primary significance to legislators, law reformers, and teachers of law, although social issues often come up in litigation and negotiation.

Fifty years ago the term "Analytic Jurisprudence" stood for a narrower topic: the examination of particular verbal concepts in the law, such as right, duty, privilege, and ownership—what was called Hohfeldian analysis. Although the present book includes Hohfeldian analysis, it includes a lot more. All the readings herein serve the same purpose that Wesley N. Hohfeld ascribed to his narrower version of analytic jurisprudence: "to gain an accurate understanding of the fundamental working conceptions of all legal reasoning."

Analytic Jurisprudence is general in conception; it applies to any legal system anywhere in the world. In contrast, Social Jurisprudence derives its content from particular legal systems. I hope that in the near future a Social Jurisprudence Anthology will be published that covers current social concerns in American law, one that might serve as a companion volume to the present Analytic Jurisprudence Anthology.

Analytic and Social Jurisprudence are not wholly separate from each other. Indeed, any account of the internalities of law would have to be grounded in the context of existing externalities. However, I think efficiency in legal instruction is served by treating separately law's internal and external logics, leaving it to the student to build bridges between them. A student who takes a course in Analytic Jurisprudence should be able to "plug in" to substantive social or policy issues in other courses. In this respect, Analytic Jurisprudence is like a tool that can be used to build many different things.

* * * * * * * * * *

My motivation for assembling the present materials is a long-standing dissatisfaction with the texts on jurisprudence that are currently available in the market. There is no doubt that Jurisprudence has proved to be the most intractable subject in the law-school curriculum. Although universally regarded as one of the most important subjects in legal education, Jurisprudence these days has become a sprawling, formless, kitchen-sink, idiosyncratic, anything-counts field.

In my own Jurisprudence courses over the past thirty years I have shifted uneasily from one set of teaching materials to another, most of the time winding up with a temporary mix of reproduced articles. Gradually I began to see the outlines of the present enterprise: to approach the study of law from the major jurisprudential vantage points (positivism, natural law, formalism, realism, pragmatism, and justice), give each of these theories breathing room so that they extend to the limits of their logic, and leave to the student (and classroom dialogue) the challenge of reconciling the theories or using one to combat another. A few years ago Glen Weissenberger, series editor of the Anderson Publishing Company's anthologies, bravely encouraged me to assemble materials on analytic jurisprudence for a new anthology in the series.

By the fall of 1994 I had assembled enough of the materials in a logically progressive form that I was ready to try them in class. To discourage enrollment and thus contain the inevitable damage, I changed the title of the course from "Jurisprudence" to "Analytic Jurisprudence." The course duly started with a low enrollment, but to my surprise word-of-mouth was strong. Over the first two weeks of class the classroom overfilled and we had to bring in extra chairs that students were willing to use even though they lacked desks. The class discussions were exhilarating. I began to sense that law students these days seem to be suffering from an overdose of substantive rules and policy articulation. They apparently found "pure theory" refreshingly attractive.

* * * * * * * * *

This book contains more than enough material for an intensive 15-week semester course in Jurisprudence. However a professor may wish to supplement it with copies of other articles or cases. Sometimes a complete copy of an article that is excerpted in this Anthology is a a desirable supplement.

I have included numerous Questions and Comments throughout the book. I remember, as a high school student, dreading the "questions" that came at the end of a math chapter because it meant that I had to answer them at home and hand in my work the next morning. Since then, I've come to see that well-formed questions can serve a useful interactive purpose. A good question can reveal a way of thinking that the reader might not have considered. It can point the way to a new understanding of the text. And, unlike a math text, here the questions have no definitive answers. No one is going to check the student to see if her answers are correct, or in that quaint high school phrase, "mark her papers." Indeed, the absence of definitive answers is a hallmark of the practice of law. If you're in practice and a client asks you what the law is on a particular problem the client has, the last thing you should do is to reply with the same definitive assurance that you might have in solving a math problem. Instead, you should convey to your client your degree of confidence in what the law may be. Your degree of confidence can never be 100% because no one can predict exactly what a judge (or jury) might eventually decide if the client's situation ends up in litigation. We have to settle for uncertainty in law, and regard the life of the law as an endless unfolding of questions. Beginning law students are often dismayed when they begin to sense the uncertainty of law, but I would venture to suggest that it is this very uncertainty that makes the study of law an endlessly fascinating intellectual endeavor.

* * * * * * * * *

I've not selected readings on the basis either of the importance of the authors or as a fair sample of what's available in the field of jurisprudence. Rather, my decision for each selection in this Anthology was based solely on whether it contributes a new and challenging idea to the chapter in which it is located. Naturally I've missed items that should have been included. I hope very much that when you spot such an item, you will send me a note about it so that I can consider it for the second edition. I thank you in advance for this courtesy.

* * * * * * * * *

My initial attraction to the (economically irrational) career of teaching law was when I realized that it was a genuine field of study, that it had an "internal logic." I can locate the precise time: when I read, in my first year of law school, Lon L. Fuller's The Law in Quest of Itself. The book opened up for me a wholly new world. It introduced matters that were deeper and more intellectually stimulating than anything I had previously encountered in my college courses. I began to see that law is an artificial, invented system that tries to hook onto the real world, like mathematics. Yet, unlike mathematics, it affects people's lives directly. Is there anything that has a greater personal impact on individual lives than a court's decision awarding custody of a child to one parent and not to the other, or a verdict of guilty or innocent in a capital punishment case? Indeed, I ask, how can anyone resist studying law? ("No problem," my wife says.)

To the extent that law is an academic discipline (like mathematics, economics, anthropology), it must have its own logic. Otherwise it would just be a species of technical training. I contend that law does have an internal logic. This book is an expression of that faith. But not just one internal logic. Rather, there appear to be several competing comprehensive logics—such as positivism, natural law, realism, formalism, pragmatism, justice—as well as a number of subsidiary logical derivations within and among these comprehensive logics. (If theoretical pluralism does not appeal to you, you are free to choose one of the logics as the True Internal Logic of the law and reject the others as failed attempts at displacement.)

Analytic jurisprudence has historically been an important part of a good law-school education not only because it provides an insight into the structure of legal reasoning and argumentation but also because it stimulates the mind. It is a direct neuronal channel to that oft-quoted goal of law schools: to train students to "think like a lawyer." Of course, we should revise that quotation somewhat and make it into a tautological truth. It should read: "train students to think like a lawyer who has had the benefit of a superior law-school education that included analytic jurisprudence."

The philosopher Michael Foucault drew a useful distinction between *connaissance* and *savoir*. Anyone can have *connaissance* of the law by reading statutes and cases and attending court trials; this is surface knowledge. To attain *savoir*, or depth knowledge of a field, would require, in Foucault's words, study of "the objects with which it deals, the types of statements and expressions that it uses, the concepts that it manipulates, and the strategies it employs." Jurisprudence is one of the courses that law school offers that helps achieve this kind of savoir.

* * * * * * * * *

It might be worthwhile to contemplate why the great legal philosophers so doggedly pursued their lonely, exhausting studies into the logical intricacies of law. Were people like John Austin, Hans Kelsen, Lon Fuller, and H.L.A. Hart driven by a desire for wealth or fame? Many of them were berated for their bookishness in their lifetimes. With their obvious talent they could have achieved great wealth as practicing attorneys. (When Lon Fuller moved from the Duke Law School faculty to join the Harvard Law School faculty, he decided to study for the Massachusetts Bar. I have heard that he holds the record as the only person ever to have achieved a perfect score on that bar exam.) I suggest that what motivated the great jurisprudential theorists was a search for Beauty. As G.F. Hardy said in A Mathematician's Apology (1940):

A painter makes patterns with shapes and colours, a poet with words. The mathematician's patterns, like the painter's or the poet's, must be beautiful; the ideas, like the colours or the words, must fit together in a harmonious way. Beauty is the first test: there is no permanent place in the world for ugly mathematics. It may be very hard to define mathematical beauty, but that is just as true of beauty of any kind—we may not know quite what we mean by a beautiful poem, but that does not prevent us from recognizing one when we read it.

I would like to believe that new generations of law students will discover in the sometimes dry, precise, and formal excerpts in this Anthology a kind of beauty. I would like to believe that my students sensed this other-worldly dimension of legal thought in the Analytic Jurisprudence course, and I take comfort in hoping that their discovery of the aesthetic in such an unlikely place will serve them well as they revisit and rethink the meaning of law throughout their professional careers.

* * * * * * * * *

For their help in assembling this Anthology, I'd like to express my gratitude to my secretary Pat Welsh, to my research assistants Dawn Hyun, Matthew Horsley, Marc Sharma and Elizabeth Wiet, and to editor Sean Caldwell. I'd also like to thank Dean David Van Zandt for his suggestions on readings for the Chapter on Legal Realism.

1

Fundamental Themes

The question "What is law?" appears abstract and inconsequential. As H.L.A. Hart once pointed out, chemists don't ask "What is chemistry?" so why should lawyers ask "What is law?" Yet there is a compelling reason for lawyers to ask this question. The reason is that the way judges decide a case is informed by their own conceptions of what the law is—not just what a statute might say, or a previous case might have held, but what the law is in the sense of how they should *interpret* those statutes or cases. In this fashion, the question of the nature of law comes up in every single case. But it usually comes up in a hidden, background sort of way. Sometimes, however, it comes up explicitly. Lon L. Fuller invented a case, which he set in the year 4300, in which the nature of law had a direct and perspicuous impact upon the reasoning of the judges and the conclusions they reached. He was inspired by a real case that had come up in the nineteenth century involving sailors marooned on a raft at sea. But Professor Fuller modified the facts considerably, because he wanted to present the jurisprudential issues in their clearest and starkest form.

The fictitious Supreme Court of Newgarth records the opinions of its individual justices in *seriatim* fashion, much like high British courts. We begin with the opinion of the Chief Justice.

The Case of the Speluncean Explorers[1]

A. The Facts

In the Supreme Court of Newgarth, 4300. The defendants, having been indicted for the crime of murder, were convicted and sentenced to be hanged by the Court of General Instances of the County of Stowfield. They bring a petition of error before this Court. The facts sufficiently appear in the opinion of the Chief Justice.

---

[1] Lon L. Fuller, The Case of the Speluncean Explorers, 62 HARVARD LAW REVIEW 616 (1949). Copyright 1949 by The Harvard Law Review Association. Reprinted by permission.

TRUEPENNY, C. J. The four defendants are members of the Speluncean Society, an organization of amateurs interested in the exploration of caves. Early in May of 4299 they, in the company of Roger Whetmore, then also a member of the Society, penetrated into the interior of a limestone cavern of the type found in the Central Plateau of this Commonwealth. While they were in a position remote from the entrance to the cave, a landslide occurred. Heavy boulders fell in such a manner as to block completely the only known opening to the cave. When the men discovered their predicament they settled themselves near the obstructed entrance to wait until a rescue party should remove the detritus that prevented them from leaving their underground prison. On the failure of Whetmore and the defendants to return to their homes, the Secretary of the Society was notified by their families. It appears that the explorers had left indications at the head-quarters of the Society concerning the location of the cave they proposed to visit. A rescue party was promptly dispatched to the spot.

The task of rescue proved one of overwhelming difficulty. It was necessary to supplement the forces of the original party by repeated increments of men and machines, which had to be conveyed at great expense to the remote and isolated region in which the cave was located. A huge temporary camp of workmen, engineers, geologists, and other experts was established. The work of removing the obstruction was several times frustrated by fresh landslides. In one of these, ten of the workmen engaged in clearing the entrance were killed. The treasury of the Speluncean Society was soon exhausted in the rescue effort, and the sum of eight hundred thousand frelars, raised partly by popular subscription and partly by legislative grant, was expended before the imprisoned men were rescued. Success was finally achieved on the thirty-second day after the men entered the cave.

Since it was known that the explorers had carried with them only scant provisions, and since it was also known that there was no animal or vegetable matter within the cave on which they might subsist, anxiety was early felt that they might meet death by starvation before access to them could be obtained. On the twentieth day of their imprisonment it was learned for the first time that they had taken with them into the cave a portable wireless machine capable of both sending and receiving messages. A similar machine was promptly installed in the rescue camp and oral communication established with the unfortunate men within the mountain. They asked to be informed how long a time would be required to release them. The engineers in charge of the project answered that at least ten days would be required even if no new landslides occurred. The explorers then asked if any physicians were present, and were placed in communication with a committee of medical experts. The imprisoned men described their condition and the rations they had taken with them, and asked for a medical opinion whether they would be likely to live without food for ten days longer. The chairman of the committee of physicians told them that

there was little possibility of this. The wireless machine within the cave then remained silent for eight hours. When communication was re-established the men asked to speak again with the physicians. The chairman of the physicians' committee was placed before the apparatus, and Whetmore, speaking on behalf of himself and the defendants, asked whether they would be able to survive for ten days longer if they consumed the flesh of one of their number. The physicians' chairman reluctantly answered this question in the affirmative. Whetmore asked whether it would be advisable for them to cast lots to determine which of them should be eaten. None of the physicians present was willing to answer the question. Whetmore then asked if there were among the party a judge or other official of the government who would answer this question. None of those attached to the rescue camp was willing to assume the role of advisor in this matter. He then asked if any minister or priest would answer their question, and none was found who would do so. Thereafter no further messages were received from within the cave, and it was assumed (erroneously, it later appeared) that the electric batteries of the explorers' wireless machine had become exhausted. When the imprisoned men were finally released it was learned that on the twenty-third day after their entrance into the cave Whetmore had been killed and eaten by his companions.

From the testimony of the defendants, which was accepted by the jury, it appears that it was Whetmore who first proposed that they might find the nutriment without which survival was impossible in the flesh of one of their own number. It was also Whetmore who first proposed the use of some method of casting lots, calling the attention of the defendants to a pair of dice he happened to have with him. The defendants were at first reluctant to adopt so desperate a procedure, but after the conversations by wireless related above, they finally agreed on the plan proposed by Whetmore. After much discussion of the mathematical problems involved, agreement was finally reached on a method of determining the issue by the use of the dice.

Before the dice were cast, however, Whetmore declared that he withdrew from the arrangement, as he had decided on reflection to wait for another week before embracing an expedient so frightful and odious. The others charged him with a breach of faith and proceeded to cast the dice. When it came Whetmore's turn, the dice were cast for him by one of the defendants, and he was asked to declare any objections he might have to the fairness of the throw. He stated that he had no such objections. The throw went against him, and he was then put to death and eaten by his companions.

After the rescue of the defendants, and after they had completed a stay in a hospital where they underwent a course of treatment for malnutrition and shock, they were indicted for the murder of Roger Whetmore. At the trial, after the testimony had been concluded, the foreman of the jury (a lawyer by profession) inquired of the court whether the jury might not find a special verdict, leaving it to the court to say whether on the facts as found the defendants were guilty. After some discussion, both the Prosecutor and counsel for the defendants indicated their acceptance of this procedure, and it was adopted by the court. In a lengthy special verdict the jury found the facts as I have related them above, and found further that if on these facts the defendants were guilty of the crime charged against them, then they found the defendants guilty. On the basis of this verdict, the trial judge ruled that the defendants were guilty of murdering Roger Whetmore. The judge then sentenced them to be hanged, the law of our Commonwealth permitting him no discretion with respect to the penalty to be imposed. After the release of the jury, its members joined in a communication to the Chief Executive asking that the sentence be commuted to an imprisonment of six months. The trial judge addressed a similar communication to the Chief Executive. As yet no action with respect to these pleas has been taken, as the Chief Executive is apparently awaiting our disposition of this petition of error.

It seems to me that in dealing with this extraordinary case the jury and the trial judge followed a course that was not only fair and wise, but the only course that was open to them under the law. The language of our statute is well known: "Whoever shall willfully take the life of another shall be punished by death." N.C.S.A. (N.S.) §12-A. This statute permits of no exception applicable to this case, however our sympathies may incline us to make allowance for the tragic situation in which these men found themselves.

In a case like this the principle of executive clemency seems admirably suited to mitigate the rigors of the law, and I propose to my colleagues that we follow the example of the jury and the trial judge by joining in the communications they have addressed to the Chief Executive. There is every reason to believe that these requests for clemency will be heeded, coming as they do from those who have studied the case and had an opportunity to become thoroughly acquainted with all its circumstances. It is highly improbable that the Chief Executive would deny these requests unless he were himself to hold hearings at least as extensive as those involved in the trial below, which lasted for three months. The holding of such hearings (which would virtually amount to a retrial of the case) would scarcely be compatible with the function of the Executive as it is usually conceived. I think we may therefore assume that some form of clemency will be extended to these defendants. If this is done, then justice will be accomplished without impairing either the letter or spirit of our statutes and without offering any encouragement for the disregard of law.

QUESTIONS AND COMMENTS FOR YOUR CONSIDERATION

1. Does Chief Justice Truepenny's opinion persuade you?

2. How heavily does he rely on his expectation that the Chief Executive will pardon the defendants?

3. How much does his expectation of this pardon affect his reasoning?

4. Shouldn't a court of law decide its own cases instead of relying on the intervention of another branch of government? Is there anything that would *compel*

a court to decide its own cases? What, if anything, *ever* compels a court to do (or not do) something? The court itself?

B. Natural Law

We now turn to the opinion of Justice Foster. It has often been suspected that Professor Fuller used the name "Foster" because it was close to his own name, and he wanted to associate himself most strongly with "Foster's" views. While there may be some truth in this story, Professor Fuller in his other writings never took as uncompromising a position regarding "Natural Law" as that depicted in Justice Foster's account.

Natural Law is one of the fundamental themes in jurisprudence. For many scholars of law, from the times of Cicero and St. Thomas Aquinas to the present day, "natural law" is the ultimate reference point for all law. Strict natural lawyers might say, for example, that a statute that violates natural law *ipso facto* violates the Constitution and hence has no force and effect. Many natural lawyers go almost that far when they interpret statutes and precedents so as to conform to "natural law" even if in so doing they appear to stretch the words of those statutes and precedents almost to the breaking point.

What is "Natural Law"? St. Thomas said it is "right reason." But substituting one strange phrase for another doesn't help. Let us see what content Justice Foster gives to his idea of natural law:

FOSTER, J. I am shocked that the Chief Justice, in an effort to escape the embarrassments of this tragic case, should have adopted, and should have proposed to his colleagues, an expedient at once so sordid and so obvious. I believe something more is on trial in this case than the fate of these unfortunate explorers; that is the law of our Commonwealth. If this Court declares that under our law these men have committed a crime, then our law is itself convicted in the tribunal of common sense, no matter what happens to the individuals involved in this petition of error. For us to assert that the law we uphold and expound compels us to a conclusion we are ashamed of, and from which we can only escape by appealing to a dispensation resting within the personal whim of the Executive, seems to me to amount to an admission that the law of this Commonwealth no longer pretends to incorporate justice.

For myself, I do not believe that our law compels the monstrous conclusion that these men are murderers. I believe, on the contrary, that it declares them to be innocent of any crime. I rest this conclusion on two independent grounds, either of which is of itself sufficient to justify the acquittal of these defendants.

The first of these grounds rests on a premise that may arouse opposition until it has been examined candidly. I take the view that the enacted or positive law of this Commonwealth, including all of its statutes and precedents, is inapplicable to this case, and that the case is governed instead by what ancient writers in Europe and America called "the law of nature."

This conclusion rests on the proposition that our positive law is predicated on the possibility of men's coexistence in society. When a situation arises in which the coexistence of men becomes impossible, then a condition that underlies all of our precedents and statutes has ceased to exist. When that condition disappears, then it is my opinion that the force of our positive law disappears with it. We are not accustomed to applying the maxim *cessante ratione legis, cessat et ipsa lex* to the whole of our enacted law, but I believe that this is a case where the maxim should be so applied.

The proposition that all positive law is

based on the possibility of men's coexistence has a strange sound, not because the truth it contains is strange, but simply because it is a truth so obvious and pervasive that we seldom have occasion to give words to it. Like the air we breathe, it so pervades our environment that we forget that it exists until we are suddenly deprived of it. Whatever particular objects may be sought by the various branches of our law, it is apparent on reflection that all of them are directed toward facilitating and improving men's coexistence and regulating with fairness and equity the relations of their life in common. When the assumption that men may live together loses its truth, as it obviously did in this extraordinary situation where life only became possible by the taking of life, then the basic premises underlying our whole legal order have lost their meaning and force.

Had the tragic events of this case taken place a mile beyond the territorial limits of our Commonwealth, no one would pretend that our law was applicable to them. We recognize that jurisdiction rests on a territorial basis. The grounds of this principle are by no means obvious and are seldom examined. I take it that this principle is supported by an assumption that it is feasible to impose a single legal order upon a group of men only if they live together within the confines of a given area of the earth's surface. The premise that men shall coexist in a group underlies, then, the territorial principle, as it does all of law. Now I contend that a case may be removed morally from the force of a legal order, as well as geographically. If we look to the purposes of law and government, and to the premises underlying our positive law, these men when they made their fateful decision were as remote from our legal order as if they had been a thousand miles beyond our boundaries. Even in a physical sense, their underground prison was separated from our courts and writ-servers by a solid curtain of rock that could be removed only after the most extraordinary expenditures of time and effort.

I conclude, therefore, that at the time Roger Whetmore's life was ended by these defendants, they were, to use the quaint language of nineteenth-century writers, not in a "state of civil society" but in a "state of nature." This has the consequence that the law applicable to them is not the enacted and established law of this Commonwealth, but the law derived from those principles that were appropriate to their condition. I have no hesitancy in saying that under those principles they were guiltless of any crime.

What these men did was done in pursuance of an agreement accepted by all of them and first proposed by Whetmore himself. Since it was apparent that their extraordinary predicament made inapplicable the usual principles that regulate men's relations with one another, it was necessary for them to draw, as it were, a new charter of government appropriate to the situation in which they found themselves.

It has from antiquity been recognized that the most basic principle of law or government is to be found in the notion of contract or agreement. Ancient thinkers, especially during the period from 1600 to 1900, used to base government itself on a supposed original social compact. Skeptics pointed out that this theory contradicted the known facts of history, and that there was no scientific evidence to support the notion that any government was ever founded in the manner supposed by the theory. Moralists replied that, if the compact was a fiction from a historical point of view, the notion of compact or agreement furnished the only ethical justification on which the powers of government, which include that of taking life, could be rested. The powers of government can only be justified morally on the ground that these are powers that reasonable men would agree upon and accept if they were faced with the necessity of constructing anew some order to make their life in common possible.

Fortunately, our Commonwealth is not bothered by the perplexities that beset the ancients. We know as a matter of historical truth that our government was founded upon a contract or free accord of men. The archeological proof is conclusive that in the first period following the Great Spiral the survivors of that holocaust voluntarily came together and drew up a charter of government. Sophistical writers have raised questions as to the power of those remote contractors to bind future generations, but the fact remains that our government traces itself back in an unbroken line to that original charter.

If, therefore, our hangmen have the power to end men's lives, if our sheriffs have the power to put delinquent tenants in the street, if our police have the power to incarcerate the inebriated reveler, these powers find their moral justification in that original compact of our forefathers. If we can find no higher source for our legal order, what higher source should we expect these starving unfortunates to find for the order they adopted for themselves?

I believe that the line of argument I have just expounded permits of no rational answer. I realize that it will probably be received with a certain discomfort by many who read this opinion, who will be inclined to suspect that some hidden sophistry must underlie a demonstration that leads to so many unfamiliar conclusions. The source of this discomfort is, however, easy to identify. The usual conditions of human existence incline us to think of human life as an absolute value, not to be sacrificed under any circumstances. There is much that is fictitious about this conception even when it is applied to the ordinary relations of society. We have an illustration of this truth in the very case before us. Ten workmen were killed in the process of removing the rocks from the opening to the cave. Did not the engineers and government officials who directed the rescue effort know that the operations they were undertaking were dangerous and involved a serious risk to the lives of the workmen executing them? If it was proper that these ten lives should be sacrificed to save the lives of five imprisoned explorers, why then are we told it was wrong for these explorers to carry out an arrangement which would save four lives at the cost of one?

Every highway, every tunnel, every building we project involves a risk to human life. Taking these projects in the aggregate, we can calculate with some precision how many deaths the construction of them will require; statisticians can tell you the average cost in human lives of a thousand miles of a four-lane concrete highway. Yet we deliberately and knowingly incur and pay this cost on the assumption that the values obtained for those who survive outweigh the loss. If these things can be said of a society functioning above ground in a normal and ordinary manner, what shall we say of the supposed absolute value of a human life in the desperate situation in which these defendants and their companion Whetmore found themselves?

This concludes the exposition of the first ground of my decision. My second ground proceeds by rejecting hypothetically all the premises on which I have so far proceeded. I concede for purposes of argument that I am wrong in saying that the situation of these men removed them from the effect of our positive law, and I assume that the Consolidated Statutes have the power to penetrate five hundred feet of rock and to impose themselves upon these starving men huddled in their underground prison.

Now it is, of course, perfectly clear that these men did an act that violates the literal wording of the statute which declares that he who "shall willfully take the life of another" is a murderer. But one of the most ancient bits of legal wisdom is the saying that a man may break the letter of the law without breaking the law itself. Every proposition of positive law, whether contained in a statute or a judicial precedent, is to be interpreted reasonably, in the light of its evident purpose. This is a truth so elementary that it is hardly necessary to expatiate on it. Illustrations of its application are numberless and are to be found in every branch of the law. In *Commonwealth v. Staymore* the defendant was convicted under a statute making it a crime to leave one's car parked in certain areas for a period longer than two hours. The defendant had attempted to remove his car, but was prevented from doing so because the streets were obstructed by a political demonstration in which he took no part and which he had no reason to anticipate. His conviction was set aside by this Court, although his case fell squarely within the wording of the statute. Again, in *Fehler v. Neegas* there was before this Court for construction a statute in which the word "not" had plainly been transposed from its intended position in the final and most crucial section of the act. This transposition was contained in all the successive drafts of the act, where it was apparently overlooked by the draftsmen and sponsors of the legislation. No one was able to prove how the error came about, yet it was apparent that, taking account of the contents of the statute as a whole, an error had been made, since a literal reading of the final clause rendered it inconsistent with everything that had gone before and with the object of the enactment as stated in its preamble. This Court refused to accept a literal interpretation of the statute, and in effect rectified its language by reading the word "not" into the place where it was evidently intended to go.

The statute before us for interpretation has never been applied literally. Centuries ago it was established that a killing in self-defense is excused. There is nothing in the wording of the statute that suggests this exception. Various attempts have been made to reconcile the legal treatment of self-defense with the words of the statute, but in my opinion these are all merely ingenious sophistries. The truth is that the exception in favor of self-defense cannot be reconciled with the *words* of the statute, but only with its *purpose*.

The true reconciliation of the excuse of self-defense with the statute making it a crime to kill another is to be found in the following line of reasoning. One of the principal objects underlying any criminal legislation is that of deterring men from crime. Now it is apparent that if it were declared to be the law that killing in self-defense is murder such a rule could not operate in a deterrent manner. A man whose life is threatened will repel his aggressor, whatever the law may say. Looking therefore to the broad purposes of criminal legislation, we may safely declare that this statute was not intended to apply to cases of self-defense.

When the rationale of the excuse of self-defense is thus explained, it becomes apparent that precisely the same reasoning is applicable to the case at bar. If in the future any group of men ever find themselves in the tragic predicament of these defendants, we may be sure that their decision whether to live or die will not be controlled by the contents of our criminal code. Accordingly, if we read this statute intelligently it is ap-

parent that it does not apply to this case. The withdrawal of this situation from the effect of the statute is justified by precisely the same considerations that were applied by our predecessors in office centuries ago to the case of self-defense.

There are those who raise the cry of judicial usurpation whenever a court, after analyzing the purpose of a statute, gives to its words a meaning that is not at once apparent to the casual reader who has not studied the statute closely or examined the objectives it seeks to attain. Let me say emphatically that I accept without reservation the proposition that this Court is bound by the statutes of our Commonwealth and that it exercises its powers in subservience to the duly expressed will of the Chamber of Representatives. The line of reasoning I have applied above raises no question of fidelity to enacted law, though it may possibly raise a question of the distinction between intelligent and unintelligent fidelity. No superior wants a servant who lacks the capacity to read between the lines. The stupidest housemaid knows that when she is told "to peel the soup and skim the potatoes" her mistress does not mean what she says. She also knows that when her master tells her to "drop everything and come running" he has overlooked the possibility that she is at the moment in the act of rescuing the baby from the rain barrel. Surely we have a right to expect the same modicum of intelligence from the judiciary. The correction of obvious legislative errors or oversights is not to supplant the legislative will, but to make that will effective.

I therefore conclude that on any aspect under which this case may be viewed these defendants are innocent of the crime of murdering Roger Whetmore, and that the conviction should be set aside.

QUESTIONS AND COMMENTS FOR YOUR CONSIDERATION

1. How important is Justice Foster's assumption of a "state of nature"? Does Natural Law apply in a state of nature?

2. Would Natural Law prohibit murder, for example, even if there were no murder statute on the books—even if a case of murder is a case of first impression in that particular jurisdiction?

3. The second half of Justice Foster's opinion applies natural-law reasoning to the statutes of the Commonwealth of Newgarth. Hence, he is using natural law as an interpretive tool. One of his examples has been cited frequently ever since

Professor Fuller published this case. It is the example of a statute mistakenly containing the word "not." If the statute had to be applied literally, then it would defeat its own purpose! Back in 1949, when Professor Fuller published this case, personal computers and word processors did not exist. Nowadays, most people are well acquainted with the literalness of computers. If you command the computer NOT to do something, it won't do it, period. So imagine if our society were run by computers (something which some sci-fi writers have postulated from time to time). An error gets into the computer program, and suddenly—chaos! A power station blows up; traffic goes the wrong way; all the lights start blinking; missiles get fired at other countries; a bank sends you a check for a billion dollars. Is this a reason why law should be applied by judges and not by computers?

4. Should judges take error into account in interpreting statutes? If they do, isn't it just a short move to a system where judges constantly find "errors" in statutes and begin rewriting them according to the judge's own ideas of what the statutes really should contain? In other words, assuming Justice Foster is right that the statute that erroneously contained the word "not" should not be interpreted and applied literally, what then? How do we *know* that any word in a statute is a *mistake*? How can we be sure that the legislature did not *intend* that word to be there? Isn't a statute a command based on its words—and not the words that some unelected judge might insert into the statute? Justice Foster said that his approach often gives rise to the "cry of judicial usurpation." Do you agree with that criticism?

C. Legal Indeterminacy

Many writers argue that law is necessarily indeterminate—that a given decision in a given case does not necessarily "follow" from legal rules or precedents. We shall examine legal indeterminacy in Chapters 4, 5, and 6. Justice Tatting's *indecision* is a form of indeterminacy.

TATTING, J. In the discharge of my duties as a justice of this Court, I am usually able to dissociate the emotional and intellectual sides of my reactions, and to decide the case before me entirely on the basis of the latter. In passing on this tragic case I find that my usual resources fail me. On the emotional side I find myself torn between sympathy for these men and a feeling of abhorrence and disgust at the monstrous act they committed. I had hoped that I would be able to put these contradictory emotions to one side as irrelevant, and to decide the case on the basis of a convincing and logical demonstration of the result demanded by our law. Unfortunately, this deliverance has not been vouchsafed me.

As I analyze the opinion just rendered by my brother Foster, I find that it is shot through with contradictions and fallacies. Let us begin with his first proposition: these men were not subject to our law because they were not in a "state of civil society" but in a "state of nature." I am not clear why this is so, whether it is because of the thickness of the rock that imprisoned them, or because they were hungry, or because they had set up a "new charter of government" by which the usual rules of law were to be supplanted by a throw of the dice. Other difficulties intrude themselves. If these men passed from the jurisdiction of our law to that of "the law of nature," at what moment did this occur? Was it when the entrance to the cave was blocked, or when the threat of starvation reached a certain undefined degree of intensity, or when the agreement for the throwing of the dice was made? These uncertainties in the doctrine proposed by my brother are capable of producing real difficulties. Suppose, for example, one of these men had had his twenty-first birthday while he was imprisoned within the mountain. On what date would we have to consider that he had attained his majority—when he reached the age of twenty-one, at which time he was, by hypothesis, removed from the effects of our law, or only when he was released from the cave and became again subject to what my brother calls our "positive law"? These difficulties may seem fanciful, yet they only serve to reveal the fanciful nature of the doctrine that is capable of giving rise to them.

But it is not necessary to explore these niceties further to demonstrate the absurdity of my brother's position. Mr. Justice Foster and I are the appointed judges of a court of the Commonwealth of Newgarth, sworn and empowered to administer the laws of that Commonwealth. By what authority do we resolve ourselves into a Court of Nature? If these men were indeed under the law of nature, whence comes our authority to expound and apply that law? Certainly we are not in a state of nature.

Let us look at the contents of this code of nature that my brother proposes we adopt as our own and apply to this case. What a topsy-turvy and odious code it is! It is a code in which the law of contracts is more fundamental than the law of murder. It is a code under which a man may make a valid agreement empowering his fellows to eat his own body. Under the provisions of this code, furthermore, such an agreement once made is irrevocable, and if one of the parties attempts to withdraw, the others may take the law into their own hands and enforce the contract by violence—for though my brother passes over in convenient silence the effect of Whetmore's withdrawal, this is the necessary implication of his argument.

The principles my brother expounds contain other implications that cannot be tolerated.

He argues that when the defendants set upon Whetmore and killed him (we know not how, perhaps by pounding him with stones) they were only exercising the rights conferred upon them by their bargain. Suppose, however, that Whetmore had had concealed upon his person a revolver, and that when he saw the defendants about to slaughter him he had shot them to death in order to save his own life. My brother's reasoning applied to these facts would make Whetmore out to be a murderer, since the excuse of self-defense would have to be denied to him. If his assailants were acting rightfully in seeking to bring about his death, then of course he could no more plead the excuse that he was defending his own life than could a condemned prisoner who struck down the executioner lawfully attempting to place the noose about his neck.

All of these considerations make it impossible for me to accept the first part of my brother's argument. I can neither accept his notion that these men were under a code of nature which this Court was bound to apply to them, nor can I accept the odious and perverted rules that he would read into that code. I come now to the second part of my brother's opinion, in which he seeks to show that the defendants did not violate the provisions of N.C.S.A. (N.S.) §12-A. Here the way, instead of being clear, becomes for me misty and ambiguous, though my brother seems unaware of the difficulties that inhere in his demonstrations.

The gist of my brother's argument may be stated in the following terms: No statute, whatever its language, should be applied in a way that contradicts its purpose. One of the purposes of any criminal statute is to deter. The application of the statute making it a crime to kill another to the peculiar facts of this case would contradict this purpose, for it is impossible to believe that the contents of the criminal code could operate in a deterrent manner on men faced with the alternative of life or death. The reasoning by which this exception is read into the statute is, my brother observes, the same as that which is applied in order to provide the excuse of self-defense.

On the face of things this demonstration seems very convincing indeed. My brother's interpretation of the rationale of the excuse of self-defense is in fact supported by a decision of this court, *Commonwealth v. Parry*, a precedent I happened to encounter in my research on this case. Though *Commonwealth v. Parry* seems generally to have been overlooked in the texts and subsequent decisions, it supports unambiguously the interpretation my brother has put upon the excuse of self-defense.

Now let me outline briefly, however, the perplexities that assail me when I examine my brother's demonstration more closely. It is true that a statute should be applied in the light of its purpose, and that one of the purposes of criminal legislation is recognized to be deterrence. The difficulty is that other purposes are also ascribed to the law of crimes. It has been said that one of its objects is to provide an orderly outlet for the instinctive human demand for retribution. *Commonwealth v. Scape.* It has also been said that its object is the rehabilitation of the wrongdoer. *Commonwealth v. Makeover.* Other theories have been propounded. Assuming that we must interpret a statute in the light of its purpose, what are we to do when it has many purposes or when its purposes are disputed?

A similar difficulty is presented by the fact that although there is authority for my brother's interpretation of the excuse of self-defense, there is other authority which assigns to that excuse a different rationale. Indeed, until I happened on *Commonwealth v. Parry* I had never heard of the explanation given by my brother. The taught doctrine of our law schools, memorized by generations of law students, runs in the following terms: The statute concerning murder requires a "willful" act. The man who acts to repel an aggressive threat to his own life does not act "willfully," but in response to an impulse deeply ingrained in human nature. I suspect that there is hardly a lawyer in this Commonwealth who is not familiar with this line of reasoning, especially since the point is a great favorite of the bar examiners.

Now the familiar explanation for the excuse of self-defense just expounded obviously cannot be applied by analogy to the facts of this case. These men acted not only "willfully" but with great deliberation and after hours of discussing what they should do. Again we encounter a forked path, with one line of reasoning leading us in one direction and another in a direction that is exactly the opposite. This perplexity is in this case compounded, as it were, for we have to set off one explanation, incorporated in a virtually unknown precedent of this Court, against another explanation, which forms a part of the taught legal tradition of our law schools, but which, so far as I know, has never been adopted in any judicial decision.

I recognize the relevance of the precedents cited by my brother concerning the displaced "not" and the defendant who parked overtime. But what are we to do with one of the landmarks of our jurisprudence, which again my brother passes over in silence? This is *Commonwealth v. Valjean.* Though the case is somewhat obscurely reported, it appears that the defendant was indicted for the larceny of a loaf of bread, and offered as a defense that he was in a condition approaching starvation. The court refused to accept this defense. If hunger cannot justify the theft of wholesome and natural food, how can it justify the killing and eating of a man? Again, if we look at the thing in terms of deterrence, is it likely that a man will starve to death to avoid a jail sentence for the theft of a loaf of bread? My brother's demonstrations would compel us to overrule *Commonwealths v. Valjean*, and many other precedents that have been built on that case.

Again, I have difficulty in saying that no deterrent effect whatever could be attributed to a decision that these men were guilty of murder. The stigma of the word "murderer" is such that it is quite likely, I believe, that if these men had known that their act was deemed by the law to be murder they would have waited for a few days at least before carrying out their plan. During that time some unexpected relief might have come. I realize that this observation only reduces the distinction to a matter of degree, and does not destroy it altogether. It is certainly true that the element of deterrence would be less in this case than is normally involved in the application of the criminal law.

There is still a further difficulty in my brother Foster's proposal to read an exception into the statute to favor this case, though again a difficulty not even intimated in his opinion. What shall be the scope of this exception? Here the men cast lots and the victim was himself originally a party to the agreement. What would we have to decide if Whetmore had refused from the beginning to participate in the plan? Would a majority be permitted to overrule him? Or, suppose that no plan were adopted at all and the others simply conspired to bring about Whetmore's death, justifying their act by saying that he was in the weakest condition.

Or again, that a plan of selection was followed but one based on a different justification than the one adopted here, as if the others were atheists and insisted that Whetmore should die because he was the only one who believed in an afterlife. These illustrations could be multiplied, but enough have been suggested to reveal what a quagmire of hidden difficulties my brother's reasoning contains.

Of course I realize on reflection that I may be concerning myself with a problem that will never arise, since it is unlikely that any group of men will ever again be brought to commit the dread act that was involved here. Yet, on still further reflection, even if we are certain that no similar case will arise again, do not the illustrations I have given show the lack of any coherent and rational principle in the rule my brother proposes? Should not the soundness of a principle be tested by the conclusions it entails, without reference to the accidents of later litigational history? Still, if this is so, why is it that we of this Court so often discuss the question whether we are likely to have later occasion to apply a principle urged for the solution of the case before us? Is this a situation where a line of reasoning not originally proper has become sanctioned by precedent, so that we are permitted to apply it and may even be under an obligation to do so?

The more I examine this case and think about it, the more deeply I become involved. My mind becomes entangled in the meshes of the very nets I throw out for my own rescue. I find that almost every consideration that bears on the decision of the case is counterbalanced by an opposing consideration leading in the opposite direction. My brother Foster has not furnished to me, nor can I discover for myself, any formula capable of resolving the equivocations that beset me on all sides.

I have given this case the best thought of which I am capable. I have scarcely slept since it was argued before us. When I feel myself inclined to accept the view of my brother Foster, I am repelled by a feeling that his arguments are intellectually unsound and approach mere rationalization. On the other hand, when I incline toward upholding the conviction, I am struck by the absurdity of directing that these men be put to death when their lives have been saved at the cost of the lives of ten heroic workmen. It is to me a matter of regret that the Prosecutor saw fit to ask for an indictment for murder. If we had a provision in our statutes making it a crime to eat human flesh, that would have been a more appropriate charge. If no other charge suited to the facts of this case could be brought against the defendants, it would have been wiser, I think, not to have indicted them at all. Unfortunately, however, the men have been indicted and tried, and we have therefore been drawn into this unfortunate affair.

Since I have been wholly unable to resolve the doubts that beset me about the law of this case, I am with regret announcing a step that is, I believe, unprecedented in the history of this tribunal. I declare my withdrawal from the decision of this case.

QUESTIONS AND COMMENTS FOR YOUR CONSIDERATION

1. Does Justice Tatting represent any coherent philosophical point of view? Can his view of the case be easily summarized? Does he sound a bit like the classroom professor who pokes holes in everyone's legal arguments and then simply goes on to the next case without resolving anything? But isn't that a good way to help students see "the other side" of a case? If so, should a judge behave like a law professor—a judge who is, after all, paid to reach decisions?

2. Justice Tatting appears to be the very model of a judge who can't make up his mind! Yet we can read his opinion in a different way. We can read it as an illustration of Legal Indeterminacy. When Professor Fuller invented this case in 1949, the terms "legal indeterminacy" and "legal uncertainty" had not become focal points for jurisprudence. Today, many legal scholars have claimed that there is *inherent* uncertainty in legal directives. At the extreme, some believe that *no*

case is an "easy" case—that all cases are fundamentally indeterminate as far as the applicability of the law to their facts is concerned. They believe, in short, that any judge can decide any case either way. Is this what Justice Tatting is saying?

3. The middle position among legal scholars is one that has been called "moderate indeterminacy." Scholars who hold this position believe that some cases are "hard"—that is, they might be decided either way by a judge, while other cases are "easy"—they can only be decided one way under the applicable law. Professor Fuller not only was ahead of his time in presenting the opinion of Justice Tatting that exemplified total legal indeterminacy, but also, by the obvious sharp differences among the other judges in the case, Fuller has conveyed the message that each judge believes that his solution is the only possible one and that it is "easy." Thus, the reader is left with one of two possible choices. Either the reader can agree with the reasoning of one judge in the case, simply decide that all the other judges are *wrong*, and conclude that it is an "easy case." Or the reader can conclude that the case is truly indeterminate.

4. If the case is truly indeterminate, then what about all other cases that come up every day? Are they also indeterminate, except that their indeterminacy is well *disguised* by the judges? Or are they determinate? Or are some of them determinate? This first Chapter, of course, simply introduces this theme and other themes in the jurisprudential literature. Later chapters will deal with these themes in more detail.

5. If all—or most—cases are indeterminate, then why do we have judges who are trained in the law? After all, if law is indeterminate, it can't help judges reach the right decision. Why not just pick judges from all walks of life—whether they know anything about law or not? What's wrong with this idea? What's right with it?

D. Positivism

Now we encounter the opinion of Justice Keen. Here, at last, we find the kind of analytical purity that is often held up as the best model of legal reasoning in law school. For Justice Keen reflects the jurisprudential theory of "positivism." What exactly is positivism? According to John Austin, writing in the nineteenth century, positivism is the command of the sovereign. What "command"? What "sovereign"? Aren't we again substituting one vague phrase for another? Not quite. By "command" Austin meant *statutes*. (Positivists, as you will see, wish to trace all of law to statutes; they have some difficulty with judicial *precedents* as a source of law.) And by "sovereign" he meant the government, or governing body, that makes laws. Is there something circular in these two definitions taken together? Natural lawyers would reject the notion that law is nothing other than a legislature's *command*.

Let us now look at the product of the sharp analytical mind of the aptly named Justice Keen:

KEEN, J. I should like to begin by setting to one side two questions which are not before this Court.

The first of these is whether executive clemency should be extended to these defendants if the conviction is affirmed. Under our system of government, that is a question for the Chief Executive, not for us. I therefore disapprove of that passage in the opinion of the Chief Justice in which he in effect gives instructions to the Chief Executive as to what he should do in this case and suggests that some impropriety will attach if these instructions are not heeded. This is a confusion of governmental functions—a confusion of which the judiciary should be the last to be guilty. I wish to state that if I were the Chief Executive I would go farther in the direction of clemency than the pleas addressed to him propose. I would pardon these men altogether, since I believe that they have already suffered enough to pay for any offense they may have committed. I want it to be understood that this remark is made in my capacity as a private citizen who by the accident of his office happens to have acquired an intimate acquaintance with the facts of this case. In the discharge of my duties as judge, it is neither my function to address directions to the Chief Executive, nor to take into account what he may or may not do, in reaching my own decision, which must be controlled entirely by the law of this Commonwealth.

The second question that I wish to put to one side is that of deciding whether what these men did was "right" or "wrong," "wicked" or "good." That is also a question that is irrelevant to the discharge of my office as a judge sworn to apply, not my conceptions of morality, but the law of the land. In putting this question to one side I think I can also safely dismiss without comment the first and more poetic portion of my brother Foster's opinion. The element of fantasy contained in the arguments developed there has been sufficiently revealed in my brother Tatting's somewhat solemn attempt to take those arguments seriously.

The sole question before us for decision is whether these defendants did, within the meaning of N.C.S.A. (N.S.) §12-A, willfully take the life of Roger Whetmore. The exact language of the statute is as follows: "Whoever shall willfully take the life of another shall be punished by death." Now I should suppose that any candid observer, content to extract from these words their natural meaning, would concede at once that these defendants did "willfully take the life" of Roger Whetmore.

Whence arise all the difficulties of the case, then, and the necessity for so many pages' of discussion about what ought to be so obvious? The difficulties, in whatever tortured form they may present themselves, all trace back to a single source, and that is a failure to distinguish the legal from the moral aspects of this case. To put it bluntly, my brothers do not like the fact that the written law requires the conviction of these defendants. Neither do I, but unlike my brothers I respect the obligations of an office that requires me to put my personal predilections out of my mind when I come to interpret and apply the law of this Commonwealth.

Now, of course, my brother Foster does not admit that he is actuated by a personal dislike of the written law. Instead he develops a familiar line of argument according to which the court may disregard the express language of a statute when something not contained in the statute itself, called its "purpose," can be employed to justify the result the court considers proper. Because this is an old issue between myself and my colleague, I should like, before discussing his particular application of the argument to the facts of this case, to say something about the historical background of this issue and its implications for law and government generally.

There was a time in this Commonwealth when judges did in fact legislate very freely, and all of us know that during that period some of our statutes were rather thoroughly made over by the judiciary. That was a time when the accepted principles of political science did not designate with any certainty the rank and function of the various arms of the state. We all know the tragic issue of that uncertainty in the brief civil war that arose out of the conflict between the judiciary, on the one hand, and the executive and the legislature, on the other. There is no need to recount here the factors that contributed to that unseemly struggle for power, though they included the unrepresentative character of the Chamber, resulting from a division of the country into election districts that no longer accorded with the actual distribution of the population, and the forceful personality and wide popular following of the then Chief Justice. It is enough to observe that those days are behind us, and that in place of the uncertainty that then reigned we now have a clear-cut principle, which is the supremacy of the legislative branch of our government. From that principle flows the obligation of the judiciary to enforce faithfully the written law, and to interpret that law in accordance with its plain meaning without reference to our personal desires or our individual conceptions of justice. I am not concerned with the question whether the principle that forbids the judicial revision of statutes is right or wrong, desirable or undesirable; I observe merely that this principle has become a tacit premise underlying the whole of the legal and governmental order I am sworn to administer.

Yet though the principle of the supremacy of the legislature has been accepted in theory for centuries, such is the tenacity of professional tradition and the force of fixed habits of thought that many of the judiciary have still not accommodated themselves to the restricted role which the new order imposes on them. My brother Foster is one of that group; his way of dealing with statutes is exactly that of a judge living in the 3900s.

We are all familiar with the process by which the judicial reform of disfavored legislative enactments is accomplished. Anyone who has followed the written opinions of Mr. Justice Foster will have had an opportunity to see it at work in every branch of the law. I am personally so familiar with the process that in the event of my brother's incapacity I am sure I could write a satisfactory opinion for him without any prompting whatever, beyond being informed whether he liked the effect of the terms of the statute as applied to the case before him.

The process of judicial reform requires three steps. The first of these is to divine some single "purpose" which the statute serves. This is done although not one statute in a hundred has any such single purpose, and although the objectives of nearly every statute are differently interpreted by the different classes of its sponsors. The second step is to discover that a mythical being called "the legislator," in the pursuit of this imagined "purpose," overlooked something or left some gap or imperfection in his work. Then comes the final and most refreshing part of the task, which is, of course, to fill in the blank thus created. *Quod erat faciendum.*

My brother Foster's penchant for finding holes in statutes reminds one of the story told by an ancient author about the man who ate a pair of shoes. Asked how he liked them, he replied that the part he liked best was the holes. That is the way my brother feels about statutes; the more holes they have in them the better he likes them. In short, he doesn't like statutes.

One could not wish for a better case to illustrate the specious nature of this gap-filling process than the one before us. My brother thinks he knows exactly what was sought when men made murder a crime, and that was something he calls "deterrence." My brother Tatting has already shown how much is passed over in that interpretation. But I think the trouble goes deeper. I doubt very much whether our statute making murder a crime really has a "purpose" in any ordinary sense of the term. Primarily, such a statute reflects a deeply-felt human conviction that murder is wrong and that something should be done to the man who commits it. If we were forced to be more articulate about the matter, we would probably take refuge in the more sophisticated theories of the criminologists, which, of course, were certainly not in the minds of those who drafted our statute. We might also observe that men will do their own work more effectively and live happier lives if they are protected against the threat of violent assault. Bearing in mind that the victims of murders are often unpleasant people, we might add some suggestion that the matter of disposing of undesirables is not a function suited to private enterprise, but should be a state monopoly. All of which reminds me of the attorney who once argued before us that a statute licensing physicians was a good thing because it would lead to lower life insurance rates by lifting the level of general health. There is such a thing as overexplaining the obvious.

If we do not know the purpose of §12-A, how can we possibly say there is a "gap" in it? How can we know what its draftsmen thought about the question of killing men in order to eat them? My brother Tatting has revealed an understandable, though perhaps slightly exaggerated revulsion to cannibalism. How do we know that his remote ancestors did not feel the same revulsion to an even higher degree? Anthropologists say that the dread felt for a forbidden act may be increased by the fact that the conditions of a tribe's life create special temptations toward it, as incest is most severely condemned among those whose village relations make it most likely to occur. Certainly the period following the Great Spiral was one that had implicit in it temptations to anthropophagy. Perhaps it was for that very reason that our ancestors expressed their prohibition in so broad and unqualified a form. All of this is conjecture, of course, but it remains abundantly clear that neither I nor my brother Foster knows what the "purpose" of §12- A is.

Considerations similar to those I have just outlined are also applicable to the exception in favor of self-defense, which plays so large a role in the reasoning of my brothers Foster and Tatting. It is of course true that in *Commonwealth v. Parry* an *obiter dictum* justified this exception on the assumption that the purpose of criminal legislation is to deter. It may well also be true that generations of law students have been taught that the true explanation of the exception lies in the fact that a man who acts in self-defense does not act "willfully," and that the same students have passed their bar examinations by repeating what their professors told them. These last observations I could dismiss, of course, as irrelevant for the simple reason that professors and bar examiners have not as yet any commission to make our laws for us. But again the real trouble lies deeper. As in dealing with the statute, so in dealing with the exception, the question is not the conjectural *purpose* of the rule, but its *scope*. Now the scope of the exception in favor of self-defense as it has been applied by this Court is plain: it applies to cases of resisting an aggressive threat to the party's own life. It is therefore too clear for argument that this case does not fall within the scope of the exception, since it is plain that Whetmore made no threat against the lives of these defendants.

The essential shabbiness of my brother Foster's attempt to cloak his remaking of the written law with an air of legitimacy comes tragically to the surface in my brother Tatting's opinion. In that opinion Justice Tatting struggles manfully to combine his colleague's loose moralisms with his own sense of fidelity to the written law. The issue of this struggle could only be that which occurred, a complete default in the discharge of the judicial function. You simply cannot apply a statute as it is written and remake it to meet your own wishes at the same time.

Now I know that the line of reasoning I have developed in this opinion will not be acceptable to those who look only to the immediate effects of a decision and ignore the long-run implications of an assumption by the judiciary of a power of dispensation. A hard decision is never a popular decision. Judges have been celebrated in literature for their sly prowess in devising some quibble by which a litigant could be deprived of his rights where the public thought it was wrong for him to assert those rights. But I believe that judicial dispensation does more harm in the long run than hard decisions. Hard cases may even have a certain moral value by bringing home to the people their own responsibilities toward the law that is ultimately their creation, and by reminding them that there is no principle of personal grace that can relieve the mistakes of their representatives.

Indeed, I will go farther and say that not only are the principles I have been expounding those which are soundest for our present conditions, but that we would have inherited a better legal system from our forefathers if those principles had been observed from the beginning. For example, with respect to the excuse of self-defense, if our courts had stood steadfast on the language of the statute the result would undoubtedly have been a legislative revision of it. Such a revision would have drawn on the assistance of natural philosophers and psychologists, and the resulting regulation of the matter would have had an understandable and rational basis, instead of the hodgepodge of verbalisms and metaphysical distinctions that have emerged from the judicial and professorial treatment.

These concluding remarks are, of course, beyond any duties that I have to discharge with relation to this case, but I include them here because I feel deeply that my colleagues are insufficiently aware of the dangers implicit in the conceptions of the judicial office advocated by my brother Foster. I conclude that the conviction should be affirmed.

QUESTIONS AND COMMENTS FOR YOUR CONSIDERATION

1. Does Justice Keen's opinion hit you with the force of a clean breath of fresh air?

2. Aren't there deep hidden difficulties in Justice Keen's apparently straightforward approach? How, for example, does he explain the origin of the self-defense exception? Does he feel that its origin needs explanation? If not, why is he willing to live with self-defense as a legally justified exception?

3. Positivists, such as Justice Keen, have often been criticized as cold, impersonal, machine-like individuals. They have been accused of being people who follow orders, "like a good Nazi," without questioning those orders. If the law says something, according to this critique of positivism, a positivist judge will say "yours is not to reason why, yours is but to do or die." Does Justice Keen strike you as this sort of person? Does he have the same humanistic feelings as the other judges, but only hides them better?

4. Of course, we really don't care about Justice Keen, who is after all a wholly fictitious judge. But Keen so well embodies the spirit of positivistic jurisprudence that, in a very real sense, the personal attributes that we can infer from Keen's opinion are very much like the philosophical attributes that we can infer from positivistic theory. No legal theory is a disembodied philosophy floating in outer space. Legal theories such as natural law, positivism, and realism were invented in the first instance by real people to solve real legal problems.

5. Note the critical importance of role-playing in Justice Keen's opinion. Justice Keen plays two roles: his role as a private citizen, and his role as a judge. In the first of these roles, he would acquit the defendants; in the second, he convicts them. Are you satisfied with this self-imposed bifurcation, this self-inflicted dual personality? Does Justice Keen believe that he is in a play, playing the role of a judge—a role where the script requires him to say "guilty"? Or does he believe that the "play" happens in what we call "real life," and his *real* role is that of judge? Which of these two roles, from the point of view of the defendants, is the real one? When the defendants ascend the scaffold, would it comfort them to know that Justice Keen, in his private life role, would have acquitted them? Or would this fact not make the defendants even more angry? What, ultimately, *requires* Justice Keen to divide his conscience into two parts? What requires him to cast aside his private views? Have the other judges asked him to do this? Or does the "requirement" simply come from Justice Keen's view of the law—from positivism?

6. Note also the approach that could be called Legislative Flagellation. It might be defined as follows: "If the legislature enacts a statute that, when applied in a particular case, may lead to an absurd or unjust or immoral result, the court should indeed reach that result and in so doing punish the legislature for enacting an unwise or unjust statute! The court indeed is so intent on inflicting political pain upon the legislature for its bad statute that it ignores the fact that the real person or persons who will suffer are the defendants." Is Justice Keen a legislative flagellator?

7. Reconsider Question 6. What is so "bad" about N.C.S.A. (N.S.) §12-A? Is it only "bad" if it leads to conviction of the defendants? Does Justice Foster regard it as a "bad" statute? Is there something *ironic* about a natural law judge like Foster being more willing to "apply" the statute than a positivist like Keen who dislikes (if we believe his "private role") the statute? Or does this Question put the cart before the horse? (Does Foster like the statute *only* because his "application" of it leads to acquittal?)

E. Realism

"Realism" is another jurisprudential position. In law schools today, it is called by another name and has been somewhat transformed in the process. Today's legal realists go by the name "critical legal studies." Professor Fuller invented the ultimate realist judge, Justice Handy:

HANDY J. I have listened with amazement to the tortured ratiocinations to which this simple case has given rise. I never cease to wonder at my colleagues' ability to throw an obscuring curtain of legalisms about every issue presented to them for decision. We have heard this afternoon learned disquisitions on the distinction between positive law and the law of nature, the language of the statute and the purpose of the statute, judicial functions and executive functions, judicial legislation and legislative legislation. My only disappointment was that someone did not raise the question of the legal nature of the bargain struck in the cave—whether it was unilateral or bilateral, and whether Whetmore could not be considered as having revoked an offer prior to action taken thereunder.

What have all these things to do with the case? The problem before us is what we, as officers of the government, ought to do with these defendants. That is a question of practical wisdom, to be exercised in a context, not of abstract theory, but of human realities. When the case is approached in this light, it becomes, I think, one of the easiest to decide that has ever been argued before this Court.

Before stating my own conclusions about the merits of the case, I should like to discuss briefly some of the more fundamental issues involved—issues on which my colleagues and I have been divided ever since I have been on the bench.

I have never been able to make my brothers see that government is a human affair, and that men are ruled, not by words on paper or by abstract theories, but by other men. They are ruled well when their rulers understand the feelings and conceptions of the masses. They are ruled badly when that understanding is lacking.

Of all branches of the government, the judiciary is the most likely to lose its contact with the common man. The reasons for this are, of course, fairly obvious. Where the masses react to a situation in terms of a few salient features, we pick into little pieces every situation presented to us. Lawyers are hired by both sides to analyze and dissect. Judges and attorneys vie with one another to see who can discover the greatest number of difficulties and distinctions in a single set of facts. Each side tries to find cases, real or imagined, that will embarrass the demonstrations of the other side. To escape this embarrassment, still further distinctions are invented and imported into the situation. When a set of facts has been subjected to this kind of treatment for a sufficient time, all the life and juice have gone out of it and we have left a handful of dust.

Now I realize that wherever you have rules and abstract principles lawyers are going to be able to make distinctions. To some extent the sort of thing I have been describing is a necessary evil attaching to any formal regulation of human affairs. But I think that the area which really stands in need of such regulation is greatly overestimated. There are, of course, a few fundamental rules of the game that must be accepted if the game is to go on at all. I would include among these the rules relating to the conduct of elections, the appointment of public officials, and the term during which an office is held. Here some restraint on discretion and dispensation, some adherence to form, some scruple for what does and what does not fall within the rule, is, I concede, essential. Perhaps the area of basic principle should be expanded to include certain other rules, such as those designed to preserve the free civilmoign system. But outside of these fields I believe that all government officials, including judges, will do their jobs best if they treat forms and abstract concepts as instruments. We should take as our model, I think, the good administrator, who accommodates procedures and principles to the case at hand, selecting from among the available forms those most suited to reach the proper result.

The most obvious advantage of this method of government is that it permits us to go about our daily tasks with efficiency and common sense. My adherence to this philosophy has, however, deeper roots. I believe that it is only with the insight this philosophy gives that we can preserve the flexibility essential if we are to keep our actions in reasonable accord with the sentiments of those subject to our rule. More governments have been wrecked, and more human misery caused, by the lack of this accord between ruler and ruled than by any other factor that can be discerned in history. Once drive a sufficient wedge between the mass of people and those who direct their legal, political, and economic life, and our society is ruined. Then neither Foster's law of nature nor Keen's fidelity to written law will avail us anything.

Now when these conceptions are applied to the case before us, its decision becomes, as I have said, perfectly easy. In order to demonstrate this I shall have to introduce certain realities that my brothers in their coy decorum have seen fit to pass over in silence, although they are just as acutely aware of them as I am.

The first of these is that this case has aroused an enormous public interest, both here and abroad. Almost every newspaper and magazine has carried articles about it; columnists have shared with their readers confidential information as to the next governmental move; hundreds of letters-to-the-editor have been printed. One of the great newspaper chains made a poll of public opinion on the question, "What do you think the Supreme Court should do with the Speluncean explorers?" About ninety per cent expressed a belief that the defendants should be pardoned or let off with a kind of token punishment. It is perfectly clear, then, how the public feels about the case. We could have known this without the poll of course, on the basis of common sense, or even by observing that on this Court there are apparently four-and-a-half men, or ninety per cent, who share the common opinion.

This makes it obvious, not only what we should do, but what we must do if we are to preserve between ourselves and public opinion a reasonable and decent accord. Declaring these men innocent need not involve us in any undignified quibble or trick. No principle of statutory construction is required that is not consistent with the past practices of this Court. Certainly no layman would think that in letting these men off we had stretched the statute any more than our ancestors did when they created the excuse of self-defense. If a more detailed demonstration of the method of reconciling our decision with the statute is required, I should be content to rest on the arguments developed in the second and less visionary part of my brother Foster's opinion.

Now I know that my brothers will be horrified by my suggestion that this Court should take account of public opinion. They will tell you that public opinion is emotional and capricious, that it is based on half-truths and listens to witnesses who are not subject to cross-examination. They will tell you that the law surrounds the trial of a case like this with elaborate safeguards, designed to insure that the truth will be known and that every rational consideration bearing on the issues of the case has been taken into account. They will warn you that all of these safeguards go for naught if a mass opinion formed outside this framework is allowed to have any influence on our decision.

But let us look candidly at some of the realities of the administration of our criminal law. When a man is accused of crime, there are, speaking generally, four ways in which he may escape punishment. One of these is a determination by a judge that under the applicable law he has committed no crime. This is, of course, a determination that takes place in a rather formal and abstract atmosphere. But look at the other three ways in which he may escape punishment. These are: (1) a decision by the Prosecutor not to ask for an indictment; (2) an acquittal by the jury; (3) a pardon or commutation of sentence by the executive. Can anyone pretend that these decisions are held within a rigid and formal framework of rules that prevents factual error, excludes emotional and personal factors, and guarantees that all the forms of the law will be observed?

In the case of the jury we do, to be sure, attempt to cabin their deliberations within the area of the legally relevant, but there is no need to deceive ourselves into believing that this attempt is really successful. In the normal course of events the case now before us would have gone on all of its issues directly to the jury. Had this occurred we can be confident that there would have been an acquittal or at least a division that would have prevented a conviction. If the jury had been instructed that the men's hunger and their agreement were no defense to the charge of murder, their verdict would in all likelihood have ignored this instruction and would have involved a good deal more twisting of the letter of the law than any that is likely to tempt us. Of course the only reason that didn't occur in this case was the fortuitous circumstance that the foreman of the jury happened to be a lawyer. His learning enabled him to devise a form of words that would allow the jury to dodge its usual responsibilities.

My brother Tatting expresses annoyance that the Prosecutor did not, in effect, decide the case for him by not asking for an indictment. Strict as he is himself in complying with the demands of legal theory, he is quite content to have the fate of these men decided out of court by the Prosecutor on the basis of common sense. The Chief Justice, on the other hand, wants the application of common sense postponed to the very end, though like Tatting, he wants no personal part in it.

This brings me to the concluding portion of my remarks, which has to do with executive clemency. Before discussing that topic directly, I want to make a related observation about the poll of public opinion. As I have said, ninety per cent of the people wanted the Supreme Court to let the men off entirely or with a more or less nominal punishment. The ten per cent constituted a very oddly assorted group, with the most curious and divergent opinions. One of our university experts has made a study of this group and has found that its members fall into certain patterns. A substantial portion of them are subscribers to "crank" newspapers of limited circulation that gave their readers a distorted version of the facts of the case. Some thought that "Speluncean" means "cannibal" and that anthropophagy is a tenet of the Society. But the point I want to make, however, is this: although almost every conceivable variety and shade of opinion was represented in this group, there was, so far as I know, not one of them, nor a single member of the majority of ninety per cent, who said, "I think it would be a fine thing to have the courts sentence these men to be hanged, and then to have another branch of the government come along and pardon them." Yet this is a solution that has more or less dominated our discussions and which our Chief Justice proposes as a way by which we can avoid doing an injustice and at the same time preserve respect for law. He can be assured that if he is preserving anybody's morale, it is his own, and not the public's, which knows nothing of his distinctions. I mention this matter because I wish to emphasize once more the danger that we may get lost in the patterns of our own thought and forget that these patterns often cast not the slightest shadow on the outside world. I come now to the most crucial fact in this case, a fact known to all of us on this Court, though one that my brothers have seen fit to keep under the cover of their judicial robes. This is the frightening likelihood that if the issue is left to him, the Chief Executive will refuse to pardon these men or commute their sentence. As we all know, our Chief Executive is a man now well advanced in years, of very stiff notions. Public clamor usually operates on him with the reverse of the effect intended. As I have told my brothers, it happens that my wife's niece is an intimate friend of his secretary. I have learned in this indirect, but, I think, wholly reliable way, that he is firmly determined not to commute the sentence if these men are found to have violated the law.

No one regrets more than I the necessity

for relying in so important a matter on information that could be characterized as gossip. If I had my way this would not happen, for I would adopt the sensible course of sitting down with the Executive, going over the case with him, finding out what his views are, and perhaps working out with him a common program for handling the situation. But of course my brothers would never hear of such a thing.

Their scruple about acquiring accurate information directly does not prevent them from being very perturbed about what they have learned indirectly. Their acquaintance with the facts I have just related explains why the Chief Justice, ordinarily a model of decorum, saw fit in his opinion to flap his judicial robes in the face of the Executive and threaten him with excommunication if he failed to commute the sentence. It explains, I suspect, my brother Foster's feat of levitation by which a whole library of law books was lifted from the shoulders of these defendants. It explains also why even my legalistic brother Keen emulated Pooh-Bah in the ancient comedy by stepping to the other side of the stage to address a few remarks to the Executive "in my capacity as a private citizen." (I may remark, incidentally, that the advice of Private Citizen Keen will appear in the reports of this court printed at taxpayers' expense.)

I must confess that as I grow older I become more and more perplexed at men's refusal to apply their common sense to problems of law and government, and this truly tragic case has deepened my sense of discouragement and dismay. I only wish that I could convince my brothers of the wisdom of the principles I have applied to the judicial office since I first assumed it. As a matter of fact, by a kind of sad rounding of the circle, I encountered issues like those involved here in the very first case I tried as Judge of the Court of General Instances in Fanleigh County.

A religious sect had unfrocked a minister who, they said, had gone over to the views and practices of a rival sect. The minister circulated a handbill making charges against the authorities who had expelled him. Certain lay members of the church announced a public meeting at which they proposed to explain the position of the church. The minister attended this meeting. Some said he slipped in unobserved in a disguise; his own testimony was that he had walked in openly as a member of the public. At any rate, when the speeches began he interrupted with certain questions about the affairs of the church and made some statements in defense of his own views. He was set upon by members of the audience and given a pretty thorough pommeling, receiving among other injuries a broken jaw. He brought a suit for damages against the association that sponsored the meeting and against ten named individuals who he alleged were his assailants.

When we came to the trial, the case at first seemed very complicated to me. The attorneys raised a host of legal issues. There were nice questions on the admissibility of evidence, and, in connection with the suit against the association, some difficult problems turning on the question whether the minister was a trespasser or a licensee. As a novice on the bench I was eager to apply my law school learning and I began studying these questions closely, reading all the authorities and preparing well-documented rulings. As I studied the case I became more and more involved in its legal intricacies and I began to get into a state approaching that of my brother Tatting in this case. Suddenly, however, it dawned on me that all these perplexing issues really had nothing to do with the case, and I began examining it in the light of common sense. The case at once gained a new perspective, and I saw that the only thing for me to do was to direct a verdict for the defendants for lack of evidence.

I was led to this conclusion by the following considerations. The melee in which the plaintiff was injured had been a very confused affair, with some people trying to get to the center of the disturbance, while others were trying to get away from it; some striking at the plaintiff, while others were apparently trying to protect him. It would have taken weeks to find out the truth of the matter. I decided that nobody's broken jaw was worth that much to the Commonwealth. (The minister's injuries, incidentally, had meanwhile healed without disfigurement and without any impairment of normal faculties.) Furthermore, I felt very strongly that the plaintiff had to a large extent brought the thing on himself. He knew how inflamed passions were about the affair, and could easily have found another forum for the expression of his views. My decision was widely approved by the press and public opinion, neither of which could tolerate the views and practices that the expelled minister was attempting to defend.

Now, thirty years later, thanks to an ambitious Prosecutor and a legalistic jury foreman, I am faced with a case that raises issues which are at bottom much like those involved in that case. The world does not seem to change much, except that this time it is not a question of a judgment for five or six hundred frelars, but of the life or death of four men who have already suffered more torment and humiliation than most of us would endure in a thousand years. I conclude that the defendants are innocent of the crime charged, and that the conviction and sentence should be set aside.

TATTING, J. I have been asked by the Chief Justice whether, after listening to the two opinions just rendered, I desire to reexamine the position previously taken by me. I wish to state that after hearing these opinions I am greatly strengthened in my conviction that I ought not to participate in the decision of this case.

The Supreme Court being evenly divided, the conviction and sentence of the Court of General Instances is *affirmed*. It is ordered that the execution of the sentence shall occur at 6 A.M., Friday, April 2, 4300, at which time the Public Executioner is directed to proceed with all convenient dispatch to hang each of the defendants by the neck; until he is dead.

QUESTIONS AND COMMENTS FOR YOUR CONSIDERATION

1. Are you happy with the result reached by the Supreme Court of Newgarth? If so, do you believe justice was done?
2. Or do you believe that as much justice *as was available to the Court* was done?
3. Are these very different questions?

F. Formalism

Professor Fuller's *Case of the Speluncean Explorers* has continued to fascinate me over the years. But I had several uneasy feelings about it. In the first place, I was not sure that Professor Fuller had given sufficient attention to the murder case against the explorers. There was a feeling throughout the opinion that what the defendants did was not quite murder—perhaps, not quite in the *self-interested* sense that we think motivates true murderers. I thought that more attention might have been paid to this aspect of the case. Secondly, I thought that not enough attention was paid to justice. Of course, in one sense, justice is what the case is all about. Yet the actual result seems quite unjust! This situation posed a real paradox for me the more I thought about it.

And so I sat down to write additional opinions in the case. I couldn't invent any more judges, so I viewed further opinions in the case as coming from a panel of law professors at Newgarth Law School. The Chief Executive of Newgarth, having received the opinion of the Supreme Court, now wants guidance as to what to do. The Chief Executive does not want to proceed with the execution of these defendants without being on firmer ground than just a divided opinion from the

Supreme Court. And so the law professors are asked to write their own views on the case for the guidance of the Chief Executive.

I say that I "sat down" to write these additional opinions, but in fact it took me five years. I've never spent so much time on any single writing project. But I needed the time to contemplate in leisure the many dimensions of the case and to assemble the thoughts that occurred to me about it. My opinions in the case were published in 1980. Alas, Professor Fuller had passed away, and so the one person I most wanted to see what I had written was no longer with us.

Here, then, are the three individual opinions of the professors at Newgarth Law School.[2]

PROFESSOR WUN. When I received news of the decision in this case, I was relieved that the Court had reached the only proper result. But later, as I read the opinion of the Justices, I realized how fragile the Court's decision really was. To recap the vote, Justices Handy and Foster voted for acquittal, Tatting withdrew from the case, and although Keen and Truepenny voted to affirm the finding of guilty they engaged in powerful pleas to the Chief Executive to extend clemency to the convicted defendants. Not one of them came even close to believing, as I do, that the defendants were clearly guilty of murder. Perhaps the most egregiously bankrupt opinion illustrating the Court's true feeling is that of Justice Keen, who found it necessary to resort to the old and discredited theory of positivism to prop up his conclusion. He insisted upon a separation between law and morality, holding that "the law" required a finding of utility even though his own morality would lead to a different result. Without repeating familiar arguments against this positivistic stance, it may suffice to ask what morality compels Justice Keen to insist upon a separation between law and morality.

Since I believe that matters of right cannot be separated from matters of law, I might most efficiently begin by showing that what these defendants did is murder as a matter of morality, and only after that turn to the legal conclusion that murder was committed. As moral arguments are often best proved by analogies, let us consider four per-

sons on the brink of death due to, respectively, a defective heart, diseased lungs, a destroyed liver, and a nonfunctioning kidney. Since their lives are at stake their "need" to have these organs replaced by healthy ones could not possibly be greater. We will assume that there are no replacement organs available. The four persons thereupon decide that they will kidnap a stranger who is in good health, take him to a medical office where they have several highly paid doctors waiting, kill the stranger, and have the doctors transplant his four healthy organs into the four conspirators. Four lives will thus be saved at the cost of only one, and the result can be said to have been objectively compelled by "necessity" and not by any personal malice toward the stranger or any wish to harm him.

I will assume that anyone would immediately conclude that these four persons would be morally guilty of murdering the stranger (and, consequently, that they should be prosecuted under the law for murder). But then, of course, we must ask whether there is any significant difference between the hypothetical and the speluncean explorers. Certainly not because the victim was a stranger whereas Whetmore was known to the explorers. For the case would not be morally improved if the four persons needing organ transplants had instead selected a victim who had been friendly with them. But, one might object, Whetmore was involved in the same enterprise as the other explorers; that surely makes a difference. Yet consider the following alteration: The four persons, partners in a research team, had their vital organs damaged because their machine had broken and emitted omicron rays. A fifth coworker was also present, but miraculously she was not hurt. Are the four damaged indi-

[2] Anthony D'Amato, *The Speluncean Explorers—Further Proceedings*, 32 STANFORD LAW REVIEW 467 (1980). Copyright Anthony D'Amato 1980.

viduals thereby entitled to kill her and transplant her organs simply because she was involved in the same enterprise and at the same time as they?

What of another possible distinction: that Whetmore was going to die shortly of malnutrition anyway, whereas the Stranger in the hypothetical case was in good health? Does that fact give the explorers a moral right to kill Whetmore? What if the persons needing transplants read in the papers that doctors had informed a certain individual that he had only six more months left to live? Would they be justified in kidnapping and killing that individual because his interest in living only six months is negligible in comparison with the four of them surviving for many years if they can have his organs? But even the six months can be questioned. The doctors might have been in error as to his good health; or the doctors may have been correct but a month later a cure could be discovered. Possibilities always exist, and analogous ones existed for Whetmore. For the explorers trapped in the cave could not be certain that they would not be rescued the next day or even the next hour. Suppose the engineers had been wrong or that another entrance to the cave had been found and the defendants had been rescued two hours after they had killed and eaten Whetmore; would the Justices of our Supreme Court have been as sympathetic about the murder?

Let us look more deeply at estimating the possibility of survival for the four defendants trapped in the cave and the four persons needing organ transplants in the hypothetical case. Surely we cannot coerce them to be optimistic about the chance of rescue or of some dramatic medical breakthrough. They have the right to assess the odds for themselves. My contention is simply that they cannot force their version of the odds for survival upon Whetmore or upon the individual who was told he had six months to live.

But such a conclusion does not mean that we should give them a privilege of acting "out of necessity" to harm or kill someone else. At the very most they might decide upon a procedure to save most of their own lives at the expense of one or more of their own number. For example, since each of the four persons needing transplants needed a different organ, any three of them could survive with the healthy organs of the fourth. Suppose the four of them are in the medical office and they put on the table four identical looking pills, three of which are placebos and the fourth an instantaneous deadly poison. If each selects a pill, one would die and his or her organs could immediately be transplanted to the others. Such a procedure, incidentally, would not involve any of them actually killing any of the others; at worst they would each be guilty of attempted suicide and the victim would be guilty of actual suicide. But from a moral point of view, I tend to believe at the present time—unless someone persuades me that I have not refined my personal code of morality sufficiently and that further thought would lead to a different conclusion—that the four persons would have a moral right to decide that three survivors would be better than no survivors and that such a procedure would thus be justifiable. Note that the decision to go ahead with the pill-taking was the result of the informed consent of all four persons, each of whom arrived independently at the conclusion that the odds of survival if no action was taken were negligible. The willingness to go ahead with this desperate procedure would prove the genuineness of each individual's decision as to the odds of survival.

Let us apply analogous reasoning to the explorers. Roger Whetmore, for his own reasons, which may have included optimism in a greater degree than any of the other explorers about the chances of an early rescue, did not want to participate in the cannibalism scheme. To be sure there are complicating elements: Whetmore first proposed such a scheme, he carried the dice used to cast lots, and he initially agreed to participate. Yet surely none of these points either in themselves or when taken together estops Whetmore to withdraw, or sets up some sort of reliance by the others such that Whetmore could not fairly withdraw from the scheme. Their charging him with a "breach of faith" is outrageous. Such a charge might properly be levelled at one who attempted to withdraw from the scheme after being designated the victim, but it cannot be applied to a person who withdrew prior to the throw. Although the Justices of our Supreme Court have glossed over the significance of Whetmore's withdrawal, to me the point is of critical importance. By withdrawing, Whetmore both avoided the risk of being killed by the others and denied himself the chance to survive if the others went ahead with their plan. He chose to risk nothing and had nothing to gain. Certainly such an action cannot be labelled as unfair to others.

The others, however, did have something to gain by including Whetmore. To be sure, by including Whetmore, the others were taking a risk that Whetmore might end a winner.

Curiously, however, when we examine the odds involved, the fact that Whetmore could be a winner is not as significant as the fact that he could be the loser. Consider the four men only. If one of them is to die so that the others will be saved, then each man's chance of dying is one in four, or 25%. If we include Whetmore, each man's chance of dying now becomes one in five, or 20%. In short, each of the four defendants in this case calculated—and they certainly did so calculate, for we know from the testimony that there was much discussion of the mathematical problems involved—that his own chance of survival increased by five percentage points from 75% to 80% if Whetmore was included. The forcible inclusion of Whetmore was distinctly in their self-interest. The motive for murder is clear.

Additionally we should not lose sight of the fact that the others had to kill Whetmore. A suicide procedure analogous to the pill taking hypothetical might have been preferable in itself, but such a procedure was not available to them. We know Whetmore refused to throw the dice. Clearly he would have refused to take a pill. By his refusal to participate, Whetmore placed the burden of action upon the others. They had to kill him. In fact, they murdered him.

Although I believe that the preceding arguments establish the defendants' moral guilt, I recognize the possible objection that my position against the "necessity" excuse in criminal law proves too much. Surely there are situations where necessity is a legitimate excuse. What if Whetmore discovered on the twentieth day that his pickaxe, which he purchased with his own money, had a hollow handle filled with condensed food pills to be used in case of emergency. Assume that there are enough pills so that Whetmore and his companions could survive for another two weeks. Assume further that

Whetmore had come to loathe his companions and offers only to sell them food pills at astronomical prices. When his companions accept his price, Whetmore decides that they could not be trusted to pay once they are freed from the cave, and so he asks for immediate payment in cash. At this point, would his companions have the moral right to take some of the pills away from Whetmore by force? I would say yes. But the distinguishing feature of this hypothetical is that a property right is being sacrificed to save one or more lives, whereas in the real case, we are considering that a life can be sacrificed to save other lives. In short, property-for-life involves rights on a different level whereas life-for-life involves rights on the same level. And when we operate on the same level, necessity is not a justification. Even in a property-for-property case, for example, a man facing bankruptcy cannot justifiably steal money from someone else so that he can save his own property.

At first blush my analysis may appear to be challenged by Commonwealth v. Valjean, a case cited by Justice Tatting, which refused to accept the excuse that the defendant stole a loaf of bread because he was starving. I suppose the court paused seriously over the trade between property and life in that case, but must have decided as it did because a decision in the defendant's favor would have had enormously disruptive consequences for society. For if the law were to allow the theft of property by a starving man, many people might soon put themselves into a condition approaching starvation (for example, by first squandering their money in a gambling parlor) and then use that condition as an excuse for stealing food or money without restraint. Thus the harshness of the result to the defendant in Valjean is dictated by the need to deter others from exploiting such an "excuse." In contrast, the facts of the speluncean explorers clearly preclude the possibility of general exploitation for the purpose of obtaining nutriment.

Suppose we alter my hypothetical so that Whetmore finds enough pills only to keep one person alive for two weeks. Then if the others force him to share the pills, each will be kept alive for two or three days, but not until the rescue team breaks in ten days later. In that case, Whetmore would be justified in keeping all the pills for himself. But then this is not a case of property winning over lives, it is still a life-for-life case. For if the others forcibly took away from Whetmore the pills he needed to survive, they would be killing him, even though they may have then redistributed to Whetmore a two- or three-day supply equal to each of theirs. Thus even the Valjean case, upon further refection, may be seen as a life-for-life case and thus explainable as directly analogous to the real case of the speluncean explorers. For if hungry people could steal loaves of bread, farmers would not grow as much wheat and bakers would not make loaves of bread for sale to others. The shortage of food would mean that all would starve, including the farmer, since starving men would take away all of his wheat. Allowing theft not only destroys the incentive to produce in order to sell to others, but also destroys the ability to grow wheat for one's own consumption, since as soon as it is grown it will be stolen by hordes of starving people. In brief, it may be very hard to find a true "necessity" case. And if my first pickaxe hypothetical example is such a case, it is different from that of the speluncean explorers.

Let us turn now to the legal analysis, which is coincident with the moral argument previously given. Clearly the statute under which the defendants were convicted covers the present case. Section 12-A of the Consolidated Statutes of Newgarth, N.C.S.A. (N.S.) §12-A, provides: "Whoever shall willfully take the life of another shall be punished by death." I do not have to explore the question whether this statute admits of exceptions, and I need not repeat the arguments of the Justices of our Supreme Court on the question whether self-defense is one such exception. Suffice it to say that if the statute does allow for exceptions, "necessity" is not one of them since it is a life-for-life and not a property-for-life case.

Nor am I troubled by Justice Foster's argument that the explorers, trapped in the cave, were removed from the jurisdiction of Newgarth and hence the law cannot be applied to them. For one thing, the explorers are nationals and citizens of Newgarth, and on that basis our criminal laws may be extended to them even if they were outside the territorial limits of Newgarth. (Of course they were not; they were in a cave within the Commonwealth.) Second, they killed a national of Newgarth and thereby harmed the Commonwealth itself; accordingly Newgarth has a right of vindication through its criminal law process. Third, the defendants expected to be rescued by citizens of Newgarth, and hence their "captors"—the first persons who would have jurisdiction over them—would be persons subject to our laws. Fourth, the taking of the life of another is the gravest possible violation of a human right enjoyed by everyone wherever located. Even if Judge Foster were correct that legislative power did not reach these explorers in their cave, our laws would provide a statutory and administrative basis for enforcing the universal prohibition against murder wherever perpetrated.

Finally, legal analysis requires us to consider the purpose of the statute. The purpose of this or any other criminal statute is not primarily to punish someone for a past act, but to deter the act from ever taking place. Such statutes institutionalize rights—the rights accorded to every person to not be the victim of criminal acts. The purpose of the statute in the present case, therefore, is to give to potential murder victims the protective power of the state. We might imagine Roger Whetmore saying something like the following to the four explorers as they advance upon him: "What you are about to do is to commit murder. If you do so, and you survive and are rescued from this cave, the Commonwealth of Newgarth will try, convict, and execute you for murder. So do not attempt to kill me. I have not participated in your casting of lots, and you have no rights against me. Either try to hold out a while longer, as I have decided to do, or else do whatever you feel you must among the four of you alone. But do not include me; the law protects me against death at your hands."

Some such statement, I submit, is the only protection that the Whetmores of this Commonwealth may have when they are outnumbered and cannot protect themselves. As I have said earlier, the situation need not be so rare as explorers trapped in a cave; it includes my organ-transplant hypothetical, and any situation where a potential victim must rely on the law for protection. Our Supreme Court has upheld the law. Certainly as Chief Executive you should not undercut the sanction provided by the statute by commuting the sentence. What the defendants did in this case they did willfully. They acted out of self-interest, to increase the odds of their individual survival by forcibly including Whetmore. Now each defendant should pay fully for the murder he committed to advance his self-interest at the expense of the life of another.

QUESTIONS AND COMMENTS FOR YOUR CONSIDERATION

1. Professor Wun attempted to draw logical conclusions from hypothetical and counterfactual cases. Is this form of reasoning persuasive?

2. As you can imagine, Professor Wun's opinion was the hardest for me to write of the three professors' opinions. The analogy to body transplants was one of the first things I thought of; without *that* analogy I probably would not have been able to proceed with the rest of the essay. The really hard thing was figuring out that the mathematical probabilities could be different depending on whether Roger Whetmore participated or didn't participate. Of course, calculating those probabilities was simple—a matter of a minute's time. The hard thing was figuring out what *questions* to ask. For it often comes up in legal practice that the most important thing a lawyer can do is figure out what the question is. That's why so much of law-school education in the classroom is a matter of question-and-answer. The answers are usually easy once you've figured out what question to ask. In addition, once you've figured out what question to ask, and answered it, your client will probably say, "Why, that's simple. Anyone could have thought of it!" And so it may seem to many readers of Professor Wun's inquiry into the mathematical probabilities involved in the case. The idea that the speluncean explorers had something to gain for themselves by *including* Roger Whetmore in the throw of the dice seems rather simple once the little exercise in deductive logic takes place. Yet I can report that until my essay was published in 1980, no one as far as I know (including Professor Fuller himself) had ever thought of asking whether the probabilities would change if Roger Whetmore were included in the throw of the dice. I also have the feeling—although who can ever know?—that Professor Fuller would have included the argument about mathematical probabilities in his original Case if it had occurred to him. Of course, in speculating about this, I don't mean to criticize his invention of the case. It is to my mind the greatest work of art in the legal literature; to criticize it would be like saying that Michelangelo should have improved the drawing of one of the minor figures at the lower border of his painting at the Sistine Chapel.

3. Would we *want* law to be entirely logical? Another way of asking this question is: Do we *agree* with Professor Wun's reasoning and with his conclusion? Are we willing to live with the result that Wun reached?

G. Pragmatism

PROFESSOR TIEU. As my colleague Professor Wun knows, I have always found it difficult to accept any conclusion he reaches. The present case is the clearest example so far. I believe that the four defendants are innocent of any crime. Since I disagree with Professor Wun's conclusion but not his logic, the difficulty must lie in his premises. His position rests upon a common, unstated, and usually unchallenged assumption that we are all discrete individuals and that the laws of murder provide an essentially nonrational zero-sum game rule for individual players competing with each other. I disagree with nothing less than his implied definition of human life.

At the most fundamental level, the possibility of human life on earth rests upon the fate of the group, not the individual. The truism that "man is a social animal" tends to hide under a mask of triviality the ultimate fact that for the human species to survive, the individual must be subordinated to the welfare of the group. If, for example, a terrible disease destroyed all but a thousand members of the human race, and left only a hundred of these capable of reproduction, nothing would be more immoral than to sacrifice these fertile survivors before the others, if sacrifice of a substantial number of the thousand were required by the exigencies of the situation.

Because people have minds of their own, they tend to think that their own welfare has supreme value. Yet the desire for group preservation, over and above individual preservation, has stronger roots. To fully appreciate this point, we might profitably consider two kinds of behavior observed in other species: the warning behavior and the leadership phenomenon.

An impala will warn the rest of the herd if it spots a nearby lion; the repeated warning snorts enable the herd to run away, but the warner risks its life. A gazelle warns its fellows by leaping repeatedly stifflegged on all four feet. Yet this permits an approaching pack of predatory dogs to catch up with the warning gazelle even though the rest of the herd escapes. What is noteworthy about these and other instances that have been reported of the "warning" function is that, under standard evolutionary theory, the warners should have been "selected out" eons ago since the function "giving warning" is inimical to the survival of the warner, much the same as being born with a mutation is inimical to the ability of an individual to survive. Clearly what is happening is that the group is being saved by an hereditary characteristic that causes the death of some of the members of the group. Species survival exceeds the survival of individuals, and it is not extinguished even though the individuals who give the warning are sacrificed.

A "group gene" is at work here, not an "individual" gene.

As a further behavioral example, within a given territory or grouping of like animals a particular animal is deferred to as the leader of the group. The leader is easy to identify; it is usually given the best food, choice of mate or mates, and the other animals respond to its movements as if they are commands. Should the leader be killed, the group will find an individual animal—who previously had only been a follower—to inherit the leadership mantle.[3] From an evolutionary point of view, the problem here is not the extinction of the leadership characteristic (as it was in the case of warners), but rather why the leadership trait has not become dominant. The leader of the group typically has the most offspring (due to choice of mates and other perquisites of leadership) and yet, over the centuries, the group's "follower" characteristic has not been extinguished. The answer, again, must be that leading and following are not individual characteristics but rather are evolutionarily inherited functions of the group.

The "warning" and "leadership" behaviors have always been a part of human society. We have many words that indicate behaviors similar to the sacrificial warning behavior of animals: courage, heroism, martyrdom, nobility, gallantry, altruism, and so forth. When a group of people—or a nation—is endangered, these traits blossom forth in some individuals so that the group may be protected. Yet self-sacrifice itself is not selected out; courage and heroism never die. Similarly, leadership—not only political but also in the arts and sciences and in social groupings—is a commonplace event. We are in fact so accustomed to these behaviors that their importance has to be stressed here.

One could object at this point that I have only described behavior in some animals and some humans that points to the paramountcy of group survival, and that we cannot derive from this description a normative statement that would govern how all humans ought to behave. In other words, an "is" cannot produce an "ought." My reply is twofold. First, I deny that an "ought" does not follow from an "is." Our entire normative

---

[3] This is known as the "alpha principle."

mode of reasoning rests upon our conviction that some things, as a consequence of their existence, should be maintained. For example, our life-supporting environment is a fact; from it we derive the proposition that we have a duty to maintain the environment not only for all humans in existence but for future generations as well. The very notion of a normative principle can have no meaning if it excludes the most fundamental imperative of all: that since human life exists, it ought to be maintained. If we cannot conclude from the fact that human life exists the proposition that it ought to continue to exist, then, I submit, we do not really know what is valuable, and without this, we cannot know the meaning of the term "ought" at all. In my previous examples, we saw that a group of animals could owe its continued existence to the genetic trait manifested in some of them who, at sacrificial cost, warned the others of imminent danger. The only one who could conclude that the warning behavior was valueless would be one who denies that there is any value whatsoever in living. Such a person could not give any meaning to the term "morality," much less comment on whether morality can be derived from fact. Those who understand what "morality" means ultimately trace their understanding to observations of fact. Second, even if I must assume for the moment that "ought" cannot be derived from "is," my previous examples reduce to highly suggestive claims. Anyone looking dispassionately at the warning behavior in a social grouping of animals would have to concede that nature is trying to tell us something! And what nature is saying, rather unambiguously, is that "life" consists of the continued existence of the group rather than any of its members.

So far I have been somewhat abstract in defining the "life" of a group; the definition should be made precise. Each particular animal is the manifestation of the blueprints of its genes, and the carrier of those genes. Bodies are in reality only large and temporary carriers of the genes. The living genes are truly immortal, so long as the species which supports them continues to survive.

From this last observation I derive the ultimate moral imperative: that one may not destroy the possibility of reproduction. I think we have always perceived this fact even though it tends to go unnoticed in the routine of our lives. What are our laws but expressions of concern for group survival? From the lowliest traffic ordinance to the prohibition against genocide, the laws bespeak social preservation. If the perceptions of how society is best preserved change, the laws will surely change as well—even law which seems clear and unchangeable. As an example, we might briefly reflect upon the history of abortion.

In the period following the Great Spiral, there was a perceived fear that human life might be snuffed out completely. Our numbers were small and the conditions of living were harsh. At that time a human fetus was considered a "life in being" and hence abortion was universally condemned as "murder" under the laws. But after several centuries of population growth and normal conditions, the laws against abortion were honored more in the breach than in the observance. Although religions continued to consider abortion a grave sin, hardly anyone was criminally prosecuted. Finally, in the modern era, overpopulation, and not underpopulation, is considered a grave threat to human survival. As the peril of overpopulation has become perceived and absorbed by the public and by the lawmakers, we have witnessed the total legalization of abortion. We have witnessed an historic change in the popular conception of a human fetus; it is no longer a "life," but rather, the mere possibility of one. Although religious institutions have been the slowest to react, we are also seeing changes in their doctrine. The very definition of "life" for the purpose of our laws against murder thus reflects a differential societal perception of the danger to human survival.

What of the more typical case of "murder"? Why does our statute provide that a human being who kills another shall forfeit his own life? If capital punishment is appropriate in our modern age of an overpopulated world, how could it ever have been appropriate in conditions of perceived underpopulation? Capital punishment was conceived for the purpose of deterrence.

Even in an underpopulated society, the best way to ensure the minimum number of intentional killings is to threaten the killer with the loss of his own life. Unfortunately, in those few cases where the threat fails, society must exact capital punishment not because it has "promised" to do so or because

Doesn't this stem from valuing autonomy rather than a concern about overpopulation vengeance is necessary, but rather—and only—to ensure the threat's credibility to future potential murderers. In any event, there have been historical examples where, despite the statute, the penalty was not exacted. In time of war, when there have been severe shortages of military personnel, a convicted murderer will not be executed but will be sent to the front lines. Society does not want to "waste" even convicted murderers when, by being sent to the front fighting lines, they will contribute to its survival.

The foregoing considerations serve to indicate the narrowness of my colleague Professor Wun's individualistic approach to the present case. He views the law of murder as analogous to the rules of a game. He is afraid that the game will be impaired if the game rule is not applied to the four men who killed Whetmore. But why does he not inquire into the purpose of this game? Why do we have a law against murder? What values are at stake? These are the questions that go totally ignored in the one-dimensional approach of my colleague.

Under the view that I have outlined, we should consider the five explorers trapped in the cave as a total society. We do not have to do this in the somewhat artificial sense expressed by Judge Foster. Rather, we can consider as a fact that the group existence of the five men would be terminated entirely unless they undertook strong action.

To survive, they had to kill and eat one of their number. We might draw an analogy to an individual who has to amputate a diseased limb that would otherwise threaten to destroy his body. (Similarly, the "body politic" in the cave had to kill one of its members to preserve the corpus.) As important as a leg or arm is to an individual, he or she should not hesitate to amputate it if that is the only way to preserve the life of the body. And, I might add, it is not essential to my analogy that the arm or leg be diseased. If one's limb were hopelessly trapped beneath a railroad trestle, amputation to avoid being killed by an oncoming train would be gruesome, but entirely rational. No religious prohibition of self-mutilation could make any sense in such a case. But then how can Professor Wun think that what the explorers did was in any sense immoral?

To the contrary, the most immoral act that we can conceive would be to terminate the life of the group. Conversely, one of the highest acts of morality is to preserve the life of a group. The explorers trapped in the cave must have sensed the force of this moral imperative. Despite all their previous training and all their previous social experiences and learned taboos, they had to reach the decision to engage in cannibalism in order to survive.

I could end my argument at this point, but perhaps it might be helpful for avoiding misunderstanding to spell out the acceptable procedures for implementing this moral imperative. Had one of the explorers been the "leader" in the cave, I would see nothing wrong with that leader selecting the victim whose flesh would provide the life saving nutriment to the others. I would not second-guess the selection. Fairness in selection is as unimportant when the life of the group is at stake as it would be absurd, in my self-mutilation hypothetical, to have to be "fair" to all one's fingers if one of them has to be sacrificed. Thus the leader in the cave might base his selection of a victim on a ground as arbitrary as that suggested by Judge Tatting: Kill the one person who believes in afterlife, since the harm to him would be the least. Or it might be to kill the oldest, or the poorest, or—I hesitate to say it—the fattest. Or—to take care of Professor Wun's position—the decision might be to kill any individual who did not want to participate in the plan for group survival. Indeed, it would make no difference to me if the leader were to "reward" the person who first proposed the idea of cannibalism as a means of saving four out of five lives by selecting him as the victim.

Now, in fact, there was a "leadership" principle working in the cave, manifesting itself in the form of a democracy rather than an autocracy. The leadership was that of the group; its will became the ruling principle. It decided, in its wisdom, to give Roger Whetmore an even chance with the others in the throw of the dice. I do not consider that to have been a necessary part of the selection procedure, but the democratic nature of the proceedings in the cave certainly does not hurt my overall argument. Perhaps the "leadership" that emerged in the cave could only have emerged if it were grounded, as it was, upon conditions of fairness and equality. No matter. The fact is that four men survived. Had the leadership principle not emerged, the rescue party would have found in the cave five dead speluncean explorers. Would such a scene have been fair repayment for the tremendous efforts of the rescue party? Yet those who now want to execute the group for the crime of self-preservation would essentially recreate such a scene.

There has been no violation of N.C.S.A. (N.S.) §12-A stating that "[w]hoever shall willfully take the life of another shall be pun-ished by death," since we must construe "life" as the life of the group in the cave, as we would in a situation where the entire society's future existence is imperiled. It is with the greatest irony, then, that we must conclude that the only person in this case who could violate the statute would be the public executioner, if he is allowed to proceed to execute the four defendants. He would be "willfully taking the life of another." As Chief Executive, you need not be an instrumentality in the derivation of an immoral conclusion from absurd premises. I urge you to pardon the defendants.

QUESTIONS AND COMMENTS FOR YOUR CONSIDERATION

1. Inductive logic proceeds from observed facts and attempts to derive from them a prediction. The prediction "the sun will rise tomorrow" is a famous inductive conclusion from the repeated observations that the sun has arisen each day in the past for as long as anyone can remember. An inductive logician might say that the prediction "the sun will rise tomorrow" is *true.* Clearly this notion of "truth" is not the same as truth derived from stated premises in the process called "deductive logic." But that does not mean that an inductively derived "truth" is not a true statement. An inductive truth is capable of being falsified; if the sun does not arise tomorrow (surely this is a possibility, however remote),[4] then the statement will have been falsified. But since inductive "truths" are the truths of our daily existence, they are as close to "truth" as nature will allow. If you want to be accurate, of course, you could call them "extremely likely hypotheses about the future."

2. Professor Tieu takes the observed fact of human survival and derives "truths" from it that she says will resolve the case of the speluncean explorers. She also takes observations from the field now known as sociobiology. Yet a mere inductive "truth" may not have enough force in it to compel a judge to decide a case a certain way. For a judge might say: "Why *should* I decide this case according to your demonstration of inductive truth?" Accordingly, Professor Tieu tries to make the greatest inductive leap of them all—to derive an "ought" from an "is." She is attempting to argue that *what is* is *what morally there ought to be.* This leap of inductive logic was first noticed, and condemned, by the great philosopher David Hume. Here is what Hume said about it in 1739:

> I cannot forbear adding to these reasonings an observation which may, perhaps, be found of some importance. In every system of morality which I have hitherto met with, I have always remarked that the author proceeds for some time in the ordinary way of reasoning, and establishes the being of a god, or makes observations concerning human affairs; when of a sudden I am surprised to find that instead of the usual copulations of propositions *is* and *is*

---

[4] The assertion is inconsistent if by the word "tomorrow" we *mean* "the day that begins at sunrise"! But the assertion is capable of falsification if by the word "tomorrow" we mean "twenty-four hours from now as measured by an atomic clock."

not, I meet with no proposition that is not connected with an *ought* or an *ought not*. This change is imperceptible, but is, however, of the last consequence. For as this *ought* or *ought not* expresses some new relation or affirmation, it is necessary that it should be observed and explained; and at the same time that a reason should be given for what seems altogether inconceivable, how this new relation can be a deduction from others which are entirely different from it. But as authors do not commonly use this precaution, I shall presume to recommend it to the readers; and am persuaded that this small attention would subvert all the vulgar systems of morality and let us see that the distinction of vice and virtue is not founded merely on the relations of objects, or is perceived by reason.[5]

Do you agree with Hume? Or with Professor Tieu?

3. At the point in Professor Tieu's opinion where she says, "I could end my argument at this point, but . . ." I intended to signal that her argument is in fact complete at that moment. But I felt compelled to go on because I wanted to draw some of the implications of her argument. I was in fact trying to follow in the footsteps of Professor Fuller when he *added* to Justice Handy's opinion the example of a religious sect that unfrocked a minister. Many of my students in past years, reading Handy's opinion, had been persuaded by everything Handy said up to the point that he revealed how he had decided the case of the religious sect. That example shocked them. They then saw the *excesses* and *injustices* that could derive from what up until then seemed a quite refreshing, realistic view of the law. I hoped to do the same thing with the examples given by Professor Tieu of how her views work out in practice. How did these examples strike you? Did it have the effect—which I admit I tried to achieve—of calling into question everything she had said up to that point? If so, I will have achieved in a small way what Professor Fuller obviously tried to achieve in Justice Handy's approach to the speluncean explorers. Professor Fuller was attempting to convey one of the most important lessons of the law—that the principles we apply to the case at hand may cause problems for us in other cases. No matter how reasonable it may appear to a reader to read the principles as applied to the case at hand, a judge must always be concerned with the precedential value of those same principles. Or, in other words, don't fall in love with a theory too readily, because some day that same theory might come back to haunt you.

4. Aren't the *implications* of Professor Tieu's theories quite positivistic? Consider, for example, that the leading principle in Thomas Hobbes great book, *The Leviathan*, was the necessity for social survival. From that principle, Hobbes derived the entire logic of the state. Consider, also, that H.L.A. Hart, one of the greatest modern proponents of legal positivism, also elevates survival of society to the highest principle. Hart even calls it a "moral" principle![6]

5. Consider, also, the theory of state supremacy, suggested in the philosophy of Hegel and in the writings of proponents of fascism. In the extreme fascist view, a state can do no wrong because a state invents what is right and wrong. It has the power to invent right and wrong because it, and it alone, must survive. The imperative of survival becomes transformed into statist totalitarianism. Some posi-

---

[5] DAVID HUME, A TREATISE OF HUMAN NATURE, BOOK III, Pt. 1, Sect. 2 (1739).

[6] H.L.A. HART, THE CONCEPT OF LAW 189 (1961). Indeed, Hart calls "the minimum purpose of survival" a principle of natural law! In my view, this may be the way a *positivist* looks at natural law, but it's not the way a natural lawyer would look at it. If survival were "everything," then wouldn't it justify the grossest violations of morality? Charles de Gaulle reportedly said, "*Apres moi, le deluge!*"

tivists like to say that there is no such things as a "right" unless it is enforced by the state. Isn't it a small step from there to say that the state is the *source* of all our rights? And isn't it a small additional step to say that if the state chooses to take our rights away, then we simply lose them—end of story? Finally, is this chain of reasoning implicit in Professor Tieu's opinion?

H. Justice

PROFESSOR THRI. I recommend that you commute the sentence of the four defendants to several years' compulsory service in a hospital or similar place where they can help save the lives of others, for I believe that the defendants are neither guilty nor innocent of the crime of murder. Lest my position appear a compromise between those of my colleagues, I hasten to point out at the outset that no true compromise between their extreme positions appears possible. They present a thesis and an antithesis on what constitutes "life." Even so, I want to draw upon aspects of each of their separate opinions in constructing my own synthesis.

Let me start with Professor Tieu's argument that the relevant unit in this case is the group and not the individual. As she well knows from our many discussions, I reject the metaphysics upon which she leans in fashioning a larger-than-life portrait of the group or the state. But metaphysics aside, I find her present argument nothing other than the old, and I should have thought discredited, philosophy of utilitarianism. A classic objection to this form of utilitarianism is that in practice it becomes the tyranny of the majority. A society may, for example, enslave members of a different race, and then justify the continued system of slavery on the ground that the harm to a minority (the enslaved) is outweighed by the happiness and luxury afforded to the majority (the citizenry). There is a similar danger in Professor Tieu's espousal of arbitrary grounds for selecting the explorers' victim. If Whetmore were selected arbitrarily, the procedure would be as morally unjustifiable as the perversion of utilitarianism that justifies slavery. I think Professor Tieu's argument would be improved if she required that each person in the cave be subjected to an equal chance of being killed. In that permutation we might see utilitarianism in its pure form.

But even with the proviso of fairness in the selection of the victim, her argument would still be vulnerable. Suppose a crime is committed which causes great public outrage, and many lives will be lost in riots if the killer is not apprehended and brought to justice quickly. If the police cannot find the killer, utilitarianism requires that the authorities select an innocent person as a scapegoat, manufacture evidence, and convict him. Many lives would be saved at the expense of one, although the law is perverted. Similarly, utilitarianism would condone Professor Wun's organ-transplant hypotheticals, which save several lives at the expense of one. Since all these examples are logically required by utilitarianism, we can only conclude that the philosophy does not express a moral system.

But despite my criticisms of Professor Tieu's philosophical premises, I want now to derive an important argument from her insistence upon the group as the relevant unit. Her simplistic vision of the "group" usefully summarizes a complex set of mutual reliances. The explorers were in fact engaged in a cooperative enterprise. In general, when a person decides to join a society to go spelunking in the company of its members he knows by the very nature of its being a joint expedition that the others will support him if a common danger or emergency arises. Indeed, this is why explorers tend to work in groups. A solitary explorer would be taking enormous risks of being disabled and being unable to summon help. Even in a two-person exploring team, if one is hurt and needs continuous attention, there would be no third person to summon assistance. We can readily see that important safety increments may be added as each marginal person joins the group. We might well infer that in the absence of any other evidence, Whetmore's decision to go exploring with the others may have been critical in their decision to go exploring at all. They may have decided that safety considerations required five; and, by inference, all five would have to undertake to pitch in to ensure group safety. In short, Professor Tieu is right in her criticism of Professor Wun's "zero-sum game" approach. Clearly the explorers were not engaged in a mutually antagonistic or competitive enterprise going into the cave or even when the landslide sealed off the passage.

It is in this sense that a coherent meaning can be given to the charge by the four defendants that Whetmore was guilty of a "breach of faith" when he withdrew from the lottery. Professor Wun assumes the charge was based solely upon Whetmore's withdrawing from the lottery after having suggested it was the right thing to do. But a more reasonable explanation of their charge is that Whetmore had no right not to contribute to the solution of the emergency that threatened all of them, just as he would have had no right to refuse to take his turn at chopping through the wall of the cave if that had been a feasible means of escape. When he joined the group, Whetmore knew that he was committing himself to full participation in the event of emergency. If Whetmore at the outset of the exploration had declared that if he was not in the mood when an emergency arose he would feel no obligation to do his share in helping to meet it, we can be quite certain that the others would not have accepted him as part of their group.

If Whetmore had no right to withdraw from the group's attempt to meet the emergency, does it follow that the defendants had a right to include him in their lottery and to kill him when he emerged the loser? If I could answer this question affirmatively, I would reach the same result as Professor Tieu and conclude that the defendants are innocent of any crime. However, the argument stops short of fully convincing me because of the following objection.

In joining the group Whetmore implicitly agreed to do his share of the work and to participate in the handling of emergency situations. Thus if the combined effort of five men could have moved the boulders that sealed the cave, he would have had no right to refuse to participate. But there are two limits, each decisive, to the inferred agreement to participate in an emergency. First, joint exploration does not require that any person be required to risk his life to save the others. Such an act of moral altruism is rare in any circumstance and certainly has never been a part of normal expected behavior. A mountain climber, for example, might slip and be placed in mortal danger; the others in the group must do everything to help her save herself, but they are not expected to risk their lives to save hers. (Of course, I am talking of a meaningful risk of life, and not a negligible one which might indeed be present in any exploring venture; in fact, I am talking about no less than a 20% risk of life, which was the chance in the lottery in the present case.) Second, even if we concede that the explorers agreed to risk their lives to save another in an emergency, the situation in the cave was entirely beyond their agreement. In the normal case a risk is undertaken in which all might be saved. Rescuer and rescued combine to overcome a situation so that both will survive. But in the cave the explorers had passed that point. The boulders were unmovable. Nature had already won. Indeed, the exploring enterprise was over, for no amount of effort, no degree of risk against nature could make any difference. It is inconsistent with the idea of a lottery that everyone could survive. Therefore such a situation was not at all contemplated in the agreement to go exploring. Whetmore had not lost the right to choose not to be a part of a pact that would result in certain death "by inference" when he originally agreed to go exploring. It is clear that unless another argument is made on behalf of the defendants, the "group" argument is insufficient to exonerate them.

But such an argument can be made, I believe, if we examine closely the reasoning relating to the defense of "necessity" in Professor Wun's opinion. Professor Wun disclaims total opposition to the "necessity" argument. Clearly his own hypothetical example of Whetmore finding food pills in the pickaxe handle is a compelling case for allowing such a defense. This Commonwealth certainly recognizes that each human being has a privilege, if survival is at stake, to appropriate the property of another. It is a property-for-life case, and the defendants in the pickaxe hypothetical would have a legal right to take the pills by force, so long as they left Whetmore enough pills so that he could survive.

The problem that I have with my colleague's reasoning is his easy assumption that the speluncean explorers is a life-for-life case. My colleague argues that when Whetmore told the others that he had withdrawn from the scheme, they could have excluded Whetmore and proceeded to work out a suicide pact among themselves. Accordingly, one of the four would lose and would have killed himself. The three would be entitled to eat his dead flesh, and Whetmore, having excluded himself from the total arrangement, would not be so entitled. But here is the flaw in my colleague's reasoning. At that point Whetmore would be entitled to eat the nutriment, since it is no longer a "life" but is merely the "property" of the other three explorers. The fact that his withdrawal from the lottery was conditioned upon his subsequent disentitlement to partake of the nutriment is nothing other than a statement that the other three explorers have a property interest in the dead body. Yet this interest can legally be overcome when a life (Whetmore's) is at stake, just as in the pick-axe example a property interest in the pills can be overcome when survival is at stake. In short, what started out as a "life" interest becomes transformed, after the death of one explorer, into a "property" interest.

We can well imagine what would happen a day or two after one of the four explorers died and the others are surviving on his dead flesh. Whetmore might beg for food, he might repent his "ill-advised" decision not to participate in the lottery, he would surely point out that there is ample food for all to survive for ten more days, and that their insistence upon excluding him now would mean that he would die when he could otherwise survive at no cost to them. An argument exists for Whetmore to the effect that the others will be guilty of murder if they deprive him of the nutriment. For if he has a legal right to the nutriment—a right based upon the property-for-life argument from "necessity"—then they have no right to deprive him of it. Such a deprivation would in fact amount to murder.

Thus we arrive at the conclusion that there was no way legally for the others to exclude Whetmore from surviving on the dead flesh of one of their number. Or to put it differently, at the moment Whetmore withdrew from the lottery, he was in effect, if not consciously, trying to ensure his own survival at no risk to himself. Clearly the law cannot single out one person for special treatment, requiring the others to risk their own lives to save Whetmore. Conversely, the others were legally justified in forcibly including him in their lottery.

We now have the argument in behalf of the defendants. First, the "group" argument operates to show that they had a right to some extent to rely upon Whetmore's participation.

Second, the "necessity" argument indicates that there was no reasonable nor fair alternative to their forcibly including Whetmore in the lottery. But while these two arguments distinguish the present case from Professor Wun's organ-transplant hypotheticals, the defendants are not completely innocent. They took a life, and they profited from it; technically, they violated the statute. Yet if it ever made sense to have a pardoning power, it makes sense to have it in a case of technical violation of statute where a substantial justification can be advanced for the violation. And the pardoning power is not an all-or-nothing tool. The defendants' sentences can be commuted to lesser penalties. I would urge that the defendants be sentenced to three or four years' compulsory service in a hospital or similar institution where they may be in a position to save the lives of people who need help. In that fashion, I believe, exact justice will have been achieved.

QUESTIONS AND COMMENTS FOR YOUR CONSIDERATION

1. Professor Thri wants to achieve "exact justice." The word "justice" seems to suggest to some people a matter that is vast and overly theoretical. For present purposes, let's use "fairness" in its everyday sense as a synonym for justice. In your opinion, is Thri's conclusion the fairest opinion among all that you have read (Truepenny, Foster, Tatting, Keen, Handy, Wun, Tieu, and Thri)?

2. What, structurally, allows Thri to be "fair"? Is he doing something that Truepenny, Foster, Tatting, Keen, and Handy were not in a position to do? Think about this before looking at the next question.

3. As you have realized in answering the previous question, Professor Thri's mandate is to advise the Chief Executive of Newgarth. The Chief Executive is not legally bound by statutes or precedents; he may commute the court's sentence entirely, or modify it in a manner such as that suggested by Thri. In contrast, the Justices of the Supreme Court of Newgarth (given the special verdict of the jury) can only make an all-or-nothing (a yes-or-no) decision; they can either acquit the defendants or sentence them to death. Is it therefore not substantially easier for Professor Thri to reach a "justice" conclusion than it would be for the Justices of the Supreme Court? Legally easier? Logically easier? Psychologically easier?

4. Have we now reached the ultimate, bedrock issue in the Case of the Speluncean Explorers—namely, whether the judicial system can ever be said to be incapable of achieving justice? If the Supreme Court of Newgarth was unable to achieve justice in this case (assuming that you agree with Professor Thri as to the dictates of justice in this case), do we not open the door to admitting that any real court at any time in any place may be so bound by a felt need to render a yes-or-no decision that it may be unable to do exact justice to the parties?

5. If so, are courts disabled because they are courts? Or is it law that is disabling the courts from achieving exact justice (in at least some cases)? Or is it the judges' own philosophies of law?

6. If it is the law, then is there an inherent conflict between law and justice? The tension between law and justice is a recurrent theme in this Anthology, but we will focus upon it specifically in Chapter 7.

2
Positivism

A. The Command Theory of Law

It was Thomas Hobbes who first announced, in his famous *The Leviathan* (1651), that law is the command of the sovereign. But the command theory of law did not receive extended legal consideration until 1789 in the writings of Jeremy Bentham. And it did not receive extended jurisprudential analysis until 1832 in the lectures of John Austin.

Jeremy Bentham was one of Sir William Blackstone's students at Oxford (Blackstone's *Commentaries* was probably the most influential legal treatise of all time). But Bentham was repelled by his professor's veneration of the common law. Bentham denounced his teacher's approval of "legal fictions" by which judges changed the law while making it appear to conform to precedent. "Fictions are falsehoods," Bentham proclaimed, "and the judge who invents a fiction ought to be sent to jail." The purpose of legal fictions, he said, was "to deceive, and by deception, to govern, and by governing to promote the interest" of the English ruling classes and the gentry.

Bentham sought to enhance rule by Parliament at the expense of rule by the British judiciary. The legislature at least represented the will of the people, and legislators who failed to respond to the popular will could be voted out of office. Bentham worked tirelessly on drafting detailed legislative codes to replace the common law. He believed that codes made law easily accessible to the average person, and that the detail in the codes would ensure that they would be applied by the judges to specific cases.

Positivism received its earliest and most complete expression in the writings of Jeremy Bentham. Bentham championed the causes of the poor and the dispossessed at a time when the English aristocracy and landed gentry were busy manipulating government and the laws to further their own class interests. Bentham was one of the earliest spokespersons for animal rights. He viewed existing law as a creature of the judicial class, whose sympathies were with the aristocracy and landed gentry. Judges made up law, judges invented law, judges manipulated law (Bentham charged) so as to favor their own interests and the interests of their friends. Bentham saw that the way to change this was to emphasize the role of Parliament, because at least Parliament was an elected body and hence was more likely to be fair to all the people. To emphasize the role of Parliament, Bentham revised the entire way we look at "law." To Bentham, real law was statutory law. Judges had no right to change it.

1. Jeremy Bentham: Positivism and Common Law[1]

The term *law* should be applied to every expression of will, the uttering of which was an act of legislation, an exertion of legislative power.

What is the nature of common law?[2] It is nothing but so many particular autocratic acts or orders, which in virtue of the more extensive interpretation which the people are disposed to put upon them, have somewhat of the effect of general laws. A magistrate exercises some act of power over a particular individual; the assemblage of acts by which this is done serves as a sign to the people at large expressing that the like act of power will probably be exercised in future in a like case. A Cadi [a magistrate among the Turks, Arabs, etc.] comes by a baker's shop, and finds the bread short of weight: the baker is hanged in consequence. This, if it be part of the design that other bakers should take notice of it, is a sort of law forbidding the selling of bread short of weight under the pain of hanging. Whether the Cadi makes a record in writing attesting that the baker has sold bread short of weight, and issues an order to a public executioner to strangle him, or whether the Cadi himself without saying a word strangles him on the spot with his own hands, is what to this purpose makes no difference. The silent act of hanging when thus made a consequence of the offense has as good a title in point of extent to the appellation of a law as anything that could be made out of a whole shelf full of pleadings put together. Written law [statutory law] then is the law of those who can both speak and write: traditional law, of those who can speak but can not write: common law, of those who neither know how to write, nor how to speak. Written law is the law for civilized nations; traditional law, for barbarians; common law, for brutes.

The common law, you say, punishes theft with hanging: be it so. But by what law is this done? who made it? when was it made? where is it to be found? what are the parts that it contains? by what words is it expressed? Theft, you say, is taking under certain circumstances: but taking by whom? taking of what? under what circumstances? taking by a person of such a sort, taking a thing of such a sort, taking under such and such circumstances. But how know you this?—because so it has been adjudged. What then? Not if it be a taking by any other person, nor if of any other thing, nor if under any other circumstances. O yes, in many other cases: if *by* a person of such another sort, if *of* a thing of such another sort, if *under* such and such circumstances? But how do you know this is the case? because I think it ought to be so, because I believe it would be so: because such and such persons believe it ought to be so or would be so. But how *came* you to think so? and how came *they* to think so? and what if I think differently and as many people with me?

If there be still a man who will stand up for the existence and certainty of a rule of common law, give him everything he asks, he must still have recourse to fiction to produce any such rule: if it appears in any shape it must clothe itself in the similitude of some particular provision of the nature of statute law: it must purport to be, it must pretend to be a provision of statute law, although it be no such thing. To enable ourselves to conceive and express the influence which a rule of this sort may have over the whole system of law and at the same time to distinguish it from the real entity whose semblance it usurps, it may be called after the name of that which it would be if it were anything, with the particle *quasi* prefixed to it; according to the usage of the Roman Law. Upon this plan a rule of common law describing for example, what is to be looked upon as theft, may be styled a *quasi*-law against theft: which *quasi*-law will accordingly have its *quasi*-imperative, *quasi*-limitive, *quasi*-exceptive provisions, and so on.

[1] JEREMY BENTHAM, OF LAWS IN GENERAL (H.L.A. Hart, ed., 1970).

[2] *Editor's Note:* Bentham used the terms "common law" and "customary law" interchangeably. Today, the "common law" is the more familiar term, and I will use it in the text in some places where Bentham used the term "customary law."

QUESTIONS AND COMMENTS FOR YOUR CONSIDERATION

1. From Bentham's writings as a whole, a basic diagram of legal positivism

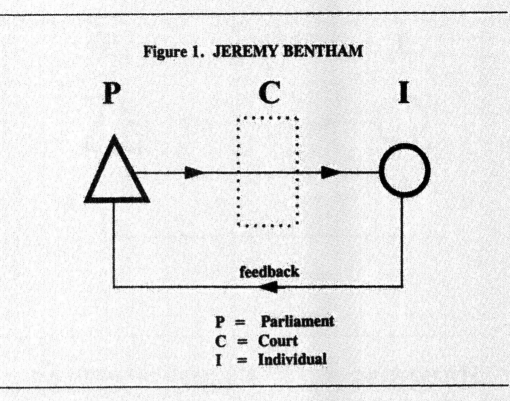

Figure 1. JEREMY BENTHAM

P = Parliament
C = Court
I = Individual

might look like Figure 1.[a] This diagram shows that a message, or communication, is issued by the legislature (Parliament). Positivists call this message a "command." The command is directed to an individual (to you and to me). The command filters through a subsystem called a court. The court's job is to apply the command to specific individuals. The court is represented by dots to show that the legislature's command is essentially transmitted intact through the court to the individual subject. This depiction indicates Bentham's purpose in minimizing the role of the court. Bentham could not eliminate the court entirely, because some subsystem is necessary to apply the legislative command to individuals. Since the legislature's commands are general, a specific fact-finder-and-applier is needed. The court, therefore, serves as a subsystem whose function is to faithfully apply a general command to all those individuals whose factual situation brings them within the ambit of the general command.

2. The feedback mechanism depicted above, which runs from the individual back to Parliament, represents Bentham's overriding concern about democratic government: that Parliament must be responsible to the citizenry. Through periodic elections, individuals are able to vote to retain some legislators and vote others out of office. This ability ensures that legislation will be responsive to popular needs. Note the important role that this aspect of Bentham's theory played in the opinion of Justice Keen in the Case of the Speluncean Explorers. Justice Keen

[a] This and subsequent diagrams are quoted from Anthony D'Amato, *Towards a Reconciliation of Positivism and Naturalism: A Cybernetic Approach to a Problem of Jurisprudence*, 14 Western Ontario Law Review 171 (1975). Reprinted by permission.

felt that it was his job to apply the legislature's command exactly as it was written (*i.e.*, a court should not alter the legislative message), and that the cure for any injustices that might result from this application of the legislature's command consists of public demand upon the legislature to amend or revise its statutes. Of course, since a legislature can only act *prospectively*, any amendment by the legislature of its statute would be too late to do any good for the four speluncean explorers. But Justice Keen felt strongly that this process was the only way to ameliorate harsh results that might from time to time arise from judicial applications of statutes to individuals.

3. In contrast to Bentham's highly visible life as an indefatigable social reformer, John Austin lived his life in obscurity and poverty. Austin began teaching law courses at the University of London in 1828. In those days, professors did not receive a salary; they were totally dependent upon student fees. Austin's classes steadily dwindled in attendance, and he resigned in 1832 when he only had five students left. He remained poor through most of his life, supported mainly by his wife who worked as a writer and translator. Austin died in 1859. At the end, he said, "I was born out of time and place. I ought to have been a schoolman of the twelfth century or a German professor."

4. Austin's prose seems heavy and stilted. But what stimulating ideas come shining through! His few devoted students must have fanatically admired his powerful and incisive mind. The following are excerpts from Austin's major work, *The Province of Jurisprudence Determined* (1832), interpolated with some sections from his posthumously published *Lectures on Jurisprudence*:

2. John Austin: Jurisprudential Positivism[4]

Laws proper, or properly so called, are commands; laws which are not commands, are laws improper or improperly so called.

The matter of jurisprudence is positive law: law, simply and strictly so called: or law set by political superiors to political inferiors. But positive law (or law, simply and strictly so called) is often confounded with objects to which it is related by resemblance, and with objects to which it is related in the way of analogy: with objects which are also signified, properly and improperly, by the large and vague expression *law*.

A law, in the most general and comprehensive acceptation in which the term, in its literal meaning, is employed, may be said to be a rule laid down for the guidance of an intelligent being by an intelligent being having power over him.

The aggregate of the rules established by political superiors is frequently styled *positive law*. These are contradistinguished to the rules which are improperly called *laws*, being rules set and enforced by mere opinion, that is, by the opinions or sentiments held or felt by an indeterminate body of men in regard to human conduct. Instances of such a use of the term *law* are the expressions "The law of honor"; "The law set by fashion"; and rules of this species constitute much of what is usually termed "International law."

Besides the various sorts of rules which are included in the literal acceptation of the term law, and those which are by a close and striking analogy, though improperly, termed laws, there are numerous applications of the term law which rest upon a slender analogy and are merely metaphorical or figurative. Such is the case when we talk of laws observed by the lower animals; of laws regulating the growth or decay of vegetables; of laws determining the movements of inanimate

4 JOHN AUSTIN, THE PROVINCE OF JURISPRU-
DENCE DETERMINED (1832) and LECTURES ON JURIS-
PRUDENCE, excerpts.

bodies or masses. For where intelligence is not, or where it is too bounded to take the name of reason, and therefore is too bounded to conceive the purpose of a law, there is not the will which law can work on, or which duty can incite or restrain. Yet through these misapplications of a name, flagrant as the metaphor is, has the field of jurisprudence and morals been deluged with muddy speculation.

I shall now state the essentials of a law or rule properly so called. Every law or rule is a command. Or rather, laws or rules, properly so called, are a species of commands.

Accordingly I shall endeavor, in the first instance, to analyze the meaning of *command*. If you express or intimate a wish that I shall do or forbear from some act, and if you will visit me with an evil in case I comply not with your wish, the expression or intimation of your wish is a *command*. A command is distinguished from other significations of desire, not by the style in which the desire is signified, but by the power and the purpose of the party commanding to inflict an evil or pain in case the desire be disregarded. If you cannot or will not harm me in case I comply not with your wish, the expression of your wish is not a command, although you utter your wish in imperative phrase. If you are able and willing to harm me in case I comply not with your wish, the expression of your wish amounts to a command, although you are prompted by a spirit of courtesy to utter it in the shape of a request.

Being liable to evil from you if I comply not with a wish which you signify, I am *bound* or *obliged* by your command, or I lie under a *duty* to obey it. If, in spite of that evil in prospect, I comply not with the wish which you signify, I am said to disobey your command, or to violate the duty which it imposes.

Command and duty are, therefore, correlative terms: the meaning denoted by each being implied or supposed by the other. Or (changing the expression) wherever a duty lies, a command has been signified; and wherever a command is signified, a duty is imposed.

Commands are of two species. Some are *laws* or *rules*. The others have not acquired an appropriate name, nor does language afford an expression which will mark them briefly and precisely. I must, therefore, note them as well as I can by the ambiguous name of "*occasional or particular* commands."

By every command, the party to whom it is directed is obliged to do or to forbear.

Now where it obliges *generally* to acts or forbearances of a class, a command is a law or rule. But where it obliges to a *specific* act or forbearance, or to acts or forbearances which it determines specifically or individually, a command is occasional or particular. An example which best illustrates the distinction is that *judicial commands* are commonly occasional or particular, although the commands which they are calculated to enforce are commonly laws or rules. Thus, while the legislator prohibits acts of the class generally and indefinitely [such as prohibitions against murder, theft, or arson], the judge orders a specific punishment, as the consequence of a specific offense.

It may happen that the author of a statute, when he is making the statute, conceives and expresses exactly the intention with which he is making it, but conceives imperfectly and confusedly the end which determines him to make it. Now, since he conceives its scope inadequately and indistinctly, he scarcely pursues its scope with logical completeness, or he scarcely adheres to its scope with logical consistency. Consequently, though he conceives and expresses exactly the intention with which he is making it, the statute, in respect of its reason, is defective or excessive. Some class of cases which the reason of the statute embraces is not embraced by the statute itself; or the statute itself embraces some class of cases which a logical adherence to its reason would determine its author to exclude from it.

But, in pursuance of a power which often is exercised by judges, (and, where they are subordinate to the State, with its express or tacit authority,) the judge who finds that a statute is thus defective or excessive, usually fills the chasm, or cuts away the excrescence. In order to the accomplishment of the end for which the statute was established, the judge completes or corrects the faulty or exorbitant intention with which it actually was made. He enlarges the defective, or reduces the excessive statute, and adjusts it to the reach of its ground. For he applies it to a case of a class which it surely does not embrace, but to which its reason or scope should have made the lawgiver extend it; or he withholds it from a case of a class which it embraces indisputably, but which its reason or scope should have made the lawgiver exclude from it. His adjustment of the statute to the reach or extent of its ground is a palpable act of judicial legislation, and is not interpretation or construction (in the proper acceptation of the term).

I by no means disapprove of what Mr. Bentham has chosen to call by the disrespectful, and therefore, as I conceive, injudicious, name of judge-made law. I cannot understand how any person who has considered the subject can suppose that society could possibly have gone on if judges had not legislated, or that there is any danger whatever in allowing them that power which they have in fact exercised, to make up for the negligence or the incapacity of the avowed legislator.

Being a *command*, every law properly so called flows from a *determinate* source, or emanates from a determinate author. In other words, the author from whom it proceeds is a determinate rational being, or a determinate body or aggregate of rational beings. Every *sanction* properly so called is an eventual evil annexed to a command. Any eventual evil may operate as a motive to conduct; but, unless the conduct be commanded and the evil be annexed to the command purposely to enforce obedience, the evil is not a *sanction* in the proper acceptation of the term. Every *duty* properly so called supposes a *command* by which it is created. For every sanction properly so called is an eventual evil annexed to a command. And duty properly so called is obnoxiousness to evils of the kind.

Now it follows from these premises that the laws of God, and positive laws, are laws proper, or laws properly so called.

The laws of God are laws proper, inasmuch as they are *commands*, express or tacit, and therefore emanate from a *certain* source.

Positive law, or law strictly so called, is a direct or circuitous command of a monarch or sovereign number to a person or persons in a state of subjection to its author. And being a command (and therefore flowing from a determinate source), every positive law is a law proper, or a law properly so called.

The sanctions annexed to the laws of God may be styled *religious*. The sanctions annexed to positive laws, may be styled *legal*. The duties imposed by the laws of God may be styled *religious*. The duties imposed by positive laws may be styled *legal*.

The existence of law is one thing; its merit or demerit is another. Whether it be or be not is one enquiry; whether it be or not be comfortable to an assumed standard is a different enquiry. A law which actually exists is a law, though we happen to dislike it. This truth, when formally announced as an abstract proposition, is so simple and glaring that it seems idle to insist upon it. Yet the enumeration of the instances in which it has been forgotten would fill a volume.

Sir William Blackstone, for example, says in his "Commentaries" that the laws of God are superior in obligation to all other laws; that no human laws should be suffered to contradict them; that human laws are of no validity if contrary to them; and that all valid laws derive their force from that Divine original.

Now he *may* mean that all human laws ought to conform to the Divine laws. If this be his meaning, I assent to it without hesitation. The evils which we are exposed to suffer from the hands of God as a consequence of disobeying His commands are the greatest evils to which we are obnoxious; and if human commands conflict with the Divine law, we ought to disobey the command which is enforced by the less powerful sanction; this is implied in the term *ought*; it is our interest to choose the smaller and more uncertain evil, in preference to the greater and surer. If this be Blackstone's meaning, I assent to his proposition, and have only to object to it that it tells us just nothing.

But the meaning of this passage of Blackstone, if it has a meaning, seems rather to be this: that no human law which *conflicts* with the Divine law is obligatory or binding; in other words, that no human law which conflicts with the Divine law *is a law*, for a law without an obligation is a contradiction in terms.

Now, to say that human laws which conflict with the Divine law are not binding, that is to say, are not laws, is to talk stark nonsense. The most pernicious laws, and therefore those which are most opposed to the will of God, have been and are continually enforced as laws by judicial tribunals.

Suppose an act innocuous, or positively beneficial, be prohibited by the sovereign under the penalty of death; if I commit this act, I shall be tried and condemned, and if I object to the sentence that it is contrary to the law of God, the Court of Justice will demonstrate the inconclusiveness of my reasoning by hanging me up. An exception, demurrer, or plea, founded on the law of God was never heard in a Court of Justice, from the creation of the world down to this present moment.

Figure 2. JOHN AUSTIN

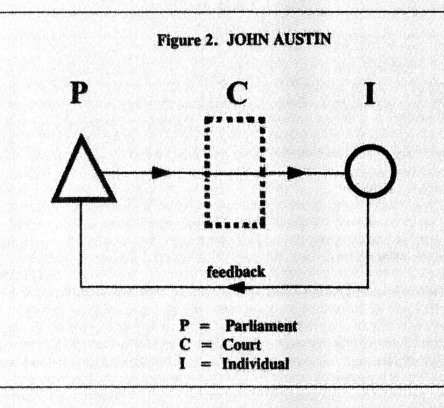

P = Parliament
C = Court
I = Individual

QUESTIONS AND COMMENTS FOR YOUR CONSIDERATION

1. A diagram of John Austin's theory of law would very closely resemble Bentham's (see Figure 2). The only difference is that the dots around *C* have been replaced by dashes. This indicates that Austin approved of courts altering the legislative message before applying it to litigants. Austin had more faith in courts than Bentham had; he was willing to allow judges a degree of latitude in interpreting and even modifying the legislative message, as you have seen from passages in the above reading where Austin referred to *judicial legislation*.

While this seems like only a minor *jurisprudential* difference between Bentham and Austin, it was a major *political* difference in their philosophies. Jeremy Bentham died in the year that John Austin published in his major book (1832). It is possible that the two men may have had some contact in the last years of Bentham's life, if only indirectly through Austin's students. But it is clear that the political differences between them were so great that Bentham surely would have repudiated Austin's version of positivism. Students who were fans of Bentham's writings were initially attracted to Austin, who seemed to be following up on Bentham's theories of law.

But these students began abandoning Austin's classes when they found that Austin repudiated Bentham's most important goal—to minimize the power of judges. Bentham indeed had embraced positivism because of its usefulness as a theory for downplaying—to the vanishing point if possible—the role of courts. He would have felt frontally challenged by another positivist who was willing to give courts a degree of legislative freedom. For Bentham, this would be like allowing the camel's nose under the tent; the whole structure could collapse in short order.

2. In discussing a legal system, we can make good use of the Positivist conception that the legislature issues commands (to courts, to us) without normally adverting to the question of the constitutionality of the commands themselves. All we need in order to make sense of the notion of command is a commander and a subordinate. For instance, a captain may issue a command to a lieutenant, and normally the lieutenant simply follows the command without adverting to the question whether the captain is authorized to issue it. Only in rare cases might the lieutenant have some reason to believe that the captain's command itself violates the higher command of a major or a general and therefore might be invalid.

But in jurisprudence, especially decades ago, legal philosophers often turned to the question: who is the highest commander? They referred to this as the problem of "sovereignty." If you read Austin's works, you will find that he devotes more space to the conception of sovereignty than to anything else. In this Anthology we are only giving a passing mention to this extensive part of Austin's jurisprudence because Austin's own elaborate discussion of sovereignty seems to have boiled down to a self-refuting argument! (This is no major indictment against Austin, because he was the first positivist thinker to pursue the notion of sovereignty to the limit of its logic.)

Let us briefly consider Austin's reasoning on the vexed question of sovereignty. He starts by insisting that a commander must be a determinate person or persons, rightfully disdaining the view that vague concepts, like "the public" or "the general will" can issue commands.[5] So far so good.

Austin's next step is to posit that in any state there must be an uncommanded commander. He believes that there must be some definable, determinate person or persons who commands others but is not *legally* subject to anyone else's commands. That determinate person or persons is the "sovereign."

But then Austin comes up against a hard case. What about the United States of America? Who is the "sovereign" of the United States in Austin's sense of that term? Austin does not take the easy way out, which would be to say that the United States Constitution is the "sovereign." The Constitution is, after all, words on parchment, and not a determinate person or persons capable of issuing commands. So who is the sovereign in the United States? See if you can figure out the answer before looking at the following comment.

3. Austin managed to locate the uncommanded commander in the United

---

[5] Rousseau's elaborate SOCIAL CONTRACT was an ingenious (but vague) attempt to have the "general will" in a state actually issue commands.

States, but in so doing he may have refuted his own argument about sovereignty. The self-refutation is not a logical one, because, as you will see if you haven't already thought of the answer, Austin was consistent and precise in his logic. His "United States Sovereign" clearly fits his own definition of a sovereign. Yet he refuted his own argument in a practical sense: once he "located" this elusive sovereign, a reader can tell at a glance that there must be something gravely wrong with Austin's entire conception of "sovereignty" if it leads to finding this particular sovereign.

Austin's United States Sovereign is none other then the person or persons who have the power to *amend* the Constitution. The power of amendment is legally unrestrained.[6] Thus, the "amenders" of the United States Constitution are, in Austin's theory, the uncommanded commanders—the sovereign.

Who are these sovereign persons? We look at Article V of the Constitution, which sets forth the amendment procedure. We note that an amendment can be "proposed" in two different ways. But surely the mere proposers of an amendment are not the sovereign that Austin was looking for. Austin regarded the true sovereign as those persons who can *ratify* or *not ratify* a proposed amendment. Thus, the United States Sovereign consists of the "ratifiers"! Who are these persons? Article V provides that a constitutional amendment may be ratified by

> the legislatures of three-fourths of the several states, or by conventions in three fourths thereof, as the one or other mode of ratification may be proposed by the Congress.

So now we are getting close to finding the sovereign. It turns out that the sovereign can be one of two different groups of people. Group (a) is "the legislatures of three-fourths of the several states." But obviously we don't need to count all the individual legislators who make up the legislatures of those states; we need only to count the majority of legislators in each of those legislatures, since the majority can pass upon the proposed Constitutional amendment. So one of the two "sovereigns" turns out to be: *the majority of legislators who are serving in three-fourths of the legislatures of the states.* As for group (b), similar reasoning locates the "sovereign" as *the majority of persons voting at amendment-ratification conventions in three fourths of the several states.*

Group A

Group B

Can you name any significant number of the actual persons in either group (a) or group (b)? Are these the real people who are running the United States, the "uncommanded commanders"? Or did Austin manage to end up with a practical refutation of his own intricate demonstration about sovereignty?

4. If Bentham would not have liked Austin's version of positivism, he would

---

[6]Actually, the United States Constitution places two minor restrictions on the amendment power. This gives rise to a paradox known to many legal systems: an apparent disability to amend a constitution on a statue that is written in to the constitution of statute. The notion behind these self-limitations is analogous to the ancient military practice known as "burning one's bridges." A military commander would often issue orders to his army to burn the bridges behind them, thus cutting off any possible retreat. The result would be that the army, with no escape possible, would fight to the death. This was often a highly productive (though brutal) policy; soldiers with *that* amount of incentive often won the war.

Theoretically, it would be possible for the army to repair the bridges that they had burned (though usually not in the heat of battle). Is there an analogous strategy for dealing with an unwanted Constitutional restriction on the amendment power?

have positively hated the version contributed by the American law professor John Chipman Gray. Gray's theory of jurisprudence, contained in his book, *The Nature and Sources of the Law* (1909), took Austin's tentative steps toward investing courts with a lawmaking function, and pushed the idea to its extreme. While Gray is squarely within the positivist tradition because he believes that law is a legislative command, he takes the extreme position that *judges* are the legislators!

5. Gray's guiding principle was Bishop Hoadly's remark, "Nay, whoever hath an absolute authority to interpret any written or spoken laws it is he who is the lawgiver to all intents and purposes and not the person who first wrote or spake them." Gray argued that a statute is a source of the law, similar to other sources a judge might consult before deciding a case. Although Gray conceded that there are "undoubtedly" limits upon a court's power of interpretation, "these limits are almost as undefined as those which govern [courts] in their dealing with the other sources".

Gray's view of law may be depicted as shown in Figure 3. In this diagram, the solid box around the Court indicates that the court is, for all intents and purposes, a "black box." To be sure, the court hears the legislative message. But then the court has the discretion to *transform* the legislative message. An observer cannot predict with any reasonable degree of certainty what the legislative message will look like when it comes out of the court. In effect, what Gray is saying is that Parliament *delegates* the legislative function to the courts. Thus, although a statute may indicate what the legislature wants in the way of a command, it is the court that actually legislates. It is the court that tells the litigants—and through them, the public—what the statute means. The way the court has "construed" the statute becomes more important than the statute's own language. (Indeed, one might say that it is consistent with Gray's philosophy to assume that a legislature's statute in some sense does not exist until a court actually construes it.)

6. John Chipman Gray, in effect, goes back to the very common law system that Bentham excoriated. What Bentham disliked most about common law was freewheeling judicial legislation. With Gray, we have come full circle back to the freewheeling judicial legislation that Bentham invoked the theory of positivism to destroy. One might quarrel that Gray is really a positivist. From Bentham's point of view, Gray is an anti-positivist. Yet Gray accepts the central tenet of Hobbes that law is a command. In this critical aspect, therefore, Gray is indeed a positivist.

7. Let us test Gray's model against an everyday statute. Suppose that the legislature in a state changes the maximum vehicle speed on highways from 70 mph to 60 mph. Can it realistically be said that this is not a "law" until a driver gets arrested for driving in excess of 60 mph and a judge applies the statute to him in a courtroom and convicts him of a misdemeanor?

Surely we cannot say that no "law" exists until a judge interprets it, because we can well imagine the new law operating to "slow down" many drivers on the highway. For them the law is quite real. Indeed, in the extreme case, we could imagine a state whose citizens comply so fully with the law that no one drives over 60 mph and hence no one is arrested for speeding. We could not fairly conclude from the fact that no one breaks the law (and that therefore no judge gets an opportunity to construe the statute) that there is no law.

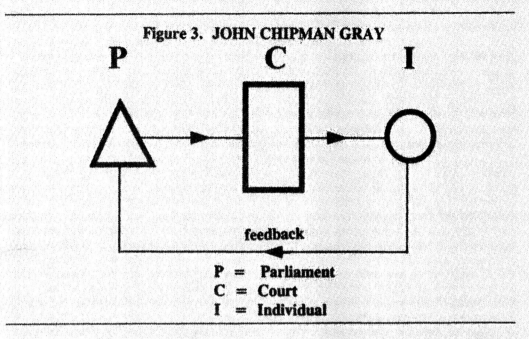

Figure 3. JOHN CHIPMAN GRAY

P = Parliament
C = Court
I = Individual

8. Isn't Gray correct in one respect: judge-made law is truly law for the litigant before the court? Suppose a driver is arrested for driving at 65 mph, and he explains to the judge in traffic court—quite accurately—that drivers routinely assume that they have a bit of a margin to drive over the speed limit without being arrested. If the judge says, "That may be true, but since you drove over 60 miles per hour, you're guilty no matter what the other drivers think." The "law" that has been applied to this driver may thus be stricter than the operative law that drivers assume applies to them. Yet traffic court decisions are not widely publicized, and it is safe to assume that other drivers will continue to interpret the 60 mph speed limit sign in a more liberal fashion. Indeed, some other traffic court judge might acquit a driver who was only driving five miles per hour above the speed limit (and might even lecture the arresting officer not to be so rigid in interpreting highway rules).

9. Although Gray vividly reminds us that statutes have a degree of uncertainty, positivist theory might reply that all rules that look to the future are inherently uncertain. A statutory rule looks to the future in its attempt to shape and channel human conduct to conform to its prescriptions. A court's judgment, in contrast, is backward-looking. The court "applies" a rule to an event that occurred prior to the court's decision. Therefore, as far as the litigant is concerned, the court's decision can have no effect upon shaping or channeling her behavior. Her behavior regarding the event that led to the case occurred in the past, and the only thing a court can do now is possibly to attach a penalty to that behavior.

Thus is it not absurd to deny to future-oriented rules the title "law," since those rules shape most of the behavior in a society? Gray's model must be rejected as incomplete. His theory over the years has certainly not attracted notable adherents. Yet it is an interesting theory. It reminds us that the difficulty positivists have of explaining a court's role led at least one positivist to try for an "explanation" that would replace the legislature with judges who legislate. Perhaps Gray's has its best use as a straightforward critique of legislative supremacy. Perhaps Gray's theory tells us that Bentham's invocation of Hobbes' idea that law is a command was not philosophically sufficient to accomplish Bentham's real aim—to elevate the role of Parliament and to downgrade the role of courts.

10. Is the *sine qua non* of legislation its generality? Is the following statement enlightening or superficial: "Statutes must be general in applicability; if they are so specific as to name persons, then they are void as bills of attainder. Decisions of courts are the opposite. They must be specific in applicability; they must apply to a particular person or persons"?

11. If legislation must be general, does the "command" theory really capture its essence? Don't we normally think of commands as being addressed to particular persons?

12. Can a statute be so general as to be useless? Consider a statute that says "Behave in an orderly fashion." Is this vacuous? Useless? Or just highly indeterminate?

13. Is there a way for a legislature to control the population generally and specifically at the same time? Consider the two-way television set in George Orwell's novel, 1984. At the beginning of the novel, Winston Smith is performing his health exercises in front of his television when suddenly the woman demonstrating the exercises points her finger at the camera and by name instructs Smith to bend lower and try harder. Her instruction to him is an example of a totally specific legislative rule. Orwell has captured an important characteristic of legislation—that it represents the voice of the few commanding the many. What is the problem with Orwell's illustration? Think about this before looking at the next question.

14. Addressing the problem raised in the previous question, I wrote:[7]

> What is lacking in Orwell's image is how the situation would bog down in practice. If five million citizens are all dutifully doing their morning exercises, the instructor would have to have five million TV monitors in her studio to be able to single out those who like Winston Smith were not performing adequately. Once her attention is given to Smith, several hundred thousand other disgruntled exercisers would begin a mild form of civil disobedience—taking a break while Winston is being verbally disciplined. Then presumably the instructor would start screaming at them one by one, to the eventual breakdown of the entire program. An obvious but enormously expensive way to cure the problem would be to have five million legislator-instructors at the studio each watching a single TV monitor so that a one-to-one observational situation may be maintained. But who would guard so many guardians?

15. Two decades after the death of John Austin, his successor was born in Prague, Czechoslovakia. Hans Kelsen became the greatest legal positivist of the twentieth century. Kelsen began teaching public law and jurisprudence at the University of Vienna in 1911, then at the University of Cologne from 1930 to 1933, and at the University of Geneva from 1933 to 1940. He emigrated to the United States and served as a lecturer at Harvard Law School in 1940, at the urging of Professor Lon L. Fuller. The Harvard faculty declined to extend Kelsen a permanent offer, and so he left in 1941 to join the faculty of the University of California School of Law at Berkeley. One may wonder why Harvard Law School let Kelsen go. His lasting reputation today exceeds the combined fame of the entire Harvard Law

---

[7] Anthony D'Amato, *Legal Uncertainty*, 71 CAL. L. REV. 1, 39 n.78 (1983).

faculty of 1940, with the possible exception of its most illustrious member Lon L. Fuller. In fact, Professor Fuller was not valued at the time for his jurisprudence; his colleagues simply regarded him as a good teacher of contracts. In those days of rampant legal realism, law professors tended to sneer at philosophers of law. Even when I was a student at Harvard Law School, in the late 1950s, the atmosphere was still laden with off-putting remarks like "that's a philosophical argument, not a *legal* argument," or "real lawyers argue about legal interests, jurisprudential lawyers argue about how many angels can dance on the head of a pin." (As a natural-born dissenter, these remarks encouraged me to read more legal philosophy.)

16. What *is* the role of large theories in the solution of particular legal problems? One reason the legal realists sneered at "philosophical" arguments was not that they were opposed to philosophy, but rather that they believed cases were decided on *particular* contested facts and *specific detailed* legal rules. They simply did not see the *relevance* of broad legal theories (such as "positivism" or "natural law") in the solution of concrete cases.

The legal realists on the Harvard faculty when I was a student there have their disciples on many law faculties today. Are they right about the irrelevance of large jurisprudential theories to the solution of particular cases?

Consider, in this connection, the "Case of the Speluncean Explorers." Was there any dispute whatsoever about the facts of the case? Was there any dispute whatsoever about the content of N.C.S.A (N.S.) §12-A of The Consolidated Laws of Newgarth? Was there any dispute whatsoever that this statute, and this statute alone, was the controlling statute in the case? Was there any dispute whatsoever that the cases cited by the individual judges were in fact legally authoritative and binding precedents? If your answer to all of these questions is "no," then what force is there in the legal realists' contention that cases are decided on the specifics of their facts and applicable rules? Should we not say, instead, that for each individual judge, as well as for the Supreme Court of Newgarth as a whole, that the Speluncean Explorers' Case was decided according to the jurisprudential theories of the judges?

17. To be sure, one might argue that the Speluncean Explorers' Case is (a) fictional, and (b) not representative of most litigation. Surely one must concede, at the very least, that most judges in most cases do not make their jurisprudential orientations explicit in their written opinions. Moreover, some judges may not have a very clear idea of their own jurisprudential orientation! Yet, is this the same as saying that these large jurisprudential orientations don't count? Do we have any way to show or prove that (apart from the explicitness of the opinions) the average case is *so different* from the Speluncean Explorers' Case that jurisprudential orientations and motivations are inapplicable? Even if we think so, can we be sure?

18. The question whether "large" issues or "small, concrete" ones drive particular cases is analogous to a question that comes up in scientific research all the time. In a recent book on Darwinian evolution theory, Daniel Dennett raises the question whether we can perceive and understand evolutionary development if we focus too much on the micro-details of causation within the genetic structure of any given organism. He says that good science is "an invitation to cut through

the Gordian knot of tangled causation with an abstract formulation that is predictive precisely *because* it ignores all those complications."[8] He adds: "It is the glory of science that it can find the patterns in spite of the noise."

Do you agree? Wouldn't the legal realist reply: "Fine, but how can we tell what is noise and what is data?"

Is it sufficient to reply: "We do it all the time. It's what we call 'living.' It is the only way we can make sense out of the world."

Or is a better answer to the legal realist the following: "No one can ever tell definitively the difference between noise and data. Physicists prior to Einstein regarded the slight deviation of their astronomical observations from Newton's theory of gravitation as 'noise' or 'measurement error.' Einstein reinterpreted this 'noise' and constructed it into a general Theory of Relativity that made sense out of the noise, reinterpreted it as data and thus removed it as measurement error, and in the end dethroned Newton's theory of gravitation. This and many similar examples in the history of science caution us to be forever *tentative* about the distinctions we draw between noise and data. We may have to draw these distinctions to get along—to make sense out of the world as we live our daily lives—but we should always regard the distinctions as *heuristics*—heuristics that can be reinterpreted as soon as we have a good reason to do so."

Finally, isn't this latter statement just another way of describing the process of the common law?

---

[8] DANIEL C. DENNETT, DARWIN'S DANGEROUS IDEA: EVOLUTION AND THE MEANINGS OF LIFE 358 (1995).

3. Hans Kelsen: The Pure Theory of Law[9]

Law is a social technique which consists in bringing about the desired social conduct of men through the threat of a measure of coercion which is to be applied in case of contrary conduct. The law is a coercive order.

The element of "coercion" which is essential to law consists in the fact that specific acts of coercion, as sanctions, are provided for in specific cases by the rules which form the legal order. Whether or not men do actually behave in a manner to avoid the sanction threatened by the legal norm, and whether or not the sanction is actually carried out in case its conditions are fulfilled, are issues concerning the efficacy of the law. But it is

not the efficacy, it is the validity of the law which is in question here.

What is the nature of the validity, as distinguished from the efficacy of law? The difference may be illustrated by an example: A legal rule forbids theft, prescribing that every thief must be punished by the judge. This rule is "valid" for all people, to whom theft is thereby forbidden, the individuals who have to obey the rule, the "subjects." The legal rule is "valid" particularly for those who actually steal and in so doing "violate" the rule. That is to say, the legal rule is valid even in those cases where it lacks "efficacy." It is precisely in those cases that it has to be "applied" by the judge.

By "validity" we mean the specific existence of norms. To say that a norm is valid, is to assume that it has "binding force" for those whose behavior it regulates. Rules of law, if valid, are norms. They are, to be more precise, norms stipulating sanctions. But what is a norm?

Let us provisionally assume that a norm is a command. This is how Austin character-

---

[9] HANS KELSEN, THE PURE THEORY OF LAW (1924; Max Knight, tr. 1967); excerpts also taken from HANS KELSEN, GENERAL THEORY OF LAW AND STATE (1945).

izes law. A command is the expression of an individual's will (or wish) the object of which is another individual's behavior. But not every command is a valid norm. A command is a norm only if it is binding upon the individual to whom it is directed, only if this individual ought to do what the command requires. Whether or not a command is binding depends upon whether or not the individual commanding is "authorized" to issue that command. Austin identifies the two concepts "command" and "binding command." But that is incorrect, since not every command issued by somebody superior in power is of a binding nature. The command of a bandit to deliver my cash is not binding, even if the bandit actually is able to enforce his will. To repeat: A command is binding, not because the individual commanding has an actual superiority in power, but because he is "authorized" or "empowered" to issue commands of a binding nature. And he is "authorized" or "empowered" only if a normative order, which is presupposed to be binding, confers on him this capacity, the competence to issue binding commands. The binding force of a command is not "derived" from the command itself but from the conditions under which the command is being issued. Supposing that the rules of law are binding commands, it is clear that binding force resides in those commands because they are issued by competent authorities.

Austin draws an explicit distinction between "laws" and "particular commands." But law does not consist of general norms only. Law includes individual norms, i.e. norms which determine the behavior of one individual in one non-recurring situation and which therefore are valid only for one particular case and may be obeyed or applied only once. Such norms are "law" because they are parts of the legal order as a whole in exactly the same sense as those general norms on the basis of which they have been created. Examples of such particular norms are the decisions of courts as far as their binding force is limited to the particular case at hand. Suppose that a judge orders a debtor A to return $1000 to his creditor B. The decision of the judge is a legal norm in the same sense and for the same reasons as the general principle that if somebody does not return a loan then a civil sanction ought to be inflicted upon him on the motion of the creditor.

General legal norms always have the form of hypothetical statements. The sanction stipulated by the norm is stipulated under certain conditions. The court decision just mentioned provides an example. The civil sanction is stipulated on the condition that the defendant does not observe the conduct prescribed by the court.

A legal norm does not refer to the behavior of one individual only, but to the behavior of two individuals at least: the individual who commits or may commit the delict [the prohibited act], and the individual who ought to execute the sanction. The legal norm is split into two separate norms, two "ought" statements: one to the effect that a certain individual "ought" to observe certain conduct, and one to the effect that another individual ought to execute a sanction in case the first norm is violated. An example: One shall not steal; if somebody steals, he shall be punished. If it is assumed that the first norm which forbids theft is valid only if the second norm attaches a sanction to theft, then the first norm is certainly superfluous in an exact exposition of law. If at all existent, the first norm is contained in the second, which is the only genuine legal norm.

QUESTIONS AND COMMENTS FOR YOUR CONSIDERATION

1. Has Kelsen taken positivism to the extreme of its logic? Consider the diagram in Figure 4. In this diagram, the individual is left out in the cold, to fend for herself. The legislature is not "commanding" her to do anything. The legislature is only "talking" to courts, police officers, and other administrative and enforcement officials. What the legislature is telling these officials is how they should behave if they see an individual doing something (or failing to do something). To put it crudely, the legislature is telling all these government officials something like: "if you see anyone stealing anything, arrest that person, prosecute her, sentence

Figure 4. HANS KELSEN

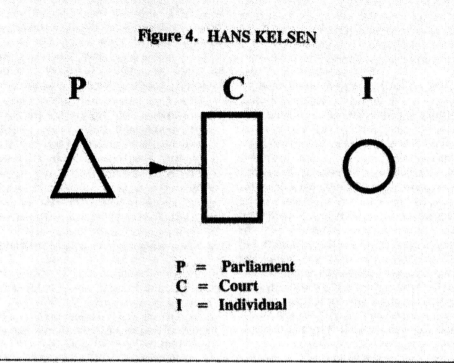

P = Parliament
C = Court
I = Individual

her, and send her to prison for a term of one to five years, the exact amount of the sentence to be determined by you in your discretion." And that is all there is to the legal system! It has been reduced to one "genuine norm," in Kelsen's terms: a norm prescribing a sanction for a certain specified behavior.

If this seems fanciful, look at any modern penal code and see if it doesn't bear out Kelsen's theory. For example, Chapter 38 of the Illinois Revised Statutes has the following provisions regarding theft:

§16-1. Theft.
  (a) A person commits theft when he knowingly:
    (1) Obtains or exerts unauthorized control over property of the owner; or
    (2) Obtains by deception control over property of the owner; or
    (3) Obtains control over stolen property knowing the property to have been stolen or under such circumstances as would reasonably induce him to believe that the property was stolen; and
      (A) Intends to deprive the owner permanently of the use or benefit of the property; or
      (B) Knowingly uses, conceals or abandons the property in such manner as to deprive the owner permanently of such use or benefit; or
      (C) Uses, conceals, or abandons the property knowing such use, concealment, or abandonment probably will deprive the owner permanently of such use or benefit; or
    (5) Obtains or exerts control over property in the custody of any law enforcement agency which is explicitly represented to him by any law enforcement officer or any individual acting in behalf of a law enforcement agency as being stolen.
  (b) Sentence.
    (1) Theft of property, other than a firearm, not from the person and not exceeding $300 in value is a Class A misdemeanor. . .
    (4) Theft of property from the person not exceeding $300 in value, or theft of property exceeding $300 and not exceeding $10,000 in value, is a Class 3 felony. . .

§1005-8-1. Sentences of Imprisonment for Felony.
   (a) Except as otherwise provided in the statute defining the offense, a sentence of imprisonment for a felony shall be a determinate sentence set by the court under this Section, according to the following limitations:
      (6) for a Class 3 felony, the sentence shall be not less than 2 years and not more than 5 years;

This portion of the Illinois penal code is clearly not addressed to the average citizen. Instead, it reads as if it is a set of instructions to judges and police officers. As statutes grow in complexity in our modern age, Kelsen's theory seems to be increasingly vindicated. In the United States today, there probably isn't one taxpayer out of a hundred thousand (other than lawyers, accountants, or judges) who actually reads any provision of the Internal Revenue Code. And if the taxpayer *tried* to read the tax code, it would probably seem incomprehensible. The Internal Revenue Code seems deliberately to be written only for lawyers, accountants, Internal Revenue agents, and judges.

2. Hans Kelsen was born in Prague in 1881; Franz Kafka was born in Prague in 1883. In 1914, when Kelsen was thinking about the meaning of law leading up to his publication of *The Pure Theory of Law* in 1924, Franz Kafka started writing *The Trial*, which was eventually published in 1925, a year after Kafka's death. Kelsen taught law at the University of Prague; Kafka studied law at that university. Is it possible that Kafka studied law under Kelsen? I hope someone can find out and let me know.

The reason this question is so interesting to me is that in an important sense Kafka's *The Trial* is a novelization of precisely the picture that Kelsen paints of the citizen "out in the cold" who wants to discover what the what the law is. In Kafka's novel, Josef K tries to discover what the charges (if any) are against him. No other book that I know of can be so funny, absurd, startling, and nightmarish to a law student than *The Trial!* If you've spent hours in the library or surfing on the computer network to find a case or a statute in point, and later that night have a nightmare about your search, you will discover in *The Trial* Josef K's nightmare in real life. Joseph K physically tries to discover the law in a world of weird courtrooms, offices, closets, and doors that are the side-splitting analogues of a long library search or a computer retrieval.

I've said that *The Trial* is very funny. Most "serious" literary critics would vehemently disagree. Kafka is generally reputed as a neurotic, introspective, pre-existentialist Freudian modernist author. But these critics may not understand law; they may not understand positivism; they may not understand Kelsen; and they may not grok outrageous humor when they encounter it. Few people know that Kafka used to invite a small circle of friends to his home in the evening and read to them what he had written that day. After nearly every sentence, they laughed at the outrageousness of the humor. These were immensely joyous gatherings–quite unlike the dreary portrait that many biographers have painted of Franz Kafka.

All of this is almost like asking: "What happens if you take positivism to the absolute, inevitable limit of its logic?" Answer: "You laugh."

What about Kelsen (who, for all I know, may have been Kafka's *teacher*)? I confess that I have found nothing humorous in all of his voluminous writings. They are almost *too* dry. However, a few years ago, I buttonholed one, and then another, of Kelsen's former students (now law professors). I asked them what sort of a person Kelsen was. They told me: "One of the most lively, fun-loving, boisterous people you'll ever meet. Full of jokes. And his classes were an unforgettable delight."

3.   Does Kelsen's theory that law comes to us in the form of a conditional statement ("if you choose to do X, you will be sanctioned") truly capture the intent and spirit of modern legislation? If so, there are at least five important implications of his theory that should be considered:

(a) An enormous new private industry, which we could call the "translating industry," has arisen. Its job is to translate the legislative message to the average citizen so that the citizen can be informed about the content of the law. This translating industry includes lawyers, accountants, writers of books with titles like "Your Federal Income Tax Simplified" and "Estate Planning Self-Taught," makers of software packages like Turbo Tax, government agencies that print legal forms like Form 1040 for paying your annual income tax, "legal" columnists and media persons, and so forth. The citizen invariably gets her legal information second-hand through these sources. There is nothing "guaranteed" about the accuracy of the translations.

Some government agencies even print a disavowal on the very forms they promulgate to the public, to the effect that "if anything on this form conflicts with the requirements of the law, you shall have no right to cite the form as a complete defense to your obligations under the law." In short, says the official government agency: if we've misled you, it's your problem. As far as a lawyer is concerned, her role in Kelsen's universe is to read the statutes and codes, figure out what the judges and police are likely to do when *they* read the same statutes and codes, and then advise her client about what the client *shouldn't* do in order to avoid the wrath of judges and police officers.

(b) Kelsen's theory would allow secret legislation. For example, during the Third Reich, a Gestapo agent might arrest a citizen for violating the law. When the citizen asked what he did to violate what law, the police officer replied "you violated Section 22, whose contents are an official secret." If you look at the diagram above, Kelsen's view of the law is complete when judges and other officials receive the message from the legislature. There is no requirement of promulgation of the message to the citizenry. (Even so, a "translating industry" could develop that would look at arrest patterns and attempt to *infer* the contents of Section 22.) Do you recall that Bentham's example of the Cadi who strangled the baker without saying a word and without invoking any legislation? Bentham said that executing the baker for giving short weight constituted the law. This example seems to indicate (though obviously Bentham didn't approve of it) that positivist theory allows for secret legislation.

(c) The *citizen* may become aware of the legislative message: "If you do X, you will be sanctioned," but what about the sanctioner? Is there *another* implicit message from the legislator to the sanctioner, saying "If you fail to punish the citizen who did X, then you yourself will be sanctioned." But then, who will sanction the sanctioner of the sanctioner? Doesn't Kelsen's theory recede backwards into an infinite regress? Or is Kelsen simply saying, "The government will act in ways to make sure that citizens are punished if they commit illegal acts, and it is unimportant *how* the government does this." But isn't it important whether under Kelsen's theory we can tell whether government officials are themselves acting legally? Suppose the punisher over-punishes, using "excessive force." Would the punisher then be acting illegally? Or is there no room in Kelsen's theory for "law" among government officials? Consider the following puzzling question: if the Gestapo officer is acting pursuant to a secret law, how could the public ever tell whether or not the Gestapo agent has used excessive force?

(d) The lack of a feedback loop in Kelsen's theory could mean one of three things. First, it could simply indicate that Kelsen's theory is more universal than those of Bentham and Austin: it applies to dictatorships and totalitarian regimes as well as democracies. Second, it could tell us something negative about positivism: that positivism is not necessarily a democratic theory, but rather has tendencies toward becoming totalitarian. Third, it could serve as a critique of Kelsen's theory of law: how can something be "law" at all if it is kept secret from the public?

(e) Kelsen's theory could be interpreted as a strong endorsement of libertarianism. The roots of libertarianism can be found in the free-market writings of Friedrich Hayek and other leading economists, which emphasize individual freedom of choice as a primary good. In accordance with the libertarian tradition, Kelsen seems to be saying: "the law doesn't command any individual member of society to do anything. The law simply presents people with a choice. The choice is: if you want to do *X*, then you're looking at a prison sentence of 2 to 5 years. If you believe, in the exercise of your individual autonomy, that doing *X* is *worth* spending 2 to 5 years in prison, then go ahead and do it." This is what Kelsen means when he says that "If it is assumed that the first norm which forbids theft is valid only if the second norm attaches a sanction to theft, then the first norm is certainly superfluous in an exact exposition of law. If at all existent, the first norm is contained in the second, which is the only genuine legal norm." The law, in short, comes to us in the form of a conditional statement: if you want to do *X*, then you can expect the state's officials to punish you for it in a certain prescribed way. And even this conditional statement of Kelsen's is not directly communicated to the public. Rather, the communication takes place entirely within the circle of government officials: from the legislature to judges and enforcement officials. We only *infer* conditional statements from these commands.

4. If Kelsen's theory of positivism is a *transformation* of *the* command theory of law as presented by Bentham and Austin—and if as a transformation it also serves as a critique of the Bentham-Austin view—the writings of H.L.A. Hart are more conspicuously designed as a critique of the command theory with the purpose of *refining* it rather than transforming it:

4. H.L.A. Hart: Positivism and the Separation of Law and Morals[10]

Austin's command theory, viewed as an effort to identify even the quintessence of law, let alone the quintessence of morals, seems breathtaking in its simplicity and quite inadequate. There is much, even in the simplest legal system, that is distorted if presented as a command—even if the notion of a command were supplemented by that of a habit of obedience. The simple scheme was this: What is a command? It is simply an expression by one person of the desire that another person should do or abstain from some action, accompanied by a threat of punishment which is likely to follow disobedience. Commands are laws if two conditions are satisfied: first, they must be general; second, they must be commanded by what (as both Bentham and Austin claimed) exists in every political society whatever its constitutional form, namely, a person or a group of persons who are in receipt of habitual obedience from most of the society but pay no such obedience to others. These persons are its sovereign. Thus law is the command of the uncommanded commanders of society—the creation of the legally untrammeled will of the sovereign who is by definition outside the law.

It is easy to see that this account of a legal system is threadbare. One can also see why it might seem that its inadequacy is due to the omission of some essential connection with morality. The situation which the simple trilogy of command, sanction, and sovereign avails to describe, if you take these notions at all precisely, is like that of a gunman saying to his victim, "Give me your money or your life." The only difference is that in the case of a legal system the gunman says it to a large number of people who are accustomed to the racket and habitually surrender to it. Law is surely not the gunman situation writ large, and legal order is surely not to be thus simply identified with compulsion.

This scheme, despite the points of obvious analogy between a statute and a command, omits some of the most characteristic elements of law. Let me cite a few. It is wrong to think of a legislature (and *a fortiorari* an electorate) with a changing membership, as a group of persons habitually obeyed: this simple idea is suited only to a monarch sufficiently long-lived for a "habit" to grow up. Even if we waive this point, nothing which legislators do makes law unless they comply with fundamental accepted rules specifying the essential lawmaking procedures. This is true even in a system having a simple unitary constitution like the British. These fundamental accepted rules specifying what the legislature must do to legislate are not commands habitually obeyed, nor can they be expressed as habits of obedience to persons. They lie at the root of a legal system.

[10] H.L.A. Hart, *Positivism and the Separation of Law and Morals*, 71 HARVARD LAW REVIEW 90 (1958). Copyright 1971 Harvard Law Review Association. Excerpts reprinted by permission.

QUESTIONS AND COMMENTS FOR YOUR CONSIDERATION

1. In his book, *The Concept of Law*, published three years after the above article in 1961, Professor Hart invented the term "rule of recognition" to apply to the aggregate of fundamental accepted rules specifying what the legislature must do to legislate. The "rule of recognition" for the United States, for example, is simply its Constitution. Clearly, Professor Hart has effectively criticized the deficiencies of the command theory of law. But what does he offer in his place? He offers a "rule of recognition" which the people of a state accept as the legitimizing, constitutional rules of the system. Thus, is he simply moving Austin's command theory to a higher, more abstract level? Is he saying that people habitually obey a set of constitutional rules? Is he saying that these constitutional rules are a form of "command"? Are they commands that issue not from real commanders but from an abstract conception called a constitution?

2. How intellectually satisfying is this aspect of Hart's version of positivism? As the twentieth century draws to a close, and as we look back on the enormous contributions of Hans Kelsen and H.L.A. Hart to positivist theory, should we conclude that positivism has had its day in court? Or should we conclude that much work needs to be done to improve and refine the positivist theory?

B. The Central Role of Language

Because of its insistence on the integrity of the legislative message, positivism seems preeminently a theory of language. The real output of the legislature is *words*. These words are critically important in positivist theory. H.L.A. Hart gave the following positivistic analysis of statutory language:

1. H.L.A. Hart: On Core and Penumbra[11]

Consider the following example. A legal rule forbids you to take a vehicle into the public park. Plainly this forbids an automobile, but what about bicycles, roller skates, toy automobiles? What about airplanes? Are these, as we say, to be called "vehicles" for the purpose of the rule or not? If we are to communicate with each other at all, and if, as in the most elementary form of law, we are to express our intentions that a certain type of behavior be regulated by rules, then the general words we use—like "vehicle" in the case I consider—must have some standard instance in which no doubts are felt about its application. There must be a core of settled meaning, but there will be, as well, a penumbra of debatable cases in which words are neither obviously applicable nor obviously ruled out. These cases will each have some features in common with the standard case; they will lack others or be accompanied by features not present in the standard case. Human invention and natural processes continually throw up such variants on the familiar, and if we are to say that these ranges of facts do or do not fall

under existing rules, then the classifier must make a decision which is not dictated to him, for the facts and phenomena to which we fit our words and apply our rules are as it were *dumb*. The toy automobile cannot speak up and say, "I am a vehicle for the purpose of this legal rule," nor can the roller skates chorus, "We are not a vehicle." Fact situations do not await us neatly labeled, creased, and folded, nor is their legal classification written on them to be simply read off by the judge. Instead, in applying legal rules, someone must take the responsibility of deciding that words do or do not cover some case in hand with all the practical consequences involved in this decision.

We may call the problems which arise outside the hard core of standard instances or settled meaning "problems of the penumbra"; they are always with us whether in relation to such trivial things as the regulation of the use of the public park or in relation to the multidimensional generalities of a constitution.

As to the cases which we did not, or perhaps could not, initially envisage (perhaps a toy motorcar electrically propelled) our aim is indeterminate. We have not settled, because we have not anticipated, the question which will be raised by the unenvisaged case when it occurs: whether some degree of peace in the park is to be sacrificed to, or defended against, those children whose pleasure or interest it is to use these things. When the unenvisaged case does arise, we confront the issues at stake and can then settle the question by choosing between the competing interests in the way which best satisfies us.

---

[11] H.L.A. Hart, *Positivism and the Separation of Law and Morals*, 71 Harvard Law Review 90 (1958). Copyright 1971 Harvard Law Review Association. Excerpts reprinted by permission.

H.L.A. Hart. The Concept of Law 124-26 (1961). Copyright Oxford University Press 1961. Excerpts reprinted by permission.

In so doing we shall have rendered more determinate our initial aim, and shall incidentally have settled a question as to the meaning, for the purposes of this rule, of a general word.

The discretion [that is left to the judge] by language may be very wide; so that if he applies the rule, the conclusion, even though it may not be arbitrary or irrational, is in effect a choice. He chooses to add to a line of cases a new case because of resemblances which can reasonably be defended as both legally relevant and sufficiently close.

Of course, it is good to be occupied with the penumbra. Its problems are rightly the daily diet of the law schools. But to be occupied with the penumbra is one thing, to be preoccupied with it is another.

Figure 5. H.L.A. HART

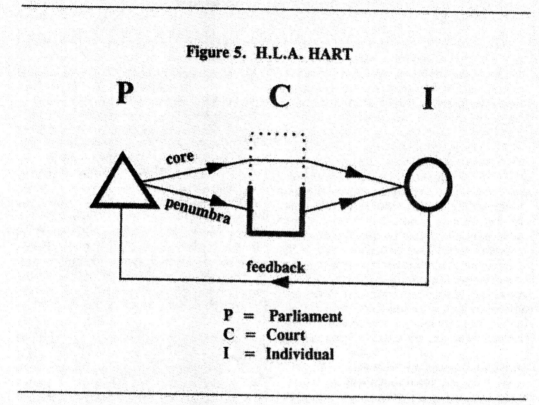

P = Parliament
C = Court
I = Individual

QUESTIONS AND COMMENTS FOR YOUR CONSIDERATION

1. In line with his positivist predecessors, we see that Hart considers the court's ability to transform the penumbral part of the message as authorized by delegation from the legislature. Or to put the point more precisely: when a legislature passes a statute, it is saying to the court "You are commanded to apply the core portion of this message intact, but you are delegated to be a mini-legislature with respect to the penumbral portion of this message."

2. Since Hart appears to view penumbral situations (situations that raise the question whether "vehicle" applies to toy cars, scooters, baby carriages) as applications that the legislature left "open," the judge has no choice but to legislate within the area of the penumbra. Inasmuch as the legislature itself had no intention with respect to these penumbral cases, we can assume that it was content

to leave it to the judge to fill in the penumbral blanks. If the legislature is at any time unhappy with a specific piece of judicial legislation within the penumbral area of one of its statutes, it can simply enact an amendment to the statute reversing the judge's decision (for example, by providing that "No vehicles, no bicycles allowed in the park; baby carriages are permitted.")

3. Consider a line of cases. Assume that the first judge is presented with a case where someone has taken a toy self-propelled automobile into the park. Whichever way the judge decides the case, she has in fact legislated within the penumbra. Now what happens when a different park official arrests a person in a different park (in the same jurisdiction) for attempting to take a toy automobile into the park? Another judge, hearing this second case, no longer has legislative discretion. Since the first judge has already "legislated" with respect to toy automobiles, the second judge must follow the ruling in the first case. And this is what positivists, following Hart, mean by judicial precedent and *stare decisis*.

A diagram of Hart's scheme would show the legislature's output (its statute) bifurcating into two components: a core and a penumbra. The core message must be applied by the court without modification. Thus, as to the core message, Hart's diagram looks the same as Bentham's. But the penumbral part of the legislative message—giving the first court to apply the penumbra the freedom to legislate—must look a lot like John Chipman Gray's diagram. So, in effect, Hart's diagram depicts the court as having a split personality—Bentham's and Gray's:

This diagram tells us that *if* a case falls within the core of the statute, the court must apply the statute directly to the case; and *if* a case falls within the penumbra of the statute, then the court has full discretion whether or not to apply the statute to the case. But who is supposed to determine *whether* a case falls within the court or the penumbra? Clearly the court must make this determination. But how can we tell, from the statute, whether the court has made the correct determination? Suppose, for example, that a person in the park has a heart attack (not a Hart attack) and someone calls for an ambulance. The ambulance pulls up to the gate of the park, sees the "No vehicles allowed" sign, and refuses to enter the park. The result is that the person dies, and his family brings a wrongful death action against the ambulance company. How should a court decide this case? Should the court say, "An ambulance is clearly a vehicle, and therefore, unless and until the legislature amends the statute, the ambulance driver made the correct decision. The ambulance company is not liable." Or could the court rule that an ambulance falls within the penumbra of the statute because the legislature clearly could not have intended to exclude ambulances? Hart's text, quoted above, has little to say that could be applicable to the ambulance case. As you recall, he dealt with the "unenvisaged case" of the toy motorcar by saying that the issue facing the judge is "whether some degree of peace in the park is to be sacrificed to, or defended against, those children whose pleasure or interest it is to use these things." But if "peace in the park" is the aim of the statute, as Hart assumes it is (without quite saying how he knows this), surely a speeding ambulance with sirens blaring will shatter the peace in the park.

Thus, we may be left with the uncomfortable position that the question whether an ambulance falls within the core or the penumbra of the statute is a question that can not be solved by looking at the statute that forbids vehicles in the park.

Within the positivist framework, anyone's guess is as good as anyone else's. To be sure, we can leave the ultimate resolution of this issue to the first judge who is presented with an actual case; *that* judge will legislate a solution so that forever afterwards (unless the legislature intervenes with an amended statute) the judge's decision will control whether an ambulance is or is not prohibited within the park. But perhaps leaving the initial determination to a judge is not good enough. If the first case involves a person who has just had a heart attack in the park, we may not want to leave it to the ambulance driver to *guess* what a judge will hold. Indeed, the ambulance driver (or the ambulance company) may be risk-averse. The ambulance company may instruct its drivers not to risk breaking the law even if a stranger's life is at stake.

4. What would Justice Foster say about such a case? Foster was not a positivist; hence, he would not be constrained by the positivist distinction between core and penumbra. Is it not quite likely that Foster would say something like, "Of course the ambulance should go into the park to save a human life. Any judge who would say otherwise, on the basis of the vehicles-are-prohibited statute, simply would be a judge who neither knows nor cares anything about real people in the real world." Indeed, might not Foster say that any judge who would "apply" the "core" of the statute to exclude the ambulance would resemble a computer more than a real person?

5. Is the following example fair?[12]

SCENE: A pleasant Sunday afternoon at the entrance to a public park. Professor H.L.A. Hart, with a book tucked under his arm, attempts to enter the park.

GUARD: Good afternoon, sir. May I ask what you have tucked under your arm.

HART: It's a book. As a matter of fact, it's my book, *The Concept of Law*.

GUARD: That's very nice, sir, but you know you cannot take that book into the park.

HART: And why not?

GUARD: You see the sign right there? It says, "No vehicles allowed in the park."

HART: Certainly. It is a valid ordinance.

GUARD: And you agree that I must go by the exact words of the statute?

HART: Of course I agree. But surely this book is not a vehicle.

GUARD: I beg to differ with you. I have become an expert in these matters, and I can assure you that the book is, in fact, a vehicle.

HART: But, look. One opens it up and one does not find a motor in it. Moreover, it does not consume petrol. It does not emit harsh noisy sounds. If I were to place it on the ground and stand on it, it would not transport me from here to there.

GUARD (*taking a notebook from his pocket*): Well, this is what I have copied from several dictionaries. It is a list of standard uses of the word "vehicle." One of the items on the list says that a book is a vehicle for ideas.

---

[12] Excerpted from Anthony D'Amato, *Can Legislatures Constrain Judicial Interpretations of Statutes?* 75 VIRGINIA LAW REVIEW 561, 596 n.93 (1989). Copyright 1989 Anthony D'Amato.

6. Was this a fair example to use against Hart's positivism? Is the ambulance case a fairer example? In the extreme, does positivism aspire to replace human decision-makers (guards at public parks, administrators, judges) with literal-minded automatons in order to achieve definitive clarity in the law? Is the ultimate goal of positivism to replace judicial decision-making by computerized decision-making?

7. Professor Fuller wrote a famous reply to Professor Hart. Fuller's critique of core and penumbra went beyond the objections given in the preceding questions. Fuller in fact constructed a Gödellian "undecidable"—a case that fits exactly Hart's example and yet cannot be decided within it. (The twentieth century's most important mathematical proof was Gödel's theorem of 1931—that within the apparently formalist deductive system of ordinary arithmetic there existed undecidable propositions—theorems whose truth or falsity could not be resolved within the axioms of the system.)

2. Lon Fuller: Hart's Core and Penumbra[13]

It is essential that we be just as clear as we can be about the meaning of Professor Hart's doctrine of "the core and the penumbra,"[14] because I believe the casual reader is likely to misinterpret what he has to say. Such a reader is apt to suppose that Professor Hart is merely describing something that is a matter of everyday experience for the lawyer, namely, that in the interpretation of legal rules it is typically the case (though not universally so) that there are some situations which will seem to fall rather clearly within the rule, while others will be more doubtful. Professor Hart's thesis takes no such jejune form. His extended discussion of the core and the penumbra is not just a complicated way of recognizing that some cases are hard, while others are easy. Instead, on the basis of a theory about language meaning generally, he is proposing a theory of judicial interpretation which is, I believe, wholly novel. Certainly it has never been put forward in so uncompromising a form before.

As I understand Professor Hart's thesis (if we add some tacit assumptions implied by it, as well as some qualifications he would no doubt wish his readers to supply) a full statement would run something as follows: The task of interpretation is commonly that of determining the meaning of the individual words of a legal rule, like "vehicle" in a rule excluding vehicles from a park. More particularly, the task of interpretation is to determine the range of reference of such a word, or the aggregate of things to which it points. Communication is possible only because words have a "standard instance," or a "core of meaning" that remains relatively constant, whatever the context in which the word may appear. Except in unusual circumstances, it will always be proper to regard a word like "vehicle" as embracing its "standard instance," that is, that aggregate of things it would include in all ordinary contexts, within or without the law. This meaning the word will have in any legal rule, whatever its purpose. In applying the word to its "standard instance," no creative role is assumed by the judge. He is simply applying the law "as it is."

In addition to a constant core, however, words also have a penumbra of meaning which, unlike the core, will vary from context to context. When the object in question (say, a tricycle) falls within this penumbral area, the judge is forced to assume a more creative role. He must now undertake, for the first time, an interpretation of the rule in the light of its purpose or aim. Having in mind what was sought by the regulation concerning parks, ought it to be considered as barring tricycles? When questions of this sort

---

[13] Lon L. Fuller, *Positivism and Fidelity to Law—A Reply to Professor Hart*, 71 HARVARD LAW REVIEW 593 (1958). Reprinted by permission of the Harvard Law Review Association.

[14] Hart, *Positivism and the Separation of Law and Morals*, 71 HARV. L. REV. 606-08 (1958).

are decided there is at least an "intersection" of "is" and "ought," since the judge, in deciding what the rule "is," does so in the light of his notions of what "it ought to be" in order to carry out its purpose.

If I have properly interpreted Professor Hart's theory as it affects the "hard core," then I think it is quite untenable. The most obvious defect of his theory lies in its assumption that problems of interpretation typically turn on the meaning of individual words. Surely no judge applying a rule of the common law ever followed any such procedure as that described (and, I take it, prescribed) by Professor Hart; indeed, we do not normally even think of his problem as being one of "interpretation." Even in the case of statutes, we commonly have to assign meaning, not to a single word, but to a sentence, a paragraph, or a whole page or more of text. Surely a paragraph does not have a "standard instance" that remains constant whatever the context in which it appears. If a statute seems to have a kind of "core meaning" that we can apply without a too precise inquiry into its exact purpose, this is because we can see that, however one might formulate the precise objective of the statute, *this* case would still come within it.

Even in situations where our interpretive difficulties seem to head up in a single word, Professor Hart's analysis seems to me to give no real account of what does or should happen. In his illustration of the "vehicle," although he tells us this word has a core of meaning that in all contexts defines unequivocally a range of objects embraced by it, he never tells us what these objects might be. If the rule excluding vehicles from parks seems easy to apply in some cases, I submit this is because we can see clearly enough what the rule "is aiming at in general" so that we know there is no need to worry about the difference between Fords and Cadillacs. If in some cases we seem to be able to apply the rule without asking what its purpose is, this is not because we can treat a directive arrangement as if it had no purpose. It is rather because, for example, whether the rule be intended to preserve quiet in the park, or to save carefree strollers from injury, we know, "without thinking," that a noisy automobile must be excluded.

What would Professor Hart say if some local patriots wanted to mount on a pedestal in the park a truck used in World War II, while other citizens, regarding the proposed memorial as an eyesore, support their stand by the "no vehicle" rule? Does this truck, in perfect working order, fall within the core or the penumbra?

Professor Hart seems to assert that unless words have "standard instances" that remain constant regardless of context, effective communication would break down and it would become impossible to construct a system of "rules which have authority." If in every context words took on a unique meaning, peculiar to that context, the whole process of interpretation would become so uncertain and subjective that the ideal of a rule of law would lose its meaning. In other words, Professor Hart seems to be saying that unless we are prepared to accept his analysis of interpretation, we must surrender all hope of giving an effective meaning to the ideal of fidelity to law. This presents a very dark prospect indeed, if one believes, as I do, that we cannot accept his theory of interpretation. I do not take so gloomy a view of the future of the ideal of fidelity to law.

An illustration will help to test, not only Professor Hart's theory of the core and the penumbra, but its relevance to the ideal of fidelity to law as well. Let us suppose that in leafing through the statutes, we come upon the following enactment: "It shall be a misdemeanor, punishable by a fine of five dollars, to sleep in any railway station." We have no trouble in perceiving the general nature of the target toward which this statute is aimed. Indeed, we are likely at once to call to mind the picture of a disheveled tramp, spread out in an ungainly fashion on one of the benches of the station, keeping weary passengers on their feet and filling their ears with raucous and alcoholic snores. This vision may fairly be said to represent the "obvious instance" contemplated by the statute, though certainly it is far from being the "standard instance" of the physiological state called "sleep."

Now let us see how this example bears on the ideal of fidelity to law. Suppose I am a judge, and that two men are brought before me for violating this statute. The first is a passenger who was waiting at 3 a.m. for a delayed train. When he was arrested he was sitting upright in an orderly fashion, but was heard by the arresting officer to be gently snoring. The second is a man who had brought a blanket and pillow to the station and had obviously settled himself down for the night. He was arrested, however, before he had a chance to go to sleep. Which of these cases presents the "standard instance" of the word "sleep"? If I disregard that question, and decide to fine the second man and set free the first, have I violated a duty of fidelity to law? Have I violated that duty if I interpret the word "sleep" as used in this statute to mean something like "to spread oneself out on a bench or floor to spend the night, or as if to spend the night"?

Testing another aspect of Professor Hart's theory, is it really ever possible to interpret a word in a statute without knowing the aim of the statute? Suppose we encounter the following incomplete sentence: "All improvements must be promptly reported to ... " Professor Hart's theory seems to assert that even if we have only this fragment before us we can safely construe the word "improvement" to apply to its "standard instance," though we would have to know the rest of the sentence before we could deal intelligently with "problems of the penumbra." Yet surely in the truncated sentence I have quoted, the word "improvement" is almost as devoid of meaning as the symbol "X."[15]

The word "improvement" will immediately take on meaning if we fill out the sentence with the words, "the head nurse," or, "the Town Planning Authority," though the two meanings that come to mind are radically dissimilar. It can hardly be said that these two meanings represent some kind of penumbral accretion to the word's "standard instance." And one wonders, parenthetically, how helpful the theory of the core and the penumbra would be in deciding whether, when the report is to be made to the planning authorities, the word "improvement" includes an unmortgageable monstrosity of a house that lowers the market value of the land on which it is built.

It will be instructive, I think, to consider the effect of other ways of filling out the sentence. Suppose we add to, "All improvements must be promptly reported to ..." the words, "the Dean of the Graduate Division." Here we no longer seem, as we once did, to be groping in the dark; rather, we seem now to be reaching into an empty box. We achieve a little better orientation if the final clause reads, "to the Principal of the School," and we feel completely at ease if it becomes, "to the Chairman of the Committee on Relations with the Parents of Children in the Primary Division."

It should be noted that in deciding what the word "improvement" means in all these cases, we do not proceed simply by placing the word in some general context, such as hospital practice, town planning, or education. If this were so, the "improvement" in the last instance might just as well be that of the teacher as that of the pupil. Rather, we ask ourselves, What can this rule be for? What evil does it seek to avert? What good is it intended to promote? When it is "the head nurse" who receives the report, we are apt to find ourselves asking, "Is there, perhaps, a shortage of hospital space, so that patients who improve sufficiently are sent home or are assigned to a ward where they will receive less attention?" If "Principal" offers more orientation than "Dean of the Graduate Division," this must be because we know something about the differences between primary education and education on the postgraduate university level. We must have some minimum acquaintance with the ways in which these two educational enterprises are conducted, and with the problems encountered in both of them, before any distinction between "Principal" and "Dean of the Graduate Division" would affect our interpretation of "improvement." We must, in other words, be sufficiently capable of putting ourselves in the position of those who drafted the rule to know what they thought "ought to be." It is in the light of this "ought" that we must decide what the rule "is."

Turning now to the phenomenon Professor Hart calls "preoccupation with the penumbra," we have to ask ourselves what is actually contributed to the process of interpretation by the common practice of supposing various "borderline" situations. Professor Hart seems to say, "Why, nothing at all, unless we are working with problems of the

---

[15] *Editor's Note:* Professor Fuller, who was so fond of anecdotes, might have enjoyed the following (with apologies to residents of the Garden State): "Flash! Hurricane Jezebel hit New Jersey last night, causing an estimated twenty million dollars worth of improvements."

penumbra." If this is what he means, I find his view a puzzling one, for it still leaves unexplained why, under his theory, if one is dealing with a penumbral problem, it could be useful to think about other penumbral problems.

Throughout his whole discussion of interpretation, Professor Hart seems to assume that it is a kind of cataloguing procedure. A judge faced with a novel situation is like a library clerk who has to decide where to shelve a new book. There are easy cases: the *Bible* belongs under Religion, *The Wealth of Nations* under Economics, etc. Then there are hard cases, when the librarian has to exercise a kind of creative choice, as in deciding whether *Des Kapital* belongs under Politics or Economics, *Gulliver's Travels* under Fantasy or Philosophy. But whether the decision where to shelve is easy or hard, once it is made all the librarian has to do is to put the book away. And so it is with judges, Professor Hart seems to say, in all essential particulars. Surely the judicial process is something more than a cataloguing procedure. The judge does not discharge his responsibility when he pins an apt diagnostic label on the case. He has to do something about it, to treat it, if you will. It is this larger responsibility which explains why interpretative problems almost never turn on a single word, and also why lawyers for generations have found the putting of imaginary borderline cases useful, not only "on the penumbra," but in order to know where the penumbra begins.

These points can be made clear, I believe, by drawing again on our example of the statutory fragment which reads, "All improvements must be promptly reported to ..." Whatever the concluding phrase may be, the judge has not solved his problems simply by deciding what kind of improvement is meant. Almost all of the words in the sentence may require interpretation, but most obviously this is so of "promptly" and "reported." What kind of "report" is contemplated: a written note, a call at the office, entry in a hospital record? How specific must it be? Will it be enough to say "a lot better," or "a big house with a bay window" ?

Now it should be apparent to any lawyer that in interpreting words like "improvement," "prompt," and "report," no real help is obtained by asking how some extralegal "standard instance" would define these words. But, much more important, when these words are all parts of a single structure of thought, they are in interaction with one another during the process of interpretation. "What is an 'improvement'? Well, it must be something that can be made the subject of a report. So, for purposes of this statute 'improvement' really means 'reportable improvement.' What kind of 'report' must be made? Well, that depends upon the sort of 'improvement' about which information is desired and the reasons for desiring the information."

When we look beyond individual words to the statute as a whole, it becomes apparent how the putting of hypothetical cases assists the interpretative process generally. By pulling our minds first in one direction, then in another, these cases help us to understand the fabric of thought before us. This fabric is something we seek to discern, so that we may know truly what it is, but it is also something that we inevitably help to create as we strive (in accordance with our obligation of fidelity to law) to make the statute a coherent, workable whole.

I should have considered all these remarks much too trite to put down here if they did not seem to be demanded in an answer to the theory of interpretation proposed by Professor Hart, a theory by which he puts such store that he implies we cannot have fidelity to law in any meaningful sense unless we are prepared to accept it. Can it be possible that the positivistic philosophy demands that we abandon a view of interpretation which sees as its central concern, not words, but purpose and structure? If so, then the stakes in this battle of schools are indeed high.

3. Ronald Dworkin: Rules and Principles[16]

When lawyers reason or dispute about legal rights and obligations, particularly in those hard cases when our problems with

---

[16] Ronald Dworkin, *Is Law a System of Rules?* 35 U. CHICAGO LAW REVIEW 14, 22-28, 41, 45 (1967). Copyright 1967 Ronald Dworkin. Excerpts reprinted by permission of the author.

these concepts seem most acute, they make use of standards that do not function as rules, but operate differently as principles, policies, and other sorts of standards. Positivism, I shall argue, is a model of and for a system of rules, and its central notion of a single fundamental test for law forces us to miss the important roles of these standards that are not rules.

In 1889, a New York court, in the famous case of *Riggs v. Palmer*,[17] had to decide whether an heir named in the will of his grandfather could inherit under that will, even though he had murdered his grandfather to do so. The court began its reasoning with this admission: "It is quite true that statutes regulating the making, proof and effect of wills, and the devolution of property, if literally construed, and if their force and effect can in no way and under no circumstances be controlled or modified, give this property to the murderer." But the court continued to note that "all laws as well as all contracts may be controlled in their operation and effect by general, fundamental maxims of the common law. No one shall be permitted to profit by his own fraud, or to take advantage of his own wrong, or to found any claim upon his own iniquity, or to acquire property by his own crime." The murderer did not receive his inheritance.

In 1960, a New Jersey court was faced, in *Henningsen v. Bloomfield Motors, Inc.*,[18] with the important question of whether (or how much) an automobile manufacturer may limit his liability in case the automobile is defective. Henningsen had bought a car, and signed a contract which said that the manufacturer's liability for defects was limited to "making good" defective parts—"this warranty being expressly in lieu of all other warranties, obligations or liabilities." Henningsen argued that, at least in the circumstances of his case, the manufacturer ought not to be protected by this limitation, and ought to be liable for the medical and other expenses of persons injured in a crash. He was not able to point to any statute, or to any established rule of law, that prevented the manufacturer from standing on the contract. The court nevertheless agreed with

Henningsen. At various points in the court's argument the following appeals to standards are made: (a) "We must keep in mind the general principle that, in the absence of fraud, one who does not choose to read a contract before signing it cannot later relieve himself of its burdens." (b) "In applying that principle, the basic tenet of freedom of competent parties to contract is a factor of importance." (c) "Freedom of contract is not such an immutable doctrine as to admit of no qualification in the area in which we are concerned." (d) "In a society such as ours, where the automobile is a common and necessary adjunct of daily life, and where its use is so fraught with danger to the driver, passengers and the public, the manufacturer is under a special obligation in connection with the construction, promotion and sale of his cars. Consequently, the courts must examine purchase agreements closely to see if consumer and public interests are treated fairly." (e) "Is there any principle which is more familiar or more firmly embedded in the history of Anglo-American law than the basic doctrine that the courts will not permit themselves to be used as instruments of inequity and injustice?" (f) More specifically, "the courts generally refuse to lend themselves to the enforcement of a 'bargain' in which one party has unjustly taken advantage of the economic necessities of another." The standards set out in these quotations are not the sort we think of as legal rules. They seem very different from propositions like "The maximum legal speed on the turnpike is sixty miles an hour" or "A will is invalid unless signed by three witnesses." They are different because they are legal principles rather than legal rules.

The difference between legal principles and legal rules is a logical distinction. Both sets of standards point to particular decisions about legal obligation in particular circumstances, but they differ in the character of the direction they give. Rules are applicable in an all-or-nothing fashion. If the facts a rule stipulates are given, then either the rule is valid, in which case the answer it supplies must be accepted, or it is not, in which case it contributes nothing to the decision.

This all-or-nothing is seen most plainly if we look at the way rules operate, not in law, but in some enterprise they dominate—a

[17] 115 N.Y. 506, 22 N.E. 188 (1889).
[18] 32 N.J. 358, 161 A.2d 69 (1960).

game, for example. In baseball a rule provides that if the batter has had three strikes, he is out. An official cannot consistently acknowledge that this is an accurate statement of a baseball rule, and decide that a batter who has had three strikes is not out. Of course, a rule may have exceptions (the batter who has taken three strikes is not out if the catcher drops the third strike). However, an accurate statement of the rule would take this exception into account, and any that did not would be incomplete. If the list of exceptions is very large, it would be too clumsy to repeat them each time the rule is cited; there is, however, no reason in theory why they could not all be added on, and the more that are, the more accurate is the statement of the rule.

If we take baseball rules as a model, we find that rules of law, like the rule that a will is invalid unless signed by three witnesses, fit the model well. If the requirement of three witnesses is a valid legal rule, then it cannot be that a will has been signed by only two witnesses and is valid. The rule might have exceptions, but if it does then it is inaccurate and incomplete to state the rule so simply, without enumerating all the exceptions. In theory, at least, the exceptions could all be listed, and the more of them that are, the more complete is the statement of the rule.

But this is not the way the sample principles in the quotations operate. Even those which look most like rules do not set out legal consequences that follow automatically when the conditions provided are met. We say that our law respects the principle that no man may profit from his own wrong, but we do not mean that the law never permits a man to profit from wrongs he commits. In fact, people often profit, perfectly legally, from their legal wrongs. The most notorious case is adverse possession—if I trespass on your land long enough, some day I will gain a right to cross your land whenever I please. There are many less dramatic examples. If a man leaves one job, breaking a contract, to take a much higher paying job, he may have to pay damages to his first employer, but he is usually entitled to keep his new salary. If a man jumps bail and crosses state lines to make a brilliant investment in another state, he may be sent back to jail, but he will keep his profits.

We do not treat these—and countless other counter-instances that can easily be imagined—as showing that the principle about profiting from one's wrongs is not a principle of our legal system, or that it is incomplete and needs qualifying exceptions. We do not treat counter-instances as exceptions (at least not exceptions in the way in which a catcher's dropping the third strike is an exception) because we could not hope to capture these counter-instances simply by a more extended statement of the principle. They are not, even in theory, subject to enumeration, because we would have to include not only those cases (like adverse possession) in which some institution has already provided that profit can be gained through a wrong, but also those numberless imaginary cases in which we know in advance that the principle would not hold. Listing some of these might sharpen our sense of the principle's weight (I shall mention that dimension in a moment), but it would not make for a more accurate or complete statement of the principle.

A principle like "No man may profit from his own wrong" does not even purport to set out conditions that make its application necessary. Rather, it states a reason that argues in one direction, but does not necessitate a particular direction. If a man has or is about to receive something as a direct result of something illegal he did to get it, then that is a reason which the law will take into account in deciding whether he should keep it. There may be other principles or policies arguing in the other direction—a policy of securing title, for example, or a principle limiting punishment to what the legislature has stipulated. If so, our principle may not prevail, but that does not mean that it is not a principle of our legal system, because in the next case, when these contravening considerations are absent or less weighty, the principle may be decisive. All that is meant, when we say that a particular principle is a principle of our law, is that the principle is one which officials must take into account, if it is relevant, as a consideration inclining in one direction or another.

The logical distinction between rules and principles appears more clearly when we consider principles that do not even look like rules. Consider the proposition, set out under "d" in the excerpts from the *Henningsen opinion,* that "the manufacturer is under a special obligation in connection with the construction, promotion, and sale of his cars." This does not even purport to define the specific duties such a special obligation entails, or to tell us what rights automobile consumers acquire as a result. It merely states—and this is an essential link in the *Henningsen* argument—that automobile manufacturers must be held to higher standards than other manufacturers, and are less entitled to rely on the competing principle of freedom of contract. It does not mean that they may never rely on that principle, or that courts may rewrite automobile purchase contracts at will; it means only that if a particular clause seems unfair or burdensome, courts have less reason to enforce the clause than if it were for the purchase of neckties. The "special obligation" counts in favor, but does not in itself necessitate, a decision refusing to enforce the terms of an automobile purchase contract.

This first difference between rules and principles entails another. Principles have a dimension that rules do not—the dimension of weight or importance. When principles intersect (the policy of protecting automobile consumers intersecting with principles of freedom of contract, for example), one who must resolve the conflict has to take into account the relative weight of each. This cannot be, of course, an exact measurement, and the judgment that a particular principle or policy is more important than another will often be a controversial one. Nevertheless, it is an integral part of the concept of a principle that it has this dimension, that it makes sense to ask how important or how weighty it is.

Rules do not have this dimension. We can speak of rules as being *functionally* important or unimportant (the baseball rule that three strikes are out is more important than the rule that runners may advance on a balk, because the game would be much more changed with the first rule altered than the second). In this sense, one legal rule may be more important than another because it has a greater or more important role in regulating behavior. But we cannot say that one rule is more important than another within the system of rules, so that when two rules conflict one supersedes the other by virtue of its greater weight. If two rules conflict, one of them cannot be a valid rule. The decision as to which is valid, and which must be abandoned or recast, must be made by appealing to considerations beyond the rules themselves. A legal system might regulate such conflicts by other rules, which prefer the rule enacted by the higher authority, or the rule enacted later, or the more specific rule, or something of that sort. A legal system may also prefer the rule supported by the more important principles. (Our own legal system uses both of these techniques.)

It is not always clear from the form of a standard whether it is a rule or a principle. "A will is invalid unless signed by three witnesses" is not very different in form from "A man may not profit from his own wrong," but one who knows something of American law knows that he must take the first as stating a rule and the second as stating a principle. In many cases the distinction is difficult to make—it may not have been settled how the standard should operate, and this issue may itself be a focus of controversy.

Sometimes a rule and a principle can play much the same role, and the difference between them is almost a matter of form alone. The first section of the Sherman Act states that every contract in restraint of trade shall be void. The Supreme Court had to make the decision whether this provision should be treated as a rule in its own terms (striking down every contract "which restrains trade," which almost any contract does) or as a principle, providing a reason for striking down a contract in the absence of effective contrary policies. The Court construed the provision as a rule, but treated that rule as containing the word "unreasonable," and as prohibiting only "unreasonable" restraints of trade.[19] This allowed the provision to function logically as a rule (whenever a court finds that the restraint is "unreasonable" it is bound to hold the contract invalid) and substantially as a principle (a court must take into account a variety of other principles and policies in determining whether a particular restraint in particular economic circumstances is "unreasonable").

---

[19] Standard Oil v. United States, 221 U.S. 1, 60 (1911); United States v. American Tobacco Co., 221 U.S. 106, 180 (1911).

Most rules of law, according to Hart, are valid because some competent institution enacted them. Some were created by a legislature, in the form of statutory enactments. Others were created by judges who formulated them to decide particular cases, and thus established them as precedents for the future. But this test of pedigree will not work for the *Riggs* and *Henningsen* principles. The origin of these as legal principles lies not in a particular decision of some legislature or court, but in a sense of appropriateness developed in the profession and the public over time. Their continued power depends upon this sense of appropriateness being sustained. If it no longer seemed unfair to allow people to profit by their wrongs, or fair to place special burdens upon oligopolies that manufacture potentially dangerous machines, these principles would not longer play much of a role in new cases, even if they had never been overruled or repealed. (Indeed, it hardly makes sense to speak of principles like these as being "overruled" or "repealed." When they decline they are eroded, not torpedoed.)

True, if we were challenged to back up our claim that some principle is a principle of law, we would mention any prior case in which that principle was cited, or figured in the argument. We would also mention any statute that seemed to exemplify that principle (even better if the principle was cited in the preamble of the statute, or in the committee reports or other legislative documents that accompanied it). Unless we could find some such institutional support, we would probably fail to make out our case, and the more support we found, the more weight we could claim for the principle. Yet we could not devise any formula for testing how much and what kind of institutional support is necessary to make a principle a legal principle, still less to fix its weight at a particular order of magnitude.

The positivist's picture of law as a system of rules has exercised a tenacious hold on our imagination, perhaps through its very simplicity. If we shake ourselves loose from this model of rules, we may be able to build a model truer to the complexity and sophistication of our own practices.

QUESTIONS AND COMMENTS FOR YOUR CONSIDERATION

1. As we saw earlier in this Chapter, one of the difficulties of Hans Kelsen's view of law as a conditional statement ("If you choose to do X, you will be sanctioned") is that, if infinite regress ("Who will sanction the sanctioner?") is to be avoided, then Kelsen's theory does not seem to provide rules for constraining judges, sheriffs, or other governmental officials. These officials simply mete out sanctions without being legally constrained by rules. But is this a drawback of Kelsen's theory, or is it a drawback of our usual understanding of the term "rules"? Are "rules," in the sense of clear verbal prescriptions, inherently incapable in themselves of constraining government officials? When a group (like the group of officials) holds the *power* in a state, do we delude ourselves that mere words ("rules") can force them to behave according to the words?

2. Do you find that Dworkin's distinction between a rule and a principle to be a clear difference in kind? Or does it seem to be a matter of degree? Consider a rule that is only tangentially applicable to the case at hand—a rule that does not "determine" the result of the case, but appears to be marginally relevant. Does such a rule act as a "rule" or a "principle"?

3. Are there situations where rules and principles work side-by-side, almost to the point where one cannot distinguish between them? Consider professional basketball. There are obvious "fouls"—so-called "flagrant fouls"—but there are many other contacts between players that might or might not be called a "foul." In this gray area, do referees blow the whistle according to a rule-like definition

of "foul" or do they use their discretion in deciding whether a contact amounts to a foul? Does the discretion of referees depend on the pace of the game? On the importance of the game? Consider the basketball playoffs at the end of the season. Toward the end of a close game, referees display an enormous reluctance to call fouls, even obvious ones. Knowledgeable fans realize that referees are reluctant to call fouls in such situations because it would look bad for the sport of basketball to have important games be decided on the basis of foul shots. Now, if the statement in the previous sentence is accurate, is it a "rule" or a "principle"?

4. Could we recharacterize Dworkin's distinction between rules and principles as a distinction between digital and analogue forms of information? A digital computer works on a "yes-or-no" system for each bit of information. (The "yes" answer is characterized by the binary notation 1, which means that the electrical impulse is allowed to go through the gate, and the "no" answer is characterized by the binary notation 0, which means that the electrical impulse cannot pass through the gate.) Analogue computers are rarer; a slide-rule is a mechanical illustration of an analogue device. Analogue devices work on a "more or less" system. If Dworkin's "principles" could be given quantitative "weight" on an analogue computer decisional program, would they, over time, achieve a degree of accuracy and determinacy that they presently lack?

5. Are principles always moral? Consider the principle that a man is entitled to greater legal consideration than a woman. Or that a slave should be treated not as a human but as a chattel. Would Dworkin have to accept such "principles" if they happen to comport with some judge's sense of appropriateness?

6. Where do principles come from? Does Dworkin claim that they are made up out of the blue? He talks about "a sense of appropriateness." Is that the same as saying that principles are made up out of the blue? If that's what he means, would you characterize his position as non-positivistic? Would you say it is close to natural law?

7. But note how Dworkin cuts back on his "sense of appropriateness" position. He says that unless the principle in question can be found in *legal materials—i.e.*, prior cases, statutes, legislative history—then "we would probably fail to make out our case." What does Dworkin mean here? Is he saying that a court *should* disregard the alleged principle unless it can be found in legal materials? Or that a court *may* do so? Or *might* do so? Or that Professor Dworkin himself has no idea one way or the other?

8. Is Dworkin's theory of "principles" a theory? Or is it the absence of theory? As a purely descriptive (non-theoretical) matter, Dworkin *may* be describing judicial behavior with some accuracy—*i.e.*, when a judge doesn't like the result that the rules seem to dictate, the judge can pull, out of the air, a "principle" that allows the case to be decided differently. Yet Dworkin appears to be claiming that his notion of "principles" is part of a legal theory, a theory of sophisticated positivism.

4. Stanley Fish: A Broader Notion of "Rule"[20]

Suppose you were a basketball coach and had taught someone how to shoot baskets and how to dribble the ball, but had imparted these skills without reference to the playing of an actual basketball game. Now you decide to insert your student into a game, and you equip him with some rules. You say to him, for instance, "Take only good shots." "What," he asks reasonably enough, "is a good shot?" "Well," you reply, "a good shot is an 'open shot,' a shot taken when you are close to the basket (so that the chances of success are good) and when your view is not obstructed by the harassing efforts of opposing players." Everything goes well until the last few seconds of the game; your team is behind by a single point; the novice player gets the ball in heavy traffic and holds it as the final buzzer rings. You run up to him and say, "Why didn't you shoot?" and he answers, "It wasn't a good shot."[21] Clearly, the rule must be amended, and accordingly you tell him that if time is running out, and your team is behind, and you have the ball, you should take the shot even if it isn't a good one, because it will then *be* a good one in the sense of being the best shot in the circumstances. (Notice how both the meaning of the rule and the entities it covers are changing shape as this "education" proceeds.) Now suppose there is another game, and the same situation develops. This time the player takes the shot, which under the circumstances is a very difficult one; he misses, and once again the final buzzer rings. You run up to him and say, "Didn't you see that John (a teammate) had gone 'back door' and was perfectly positioned under the basket for an easy shot?" and he answers "But you said..." Now obviously it would be possible once again to amend the rule, and just as obviously there would be no real end to the sequence and number of emendations that would be necessary. Of course, there will eventually come a time when the novice player (like the novice judge) will no longer have to ask questions; but it will not be because the rules have finally been made sufficiently explicit to cover all cases, but because explicitness will have been rendered unnecessary by a kind of knowledge that informs rules rather than follows from them.

No set of rules could be made explicit enough to cover all the possible situations that might emerge within a field of practice; no matter how much was added to the instruction "Take only good shots," it could never be descriptive of all the actions it was supposed to direct, since every time the situation changes, what is or is not a "good" shot will change too. On the other hand, for someone already embedded in a field of practice, the briefest of instructions will be sufficient and perhaps even superfluous, since it will be taken as referring to courses of action that are already apparent to the agent; upon hearing or remembering the rule, "Take only good shots," a player will glance around a field already organized in terms of relevant pieces of possible behavior. A rule can never be made explicit in the sense of demarcating the field of reference independently of interpretation, but a rule can always be received as explicit by someone who hears it within an interpretive preunderstanding of what the field of reference could possibly be.

The moral of the story, then, is not that you could never learn enough to know what to do in every circumstance, but that what you learn cannot finally be reduced to a set of rules. Or, to put the case another way (it amounts to the same thing), insofar as the requisite knowledge *can* be reduced to a set of rules ("Take only good shots," "Consult history"), it will be to rules whose very intelligibility depends on the practices they supposedly govern.

Consider what happens in the first year of law school (or, for that matter, in the first year of graduate study in English). The student studies not rules but cases, pieces of practice, and what he or she acquires are not abstractions but something like "know-how" or "the ropes," the ability to identify (not upon reflection, but immediately) a crucial issue, to ask a relevant question, and to propose an appropriate answer from a range of appropriate answers. Somewhere along

---

[20] Excerpts from STANLEY FISH, DOING WHAT COMES NATURALLY 123-28 (1989). Copyright 1989 Duke University Press. Excerpts reprinted by permission.

[21] *Editor's Note:* Note the similarity so far to the example used by Justice Foster in the Case of the Speluncean Explorers, *supra* Chapter 1.

the way the student will also begin to formulate rules or, more properly, general principles, but will be able to produce and understand them only because he or she is deeply inside—indeed, is a part of—the context in which they become intelligible.

What holds for rules holds too for every other "text" encountered in a field of practice, including the Constitution. Formal linguistics [is] the project of specifying the properties of sentences as they exist in an acontextual state, so that one could finally distinguish in a principled way between sentences that were straightforward, ambiguous, multiply ambiguous, etc. But [I argue that] sentences never appear in any but an already contextualized form, and a sentence one hears as ambiguous is simply a sentence for which one is imagining, at the moment of

hearing, more than one set of contextual circumstances. The conditions (of ambiguity and straightforwardness) are not linguistic, but contextual or institutional. That is to say, a sentence does not ask to be read in a particular way because it is a particular kind of sentence; rather, it is only in particular sets of circumstances that sentences are encountered at all, and the properties that sentences display are always a function of those circumstances. If there are debates about what the Constitution means, it is not because the Constitution "provokes" debate, not because it is a certain *kind* of text, but because for persons reading (constituting) it within the assumption of different circumstances, **different** meanings will seem obvious and inescapable.

QUESTIONS AND COMMENTS FOR YOUR CONSIDERATION

1. As we have seen, the goal of positivism is to achieve a determinate legal system. The command theory of law, elaborated by Bentham and Austin, had the (apparent) virtue of enabling us to determine the content of the law simply by referring to statutes enacted by the legislature. Later positivists such as Kelsen and Hart, and later writers in the positivist tradition such as Dworkin and Fish, have tried to make law even more determinate by linguistic analysis of the content of statutes and rules. Would the ultimate realization of positivism be a system of laws so determinate that it could be completely programmed into a computer and accessed by any person wishing to know what the law says?

2. In 1977, I wrote an article that attempted to realize a version of such a computerized system of law. In the system I outlined, courts would be replaced by computers. Lawyers would still be necessary, but only for the purpose of meeting with clients. A lawyer would listen to the client's story, and then enter the relevant facts of the client's story into a computer. The computer would then answer the question *whether the client would win* if the client brought a legal action based on those facts. The lawyer would then send the computer print-out (or modem the analysis) to the lawyer for the opposing party. The lawyer for the opposing party would presumably check the analysis by plugging the facts into *her* computer. But since all computers in all lawyers' offices will have the *same* law programmed into them, all lawyers will come up with the same result! Thus, there would be no need to have any litigation. The computer will simply say whether, under the law and under the facts that have been programmed into the computer, the defendant must pay a certain specified sum to the plaintiff or whether the defendant is not liable. Anything after that would simply be a matter of enforcing the "judgment" reached by the computer. (See the excerpt from this article, below.)

3. How could the "law" of a jurisdiction be turned into a computer program?

One could easily enter all the statutes of a jurisdiction into the computer, and then use a word-search (retrieval) function to access particular statutes. Such retrieval systems are already available. But statutes are *general* in their content. If we simply recount the facts of a particular case, the words we use in recounting those facts are not likely to be the same words that appear in the relevant statutes. And in any event, what about the *case law* of the jurisdiction? Courts, after all, *interpret* and *apply* statutes, and in addition apply *precedents* and *common law* to specific cases. A fully computerized legal system would have to include the court decisions.

5. Anthony D'Amato: Computerizing Substantive Law[22]

Let us suppose that in a given jurisdiction a team of legal researchers is hired to program a computer so that its output will be decisions involving questions of choice of law in cases where one party alleges that a tort took place in a state other than the forum state. Roughly, what the legal team would do would be to extract the facts of all the cases involving this question that have been reported in judicial opinions in the jurisdiction. These facts would be plugged into the computer on a case-by-case basis, indicating for each case's set of facts the *name* of the court and which *side* won the case. The name of the court is important because the highest court in the jurisdiction would be controlling; the Law Computer would be instructed to "scan" all the highest court's cases first and only move to the lower level courts, each level in turn, if the highest court's decision did not resolve the question at hand. The designation of which side won the case is important because clusters of facts will be correlated (as I will indicate) with the prevailing side.

One immediate problem presents itself with the rough summary I have just given: How does the team of researchers know, for instance, what a "tort" is, inasmuch as there are some areas of law (*quasi* contract, for example) where it may be unclear if a "tort" is involved? The way around this problem is to have the team of researchers program *all*

the cases ever decided in the jurisdiction. An eventual computer program would do precisely that. Then, preliminary distinctions would not have to be made; an organizing fact might be something like "personal physical injury" rather than "tort," but such organizing facts would simply be part of the facts plugged into the Law Computer by the research team and not a preliminary category that would serve to select among cases to be programmed.

A more difficult task for the research team is choosing the relevant facts of a given case. The initial determination of relevancy has, fortunately, already been made by the court. If it were not for this initial determination, the attempt to program facts into a computer might almost be impossible (how could we know, for example, whether the color of the plaintiff's eyes, or the fact that there was an eclipse of the moon three days after the accident—facts that we might discover from the pleadings—are "relevant"?). The statement of the facts that a court will include in its published opinion serves as the first filter from all the possibly relevant facts, one that narrows the facts enormously. But even that filter is not fine enough, for certain facts, even though reported by the court, will be irrelevant. Here, the question of irrelevancy is a matter for trained legal discernment, but I would not anticipate much difficulty in this regard. Lawyers can easily agree, for instance, that the names of the parties are irrelevant. Thus, the names would not be plugged into the computer. But what about the ages of the parties, if the court mentions their age? It is not immediately clear that the ages are irrelevant; one must look further in the opinion. If anything said by the court in support of its judgment refers to the age of the parties—such as the fact that one party

[22] Anthony D'Amato, *Can/Should Computers Replace Judges?* 11 GEORGIA LAW REVIEW 1277 (1977), copyright 1977 Anthony D'Amato. Minor revisions have been made to the original essay.

is a minor—then that fact (of minority) should be plugged in.

The reason it is important for the computing team to discard irrelevant facts is that the Law Computer, when it is finally used for current cases and situations, will be instructed to take all the facts into consideration. We want to avoid the possibility that the computer will find a correlation between, say, the number of letters in a party's name and whether persons of that many letters tend to win cases. Such a correlation would skew the computer's output in a new case where one of the parties might have the same number of letters in his or her name. Computers cannot determine the "meaning" of the facts that are plugged in, and therefore a computer could spew out absurd factual correlations unless we exercise some discipline in programming the computer in the first place.

Let me be more specific about the kinds of facts that are relevant. In choice-of-law cases relating to tort, the Restatement (Second) of Conflict of Laws says that the following contacts should be taken into account:

(a) the place where the injury occurred,
(b) the place where the conduct causing the injury occurred,
(c) the domicile, residence, nationality, place of incorporation and place of business of the parties, and
(d) the place where the relationship, if any, between the parties is centered.[23]

All facts bearing on these matters that are mentioned in the court's statement of facts must be fed into the computer.

So far, the Law Computer has been programmed to count certain collections of facts as constituting a "win" on the part of the plaintiff or defendant. But what about intangible weights to be accorded to various facts? The Restatement itself, after listing the facts above quoted, states that "these contacts are to be evaluated according to their relative importance with respect to the particular issue." This sentence is an important illustration of the "judgmental" factor in decision-making. How can a computer decide questions of the relative importance of facts in

cases where torts are alleged? If a person is injured in an airplane, how can the computer know whether it is less important what state the plane was flying over at the time of the injury than whether a person received the same injury that a guest might receive in a car driven on the roads of that state?

In the first place, the correlation of facts with winning sides will take into account many more facts than those suggested by the Restatement. Indeed, if two cases are roughly the same but the law of the foreign jurisdiction (the non-forum law) was applied because the injury took place in an automobile that was in the foreign jurisdiction at the time, the Law Computer will automatically find that a difference—if a difference in result exists—turns on the plane-automobile distinction. The computer is not judging "relative importance," but rather is specifying exactly what counts; the computer in this sense is more precise than the Restatement's general formula.

Second, the facts plugged into the Law Computer need not necessarily be confined to automobile-plane with respect to the differences between the two cases I have just mentioned. The court's opinions in those cases may mention: the amount of time spent by the parties in the other state where the accident occurred (a very brief amount of time for the airplane case), the relation between the injury and the laws of that state (a stronger relation might exist in an automobile accident because the state's rules of the road apply directly, whereas in an airplane there are not many relevant "rules" that differ as the plane crosses state boundaries), facts involving the particular geographical conditions of the foreign state (again, road facts may count more heavily than shifting wind currents for airplanes), and so forth. All these facts, properly plugged in, will help the Law Computer make distinctions even between other kinds of vehicles (helicopters vs. motorcycles, for instance).

Third, we might concede that in some cases a human judge might be able to make a more refined determination than a computer. A human judge might know from intuition that it is somehow more "important" that a certain contact with the foreign state should count with respect to the particular alleged tort at issue than would other con-

---

[23] RESTATEMENT (SECOND) OF CONFLICT OF LAWS 145 (1971).

tacts. But is this degree of refinement enough to warrant protracted litigation over the issue? Should lawyers engage in lengthy arguments as to the quality of certain contacts with the foreign state, or the nature of the alleged tort, and similar almost medievally intractable problems? Or would it be better to eschew further refinement in this area and instead "freeze" the law to reflect only those factors already programmed into the computer from all existing precedents?

Of course, we are only assuming that a human judge would refine and improve the law. In fact, he may misunderstand existing law and succeed only in muddying it up. His own biases might intrude; he might "want" the plaintiff to win and thus might find that the state having the more "important" contact with the parties is the one that in fact "has" the law more favorable to the plaintiff. Even the best intentioned and most impartial judge might simply be confused by the welter of precedents impinging upon a choice-of-law case. It might be very difficult for him to keep all the factors in mind and to remember what combinations of what factors led previous courts to rule what way. He might not be aided by the arguments of counsel, who themselves might not fully understand the relation of factors to decisions in previous cases or who may be trying to suggest different weight distributions because existing precedents might not help their own case. But a computer would not have any such biases unless they were programmed in, and we can expect that a team of legal researchers—appointed by the legislature and including perhaps prominent judges—would not program in actual biases. Moreover, a computer would remember everything and would always rule consistently. In practice, it could be far more faithful to existing precedents than any judge is humanly capable of being.

Another aspect of the question of what weight should be given to various facts in determining choice of law can be handled by the way the computer program is set up. I have said previously that all of the facts of a given case are programmed into the computer and correlated with the decision in that case. Let us now look at this process in more detail. The computer program essentially is that of a multiple regression analy-sis.[24] The dependent variables are "plaintiff wins" (+1) and "defendant wins" (-1); the facts of the case are independent variables. Facts will differ from case to case. The result of plugging in thousands of cases, each having, say, about fifty facts, will be enormous clusters of facts associated loosely with whether the plaintiff or the defendant wins. Now suppose a lawyer types in a new set of facts—the facts that she hopes to establish for her client in a contemplated legal action. The facts will consist of the kind of tort, where it (or most of it) occurred, residential questions, the kind of relationship between the parties, and many other facts commonly cited by courts in this kind of case. Suppose a lawyer does not know what facts to plug in. As soon as she types in any facts at all (for example, the most rudimentary description of what allegedly occurred) the computer can be programmed to ask further relevant questions. In this question-and-answer manner, all the potentially relevant facts can be elicited. This refinement further reduces the role of the lawyer (and her fees), but the overall purpose here is to deliver clear "law" to the consumer at the lowest cost.

The computer will perform a complex multivariate analysis on all the facts that are programmed in, including the answers to factual questions asked by the computer itself. Then the facts will be "regressed" to "fit" other clusters of facts previously programmed into the computer. The fit will never be exact; the only question the computer decides is whether the new facts as programmed fit more closely to facts that cluster around the dependent variable "plaintiff wins" or to facts that cluster around the dependent variable "defendant wins." The measure of their fitness ("least squares" distance or "regression") will be expressed numerically. Thus, if some of the facts lead to the plaintiff winning and other facts support the defendant, the final numerical value can be closer to zero. It will never be exactly zero, because in the (extremely unlikely) event that the facts cluster equally around the dependent variables "plaintiff

---

[24] See W. COOLEY & P. LOHNES, MULTIVARIATE PROCEDURES FOR THE BEHAVIORAL SCIENCES (1962), and bibliography therein.

wins" and "defendant wins," the computer's answer will be "defendant wins." This follows from the legal proposition that in order for a plaintiff to win any civil case, the plaintiff has the burden of evidentiary proof. If the evidence turns out to be 50-50, the plaintiff has not sustained that burden and the defendant wins.

The dependent variables need not be "plaintiff wins" or "defendant wins." They could just as easily be (and in the foregoing case probably would be) "use the foreign law" or "use the law of the forum state." Or they could be "the court has jurisdiction" or "the court lacks jurisdiction."

A further refinement might be introduced when the facts are programmed into the Law Computer. Some facts might be noted by the court in its opinion as having primary importance; for example, the place of domicile of the parties. Other facts might have secondary importance; for example, a corporation's principal place of business might exceed in importance its place of incorporation. Nonmetric data analysis can be used to rank these facts in the order of importance accorded them by the court;[25] these preference-order rankings can be given weight in the construction of the computer's multivariate equations. The mathematics involved can become extremely complex, since the "fit" in the fact clusters will be multidimensional. However, existing techniques can generate adequate programs for this purpose.[26]

But are there not some aspects of choice-of-law problems that remain intractable for a computer? What about, for example, the public policy of the forum? In a typical case where this factor made a great difference, the Supreme Court of Wisconsin overruled a long line of precedents that had held that the law of the place of the tort or injury determined the law to be applied to the case, and substituted the law of the forum state on the grounds of the public policy of the forum.[27] Under the law of the place of injury, the guest statute probably would have barred the plaintiff from recovering for an automobile injury, but under the law of the forum recovery was probable. All of the parties, including the liability insurer, were domiciled in Wisconsin, the forum state. The court saw no reason why Nebraska had any overriding interest in preventing the plaintiff from recovering against the Wisconsin insurer and thus held that the *lex loci delicti* (of Nebraska) was repugnant to the public policy of the *lex fori*. How would such a case be programmed into the computer?

The case itself could easily be programmed. Where a guest is suing the driver and the driver's insurance company, where all parties are domiciled in the forum state, and where the accident is an automobile accident, those facts are correlated with a "win" for the plaintiff even though the accident took place in a foreign state.

What, then, happened to the "public policy" argument? Wasn't it determinative of the result?

In the first place, we cannot be sure that the court was *correct* in applying "public policy." Perhaps the court did not take into account the "public policy" which cautions against charging someone twice for the same product. The insurance company, after all, may have reduced its rates to Wisconsin drivers because it was aware that other states had more restrictive statutes regarding guests in automobiles, and therefore accidents that took place out of state involving Wisconsin drivers traveling in those states would not require the Wisconsin insurer to pay compensation. By foregoing the premium it would have charged (and would now have to charge if the court overturns the precedents relied upon by the insurance company), is it not against "public policy" to force the company to pay the insured in this case? If so, an argument can be made that the Wisconsin court misread or misapplied "public policy" in this case.

But mistakes aside, could we program in

---

[25] For a discussion of nonmetric statistical data, *see* C. Coombs, A Theory of Data 444-95 (1964).

[26] *Editor's Note:* This was true in 1977. Today, with parallel processing computers, the entire case law of the fifty American states could be programmed into a giant multivariate program. Thus if a lawyer plugged in a conflicts-of-law case involving Pennsylvania and New York, the computer would not only process the laws of these two jurisdictions, but would also refer to the laws of the forty-eight other states as subsidiary data.

[27] Wilcox v. Wilcox, 26 Wis. 2d 617, 133 N.W. 2d 408 (1965).

"public policy" if we wanted to? Certainly whenever the term "public policy" showed up in any prior judicial decision, it would be programmed in the same way a statute might be. Then public policy, just like expressions found in statutes, would be correlated with certain facts and outcomes in the computer's multiple regression analysis. Thus, the outcome of a particular case might be: "defendant wins; reason is public policy."

But "public policy," like all legal expressions such as "contract," "tort," "due care," "cheapest cost avoider," "entrapment," "third-party beneficiary," and "best interests of the child," to name a few among thousands, are really *conclusions* that the law attaches to certain fact situations. The facts are primary; the attachment of legal expressions to certain configurations of facts are nothing more than the artificial imposition of the language of the law upon those facts. These expressions are indeed vague and indeterminate. They seem to convey information to us because they are no less subjective than many of the other factors that enter into cases decided by human judges. If in the future we achieve a computerized legal system, we may find that many or most of these cherished legal expressions are in fact superfluous.

The multiple regression program I have outlined—where just the facts are entered into the computer, and the computer program decides how they "cluster" and correlate with particular judicial outcomes—is all we really need to fully capture the "law" of a jurisdiction. If there is a further need to attach legal labels to the outcomes, then it would be a simple extra task for the computer to attach whichever legal expression (such as "public policy") turns out to be the closest fit to the cluster of facts. This additional legal expression will add nothing to the outcome of the case. In time, as society gets more used to the computer, many of the legal expressions might become extinct.

So far, the system I have described will "freeze" the law as it is on the day that the Law Computer is programmed with all the facts from all the reported cases in a given jurisdiction. How can the law change? In the past, law was changed either by the court or by the legislature. Under a computerized system of law, there are no courts, and the computer itself is not "creative"—it cannot

change existing law. But there is still a legislature. The task of continuously revising the content of the law, then, is left to the legislature.

But the legislature would not need to enact "statutes" as we know them. Instead, the legislature can revise as much or as little of existing law as it wishes simply by adding new inputs to the computer. There are some instances where this is already happening. For example, many accountants now submit their clients' income taxes by "electronic filing." They simply modem in the data to be entered on the various lines of an income tax return. When the Internal Revenue Service receives the data, its computers recompute the tax. Thus, if Congress raises the tax on the highest income bracket from 36% to 39%, all that needs to be done is to change the appropriate numerical inputs into the IRS computer so that the tax is recomputed at 39% instead of 36%. Obviously, tax preparers will also be notified of the change, but this notification is not essential to effectuate the law.[28] Indeed, in the future, we might expect the IRS to simply make its own software available by modem to any income tax filer. When that happens, the tax bracket and percentage figures will simply be part of the software that the filer imports from the IRS. Any changes in the law will then simply be a matter of Congress deciding on the change and then instructing its in-house programmer to change the IRS software tax program.

In the Law Computer system I have outlined in this essay, Congress's task would only be slightly more difficult than in the tax example. Suppose that a dispute arises between a biological parent and an adopting parent over temporary custody of a child. The computer, which has been programmed with the law of the jurisdiction, will search for the closest correlation between certain facts of the case and the programmed facts. Suppose that the programmed facts emphasize matters that correlate with "the best interests of the child." These matters would include, for example, the comparative home situations of the biological and adopting par-

---

[28] *Editor's Note:* Recall here the discussion of "secret laws" following the excerpt from Hans Kelsen.

ents. So, if the adopting parents are more affluent than the biological parents, have a higher education, have no history of drug abuse, etc., then the computer will "count" these home-situation facts and award custody to the adopting parents. Now suppose that the legislature wishes to change the law so that temporary custody is awarded in this type of case to the biological parents *unless* they are shown to be unfit parents; if they are unfit, then custody is awarded to the adopting parents. What the legislature will do is to instruct its computer programming expert to adjust the program in order to move the clustering points on the hard drive's database by changing the loads (or weights) assigned to different facts. The programmer will subtract weights from factors relating to the comparative home situations of the parties, and add weights to factors relating solely to the question of fitness of the biological parents. These factors would include the care and concern already shown (or not shown) to the child by the biological parents, whether the biological parents have ever abused this child or other children, whether the biological parents are users of or are addicted to drugs, and so forth. Once the Law Computer is reprogrammed in this fashion, there will be a change in the outcomes of contested cases of temporary child custody when the contesting parties are biological parents and adopting parents.

Because some of the factors in the preceding example overlap (for example, it is not in the child's best interests to be given to unfit parents), adjusting the weights in the computer program is a much more refined and precise way of assessing all the facts. A human judge who must take into account overlapping factors may ultimately be swayed by subliminal impressions (such as, which set of competing parents have more characteristics in common with the judge's neighbors and friends). Moreover, different human judges could reach different results in the same case (as every practicing lawyer can attest). The Law Computer, on the other hand, will always reach the same result on the facts of any case no matter who operates the computer or how many times it is operated.

The system could also have a human "Supreme Court." The function of that court would be to review Law Computer decisions and change the law retroactively if necessary. (Any judicial change in the law that affects the parties to the litigation is retroactive by definition.) Perhaps, in order to avoid judicial changes in the law that are too abrupt, the Supreme Court's constitutional mandate could be set at allowing changes not to exceed a certain fixed amount in the load factor of any facts already programmed in. Thus the Supreme Court's jurisdiction would be limited to changing the result in "close" cases but not being allowed to change the result in cases which the computer designates as clear wins for one side. Changes of that magnitude can only be made by the legislature, and then only prospectively.

Since the Supreme Court's limited jurisdiction is known to all attorneys using the Law Computer, the computer's output itself can reflect the possibility of review by the Supreme Court. Thus, after the entry of the facts of a current case, the computer can respond: "On these facts plaintiff wins, by a margin of 0.8. Since this margin is less than 1.0, the defendant may decide to appeal the decision to the Supreme Court. The defendant has 90 days to appeal, and then the Supreme Court has 90 days to decide whether to take the appeal."

Any state may decide for itself whether to give a human Supreme Court this kind of limited jurisdiction to review close cases. Obviously, it can expand or contract the Court's jurisdiction by increasing or decreasing the numerical amount measuring the closeness of the case. However, I would speculate that litigants who win by computer and then lose in the Supreme Court would be mightily disappointed, and would lobby to abolish the Supreme Court entirely. Their best argument would be the undesirability of uncertainty in the law resulting from the existence of a human reviewing court. They will argue, "Why keep even this level of uncertainty when we can have a perfectly determinate legal system?"

As the general public becomes knowledgeable about entering facts into the Law Computer, there will be a decrease in demand for lawyers. The public will begin to say that successful lawyers were only people who had the ability to fool judges. Now that we don't have judges, and now that no one can fool the computer, we don't need lawyers.

QUESTIONS AND COMMENTS FOR YOUR CONSIDERATION

1. Have we now come full circle in our consideration of positivism? By replacing courts with computers, and by considering the legislature as a body charged with modifying the computer program, we are back to Bentham's diagram of the legal system. Nothing is changed from that first diagram except what the letters stand for (See Figure 6). The reason the Computer is indicated by dotted lines is that the Computer faithfully obeys the instructions programmed into its hard drive by the Programmer. The Computer does not have a mind of its own.[29] If computers had been around during Bentham's time, would he not have preferred them to any living judge?

2. Does the Law Computer constitute a "Brave New World" for the law? Do we want a society without judges and lawyers? Presumably you, the reader of these words, are a law student; is the idea of a Law Computer that would largely take over the job of lawyers a frightening one to you? If you are apprehensive about it, could you put aside your own interests in reaching a judgment as to the merits or demerits of the Law Computer idea as far as the general public is concerned?

3. If we have a society without lawyers and judges, we will also have a society without law journals, books about law, law schools, and college courses in law. Is the loss of all this venerable scholarship a price worth paying to achieve legal determinacy at a low cost to the public?

4. Will the Law Computer become the master of our society, and we, the public, its servants? Will we have dehumanized government? Should we insist at least on a Supreme Court of limited jurisdiction to review the Law Computer's decisions? Should it have unlimited jurisdiction?

5. Is there a fundamental flaw in the idea of a Law Computer? After I wrote and published the article, I began to think that there is such a flaw. Consider what happens when a lawyer word-processes into the computer the facts of the client's situation. Suppose the computer replies that, on these facts, the other side wins. Would the lawyer stop here? No, the lawyer would "tinker" with the description of the facts. She would restate some of the key facts and try that out on the computer. If the computer persists in finding that the other side wins, the lawyer would then try to add some new facts (perhaps eliciting these new facts from further interviews with the client or with other possible witnesses) and see what the computer's result would be. The lawyer could also try omitting some facts, perhaps on the ground that the other side may not think of them. Sooner

---

[29] The closest simulation to a mind is to program a computer with a random-number generator. In that way, one might expect that the computer's output would not be a predictable function of its input. Alas, it is impossible to program a computer with a random-number generator. Although a computer might issue a stream of numbers that appear random, the numbers cannot be truly random because any program is itself determinate. For example, if you take the cube root of seven and divide it by the square root of eleven, omit the first one hundred decimal digits, and then proceed with the decimal digits after that, it would be exceedingly difficult (but not impossible) for anyone to figure out that the number stream thus generated is not random. Yet of course it is not in fact random because we can duplicate it exactly if we know, or deduce, the original formula. From the computer's point of view, the stream of apparently "random numbers" is completely determined by the software program that generates it.

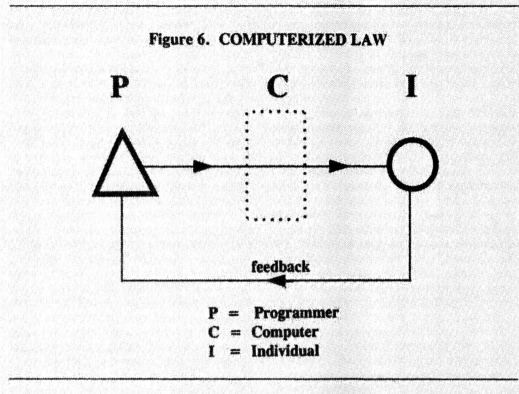

Figure 6. COMPUTERIZED LAW

P = Programmer
C = Computer
I = Individual

or later, there will be a configuration of facts presented to the computer that will result in a verdict for the lawyer's client. (This is a logical necessity; if you keep changing the facts, sooner or later there will be a version of the facts that will result in your winning this or any case.)

The lawyer thus has an exact set of programmable facts that results in a win for her client. She will modem this set of facts to the lawyer for the opposing party. If the lawyer for the opposing party plugs this set of facts into his own computer, the result will be that his client loses.

Of course, the lawyer will not be happy with a set of facts that causes a loss to his client. So he will proceed to tinker with the facts—downplaying some, adding or substituting others, omitting some. Sooner or later his revised set of facts will result in a decision by the Law Computer that his client wins.

If he modems this set of facts back to the first lawyer, she will see that the opposing sides are now engaged in a battle over what relevant facts will be programmed into the computer. Since *this* is a battle that a computer cannot solve, there is—I argue—a fundamental flaw in the idea of a Law Computer—not in just my version, but in any conceivable version of a law computer. Do you agree? Is there a way of overcoming this problem? Would anyone want to?

3
Natural Law

A. Procedural Natural Law

1. Lon Fuller: The Internal Morality of Law[1]

This is an allegory of the unhappy reign of a monarch who bore the convenient, but not very imaginative and not even very regal sounding name of Rex. Rex came to the throne filled with the zeal of a reformer. He considered that the greatest failure of his predecessors had been in the field of law. For generations the legal system had known nothing like a basic reform. Procedures of trial were cumbersome, the rules of law spoke in the archaic tongue of another age, justice was expensive, the judges were slovenly and sometimes corrupt. Rex was resolved to remedy all this and to make his name in history as a great lawgiver. It was his unhappy fate to fail in this ambition. Indeed, he failed spectacularly, since not only did he not succeed in introducing the needed reforms, but he never even succeeded in creating any law at all, good or bad.

His first official act was, however, dramatic and propitious. Since he needed a clean slate on which to write, he announced to his subjects the immediate repeal of all existing law, of whatever kind. He then set about drafting a new code. Unfortunately, trained as a lonely prince, his education had been very defective. In particular he found himself incapable of making even the simplest generalizations. Though not lacking in confidence when it came to deciding specific controversies, the effort to give articulate reasons for any conclusion strained his capacities to the breaking point.

[1] Lon L. Fuller, The Morality of Law 33-41 (rev. ed. 1969). Copyright 1969 by Yale University. Reprinted by permission of Yale University Press.

Becoming aware of his limitations, Rex gave up the project of a code and announced to his subjects that henceforth he would act as a judge in any disputes that might arise among them. In this way under the stimulus of a variety of cases he hoped that his latent powers of generalization might develop and, proceeding case by case, he would gradually work out a system of rules that could be incorporated in a code. Unfortunately the defects in his education were more deepseated than he had supposed. The venture failed completely. After he had handed down literally hundreds of decisions neither he nor his subjects could detect in those decisions any pattern whatsoever. Such tentatives toward generalization as were to be found in his opinions only compounded the confusion, for they gave false leads to his subjects and threw his own meager powers of judgment off balance in the decision of later cases.

After this fiasco Rex realized it was necessary to take a fresh start. His first move was to subscribe to a course of lessons in generalization. With his intellectual powers thus fortified, he resumed the project of a code and, after many hours of solitary labor, succeeded in preparing a fairly lengthy document. He was still not confident, however, that he had fully overcome his previous defects. Accordingly, he announced to his subjects that he had written out a code and would henceforth be governed by it in deciding cases, but that for an indefinite future the contents of the code would remain an official state secret, known only to him and his scrivener. To Rex's surprise this sensible plan was deeply resented by his subjects. They declared it was very unpleasant to have one's case decided by rules when there was no way of knowing what those rules were.

Stunned by this rejection, Rex undertook an earnest inventory of his personal strengths and weaknesses. He decided that life had taught him one clear lesson, namely, that it is easier to decide things with the aid of hindsight than it is to attempt to foresee and control the future. Not only did hindsight make it easier to decide cases, but— and this was of supreme importance to Rex—it made it easier to give reasons. Deciding to capitalize on this insight, Rex hit on the following plan. At the beginning of each calendar year he would decide all the controversies that had arisen among his subjects during the preceding year. He would accompany his decisions with a full statement of reasons. Naturally, the reasons thus given would be understood as not controlling decisions in future years, for that would be to defeat the whole purpose of the new arrangement, which was to gain the advantages of hindsight. Rex confidently announced the new plan to his subjects, observing that he was going to publish the full text of his judgments with the rules applied by him, thus meeting the chief objection to the old plan. Rex's subjects received this announcement in silence, then quietly explained through their leaders that when they said they needed to know the rules, they meant they needed to know them *in advance* so they could act on them. Rex muttered something to the effect that they might have made that point a little clearer, but said he would see what could be done.

Rex now realized that there was no escape from a published code declaring the rules to be applied in future disputes. Continuing his lessons in generalization, Rex worked diligently on a revised code, and finally announced that it would shortly be published. This announcement was received with universal gratification. The dismay of Rex's subjects was all the more intense, therefore, when his code became available and it was discovered that it was truly a masterpiece of obscurity. Legal experts who studied it declared that there was not a single sentence in it that could be understood either by an ordinary citizen or by a trained lawyer. Indignation became general and soon a picket appeared before the royal palace carrying a sign that read, "How can anybody follow a rule that nobody can understand?"

The code was quickly withdrawn. Recognizing for the first time that he needed assistance, Rex put a staff of experts to work on a revision. He instructed them to leave the substance untouched but to clarify the ex-

pression throughout. The resulting code was a model of clarity, but as it was studied it became apparent that its new clarity had merely brought to light that it was honeycombed with contradictions. It was reliably reported that there was not a single provision in the code that was not nullified by another provision inconsistent with it. A picket again appeared before the royal residence carrying a sign that read, "This time the king made himself clear—in both directions."

Once again the code was withdrawn for revision. By now, however, Rex had lost his patience with his subjects and the negative attitude they seemed to adopt toward everything he tried to do for them. He decided to teach them a lesson and put an end to their carping. He instructed his experts to purge the code of contradictions, but at the same time to stiffen drastically every requirement contained in it and to add a long list of new crimes. Thus, where before the citizen summoned to the throne was given ten days in which to report, in the revision the time was cut to ten seconds. It was made a crime, punishable by ten years' imprisonment, to cough, sneeze, hiccough, faint or fall down in the presence of the king. It was made treason not to understand, believe in, and correctly profess the doctrine of evolutionary, democratic redemption.

When the new code was published a near revolution resulted. Leading citizens declared their intention to flout its provisions. Someone discovered in an ancient author a passage that seemed apt: "To command what cannot be done is not to make law; it is to unmake law, for a command that cannot be obeyed serves no end but confusion, fear and chaos." Soon this passage was being quoted in a hundred petitions to the king.

The code was again withdrawn and a staff of experts charged with the task of revision.

Rex's instructions to the experts were that whenever they encountered a rule requiring an impossibility, it should be revised to make compliance possible. It turned out that to accomplish this result every provision in the code had to be substantially rewritten. The final result was, however, a triumph of draftsmanship. It was clear, consistent with itself, and demanded nothing of the subject that did not lie easily within his powers. It was printed and distributed free of charge on every street corner.

However, before the effective date for the new code had arrived, it was discovered that so much time had been spent in successive revisions of Rex's original draft, that the substance of the code had been seriously overtaken by events. Ever since Rex assumed the throne there had been a suspension of ordinary legal processes and this had brought about important economic and institutional changes within the country. Accommodation to these altered conditions required many changes of substance in the law. Accordingly as soon as the new code became legally effective, it was subjected to a daily stream of amendments. Again popular discontent mounted; an anonymous pamphlet appeared on the streets carrying scurrilous cartoons of the king and a leading article with the title: "A law that changes every day is worse than no law at all."

Within a short time this source of discontent began to cure itself as the pace of amendment gradually slackened. Before this had occurred to any noticeable degree, however, Rex announced an important decision. Reflecting on the misadventures of his reign, he concluded that much of the trouble lay in bad advice he had received from experts. He accordingly declared he was reassuming the judicial power in his own person. In this way he could directly control the application of the new code and insure his country against another crisis. He began to spend practically all of his time hearing and deciding cases arising under the new code.

As the king proceeded with this task, it seemed to bring to a belated blossoming his long dormant powers of generalization. His opinions began, indeed, to reveal a confident and almost exuberant virtuosity as he deftly distinguished his own previous decisions, exposed the principles on which he acted, and laid down guide lines for the disposition of future controversies. For Rex's subjects a new day seemed about to dawn when they could finally conform their conduct to a coherent body of rules.

This hope was, however, soon shattered. As the bound volumes of Rex's judgments became available and were subjected to closer study, his subjects were appalled to discover that there existed no discernible relation between those judgments and the code they purported to apply. Insofar as it found expression in the actual disposition of con-

troversies, the new code might just as well not have existed at all. Yet in virtually every one of his decisions Rex declared and redeclared the code to be the basic law of his kingdom. Leading citizens began to hold private meetings to discuss what measures, short of open revolt, could be taken to get the king away from the bench and back on the throne. While these discussions were going on Rex suddenly died, old before his time and deeply disillusioned with his subjects.

The first act of his successor, Rex II, was to announce that he was taking the powers of government away from the lawyers and placing them in the hands of psychiatrists and experts in public relations. This way, he explained, people could be made happy without rules.

Rex's bungling career as legislator and judge illustrates that the attempt to create and maintain a system of legal rules may miscarry in at least eight ways; there are in this enterprise, if you will, eight distinct routes to disaster. The first and most obvious lies in a failure to achieve rules at all, so that every issue must be decided on an *ad hoc* basis. The other routes are: (2) a failure to publicize, or at least to make available to the affected party, the rules he is expected to observe; (3) the abuse of retroactive legislation, which not only cannot itself guide action, but undercuts the integrity of rules prospective in effect, since it puts them under the threat of retrospective change; (4) a failure to make rules understandable; (5) the enactment of contradictory rules or (6) rules that require conduct beyond the powers of the affected party; (7) introducing such frequent changes in the rules that the subject cannot orient his action by them; and, finally, (8) a failure of congruence between the rules as announced and their actual administration.

A total failure in any one of these eight directions does not simply result in a bad system of law; it results in something that is not properly called a legal system at all, except perhaps in the Pickwickian sense in which a void contract can still be said to be one kind of contract. Certainly there can be no rational ground for asserting that a man can have a moral obligation to obey a legal rule that does not exist, or is kept secret from him, or that came into existence only after he had acted, or was unintelligible, or was contradicted by another rule of the same system, or commanded the impossible, or changed every minute. It may not be impossible for a man to obey a rule that is disregarded by those charged with its administration, but at some point obedience becomes futile—as futile, in fact, as casting a vote that will never be counted. As the sociologist Simmel has observed, there is a kind of reciprocity between government and the citizen with respect to the observance of rules.[2] Government says to the citizen in effect, "These are the rules we expect you to follow. If you follow them, you have our assurance that they are the rules that will be applied to your conduct." When this bond of reciprocity is finally and completely ruptured by government, nothing is left on which to ground the citizen's duty to observe the rules.

The citizen's predicament becomes more difficult when, though there is no total failure in any direction, there is a general and drastic deterioration in legality, such as occurred in Germany under Hitler. A situation begins to develop, for example, in which though some laws are published, others, including the most important, are not. Though most laws are prospective in effect, so free a use is made of retrospective legislation that no law is immune to change *ex post facto* if it suits the convenience of those in power. For the trial of criminal cases concerned with loyalty to the regime, special military tribunals are established and these tribunals disregard, whenever it suits their convenience, the rules that are supposed to control their decisions. Increasingly the principal object of government seems to be, not that of giving the citizen rules by which to shape his conduct, but to frighten him into impotence. As such a situation develops, the problem faced by the citizen is not so simple as that of a voter who knows with certainty that his ballot will not be counted. It is more like that of the voter who knows that the odds are against his ballot being counted at all, and that if it is counted, there is a good chance that it will be counted for the side against which he actually voted. A citizen in this predicament has to decide for himself whether to stay with the system and cast his ballot as a kind of symbolic act expressing the hope of a better day. So it was with the German citizen under Hitler faced with deciding whether he had an obligation to obey such portions of the laws as the Nazi terror had left intact.

In situations like these there can be no simple principle by which to test the citizen's obligation of fidelity to law, any more than there can be such a principle for testing his right to engage in a general revolution. One thing is, however, clear. A mere respect for constituted authority must not be confused with fidelity to law. Rex's subjects, for example, remained faithful to him as king throughout his long and inept reign. They were not faithful to his law, for he never made any.

2. H.L.A. Hart: Reply to Professor Fuller[3]

Professor Fuller's eight principles for carrying out the purposive activity of subjecting human conduct to rules are designated as "the inner morality of law." It should be noted that the force of the word "inner" is to stress the fact that these forms of legal excellence are derived, not from principles of justice or other "external" moral principles relating to the law's substantive aims or content, but are reached solely through a realistic consideration of what is necessary for the efficient execution of the purpose of guiding human conduct by rules. We see what they are by occupying the position of the conscientious legislator bent on this purpose, and they are essentially principles of good craftsmanship. They are independent of the law's substantive aims just as the principles of carpentry are independent of whether the carpenter is making hospital beds or torturer's racks.

The author's insistence on classifying these principles of legality as a "morality"

[2] THE SOCIOLOGY OF GEORG SIMMEL (1950), trans. Wolff, § 4, "Interaction in the Idea of 'Law,'" pp. 186-89; *see also* Chapter 4, "Subordination under a Principle," pp. 250-67.

[3] H.L.A. Hart, *Book Review: The Morality of Law*, 78 HARVARD LAW REVIEW 1281, 1284-86 (1965). Copyright 1965 Harvard Law Review Association. Excerpts reprinted by permission.

perpetuates a confusion between two notions that it is vital to hold apart: the notions of purposive activity and morality. Poisoning is no doubt a purposive activity, and reflections on its purpose may show that it has internal principles. ("Avoid poisons however lethal if they cause the victim to vomit," or "Avoid poisons however lethal if their shape, color, or size is likely to attract notice.") But to call these principles of the poisoner's art "the morality of poisoning" would simply blur the distinction between the notions of efficiency for a purpose and those final judgments about activities and purposes with which morality in its various forms is concerned.

3. Lon Fuller: Rejoinder to Professor Hart[4]

I must confess that Professor Hart's line of argument struck me at first as being so bizarre and even perverse, as not to deserve an answer. Reflection has, however, convinced me that I was mistaken in this.

I perceive two assumptions underlying my critic's rejection of the "internal morality of law." The first of these is a belief that the existence or non-existence of law is, from a moral point of view, a matter of indifference. The second is an assumption characteristic of legal positivism generally: that law should be viewed not as the product of an interplay of purposive orientations between the citizen and his government but as a one-way projection of authority, originating with government and imposing itself upon the citizen.

In the literature of legal positivism it is of course standard practice to examine at length the relations of law and morals. With respect to the influence of morals on law it is common to point out that moral conceptions may guide legislation, furnish standards for the criticism of existing law, and may properly be taken into account in the interpretation of law. The treatment of the converse influence—that of law on morality—is generally more meager, being confined chiefly

to the observation that legal rules long established tend, through a kind of cultural conditioning, to be regarded as morally right.

What is generally missing in these accounts is any recognition of the role legal rules play in making possible an effective realization of morality in the actual behavior of human beings. Moral principles cannot function in a social vacuum or in a war of all against all. To live the good life requires something more than good intentions, even if they are generally shared: it requires the support of firm base lines for human interaction, something that—in modern society at least—only a sound legal system can supply.

Two forms of social ordering are often confounded. One of these is *managerial direction*, the other is *law*. Both involve the direction and control of human activity; both imply subordination to authority. An extensive vocabulary is shared by the two forms: "authority," "orders," "control," "jurisdiction," "obedience," "compliance," "legitimacy"—these are but a few of the terms whose double residence is a source of confusion.

A general and summary statement of the distinctions between the two forms of social ordering might run somewhat as follows. The directives issued in a managerial context are *applied* by the subordinate in order to serve a purpose set by his superior. The law-abiding citizen, on the other hand, does not *apply* legal rules to serve specific ends set by the lawgiver, but rather *follows* them in the conduct of his own affairs, the interests he is presumed to serve in following legal rules being those of society generally. The directives of a managerial system regulate primarily the relations between the subordinate and his superior and only collaterally the relations of the subordinate with third persons. The rules of a legal system, on the other hand, normally serve the primary purpose of setting the citizen's relations with other citizens and only in a collateral manner his relations with the seat of authority from which the rules proceed.

Five of the eight principles of legality are quite at home in a managerial context. If the superior is to secure what he wants through the instrumentality of the subordinate he must, first of all, communicate his wishes, or "promulgate" them by giving the subordinate a chance to know what they are, for example, by posting them on a bulletin

[4]Lon L. Fuller, The Morality of Law, 201-02, 204-05, 207-09, 213-14 (rev. ed. 1969). Copyright 1969 Yale University. Reprinted by permission of Yale University Press.

board. His directives must also be reasonably clear, free from contradiction, possible of execution and not changed so often as to frustrate the efforts of the subordinate to act on them. Carelessness in these manners may seriously impair the "efficacy" of the managerial enterprise.

What of the three other principles? With respect to the requirement of generality, this becomes, in a managerial context, simply a matter of expediency. In actual practice managerial control is normally achieved by standing orders that will relieve the superior from having to give a step-by-step direction to his subordinate's performance. But the subordinate has no justification for complaint if, in a particular case, the superior directs him to depart from the procedures prescribed by some general order. This means, in turn, that in a managerial relation there is no room for a formal principle demanding that the actions of the superior conform to the rules he has himself announced; in this context the principle of "congruence between official action and declared rule" loses its relevance. As for the principle against retroactivity, the problem simply does not arise; no manager retaining a semblance of sanity would direct the subordinate today to do something on his behalf yesterday.

From the brief analysis just presented it is apparent that the managerial relation fits quite comfortably the picture of a one-way projection of authority. Insofar as the principles of legality are here applicable they are indeed "principles of efficacy"; they are instruments for the achievement of the superior's ends. This does not mean that the elements of interaction or reciprocity are ever wholly absent in a managerial relation. If the superior habitually overburdens those under his direction, confuses them by switching signals too frequently, or falsely accuses them of departing from instructions they have in fact faithfully followed, the morale of his subordinates will suffer and they may not go a good job for him; indeed, if his inconsiderateness goes too far, they may end by deserting his employ or turning against him in open revolt. But this tacit reciprocity of reasonableness and restraint is something collateral to the basic relation of order-giver and order-executor.

With a legal system the matter stands quite otherwise, for here the existence of a relatively stable reciprocity of expectations between lawgiver and subject is part of the very idea of a functioning legal order.

In a bureaucratic context, managerial direction is often accompanied by, and intertwined with miniature legal systems affecting such matters as discipline and special privileges. In such a context it is a commonplace of sociological observation that those occupying posts of authority will often resist not only the clarification of rules, but even their effective publication.

Knowledge of the rules, and freedom to interpret them to fit the case at hand, are important sources of power. One student in this field has even concluded that the "toleration of illicit practices actually enhances the controlling power of superiors, paradoxical as it may seem."[5] It enhances the superior's power, of course, by affording him the opportunity to obtain gratitude and loyalty through the grant of absolutions, at the same time leaving him free to visit the full rigor of the law on those he considers in need of being brought into line. This welcome freedom of action would not be his if he could not point to rules as giving significance to his actions; one cannot, for example, forgive the violation of a rule unless there is a rule to violate. This does not mean, however, that the rule has to be free from obscurity, or widely publicized, or consistently enforced. Indeed, any of these conditions may curtail the discretion of the man in control—a discretion from which he may derive not only a sense of personal power but also a sense, perhaps not wholly perverse, of serving well the enterprise of which he is a part.

It may seem that in the broader, more impersonal processes of a national or state legal system there would be lacking any impulse toward deformations or accommodations of the sort just suggested. This is far from being the case. It should be remembered, for example, that in drafting almost any statute, particularly in the fields of criminal law and economic regulation, there is likely to occur a struggle between those who want to preserve for government a broad freedom of action and those whose primary

---

[5] BLAU, THE DYNAMICS OF BUREAUCRACY 215 (2d ed. 1963).

concern is to let the citizen know in advance where he stands. In confronting this kind of problem there is room in close cases for honest differences of opinion, but there can also arise acute problems of conscience touching the basic integrity of legal processes. Over wise areas of governmental action a still more fundamental question can be raised: whether there is not a damaging and corrosive hypocrisy in pretending to act in accordance with preestablished rules when in reality the functions exercised are essentially managerial and for that reason demand and on close inspection are seen to exhibit a rule-free response to changing conditions.

What has just been said can offer only a fleeting glimpse of the responsibilities, dilemmas, and temptations that confront those concerned with the making and administering of laws. These problems are shared by legislators, judges, prosecutors, commissioners, probation officers, building inspectors, and a host of other officials, including—above all—the patrolman on his beat. To attempt to reduce these problems to issues of "efficacy" is to trivialize them beyond recognition.

4. Philip Mullock: The Inner Morality of Law[6]

That legal systems have practically necessary moral features is the insight to be gleaned from Fuller's notion of the inner morality of law. This does not mean that all practical principles are moral principles. Whether the principles of a practice are moral or otherwise depends on the assumptions we make about the end envisaged in the means-end relation; that the craft of the poisoner has its principles does not entail that they are moral principles.

Some of Fuller's practical principles are moral principles. The requirement that rules must be promulgated (2), that rules must be understandable (4), that they must be consistent (5), and that they must not require the impossible (6), are clearly moral in their own right. To be punished for viola-

tions of directives we are unaware of, or cannot understand, or that require us to do inconsistent things or impossible things, would be morally unsatisfactory. Generally speaking the same may be said of principle (3), the need for rules to be prospective in their applicability. However, Fuller's principle (1) that rules must be general goes to the nature of a rule regardless of the end in view, and is not of itself a moral matter.

On the other hand, it is true, as Hart suggests, that there is more to the connection between law and morality than is covered by Fuller's notion of the inner morality of law. How laws impose and create rights and duties is not answered either by Hart or Fuller. Fuller's principles go to the form rather than the substance of laws. Any further morality must be regarded as external to the means-end relation between law and social ordering covered by Fuller's internal morality of law.

When Fuller says, somewhat obscurely, that law is the purposive enterprise of subjecting human conduct to the governance of rules and having its inner morality, we may interpret this to mean that the practice of making and maintaining a legal system that creates a social order has practically necessary moral principles that impart practically necessary moral characteristics to the laws of that legal system and limit the powers of the governors by ensuring a minimum of justice and fairness as between governors and governed.

5. Robert Summers: A Moral Aspect of Procedural Natural Law[7]

Fuller sought to set forth several affirmative arguments in favor of his claim that the principles of legality somehow constitute a "morality" (i.e., necessarily translate into principles or values of moral worth). But since he did not explicitly set forth the argument that seems to support this characterization most fully, let me present it here.

---

[6] Philip Mullock, *The Inner Morality of Law*, 84 ETHICS 327, 329-31 (1973-74). Excerpted and paraphrased with the permission of the author.

[7] ROBERT SUMMERS, LON L. FULLER 37-38 (Stanford U. Press, 1984). Copyright 1984 by Robert S. Summers. Reprinted by permission.

Sufficient compliance with the principles of legality necessarily guarantees, to the extent of that compliance, the realization of a moral value, even when the content of the law involved happens to be bad. That moral value is this: the principles of generality, clarity, prospectivity, and so forth, secure that the citizen will have a *fair* opportunity to obey the law. Admittedly, the choice may be a choice to obey an evil law, but the citizen will at least have had a fair chance to decide whether to do so or not, and to act accordingly. This is in itself moral, even though, overall, what the state happens to be doing to the citizen through the substance of the law is immoral.

QUESTIONS AND COMMENTS FOR YOUR CONSIDERATION

1. Professor Fuller has described positivism as a "one-way projection of authority, originating with government and imposing itself upon the citizen," and natural law as "the product of purposive orientations between the citizen and his government." Is this fair? Simplistic?

2. Is the following a fair criticism: "Hart warns against confusing law and morality; Fuller goes out of his way to confuse the two"?

3. In the previous Chapter we studied the attempts by positivists to work out a determinate—or at least a "core"—meaning to the term "vehicle" in the statute "No vehicles allowed" in an entranceway to a public park. How would a natural lawyer interpret the same statute? Is there any doubt that a natural lawyer would allow an ambulance into the park? A baby carriage? If not, how would the natural lawyer construe the statute to allow for such interpretations?

4. Professor Fuller answered the preceding question as follows, in his much neglected book, *Anatomy of the Law*:

> It is not by looking at the word "vehicle" that we reach these conclusions, but by considering what is implicit in the notion of a park. This is true even though the word "park" nowhere appears in the statute; its language may speak not of the "city park" but of "all that area bounded on the north by Adams Boulevard, on the east by Third Street," etc. What we are basically interpreting, then, is not a word, but an institution and its meaning for the lives of human begins affected by it.
>
> It follows that the proper interpretation of the ordinance will depend on the meaning attributed to the institution "park" by the practices and attitudes of the society in question. In some countries—in the cooler latitudes, for example—a park tends to be a place of quiet and repose, where the citizen may escape the tumult of the city. In the warmer latitudes it may be a place of music and gaiety, to which the citizen will betake himself after his need for repose has been satisfied by a *siesta*. Now this difference in the meaning of the institution may have an important bearing on the interpretation of the word "vehicle." A steam calliope may be welcomed to one kind of park, for example, as a contribution to its merriment; indeed, an ingenious police sergeant might justify a ruling that it may come in by reasoning that the calliope is not really a "vehicle" at all, since it carries nothing but itself, being a musical instrument mounted on wheels. By the same token a hearse—with its sinister burden—would be definitely excluded. In another clime, where parks mean something quite different, these rulings might be reversed.

If you object to all or part of Professor Fuller's arguments, note your objections before proceeding to the next question/comment.

5. Wouldn't a *reasonable* positivist answer Professor Fuller as follows: "Of course judges should interpret statutes in light of the meaning they have in their own cultures. Thus a 'park' refers to its general meaning in the culture that enacts the statute; it would be an error to use a dictionary definition that might utilize the meaning given to the term in a different culture."

(a) But hasn't Professor Fuller anticipated this objection by noting that the word "park" isn't necessarily in the statute at all?

(b) But why would a positivist be bound by statutory words? Can't a positivist use words that are *implied* in the statute—in this case, the word "park"?

(c) But isn't one of the original purposes of positivism—going back to Jeremy Bentham—to make sure that courts do not read into legislation words that aren't there? Wasn't Bentham's main goal to avoid having the courts usurp Parliamentary authority? Didn't he fear that this is exactly what the common-law courts had done over the years as they proceeded to construe and twist statutes? Would Bentham have allowed a court to read into a statute the word "park" if that word were not there? Even if he would allow it in a particular case, wouldn't he have feared the enormous loophole for statutory interpretation that such a procedure might open up?

6. Isn't a *clear* difference between positivism and natural law the following: that positivism regards a statute as static, whereas natural law regards it as dynamic (or interactive)? Is this a better way of explaining the difference than the explanation given by Professor Fuller in Question 1, above? If so, it is derived from Fuller's own continuing argument in *Anatomy of the Law:*

> The troublesome cases [here we can refer to Hart's "penumbral" cases] are in reality resolved not in advance by the legislator, but at the point of application. This means that in applying the statute the judge or police sergeant must be guided not simply by its words but also by some conception of what is fit and proper to come into a park; conceptions of this sort are implicit in the practices and attitudes of the society of which he is a member. Finally, the social institution "park" and the legal regulations relevant to it may be expected with the passage of time to influence one another reciprocally. A lax administration of the law excluding "vehicles" may gradually change the cultural meaning of the park. Conversely, a wholly extralegal change in the uses made of parks may gradually bring about an alteration in the meaning of the statute. All this adds up to the conclusion that an important part of the statute in question is not made by the legislator, but grows and develops as an implication of complex practices and attitudes which may themselves be in a state of development and change.

Think of *any* appellate court decision that you have read involving the interpretation of a statute. Can you recharacterize the opposing arguments in the case in terms of a word-bound positivist approach and an interactive-cultural natural law approach? Would such a recharacterization help you to anticipate arguments that could have been more forcefully made by either side?

7. Reconsider the previous Question in economic terms. Can we not say that positivism is *cheaper* to apply than natural law? But if so, cheaper for whom? For the applier? For society?

8. If positivism is cheaper for judges to apply, then in a judicial system that is overcrowded with cases, can we expect judges to lean toward positivism? Can we "explain" the natural law tendency of judges centuries ago by the fact that their dockets were less crowded, and that they had more time to delve into the facts and circumstances of the cases that were brought before them?

B. Substantive Natural Law

1. H.L.A. Hart: The Case of the Grudge Informer[8]

Gustav Radbruch was a German legal philosopher who had shared the "positivist" doctrine until the Nazi tyranny. Prior to his recantation of positivism, he held that resistance to law was a matter for the personal conscience, to be thought out by the individual as a moral problem, and the validity of a law could not be disproved by showing that its requirements were morally evil or even by showing that the effect of compliance with the law would be more evil than the effect of disobedience. Austin, it may be recalled, was emphatic in condemning those who said that if human laws conflicted with the fundamental principles of morality then they cease to be laws, as talking "stark nonsense." But Austin also believed that if laws reached a certain degree of iniquity then there would be a plain moral obligation to resist them and to withhold obedience. We shall see, when we consider the alternatives, that this simple presentation of the human dilemma which may arise has much to be said for it.

Radbruch, however, had concluded from the ease with which the Nazi regime had exploited subservience to mere law—or expressed, as he thought, in the "positivist" slogan "law is law"—and from the failure of the German legal profession to protest against the enormities which they were required to perpetrate in the name of law, that "positivism" (meaning here the insistence on the separation of law as it is from law as it ought to be) had powerfully contributed to the horrors.

After the war Radbruch's conception of law as containing in itself the essential moral principle of humanitarianism was applied in practice by German courts in certain cases in which local war criminals, spies, and informers under the Nazi regime were punished. The special importance of these cases is that the persons accused of these

crimes claimed that what they had done was not illegal under the laws of the regime in force at the time these actions were performed. This plea was met with the reply that the laws upon which they relied were invalid as contravening the fundamental principles of morality. Let me cite briefly one of these cases.

In 1944 a woman, wishing to be rid of her husband, denounced him to the authorities for insulting remarks he had made about Hitler while home on leave from the German army. The wife was under no legal duty to report his acts, though what he had said was apparently in violation of statutes making it illegal to make statements detrimental to the government of the Third Reich or to impair by any means the military defense of the German people. The husband was arrested and sentenced to death, apparently pursuant to these statutes, though he was not executed but was sent to the front. In 1949 the wife was prosecuted in a West German court for an offense which we would describe as illegally depriving a person of his freedom. This was punishable as a crime under the German Criminal Code of 1871 which had remained in force continuously since its enactment. The wife pleaded that her husband's imprisonment was pursuant to the Nazi statutes and hence that she had committed no crime. The court of appeal to which the case ultimately came held that the wife was guilty of procuring the deprivation of her husband's liberty by denouncing him to the German courts, even though he had been sentenced by a court for having violated a statute, since, to quote the words of the court, the statute "was contrary to the sound conscience and sense of justice of all decent human beings." This reasoning was followed in many cases which have been hailed as a triumph of the doctrines of natural law and as signaling the overthrow of positivism. The unqualified satisfaction with this result seems to me to be hysteria. Many of us might applaud the objective—that of punishing a woman for an outrageously immoral act—but this was secured only by declaring a statute established since 1934 not to have the force of law, and at least the wisdom of this course must be doubted. There were, of course, two other choices. One was to let the woman go unpunished; one can sympathize with and endorse the view

[8] H.L.A. Hart, *Positivism and the Separation of Law and Morals*, 71 Harvard Law Review 90, 616-20 (1958). Copyright 1958 by the Harvard Law Review. Excerpts reprinted by permission of the Harvard Law Review Association.

that this might have been a bad thing to do. The other was to face the fact that if the woman were to be punished it must be pursuant to the introduction of a frankly retrospective law and with a full consciousness of what was sacrificed in securing her punishment in this way. Odious as retrospective criminal legislation and punishment may be, to have pursued it openly in this case would at least have had the merits of candor. It would have made plain that in punishing the woman a choice had to be made between two evils, that of leaving her unpunished and that of sacrificing a very precious principle of morality endorsed by most legal systems. Surely if we have learned anything from the history of morals it is that the thing to do with a moral quandary is not to hide it. Like nettles, the occasions when life forces us to choose between the lesser of two evils must be grasped with the consciousness that they are what they are.

2. Lon Fuller: The Grudge Informer[9]

After the collapse of the Nazi regime the German courts were faced with a truly frightful predicament. It was impossible for them to declare the whole dictatorship illegal or to treat as void every decision and legal enactment that had emanated from Hitler's government. Intolerable dislocations would have resulted from any such wholesale outlawing of all that occurred over a span of twelve years. On the other hand, it was equally impossible to carry forward into the new government the effects of every Nazi perversity that had been committed in the name of law; any such course would have tainted an indefinite future with the poisons of Nazism.

This predicament—which was, indeed, a pervasive one, affecting all branches of law—came to a dramatic head in a series of cases

---

[9] Lon F. Fuller, *Positivism and Fidelity to Law—A Reply to Professor Hart*, 71 HARVARD LAW REVIEW 630, 648-57 (1958). Copyright 1958 by the Harvard Law Review. Excerpts reprinted by permission of the Harvard Law Review Association.

involving informers who had taken advantage of the Nazi terror to get rid of personal enemies or unwanted spouses. If all Nazi statutes and judicial decisions were indiscriminately "law," then these despicable creatures were guiltless, since they had turned their victims over to processes which the Nazis themselves knew by the name of law. Yet it was intolerable, especially for the surviving relatives and friends of the victims, that these people should go about unpunished, while the objects of their spite were dead, or were just being released after years of imprisonment, or, more painful still, simply remained unaccounted for.

The urgency of this situation does not by any means escape Professor Hart. Indeed, he is moved to recommend an expedient that is surely not lacking itself in a certain air of desperation. He suggests that a retroactive criminal statute would have been the least objectionable solution to the problem. This statute would have punished the informer, and branded him as a criminal, for an act which Professor Hart regards as having been perfectly legal when he committed it.

On the other hand, Professor Hart condemns without qualification those judicial decisions in which the courts themselves undertook to declare void certain of the Nazi statutes under which the informer's victims had been convicted. One cannot help raising at this point the question whether the issue as presented by Professor Hart himself is truly that of fidelity to law. Surely it would be a necessary implication of a retroactive criminal statute against informers that, for purposes of that statute at least, the Nazi laws as applied to the informers or their victims were to be regarded as void. With this turn the question seems no longer to be whether what was once law can now be declared not to have been law, but rather who should do the dirty work, the courts or the legislature. But, as Professor Hart himself suggests, the issues at stake are much too serious to risk losing them in a semantic tangle. Even if the whole question were one of words, we should remind ourselves that we are in an area where words have a powerful effect on human attitudes. I should like, therefore, to undertake a defense of the German courts, and to advance reasons why, in my opinion, their decisions do not represent the abandonment of legal principle that Professor Hart sees in them. Let us turn to the actual case discussed by Professor Hart.

In 1944, a German soldier paid a short visit to his wife while under travel orders on a reassignment. During the single day he was home, he conveyed privately to his wife something of his opinion of the Hitler government. He expressed disapproval of Hitler and other leading personalities of the Nazi party. He also said it was too bad Hitler had not met his end in the assassination attempt that occurred on July 20th of that year. Shortly after his departure, his wife, who wished to get rid of him, reported his remarks to the local leader of the Nazi party, observing that "a man who would say a thing like that does not deserve to live." The result was a trial of the husband by a military tribunal and a sentence of death. After a short period of imprisonment, instead of being executed, he was sent to the front again. After the collapse of the Nazi regime, the wife was brought to trial for having procured the imprisonment of her husband. Her defense rested on the ground that her husband's statements to her about Hitler and the Nazis constituted a crime under the laws then in force. Accordingly, when she informed on her husband she was simply bringing a criminal to justice.

Let us turn now to the statute upon which Professor Hart relies in assuming that the husband's utterance was unlawful. This is the act of 1934, the relevant portions of which are translated below:

(I) Whoever publicly makes spiteful or provocative statements directed against, or statements which disclose a base disposition toward the leading personalities of the nation or of the National Socialist German Workers' Party, or toward measures taken or in situations established by them, and of such a nature as to undermine the people's confidence in their political leadership, shall be punished by imprisonment. (2) Malicious utterances not made in public shall be treated in the same manner as public utterances when the person making them realized or should have realized they would reach the public. (3) Prosecution for such utterances shall be only on the order of the National Minister of Justice; in case the utterance was directed against a lead-

ing personality of the National Socialist German Workers' Party, the Minister of Justice shall order prosecution only with the advice and consent of the Representative of the Leader. (4) The National Minister of Justice shall, with the advice and consent of the Representative of the Leader, determine who shall belong to the class of leading personalities for purposes of Section I above.

Extended comment on this legislative monstrosity is scarcely called for, overlarded and undermined as it is by uncontrolled administrative discretion. We may note only: first, that it offers no justification whatever for the death penalty actually imposed on the husband, though never carried out; second, that if the wife's act in informing on her husband made his remarks "public," there is no such thing as a private utterance under this statute. I should like to ask the reader whether he can actually share Professor Hart's indignation that, in the perplexities of the postwar reconstruction, the German courts saw fit to declare this thing not a law. Can it be argued seriously that it would have been more beseeming to the judicial process if the postwar courts had undertaken a study of "the interpretative principles" in force during Hitler's rule and had then solemnly applied those "principles" to ascertain the meaning of this statute? On the other hand, would the courts really have been showing respect for Nazi law if they had construed the Nazi statutes by their own, quite different, standards of interpretation?

Professor Hart castigates the German courts and Radbruch, not so much for what they believed had to be done, but because they failed to see that they were confronted by a moral dilemma of a sort that would have been immediately apparent to Bentham and Austin. By the simple dodge of saying, "When a statute is sufficiently evil it ceases to be law," they ran away from the problem they should have faced.

This criticism is, I believe, without justification. So far as the courts are concerned, matters certainly would not have been helped if, instead of saying, "This is not law," they had said, "This is law but it is so evil we will refuse to apply it." Surely moral confusion reaches its height when a court refuses to apply something it admits to be law, and Professor Hart does not recommend any such "facing of the true issue" by the courts themselves. He would have preferred a retroactive statute.

I hope I am not being unjust to Professor Hart when I say that I can find no way of describing the dilemma as he sees it but to use some such words as the following: On the one hand, we have an amoral datum called law, which has the peculiar quality of creating a moral duty to obey it. On the other hand, we have a moral duty to do what we think is right and decent. When we are confronted by a statute we believe to be thoroughly evil, we have to choose between those two duties.

If this is the positivist position, then I have no hesitancy in rejecting it. The "dilemma" it states has the verbal formulation of a problem, but the problem it states makes no sense. It is like saying I have to choose between giving food to a starving man and being mimsy with the borogoves. I do not think it is unfair to the positivistic philosophy to say that it never gives any coherent meaning to the moral obligation of fidelity to law. This obligation seems to be conceived as *sui generis*, wholly unrelated to any of the ordinary, extralegal ends of human life. The fundamental postulate of positivism—that law must be strictly severed from morality—seems to deny the possibility of any bridge between the obligation to obey law and other moral obligations. No mediating principle can measure their respective demands on conscience, for they exist in wholly separate worlds.

While I would not subscribe to all of Radbruch's postwar views—especially those relating to "higher law"—I think he saw, much more clearly than does Professor Hart, the true nature of the dilemma confronted by Germany in seeking to rebuild her shattered legal institutions. Germany had to restore both respect for law and respect for justice. Though neither of these could be restored without the other, painful antinomies were encountered in attempting to restore both at once, as Radbruch saw all too clearly. Essentially Radbruch saw the dilemma as that of meeting the demands of order, on the one hand, and those of good order, on the other. Of course no pat formula can be derived from this phrasing of the problem. But, unlike legal positivism, it does not present us with

opposing demands that have no living contact with one another, that simply shout their contradictions across a vacuum. As we seek order, we can meaningfully remind ourselves that order itself will do us no good unless it is good for something. As we seek to make our order good, we can remind ourselves that justice itself is impossible without order, and that we must not lose order itself in the attempt to make it good.

Professor Hart and others have been understandably distressed by references to a "higher law" in some of the decisions concerning informers and in Radbruch's postwar writings. I suggest that if German jurisprudence had concerned itself more with the inner morality of law, it would not have been necessary to invoke any notion of this sort in declaring void the more outrageous Nazi statutes.

To me there is nothing shocking in saying that a dictatorship which clothes itself with a tinsel of legal form can so far depart from the morality of order, from the inner morality of law itself, that it ceases to be a legal system. When a system calling itself law is predicated upon a general disregard by judges of the terms of the laws they purport to enforce, when this system habitually cures its legal irregularities, even the grossest, by retroactive statutes, when it has only to resort to forays of terror in the streets, which no one dares challenge, in order to escape even those scant restraints imposed by the pretense of legality—when all these things have become true of a dictatorship, it is not hard for me, at least, to deny to it the name of law.

I believe that the invalidity of the statutes involved in the informer cases could have been grounded on considerations such as I have just outlined. But if you were raised with a generation that said "law is law" and meant it, you may feel the only way you can escape one law is to set another off against it, and this perforce must be a "higher law." Hence these notions of "higher law," which are a justifiable cause for alarm, may themselves be a belated fruit of German legal positivism.

It should be remarked at this point that it is chiefly in Roman Catholic writings that the theory of natural law is considered, not simply as a search for those principles that will enable men to live together successfully, but as a quest for something that can be called a "*higher law.*" This identification of natural law with a law that is above human laws seems in fact to be demanded by any doctrine that asserts the possibility of an *authoritative* pronouncement of the demands of natural law. In those areas affected by such pronouncements as have so far been issued, the conflict between Roman Catholic doctrine and opposing views seems to me to be a conflict *between two forms of positivism.* Fortunately, over most of the area with which lawyers are concerned, no such pronouncements exist. In these areas I think those of us who are not adherents of its faith can be grateful to the Catholic Church for having kept alive the rationalistic tradition in ethics.

I do not assert that the solution I have suggested for the informer cases would not have entailed its own difficulties, particularly the familiar one of knowing where to stop. But I think it demonstrable that the most serious deterioration in legal morality under Hitler took place in branches of the law like those involved in the informer cases; no comparable deterioration was to be observed in the ordinary branches of private law. It was in those areas where the ends of law were most odious by ordinary standards of decency that the morality of law itself was most flagrantly disregarded. In other words, where one would have been most tempted to say, "This is so evil it cannot be a law," one could usually have said instead, "This thing is the product of a system so oblivious to the morality of law that it is not entitled to be called a law." I think there is something more than accident here, for the overlapping suggests that legal morality cannot live when it is severed from a striving toward justice and decency.

But as an actual solution for the informer cases, I, like Professors Hart and Radbruch, would have preferred a retroactive statute. My reason for this preference is not that this is the most nearly lawful way of making unlawful what was once law. Rather I would see such a statute as a way of symbolizing a sharp break with the past, as a means of isolating a kind of cleanup operation from the normal functioning of the judicial process. By this isolation it would become possible for the judiciary to return more rapidly to a condition in which the demands of legal morality could be given proper respect. In other words, it would make it possible to plan more effectively to regain for the ideal of fidelity to law its normal meaning.

QUESTIONS AND COMMENTS FOR YOUR CONSIDERATION

1. Look again at the Nazi statute quoted by Professor Fuller. Does it literally apply to what a husband said to his wife in the privacy of their home? Should the husband reasonably have believed that his comments would reach the public? How would they reach the public? Does the way in which they might reach the public make a major difference?

2. Is the Nazi judge's fidelity to Hitler's legislation a triumph of positivism? Does it represent the apotheosis of the separation of law and morality?

3. Is it fair to criticize positivism as applied to judges? Isn't positivism only supposed to apply to the public, and not to judges (who are after all state officials)?

4. Did Professor Fuller make a mistake, in terms of his own theory, in concluding that a retroactive statute might have been the best way to handle the "grudge informer" situation?

3. Anthony D'Amato: Comment on the Grudge Informer[10]

Hart's position is that although the Nazi laws were morally iniquitous, they were nevertheless valid laws and cannot later be declared invalid. Thus Hart would either let the informer go unpunished or face up to the moral dilemma implicit in the situation and pass a retrospective law to cover the case. But the retroactive solution is a "Nazi" type approach to the problem. Why should Hart's theory that a valid retroactive statute is "law" prevail when it could just as well be argued that retroactivity destroys the lawfulness of a statute?

Let us test the situation by imagining that the wife in 1944 actually consults an attorney to see whether she would be perfectly safe in denouncing her husband:

ATTORNEY: The statutes and practices regarding informing on subversives are valid statutes and all officials probably will adhere to them.

CLIENT: But are there any German officials who might not act in the way you predict?

ATTORNEY: The only German officials who might find you guilty of a crime would be those who might come into power if the entire Nazi regime were deposed.

CLIENT: What are the chances of that happening?

ATTORNEY: The war is going badly. Germany may lose. A new German government might decide to prosecute you for what you intend to do. After all, you and I know that you are not exactly being patriotic in denouncing your husband. Maybe a new set of officials will find a personal motive in what you intend to do, and prosecute you for it.

If this is a *possible* reconstruction of advice that *could have been* available to the wife, *then* it suggests that she had some notice of what *might* happen to her in the event that the entire German regime were replaced by a new regime. And if she had, or

reasonably should have had, such notice, then we don't need a wholly new retroactive statute to make what she did a crime. Under the scenario I have just constructed, she was, or reasonably should have been, placed on notice that what she was doing was a crime at the time she was doing it! The main reason she thought she could get away with it was her prediction about what the present German officials would probably do if she denounced her husband. But she could have had no similar degree of confidence in predicting what a future set of new officials might do.

Yet this argument proves too much. If in any given case we can imagine the replacement of all of our country's officials with a new set of officials, then everything we do is potentially questionable. If you buy a house, are you risking a future takeover by a communist regime that prosecutes you for engaging in an act of *bourgeois* capitalism? Surely there is a vanishingly small but nevertheless positive risk that this might happen. Thus the "structural" solution to the problem of the grudge informer—conjuring up a new regime of officials—is not a tidy solution to the problem of the grudge informer.

But maybe we can amend it so that it works. We begin with our instinctive notion that the wife in 1944 had reason to know that her act would be justifiably be regarded by many people as immoral. True, she would avoid prosecution by the current regime. But that is only to say that she lived at a time and a place where there was a separation between the moral requirement of not procuring the murder of another person and the legal requirement of informing on persons saying unpatriotic things. This separation between morality and law was simply due to the kind of government at that time and place.

We do not have the same instinctive reaction to the case of buying a house in the United States today. We do not have the feeling that some people regard it as wrong. Even a full-fledged communist would have to view the act of buying a house as fair within the capitalist context in which it occurs, for after all it only involves the exchange of money for a marketable commodity. Indeed there is something irrational and probably wrong with a person who, in a capi-

---

[10] Based on Anthony D'Amato, *The Limits of Legal Realism*, 87 YALE LAW JOURNAL 468 (1978). Copyright 1978 by Anthony D'Amato.

talist system, needs a house and has the money to buy it but (perhaps out of fear that someday a communist government might take over the country) refrains from buying it. Similarly, if I don't show up for work tomorrow and explain to my employer that I stayed home because I feared that a new government might take over the country and punish me for having gone to work, I would probably be advised to see a psychotherapist.

In short, the idea that anything we do can be punished someday is grossly overinclusive. A much more limited, and manageable, notion is that if we do something that is morally wrong but not punished because of the particular kind of legal regime we are living under, we might someday be punished for it if a new regime takes over. In other words, we may do something that is wrong now and "get away with it" but we have no guarantee that we will never see a day of reckoning. Even more crucial to this analysis is the prediction that the new set of officials may in their minds be doing what is morally right in punishing us. Thus, we have a good basis for predicting that a new set of officials might act in that way. The commission of an immoral act today, in the context of a regime that does not punish us for doing it, puts us on reasonable notice that a new regime might someday punish us.

Let us return to the hypothetical dialogue between the lawyer and the grudge-informer wife in 1944. The lawyer is giving the client the best possible advice that a lawyer can give, which is not just a prediction of what "the law" might do but rather is a more comprehensive prediction of what might in fact happen to the client. In the lawyer-client relationship, any lawyer has a professional obligation to advise the client broadly, including but not limited to what "the law" says. In the case of our hypothetical lawyer, the lawyer took up an issue that was "extrinsic" to the legal system of Germany in 1944, namely, the issue of morality. The issue of morality then served as the basis for a prediction about what might happen if a new set of officials took over the government.

In the preceding paragraph I've placed quotation marks around certain key terms. Under the theory of natural law, the quotation marks are critical. The natural-law view of law is much more expansive and comprehensive than the positivist view. Indeed, the

natural-law view of law is reflected by the advice given by our hypothetical lawyer. Our hypothetical lawyer is, after all, a *lawyer*. The lawyer is not giving the client medical advice, or theological advice, or simply the practical advice of a person on the street. The lawyer is giving *legal* advice. But that legal advice is not restricted to "the law" on the books in the particular German regime of 1944. Rather, the advice is a broader prediction of what *the law* might do to the client, including *the law* that a new regime might impose upon the client. To predict what a new regime might do, the lawyer needs to bring in moral principles. In the expansive view of law that I am talking about—and that our hypothetical lawyer is practicing—these moral principles are not "extrinsic" to the legal advice. Rather, they form a necessary, and critical, part of the legal advice.

Or, to put it a different way, consider the perspective of the client. Her view of law is simply *a prediction of what officials will do to her*.[11] She doesn't care about law as a subject in itself, the way an academician might care about law. She does not care about law as a practice, the way a lawyer might care about law. She is only interested in what legal officials will do to her if she carries out her plan. Moreover, she doesn't simply want advice about a certain set of named legal officials. She wants to know what *all* legal officials might do to her. Thus, her lawyer is professionally obligated to give her this advice. Her lawyer cannot simply restrict the advice to what the present set of officials in Germany might do, because personnel can change. New officials even in the Hitler regime, and certainly new officials in a takeover government, might look upon the facts differently from the way officials now in place might look upon those facts. The lawyer is under an obligation to predict the behavior of all officials, simply because the client can be at different degrees of risk depending upon who the officials are and who they will be.

Thus, under natural law theory, morality

---

[11] *Editor's Note:* The idea of law as a prediction of what officials will do is examined more fully later in the Chapter on Legal Realism.

is not "extrinsic" to the legal system.[12] Morality always furnishes a basis for predicting what officials may do. The probability can range from very small to very large, but it is not zero. The probability was not zero even for the officials in Germany in 1944! When the attorney said that all German officials "probably" will adhere to the statutes on subversives, the statement was accurate. If the attorney had said officials will "certainly" adhere to the statutes, it would have been inaccurate. For there was always a possibility, however small, that a German official would listen to the wife's story and be outraged by it, regarding her attempt to inform on her husband as a perversion of Nazi ideology and a misuse of the statute on subversives. The official might order that the wife be prosecuted for attempted murder. The attorney had to have in mind this possibility, even if it had an extremely low probability of happening. From this starting point, it is only a matter of increasing the numerical value of the probability as one contemplates the overthrow of the present regime and its replacement by a new set of officials. Hence, morality was never entirely "extrinsic" to the legal system in place in 1944, and certainly not "extrinsic" to the legal system as it would be projected into the future which would include the possibility of wholesale changes in official personnel.

The day-to-day practice of law certainly does not involve cases as exotic as the grudge informer case where all the officials of a state are replaced by an entirely new government. But the reasoning can be exactly the same. A client's fortunes may change with the change of just one official. Suppose a defendant charged with assault arranges to bribe the judge assigned to his case. The bribe money is delivered and the judge assures the defendant he will be acquitted. Then comes the day of the trial and the defendant is surprised to see that the judge he expected has been replaced by a different judge. Not only is the defendant now likely to be convicted of assault, but if he complains about the change in judges and explains the basis

for his complaint, he will also be indicted and convicted of bribery.

4. Arthur Leff: Universal Ethics?[13]

Only if ethics was something unspeakable by us, could law be unnatural, and therefore unchallengeable. As things now stand, everything is up for grabs.
Nevertheless:
Napalming babies is bad.
Starving the poor is wicked.
Buying and selling each other is depraved.
Those who stood up to and died resisting Hitler, Stalin, Amin, and
Pol Pot—and General Custer too—have earned salvation. Those who acquiesced deserve to be damned.
There is in the world such a thing as evil.
[All together now:] Sez who?
God help us.

5. Anthony D'Amato: Universal Morality[14]

Professor Fuller's jurisprudence is one of procedural natural law; it concerns what Fuller calls the "internal morality of law." He had the faith, as he put it himself, that "if we do things the right way, we'll do the right things."[15] Substantive natural law is different; it uses as a test for the validity of law the congruence of the content (not only the form)[16] of law with substantive principles of morality. This was the test offered by Cicero. Although the works of Cicero are no longer taught as part of everyone's liberal

---

[12] *Editor's Note:* The same holds true for "Justice," as I shall contend in Chapter 7.

[13] Arthur Leff, *Unspeakable Ethics, Unnatural Law,* 1979 DUKE L.J. 1229, 1249.
[14] Based on Anthony D'Amato, *Lon Fuller and Substantive Natural Law,* 26 AMERICAN JOURNAL OF JURISPRUDENCE 202 (1981). Copyright 1981 Anthony D'Amato.
[15] Lon L. Fuller, *What the Law Schools Can Contribute to the Making of Lawyers,* 1 J. LEG. EDUC. 189, 204 (1948).
[16] *Editor's Note: See supra,* Section A, "Commentary" by Philip Mullock.

education the way they were in high schools and colleges a century ago, we should revisit Cicero as the best historical exemplar of the true substantive natural lawyer. True laws, according to Cicero, were those laws consistent with justice and natural law. If a law duly enacted was inconsistent with justice or morality, then it was a law in name only, not deserving of the title "law" any more than a harmful chemical packaged by a non-druggist is entitled to be called a "prescription."[17] Under Cicero's view, citizens and judges only have an obligation to obey true laws; they have no obligation to obey commands that might just as well have issued from a gang of thieves as from the government. Of course, this theory of jurisprudence will probably not help a citizen who refuses to obey an unjust law and is arrested. Quoting Cicero in jail may avail him nought. Nevertheless the Ciceronian view has considerable power if it is accepted by judges (or by a majority of the population). A judge who refuses to apply an immoral law would frustrate the state's intent in enacting it. Dictators like Hitler would not have had an easy time in subjugating the populace if they had been resisted by judges who believed in substantive natural law. Hitler was lucky to have inherited a legal system that was populated by positivist judges, and a citizenry that had been taught that law is what the government commands.

If substantive natural law requires that the validity of law be checked by its congruence with principles of morality, it follows that these principles of morality must be fixed principles. If the principles of morality were to change from time to time or from place to place, then they could hardly serve as a reference point for the validity of law. Or, to put this matter more succinctly, substantive natural law rules out the notion of moral relativism.

The substantive natural law position holds that some things are right for all times and all places, that other things are always wrong no matter when and no matter where, and that two reasonable people cannot honestly differ about what is right and what is wrong because if they differed then one of them would not be reasonable. Clearly, this position seems unscientific in the popular scientistic culture of the twentieth century. It seems universalistic, absolutistic, and intellectually arrogant. Let me try to defend it.

Let me stipulate two definitions. I will define one type of morality, which I call M-1, as that morality which you, the reader, consider universally valid. For example, you would probably condemn as wrong the deliberate infliction of severe pain upon an innocent child. You would condemn this as wrong whether it occurred in ancient Rome or today, whether it occurs in a remote country or in Washington D.C. Equally, you would condemn as wrong the deliberate killing of a person for the killer's own personal financial profit. You would condemn as wrong a student's cheating on a final exam. You would condemn as wrong the adulteration of the food of the opposing football team the night before the game so as to give each player an upset stomach. If you condemn all, or even some, of these things, you are condemning them in general—whenever or wherever they occur. M-1 constitutes "absolute morality."

In contrast, let me define a second type of morality, which I call M-2, as an act (or forbearance) that you would label as "moral" in some times or places and "immoral" at other times or places. To give an example, you might say that extramarital sexual intercourse was viewed as immoral a hundred years ago in the city you are living in now. But you might also say that extramarital sexual intercourse was not considered immoral among the Pueblos of New Mexico as reported by anthropologist Ruth Benedict[18] or among the teenagers of Samoa as reported by Margaret Mead.[19] M-2 can be called "relative morality."

There are some practices or customs that vary from place to place or from time to time that we call "mores." For example, it is a breach of etiquette to eat with one's fingers in this country and a breach of etiquette not to eat with one's fingers in some other countries. Or, to take a temporal example, fifty

---

[17] CICERO, DE LEGIBUS II. v. 11-13.

[18] RUTH BENEDICT, PATTERNS OF CULTURE (1934).

[19] MARGARET MEAD, COMING OF AGE IN SAMOA (1928).

years ago a gentleman was expected to open a door for a lady; today, such an action is not considered a sign of good manners so much as a sign of male chauvinism. "When in Rome, do as the Romans do," is a saying that captures this relativity of mores.

We could say that mores are part of M-2. But I want to make a much stronger assertion. I claim that mores are all that we mean by M-2. In short, "relative morality" is simply a matter of mores, nothing more. M-2, or "relative morality," is not morality at all.

My assertion that "relative morality" is not "morality" can be expressed in a different way. I claim that the notion of "relative morality" is incoherent. For proof of this assertion, I ask the reader to make a simple introspective test. Would you feel morally obliged to do something (or refrain from doing something) not because you think it's the right thing to do, but only because the people around you are doing it and you don't want to hurt their feelings? For instance, you're in a mid-Eastern country and the people at the dinner table are eating with their fingers. You may do so as well, not because you feel morally obliged, but because you don't want to hurt their feelings. The real test is, what would you do when you are back home? What if you were still in the mid-Eastern country, eating breakfast in the privacy of your single hotel room? Would you continue to eat with your fingers? If not, then eating-with-one's-fingers cannot possibly be a matter of "morality."

The same thing can be true of extramarital sexual intercourse. *If* you feel morally obliged to refrain from doing it because you think that it would be wrong to do it—even in situations where you could "get away with it" without anyone knowing—then for *you* it's a matter of morality, or M-1. But if you feel that you would only refrain from extramarital intercourse at a time or a place where everyone would condemn it as immoral, but that you would do it if you could "get away with it" without anyone knowing, then for *you* it's just a more, or M-2. Suppose you were to say that extramarital intercourse was immoral in Puritan New England in the eighteenth century, but not immoral on the island of Samoa in the twentieth century. Then this is another way of proving that it's just a matter of M-2 for you. You might use the term "immoral" in describing the proscribed behavior in Puritan New England, but actually that would be a misuse of the word for *you*. Although it might describe what the New England Puritans themselves felt about the practice, it doesn't describe what *you* feel about it.

Morality is a very personal thing. If you feel that something is immoral, then the fact that some islanders do it doesn't shake your belief that it is immoral. On the other hand, if you think that something is just a matter of mores, it doesn't become a matter of morality for you simply because some other people at some other time or place believe it is a matter of morality. No one else can make moral decisions for you. As R. M. Hare puts it:

> A man who is faced with [a moral] problem knows that it is his own problem, and that nobody can answer it for him. He may, it is true, ask the advice of other people; and he may also ascertain more facts about the circumstances and consequences of a proposed action, and other facts of this sort. But there will come a time when he does not hope to find out anything else of relevance by factual inquiry, and when he knows that, whatever others may say about the answer to his problem, *he* has to answer it. If any one were to suggest that the answer must be such and such, because everybody says so—or that, even, he would be abusing the English language if he gave any other answer—he will, if he understands what moral questions are, feel that to accept these suggestions would be to accept a diminution of his own freedom. For one of the most important constituents of our freedom, as moral agents, is the freedom to form our own opinions about moral questions, even if that involves changing our language.[20]

Although we can describe what other people think by saying that they thought that something was a matter of morality, we don't accept the proposition that it *was indeed* a matter of morality unless we ourselves believe that it is a matter of morality. And we ourselves won't believe it unless we regard it as a matter of morality for all times and all places. This conclusion, after all, accords

---

[20] RICHARD M. HARE, FREEDOM AND REASON 1-2 (1963).

with common sense. Why would we feel *personally bound* to do something if we did not feel that doing it is an obligation that humankind in general has? If, for example, murder or child abuse are things we regard as contrary to morality, then we would have to regard them as contrary to morality whenever or wherever they occur.[21]

I believe that we hear so much about "moral relativism," despite what I claim is its incoherence, because famous comparative anthropologists of the twentieth century—such as William Graham Sumner, Raymond Firth, Ruth Benedict, Kroeber and Kluckhohn, and Margaret Mead—succeeded so well in teaching generations of college students that morality is relative to a particular culture. In their studies of remote, primitive, or isolated communities, they urged their readers to be tolerant of foreign practices. Ruth Benedict wrote, for instance, "We recognize that morality differs in every society, and is a convenient term for socially approved habits."[22] She called upon her readers to get rid of their cultural ethnocentrism, and to tolerate not only the behavior of people in other societies but also the abnormal behavior of people in our own society.[23] By linking moral relativism with tolerance, the pleas of these comparative anthropologists fell upon receptive ears.

---

[21] COLIN M. TURNBULL, in his book THE MOUNTAIN PEOPLE (1972), describes child abuse among the Ik community in the mountains separating Uganda and Kenya. In one of many incidents, a father laughed when his ten-year-old son developed an intestinal blockage, and joked about the distended belly. The author offered to drive the boy to a hospital, but the father stalled because he wanted to go instead (to get a ride in the author's Land Rover). The father stole food from the boy, and the boy finally died. *Id.* at 218-19. The book attracted unusual interest among comparative anthropologists because the author stated his disapproval of the Ik practices, and on occasion interfered with those practices. Academicians criticized the author for interfering with, and passing judgment upon, the subjects of his study. In our terms, the author refused to make an M-1 into an M-2.

[22] Ruth Benedict, *Anthropology and the Abnormal*, in D. Haring (ed.), PERSONAL CHARACTER AND CULTURAL MILIEU 195.

[23] RUTH BENEDICT, PATTERNS OF CULTURE (1934.)

But if we reexamine their works from the unemotional perspective allowed by the passage of half a century's time, we find that their generalizations stemmed from a single example of practice in the remote or primitive communities they studied. This example was extramarital sexual intercourse. From this practice, which they deemed moral for those societies but immoral for our own, they reached their conclusions that we should be tolerant of behavior *we* consider immoral if the people who engage in that behavior consider it moral. But the comparative anthropologists did not adduce any other examples of this so-called moral relativism. To be sure, they found many examples of folkways, mores, and customs that were different in the societies they studied. But these were not practices that Americans at the time would have considered to be *immoral*. The only example they gave of a practice that *we* considered to be immoral and the *remote communities* considered to be moral was extramarital sexual intercourse.

Indeed, as the philosopher John W. Cook has found after a careful study of the writings of these comparative anthropologists, the basic things that *we* consider immoral were also considered immoral in the communities they studied.[24] To be sure, reaching this conclusion requires some digging. One of the practices Professor Cook had to explain was human sacrifice to appease the rain god. Is this murder? If we examine what those people *believe*—that sacrificing a human being is the only way to appease the god, bring rain, and avert starvation from crop failure—then the sacrifice itself, no matter how superstitious or regrettable it appears to us, is not murder. Our own society might appear to be engaged in a similar superstition from the vantage point of a far more advanced culture—for example, from the standpoint of extraterrestrials who visit Earth from another galaxy. They might accuse us of "murder" because we engage in

---

[24] *Editor's Note:* Professor Cook kindly lent me his unpublished manuscripts and notes on moral relativism when I met with him in 1973. He resigned from the Philosophy Department at the University of Oregon which he headed at that time, and now lives and writes from Captiva, Florida. His latest book is WITTGENSTEIN'S METAPHYSICS (1994).

capital punishment, a practice which they might regard as superstitious and barbaric. They would regard our belief that capital punishment deters murder as statistically false, just as we might regard human sacrifices to appease the rain gods as statistically false (even though, in some cases, it rained right after the sacrifices took place). But we are not all murderers because our society condones capital punishment, any more than members of a society more primitive than ours are murderers because they condone human sacrifice.

By the same token, the primitive societies regard actual murder as immoral, just as we do. Suppose someone in our society, in order to get rid of a business rival, falsely accuses the rival of murder and plants incriminating evidence that the jury believes. Then even though the state accomplishes the actual killing (via capital punishment), if the facts later are revealed the person who made the false accusation will be prosecuted as the real murderer. The same thing is true of the primitive society if someone falsely maneuvers a rival into the position of being the one who is sacrificed to appease the rain god.

If we look more closely at the paradigm case offered by the comparative anthropologists of "relative morality," we will find that American society (and in particular the anthropologists' immediate audience—college students) was in the 1920s, 1930s, and 1940s in a period of transition regarding beliefs about extramarital sexual intercourse. While many people felt it was immoral, many others felt it was not immoral, and others were unsure. In that context, consider how important were the *stories* told by the comparative anthropologists of happy people in primitive communities engaging in extramarital sexual intercourse without shame or remorse. These stories helped convince the American audience that perhaps extramarital sexual intercourse was not harmful or immoral after all. In our terms, the effect of taking a comparative anthropology course might well have been to convince many students that they should regard extramarital sexual intercourse not as M-1 but as M-2. Indeed, we can take this hypothesis a step further. There is no reason for us to suppose that the anthropologists who told these stories—Sumner, Benedict, Mead, etc.—*themselves* believed that morality was relative,

even though that is what they wrote. They may instead have employed the notion of moral relativism to help "sell" college students on the idea that personal sexual habits are not the proper subjects of morality at all. In other words, the notion of moral relativism might have served for them as a transitional concept for the social move from the Puritan era to the modern.

Human conduct varies across such a broad spectrum that one should not be surprised that it cannot be divided absolutely into moral and immoral practices. Some practices are controversial. In today's society, there are people who regard the following practices as immoral and others who regard the same practices as moral: abortion, extramarital sexual intercourse, homosexuality, sodomy, public nudity, and prostitution. But I contend that the fact that some people regard certain practices as immoral and other people regard the same practices as moral does *not* mean that everyone regards these practices as proving that morality itself is relative. Rather, what naming these practices proves is simply that controversy exists over whether some practices are M-1 or M-2. The fact that people disagree whether a given practice is M-1 or M-2 does not mean that all of them believe that it is M-2. Those who believe it is M-1 remain committed to their belief. A person who believes that abortion is murder does not change her belief simply because others believe that it is not murder (although eventually she—or the others—may change their beliefs in part because of the weight of public opinion). In contrast, a person who believes that abortion is not murder simply does not believe that abortion is immoral. A belief that something is M-2 is not a belief in moral relativism; rather, it is a belief that something is not a matter of morality at all coupled with a recognition that some other people may think that it is a matter of morality.

Substantive natural law is founded upon universal morality. There *are* practices, I contend, that everyone, at all times and places, have regarded as immoral, such as murder, torture, theft, and cheating. The list becomes much longer when we include all conduct that violates the law, provided that the law is tied into, and is a part of, a regime of justice. (It would be hard to argue that one ought not to violate the law if the entire regime is unjust.) When it comes to the above-named practices, we are not tolerant of people who engage in them. Even if the murderer sincerely believes that killing his wife was commanded by God, we still punish him for murder.

The notion of absolute morality that underlies natural law precedes the existence of any particular legal system. It is prior to the legal system and operates as a restraint upon it. It is "undemocratic" in that it condemns laws passed by legislative majorities that contradict the natural law. Statutes that contradict natural law, in Cicero's view, "no more deserve to be called laws than the rules a band of robbers might pass in their assembly."[25] In his view, citizens ought not to obey such laws (and if some do, it is only because they are being coerced by the state). Moreover, natural law in Cicero's view is part of the law of a legal system even if it is not embodied in a statute. The example he gives is the rape of Lucretia. Cicero regards the rape as illegal and criminal "even if there was no written law against rape in Rome" at the time.[26]

Procedural and substantive natural law are not always compatible with each other. For example, one of Fuller's principles of the "internal morality of law" is that no man can have a moral obligation to obey a legal rule that does not exist or is kept secret from him.[27] But Cicero's rape example is a legal rule even if there was no written law against rape. Of course, Fuller might reply that if any given legal system accepts the idea of Cicero's natural law, then everyone in that system is presumably aware of its contents. Nevertheless, Fuller's insistence on proper law-making procedures appears to sit uneasily beside a robust version of substantive natural law such as Cicero's. What would Fuller say if a legislature fails to renew a criminal code after the expiration date provided in the code itself? After that date, the criminal code would not "exist" in Fuller's terms, but a philosophy of substantive natural law would have no trouble in regarding the prohibitions of that code as continuing to exist despite their formal termination.

The broadest aspect of Fuller's vision of natural law is that law effectuates the purposes and common aims of a society. But even at this philosophical level, his view can be incompatible with substantive natural law. Let me illustrate this by referring to one of Fuller's famous essays, "Reason and Fiat in Case Law."[28]

In that essay we are asked to imagine a group of shipwrecked men on an isolated island. Each man has been visited by amnesia that has wiped out all memories of previous social existence and conventions.[29] Disputes arise and the group selects one of their number to be a judge or arbitrator for all controversies. The question Fuller asks is: what standards does the judge use when there are no rules or laws on the books and no one remembers anything of life before landing on the island?

Fuller replies that such a judge or arbitrator will make his decisions conform to the group's purposes and goals. He will know that his decisions will come to be looked on as precedents, and hence can foresee that there would emerge from his decisions a body of rules that will both conform to the needs of the group and help shape the group's behavior. In short, he will believe, and will be justified in believing, "that there are external criteria, found in the conditions required for successful group living, that furnish some standard against which the rightness of his decisions should be measured." These standards, Fuller says, reflect "natural law."[30]

But do they? Certainly the standards will reflect the group's common aims and purposes, whatever those common aims and purposes might be. If Fuller means only *procedural* natural law, then one cannot quarrel

---

[25] CICERO, DE LEGIBUS II. v. 13.

[26] CICERO, DE LEGIBUS II. iv. 10.

[27] LON L. FULLER, THE MORALITY OF LAW 39 (rev. ed. 1969).

[28] Lon Fuller, *Reason and Fiat in Case Law*, 59 HARV. L. REV. 376 (1946). Professor Fuller told me that this essay was one of the two most succinct statements of his philosophy; the other one was Lon Fuller, *Human Interaction and the Law*, 14 AM. J. JURIS. 1 (1969).

[29] This is a lot like John Rawls' "original position" in his A THEORY OF JUSTICE (1971), which Fuller's essay preceded by 25 years.

[30] Lon Fuller, *Reason and Fiat in Case Law*, 59 HARV. L. REV. 376, 379 (1946).

with him. But his essay seems to be ambiguous on the point. He seems to be suggesting that the group's common aims and purposes reflect "natural law" in its classical meaning.

H.L.A. Hart has taken issue with Fuller in an individual case where Hart questions the compatibility of "purpose" with morality. Hart suggests that a poisoner may also have a purpose, and that effectuating that purpose with maximum efficiency surely cannot be compatible with morality.[31] But it seems that Hart's specific criticism cannot easily be extended to a group. Surely the group of shipwrecked men do not engage in acts such as poisoning. Perhaps Fuller is saying that when we are talking about the purposes of an entire community, a certain (substantive) natural law creeps in, simply because people by and large do not engage in immoral behavior.

Yet the following is an example of extending Hart's criticism to the behavior of a group. I was told this story by a friend who served as a midshipman in the United States Navy at the time of the Vietnam War. Two sailors aboard the ship were seen engaging in homosexual acts. The next morning, when the roll was called, the names of the two men were omitted from roll-call. No one aboard the ship ever saw or heard from them again. Presumably their parents were informed by the government of the United States that they were missing in action. My friend told me that it was common knowledge that homosexuals would be dealt with in this fashion.

Are there any significant differences between men aboard a ship and men shipwrecked on an island? In Fuller's example, the decisions of the judge or arbitrator will come to be looked upon as precedents. But this is also true of the decision that was made about the homosexuals; it was clear that this is how the Navy deals with people like that, in this case and in any future cases. What about the fact that the shipwrecked men in Fuller's example selected the judge or arbitrator, whereas the sailors did not choose their captain? While this constitutes a difference, it is not a significant one. The captain presumably was the most

experienced and knowledgeable person on the ship, and might very well have been chosen by the crew as judge or arbitrator if he had not been appointed by the United States Navy. What about group purposes and common aims? Clearly the sailors aboard the ship were engaged in a common purpose in fighting a war, a purpose which—if anything—is clearer and more cohesive than the common aims of the shipwrecked men in Fuller's example.

If there is no significant difference between the real case of the men aboard a ship and Fuller's hypothetical case of men shipwrecked on an island, then the judge or arbitrator on the island could also punish individuals for deviant conduct. Since we know nothing about the shipwrecked men—presumably whatever "morality" they used to have was forgotten—the judge might regard *dissent* as deviant conduct worthy of punishment. Dissent, after all, can upset the group's cohesiveness as well as constituting lack of respect for the judge. The island community could turn into a totalitarian state where any individual who is not of a like mind with his fellows might be tortured in order to make him recant, might be imprisoned, or might be executed. The main problem with Fuller's philosophy, as I see it, was his invocation of the terms "morality" and "natural law" to support and give extra weight to his ideas about the internal logic and efficiency of law. Fuller advanced our view of the internal logic and efficiency of law by his well-chosen examples and his analytic ingenuity. But it is hard to accept that he was really talking about natural law or morality. When Fuller says that the proper interpretation of a statute must take into account its purpose, the problem is that the purpose itself might contravene morality or natural law. His example of shipwrecked men on an island leaves open, as we have seen, the possibility that dissenters can be tortured or murdered, all in the name of promoting the group's purposes and common aims.

Substantive natural law says that torture and murder are wrong even if nearly all the members of a group (except the chosen victim) think they're right. I think that Cicero's view of natural law is a coherent alternative to positivism. Fuller's philosophy stands somewhat between positivism and natural

[31] H.L.A. Hart, *Book Review: The Morality of Law*, 78 HARV. L. REV. 1281, 1284-86 (1965).

law. Because of his frontal attacks on positivism, it is hard to call Fuller a positivist. But because he does not appear to want to accept a universal morality, it is hard to call him a natural lawyer. His insistence on purposiveness and his faith in common aims—divorced from particular moral precepts—might on balance place him closer to positivism than to natural law.

Of course, even if substantive natural law is a coherent alternative to positivism, that doesn't mean that it is descriptive of the legal system we now have. There is always a tension between theory and reality. Neither positivism nor natural law describe the legal system that exists in any country, although they may describe some of it or a large part of it depending on what the legal system is. All theories of law—positivism and natural law included—are partly descriptive and partly normative. At some times, and in some places, a given theory may be less descriptive of reality than it is at other times and other places. But the normative force of a theory of law can be used as a critique of any real legal system at any time and at any place. Even more important than its function as criticism, a legal theory can become self-fulfilling at any time and place. The more the participants in a legal system (legislators, judges, officials in general, the public) absorb any particular legal theory as the right and proper one, the more that legal theory will become descriptive of the reality of that legal system. This indeed is the power of legal theory, a power that means in effect that jurisprudence is not simply a philosophy about law but a philosophy of law that shapes the very object of its attention.

QUESTIONS AND COMMENTS FOR YOUR CONSIDERATION

1. Is moral relativism a contradiction in terms?

2. If you "agree to disagree" with your friend after a discussion about morality, are either of you really talking about morality?

3. When two moral imperatives compete with each other in a given situation, is that evidence that morality is relative? Consider the "two track" problem discussed in the recent literature of moral philosophy, originally posited by Philippa Foot. You are on an elevated train standing next to the driver. You see in front of you a group of school children playing on the tracks, oblivious to the oncoming train. If nothing is done, they will be run over and killed. You can easily pull a lever that moves the train on to a second track, thus avoiding the school children. However, on the second track are two workers repairing the tracks. Would you be committing the murder of these two repair persons if you switch the train to the second track? Does morality require that you do nothing? If you do nothing, are you responsible for the death of the schoolchildren?

Moral philosophers have agonized over this question. It is extraordinarily difficult. But does the difficulty of the question lead to the conclusion that morality is relative?

4. The morality of abortion is equally difficult, at least for many people. But the difference in the focus of attention is what makes the problem so difficult. Those who believe in "right to life" focus on the rights of the fetus; those who believe in the right of abortion focus on the rights of the mother. Should we conclude that the existence of this profound social debate means that morality is relative? Or is it a situation where people are talking about two different moralities? If so, who is to decide that the two moralities are different?

5. Is the following a fair summary: "Positivists assert that morality has a contingent relation to law; natural lawyers assert that morality has a necessary relation to law."

6. Does morality become part of law through the instrumentality of the judge? If so, must it? Or can it? What if a judge does not care about morality?

7. In arguing a case, is it ever wise to assume that the judge cares nothing about morality? Would a judge who in fact cares nothing about morality ever reveal that fact? Would it therefore be a good litigating strategy for an attorney simply to adopt the Pascalian principle: *assume* that the judge cares (a lot) about morality, because at best the assumption can help and at worst it is simply rhetoric that cannot hurt one's case? (Blaise Pascal asserted that it is prudent to believe in God: if one turns out to be right, then there may be an advantage in the hereafter; if one turns out to be wrong, then nothing has been lost.)

8. Isn't the real question of jurisprudence not whether the judge believes in morality, but rather how to get the judge to pay attention to moral considerations in a case? And isn't *this* question a function of the judge's own jurisprudential view? (A positivist judge might be inclined to pay much less attention to morality than a natural law judge: consider the dichotomy Justice Keen drew between his own personal morality and his job on the bench!)

9. Does the jurisprudential culture in which *you* are immersed favor positivist or natural law judges? Isn't it quite clear that most judges at the present time are positivists? (Maybe they are "closet" natural lawyers?)

10. One way to test the preceding question is to ask yourself which of the two arguments is more *likely* to prevail in any given case:

(a) ATTORNEY FOR PLAINTIFF: "Every dictate of morality, every notion of justice that has ever been articulated, cry out for a decision in favor of the plaintiff."

(B) ATTORNEY FOR DEFENDANT: "There is no law on the plaintiff's side, so naturally the plaintiff is calling for morality and justice. The defendant clearly wins here because the law requires it."

11. Compare Question 10 with Question 8. If you are the attorney for the Plaintiff, how do you "get" the judge to take morality and justice into consideration? Do you do it by just blurting out what the Attorney for the Plaintiff said in Question 10? (An entire coursebook published by Anderson is devoted to this particular problem: see JUSTICE AND THE LEGAL SYSTEM (1992)).

C. Legal Obligation

1. Anthony D'Amato: The Moral Dilemma of Positivism[32]

In simply *describing* what "natural law" is all about, positivists go about their description by talking about two criteria for law: the pedigree test and the content test. Thus, the positivist Neil MacCormick says that natural law consists of two criteria:

1. *The Pedigree Test.* Someone alleges that a rule is a rule of law. To test it, apply an "institutional fact" analysis.[33] Simply look at the rule's pedigree. Was the rule in fact generated by the constitutional processes of the legal system in question?

2. *The Content Test.* Now apply the test of "moral justifiability" to the rule: look at the rule, and see whether it is compatible with morality.

In contrast with natural law, positivism

---

[32]Anthony D'Amato, *The Moral Dilemma of Positivism*, 20 VALPARAISO UNIVERSITY LAW REVIEW 43 (1985). Copyright 1985 Anthony D'Amato.

[33]Neil MacCormick, *A Moralistic Case for a Moralistic Law?* 20 VAL. U. L. REV. 1 (1985).

(again as defined by the positivists themselves) applies only the first test, the test of pedigree. A given rule is in fact a rule of law if it passes the pedigree test. Step two (morality) has nothing to do with validity.

Yet, like other positivists going all the way back to Jeremy Bentham, Professor MacCormick is troubled by the notion that the pedigree test alone means that we have to call "law" even rules that are morally iniquitous or rules that are simply expressions of official abuse of power. He cites the solution provided by H.L.A. Hart:

> What surely is most needed in order to make men clear sighted in confronting the official abuse of power, is that they should preserve the sense that the certification of something as legally valid is not conclusive of the question of obedience, and that, however great the aura of majesty or authority which the official system may have, its demands must in the end be submitted to moral authority.[34]

Note the careful use of the term "legally valid" in this quotation. A legally valid rule, according to Hart (and MacCormick) is a rule that passes the pedigree test alone. Surely, then, it is *inapplicable* to the notion of validity under natural law. Under natural law (again as the positivists see it), a rule in order to be valid must pass both the pedigree and content tests. If a rule passes both tests, then it *is* conclusive of the question of obedience. We must obey it because it is part of our moral obligation.

What Professor MacCormick has done (in company with most other positivists who in some form or other make the same argument) is to use the passage from Hart to refute the natural law contention that there should be a content test in addition to a pedigree test, but in so doing reasons in a circle by adopting Hart's term "legally valid" on the basis of the pedigree test alone.

Yet even wholly circular arguments do not go away. They remain with us for psychological as distinct from logical reasons. Consider the positivist who during the day is satisfied that legal validity is conclusively proven as a factual entailment derived from constitutional processes. But he awakes suddenly at night realizing that his conception may lead to the worst kinds of official abuses of power. Any dictator's commands are "law" because the dictator is the constitutionally valid legal authority. Once labeled "law," the dictator's commands tend to be obeyed by a public that believes in obeying "the law." The public is willing to assume, for whatever reasons (perhaps a combination of a sense that one should submit to authority, plus a sense that the dictator surely knows what is right in the long run even if his commands seem arbitrary in the short run, plus a fuzzy notion that everyone "ought" to obey the law), that the dictator's commands are binding and ought to be obeyed. Of course, not all members of the public feel this way, but perhaps a majority do. They felt this way in Nazi Germany, and they have continued to feel this way in dictatorial regimes since then.

What can the positivist do about this nightmare? He must embark upon an ambitious program to change the reality of public perception in order to suit his theory. He must teach the public to erase from its mind any notion that a law carries with it a sense of obligation. Thus he begins by lecturing to law students, then writes articles, and finally publishes books aimed at a larger audience, exhorting his readers to renounce their unenlightened psychological attitudes about obedience to law.

This reminds me of a story of a director who, during rehearsals, asked the playwright to change a line of the script on the ground that the audiences would be confused and sidetracked by the line as written. The playwright responded, "If the audience doesn't like it the way I've written it, why don't you change the audience?" So too the positivist, confronted with the nightmarish possibility that the public will confuse legally valid rules with rules that ought to be obeyed, sticks to his positivist thesis and sets out to change the public.

Yet I must concede that to the extent that natural law theory is presumed to have a content test in addition to a pedigree test,[35]

---

[34] H.L.A. HART, THE CONCEPT OF LAW 106 (1961).

[35] *Editor's Note*: Not all versions of natural law, not even Professor Fuller's version, require a "content" test.

the burden is upon the natural lawyer to answer the charge that the content test is hopelessly impractical. It is impractical because obviously a citizen cannot pick and choose among the enacted rules of a society those which accord with her own feelings about morality. Let me suggest four practical criteria that we can employ in giving specific content to the content test (assuming, again, that natural law requires a content test):

(1) Morally neutral legislation passes the content test. Most laws, rules, and regulations which are addressed to facilitating the interface between citizens and government, are morally neutral.

(2) Morally supportive legislation passes the content test. This includes nearly all the criminal law, family law, and the law of torts. (Even the thief, as Diderot pointed out in his Encyclopedia, favors the law against theft; for as soon as the thief steals something, he wants to use it as his own property and wants legal protection against someone else taking it from him.)

(3) Laws that we disapprove of probably pass the content test. Here we have to employ the macro-justice concept of John Rawls and other philosophers, to the effect that in most societies there will be laws that seem unfair to particular persons or groups, and yet overall these unfairnesses tend to be canceled out. For example, a progressive income tax may seem blatantly unfair to a rich person, but there is usually a regressive sales tax that compensates for the progressive income tax. James Madison was well aware of the power of factions to promote interest-group legislation, and yet in a pluralist society many of these laws counterbalance each other. Those that do not (such as the sugar and tobacco subsidies in present-day United States) tend to come under attack and eventually can be reversed by a reformist Congress.

(4) In rare instances, a statute or judicial decision can be so egregiously immoral that it fails the content test and should be stripped of the term "law." Fine, you might say, but what difference does it make—you'll go to jail anyway if you disobey it.

Divesting the rule of the status "law" can make a difference in the following ways:

(a) It can certainly make a difference to a judge. If the judiciary in a given country believes that immoral laws are not "laws," they are more likely to strike them down than if the judiciary believes they are valid, though morally iniquitous, laws. The South African Supreme Court has in recent years displayed enormous political courage in invalidating some of the more excessive apartheid legislation of the South African Parliament, even though that legislation clearly passed the positivist pedigree test.

(b) It can make a difference to the dissenter. If your country passed a Nuremberg-type law requiring the sterilization of your ethnic group, you would be better off engaging in civil disobedience under the claim not simply that the "law" is immoral but rather that it is not a "law" at all.[36]

The positivist may reply that, even when applied only to a rare immoral law in a society, the content test is too elusive. Professor MacCormick says that "It is in fact a weakness of natural law proposals to incorporate an element of moral substance into the formal definition of valid law that there can be and is so broad and diverse a range of moral opinions and convictions."[37] Moral notions are indeed broad and diverse, but I believe that they converge according to the gravity of the moral question at issue. Consider Professor MacCormick's startling example of breadth and divergence: the Nazi claims that their legislation was "done in the name of moral duty and racial purity and such like supposed moral values."[38] Professor MacCormick seems to be proposing that we take those Nazi claims *seriously*. He seems to be suggesting that the Nazi practices constitute an example of moral diversity. True, the Nazis could claim that what they did was moral, but anyone can make such a claim about anything. What is moral is not a matter of what people claim but a matter of what we believe.

One could reply that one person's belief is as good as another's, and hence morality is relative. But moral relativism is incoher-

---

[36] For a full statement of this position, see ANTHONY D'AMATO, DISOBBEDIENZA CIVILE, ENCICLOPEDIA DELLE SCIENZE SOCIALI.

[37] MacCormick, *supra* note 32, at 29.

[38] *Ibid.*

ent. It denies meaning to the term "moral." To take an extreme case, moral relativism requires a person to believe that although she may think that torturing a child is wrong, if the torturer disagrees then the issue is a stand-off.

Clearly, if one truly believes that all morality is relative (and hence there can never be any right answer to any moral question, including the torture of children), then that person will reject anything having to do with natural law. But if one stops short of moral relativism, then natural law may be worthy of consideration.

2. John Finnis: The Moral Obligation to Obey the Law[39]

In the 1970s legal theorists began to argue that law, even good law, creates no moral reason to obey it just because it is law. There is, they have argued, no generic moral obligation, not even prima facie or presumptive, or defeasible, to obey the law.

Joseph Raz's influential denial of the law's moral authority ("there is no [moral] obligation to obey the law even in a good society whose legal system is just"[40]) goes along with two ungrudging admissions: that everyone has moral reason to cooperate in securing social goals, and that law is instrumental in securing those goals. These admissions expose Raz's case to an obvious objection: what is instrumental in securing a morally obligatory goal must itself be morally obligatory, unless there is some other instrumentality, equally or more serviceable. Raz responds unsuccessfully to that objection, and the failure of his response clarifies the way in which law serves the goods attainable by cooperation.

Raz begins by granting that law indeed has, as one of its two principal functions, the role of securing morally desirable coopera-

tion. As he points out, schemes of social cooperation are of various kinds. One of the most typical and pervasive schemes concerns acts which are useful if a sufficiently large number of people behave in appropriate ways but are without any value if nobody does or if only a few people do. Polluting the rivers is an example. If a sufficiently large number of people refrain from polluting the rivers, they will be clean, and each person has a moral reason to contribute to keeping them clean. The law, continues Raz, is indeed

> instrumental in setting up and maintaining schemes of social cooperation, and this not only by providing sanctions to motivate those who would not otherwise contribute their shares, but also through designing in an open and public way what the scheme is and what each has to do as his contribution to it, thus enabling those who are motivated by the appropriate reasons to take part in the cooperative enterprise.[41]

But, he concludes, the fact that law thus "enables" us to do what we have moral reason to do does not create for us a moral reason to comply with the law. For, he says,

> the moral reasons affecting such cases derive entirely from the factual existence of the social practice of cooperation and not at all from the fact that the law is instrumental in its institution or maintenance. Consider the examples of river pollution mentioned above. It matters not at all to one's moral reasoning whether the practice of keeping the rivers clean is sanctioned by law, is maintained by exhortations and propaganda undertaken by enthusiastic individuals, or whether it grew up entirely spontaneously.[42]

In short, the moral authority of the scheme of cooperation derives entirely from the practice of cooperation and not at all from the fact that the practice is legally stipulated. The goal, cooperation, is morally obligatory, but the law is not necessary for attaining it; other available means will do.

---

[39] John Finnis, *The Authority of Law in the Predicament of Contemporary Social Theory*, 1 NOTRE DAME JOURNAL OF LAW, ETHICS, & PUBLIC POLICY 113, 116-120, 136-137 (1984). Reprinted by permission.

[40] J. RAZ, THE AUTHORITY OF LAW 233 (1979).

---

[41] *Id.* at 248-49.
[42] *Id.* at 249.

In affirming that law has moral authority, one is contradicting Raz's claim that it "matters not at all to one's moral reasoning" whether a scheme of social cooperation is sanctioned by law, or maintained merely by the alternative means of exhortations and propaganda or spontaneous social practices. And the ground for contradicting Raz's claim is essentially that human good is complex, and conceptions of human goods are even more so. To speak to the case discussed by Raz: the benefit of having clean rivers neither is, nor is universally regarded as, the only relevant good.

It is perfectly possible for farmers or manufacturers on the banks of the river to judge that there is no sufficient reason for a national policy of eliminating river pollution. Such a view may equally be held by persons with no special personal interest, concerned only for the well-being of the national economy. They may rest their view on the heavy economic costs of the anti-pollution policy: the cost of compensating riparian owners, and the cost of providing alternative means of waste disposal, at a time of economic stringency in export industries competing with foreigners unhampered by anti-pollution laws. And so forth.

Confronted with an anti-pollution propaganda campaign, whether by pressure groups or even by Government, the farmer or manufacturer has, therefore, no sufficient reason to comply. He may well think the policy misguided; and it will damage him personally while yielding him nothing which he counts a significant benefit. Similarly, with a practice of not polluting rivers, the farmer has no reason to treat the incipient or prevailing trend as morally compelling. For, once again, he may well think the practice misguided; and, again his own immediate interests also suggest that he have no part in it.

But if and when a *law* is passed, things are changed for the farmer's practical reasoning. Now he can reason thus: "I should comply with this law, even though this law is neither in the national interest nor in my own. I should comply because I get many benefits from 'the law,' from the legal system within which I live. My farm is protected from damage; my sales of farm produce are enforceable against the purchaser for the purchase price; those prices are supported by a government policy based on the laws of taxation and of market regulation; and so forth. Getting these benefits from the law, I should accept its burdens. Even though I might be able to 'benefit' even more by my secret non-compliance, I want to be a fair and upright citizen, just as I want others to be fair and upright in their dealings with me, whether they be my employees, fellow tradesmen, bankers and insurers, or the local police and courts. Moreover, I think the votes of elected representatives a useful and fair method of resolving national issues; in this instance my view has not prevailed in that political process; but sometimes the favor is in the majority, and when that happens I expect the law to be obeyed; so I should go along with it when I'm on the losing side in the vote."

Still, it may be asked, why does the law, and not the propaganda campaign or the spontaneous social practice, get the benefit of these considerations of fairness? An answer must begin by pointing to the *wide range* of benefits which the subject derives from others' compliance with the law. This particular law, just because it is the law, lays on him the burden of avoiding river-polluting methods of farming or manufacturing. But the law (not just this particular law, but the same "law of the land"), just as law, enforces against his neighbors the obligation not to burn down his buildings, and not to build new premises in defiance of zoning regulations, and the obligation to pay the purchase price of goods bought from him. Equally, the law, just as law, imposes on countless other people the obligation to pay the taxes which make possible a farm price support policy rather beneficial to the farmer.

The law presents itself as a seamless web. Its subjects are not permitted to pick and choose among the law's prescriptions and stipulations. It links together, in a privileged way, all the persons, and all the transactions, bearing on the farmer's present and immediate future situation. It also links all the people and transactions which have borne on the farmer's well-being or interests in the past. And finally, it links too all the people and transactions that may bear on his future interests and well-being as he moves into other occupations, into retirement, old-age, illness and death. The metaphors "web" and "links" here stand for the fact that in all these differing times and situations, a common reason for action—the law—was available and peremptory.

Not all aspects of the common good are identified and protected or advanced, even purportedly, by the law. Not all the requirements of fairness or of appropriate community-mindedness are brought into play by the law's requirements. But to trace out the seamless web of the law is to gain a singularly adequate view of the breadth and *complexity* of the common good, of fairness, and of what may be involved in an appropriate *philia politike* ("friendship within the polity," good neighborliness towards the whole of society).

The law has a further significance. Apart from the law, the farmer could reasonably be relatively indifferent to the concerns and interests of persons whose activities, apart from the law, do not affect him or at least do not benefit him. To take only the most obvious example, the farmer could, apart from the law, be indifferent to the concerns and interests of all the environment-conscious enthusiasts who campaign for anti-pollution laws. But when the law forbids pollution, he cannot but recognize that those who pressed on him this burden are themselves subject to burdens which, while they have no intrinsic relation to his burden, to share with him the quality of being peremptory and imposed for the supposed common good of this same community.

There remains the question whether and how the farmer has a shared interest in complying with the anti-pollution laws. There is a shared interest, or sharing of aim, which makes a community possible and lasting despite lack of consensus on almost every practical problem. This sharing of aim has as its most directly significant component the shared willingness to treat friendship and fairness for what they are: aspects of human flourishing which provide a counter-attraction to, and *critique* of, many alternative, vividly attractive, but diminished conceptions of that well-being. Concretely, then, the farmer can judge that the regular, impartial maintenance of the legal order itself is a good which gives him sufficient shared interest in, and reason for, cooperation by compliance with the anti-pollution law. The good he thus discerns and seeks to realize is . . . the good of a fair method of relating burdens to benefits, and persons to persons, over an immensely complex and lasting but shifting set of persons and their aspirations and transactions. Nothing other than legal order can promise such a method.

QUESTIONS AND COMMENTS FOR YOUR CONSIDERATION

1. Based on the argument that Professor Finnis has just made, should we invest the trapped explorers with an obligation to obey the laws of Newgarth?

2. What good would future "benefits" of Newgarthian law be for the trapped explorers? May they not reason as follows:

   (a) If we kill one of us so that the others may survive, the only "benefit" we'll get from the laws of Newgarth is the death penalty.

   (b) If we refrain from killing one of us, the only "benefit" we'll get is an innocent but early death in this cave.

3. Is the first part of Justice Foster's opinion (the part based on the assumption that the trapped speluncean explorers were removed from Newgarth's laws) compatible with Professor Finnis's position? Why?

4. If your answer to Question 1 is "yes," how do you account for the fact that Professor Finnis is expounding a natural-law position? Is a true natural law position *incompatible* with the first part of Justice Foster's opinion? Isn't Justice Foster expounding a natural law position in both parts of his argument?

3. Joseph Raz: There Is No Moral Obligation to Obey the Law[43]

Most political theorists acknowledge that there is no general obligation to obey the law of an unjust state. But, it is contended, there is an obligation to obey the law of a reasonably just state, and the greater its justice the stricter, or at any rate the clearer, the obligation. But is this so? Isn't the reverse the case? The morality of a government's laws measures, in part, its justice. Its laws are moral only if there is a moral obligation to perform the actions which they impose a legal obligation to perform. That moral obligation cannot be due to the existence of an obligation to obey the law. To establish an obligation to obey the law one has to establish that it is relatively just. It is relatively just only if there is a moral obligation to do that which it imposes legal obligations to do. So the moral obligations on which the claim that the law is just is founded are prior to and independent of the moral obligation to obey the law. The alleged moral obligation to obey arises from these independent obligations to act as the law requires.

Since the obligation to obey the law derives from these other moral obligations, its weight or strictness reflects their weight. The stricter they are the stricter is the obligation to obey. But if so, then the obligation to obey the law is at best redundant. It may make a moral difference if it exists in an unjust state, for there it imposes a moral obligation where none exists. But in a just state, it is at best a mere shadow of other moral duties. It adds nothing to them. Since the obligation to obey exists only in a just state, it is at best redundant.

Consider the question whether there is a legal obligation to obey the law. The obligation exists, but it is hardly ever mentioned, for it is the shadow of all the specific legal obligations. The law requires one to pay tax, refrain from murder, assault, theft, libel, breach of contract, etc. Hence, tautologically, one has a legal obligation to pay tax,

refrain from murder, assault, theft, libel, breach of contract, etc. A short, though empty and uninformative, way of describing one's legal duties is to say that one has a legal duty to obey the law. One has a legal duty to obey the law because one has a legal duty to obey this law and that, and so on, until one exhausts their list. It is likewise, the paradox can be interpreted as alleging, with the moral duty to obey the law. It exists only to the extent that there are other, independent moral duties to obey each of the laws of the system. It is merely their shadow.

In fact the paradox is even worse. The obligation to obey the law is no mere shadow. It would be, were it to exist, a moral perversion. Consider legal duties such as the duty not to commit murder and not to rape. Clearly there are moral duties to refrain from murder and from rape. Equally clearly we approve, if we do, of the laws prohibiting such acts, because the acts they prohibit are morally forbidden. Moreover, we expect morally conscientious people to comply with these laws because the legally prohibited acts are immoral. I would feel insulted if it were suggested that I refrain from murder and rape because I recognize a moral obligation to obey the law. We expect people to avoid such actions whether or not they are legally forbidden, and for reasons which have nothing to do with the law.[44] If it turns out that those reasons fail, that it is only respect for the law which restrains them from such acts, then those people lose much of our respect.

But if the obligation to obey the law is not a morally correct reason by which the morally conscientious person should guide his action, at least not in such elementary and fundamental areas of the law as those mentioned, then can there be such an obligation? Can there be a moral obligation to per-

[43] Joseph Raz, *The Obligation to Obey: Revision and Tradition*, 1 NOTRE DAME JOURNAL OF LAW, ETHICS & PUBLIC POLICY 139, 140-142, 150-155 (1984). Reprinted by permission.

[44] *Editor's Note*: Professor Raz might have illustrated this point by the following observation. For soldiers fighting during a war there is no effective "law" except the commands of one's superiors. If an officer gives permission to soldiers to rape the inhabitants of the town that has just been captured, are the ensuing acts of rape less morally reprehensible because they do not violate any state law or indeed because they are carried out with the permission of the only "law" that is effectively in force?

form an action if to take the existence of the obligation as one's reason for the action it enjoins would be wrong, or ill-fitting?

So much for the apparent paradox of the just law. The more just and valuable the law is, it says, the more reason one has *to conform to it*, and the less *to obey it*. Since it is just, those considerations which establish its justice should be one's reasons for conforming with it, *i.e.*, for acting as it requires. But in acting for these reasons one would not be obeying the law, one would not be conforming because that is what the law requires. Rather one would be acting on the doctrine of justice to which the law itself conforms.

Dr. Finnis's argument exemplifies some of the confusions which pervade our reflections on the obligation to obey. His central claim is that the law presents itself as a seamless web: its subjects are not allowed to pick and choose. This certainly is the case. But Finnis does not even pause to indicate that he draws from this the conclusion that we are not allowed to pick and choose, let alone present any reason in support of it. For him, if this is how the law presents itself, then this is how we ought to take it. To be sure, if we have an obligation to obey the law, then the conclusion does indeed follow. But we cannot presuppose that we have such an obligation in order to provide the reason ("the law is a seamless web") for claiming that we have an obligation to obey. This would be a most vicious circle indeed.

Finnis tells us that, even if farmers have a duty not to pollute the river they may misguidedly dispute this, and therefore the way to get them to do their moral duty is to have a moral obligation to obey the law. They will then refrain from pollution, because the law requires them to do so. But that will be the case only if they will not make a mistake about their obligation to obey the law, and only if the law makers will not make a mistake about the obligation not to pollute the rivers. Even if these conditions are met, they constitute an argument for the existence of an obligation to obey the law only if the lawmakers are not likely to make fewer mistakes than the farmers on other issues as well. For the obligation to obey is general and what is won in the absence of pollution can easily be lost in the maltreatment of old age pensioners or of the mentally ill.

Those who emphasize the danger of every person deciding for himself whether the case for the law's authority over any range of questions is good or not, often overlook this last point. Human judgment errs. It falls prey to temptations and bias distorts it. This fact must affect one's considerations. But which way should it incline one? The only general answer which I find persuasive is that it depends on the circumstances. In some areas and regarding some people, caution requires submission to authority. In others it leads to denial of authority. There are risks, moral and other, in uncritical acceptance of authority. Too often in the past, the fallibility of human judgment has led to submission to authority from a misguided sense of duty where this was a morally reprehensible attitude.

Finnis's elegant discussion of the river pollution case illustrates one way in which the law can do good, and when it does it certainly should be obeyed. It is a good illustration of an occasion on which the existence of the law makes a difference. While some laws make a difference, I doubt that all do. One should not be so captivated by one paradigm that others go unnoticed. Consider the river pollution case itself. Finnis quite reasonably directs our attention to a time when coordination, though desirable, does not obtain and the law steps in to secure it. But travel ten years on. By now, let us simplify, either the scheme introduced by the law has taken root and is the general practice, or it has long since been forgotten and is honored only in the breach. In the second case, my conforming with the law will serve no useful purpose unless it happens to protect me from penalties, or to stop my behavior being misunderstood by others. There is then no point in obeying the law. There is reason to conform with it if the scheme is in general effective. But, as is evident by comparing this case with the previous one where the law is the same but the practice of conformity is missing, that reason is not the law but the actual practice.

Today one of the most common arguments [for obeying the law] is based on alleged considerations of fairness. It is unfair, it claims, to enjoy benefits derived from the law without contributing one's share to the production of those benefits. As has been pointed out many times before, this argument is of dubious validity when one has no choice but to accept the benefits, or even more generally, when the benefits are given to one who doesn't request them, and in circumstances which do not imply an understanding concerning the conditions attached to their donation and receipt. Besides, even where it is unfair not only to reciprocate for services received, or not to contribute one's share to the production of a good of general public value, it cannot be unfair to perform innocuous acts which neither harm any one, nor impede the provision of any public good. Many violations of law are such innocuous acts. Therefore, appeals to fairness can raise no general obligation to obey the law.

The more traditional justification of the obligation to obey the law relies on contract and consent. Hobbes wished to derive it all from enlightened self interest. Locke allowed moral reasons to enter the argument, but they are instrumental reasons.[45] Consent to obey is designed to bring greater conformity with the natural law and greater respect for the natural rights of men than is likely to be achieved in a state of nature. Rousseau was the most important eighteenth century thinker to highlight the intrinsic value of the social contract as the act which constitutes civil society, as well as the personality of those who belong to it.

Consent to obey the law of a relatively just government indeed establishes an obligation to obey the law. The well-known difficulty with consent as the foundation of political authority is that too few have given their consent. This argument in its customary form can be right and wrong at the same time. Consent or agreement requires a deliberate, performative action, and to be binding it has to be voluntarily undertaken. Many people, however, have never performed anything remotely like such an action. The only time I did was during my national military service, in circumstances where failure to take the oath would have led to being court-martialled. I would not have made the oath but for these circumstances, and I do not think I was ever bound to observe this coerced undertaking.

Nevertheless, this objection is also misguided. There are other ways of incurring voluntary or semi-voluntary obligations. Consider a family or a friendship. There are obligations which friends owe each other, and which are in a sense voluntary obligations, as it is obligatory neither to form friendships nor to continue with them once formed. Yet we do not undertake these obligations by an act of promise or consent. As does friendship, these obligations arise from the developing relations between people. Loyalty is an essential duty arising from any personal relationship. The content of this duty helps us to identify the character of the relationship. If the duty precludes your having sex with another person, then your relations are of one character; and if it precludes publicizing disagreements between you, then you have relations of another kind, and so on. In other words, duties of loyalty are semi-voluntary, because the relationship itself is not obligatory. Moreover, they are non-instrumentally justified because they are part of what makes the relationship into the kind of relationship it is. (I am assuming that having the particular relationship, friendship, is itself of intrinsic value.)

What has this excursion into the normative aspect of personal relations to do with the obligation to obey the law? It demonstrates the possibility of one kind of obligation to obey which arises out of a sense of identifying with or belonging to the community. Such an attitude, if directed to a community which deserves it, is intrinsically valuable. It is not however obligatory. One does not have a moral duty to feel a sense of belonging in a community; certainly there is no obligation to feel that one belongs to a country (rather than one's village or some other community). I talk of a feeling that one belongs, but this feeling is nothing other than a complex attitude comprising emotional, cognitive and normative elements. Feeling a sense of loyalty and a duty of loyalty constitutes, here too, an element of such an attitude.

The government and the laws are official or formal organs of the community. If they represent the community or express its will justly and accurately, then an entirely natural indication of a member's sense of belong-

---

[45] *Editor's Note*: By "instrumental reasons," Professor Raz is referring to the situation where we have our own reasons to promote or protect certain states of affairs and we regard the law as a way of promoting or protecting those states of affairs.

ing is one's attitude toward the community's organization and laws. I call such an attitude respect for law. It is a belief that one is under an obligation to obey because the law is one's law, and the law of one's country. Obeying it is a way of expressing confidence and trust in its justice. As such, it expresses one's identification with the community. Respect for law does not derive from consent. It grows, as friendships do; it develops as does one's sense of membership in a community. Nevertheless, respect for law grounds a quasi-voluntary obligation. An obligation to obey the law is in such cases part and parcel of one's attitude toward the community. One feels that one betrays the community if one breaks the law to gain advantage, or out of convenience, or thoughtlessness, and this regardless of whether the violation actually harms anyone, just as one can be disloyal to a friend without harming him or any of his interests, without even offending him.

An obligation to obey which is part of a duty of loyalty to the community is a semi-voluntary obligation, because one has no moral duty to identify with this community. It is founded on non-instrumental considerations, for it constitutes an attitude of belonging which has intrinsic value, if addressed to an appropriate object. Vindicating its existence does not therefore establish the existence of a general obligation to obey the law. For good or ill there are many who do not feel this way about their country, and many more who do not feel like this about its formal legal organizations. It is sometimes said that the denial of a general obligation is of recent vintage. It is in many ways the opposite. At the birth of modern political theory in the seventeenth and eighteenth centuries, there was one clear orthodoxy: if there is a general obligation to obey the law, it exists because it was voluntarily undertaken. That is the view I am defending. The fathers of modern political theory also believed that such obligations were indeed voluntarily undertaken. If this view is no longer true today it is because the societies we live in are less homogeneous, more troubled about their own identity, and about the role of government and the law in the social fabric. Society has changed, not political theory.

QUESTIONS AND COMMENTS FOR YOUR CONSIDERATION

1. John Finnis is a contemporary proponent of the natural law position in jurisprudence; Joseph Raz writes in the positivist tradition. Who is more persuasive to you?

2. Leora Batnitzky has called attention to the centrality of the moral authority of judges in Joseph Raz's view of law.[46] She finds this a bit strange in light of Raz's insistence on the separation of law and morality. She writes:

> It is obvious that there could be, and in fact are, corrupt judges who submit neither to the authority of the law nor to morality in making their decisions. Is Raz implying that judges must *pretend* to believe in, or consent to, the law? However undesirable this position may be, it is the consequence of Raz's separation of authority and obligation. If we find this consequence unacceptable, then we are forced to insist that Raz's separation between authority and obligation does not hold.[47]

Do you agree? Do positivists face an insuperable difficulty in maintaining that there is a necessary separation between law and morality? Between authority and obligation?

---

[46] Leora Batnitzky, *A Seamless Web? John Finnis and Joseph Raz on Practical Reason and the Obligation to Obey the Law*, 15 OXFORD J. LEG. STUDIES 153 (1995).
[47] *Id.* at 173.

4. Anthony D'Amato: Law Is Only a Fact, Not a Value[48]

To ask whether we have a *prima facie* obligation to obey the law is, I argue, the same as asking whether we have a *prima facie* obligation to obey a mountain or a river. Laws, mountains, and rivers are only facts. There is nothing about natural objects, unless you're a radical pantheist, that would invest them with normative power. Similarly, a law does not start out with any normative power. For example, a legislature can pass a statute that is unjust and causes objective harm to the people for no other reason than to reward an interested lobbyist for contributing heavily to the political campaigns of key legislators. A judge can render an unjust decision in a case because the judge was secretly bribed by one of the parties. I do not claim that these things happen often, only that they can happen. Since they can happen, it would be a category mistake to infuse normative power to statutes or decisions like these. And since we normally cannot tell as of any given statute or decision what motivated it, we should not begin by assuming that law has any normative element to it. My contention is that laws are just facts.

However, what starts out as a fact can be given an overlay of normative power depending on its content. It is perfectly possible that a legislature can enact a beneficial statute even though the legislators who enacted it did so because they were paying off a lobbyist. It is similarly possible for a judge to render a just decision even though the judge did so for corrupt reasons. Yet it is important to be clear in our minds that we only reach the decision that a given statute is beneficial or that a given legal decision is *just* after we have assessed their contents in light of our standards about morality and justice.

I believe that the reason the question comes up so often whether there is a *prima facie* obligation to obey the law is that in most societies most of the time there is a substantial overlap between law and justice.

For most people most of the time, laws (statutes, decisions, regulations, etc.) seem to comport with justice. It becomes easy—and no real harm is done—simply to assume that a given law ought to be obeyed. Even though the reason we ought to obey the law has nothing to do with the law *per se*, the law is so likely to track general societal notions of justice that making a distinction between law and justice simply becomes a cumbersome task that is not worthy of pursuit. Yet there is a danger in eliding so easily from law to justice. Once in a while a truly evil statute might be enacted, and if it is, it should not be accorded moral force just because it is a statute. The Nuremberg laws of Nazi Germany are the most perspicuous example of statutes that some otherwise conscientious citizens felt they had to obey because they were, after all, "law."

I've compared law to a mountain or a river, but a better comparison would be to a color. If we put on a pair of green sunglasses, suddenly the entire world looks as if it has a greenish tint. Law is like that; it colorizes the world we live in. When somebody acts and we want to know the legality of that action, it is as if we are looking at that action through a pair of legal glasses. Our law-tinted glasses do not change the action we see; they only assist us in interpreting the action. When an action occurs in the real world, there are usually many ways to interpret it. Elizabeth Anscombe introduced the idea of "action theory" into philosophy in 1959.[49] The following four sentences, taken from her book, describe the same action:

1. A man is moving a lever up and down.
2. He is manually pumping water into the cistern of a house.
3. He is pumping poisoned water into a country house where evil men meet for planning sessions.
4. He is poisoning the men who meet in the house.

A videotape of the man's actions would not tell us which of the four interpretations is correct. As Ian Hacking puts it, "Each successive description of the action involves a larger range of circumstances, but only one

---

[48] Based upon, and updated from, Anthony D'Amato, *On the Connection Between Law and Justice*, 26 UNIVERSITY OF CALIFORNIA AT DAVIS LAW REVIEW 527, 539-54 (1993). Copyright 1993 by Anthony D'Amato.

[49] *See* G.E.M. ANSCOMBE, INTENTION 37-44 (1959).

intentional action is being described."[50]

Suppose, to take a more benign example, we see a videotape of a woman parking her car alongside an orange grove, picking a number of ripe oranges, filling the trunk of her car with them, and driving off. Now we look at the same action through legal-tinted glasses. We find that the woman's action is colored by the specific legal topography of the situation. It could be one of several legal topographies:

1. It is her orange grove.
2. She has prepaid the owner of the orange grove for the right to fill the trunk of her car with oranges.
3. It is a communal orange grove, and anyone can take as many oranges as he or she likes.
4. It is a privately owned orange grove, not the woman's, and she has not paid for the right to pick oranges.
5. She is stealing oranges.

I contend that there is a legal fact of the matter that determines which of the above five categories (or perhaps other categories that can be imagined[51]) apply to the woman's actions. In addition, we would expect that the applicable category is known to the woman (she knows her own intentions and what she is doing). Her action, in short, takes place in a world that is already colorized by law.

My point is that the legal colorization is part of the factual depiction of the woman's case, but not necessarily part of our normative evaluation of what she has done. For example, suppose we know that description (4) is true. It does not follow that what the woman has done is wrong. She may have gathered the oranges in order to speed them to a group of children who are dying of starvation, and that she intends to pay for the oranges as soon as practicable after delivering them to the children. Suppose, instead, that description (5) is true. Here we have congruence between law and morality: "stealing" is both illegal and immoral. The fact that stealing is illegal, however, does not make it immoral. (Indeed, we suspect that historically the chain of causation was the other way around—stealing was considered immoral, and then was enacted into legal prohibitions).

QUESTIONS AND COMMENTS FOR YOUR CONSIDERATION

1. If law is a fact, does it follow that a judge is not bound to apply the law?

2. If law is a fact, does a judge have any right to disregard it in deciding a case? Does your answer to this question depend on whether you interpret "right" as meaning "legal right" or "moral right"? Does your answer depend on the moral quality of the particular law that the judge may be willing to disregard?

3. If law is a fact, does it have to be known to the parties? What about the "secret law" that was discussed in connection with Hans Kelsen in Chapter 2? If law is a fact, then should judges refuse to apply "secret laws"?

5. Lon Fuller: Legal Scholarship[52]

Positivism has an inhibiting effect upon

---

[50] Ian Hacking, Rewriting the Soul 234 (1995).

[51] For instance, none of the five categories apply because we have been watching a scene in a fictional motion picture.

[52] Lon L. Fuller, The Law in Quest of Itself 138-40 (1940). Copyright 1940 Northwestern University. Reprinted by permission.

legal scholarship because of the fear it engenders of a very simple question. Everyone who has attempted to write on the law of the cases must have been concerned by the possibility that his readers might pose this question to him: "Does this article state the law, or only your idea of what the law ought to be?" Positivism demands that this question be answered, for obviously if it cannot then the basic distinction which positivism seeks to preserve is lost. Yet the writer may feel great embarrassment in answering it. To say that he is stating the law as it is will seem to involve either a species of fraud or a kind of omniscience which he has no intention of claiming. On the other hand, he does not like to say that he is only offering for consideration a series of personal reactions to the law, for he may well feel that he has, to a degree not precisely ascertainable, only made explicit ideas which were already implicit in the cases.

Caught in this dilemma, the scholar may decide not to write at all. Or he may devote himself to problems of methodology, discussing the proper approach to law without incurring the responsibility for applying it. Or he may adopt a style so obscure that it is impossible to tell exactly what objective he seeks, and hence impossible to criticize him for having evaded his duties to positivism. That all of these things are occurring is abundantly evidenced in our law reviews.

How repressive is this demand that the legal scholar ticket precisely his own contribution can be seen if we imagine a similar demand to be made in fields outside the law. Suppose a surgeon were forbidden to operate unless he could tell of each movement of his scalpel whether it was intended to restore the organism to the condition it was in before being stricken with disease or to bring about a new condition of the organism which would enable it to survive? Suppose the artist were forbidden to paint a picture unless he could say of each stroke of his brush whether it was a true representation of nature or an imaginative interpretation of his own? No science or art could long survive such a limitation. I see no reason to think that the law is different. I have never found anyone who would not admit that there is an element of creation and discovery in the law. It seems to me as clear as anything can be that the positivist philosophy in its usual forms tends to stifle this element.

The judge or legal writer ought not to be ashamed of his inability to answer the question which positivism puts to him. Rather, he ought to be proud that his contribution is such that it cannot be said with certainty whether it is something new or only the better telling of an old story. This is the best possible guaranty that his work is at once creative and sound, and that he is playing his part in the eternal process by which the common law works itself pure and adapts itself to the needs of a new day.

D. Obligation and the Community

Recall Professor Thri's opinion in the Case of the Speluncean Explorers. According to Professor Thri, the "common enterprise" that the explorers were engaged in had certain normative implications regarding the "law" that they were required to apply in the cave. If we expand the theme of common enterprise to the community or state as a whole, can we derive binding legal obligations from the mere fact of our participation in the community or our citizenship in the state? This would be Professor Thri's opinion "writ large." Although many philosophers (including Plato, Rousseau, and Hegel) have asserted that we have some obligations to the state by virtue of our membership in it, this is a proposition that is easier to express in the abstract than to prove (or disprove) in detail.

1. John Mackie: Respect for the Law[53]

The inevitable partial conflicts of interest among human beings mean that a tolerable community of any size requires a system of law and, indeed, all actual communities of any size have such systems. The general existence of some degree of respect for the law will be a great help towards the smooth working of such a system, particularly since the more respect there is for the law, the less need there will be for actual use of sanctions.

Nevertheless, there are qualifications. First, the obligation to obey the law would only be a prima facie obligation, not an abso-

[53] Excerpted from J.L. Mackie, *Obligations to Obey the Law*, 67 Virginia Law Review 143, 151-55, 158 (1981). Copyright 1981 by the Virginia Law Review. Excerpts reprinted by permission.

lute one. Since we would regard many existing regimes and their associated bodies of law as iniquitous, and none as ideal, we cannot wish that people anywhere should have so strong a respect for the law as to feel absolutely obliged to obey it all the time, regardless of all other moral and prudential considerations. Rather, we would wish them to feel that countervailing considerations may sometimes—and with bad laws and bad regimes will quite often—make it permissible and perhaps obligatory to break the law. If anyone thinks that this proposal is incoherent, he might reflect and find that it is just such a complicated attitude that we already think appropriate with regard to the breaking of promises, the failure to pay a debt of gratitude, and perhaps even with regard to lying.

But why is it better that people should have this attitude rather than that of reserving one's judgment and examining each situation as it arises? Before we can answer this question, we must know what the alternative proposal is, that is, by what rival principles our judgment is to be guided. The standard social situation is one of a partial conflict of interests that generates problems that are of forms approximating to that of a multiperson prisoner's dilemma. Norms of various kinds can be seen as having the function of solving such dilemmas; but we can ask what sorts of norms do or can perform this task. In principle, perhaps, a norm of rational benevolence, if it were effective in controlling people's conduct, could do the trick. But in practice we find that the work is done rather by such norms as these: (1) "Make and keep mutually beneficial agreements with others." (2) "Help those who are helping, have helped, or will help you." (3) "Join in enterprises that promote public goods in which you will share, and play your part in them." (4) "Join others in refraining from activities that would produce public harms from which you, along with others, would suffer."

These norms, unlike that of rational benevolence, all build in some way on the notion of reciprocation, and some, but not all, suggest collective action and collective responsibility. It is not too difficult to see why such norms as these have psychological and sociological advantages over that of rational benevolence. They can more easily grow out of and harmonize with the prior motives and interests—often, though not always, either egoistic or self-referentially altruistic—which in themselves give rise to the initial dilemmas. Another norm that is, in effect, of the same reciprocal sort is that which prescribes honesty with regard to property or tells people not to take one another's possessions without their consent; or rather, this norm is of this reciprocal sort provided that all the persons concerned have some property that they wish others to respect. The norm that lays down a prima facie obligation to obey the law as such is a further, though more extensive, reciprocal norm, like those that prescribe gratitude and loyalty to friends, collective action or forbearance, and honesty about property. What the law (anywhere) defines and helps to maintain is *some* existing cooperative social practice, though the cooperation may be on very unequal terms, with greatly differential advantages for some groups as opposed to others. The general recognition of an obligation to obey the law therefore shares with these other reciprocal norms a feature that makes it simply more viable than the norm of rational benevolence.

But is it better that people should recognize this obligation rather than examine each situation as it arises in the light of various other norms of reciprocity and collective action? Given the fact that there is a working system of law, it may do no harm if a few people feel no obligation to obey the law as such, but instead consider each problem in the light of other norms of reciprocity and collective action, *provided that they take into account in their deliberations the fact that there is this working system of law*. But it does not follow that all would be well if nearly everyone did this; we are able to have a working system of law for such refined thinkers to take into account only because there are many who recognize the simpler immediate obligation to obey the law as such. In other words, the "reserved" attitude is acceptable only where it is parasitic upon the simple respect for the law. If everyone adopted this reserved attitude and relied only on other norms, there would be at least "coordination" problems for which legal norms, and some direct regard for them, are the obvious solution.

Whether the citizen identifies with the

legal regime and respects it depends on how good it is. Joseph Raz identifies "rule of law" features: that the laws are prospective, open, clear, and relatively stable; the making of particular legal orders is guided by open, stable, clear, and general rules; there is an independent judiciary; the procedural principles of natural justice are observed; the courts are accessible; crime-preventing agencies are not able to pervert the law; and the courts have sufficient powers of review of legislation and administrative action to be able to maintain the rule of law.[54] These features do not in themselves make a regime just or fair, but contrasting deficiencies in these respects greatly diminish the tendency of the law to fulfill the sort of function that we may see as its *raison d'etre*. The better a legal system is in this and other ways, the more closely the obligation to obey the law as such will connect with other norms of reciprocity and collective action. That which respect requires will coincide more with actions that can be seen as being in their own right contributions to cooperative practices, or the requirements of a fair compromise between conflicts of interests, or the fulfillment of reasonable expectations on which others have relied. We are not now trying to derive an obligation to obey the law as such from these other obligations; it is merely that the independent and underived obligation to obey the law will, in practice, be felt as stronger if it often coincides with similar principles of reciprocity and union instead of conflicting with them.

Respect for the law should vary in strength, being stronger where the legal system comes closer to certain definable standards of justice and the rule of law.

2. Anthony D'Amato: The Death of Socrates[55]

Socrates was accused of the capital crime of corrupting the young with his teachings, tried before a judge and jury panel of 500 or 501 members, and sentenced to death. The sentence was later effected when he was given poison to drink. At no point during the proceedings did Socrates deny that corrupting the young was a criminal act punishable by death. While the crime of corrupting the young probably derived from the various codes the Athenians considered "law" (primarily the codes of Draco, Solon, and Cleisthenes), it was in a sense a common law offense, inasmuch as no precedents were offered which even suggested that engaging in philosophical debate could be considered corruption of the young. Since trials and decisions were not formally reported in Socrates' time, the words "precedent" and "common law" should be taken in a figurative sense. At Athenian trials, both accusers and accused could and did refer to recent trials of which the tribunals were familiar. But to Socrates, and presumably to the Athenian citizenry as a whole, judging from the evidence which exists, a trial and judgment was simply an attempt by the tribunal to apply "the law," an immutable concept which somehow had a separate, independent existence unchanged by specific cases.

The careful reader of the Platonic account,[56] however, will sense a tension between this simplified description of Athenian jurisprudence and the manner in which Socrates' trial was conducted. Many of Socrates' arguments in his defense are addressed not to "facts" or to what might today be called "law-facts," but rather to the law itself. Socrates argued, for example, that his teachings in principle could not have corrupted the young.

Finding it quite natural that the state would attempt, above all, to protect its young, Socrates agreed that if he were indeed guilty of corrupting the young, he ought to be punished according to law. The poignant difficulty in Socrates' case is that the charge of corrupting the youth of the city was based upon acts that Socrates did and

[54] JOSEPH RAZ, THE AUTHORITY OF LAW 210-17 (1979). [*Editor's Note*: Some of these features are, of course, similar to Professor Fuller's.]

[55] Anthony D'Amato, *Obligation to Obey the Law: A Study of the Death of Socrates*, 49 SOUTHERN CALIFORNIA LAW REVIEW 1079 (1976), copyright by Anthony D'Amato. For present purposes, some minor changes have been made in the wording of this essay.

[56] I base this essay nearly entirely upon two Platonic dialogues: *Apology* and *Crito*. These have been retranslated and reprinted in numerous editions; the edition I used is B. JOWETT, THE DIALOGUES OF PLATO (1892).

believed in all his life: asking questions of anyone who would listen, probing their answers for weaknesses, examining their logic, and attempting to arrive at truth. By so doing, he helped his listeners to think for themselves. Moreover, he actively tried to persuade fellow citizens, young and old alike, not to care first and foremost for their bodies or for wealth, but rather for the improvement of their minds and souls. He forced no one to listen to him, nor did he charge any money for his teaching. As Plato said, Socrates strove to persuade his listeners not to concern themselves with their external possessions but rather to strive for perfection of the self in goodness and wisdom.

Since Socrates was accused of corrupting the young through the ideas he taught and the manner in which he taught them, his acts were inseparable from the crime of which he was accused. Thus, the enormity of the crime could hardly have been greater than in his particular case: it meant that everything he had done in his life was illegal, since his entire life stood for the proposition that he ought to teach his philosophy to anyone who would listen. As Plato reports, Socrates believed that "the life unexamined is not worth living." The depth of that belief made the accusation of corrupting the young almost equivalent to being charged with the crime of having lived. The asserted obligation to obey the law could hardly be presented more dramatically.

By teaching the youth of Athens to think for themselves, Socrates in the eyes of the Athenian prosecutors was teaching them to worship "false gods." For young citizens who think for themselves and examine premisses cannot be counted upon to obey the state's commands or to make good soldiers who obey orders without hesitation. The Athenian establishment recognized certain gods, certain duties, and a certain lifestyle; these institutions served as a cement keeping the society together and making it strong in battle. Socrates' disinterested pursuit of truth chipped away at this cement and therefore at the foundations of Athenian society. In this basic sense, Socrates' very life, devoted to teaching philosophy, was perceived as a threat to the state. Therefore, it was not by random accident that Socrates was prosecuted. Although the immediate cause of his prosecution may have been a petty vindictiveness on the part

of certain poets, orators, and politicians,[57] the basis for prosecuting Socrates was nothing less than this perceived threat to the entire Athenian society that could result from Socrates' own teachings. The situation is analogous to a modern dictatorship or totalitarian government silencing an individual for having addressed fellow citizens about the true nature of their political system. The compromise which the court offered to Socrates is further evidence that the real basis of his prosecution was a threat to Athenian society. Socrates was offered acquittal on the condition that he would no longer spend his time in the pursuit of philosophy. He refused the offer, saying: "As long as I breathe and have the power, I shall never abandon philosophy nor cease to admonish you and reveal the truth to anyone of you I may meet from time to time." Further evidence can be derived from the discussion surrounding his sentencing. The custom was that the prosecutor and the defendant each would offer a punishment, and the tribunal would choose between the two alternatives. Socrates considered but rejected the possibility of exile. He wanted to each the citizens of Athens and was not interested in going abroad and teaching others. Socrates sought more than a general freedom to speak, a freedom probably available in some foreign state or in the wilderness; he sought the precise liberty of speaking to his fellow citizens in the state in which he was raised. If Athenians could no longer endure his words and discourses, Socrates foresaw that citizens of other cities would have the same reaction. "A fine life mine would be if I left Athens at my age and lived like a hunted thing, constantly changing from city to city." While it is not necessarily true that Socrates would have been persecuted abroad, he was making a logical point: if his fellow citizens of Athens did not see fit to acquit him of this crime, there would be no benefit in going abroad, only to endure the same sequence of events. Once convicted by his fellow Athenians, Socrates faced profoundly unac-

---

[57] Socrates pointed out in his own defense at the trial that not a single youth whom he allegedly corrupted was complaining about him. Socrates' accusers—Meletus, Lycon, and Anytus—may have been angry because Socrates' students showed them up.

ceptable alternatives: to remain in Athens and be punished with death or to go abroad and end his life in compromised, impotent exile. If his teaching was a threat to the state, Socrates certainly did nothing to appease his accusers.

Although Socrates believed that he was innocent of the charge of corrupting the young, when he was found guilty at trial he accepted the legality of the verdict against him. He believed that the system under which the jury acted was perfectly just; the tribunal sat to dispense justice and to judge according to the laws. To question the propriety or the procedure of the trial or to suggest that the jurors acted illegally never occurred to Socrates.[56] He believed that the Athenian legal system was the backbone of the Athenian state and it had to be respected. He deferred to the interpretation of the Athenian laws that resulted in his sentence of death. Socrates personifies these laws in a crucial imaginary dialogue, making his point abundantly clear. Suppose, he said to Crito, that he is on the point of escaping, and the laws and the government come and say: "Tell us, Socrates, what are you about? Are you not going by an act of yours to overturn us—the laws and the whole state, as far as in you lies? Do you imagine that a state can subsist and not be overthrown, in which the decisions of law have no power, but are set aside and trampled upon by individuals?" He asks Crito whether he should reply, "Yes, but the state has injured us and given an unjust sentence." Crito, who was urging Socrates to escape, agreed with this last statement. We might indeed ask (along with Crito) that if the process of escaping from prison did not harm anyone (*i.e.*, Socrates' jailers would not be injured), wouldn't *remaining* in prison simply compound the injustice of Socrates' conviction?

Socrates began by eliciting from Crito assent to the proposition that if escaping were wrong, then Socrates should not escape. Even though the escape that Crito had

planned for Socrates would not harm any of the jailers, even though the plan was feasible, and despite the important fact that by escaping he would have more time to instruct people in his philosophy and thereby continue his good works, Socrates felt imprisoned by the unbreakable bond of an obligation: his obligation not to act unjustly. Hence, only if it could be demonstrated that escaping was either right or at least ethically neutral would Socrates not drink the poisoned hemlock on the appointed day.[59]

I will now take the arguments that Socra-

---

[56] Contrast this with Dimitrov's brilliant self-defense at the Reichstag Fire Trial. Dimitrov constantly attacked the court, the Gestapo, the Nazi leaders, and the witnesses. Remarkably, his defense worked; he was acquitted under the most hostile of conditions. For an account of his amazing trial, *see* F. TOBIAS, THE REICHSTAG FIRE (1964).

[59] Socrates also adduced a number of pragmatic arguments. The reader may judge whether these considerations might have been more important than the ethical ones or whether the practical considerations Socrates adduced were meant merely to mollify Crito and indeed were somewhat disingenuous given Socrates' firm decision to adhere to the dictates of morality. These are:

(1) Escaping might place Socrates' friends in danger. They might be exiled and deprived of their country or of their property.

(2) If Socrates went to a nearby city, such as Thebes or Megara, he would be viewed as an enemy to their government, as one who destroys the laws.

(3) A corrupter of the laws—that is, one who escapes, contrary to the law—would seem more than likely to be a corrupter of the young as well. Escape thereby would serve to confirm his accusation.

(4) Would life be worth living? How could Socrates continue to maintain that goodness and righteousness and laws are man's most precious possessions, if he were to avoid them himself? Additionally, people in foreign cities might regard him as a man so interested in preserving his own life that he had resorted to a ridiculous disguise to slip by the clutches of the law.

(5) What about Socrates' children? Must he take them away and make exiles of them too? Or would they be better brought up and educated in Athens even though he could not be with them?

(6) What example would be set for his pupils if he were to escape? If he were executed he would depart this life the victim of injustice wrought by men. But if he escaped, repaying injustice with injustice and evil with evil, breaking his agreements and covenants, and injuring those whom he should least injure, then posterity and the laws of Athens and the laws of all other states would not regard him well.

tes made to Crito as a point of departure[60] for considering two possible bases for a general obligation to obey the law: consent, and estoppel in the absence of consent.

a. Consent

(1) May we infer an agreement?

Socrates believed that the most important reason why escape from prison would be wrong was that it would be a breach of a "just agreement" he had with Athens. There was no explicit agreement, oral or written, in Socrates' case. Nevertheless, the ethical question is whether an agreement is properly inferable. If we think of the agreement as an implied contract between citizen and state, Socrates' duties under that contract would have been to obey the valid legislative decrees and valid judicial verdicts of the state. (Here I'm not speaking of moral validity, for that would beg the entire question. Rather I have in mind formal validity—that the legislators were elected in a fair election the statutes were properly enacted according to parliamentary rules, and so forth.[61]) If there is an implied contract between Socrates and the city of Athens, and if we require that there be "consideration" for such a contract, the "consideration" Socrates received was the benefits of Athenian citizenship: birth, nurture, education, and protection. Anticipating the objection that a minor could not be held to have impliedly consented to such a contract, Socrates argued that since each Athenian citizen was free to leave the state when he reached manhood, his own decision to remain in the city was tantamount to ratifying the contract requiring his

compliance with Athens' laws. Socrates added that in his own case the situation was even clearer: he did not leave the city to see the world except for one visit to the Isthmus, and he never traveled anywhere else except in military service. Moreover, he raised his children in Athens, proof that he liked the city. Additionally, he did not propose the penalty of exile at his trial. Thus, he was not unwillingly compelled to consent to Athenian legality nor deceived into consenting or forced to come to a quick decision to remain in Athens. But was the fact that he remained in the city the same thing as agreeing to its laws? He answered rhetorically: "Who could take pleasure in a city apart from its laws?" In sum, Socrates believed himself bound by an implied contract with the city to obey all its laws, not just those which he liked or those which might result in a good verdict for him. Having made this agreement, he would not breach it by attempting to escape.

It would be difficult to argue that no agreement can fairly be implied in Socrates' case—or indeed, in the case of most citizens with respect to their states. And certainly an implied agreement is as valid as a written one; (indeed, we might be more suspicious of a written agreement extracted from a youth of 21 by a state). But conceding the existence of an implied agreement is merely the first formal step of the argument. We must now determine the nature and scope of Socrates' duties under the agreement.

(2) To whom are Socrates' obligations owed?

Socrates considered his obligations under the implied agreement as analogous to the duties of a son toward his father. The state, like a father, begat Socrates, nurtured him, educated him, protected him, and told him when he reached the age of majority that he could either leave and escape the constraints of the city's laws or stay and be obedient to all its laws.

Conceding for a moment that the benefits conferred upon Socrates were as described, to whom were the duties then owed? If F, a father, confers such benefits upon S, his son, might not S "repay" F by conferring similar benefits upon G his son (F's grand-

---

[60] This essay is not an exegesis of Plato's Socratic dialogues, something which I happily leave to scholars of the classics. Rather, my interest is in the concepts evoked by my reading of the dialogues. Whether these concepts have validity can be judged by the reader independently from the question whether the concepts in whole or in part can fairly be attributed to Plato's account of the death of Socrates.

[61] For an important discussion of "validity" in this sense, see H.L.A. HART, THE CONCEPT OF LAW 97-107 (1961).

son)? Is it not more rational to consider family obligations as moving forward through time than to regard them as moving backward—that a son devote his energies to the care of his own son even at the expense of the needs of his father? Why shouldn't "forward repayment" be as ethical as "backward repayment"? And can't Socrates' obligations to Athens be viewed in a similar light? Although a state may be regarded simply as a collection of individuals living in a certain geographic area, Socrates' metaphor that anthropomorphizes the state makes the "forward repayment" argument all the stronger.[62]

Under the "forward repayment" argument, what the state did for Socrates—create, nurture, educate—he repaid the state by doing the same for his own sons, including the payment of taxes (to the state) to support education, and participation in military service to secure his sons against the state's external enemies. The ethical argument could be made that the preservation of future generations was in the past a condition precedent to the existence of the present generation, and hence remains a primary ethical obligation.

Suppose Socrates' "subversive" teaching resulted in a major, perhaps revolutionary, change in the life of Athens. Would this not have been Socrates' "contribution" to the state resulting from his own philosophical convictions, the same way the Parthenon was the inspired contribution of an architect? As a father, Socrates did what he thought best for his son, even if it might not have pleased the son's grandfather. Why should the state (in the role of grandfather) have a better idea of what is best for Socrates' children than the product of the state's own educational system, namely, Socrates himself? If Socrates believed that his idea of what was best was superior to that of the state, why should he have felt morally bound to obey the state rather than

follow what he believed to be the best interests of his children? Wasn't the success of Athens due to the rational contributions of all its citizens who planned for the future? Wouldn't Socrates have violated this implicit ethical responsibility of seeking progress for the state if he kowtowed to the state's own regressive view of "belief in the gods"?

(3) Did Socrates actually receive benefits?

Apart from the question of whether the repayment should be forward or backward, we might look more closely at the question whether what Athens conferred upon Socrates were actually benefits. Although Socrates gave the state credit for begetting, nurturing, and educating him, we might now ask whether he would have been born, nurtured, or educated even if the state did not exist?

Certainly the existence of a state is not necessary for people to be born; people were around for a long time before the first state was organized. The question of nurturing is slightly more complex. Although Socrates would not have claimed that the state did more to nurture him than did his own parents, he might have had in mind the protection afforded him by the state against external enemies. If other nations threatened to pounce upon Athens and enslave it, then the Athenian soldiers conferred a needed benefit on young Socrates. But it seems to me that this benefit was repaid by Socrates' own service in the military. The value that any citizen receives from the common defense is repaid when he (or his or her son) participates in military service.

Education is a more complex benefit to analyze than nurturing. Education is universally valued; the education that the state provided to Socrates must therefore count as beneficial to him. Yet, that education cannot amount to "consideration" in a contractual sense because Athens did not give Socrates a choice of rejecting his education. Instead—perhaps for reasons of instilling in young citizens a loyalty to Athens and its culture and values—education was mandatory. Since Socrates had no choice in the matter,

---

[62] Hegel's anthropomorphizing of the state as an organism persisting through time is another way of conceptualizing this "forward benefits" argument, for according to Hegelian logic the resolution of thesis and antithesis is necessarily forward-looking (in the eventual synthesis). *See* G. HEGEL, A PHILOSOPHY OF RIGHT (T.M. Knox trans. 1942).

it would not be fair to infer from the fact that he was educated by the state a duty on his part to obey all the state's laws.

(4) Does our inference extend to all laws or only to some laws?

Despite the foregoing considerations relating to the nature of Socrates' obligations, one might contend that if Socrates had an agreement with the state, he may simply have made a "bad deal" in agreeing to obey all its laws, but that's his problem. A deal is a deal, and he is obligated to obey the law under which he was convicted. Perhaps it is in the nature of what we call "contract" that obligations can arise despite a lack of equal bargaining power or roughly similar "consideration" on each side. In other words, while Socrates might discharge some of his obligations by contributing toward the education and security of other people living in the state, he might in addition have the obligation to obey all of the state's laws simply because that was part of the deal. Under this view, we do not examine the adequacy of the state's consideration, but only the fact that there was a nontrivial consideration. The basic fault in this argument is that the agreement was not explicit. Hence, whether Socrates is bound to obey the law that resulted in his conviction is the very question at issue. If that law was part of his agreement, then under the general theory, he is obligated to obey it. But was it part of the agreement? Or, would such a law have been an "unconscionable" addition? Moreover, is there not an infirmity in any "open-ended" contract, where substantive provisions depend upon future actions of one of the parties? Socrates' implied contract has as one of its terms the open ended provision that any law thereafter enacted by the state, as party to the contract, will be binding upon Socrates. This open ended provision is hard to read into Socrates' implied contract.

The state might reply that while no one can specify in advance all the laws that a state might enact, uncertainty does not mean that such a contract can never be made. Moreover, since each citizen has a chance to participate in the making of the laws, the provision is not totally one sided. How would Socrates have responded?

The Platonic dialogues do not reach this question explicitly. We might imagine one possible answer: that the open-ended contractual provision is reasonable with respect to laws that are foreseeable and related to the kinds of laws passed before the contract was signed, but not otherwise. Thus, new laws that fill in details or extend past laws to new technologies would have been reasonably within the scope of the parties' contemplations, and are therefore just. But a totally new and different law, such as one that sentences a man to death for speaking his mind as he has done all his life, would be *ultra vires* even if we assume the existence of such an open-ended contractual provision.

What if the state responds that, as a citizen, Socrates has a voice in the formulation of any new law and, indeed, that his voice at his own trial was exceptionally eloquent and was considered seriously by the entire tribunal? Although superficial, it is often said that in submitting to the majority will, a citizen must take the bad laws that are enacted by the majority along with the good. But even on the level of this apparent cliche one might inquire whether a citizen has actually agreed to accept any law passed by the majority. (Certainly, the American Bill of Rights and other individual rights provisions in the body of the 1789 Constitution were minoritarian safeguards.) What if the majority, without giving any reason, sentenced the individual's children to death? Is that within the contemplation of submission to majority rule? Or is there a deeper set of reservations—conscious or subconscious—in any individual's submission to governmental power, whether the government is a representative democracy or a benevolent dictatorship? Are there some possible acts by the government that cannot reasonably be depicted as flowing from a prior agreement to be bound by that government's enactments? If so, an implied agreement does not conclusively determine whether the scope of such an agreement includes obedience to the law making corruption of the young by the teaching of philosophy a capital crime.

Another possible qualification to the scope of Socrates' obligation is his pledge only to obey laws that are just. Thus, he cannot be said to have had an ethical duty to obey unjust laws. This superficially appealing formula, which recurs in the early stages of any argument concerning civil disobedience, has been shown by John Rawls to be perhaps a necessary, but certainly not a sufficient, standard for a potential individual dissenter. Rawls believes that "when the basic structure of society is reasonably just, as estimated by what the current state of things allows, we are to recognize unjust laws as binding provided that they do not exceed certain limits of injustice."[63] Although Socrates' Athens would not qualify as a just society under Rawls' other formulae (an immediate disqualification was its system of slavery), it nevertheless may have appeared to Socrates as "reasonably just." Rawls supports his conclusion, in terms that Socrates obviously would accept, by arguing that even in a just society there obviously will be some laws passed by a majority of legislators that will be viewed as unjust by certain groups (just as there will be some decisions of judges that will be viewed as unjust by the losing party). "Majorities (or coalitions of minorities)," he writes, "are bound to make mistakes."[64] Nevertheless, "in the long run the burden of injustice should be more or less evenly distributed over different groups in society."[65] If not, "permanent minorities that have suffered from injustice for many years" might then no longer have a duty to comply.[66] In other words, although Rawls might not accept the following way to characterize his argument, we can think of Rawls as speaking about small injustices and large injustices. Only with respect to large injustices does a member of society not have a duty of compliance.

If we apply Rawls' analysis to Socrates' situation, can we say that the law under which he was sentenced to death was a small injustice—a singular deviation from a generally just regime? In a sense, Athens excised a portion of its brain by eliminating its leading person of intellect—by finding him guilty, essentially, of having lived. Is this not a large

injustice, discharging any duty of obedience to the laws Socrates otherwise would have had? The problem with this line of reasoning, however, is that Rawls imposes his own standard of justice upon a society to determine which laws are ethically enforceable. In contrast, Socrates was unwilling to substitute forcefully his own notion of justice for that of the state ("forcefully," because although Socrates was willing to continue to criticize the state as long as he lived, he was unwilling to take the moderate yet "forceful" act of escaping from prison). Compounding Socrates' difficulty was his belief that the actual law under which he was tried, namely corruption of the young, was a just law in the sense that the law was not to blame for his execution; the injustice consisted of the tribunal's action under that law. Attributing the injustice to the 280 jurors who voted for his conviction, rather than to the law itself, Socrates probably would not have found that Rawls' distinction between large and small injustices had any application to his own case.

(5) How do we factor in the question of authoritative determination of the law?

Our consideration of Rawls' theory has moved us closer to a fundamental dilemma previously posed: that of the distinction between "the laws" and the way the laws are interpreted in the context of real cases. Does Socrates' commitment to the laws include a commitment to the institutional means by which laws are authoritatively determined?

Let us examine an extreme case, an example that we would rarely conceive as being a possibility within a rational legal system. Suppose there were a law in Athens at the time Socrates reached his maturity that guaranteed to all persons the right to speak freely and to philosophize without any interference from the state, no matter what the result of such activities. Suppose further that Socrates is brought to trial under the same circumstances as in fact occurred and that he invokes this law in his defense. The tribunal considers it, among the other laws and precedents, yet finds Socrates guilty of the capital crime of corrupting the young by

---

[63] JOHN RAWLS, A THEORY OF JUSTICE 351 (1971).

[64] Id. at 354.

[65] Id. at 355-56.

[66] Id.

virtue of his speaking and teachings. Even further, suppose the court does so without citing any reason why the statute was not a complete bar to its decision.[67] Socrates would conclude that the court had rendered a judgment directly contrary to a statute that it would admit is valid. What can Socrates do now? On the one hand, the law that he plainly has relied upon and which he believes clearly applies to his case remains a valid statute. On the other hand, the tribunal which is the authoritative determiner of the law has found him guilty. In Crito, Socrates made it clear that under similar circumstances he would not substitute his individual judgment for that of the tribunal. Although he felt the tribunal had decided unjustly,[68] it was "the law" that was speaking and which Socrates felt a moral obligation to obey. Perhaps Socrates would not have gone quite so far as Bishop Hoadly who said, many centuries later, "Whoever hath an absolute authority to interpret any written or spoken laws it is he who is the lawgiver to all intents and purposes and not the person who first wrote or spake them."[69] Perhaps he would not have fully agreed with the statement attributed to Chief Justice Hughes that "the Constitution is what the judges say it is."[70] Yet Socrates would have

to concede that at least part of what he means by "law" consists of a commitment to external authoritative interpretation.

This concept of a necessary connection between the content and application of law raises in acute form the ethical dilemma posed by the death of Socrates. As we have seen, Socrates' agreement to obey the laws included a moral commitment to an institutional structure external to himself—or, at minimum, external to himself as the defendant in a trial—as the authoritative interpreter of the laws. Socrates may have argued to the tribunal, he may have believed that they listened to him, and he may even have believed that they understood him; but in the end, the decision regarding the interpretation of the law was theirs and not his.

Accordingly, Socrates' moral commitment to obey the law seems to involve a necessary delegation of part of his own ethical standard to the tribunal. Yet at the heart of his teachings was the proposition of non-delegability of morality. Socrates taught that each man must think for himself and must discover what is the truth and what is morally right. Socrates believed that there were certain immutable standards of right and wrong discoverable through a process of logical thinking (in later dialogues these become Platonic ideals). Socrates further believed that no man should blindly follow the teachings of another even if those teachings were supported by everyone else in the world.[71] Therefore, was not Socrates inconsistent in deferring to the application of the law by the tribunal? To be sure, in his decision not to escape, Socrates certainly was deciding what he internally thought was right. But the path that led to his imprisonment consisted of Socrates' delegating a portion of his own set of ethics to the external lawmaking authorities, so that they, and not he, decided the morality of the law that condemned him to death.

In sum, even under a generously open-ended theory of the content of the implied contract between citizen and state, and even conceding that laws with minor injustices ought to be obeyed (assuming that Rawls' distinction can and should be made), Socrates did not persuasively show that the objec-

---

[67] *Compare* this *with* the Supreme Court's denial, without a single reason or explanation, of Massachusetts' motion to invoke the court's original jurisdiction for the purpose of challenging the constitutionality of the Vietnam war. *See* Massachusetts v. Laird, 400 U.S. 886 (1970) (from which Justices Harlan, Stewart, and Douglas dissented). This was the Supreme court's first denial of original jurisdiction without a reasoned opinion. ANTHONY D'AMATO & ROBERT O'NEIL, THE JUDICIARY AND VIETNAM 45 (1972). Yet there were substantial grounds for the compulsory invocation of original jurisdiction in this case. *See Brief for Constitutional Lawyers' Committee on Undeclared War As Amicus Curiae*, Massachusetts v. Laird, 17 WAYNE L. REV. 81 (1971). One suspects that the Court gave no reasons because it had no reasons to give.

[68] *See* Plato, *supra* note 56, *Apology* at [P] 41B.

[69] Quoted in H.L.A. HART, THE CONCEPT OF LAW 137 (1961). [*Editor's Note*: Refer back to the discussion in Chapter 2 of the positivist theory of John Chipman Gray.]

[70] S. HENDEL, CHARLES EVAN HUGHES AND THE SUPREME COURT 11 (1951).

[71] *See* Plato, *supra* note 56, *Crito* at [P] 48A.

tively unjust law under which he was sentenced to death could have been part of the contract. If the existence of the contract is a matter of ethical implication, it seems inconsistent to read into it such a gravely unjust law. On the other hand, if the injustice consists only of the application of the law to Socrates by the tribunal, and not the law itself, then Socrates should not have concluded that escaping would be an act of disobedience to the law. Thus, both lines of the contract argument reach results that I think are unpersuasive.

b. Estoppel

In the preceding section, we found that there were grave difficulties in inferring an agreement between Socrates and the state. But what if the notion of agreement is set aside, and we focus, instead, upon whether Socrates is estopped to disobey the law under which he was convicted because of his prior actions as a citizen? Here we are using the notion of estoppel only in its root foundation of fairness, and not in a technical sense. What actions can we say are attributable to Socrates that would, as a matter of fairness, estop him to escape from prison?[72]

The only act attributable to Socrates, for the purpose of the estoppel argument, is his decision to stay in Athens past the age of majority. On the contractual theory previously considered, we have seen that in deciding to stay in Athens, Socrates may have consented to all the laws of the state that were in force at the time of the decision to remain as well as those which were foreseeable or reasonable modifications. On that theory, if he later committed a robbery he would have no basis for dissociating himself from the state at the moment he was apprehended and charged with that crime. But when we consider an estoppel argument, we have to ask whether the mere act of staying

---

[72] *Editor's Note*: It is grammatically correct to say that you *stop* somebody *from* doing something but you *estop* somebody *to* do something. However, colloquial usage is rapidly eroding the distinction. When words sound alike, many people assume they are the same words (like "envisage" and "envision," or "leveled" and "levied").

within Athens can properly be interpreted as a continuing submission to all new laws and interpretations as enacted and applied.

(1) Scope of the estoppel.

If an estoppel existed, it must extend to the law under which Socrates was prosecuted. Socrates courageously admitted at his trial that, irrespective of the tribunal's verdict, he would continue teaching philosophy to all who would listen, until the moment of his death. By taking this stand, Socrates essentially conceded that even upon notice that his actions were illegal, he would continue to act. More importantly, Socrates expressly disavowed the alternative of exile; he would continue to teach in Athens, where presumably he would continue to derive the benefits that the state confers upon its citizens. Hence Socrates certainly would have been estopped after the tribunal pronounced its verdict. This outcome renders insignificant the inquiry into the scope of the estoppel, for the scope is, in effect, conceded to include the law under which Socrates was convicted.

One distinction should be made clear. The fact that Socrates intended to violate the law after he was given notice that his teachings would be punishable would not mean that he was estopped to deny the moral force of that law. The moral underpinnings of any law are not changed when a person is merely given notice of the law; if unjust from the beginning, the law continues to be unjust. The only difference is that the person then knows for certain that the state will punish him if he continues to resist the law. Thus, in asking next whether an estoppel existed in Socrates' case, we will not look at his planned actions in continued violation of the law in question. We will instead ask whether remaining in Athens was the kind of voluntary action which would give rise to a proper inference that Socrates should have been estopped to deny the right of the state to prosecute him for the crime of corrupting the young through his teachings.

(2) Existence of an estoppel.

We thus reach the critical question of whether Socrates' decision to remain in Athens can be construed as a voluntary act that estopped him to deny the right of the state to prosecute him for a newly formulated crime. As a starting point for analysis, consider whether a state is like a voluntary organization or club. A local fraternal organization, for instance, might tell its members that unless they obey all the rules of the club, they will be expelled from membership. The rules are a condition of continued membership, and this condition is made known to all prospective members. Is the state an example of such a voluntary organization? Such a conceptual question can obviously be the subject of endless dispute, if dealt with on a purely theoretical level. Let us instead approach it from a practical viewpoint: could someone leave the state if he no longer accepts its rules the same way that a person can resign membership in a club?

One way to leave a state is to sell one's possessions and to travel beyond the state's boundaries. Such emigration is obviously different in kind from quitting a voluntary organization, which normally would not require physical relocation of one's person and belongings. Moreover, emigrating from one state means immigrating into another. States have a monopoly over the earth's geographic surface; to the extent that states are more or less alike, the choice of leaving one state is illusory. Again, this fact is distinguishable from the voluntary organization; by leaving one you do not automatically join another.[73]

A second way to leave a state would be to "opt out" in the sense described by Robert Nozick: a person would form an apolitical, stateless enclave around his house.[74] If others did this too, the state would ultimately resemble something like political Swiss cheese, having holes wherever citizens disavowed the state. The citizen then would have no right to obtain services from the state, nor would he pay any taxes; presumably, he would negotiate for any goods or services and pay for them purely upon a barter basis. But in practice states do not allow this kind of opting-out. States typically claim "ownership" of the same land that private persons own; states assert that individuals within their geographic area merely own land vis-a-vis other individuals but do not have an absolute ownership right vis-a-vis the state. This assertion, though not necessarily correct, can be enforced. Therefore, at least from a practical standpoint, the citizen's only real option if he wants to leave the state is to leave physically, liquidating his possessions and abandoning his friends.

We are now in a position to ask the more theoretical question. Who, as a matter of justice, has a prior right to remain located in a particular geographic area—the state, or a person who wants to opt out of the state? Consider a person who owns a plot of land and a structure upon that land. Did his ownership or that of the state come first in time? Individual ownership results either from the individual's paying someone else for the rights to that plot of land or from someone's gift or devise. The transactions resulting in this chain of ownership probably were supervised and enforced by the state, but that fact alone does not give the state a supervening right of ownership of the equity. If the state originally owned the land, then the question of what the private purchaser received is a matter of interpreting what the state conveyed to him (or his ancestor) and what it retained. For example, the state may have retained the air rights or the mineral rights; it may also have retained jurisdictional rights over that land so that the owner could never opt out of the state. But in many cases, the state did not originally own the land; indeed, in the typical situation, the state arises as a collective, long after persons have staked out the land into plots. If a person owned a plot of land and later a state came into existence, then even if the state asserted rights over that plot of land, the assertion is not backed up by any ownership interest that ought to be recognized as a matter of justice.

The point of these speculations is that when a state claims that a person is estopped

---

[73] *Editor' Note*: Under present international law, there is a right to leave one's country, but there is no right to immigrate into another country. As Louis Henkin recently put it: "The refugee, one might say, has at best half a right; the right to leave his or her own country and to become a refugee, but not the right to live anywhere as a refugee." Louis Henkin, *An Agenda for the Next Century: The Myth and Mantra of State Sovereignty*, 35 VA. J. INT'L L. 115, 117 (1994).

[74] *See* R. NOZICK, ANARCHY, STATE, AND UTOPIA 290 (1974).

by his "act" of continuing to reside on a plot of land that he owns, the state is necessarily asserting that the person's moral choice is either to emigrate or to submit to the state's laws. But the state's moral position would vanish if it had no right to that plot of land as against the owner's right. The owner's decision to remain on the land could not be construed as any participation or acquiescence in the state's legal system; it would be equally consistent with opting-out.

(3) An ethical estoppel?

Socrates argued to Crito that escape from prison would serve as an example of disrespect for the law. Yet we might ask: would not his escape have brought home to the public the immorality of the law that sentences a person to death for teaching what he believes? Would not his refusal to escape have operated to inhibit others from thinking for themselves or teaching what they believe? Socrates' decision not to escape contributed to the exaltation of the state above the individual, which probably received its ultimate expression in the nineteenth-century jingoist cliche "my country, right or wrong." I suggest that Socrates' decision not to escape was not morally necessary and, hence, contributed to a depreciation and diminution of individual rights when asserted against claims made by the state.

I do not think that, as a matter of ethics, we have to accept all the laws of a state as a kind of "package deal." There are some claims that the state makes upon us that are indeed fair, but that does not mean that all the claims a state makes or may make in the future are fair. Consider the question of military service. Athens provided Socrates with the benefit of protection against external enemies. In turn, Socrates was ethically obliged to serve in the military (or to perform some alternative service). The reason for inferring an ethical obligation here is a matter of objective reasonableness: Athens did not invent its external enemies in order to justify inducting its citizens into military service. Rather, the external enemies were real, and all citizens, including Socrates, objectively benefited from the protection afforded by the Athenian army.

But I believe that service in the army is one thing and imprisonment another. If the imprisonment is a consequence of an unjust law, then the imprisonment itself is unjust. In short, differences among the state's laws necessarily lead to differences in ethical obligation. Socrates may have been ethically obliged to serve in the army, but he was not ethically obliged to submit to capital punishment for teaching philosophy. The two are different. Interestingly, the most crucial theme of the entire Apology and Crito dialogues is that they are not different.

3. Lon Fuller: The Spontaneous Ordering of Human Relations[75]

The most dangerous quality of legal positivism lies in the inhibitive effect it inevitably has upon the development of a spontaneous ordering of human relations. Kelsen asserts that it is characteristic of all forms of natural law that they are anarchistic in tendency; they assume the possibility of an ordering of society which rests upon a voluntary acceptance of guiding notions and is not dependent upon any governmental structure. He seems to assume, though apparently he hesitates at open assertion, that no such ordering is possible. As a matter of fact it is clear that it is not only possible, but exists. The bulk of human relations find their regulation outside the field of positive law, however that field may be defined. The existing body of positive law in general serves only to fill that comparatively narrow area of possible dispute where conflicts are not automatically resolved by a reference to tacitly accepted conceptions of rightness. We have cases telling us how mentally deranged a man has to be before he loses the power to make a valid will; we have statutes saying how many witnesses furnish a sufficient guaranty of the authenticity of a will. We need positive law in these cases because without it men might reasonably differ. On the other hand, we do not have cases or stat-

---

[75] Lon L. Fuller. The Law in Quest of Itself 110-23 (1940). Copyright 1940 Northwestern University. Reprinted by permission.

utes telling us whether a will is rendered invalid by the fact that the testator wore a green hat while signing it, or whether a newly marketed fountain pen, not in existence when the statutes were passed, is an effective instrument for the expression of testamentary intention. These problems find their regulation outside the positive law, a regulation so automatic that they do not appear as problems at all. In this field of autonomous order which surrounds the positive law there can be no sharp division between the rule that is and the rule that ought to be. The field, being unorganized and formless, permits of no such division. Though there are here neither sovereigns, nor sequences of judicial conduct, nor basic constitutional norms, the chaos of opinion which Hobbes so feared does not exist. Here is a combination of custom and natural law which rules, and that very effectively.

To my mind nothing is more preposterous than Kelsen's argument that natural law is inherently static, while his own view is dynamic. He argues that natural law is static because it derives the legal order, not from a vacant principle of constitutionalism, but from certain meaningful notions of justice. These notions, he asserts, hold the legal order within a frame and freeze it into rigidity. This view simply ignores the plain fact that ideas are capable of growth, and that there is a process by which the common law, to use Mansfield's magnificent phrase, "works itself pure." If one wishes to be mystic one may describe this process in Hegelian terms as the dialectic of history. But in the end it remains as obvious, and as mysterious, as the process by which an anecdote changes and generally improves in the course of being retold. As for the alleged "dynamic" quality of Kelsen's own view, it seems to me to be about as "dynamic" as an empty wheelbarrow. To be sure, you can dump anything you wish into it, and you can push it in any direction you like. But there is absolutely nothing to make it go.

The important practical question which emerges is: Should we seek to bring human relations increasingly within the field of autonomous and non-governmental control, or should our object be to reduce those relations to neat hierarchic patterns, in which every man instead of being, as Hobbes feared, wolf to another, becomes officer to another?

If Renan was right in assuming that men have the capacity for developing the illusions necessary for their survival, we ought to be seeing a revival of natural law. Though such a revival has often been heralded, and though there are distinct signs of it in the law of the cases, there is precious little evidence that it has as yet substantially affected our law schools.

There are, I think, a number of factors which tend to explain why American legal scholarship has remained so unseasonably positivistic. There is, first of all, the enormous influence of Holmes. His positivism has not been diminished by the circumstance that he did not always himself remain faithful to the program for a rigid separation of law and morals laid down in his early essays. The fact that he occasionally gave eloquent if somewhat vague expression to the human aspirations which prevent the law from ever becoming something which merely "is" actually served, I believe, to reinforce the influence of his positivism by giving it an appearance of breadth and philosophic grounding. His very inconsistencies made him a more effective advocate of the positivist philosophy than such men as Austin and Kelsen, who never let the green fields of life lure them from the gray path of logic.

Modern legal positivism also owes a great deal to the popularity of what is called the "scientific method." The current enthusiasm for this method has, I believe, led to the neglect of a rather obvious truth, which is that the question of the proper method for solving a problem depends to a large degree on the kind of problem to be solved. For example, the type of factual inquiry appropriate to determining whether our trains actually run on time is not necessarily the best way of finding out what we ought to do to make them run on time. A negative attitude which insists that judgment be suspended in the absence of controlled experiments or statistical demonstration is appropriate in many areas of research. But to project this attitude over the whole field of law and ethics is to erect a substantial taboo against any intelligent discussion of the vague and shifting forces which ultimately shape men's lives. When the "scientific method" is thus pervasively applied, the net effect is to render most "scientific" that theory which has the least to say—a circumstance from which legal positivism has drawn a large advantage in recent years.

(3)   A third factor supporting the positivistic attitude toward law is to be found, I believe, in the influence of a peculiarly modern conception of democracy. The force of this conception is not diminished, but rather increased, by the fact that it is not generally reduced to articulate expression. Here again it is Kelsen who has been willing to trace out and accept the logical implications of an idea which most men are content to leave on the periphery of consciousness, where its full implications are held in check by competing notions and sentiments. The conception to which I refer is that which finds the justification for democracy in intellectual skepticism. There is no such thing as justice. Human reason is utterly incapable of regulating the relations of men among themselves. Some purely arbitrary principle of order becomes, therefore, necessary. Since power rests ultimately on the acquiescence of the governed, the most logical principle of government is that of majority rule, since this offers the broadest base for the order set up. It must be noted how purely negative this conception of democracy is. It does not adopt the common will from any notion that is closer to the inner essence of things than the will of any particular individual. Majority rule is preferred not because it is most likely to be right, but because it is most likely to be obeyed. Democracy is rested not on an affirmation, but on a denial that government and law can in the end be anything but arbitrary.

In my opinion, democracy must be founded not on a negation of the force of ideas, but on a faith that in the long run ideas are more important than the men who form them.[76] The greatness of what we call democratic government does not lie in the mere fact that a numerical majority controls at election time, but at a point further removed from the ballot box, in the forces which are permitted to play upon the electorate. For in the world as it is now constituted, it is only in a democratic and constitutionally organized state that ideas have a chance to make their influence felt. By preserving a fluidity in the power structures of society, by making possible the peaceful liquidation of unsuccessful governments, democracy creates a field in which ideas may effectively compete with one another for the possession of men's minds. In a dictatorship, on the other hand, the chief requisite for the success of an idea is that it serve the interests of those who have enough power to make it effective.

4. Arthur Jacobson: Common Law and Reciprocity[77]

The rationality of exchange allows two persons to earn recognition of each other by working to establish an equivalence in exchange. The recognition exchange establishes is a recognition of persons as individuals. It is personal recognition, actual respect. Kant's universal legislation abstractly demands that persons treat each other with respect, not supposing they have to earn it through deals. As a consequence, the respect Kant's persons get is a respect having nothing to do with their achievements as individuals. Kant's condition of respect is that persons give up individuality. Persons thus establish individuality only by departures from universal legislation.

In contrast, Hegel's philosophy describes the passionately right-seeking creature who respects the rights of others not because it wishes to be rational or seeks self-perfection, but because only by respecting the rights of

---

[76] *Editor's Note*: Here, and throughout this Anthology, I have resisted the temptation to alter the text of authors who exclusively referred to "men" instead of "persons" and who referred to all judges, lawyers, and scholars as males. As one who believes that equal rights for women is an absolute moral imperative, I think it is important not to forget how only a few decades ago law was regarded as the exclusive province of men. Although I would like to believe that Professor Fuller and others of his generation used the pronoun "he" in an abstract and general sense without consciously intending to exclude women, I suspect that many otherwise enlightened thinkers at that time in fact accepted or shared in a somewhat patronizing attitude toward women that I regard as abhorrent just because it was so subtle and so widespread.

[77] Excerpted from Arthur J. Jacobson, *Hegel's Legal Plenum*, 10 CARDOZO LAW REVIEW 877, 897-98, 906-07 (1989). Copyright 1989 by Arthur J. Jacobson. Reprinted by permission of the author.

others can it achieve recognition. The right-seeking creatures at the beginning of Hegel's Philosophy of Right are simply not interested in court enforcement of rights for its own sake. Holmes's "bad man" is not the person these creatures would deal with in the first place. The passionately right-seeking creatures want recognition from their fellow creatures, and the goods of a deal are the occasion for recognition.

Enforcement through the legal system interests these creatures only as it supplies or corrects the failures of recognition.

Persons have a hunger for recognition because they love other persons. Without loving others, the person would have no noninstrumental need for them. We need regard only from persons we love. At the same time, loving other persons causes us to want to care for them. The recognition we get from them gives us a stake in their welfare. We feel responsible for them, not because we have legal duties towards them, but because we love them.

The goal of Hegel's jurisprudence of right is liberation of the person. The goal of Kant's jurisprudence of duty is salvation of the person. The goal of Common Law is order, liberation, and salvation—transformed through the reciprocal alliances which Common Law generates.

Common Law can achieve order—more precisely, orders—where positivism and naturalism cannot. Unlike positivism and naturalism, Common Law does not attempt to achieve a single order at one moment (positivism) or forever (naturalism). The effort to achieve a single order produces disorder instead.

In positivism, the disorder is an explosive and irreconcilable struggle over content.

Persons will always engage in this struggle, since law determines more than order. Positivism cannot hide from the fact that law tells people how to live and what to live for. Positivism works, Kelsen and Hart recognize, only if every law is a procedure, only if no law has a content. Sooner or later, however, law must have a content.

In naturalism, disorder stems from disagreement over the credentials of the rational observer. Rules that the observer perceives must in fact be the rules for participants in the system.

Common Law suffers from neither disorder—the disorder of substance or the disorder of procedure—since the jurisprudence of Common Law allows, but does not determine, a substance of orders. Nor does Common Law insist on a single procedure, or even any procedure. It foments orders, not order.

The legal systems of positivism and naturalism serve only the production of order.

Common Law serves personal goals as well as the production of order. Law is the instrument of reciprocity, of salvation and liberation in the context of order. Persons use Common Law to achieve reciprocity.

4

Formalism

A. Autonomy

1. Stanley Fish: The Law Wishes to Have a Formal Existence[1]

The law wishes to have a formal existence. That means, first of all, that the law does not wish to be absorbed by, or declared subordinate to, some other—nonlegal—structure of concern; the law wishes, in a word, to be distinct, not something else. And second, the law wishes in its distinctness to be perspicuous; that is, it desires that the components of its autonomous existence be self-declaring and not be in need of piecing out by some supplementary discourse; for were it necessary for the law to have recourse to a supplementary discourse at crucial points, that discourse would be in the business of specifying what the law is, and, consequently, its autonomy would have been compromised indirectly. It matters little whether one simply announces that the principles and mechanisms of the law exist ready-made in the articulations of another system or allows those principles and mechanisms to be determined by something they do not contain; in either case, the law as something independent and self-identifying will have disappeared.

In its long history, the law has perceived many threats to its autonomy, but two seem perennial: morality and interpretation. The dangers these two pose are, at least at first glance, different. Morality is something to which the law wishes to be related, but not too closely; a legal system whose conclusions clashed with our moral intuitions at every point so that the categories *legally valid* and *morally right* never (or almost never) coin-

cided would immediately be suspect; but a legal system whose judgments perfectly meshed with our moral institutions would be thereby rendered superfluous. The point is made concisely by the Supreme Court of Utah in a case where it was argued that the gratuitous payment by one party of the other party's mortgage legally obligated the beneficiary to repay. The court rejected the argument, saying "that if a mere moral, as distinguished from a legal, obligation were recognized as valid consideration for a contract, that would practically erode to the vanishing point the necessity for finding a consideration."[2] That is to say, if one can infer directly from one's moral obligation in a situation to one's legal obligation, there is no work for the legal system to do; the system of morality has already done it. Although it might seem (as it does to many natural law theorists) that such a collapsing of categories recommends itself if only on the basis of efficiency (why have two systems when you can make do with one?), the defender of a distinctly legal realm will quickly answer that since moral intuitions are notoriously various and contested, the identification of law with morality would leave every individual his or her own judge; in place of a single abiding standard to which disputing parties might have recourse, we would have many standards with no way of adjudicating between them. In short, many moralities would make many laws, and the law would lack its most saliently desirable properties, generality and stability.

It is here that the danger posed by morality to law, or, more precisely, to the rule (in two senses) of law intersects with the danger posed by interpretation. The link is to be found in the desire to identify a perspective

---

[1] Stanley Fish, *The Law Wishes to Have a Formal Existence*, in THE FATE OF LAW 159-162 (Austin Sarat & Thomas R. Kearns, eds., 1991).

[2] Manwill v. Oyler, 11 Utah 2d 433, 361 P. 2d 177 (1961).

larger and more stable than the perspective of local and individual concerns. Morality frustrates that desire because, in a world of more than one church, recourse to morality will always be recourse to someone's or some group's challengeable moral vision. Interpretation frustrates that desire because, in the pejorative sense it usually bears in these discussions, interpretation is the name for what happens when the meanings embedded in an object or text are set aside in favor of the meanings demanded by some angled, partisan object. Interpretation, in this view, is the effort of a morality, of a particular, interested agenda, to extend itself into the world by inscribing its message on every available space. It follows then that, in order to check the imperial ambitions of particular moralities, some point of resistance to interpretation must be found, and that is why the doctrine of formalism has proved so attractive. Formalism is the thesis that it is possible to put down marks so self-sufficiently perspicuous that they repel interpretation; it is the thesis that one can write sentences of such precision and simplicity that their meanings leap off the page in a way no one—no matter what his or her situation or point of view—can ignore; it is the thesis that one can devise procedures that are self-executing in the sense that their unfolding is independent of the differences between the agents who might set them in motion. In the presence (in the strong Derridean sense) of such a mark or sentence or procedure, the interpretive will is stopped short and is obliged to press its claims within the constraints provided by that which it cannot override. It must take the marks into account; it must respect the self-declaring reasons; it must follow the route laid down by the implacable procedures, and if it then wins it will have done so fairly, with justice, with reason.

Obviously then, formalism's appeal is a function of the number of problems it solves, or at least appears to solve: it provides the law with a palpable manifestation of its basic claim to be perdurable and general; that is, not shifting and changing, but standing as a point of reference in relation to which change can be assessed and controlled; it enables the law to hold contending substantive agendas at bay by establishing threshold requirements of procedure that force those agendas to assume a shape the system will recognize. The idea is that once a question has been posed as a *legal* question—has been put into the proper *form*—the answer to it will be generated by relations of entailment between that form and other forms in the system. As Hans Kelsen put it in a book aptly named *The Pure Theory of Law*,

> The law is an order, and therefore all legal problems must be set and solved as order problems. In this way legal theory becomes an exact structural analysis of positive law, free of all ethical-political value judgments.[3]

Kelsen's last clause says it all: the realms of the ethical, the political, and of value in general are the threats to the law's integrity. They are what must be kept out if the law is to be something more than a misnomer for the local (and illegitimate) triumph of some particular point of view.

There are at least two strong responses to this conception of law. The first, which we might call the "humanistic" response, objects that a legal system so conceived is impoverished, and that once you have severed procedures from value, it will prove enormously difficult, if not impossible, to relink them in particular cases. Since the answers generated by a purely formal system will be empty of content (that, after all, is the formalist claim), the reintroduction of content will always be arbitrary. The second response, which we might call "radical" or "critical," would simply declare that a purely formal system is not a possibility, and that any system pretending to that status is already informed by that which it purports to exclude. Value, of both an ethical and political kind, is already inside the gate, and the adherents of the system are either ignorant of its sources or are engaged in a political effort to obscure them in the course of laying claim to a spurious purity. However much the law wishes to have a formal existence, it cannot succeed in doing so, because—at any level from the most highly abstract to the most particular and detailed—any specification of what the law is will already be infected by

---

[3] P. 192. Trans. Max Knight from the 2d (rev. and enl.) German ed. (Berkeley: University of California Press, 1967).

interpretation and will therefore be challengeable.

2. Michael S. Moore: The Semantics of Judging[4]

The formalist theory of adjudication asserts that legal disputes can be, should be, and are resolved by recourse to legal rules and principles, and the facts of each particular dispute. Thus, a formalist judge has an extremely limited set of materials to consider as relevant to his decision in a particular case—the rules and the facts. His decision is to be logically deduced from these two items alone.

An example may be helpful. In *Interstate Commerce Commission v. Kroblin*,[5] a non-certificated carrier (Allen Kroblin) transported frozen, eviscerated chickens interstate. A statute required carriers to obtain certificates from the Interstate Commerce Commission (ICC) unless the carriers were transporting agricultural commodities, as opposed to manufactured products. The court decided that eviscerated chickens were agricultural commodities, not manufactured products, and that Kroblin was therefore exempt from the certification requirements. A formalist reconstruction of the court's reasoning would be as follows. The major premise (based on a simplified version of the statute which ignores those requirements not at issue) may be stated:

1. Objects that are not manufactured products may be carried without an ICC certificate.

The minor premise is obtained from the facts of the case. The court decided that eviscerated chickens were agricultural commodities, not manufactured products. Thus:

2. These things (eviscerated chickens) are not manufactured products.

From these two premises, the conclusion of the court does indeed follow—eviscerated chickens may be carried by Kroblin without obtaining an ICC certificate.

What such a theory of adjudication excludes as improper for consideration by the judge is striking. The consequences of this decision upon the parties to the action and upon the public at large are to be ignored. Ethical principles pay no part. General social policies that will be frustrated or furthered by the rule resulting from the judge's decision are not fit grist for the judicial mill. Rather, the judge's role is to decide solely on the basis of the meaning of legal rules applied to the facts before him.

Two items require further clarification in this definition of legal formalism. One is the extent to which formalism is committed to the thesis that there is a single right answer in *every* case. The other is the extent to which formalism is committed to a deductive structure existing behind positive law, so that the rules from which decisions are deduced are themselves deducible from more general principles.

"Formalism," as used in this Article, denotes a theory that a judge can deduce a single answer in at least some, if not all, cases. To argue against formalism, accordingly, one must demonstrate that there are no "easy" or "plain" cases in which a result may be deduced. The idea of a single, unique result may itself be unclear. The discussion that follows assumes that a fact-finder is presented with a simple decision: he either agrees or disagrees with some proposition about the case presented. In *Kroblin*, for example, the fact-finder either affirms or denies that eviscerated chickens are manufactured products. The lack of clarity of such an idea, and of the assumption behind it, can be quickly appreciated when it is remembered that all legal terms are dispositive in nature. That is, legal terms look to both the factual states which they describe *and* the legal consequences that they engender. For example, "not a manufactured product" is a phrase that both describes certain objects and, when used in a legal rule, prescribes that a certain legal result obtain, *i.e.*, that the item can be transported by a non-certificated carrier. This Janus-like characteristic of words used in legal rules guarantees that a judge has more to decide than whether the facts before him match some legal description. In addition, the judge must decide

---

[4] Michael S. Moore, *The Semantics of Judging*, 54 S. Cal. L. Rev. 155-60.

[5] 113 F. Supp. 599 (N.D. Iowa 1953), *aff'd*, 212 F. 2d 555 (8th Cir. 1954).

whether the contemplated remedy results in legal consequences prescribed by the rule. In *Kroblin*, even if the judge decides that eviscerated chickens are manufactured products, he still must reach the determination that enjoining Kroblin from carrying such things is *the* remedy the rule prescribed. Given both the indeterminacy of language in the description of legal consequences and the often explicit grant of discretion to judges to choose among alternative remedies, often no single remedy *can* plausibly be said to be required by the rule.

Thus, the assumption that a judge has only one choice, to which he answers yes or no, is plainly unrealistic; any adjudication in fact has a many-valued choice (of remedy), and not just a two-valued choice (of applying some description). A discussion of formalism without such a simplifying assumption is unnecessary, however. The problems of meaning faced by a formalist judge in determining whether some dispositive legal concept truthfully describes the facts before him are the same as the problems that affect his decision concerning the propriety of the remedy he proposes to give. This special assumption will thus allow the critique to proceed without unnecessary duplication of the argument.

The second item requiring further clarification in this definition of formalism is the deductive structure thought by many formalists to exist behind positive law. This is a separable aspect of formalist theory that merits special attention. C.C. Langdell, the archformalist to many, thought that law, no less than natural science, had a deductive structure behind it, in which theories using nonordinary terms lacking in any reference to physical objects—terms such as "estate," "title," and "meeting of the minds"—could be found. The justification for such terms and the theories that used them was for Langdell the same as the justification for a similar enterprise in science. Such words were necessary to predict and to explain "the data," which in law were the decisions of judges and the rules which they applied.

Langdell's classification of law as a science seems to assume that legal reasoning could be reconstructed properly to include not only rules and facts, but also more general, theoretical statements. Science, too, is concerned not only with laws connecting observable events, but also with more general theories explaining these laws. An example is the legal rule that acceptance of an offer is effective upon dispatch, whereas the revocation of an offer is effective upon receipt. Although Langdell recognized that there might be policy arguments to support such a rule, for him the true justification lay in the deducibility of the rule from a more general, theoretical principle of contract law: no contract exists until there is a meeting of the minds. The ability to deduce a rule from a more general principle rendered policy arguments irrelevant.

Although in the abstract formalists need not subscribe to this conception of theories in law, they must do so in the context of a familiar legal system. The systems with which we are familiar have such a paucity of rules that some recognition of theories behind the rules is necessary to enrich the strictly legal materials available to a judge. Accordingly, this separable claim has been included as part of a formalist theory of adjudication. So construed, formalism asserts not only that there exists, in all or some cases, one unique result deducible from the rules and the facts, but also that the rules themselves may be derived from some more general theoretical statements.

Formalism, so defined, has long been parodied and ridiculed in American jurisprudence. From Holmes' sometimes aphoristic attack,[6] through Pound's celebrated assault on "mechanical jurisprudence,"[7] to the contemptuous dismissals by the loose assemblage of persons sometimes called Legal Realists, formalism has been scorned as a theory of adjudication. Yet formalism is central in our ideas about law. Formalism is not just *a* theory of adjudication. It has all the appearances of being *the* theory of adjudication that permits faithfulness to those ideals encompassed in the concept of the rule of law.

---

[6] O.W. Holmes, The Common Law (1881); Holmes, *The Path of Law*, 10 Harv. L. Rev. 457 (1897).

[7] Pound, *Mechanical Jurisprudence*, 8 Colum. L. Rev. 605 (1908).

3. Ellen Ash Peters: The Rule of Statutes[8]

Reviewing the cases decided in my court since we started this last October [1981], I found only a scant ten percent of them to be purely common law cases. Everywhere else, statutes were relevant if not determinative of the controversy. Significantly, the role of statutes is just as crucial in the litigation involving so-called common law subjects, such as torts, contracts, property, and procedure, as elsewhere. Litigated negligence cases, when they concern accidents in the workplace, run into workers' compensation statutes; when they arise out of automobile accidents, they run into motor vehicle statutes. Contract cases are affected by the Uniform Commercial Code, by statutory liens such as mechanic's liens, and by a host of licensing statutes. Procedure is governed by judicially adopted rules of practice that are legislative in their effect even though they are judicial in their origin. Real property law is heavily influenced by local regulation in the form of zoning ordinances and by state and national regulation in the form of environmental controls.

Statutory construction seems, at first blush, to be too mundane a subject to discuss. Sutherland has, after all, written volumes,[9] volumes that one suspects are often more cited than read. Regrettably the judicial vantage point reveals some recurring trouble spots. The first of these is the difficulty that we all encounter in locating relevant statutes. I am of course particularly sensitive to cases in which the Uniform Commercial Code is overlooked,[10] which arise with dismal regularity. But the UCC is not the only statute that fails to surface. Courts and counsel frequently miss a statute that is directly in point[11] and rarely venture in search of statutes that are indirectly applicable. I can only speculate why this unhappy state of affairs should persist. Of prime importance is the fact that few of us have been trained to do statutory research. We cut our legal teeth on cases, not statutes, and we tend, therefore, to *look* for cases rather than statutes. It is almost as if a statute was not firmly planted in the legal turf until some court had found it and commented upon its scope and meaning. Furthermore, the legal materials that we use most comfortably are case oriented rather than statute oriented. When a legislature passes a statute reversing or modifying a common law line of cases, that fact is not generally noted in the case digests or in the case Shepard's. Even when one thinks to look in the legislative indices, they tend to be unhelpful for anyone without pre-knowledge of the statute's existence. The indices are, for the most part, vertically organized, by existing statutory classifications, rather than horizontally across statutory lines. To revert again to the UCC cases with which I am familiar, the general index to the Connecticut statutes contains no reference for unconscionability or for impracticability of performance. To discover, in Connecticut, that the UCC has suggestions for the law of accord and satisfaction, one would have to know to look under "reservation of rights." Perhaps electronic retrieval will remedy this situation, although even there it may well be necessary to rely on educated surmise to discover the language that the statutory author is likely to have employed. There is an urgent need for lawyers to develop greater sensitivity and better techniques for locating relevant statutory materials.

Having found a statute that may apply, a lawyer is then faced with the task of reading it. What a cheerless undertaking! Cases are fascinating; they engage our attention because of the human drama that they portray, but statutes! That is why it is much easier to read comments on statutes than statutes themselves. It takes an extraordinary act of will to work through a statute of any length. While it is clear that every word must be read, it is equally apparent that a reader cannot rely on the literal meaning of every word, without inquiring how that word is used elsewhere in the statute. In the UCC there are some sections, such as the one deal-

---

[8] Justice, Supreme Court of Connecticut. Excerpted from: Ellen Ash Peters, *Common Law Judging in a Statutory World: An Address*, 43 UNIVERSITY OF PITTSBURGH LAW REVIEW 995, 998-1000, 1006-08, 1010-11 (1982). Reprinted by permission.

[9] J. SUTHERLAND, STATUTES AND STATUTORY CONSTRUCTION (3d ed. 1943).

[10] *See, e.g.*, Bead Chain Mfg. Co. v. Saxon Prods., Inc., 439 A.2d 314 (1981).

[11] *See, e.g.*, State v. Burke, 438 A.2d 93 (1980).

ing with installment contracts, that are intrinsically unreadable, and others, such as those dealing with negotiation of negotiable instruments, that only become unreadable when read in unison with each other. In Connecticut we have an intricate mechanic's lien statute. I have had five cases dealing with it and have only now come to begin to unravel it in its entirety. With deference, I think that with all of the emphasis recently placed on teaching clinical skills, we have insufficiently noted the importance of teaching statutory skills.

Of course, some statutes come to us with helpful secondary gloss. They may have a legislative history, although in state legislation such a history is more often the exception than the rule. Many statutes are the product of compromise and tradeoff, so that the search for a single legislative intent is fruitless. Even statutes which have no history may, however, develop a present source of interpretation. Statues whose enforcement is entrusted, in the first instance, to administrative agencies often generate regulations which, once located, are enormously helpful. Regulations, because of their greater specificity and because they are frequently blessed with illustrative examples, tend, like "official comments," to be much more readable than the underlying statutes. It is clear that the Internal Revenue Code would be entirely impenetrable to any nonspecialist without Internal Revenue Service regulations. On a state level, insurance and banking regulations often serve a similar highly useful function.

What authority does a court have to *refuse* to enforce a statute that, properly interpreted, applies to the case at hand? There are clear limitations. Courts are not free simply to disregard statutes which, as legislators, they would have voted against. Legislators are not required to make policy decisions that please courts; legislators are not even required to make policy decisions that are universally fair. Unless legislative action runs into constitutional constraints, the legislative voice generally determines the demands of policy and the ultimate choice among social and fiscal responses.

Apart from unconstitutional statutes, there is the statute which a court would like to influence. Professor Calabresi is most concerned with statutory obsolescence, with statutes that continue to remain on the books although their present reenactment seems doubtful.[12] Professor Gilmore says statutes are most unsatisfactory in their middle age. In his words, as always eminently quotable, "Admittedly the statute is no longer what it once was but there is life in the old dog yet. An occasional subsection still has teeth and subparagraph (3)(b) may burn with a gem-like flame."[13] For myself, I am most troubled about what the legislature has done lately. The democratization of our political processes, the pressure for the immediate institutional responses, the spotlight cast by the media, all have the capacity for producing legislation that is, from its inception, ill-conceived. Chief Justice Rose Bird of the California Supreme Court, speaking at the national Judicial College last fall on "The Role of the Judge in the 80's," noted the extent to which we have as a nation come to place a higher value on image and on speed than on sober reflection. "Life in the fast lane," as she put it, is reflected in a headlong rush by legislators to achieve a quick fix for every social problem. Legislators feel that they need to stand up and be counted, on subjects ranging from the appropriateness of allowing physicians to prescribe marijuana for patients on chemotherapy to the desirability of requiring juries to convict, rather than acquit, criminal defendants who are found to be insane. Who can be sure that these statutes, almost always well-intentioned, may not hit an entirely unforeseen obstacle or target?

Judicial intervention may be seductively tempting because of the particular facts of an especially appealing case that may be quite unrepresentative of the legal landscape as a whole. It is still true that hard cases make bad law. For those of us who are inclined to see ourselves as judicial activists, it is nonetheless heady indeed to contemplate extension of our hegemony to the world of statutes. Only a sober recognition that we may intrude only when we must, and that we must step cautiously when we can, will help us to begin to find our way.

---

[12] GUIDO CALABRESI, A COMMON LAW FOR THE AGE OF STATUTES (1982).

[13] GRANT GILMORE, THE AGES OF AMERICAN LAW 96 (1977).

4. Lon Fuller: Legal Formalities[14]

If it were true that laymen generally regarded the ceremony of "shaking hands on it" as creating a binding contract, it would not follow that a court would have to accept this ceremony as a valid legal formality if it considered that it offered insufficient safeguards against the dangers which legal formalities are supposed to avert. Our courts probably made a mistake in following lay practice in the "liberalization" of the requirement of a seal. In this way they frittered away, perhaps irretrievably, a valuable social practice. The law has always to weigh against the advantages of conforming to life, the advantages of reshaping and clarifying life, bearing always in mind that its attempts to reshape life may miscarry, or may cost more than they achieve.

B. Deductive Logic

1. Morris R. Cohen: Logic in the Law[15]

Justice Holmes is careful to emphasize the function of general ideas in the development of the law (e.g., the idea of identity in succession after death and inter vivos), and his book [The Common Law] abounds in illustrations of how difficult legal problems can be cleared up by just logical analyses. But the new, more zealous crusaders against legal ideology are less cautious, and are inclined to deny all value to logic and general principles. Now it is a rather simple task to show the inadequacies of the proposed substitutes for the traditional principles of legal science. Sound common sense, the lessons of experience, the unspoiled sense of justice, the teachings of the as-yet-to-be-established science of sociology, or the somewhat elusive and perhaps altogether mythi-

cal will of the dominant class, cannot, without the aid of a logical legal technique, help us elaborate the laws of gifts, sales, mortgages, or determine the precise liability of a railroad company to those who use its sleeping car service. It is also easy enough to refute these new crusaders out of their own mouths and show that they themselves attach great value to a clear and logically consistent elaboration of the law. But such easy refutations, while they may be just, are seldom illuminating, unless we examine the situation with some thoroughness. This may lead us into the supposedly foreign fields of logic and metaphysics. But at the time when the foundations of our legal system are questioned both inside and outside of the legal fraternity, it would only be the wisdom of the ostrich which would counsel us to refrain from entering into these fields because, forsooth, the old tradition says that law is law, and has nothing to do with any other field of human inquiry.

The law, of course, never succeeds in becoming a completely deductive system. It does not even succeed in becoming completely consistent. But the effort to assume the form of a deductive system underlies all constructive legal scholarship.

In endeavoring to make the law systematic, jurists are not merely pursuing their own purely theoretic or scientific interest. They are performing a duty to the community by thus transforming the law. A legal system that works with general principles has powerful instruments. Just as the generalized arithmetic which we call advanced mathematics has increased manifold our power of solving physical problems, so a generalized jurisprudence enlarges the law's control over the diversity of legal situations. It is like fishing with large nets instead of single lines.

As nature has other cares besides letting us paint her deductive charm, she constantly reveals aspects that hamper or complicate our beautiful analytic equations. So, also, the affairs of practical life generate situations which mock our well-intentioned efforts to reduce the law to a rational system. In the presence of these, as of other seemingly insurmountable obstacles, human frailty is tempted to blink at the difficulties. So urgent is the need for assured first principles that most people resent the service that

[14] Lon L. Fuller, American Legal Realism, 82 UNIVERSITY OF PENNSYLVANIA LAW REVIEW 420, 460 (1934). Reprinted by permission.

[15] MORRIS R. COHEN, LAW AND THE SOCIAL ORDER (1933). Copyright 1933 Harcourt, Brace & Co. Reprinted by permission.

the skeptical-minded—the stray dogs of the intellectual world—render by showing the uninhabitableness of our hastily constructed legal or philosophic kennels. In the legal field, the blinking at the practical difficulties is facilitated by the ready assurance that if our principles are just it is none of our fault if any inconvenience results. *Fiat justitia pereat mundus*,[16] is a very edifying excuse for refusing to reexamine our principles in the light of the harsh results to which they lead.

The limitation that underlies the traditional logic shows itself in the familiar difficulty as to the presence of discretion in the law. The law is primarily directed toward certainty, which, according to the classical view, can be produced only by definite rules that leave no room for individual discretion. Individual discretion, whether of judge or of legislator acting under constitutionally limited powers, appears to this view synonymous with the absence of law. Thus in criminal law the old maxim is, Fix the offense definitely and the definite penalty. To individualize punishment seems to the old view to abandon legal security and to open the floodgates of judicial arbitrariness. This view, however, is based on an inadequate logic, which fails to appreciate the necessarily provisional character of all legal classification and the consequent necessity of discretion to make definite that which would otherwise be really indefinite. Logically the task of the law is similar to that of the wholesale manufacturer of shoes or any similar commodity. Human feet vary in size, and perhaps there is truth in the saying that no two are exactly alike. On the assumption that the shoe should fit the foot, the theoretical consequence would be that no two shoes should be made exactly alike. Experience, however, without contradicting these postulates of the perfect art of shoe making, finds that a limited number of classes of "sizes" will satisfy all normal demands. How is the number of these "sizes" determined? Obviously by striking a balance between the (very slight) inconvenience of having a shoe that may be one sixteenth of an inch too long and the inconvenience of doubling or tripling the number of sizes. The same method is at the basis of the criminal law. The number of ways and circumstances, for instance, in which the life of one person can be destroyed by another is endless. What the law does is to group them into a small number of classes, *viz.*, murder, manslaughter, etc., attempting to define the characteristics of each type in such a way that no one can take the life of a fellow-being in a way that society disapproves without falling in one or another of these groups. There is, of course, no logical reason why the division into groups should be so rough, and it is abstractly possible to carry the classification to any degree of fineness and discrimination—except that the difficulty of making juries understand the difference between murder in the first degree, murder in the second degree and manslaughter is already sufficiently great. It is foolish to attempt results more delicate than the instruments at your disposal will permit. Would we attempt to carve a delicately featured wooden statue with an ax? Judicial discretion in the individualization of punishment is simply an attempt to bring into the penal machinery a greater degree of discrimination than is practically possible by the prescription of hard and fast general rules.

The same argument applies to legislative discretion. "If the legislature has power to fix the maximum number of hours in an industry to ten, then why not nine, etc? Where are you going to draw the line?" The answer is that no such line can be drawn *a priori*, since we are dealing with a line that must necessarily vary in different industries and at different times.

Jurists, like other men, are in their attitude to the employment of logic either intellectuals or mystics. The intellectualist not only trusts implicitly all the results of reasoning, but believes that no safe result can be obtained in any other way. Hence in law he emphasizes the rule rather than the decision. This, however, leads to an ignoring of the absurd consequences to which the logical application of rules frequently leads. *Summum jus, summa injuria*. The mystics distrust reasoning. They have faith in intuition, sense, or feeling. "Men are wiser than they know," says Emerson, and the Autocrat of the Breakfast Table, who was not a stranger

---

[16] Let justice be done even if the world must perish. A similar Latinism is: *fiat justitia ruat coelum*: Let justice be done though the heavens fall asunder.

to the study of the law, adds, "You can hire logic, in the shape of a lawyer, to prove anything you want to prove." But shall we subscribe to the primitive superstition that only the frenzied and the mentally beclouded are divinely inspired? Like other useful instruments, logic is very dangerous, and it requires great wisdom to use it properly. A logical science of law can help us digest our legal material, but we must get our food before we can digest it. The law draws its sap from feelings of justice and social need. It has grown and been improved by sensitively minded judges attending to the conflicting claims of the various interests before them, and leaving it to subsequent developments to demonstrate the full wisdom or unwisdom of the decision. The intellectualist would have the judge certain of everything before deciding, but this is impossible. Like other human efforts, the law must experiment, which always involves a leap into the dark future. But for that very reason the judge's feelings as to right and wrong must be logically and scientifically trained. The trained mind sees in a flash of intuition that which the untrained mind can succeed in seeing only after painfully treading many steps. They who scorn the idea of the judge as a logical automaton are apt to fall into the opposite error of exaggerating as irresistible the force of bias or prejudice. But the judge who realizes before listening to a case that all men are biased is more likely to make a conscientious effort at impartiality than one who believes that elevation to the bench makes him at once an organ of infallible logical truth.

2. Richard A. Wasserstrom: The Role of Deductive Logic[17]

The question of the nature of the judicial decision process has been formulated by almost every legal philosopher as involving the issue of whether or not courts reach their decisions by a deductive or logical method of decision. Many legal philosophers have

come to regard the deductive theory, *i.e.*, the theory that is thought to describe (or propose) an essentially deductive or logical judicial decision procedure, as the chief impediment to clear and consistent thinking about the judicial process. Critics of the theory have given it a variety of names. It has been called "legal fundamentalism," "formalism," "deductivism," "the phonographic theory of law," "mechanical jurisprudence," "slot machine jurisprudence," and a host of comparable epithets. Yet, the proliferation of labels has not been accompanied by a clarification of the characteristics of the procedure or the reasons for its rejection. Indeed, as we have noted, the general attack upon the use of logic in the judicial decision process resolves itself into one or more of a variety of claims and suppositions.

What, for example, would a deductive decision procedure be like? What does the deductive theory entail? Many critics have thought the deductive theory to imply a judicial decision procedure in which all cases are decided by an appeal to rules that are certain and unchanging, whose application is completely predictable. It is regarded as in some sense postulating a gapless system of pre-existing law, from which a solution for every new case could be obtained by deduction. In such a system, apparently, the rule of law relevant to the case serves as the major premise of a syllogism; the statement that characterizes the particular fact situation before the court serves as the minor premise; and that conclusion which is derivable in accordance with the canons of Aristotelian logic is announced by the judge as the court's decision for this particular case. It would seem that the judge is peculiarly qualified to render decisions because he knows what many of the rules are, where the others may be readily located, and how to use the canons of logic to discern valid arguments.

Critics of the deductive theory also suggest that the theory necessarily denies the relevance of considerations of justice to the selection of the propositions that serve as the major and minor premises and to the conclusion that becomes the decision for the particular case. Concomitantly, since the judge's sole function is to apply the existing rules of law to the facts of the particular case, the deductive theory is deemed to entail the view that it is never the province of the judge

[17] RICHARD A. WASSERSTROM, THE JUDICIAL DECISION 14-17, 24 (1961). Copyright 1961 Stanford Univ. Press. Reprinted by permission.

to make rules of law. Thus when philosophers pronounce the deductive theory unacceptable, they attack, among other things, a procedure in which rules of law could never be formulated or altered by the judge, a procedure in which the judge plays no "creative" role in the decision process, a procedure that finds relevant the canons of formal logic, and a procedure in which there is seemingly no guarantee that justice will be done in all or even most cases. If the deductive theory, so interpreted, correctly describes even some of the characteristics of the English or American legal system, it surely furnishes the grounds for a harsh indictment of the way English or American courts have decided cases. In developing their criticism, opponents of the deductive theory have almost unanimously regarded the words of Justice Holmes as the most appropriate single point of departure for their attack. The dictum that "general propositions do not decide concrete cases" and the assertion that "the life of the law has not been logic: it has been experience," have been taken to signify that rules of law were not the means by which courts decided particular cases. These aphorisms have been understood at times to suggest that a logical application of rules to facts cannot have been the procedure by which adjudication actually was effected. And they have been interpreted, too, as a demand for an analysis that will realistically—and hence, accurately—study the decision process of the common-law courts.

When such an analysis is undertaken, the critics insist, one readily discovers that courts have in fact responded to novel situations and changing pressures. And how, it is asked, is it possible for courts by supposedly necessary logical deduction from non-contemporaneous premises and apparently without entering upon social and ethical inquiries, to reach conclusions well adapted to contemporary problems? The answer is simple. The deductive theory is an inadequate, quite inaccurate account of the way in which courts really have decided cases. Courts both past and present have clearly not invoked a formal procedure by which particular cases are adjudicated in accordance with rules; on the contrary, their methodology has been, and continues to be, distinctively nondeductive.

Why then has it taken so long to see the weaknesses of the deductive theory? Why, since common-law courts have been deciding cases for over 750 years, did the theory's inaccuracy remain hidden until the twentieth century? Again, the answer is soon found. If one were to look no further than the opinions that judges write to accompany their decisions, it would not occur to one that the decision process could be anything but deductive. For it is one of the curious features of Anglo-American case law that regardless of the way in which a given decision is actually reached, the judge apparently feels it necessary to make it appear that the decision was dictated by prior rules applied in accordance with canons of formal logic. One thing must be added, however. It would be incorrect to ascribe to the judiciary sinister motives of any kind. Judges do not deliberately seek to deceive the world about the nature of the decision process. The fact that their opinions obscure rather than illuminate the judicial process indicates that the departure from the deductive model is affected quite unconsciously.

I am arguing only that many legal philosophers are surely mistaken if they infer the inherent arbitrariness of the judicial decision process from the limited utility of formal, deductive logic. It may not make much sense to describe the judicial decision process as a completely deductive one. But it makes even less sense to insist that for this reason courts could not (and should not) employ a procedure or set of procedures that permits of some kind of reasoned justification for the judicial decisions reached by those courts.

3. Ronald Dworkin: Hard Cases[16]

The rights thesis holds that judicial decisions enforce existing political rights.

Institutional history acts not as a constraint on the political judgment of judges but as an ingredient of that judgment, because institutional history is part of the

---

[16] RONALD DWORKIN, TAKING RIGHTS SERIOUSLY 87-90, 110-123 (1977). Copyright 1977 Ronald Dworkin. Reprinted by permission of the author.

background that any plausible judgment about the rights of an individual must accommodate. Political rights are creatures of both history and morality: what an individual is entitled to have, in civil society, depends upon both the practice and the justice of its political institutions. Judges must make fresh judgments about the rights of the parties who come before them, but these political rights reflect, rather than oppose, political decisions of the past.

The rights thesis provides a more satisfactory explanation of how judges use precedent in hard cases than the explanation provided by any theory that gives a more prominent place to policy. Judges, like all political officials, are subject to the doctrine of political responsibility. This doctrine states, in its most general form, that political officials must make only such political decisions as they can justify within a political theory that also justifies the other decisions they propose to make. The doctrine seems innocuous in this general form; but it does, even in this form, condemn a style of political administration that might be called, following Rawls, intuitionistic. It condemns the practice of making decisions that seem right in isolation, but cannot be brought within some comprehensive theory of general principles and policies that is consistent with other decisions also thought right. Suppose a Congressman votes to prohibit abortion, on the ground that human life in any form is sacred, but then votes to permit the parents of babies born deformed to withhold medical treatment that will keep such babies alive. He might say that he feels that there is some difference, but the principle of responsibility, strictly applied, will not allow him these two votes unless he can incorporate the difference within some general political theory he sincerely holds.

The doctrine demands, we might say, articulate consistency. But this demand is relatively weak when policies are in play. Policies are aggregative in their influence on political decisions and it need not be part of a responsible strategy for reaching a collective goal that individuals be treated alike. It does not follow from the doctrine of responsibility, therefore, that if the legislature awards a subsidy to one aircraft manufacturer one month it must award a subsidy to another manufacturer the next. In the case of princi-

ples, however, the doctrine insists on distributional consistency from one case to the next, because it does not allow for the idea of a strategy that may be better served by unequal distribution of the benefit in question. If an official believes, for example, that sexual liberty of some sort is a right of individuals, then he must protect that liberty in a way that distributes the benefit reasonably equally over the class of those whom he supposes to have the right. If he allows one couple to use contraceptives on the ground that this right would otherwise be invaded, then he must, so long as he does not recant that earlier decision, allow the next couple the same liberty. He cannot say that the first decision gave the community just the amount of sexual liberty it needed, so that no more is required at the time of the second.

Legal argument, in hard cases, turns on contested concepts whose nature and function are very much like the concept of the character of a game. These include several of the substantive concepts through which the law is stated, like the concepts of a contract and of property. But they also include two concepts of much greater relevance to the present argument. The first is the idea of the "intention" or "purpose" of a particular statute or statutory clause. This concept provides a bridge between the political justification of the general idea that statutes create rights and those hard cases that ask what rights a particular statute has created. The second is the concept of principles that "underlie" or are "embedded in" the positive rules of law. This concept provides a bridge between the political justification of the doctrine that like cases should be decided alike and those hard cases in which it is unclear what that general doctrine requires. These concepts together define legal rights as a function, though a very special function, of political rights. If a judge accepts the settled practices of his legal system—if he accepts, that is, the autonomy provided by its distinct constitutive and regulative rules—then he must, according to the doctrine of political responsibility, accept some general political theory that justifies these practices. The concepts of legislative purpose and common law principles are devices for applying that general political theory to controversial issues about legal rights.

We might therefore do well to consider

how a philosophical judge might develop, in appropriate cases, theories of what legislative purpose and legal principles require. We shall find that he would construct these theories in the same manner as a philosophical referee would construct the character of a game. I have invented, for this purpose, a lawyer of superhuman skill, learning, patience and acumen, whom I shall call Hercules. I suppose that Hercules is a judge in some representative American jurisdiction. I assume that he accepts the main uncontroversial constitutive and regulative rules of the law in his jurisdiction. He accepts, that is, that statutes have the general power to create and extinguish legal rights, and that judges have the general duty to follow earlier decisions of their court or higher courts whose rationale, as lawyers say, extends to the case at bar.

One day lawyers will present a hard case to Hercules that does not turn upon any statute; they will argue whether earlier common law decisions of Hercules' court, properly understood, provide some party with a right to a decision in his favor.

Hercules must begin by asking why arguments of that form are ever, even in principle, sound. He will find that he has available no quick or obvious answer. He might, however, be tempted by this answer. Judges, when they decide particular cases at common law, lay down general rules that are intended to benefit the community in some way. Other judges, deciding later cases, must therefore enforce these rules so that the benefit may be achieved. If this account of the matter were a sufficient justification of the practices of precedent, then Hercules could decide these hard common law cases as if earlier decisions were statutes. But he will encounter fatal difficulties if he pursues that theory very far. It will repay us to consider why, in some detail, because the errors in the theory will be guides to a more successful theory.

Statutory interpretation depends upon the availability of a canonical form of words, however vague or unspecific, that set limits to the political decisions that the statute may be taken to have made. Hercules will discover that many of the opinions that litigants cite as precedents do not contain any special propositions taken to be a canonical form of the rule that the case lays down. It is true that it was part of Anglo American judicial style, during the last part of the nineteenth century and the first part of this century, to attempt to compose such canonical statements, so that one could thereafter refer, for example, to the rule in *Rylands v. Fletcher*.[19] But even in this period, lawyers and textbook writers disagreed about which parts of famous opinions should be taken to have that character. Today, in any case, even important opinions rarely attempt that legislative sort of draftsmanship. They cite reasons, in the form of precedents and principles, to justify a decision, but it is the decision, not some new and stated rule of law, that these precedents and principles are taken to justify. Sometimes a judge will acknowledge openly that it lies to later cases to determine the full effect of the case he has decided.

Of course, Hercules might well decide that when he does find, in an earlier case, a canonical form of words, he will use his techniques of statutory interpretation to decide whether the rule composed of these words embraces a novel case. He might well acknowledge what could be called an enactment force of precedent. He will nevertheless find that when a precedent does have enactment force, its influence on later cases is not taken to be limited to that force. He would urge that the earlier decision exerts a gravitational force on later decisions even when these later decisions lie outside its particular orbit.

This gravitational force is part of the practice Hercules' general theory of precedent must capture. In this important respect, judicial practice differs from the practice of officials in other institutions. In chess, officials conform to established rules in a way that assumes full institutional autonomy. They exercise originality only to the extent required by the fact that an occasional rule, like the rule about forfeiture, demands that originality. Each decision of a chess referee, therefore, can be said to be directly required and justified by an established rule of chess, even though some of these decisions must be based on an interpretation, rather than on simply the plain and unavoidable meaning, of that rule.

---

[19] L.R. 1 Ex. 265 (1866), *aff'd*, L.R. 3 H.L. 330 (1868).

Some legal philosophers write about common law adjudication as if it were in this way like chess, except that legal rules are much more likely than chess rules to require interpretation. That is the spirit, for example, of Professor Hart's argument that hard cases arise only because legal rules have what he calls "open texture."[20] In fact, judges often disagree not simply about how some rule or principle should be interpreted, but whether the rule or principle one judge cites should be acknowledged to be a rule or principle at all. In some cases both the majority and the dissenting opinions recognize the same earlier cases as relevant, but disagree about what rule or principle these precedents should be understood to have established. In adjudication, unlike chess, the argument *for* a particular rule may be more important than the argument *from* that rule to the particular case; and while the chess referee who decides a case by appeal to a rule no one has ever heard of before is likely to be dismissed or certified, the judge who does so is likely to be celebrated in law school lectures.

Nevertheless judges seem agreed that earlier decisions do contribute to the formulation of new and controversial rules in some way other than by interpretation; they are agreed that earlier decisions have gravitational force even when they disagree about what that force is. The legislator may very often concern himself only with issues of background morality or policy in deciding how to cast his vote on some issue. He need not show that his vote is consistent with the votes of his colleagues in the legislature, or with those of past legislatures. But the judge very rarely assumes that character of independence. He will always try to connect the justification he provides for an original decision with decisions that other judges or officials have taken in the past.

In fact, when good judges try to explain in some general way how they work, they search for figures of speech to describe the constraints they feel even when they suppose that they are making new law, constraints that would not be appropriate if they

were legislators. They say, for example, that they find new rules imminent in the law as a whole, or that they are enforcing an internal logic of the law through some method that belongs more to philosophy than to politics, or that they are the agents through which the law works itself pure, or that the law has some life of its own even though this belongs to experience rather than logic. Hercules must not rest content with these famous metaphors and personifications, but he must also not be content with any description of the judicial process that ignores their appeal to the best lawyers.

The gravitational force of precedent cannot be captured by any theory that takes the full force of precedent to be its enactment force as a piece of legislation. But the inadequacy of that approach suggests a superior theory. The gravitational force of a precedent may be explained by appeal, not to the wisdom of enforcing enactments but to the fairness of treating like cases alike. A precedent is the report of an earlier political decision; the very fact of that decision, as a piece of political history, provides some reason for deciding other cases in a similar way in the future. This general explanation of the gravitational force of precedent accounts for the feature that defeated the enactment theory, which is that the force of a precedent escapes the language of its opinion. If the government of a community has forced the manufacturer of defective motor cars to pay damages to a woman who was injured because of the defect, then that historical fact must offer some reason, at least, why the same government should require a contractor who has caused economic damage through the defective work of his employees to make good that loss. We may test the weight of that reason, not by asking whether the language of the earlier decision, suitably interpreted, requires the contractor to pay damages, but by asking the different question whether it is fair for the government, having intervened in the way it did in the first case, to refuse its aid in the second.

Hercules will conclude that this doctrine of fairness offers the only adequate account of the full practice of precedent. He will draw certain further conclusions about his own responsibilities when deciding hard cases. The most important of these is that he must limit the gravitational force of earlier deci-

---

[20] *Editor's Note*: Hart had referred to the "open texture" of rules in discussing cases that arise in the *penumbra* of statutory words.

sions to the extension of the arguments of principle necessary to justify those decisions. If an earlier decision were taken to be entirely justified by some argument of policy, it would have no gravitational force. Its value as a precedent would be limited to its enactment force, that is, to further cases captured by some particular words of the opinion.

Hercules' first conclusion, that the gravitational force of a precedent is defined by the arguments of principle that support the precedent, suggests a second. Hercules must develop his concept of principles that underlie the common law by assigning to each of the relevant precedents some scheme of principle that justifies the decision of that precedent. If the gravitational force of precedent rests on the idea that fairness requires the consistent enforcement of rights, then Hercules must discover principles that fit, not only the particular precedent to which some litigant directs his attention, but all other judicial decisions within his general jurisdiction and, indeed, statutes as well, so far as these must be seen to be generated by principle rather than policy. He does not satisfy his duty to show that his decision is consistent with established principles, and therefore fair, if the principles he cites as established are themselves inconsistent with other decisions that his court also proposes to uphold.

Suppose, for example, that he can justify a previous tort precedent by citing some abstract principle of equality, which argues that whenever an accident occurs then the richest of the various persons whose acts might have contributed to the accident must bear the loss. He nevertheless cannot show that that principle has been respected in other accident cases, or, even if he could, that it has been respected in other branches of the law, like contract, in which it would also have great impact if it were recognized at all. If he decides against a future accident plaintiff who is richer than the defendant, by appealing to this alleged right of equality, that plaintiff may properly complain that the decision is just as inconsistent with the government's behavior in other cases as if the precedent case itself had been ignored. The law may not be a seamless web; but the plaintiff is entitled to ask Hercules to treat it as if it were.

You will now see why I called our judge Hercules. He must construct a scheme of abstract and concrete principles that provides a coherent justification for all common law precedents and, so far as these are to be justified on principle, constitutional and statutory provisions as well.

Hercules must also face a different and greater problem. If the history of his court is at all complex, he will find, in practice, that the requirement of total consistency he has accepted will prove too strong, unless he develops it further to include the idea that he may, in applying this requirement, disregard some part of institutional history as a mistake. For he will be unable, even with his superb imagination, to find any set of principles that reconciles all standing statutes and precedents. This is hardly surprising: the legislators and judges of the past did not all have Hercules' ability or insight, nor were they men and women who were all of the same mind and opinion. Of course, any set of statutes and decisions can be explained historically, or psychologically, or sociologically, but consistency requires justification, not explanation, and the justification must be plausible and not sham. If the justification he constructs makes distinctions that are arbitrary and deploys principles that are unappealing, then it cannot count as a justification at all.

Suppose the law of negligence and accidents in Hercules' jurisdiction has developed in the following simplified and imaginary way. It begins with specific common law decisions recognizing a right to damages for bodily injury caused by very dangerous instruments that are defectively manufactured. The legislature adds a statute providing that in certain cases of industrial accident, recovery will be allowed unless the defendant affirmatively establishes that the plaintiff was entirely to blame. But it also provides that in other cases, for example, in airplane accidents, recovery will be limited to a stipulated amount, which might be much less than the actual loss; and it later adds that the guest in an automobile cannot sue his host even if the host drives negligently and the guest is injured.

If Hercules is called on to decide a specific case involving an injury in an automobile, he might concede, for example, a legal principle granting a right to recover for damages incurred within an automobile owned by the plaintiff, but deny a principle that would extend to other damages. But though he could in this way tailor his justification of institutional history to fit that history exactly, he would realize that this justification rests on distinctions that are arbitrary. He can find no room in his political theory for a distinction that concedes an abstract right if someone is injured driving his own automobile but denies it if he is a guest or if he is injured in an airplane. He has provided a set of arguments that cannot stand as a coherent justification of anything. He might therefore concede that he can make no sense of institutional history except by supposing some general abstract right to recover for negligence: but he might argue that it is a relatively weak right and so will yield to policy considerations of relatively minor force. He will cite the limiting statutes and cases in support of his view that the right is a weak one. But he will then face a difficulty if, though the statute limiting liability in airplane accidents has never been repealed, the airlines have become sufficiently secure, and the mechanisms of insurance available to airlines so efficient and inexpensive, that a failure to repeal the statute can only be justified by taking the abstract right to be so weak that relatively thin arguments of policy are sufficient to defeat it. If Hercules takes the right to be that weak then he cannot justify the various common law decisions that support the right, as a concrete right, against arguments of policy much stronger than the airlines are now able to press. So he must choose either to take the failure to repeal the airline accident limitation statute, or the common law decisions that value the right much higher, as mistakes.

In any case, therefore, Hercules must expand his theory to include the idea that a justification of institutional history may display some part of that history as mistaken. But he cannot make impudent use of this device, because if he were free to take any incompatible piece of institutional history as a mistake, with no further consequences for his general theory, then the requirement of consistency would be no genuine requirement at all. He must develop some theory of institutional mistakes, and this theory of mistakes must have two parts. It must show the consequences for further arguments of

taking some institutional event to be mistaken; and it must limit the number and character of the events than can be disposed of in that way.

He will construct the first part of this theory of mistakes by means of two sets of distinctions. He will first distinguish between the specific authority of any institutional event, which is its power as an institutional act to effect just the specific institutional consequences it describes, and its gravitational force. If he classifies some event as a mistake, then he does not deny its specific authority, but he does deny its gravitational force, and he cannot consistently appeal to that force in other arguments. He will also distinguish between embedded and corrigible mistakes; embedded mistakes are those whose specific authority is fixed so that it survives their loss of gravitational force; corrigible mistakes are those whose specific authority depends on gravitational force in such a way that it cannot survive this loss.

The constitutional level of his theory will determine which mistakes are embedded. His theory of legislative supremacy, for example, will insure that any statutes he treats as mistakes will lose their gravitational force but not their specific authority. If he denies the gravitational force of the aircraft liability limitation statute, the statute is not thereby repealed; the mistake is embedded so that the specific authority survives. He must continue to respect the limitations the statute imposes upon liability, but he will not use it to argue in some other case for a weaker right. If he accepts some strict doctrine of precedent, and designates some judicial decision, like a decision denying a right in negligence against an accountant, a mistake, then the strict doctrine may preserve the specific authority of that decision, which might be limited to its enactment force, but the decision will lose its gravitational force; it will become, in Justice Frankfurter's phrase, a piece of legal flotsam or jetsam. It will not be necessary to decide which.

That is fairly straightforward, but Hercules must take more pains with the second part of his theory of mistakes. He is required, by the justification he has fixed to the general practice of precedent, to compose a more detailed justification, in the form of a scheme of principle, for the entire body of statutes and common law decisions. But a justification that designates part of what is to be justified as mistaken is *prima facie* weaker than one that does not. The second part of his theory of mistakes must show that it is nevertheless a stronger justification than any alternative that does not recognize any mistakes, or that recognizes a different set of mistakes. That demonstration cannot be a deduction from simple rules of theory construction, but if Hercules bears in mind the connection he earlier established between precedent and fairness, this connection will suggest two guidelines for his theory of mistakes. In the first place, fairness fixes on institutional history, not just as history but as a political program that the government proposed to continue into the future; it seizes, that is, on forward-looking, not the backward-looking implications of precedent. If Hercules discovers that some previous decision, whether a statute or a judicial decision, is now widely regretted within the pertinent branch of the profession, that fact in itself distinguishes that decision as vulnerable. He must remember, second, that the argument from fairness that demands consistency is not the only argument from fairness to which government in general, or judges in particular, must respond. If he believes, quite apart from any argument of consistency, that a particular statute or decision was wrong because unfair, within the community's own concept of fairness, then that belief is sufficient to distinguish the decision, and make it vulnerable. Of course, he must apply the guidelines with a sense of the vertical structure of his overall justification, so that decisions at a lower level are more vulnerable than decisions at a higher.

Hercules will therefore apply at least two maxims in the second part of his theory of mistakes. If he can show, by arguments of history or by appeal to some sense of the legal community, that a particular principle, though it once had sufficient appeal to persuade a legislature or court to a legal decision, has now so little force that it is unlikely to generate any further such decisions, then the argument from fairness that supports that principle is undercut. If he can show by arguments of political morality that such a principle, apart from its popularity, is unjust, then the argument from fairness that supports that principle is overridden. Her-

cules will be delighted to find that these discriminations are familiar in the practice of other judges. The jurisprudential importance of his career does not lie in the novelty, but just in the familiarity, of the theory of hard cases that he has now created.

4. Kenneth Kress: Restating Dworkin's Argument[21]

Dworkin's rights thesis is able to avoid retroactive application of law because it asserts the controversial right answer thesis: there are always legally authoritative standards (for example, principles) that recommend single right answers in hard cases.

The rights thesis maintains that even in a hard case, where rules do not provide definitive guidance, there is a single preexisting right answer. The judge's problem is to determine which principles are authoritative. Dworkin's answer is that a principle is part of the law and hence authoritative if it is part of the theory that provides the best explanation and justification of the settled law.

According to Dworkin, when a judge confronts a legal question he should first determine the settled law in the jurisdiction. Settled law consists of the complete institutional history of the jurisdiction including constitution(s), enactment and repeal of statutes, judicial pronouncements, and perhaps administrative rulings. To simplify somewhat, settled law is the explicit, clear, black letter law. Some aspects of the settled law may be disregarded as mistakes. Dworkin's theory for determining which prior decisions and other parts of institutional history may be considered mistakes is quite complicated. Those parts of institutional history that are no longer persuasive to courts, legislatures, and the legal profession are particularly vulnerable to being labeled mistakes. So too are those parts that are unjust. Adjusting the settled law by deleting mis-

---

[21] Kenneth Kress, *Legal Reasoning and Coherence Theories: Dworkin's Rights Thesis, Retroactivity, and the Linear Order of Decisions*, 72 CALIFORNIA LAW REVIEW 369, 374, 377-79 (1984). Copyright 1984 by California Law Review, Inc. Reprinted by permission.

takes is a subtle process that Dworkin has described as seeking a "reflective equilibrium" between the institutional facts and a coherent theoretical structure that could justify those facts.[22] In the attempt to determine the best theory of the institutional facts, neither the judge's initial theory nor the judge's initial view of the settled law is immune from revision. Either may require revision in the attempt to obtain an equilibrium that best accommodates both. More likely, both will require revision. Put briefly, the judge should construct or determine that theory *STL* (the soundest theory of law) which best explains and justifies the settled law.

STL may be conceived as a set of basic principles *P* from which each of the propositions of settled law follows by deductive logic. However, there are some propositions of law L which will remain open in the sense that neither the proposition nor its negation will follow deductively from the basic principles *P*. The set of all such propositions *L* comprises the set *N* of nonconsequences. The set *N* of nonconsequences can be conceived as a set of ordered pairs of propositions and their contradictories. Since on Dworkin's theory there is always a single right answer, exactly one member of each pair of contradictories will be true. The class consisting of all the true members of these ordered pairs is the set of true but unsettled law, *UC*. The truth of a member of *UC* cannot consist in its following from *P*, the principles, by definition. Rather, Dworkin tells us, the members of *UC* are true by virtue of coherence. For example, if not-*L*, a member of the set *N* of nonconsequences is more coherent with *STL* than *L* is, not-*L* is true (and thus a member of *UC*), whereas *L* is false (and not a member of *UC*), and vice versa.

Thus, at any time, propositions of law that are not consequences of the basic principles *P* are true (or false) by virtue of their greater (or lesser) coherence with the soundest theory of law at the time. On the other hand, from the perspective of the theory, propositions of settled law may be said to be true

by virtue of their following logically from the basic principles of *P*.

C. Stare Decisis

1. Richard A. Wasserstrom: The Justification of Precedent[23]

The reason that undoubtedly is most often cited as constituting a justification for the doctrine of precedent is that its consistent application assures to the legal system a degree of certainty which would otherwise be impossible to attain.

It has been suggested, for example, that although an adherence to precedent may produce undesirable effects, the doctrine of *stare decisis* is clearly essential to a state of affairs in which the law will be certain. Law exists, it has been asserted, to ensure the order which the forces in control of a society desire to impose. Its object is uniformity of action, so that one member of society may know how, in certain circumstances, another is likely to behave, this being the essence of security. Similarly, it is insisted that adherence to precedent is the surest way to guarantee that the future will be certain. Because of the generality of law, men can be enabled to predict the legal consequences of situations that have not yet been litigated, and hence can plan their conduct for a future which is thereby rendered less uncertain.

Edgar Bodenheimer makes this point in even stronger terms: "By applying a uniform standard of adjudication to an indefinite number of equal or closely similar situations, we introduce an element of stability and coherence into the social order which guarantees internal peace and lays the groundwork for a fair and impartial administration of justice."[24]

And again, in one of the few really thorough treatments of the doctrine of precedent, the following summarization is presented: "The final, and from the English standpoint, the most important reason for following

---

[22] RONALD DWORKIN, TAKING RIGHTS SERIOUSLY 155, 159-68 (rev. ed. 1978). The term "reflective equilibrium" derives from JOHN RAWLS, A THEORY OF JUSTICE (1971).

[23] RICHARD A. WASSERSTROM, THE JUDICIAL DECISION, 60-61, 63-64 (1961). Reprinted by permission.

[24] Edgar Bodenheimer, *Law as Order and Justice*, 6 J. PUBLIC LAW 1994, 199 (1957).

precedent is that every judge should speculate upon improvements in it."[25]

To require certainty of a legal system or of any other institution is to impose an essentially formal structure upon its inevitable composition. To be content with certainty as the major attribute is to demand only that results be predictable prior to their occurrence.[26] It is to leave open the question of the nature of these results which are to be repeated in an orderly, ascertainable pattern. Like so many other purely formal requirements, it can all too easily be confused with those that are substantive.

The point is hardly original. But its familiarity should not be permitted to breed carelessness or contempt. Certainty of result may be a desirable attribute of any legal system; its presence does not assure the attribute of desirability to any legal system. For this reason, therefore, this discussion of certainty may be read as an implicit admonition as well as an explicit commendation. The ideal legal system is not proved to be ideal simply by virtue of the antecedent predictability of its decisions.

Nevertheless, the truth of the empirical proposition that stare decisis, if employed as the sole rule of decision, would produce certainty has been disputed. Wigmore's analysis is typical of those which reject the causative power of the rule.

Is the judge to be bound by his precedent? This part of the question ought not to trouble us overmuch. Stare decisis, as an absolute dogma, has seemed to me an unreal fetish. The French Civil Code expressly repudiates it; and, though French and other Continental judges do follow precedents to some extent, they do so presumably only to the extent that justice requires it for safety's sake. Stare decisis is said to be indispensable for securing certainty in the application of the law. But the sufficient answer is that it has not in fact secured it. Our judicial law is as uncertain as any law could well be. We possess all the detriment of uncertainty, which stare decisis concededly involves—the

government of the living by the dead, as Herbert Spencer has called it.[27]

There is one very easy answer to Wigmore's thesis. It is simply that stare decisis has probably never been given a test, that a legal system has never existed in which stare decisis was the only rule of decision and in which this rule was conscientiously adhered to in the decision of every case. This is true even in England. For, as Lord Campbell made plain in Beamish v. Beamish, a precedent of the House of Lords can be "overruled" by Parliament.

2. Felix S. Cohen: The Concept of Precedent[28]

Logic can never establish that one case is a precedent for another case. That is because no two cases can possibly be alike in all respects. (If they were alike in all respects, then, according to the principle of the identity of indiscernibles, they would be one case, not two cases.) Any two cases, however selected, are alike in some respects. (Otherwise, they would not both be "cases.") Whether the respects in which two cases are alike are important is a question not of logic but of values. Within one framework of values, it makes no difference whether the defendant in a damage suit is a helpless widow, a powerful steel corporation, a person of Japanese ancestry during a war with Japan, a pugnacious labor leader, or a government official. Under such a standard of "impartiality," the differences between the parties become irrelevancies. But to a judge who thinks that differences between defendants ought to be given weight, and to a lawyer or observer who thinks that such differences are given weight, the differences between the parties in the earlier case and the pending case may seriously change or destroy the precedent-value of the earlier case.

Consider, again, the time differential that always intervenes between the "precedent"

[25] Arthur L. Goodhart, Precedent in English and Continental Law, 50 Law Q. Rev. 40, 58 (1934).

[26] Editor's Note: Isn't the word "only" rather extravagant here?

[27] WIGMORE, PROBLEMS OF LAW, p. 79, quoted in Arthur L. Goodhart, Case Law in England and America, 15 CORNELL L.Q. 173, 185 (1930).

[28] Felix S. Cohen, Field Theory and Judicial Logic, 59 YALE L.J. 238, 245-48 (1950).

case and the case in which it is cited. Clearly the fact that a case has been decided and reported has some social significance. Perhaps others have relied on the decision. Perhaps other courts have built on it. How they have relied on it and built on it is not a question of logic. Often the later interpretation and application of a decision are such as may shock its original author. But, for better or worse, a ten-year old decision has a weight and shape that did not exist at its birth. Its weight and shape embody all sorts of subsequent social judgments. And the world that surrounds the ten-year old offspring is an older, if not a wiser, world than that into which it was born. Contract forms, political forces, and social institutions have changed perceptibly or imperceptibly. Here, again, logic will not suffice to determine whether a case is "on all fours" with any case decided ten years or a hundred years ago. Whether it is "on all fours" depends upon what we think of the years between and of their effect on the cases and affairs of men.

If significant differences between cases may flow even from differences in dates of decision and differences in the parties, the fact remains that further differences can always be found, as a practical matter, between any two cases. There is no precedent that cannot be distinguished away if you want to distinguish it. The use of a precedent always implies a value judgment, a judgment that similarities between the precedent and the following decision are important and the dissimilarities are relatively unimportant. The application of precedent thus always involves a process of selection or discrimination. But one man's pattern of selectivity is not the same as another man's. A judge who thinks that labor organization ought to be encouraged will rebel when decisions in antitrust cases involving capital are invoked against labor. To such a judge, the later decision may appear to force the processes of justice into a purely mechanical mold based upon false analogy. But a judge who thinks labor organization has gone far enough or too far may view the reluctance of his brothers on the bench to decide labor cases in accordance with the usual antitrust precedents as proof of their willingness to subordinate law and logic to mere expediency or demagoguery.

According to the common view, it is logical to follow precedents but illogical to make precedents. But even a slight acquaintance with the development of modern logic makes it clear that logic is no respecter of age. There is logic in change as well as in constancy, in relativities as well as in absolutes. If we give up the old exclusive reliance upon the form of the syllogism, we do not have to surrender to impressionism.

Disagreeing judges and opposing counsel will regularly disagree as to whether a precedent is squarely in point, not because either side is mistaken in its logical calculations but because the two sides bring to bear upon the issue different sets of value judgments. Ordinarily these value judgments are not made explicit. To make them explicit would, as Holmes has said, deprive judges of "the illusion of certainty which makes legal reasoning seem like mathematics."[29] Often the judges who make these implicit value judgments are not aware of them and would bitterly and honestly resent the imputation that they are allowing their own value judgments to enter into the decision of cases. In this respect, again, judges are like other human beings. We are none of us aware of our own prejudices.

The selectivity operation that we execute when we hold up one decision as precedent for another decision will, in general, expand the force and scope of those decisions that we agree with; at the same time it will restrict the force and scope of decisions that we think wrong and ill-advised. In dealing with decisions that we approve of we will generally, consciously or unconsciously, stress the broad principles of justice enunciated in the case. The decisions we disapprove of we may seek to restrict to "the facts of the case as it was actually decided," which is a politely circuitous way of saying that we would not give the decision any weight at all in any later case. But we do not have to go so far in order to free ourselves from the incubus of an apparent precedent. We are bound to find some points of difference, which will grow in importance as we reflect on the harm that would be done by ignoring these points of difference and applying an old decision to the situation now before the

---

[29] OLIVER W. HOLMES, COLLECTED LEGAL PAPERS 126 (1921).

court. And so we generally end up our briefs and arguments as lawyers, or our opinions as judges, with a stronger conviction of the justice of our result than we had when we started our search.

and then applied to a next similar situation. The steps are these: similarity is seen between cases; next the rule of law inherent in the first case is announced; then the rule of law is made applicable to the second case.

3. Edward H. Levi: Rule-based Similarity[30]

The basic pattern of legal reasoning is reasoning from case to case. It is a three-step process described by the doctrine of precedent in which a proposition descriptive of the first case is made into a rule of law

4. Larry Alexander: The Precedent Court as Legislator[31]

The precedent court has authority not only to decide the case before it but also to promulgate a general rule binding on courts of subordinate and equal rank. The rule will operate like a statute.

---

[30] EDWARD H. LEVI, AN INTRODUCTION TO LEGAL REASONING 1-2 (1949).

[31] Larry Alexander, *Constrained by Precedent*, 63 S. CAL. L. REV. 1, 17-18 (1989).

QUESTIONS AND COMMENTS FOR YOUR CONSIDERATION

1. Isn't a basic problem with Professor Alexander's approach that the precedent court might announce a breathtakingly broad rule that would then become binding on subsequent cases? Consider a far-fetched, but illustrative, example of a rule announced in the precedent court:

> Although the facts in this case were unclear and the witnesses uncertain, there is probably some evidence to suggest that the defendant may have been negligent in driving the car, and hence there might be some reason to affirm the jury's decision to award damages to the plaintiff. However, we see that a more compelling rule governs the disposition of this case and leads us to affirm the jury's decision. It is this: that in any and all tort cases, where the plaintiff is poor, and the defendant is rich in comparison to the plaintiff, a jury's decision in favor of the plaintiff will not be reversed on appeal. Similarly, in any and all tort cases, where the plaintiff is comparatively richer than the defendant, a decision in favor of the defendant will not be reversed on appeal.

Under Professor Alexander's view of *stare decisis*, wouldn't a subsequent court be bound by such a rule? So long as the subsequent case is a tort case and there is a financial disparity between the parties, wouldn't Professor Alexander's approach result in giving the judge in the precedent case enormous legislative power to reshape, in one bold stroke, a vast amount of tort law?

2. How much damage would be caused by Professor Levi's approach, where the judge in the subsequent case (Case *B*) decides what the rule was in the precedent case (Case *A*)? The judge in the subsequent case might say (using the rule given in the previous Question):

> This is an automobile accident case where the facts are unclear and the witnesses uncertain. There was some evidence that the defendant was negligent in driving the car. Case *A* is a precedent for this case. The rule in Case *A* is that even the slightest amount of evidence of negligence is enough to support a jury verdict for the plaintiff. To be sure, the court in Case *A* had a rather broader view of the rule it was applying, but we are only bound by our own reading of the rule in Case *A* that we find was minimally necessary to support its decision.

Yet wouldn't this kind of dodge create a problem of its own?

3. What if the "rule" that the Case *B* court attributes to the decision in Case *A* is extremely narrow? For example, suppose the court in Case *B* says that the "rule" of Case *A* is as follows: "Case *A* holds that when facts *T, U, V, W, X, Y,* and *Z* are present, then the plaintiff wins." Fact *V,* could be, for example, that the defendant's automobile was a Volvo, and fact *W* could be that the highway was wet and slippery. Under *this* narrow reading of the minimally necessary rule in Case *A,* it is highly unlikely that there will *ever* arise a "Case *B*" that has the same facts. (Indeed, one could *guarantee* that there will never be another case like Case *A* if fact *T* is the time and date of the accident: 8:30 p.m. on Wednesday, February 15, 1995.) If the statement of the "rule" of Case *A* is entirely in the discretion of the judge in Case *B,* as Professor Levi says it is, then is it not open to any judge in Case *B* to state the rule just narrowly enough so that it does not apply to Case *B*?

4. Is there a problem with the very notion of a "rule" being generated by the precedent case?

5. Anthony D'Amato: Fact-based Similarity[32]

Do our minds really need to be supplied with "rules" before we can tell whether two cases are similar to each other?

Consider the way we first learned to speak. An infant hears the word "mom" whenever his mother is present, and soon begins to associate that sound with her. The infant may think "mom" when his father or sister or grandmother appear, but soon learns that the sound "mom" does not seem to refer to them—other sounds are associated with their presence. Now, does the infant need to have imagined a "rule" in order to distinguish among these people? What could the rule possibly say? The infant at this stage does not know what "people" are; he may not even know that these images (of what we would call "faces") are detached from his own body, since he does not know the extent of his own body or whether it is separate from its surroundings. Nor does the infant know what happens to his father or mother when they leave the room. (Piaget's studies of *three*-year old children showed that many of them believe that when an object is covered up it disappears; only a minority understand that it is temporarily hidden and that they can retrieve it.)

Consider what an infant sees when his mother turns her head. Suddenly her smiling face is replaced by a wall of hair! This could be shocking and scary to the infant, except that the infant has not yet become sufficiently acquainted with the world that it could translate visual images to emotions like shock and fright. So, instead, the infant learns to associate the hair with the face, and both with the sound "mom."

At such an elementary level of understanding, we could not possibly invent a set of "rules" that would explain how the child finds his mother's face and hair sufficiently similar to the sound "mom" that he can associate both with that sound or how the child distinguishes the faces and backs of heads of other persons in its environment from "mom." The level of complexity that would be required in any formulation of such a set of rules is well beyond the infant's mental capability. More importantly, the infant at this stage does not think in terms of words at all. The word "mom" is the only word the infant knows, and the infant knows it only in a rudimentary sense of learning to associate it with some visual images and not others.

Considerations such as these undoubtedly led Rudolf Carnap, in his masterwork *The Logical Structure of the World,*[33] to for-

[32] Based on Anthony D'Amato, *Pragmatic Indeterminacy,* 85 Nw. U. L. Rev. 148 (1990).

[33] R. Carnap, The Logical Structure of the World: Pseudoproblems in Philosophy (trans. 1928 R.A. George, 1967). A brilliant, extended commentary on Carnap's work is Nelson Goodman, The

mulate as the basic unit of his system the *erleb*, which he defined as a momentary cross section of the total stream of experience. He argued that *erlebs* are related to each other by "part identity" and "part similarity."[34] The relationships of *erlebs* are preverbal.[35] A word is simply a label we learn to attach to *erleb* relationships that we notice.

It is clear that infants learn to recognize that two things are similar—and also learn that something can be different from something else—well before they learn the concept of a rule, and even well before they learn the concept of a word. Our mental ability to sense similarities is prior to our ability to learn a language. Our language ability itself could not have arisen if we lacked a prior mental ability to determine similarities and differences. The ability to notice similarities

is "wired in" to our brains, a result of evolution. The human race would not have survived were we unable to distinguish between similar and dissimilar things—for example, our ancestors would not have been able to recognize natural enemies. We could have survived without language; other primates have survived without language. But we have in common with all the higher animals (and perhaps the entire animal kingdom) a mental ability to tell when something is similar to something else.[36]

I am not dependent upon *words* to go through the mental process of similarity-comparison. Instead, a word is a sort of conclusion I reach when I have already decided that two things are more similar to each other than they are to a third thing. For example, if I call this object "red," I am saying that it is sufficiently similar to "red" objects colors I have seen in the past that the word "red" is appropriate.[37]

When we say that a case is a precedent for another case, we are not necessarily saying that the rule we extract from the first case

---

STRUCTURE OF APPEARANCE 110-189 (3d ed. 1977). For Carnap's brief reply to Goodman, *see* P.A. Schilpp (ed.), THE PHILOSOPHY OF RUDOLF CARNAP 944-47 (1963).

[34] Sections 67 to 93 of Carnap's book contain an informal account of his system, whereas Sections 108 to 120 present a formal statement of it. The *erleb* (abbreviation for *elementarerlebnisse*) is presented in § 67 and formalized in § 109. If life were a succession of unrelated *erlebs*, we would not know that we were alive. The fact is that each *erleb* can be related to preceding *erlebs* by a "Part Identity" (§ 76) or "Part Similarity" (§ 77) relationship. Thus, to continue the example given in the text, when the mother turns her head to the side, the infant sees a face being replaced by an object that is in part *similar* to the face and in part *identical* to it. Thus the initial *erleb* (frontal view of a face) is replaced by succession of *erlebs* that are related to the initial one by "part similarity" and "part identity."

[35] Suppose there are only two cases, A and B, in a jurisdiction. We could with equal plausibility claim that they are similar or dissimilar. Similarity thus turns out to require more than two instances. Once we are given a new case, C, it can be said to be "more" similar to either of A or B. And that, I would say, is all that we can ever know for sure about cases or anything else. The words we use are our imperfect attempts to pin down similarities, but they can never fully accomplish this job because nature does not oblige. Hence I would regard all language as a heuristic device: it helps our minds to advert to similarities and differences. Similarly, a common-law rule is (and is only) a heuristic device. It organizes a line of cases so that we can examine them for similarities. But (importantly) the "rule" is inevitably an imperfect means of doing this organizational work, as every litigator knows.

[36] We would not have survived as a species if we had not evolved the ability to notice similarities and dissimilarities in nature. Nor would most animals have successfully evolved if they were lacking in this ability (the ability, for instance, to distinguish between predator and prey, between a member of its own species and a member of another species). Since animals lack a verbal language, it is clear that "rules" in our sense of that term are inapplicable to animals. But the ability to notice similarities and differences is intrinsic to the animal mind, as it is intrinsic to our own mind. For an important study of the determining factor of evolution in the way our minds work, *see* GERALD M. EDELMAN, BRIGHT AIR, BRILLIANT FIRE (1992). For a skeptical view of Edelman's thesis, *see* Noam Chomsky, *Language and Nature*, 104 Mind 1, 11 (1995).

[37] Note that this is true even if I have a degree of color blindness that confuses red and green. If my brain sees red when I look at grass, and if my brain sees green when I look at the sunrise, nevertheless the labels (words) I attach to these objects will be the same as the words in popular use, because that is how I have learned how to use those words. So, I say it's a "red sunset" and "green grass" even if I am seeing something radically different from what other people see when they look at these objects. As Wittgenstein showed, there is no "private language" available to me in this matter. Regardless of what my mind sees, the words I use are determined by social convention.

is the governing rule in the second case. Rather, we make a quick mental comparison (a computer would have to take a lot of time to make a similar comparison) of the factual situations presented in the two cases. If they seem similar—even though one case may involve objects that are entirely different from the other case (such as automobiles in one case and airplanes in the other)—then we have an innate sense of justice that tells us that a judge in the second case should decide it in accordance with the decision in the first case.

If I can predict that a certain set of real-world events will, if litigated, have an eighty percent chance of obtaining a favorable judicial decision for my client, then I must have some elementary notion of *similarity* in my ability to make this prediction. I must have mentally *compared* my client's set of real-world events to other *similar* sets, and made the judgment that the result in my client's case will track the results previously obtained by similarly event-situated persons.

The importance of similarities for law study has, of course, been noted long ago.

Reasoning by analogy is said to be the basic way that we "think like a lawyer."[38] Lawyers are able to make predictions for their clients because of their ability to notice similarities across real-world situations. This may seem quite obvious and elementary, but it is a long way from the formalist [deductive logic] program that what lawyers do is to learn rules of law and then apply them to the facts of a case.

6. Herman Oliphant: A Return to Stare Decisis[39]

We are well on our way toward a shift from following decisions to following so called principles, from *stare decisis* to what I shall call "the vocal behavior of judges"; this shift has far-reaching and unfortunate consequence for both the art of judicial government and the science of law.

There seems to have been little critical study of just what it is in prior decisions which is to be followed.

In the first place, a court, in deciding a case, may throw out a statement as to how it would decide some other case. Now if that statement is a statement of another case which is as narrow and specific as the actual case before the court, it is easily recognized as dictum and given its proper weight as such. In the second place the court may throw out a broader statement, covering a whole group of cases. But so long as that statement does not cover the case before the court, it is readily recognized as being not a holding, much less the holding of the case. It is dictum, so labeled and appraised. But in the third place, a court may make a statement broad enough to dispose of the case in hand as well as to cover also a few or many other states of fact. Statements of this third sort may cover a number of fact situations ranging from one other to legion. Such a statement is sometimes called the *holding* of the case.[40] Thereby the whole ambiguity of that word is introduced and the whole difficulty presented.

If more careful usage limits the word *holding* to the *action* taken by the court in the specific case before, it, *i.e.*, to the naked judgement or order entered, the difficulty is not met; it is merely shifted. *Stare decisis* thus understood becomes useless, for no holding in that limited sense can ever be followed. No identical case can arise. All other cases will differ in some circumstance—in time, if in no other, and most of them will have differences which are not trivial. *Holding* in the sense meant in *stare decisis* must, therefore, refer to a proposition of law covering a group of fact situations of a group as a minimum, the fact situation of the instant case and at least one other.

To bring together into one class even this minimum of two fact situations however

---

[38] *See* J.M. Balkin, *Nested Oppositions*, 99 YALE L.J. 1669, 1671 (1990) ("the logic of law is to a large degree the logic of similarity and difference"); RICHARD POSNER, THE PROBLEMS OF JURISPRUDENCE 86-93 (1990) (criticizing typical examples of enthymematic reasoning from "analogy"). A superb illustration of common-law reasoning by analogy is given by Lon Fuller in this Chapter, Section E, *infra*.

[39] Herman Oliphant, *A Return to Stare Decisis*, 14 ABAJ 72-73, 75-76, 107, 159-62 (1927).

---

[40] *Editor's Note:* Professor Oliphant used the word "decision"; I have substituted the more modern and precise term "holding."

similar they may be, always has required and always will require an abstraction. If Paul and Peter are to be thought of together at all, they must both be apostles or be thought of as having some other attribute in common. Classification is abstraction. An element or elements common to the two fact situations put into one class must be drawn out from each to become the content of the category and the subject of the proposition of law which is thus applied to the two cases.

But such a grouping may include multitudes of fact situations so long as a single attribute common to them all can be found. Between these two extremes lies a gradation of groups of fact situations each with its corresponding proposition of law, ranging from a grouping subtending but two situations to those covering hosts of them. This series of groupings of fact situations gives us a parallel series of corresponding propositions of law, each more and more generalized as we recede farther and farther from the instant state of facts and include more and more fact situations in the successive groupings. It is a mounting and widening structure, each proposition including all that has gone before and becoming more general by embracing new states of fact. For example, A's father induces her not to marry B as she promised to do. On a holding that the father is not liable to B for so doing, a gradation of widening propositions can be built, a very few of which are:

1. Fathers are privileged to induce daughters to break promises to marry.

2. Parents are so privileged.

3. Parents are so privileged as to both daughters and sons.

4. All persons are so privileged as to promises to marry.

5. Parents are so privileged as to all promises made by their children.

6. All persons are so privileged as to all promises made by anyone.

There can be erected upon the action taken by a court in any case such a gradation of generalizations and this is commonly done in the opinion. Sometimes it is built up to dizzy heights by the court itself and at times, by law teachers and writers, it is reared to those lofty summits of the absolute and the infinite.

Where on that gradation of propositions are we to take our stand and say "This proposition is the holding of this case within the meaning of the doctrine of *stare decisis*"? Can a proposition of law of this third type ever become so broad that, as to any of the cases it would cover, it is mere *dictum*?

A student is told to seek the "doctrine" or "principle" of a case, but which of its welter of stairs shall he ascend and how high up shall he go? Is there some one step on some one stair which is *the* holding of the case within the meaning of the mandate *stare decisis*? That is the double difficulty. Each precedent considered by a judge and each case studied by a student rests at the center of a vast and empty stadium. The angle and distance from which that case is to be viewed involves the choice of a seat. Which shall be chosen? Neither judge nor student can escape the fact that he can and must choose. To realize how wide the possibilities and significant the consequences of that choice are is elementary to an understanding of *stare decisis*. To ask whether there exists a coercion of some logic to make that choice either inevitable or beneficent, searches the significance of *stare decisis* in judicial government and the soundness of scholarship in law. This question is real and insistent. It is one which should be asked explicitly and faced squarely.

The political virtues of *stare decisis* are difficult to exaggerate. It has two active qualities, one affording us the counsel of experience; the other, the latitude of trial and error. The first element of its strength and security is its unalterable refusal to indulge in broad speculation, and its untiring patience to keep attention pinned to the immediate problem in order that a wise solution for it may be found. It stoutly refuses to answer future questions, prudently awaiting the time when they enter the field of immediate vision and become issues of reality in order that to their solution may be brought the illumination which only immediacy affords and the judiciousness which reality alone can induce. It is indifferent to broad generalizations or is made apprehensive by them. It accepts few generalizations, narrow or broad, until they have been transmuted into the wisdom of experience by experimentation. It uses generalizations to suggest and to orient that experimentation but not to replace it. The second element in the strength and security of *stare decisis* is but another aspect of the constant immediacy of its ends. It leads us forward over untried ground, a step at a time, no step being taken until it is judged wise, and the stages of its advance are so short that the direction of march can be quickly shifted as experience dictates.

This tremendous political significance of *stare decisis* in the art of judicial government should not be overlooked and it should be seen as but one aspect of the political empiricism of English speaking peoples. The grace to drudge away on today's problem and the refusal to foreclose tomorrow's issues run all through our political endeavors. This sagacious opportunism in government has reared many of our most valuable institutions. In English statesmanship and diplomacy it made the British Empire and still holds together that structure which seems fragile only to those who do not know how it was wrought. It built the English Constitution and has shaped the evolving parts of our own. It abides in the very genius of our people and is our most important contribution to the art of modern government.

Of all those political fabrics which Anglo-Saxon opportunism has woven, that, threaded together by *stare decisis* into our common law, shows richest with the work of patience and fine skill. Its methods can be improved, but we shall find no craftsmanship more worthy. A better informed public might well inquire, "Who are these innovators among us so active even further to undermine that time-tried and priceless institution?"

We have been drifting from observation of judicial action to an excess of concern about judicial utterances. More and more we have been taking abstractions of the past—many going back to medieval scholasticism—and tracing them down, not through the holdings of the cases, but through the opinions to see how they have fared in those essays of rationalization. There has been little but lip service to the discipline of seeking the exact holdings of cases, as opposed to their generalized pronouncements, except when the cases happen to lie near the rim of some favorite theory whose precise border we want to mark out. There has been little genuine re-examination of the holdings of those cases which lie at the center of that theory in order to test the utility of the whole generalization.

Not the judges' opinions, but which way they decide cases will be the dominant subject matter of any truly scientific study of law. This is the field for scholarly work worthy of best talents because the work to be done is not the study of vague and shifting rationalizations but the study of such tough things as the accumulated wisdom of men taught by immediate experience in contemporary life—the battered experiences of judges among brutal facts. The response of their intuition of experience to the stimulus of human situations is the subject-matter having that constancy and objectivity necessary for truly scientific study. When we pin our attention to this, we may more freely criticize what courts have said but we shall more cautiously criticize what they have done realizing, as we shall, that they were exposed to the impact of more of the facts than we.

This surer thing for scholarly purpose is also the inner secret of what is soundest in the enfeebled *stare decisis* in judicial government today. With eyes cleared of the old and broad abstractions which curtain our vision, we come to recognize more and more the eminent good sense in what courts are wont to do about disputes before them. Judges are men and men respond to human situations. When the facts stimulating them to the action taken are studied from a particular and current point of view, which our present classification prevents, we acquire a new faith in *stare decisis*. From this viewpoint we see that courts are dominantly coerced, not by the essays of their predecessors but by a surer thing—by an intuition of fitness of solution to problem—and a renewed confidence in judicial government is engendered. To state the matter more concretely, the decision of a particular case by a thoughtful scholar is to be preferred to that by a poorly trained judge, but the decision of such a judge in a particular case is infinitely to be preferred to a decision of it preordained by some broad "principle" laid down by the scholar when this and a host of other concrete cases had never even occurred to him.

Stare decisis has been sapped of much of the spirit of the common law, and legal scholarship approaches an architecture of castles in the thin air of pure theory because of the breadth and antiquation of present groupings of human situations for legal treatment. Such a reclassification will help to send us about our proper business of raising the walls within which men must work and live by just laying one brick upon another, letting a keener awareness of the needs of the life and labor which they are to house guide our hands.

No reclassification can get us as near to a case as the judge who decides it, yet, about it lies a considerable field across which its currents can be felt. Each human situation has many aspects, yet somewhere in its field are points of opposite polarity charged with human concern. It is between these poles that the currents of our time flow and these currents are the prime stimuli of nonvocal judicial behavior. Our classification should bring us close to them for truly scientific observation.

We cannot come close to them without leaving many of our present remote points of view and without abandoning many present groupings of material which are sterile except for logical purposes and often confusing even for those. In our present classification, problems of getting laws observed, *i.e.*, problems of law administration, are intermingled with problems as to what conduct is desired. The illegality of a contract of sale, though raising a question as to the use of the disability to sue on the contract as an indirect deterrent of the illegal conduct in question, is treated as one of substantive law and discussed in terms of some such barren and ambiguous abstraction as title. These two widely different kinds of questions are now confused because we have only two groupings, substantive law and adjective (procedural) law, the latter being too narrow to embrace broad areas of law administration. Human relations as diverse as political relations, familial relations, and business relations are hopelessly mixed and confused in such broad and outworn categories as property, trusts, torts, and contracts. Problems as to leaseholds of dwellings and of railroads are grouped together so that practical differences are obscured. A contract to marry is grouped with a speculative contract to purchase stocks and their differences considered as relatively minor. Again, in those areas where only political relations are treated, no consistent grouping and subgrouping of greater current significance are attempted. Constitutional law embraces categories with

wide practical divergencies because the exigencies and accidents of post revolutionary government happened to get them mentioned in a single document. Where we segregate a fraction of familial relations and call it domestic relations, the subgrouping is in terms of such nonfunctional concepts as contract, property, and tort. When chance brings some business problem together for treatment, as happens in sales, divergent questions as to marketing, finance, and risk are confused under such labels as "passage of title."

We now can see that the choice between the legal principles competing to control the new human situations involved in the cases we pass upon is not dictated by logic. Neither deduction nor induction can do more than suggest the competing analogies and to indicate promising directions for trial and error testing. Neither the astuteness of legal scholarship nor the authority of judicial position can transcend these limitations inherent in logic. The final choice of analogy can be made only in reliance upon practical considerations or upon pure chance. Rejecting sheer guess as a basis of sound judicial action and of worthwhile scholarship, then discovering and marshaling decisive practical considerations inevitably constitute the essence of both an improved judicial process and of a more useful scholarly effort. A return to the sounder empiricism of *stare decisis* of former times should reckon with recent advances in scientific thought. That ancient empiricism was intuitive. It worked well because judges sat close to problems and viewed them as current problems. It would have worked better still had it been conscious and methodical. Remembering always that the final choice for both judge and scholar in deciding a case or criticizing a decision is always a practical one, whether consciously or unconsciously so, the problem, how a more conscious and methodical process can be substituted for an intuitive empiricism in making that choice, transcends in importance all other problems of legal education. Until its solution is attempted, a socialized jurisprudence will continue a mere aspiration and social engineering will be the profession of many but the occupation of none.

Our case material is a gold mine for scientific work. It has not been scientifically exploited. The science of mechanics was built up by experimentation, but geology, for example, has had to rely almost solely upon observation. In law we cannot institute suits to test judicial behavior, as the physicists make experiments to test the behavior of matter. But each case is a record of judicial behavior. And there is a wealth of such records equaling that to which geology, for instance, has had access and the individual records are no more fractional or otherwise imperfect. A sufficient number of recorded experiments, all of whose factors are not known but with the unknown factors varying, may be quite as illuminating as a limited number of controlled experiments. Why has not our study of cases in the past yielded the results now sought? The attempt has been made to show that this is largely due to the fact that we have focused our attention too largely on the *vocal behavior* of judges in deciding cases. A study with more stress on their *non-vocal behavior*, *i.e.*, what the judges actually do when stimulated by the facts of the case before them, is the approach indispensable to exploiting scientifically the wealth of material in the cases. Economists may well congratulate themselves that they have the statistical method to add objectivity to their results. The case method when used scientifically will be found to be a method fully as significant for law as statistics is for economics. It is outstanding as an objective method.

It is common for those despairing of the widespread application of scientific methods in legal study to assume that a method having the objectivity and precision of that of mathematical physics is prerequisite in order for us to have any scientific method in the study of law. Reflection reveals that objective methods having great utility in such areas as biology and geology differ widely from the methods of mathematical physics with respect to their precision and objectivity.

The word "objective" in the term "objective method" is itself pragmatic. A very gross measurement of an object may be sufficiently accurate for the purposes of a rough carpenter and hence for his purposes "true" while hopelessly inaccurate for the purposes of a physicist working upon the expansion coefficient of a metal. The personal equation and subjective elements bulk large in the first measurement, but for the purposes of a carpenter, they are unimportant. They are, of course, present in the measurements of a physicist. All that he can hope to do is reduce them to a minimum, and how far he needs to reduce them depends upon the particular purpose for which he is making a particular measurement. When this fact is fully appreciated by legal scholarship its hope for truly scientific methods may be found to be nearer to realization than it is now thought to be. Other social scientists are certainly making substantial progress in developing objective methods in many other fields.

QUESTIONS AND COMMENTS FOR YOUR CONSIDERATION

1. In the first part of his essay, Herman Oliphant shows how widely and variously a holding of a case can be interpreted. He lists six "gradations of generalizations" in the simple case of a father who induces his daughter to break a promise of marriage. Is his example persuasive, or do you find it to be too abstract to be useful?

2. How does Professor Oliphant reconcile, if at all, the second half of his essay with the first half? If the interpretation of a holding is potentially as broad as he says it is, why is he so concerned about preserving the integrity of *stare decisis*? What is left of the integrity of *stare decisis*? What is important about *stare decisis*?

3. What did Richard Wasserstrom, in the first essay in this section, find important about *stare decisis*? Do you agree with either Wasserstrom or Oliphant?

4. Many years after Professor Oliphant's path-breaking article, Julius Stone articulated many more than six gradations of generalizations that could be deduced as legitimate holdings from a single case. Professor Stone wisely chose

a real case, *Donoghue v. Stevenson*. Unfortunately, Professor Stone gave no credit to Professor Oliphant for first making the argument about the breadth of interpretations of the holding in a case. It is quite clear from an examination of the other citations in Professor Stone's book that the possibility that he never heard about Oliphant's work is highly unlikely. One might therefore conclude the Professor Stone plagiarized the idea from Professor Oliphant. The possibility of plagiarism, no matter where it might occur in academia, should be enough to discredit the work of the plagiarist. For present purposes, Professor Stone's contribution to the debate about holdings is sufficiently important in itself to be included in this Anthology even though it is seriously marred by the possibility of plagiarism. All Professor Stone would have had to do to ensure the untainted reception of his contribution in the legal literature was to give full and proper credit to Professor Oliphant's pioneering work. Had he done so, his contribution would have been forever associated with Oliphant's idea as a significant extension of it.

5. The case of *Donoghue v. Stevenson* was decided in 1932 in the House of Lords by a panel of five justices: Lord Buckmaster, Lord Atkin, Lord Tomlin, Lord Thankerton, and Lord Macmillan. The opinions were delivered *seriatim*. The drama must have been high as the opinions were read. Lord Buckmaster led off and, in a lengthy opinion decided in favor of Stevenson. Next was Lord Atkin who in an even lengthier opinion held for Donoghue. Lord Tomlin was brief; he seconded Lord Buckmaster's opinion. Lord Thankerton followed in a mid-sized opinion, holding for Donoghue, bringing the vote so far to 2-2. That left it up to Lord Macmillan whose opinion was almost as long as Lord Atkin's. He recapitulated the great diversity of views, but ended up in framing as narrowly as he could a decision in favor of Donoghue.

The case involved a pivotal question in Scottish and English law (which was admittedly the same law for these purposes)—whether to allow into that law the concept of products liability. The phrase "products liability" was not used; that terminology came into the law at a later time. The year was 1932, the time of the great world-wide depression. Many historians who blithely assume that court decisions follow the interests of the dominant business class in society would surely have predicted that the House of Lords would have held in favor of Stevenson, the manufacturer of the product; surely in the midst of the Great Depression business enterprises should not be financially discouraged by the imposition of new forms of liability. The plaintiff-appellant, Donoghue, was a pauper. What chance did she have against a manufacturer at such a time in history? If she won, a breakthrough precedent would have been created in English and Scottish law. As Lord Atkin pointedly observed in his opinion, "I do not think a more important problem has occupied your Lordships in your judicial capacity: important both because of its bearing on public health and because of the practical test which it applies to the system under which it arises."

Directly following are excerpts from the opinions of the justices, to be followed by Julius Stone's important analysis of the ways of interpreting the holding in the case:

7. Donoghue v. Stevenson

Donoghue v. Stevenson

House of Lords, 1932
[1932] Law Reports 562.

CLERK OF THE COURT. The appellant Donoghue, who was a shop assistant, sought to recover damages from the respondent Stevenson, who was a manufacturer of aerated waters, for injuries she suffered as a result of consuming part of the contents of a bottle of ginger-beer which had been manufactured by the respondent and which contained the decomposed remains of a snail. Donoghue averred that the bottle of ginger-beer was purchased for her by a friend in a cafe at Paisley, which was occupied by one Minchella; that the bottle was made of dark opaque glass and that Donoghue had no reason to suspect that it contained anything but pure ginger-beer; that on August 26, 1928, Minchella poured some of the ginger-beer out into a tumbler, and that Donoghue drank some of the contents of the tumbler; that her friend was proceeding to pour the remainder of the contents of the bottle into the tumbler when a snail, which was in a state of decomposition, floated out of the bottle; that as a result of the nauseating sight of the snail in such circumstances and in consequence of the impurities in the ginger-beer which Donoghue had already consumed, she suffered from shock and severe gastro-enteritis. She further averred that the ginger-beer was manufactured by Stevenson to be sold as a drink to the public; that it was bottled by Stevenson and labeled by him with a label bearing his name; and that the bottles were thereafter sealed with a metal cap by Stevenson.

Stevenson demurred.

The Lord Ordinary held that the averments disclosed a good cause of action.

The Second Division by a majority (the Lord Justice-Clerk, Lord Ormidale, and Lord Anderson; Lord Hunter dissenting) overruled the Lord Ordinary and dismissed the action.

LORD BUCKMASTER. The general principle of our prior cases is that "the breach of the defendant's contract with A to use care and skill in the manufacture of an article does not in itself give any cause of action to B when he is injured by reason of the article proving to be defective." Cases have fashioned an exception to this general rule when the article is dangerous in itself. In the present case no one can suggest that ginger-beer was an article dangerous in itself.

Decisions by courts in the United States can have no authority in Great Britain, for though the source of the law in the two countries may be the same, its current may well flow in different channels. In *Thomas v. Winchester*, 6 N.Y. 397, a chemist issued poison in answer to a request for a harmless drug, and he was held responsible to a third party injured by his negligence. It appears to me that the decision might well rest on the principle that he, in fact, sold a drug dangerous in itself, none the less so because he was asked to sell something else, and on this view the case does not advance the matter.

In *MacPherson v. Buick Motor Co.*, 217 N.Y. 382 (1916), where a manufacturer of a defective motor-car was held liable for damages at the instance of a third party, the learned judge appears to base his judgment on the view that a motor-car might reasonably be regarded as a dangerous article.

The present case does not involve contract. The appellant's conception is simply to misapply tort doctrine to a sale and purchase. The principle of tort lies completely outside the region where such considerations apply, and the duty, if it exists, must extend to every person who, in lawful circumstances, uses the article made. There can be no special duty attaching to the manufacture of food apart from that implied by contract or imposed by statute. If such a duty exists, it seems to me it must cover the construction of every article, and I cannot see any reason why it should not apply to the construction of a house. If one step, why not fifty? Yet if a house be, as it sometimes is, negligently built, and in consequence of that negligence the ceiling falls and injures the occupier or any one else, no action against the builder exists according to the English law, although I believe such a right did exist according to the laws of Babylon.

LORD ATKIN. My Lords, the sole question for determination in this case is legal: Do the averments made by the pursuer in her pleading, if true, disclose a cause of action?

The law of both England and Scotland appears to be that in order to support an action for negligence the complainant has to show that he has been injured by the breach of a duty owed to him in the circumstances by the defendant to take reasonable care to avoid such injury. In the present case we are solely concerned with the question whether, as a matter of law in the circumstances alleged, the defender owed any duty to the pursuer to take care.

In *Bates v. Batey & Co., Ltd.*, 3 King's Bench 351 (1913), the manufacturers of ginger-beer were sued by a plaintiff who had been injured by the bursting of a bottle. The manufacturers had bought the actual bottle from its maker, but were found by the jury to have been negligent in not taking proper means to discover whether the bottle was defective or not. The judge found that a bottle of ginger-beer was not dangerous in itself, but this defective bottle was in fact dangerous; but, as the defendants did not know that it was dangerous, they were not liable, though by the exercise of reasonable care they could have discovered the defect. This case differs from the present only by reason of the fact that it was not the manufacturers of the ginger-beer who caused the defect in the bottle; but on the assumption that the jury were right in finding a lack of reasonable care in not examining the bottle, I should have come to the conclusion that, as the manufacturers must have contemplated the bottle being handled immediately by the consumer, they owed a duty to him to take care that he should not be injured externally by explosion, just as I think they owed a duty to him to take care that he should not be injured internally by poison or other noxious thing.

As to things dangerous in themselves, I agree with Lord Justice Scrutton who said, "Personally, I do not understand the difference between a thing dangerous in itself and a thing dangerous by negligent manufacture. The latter, if anything, seems the more dangerous of the two; it is a wolf in sheep's clothing instead of an obvious wolf."

The illuminating judgment of Judge Cardozo in *MacPherson v. Buick Motor Co.* in the New York Court of Appeals, if it were authoritative in England, would undoubtedly lead to a decision in favor of the pursuer in the present case.

My Lords, if your Lordships accept the view that this pleading discloses a relevant cause of action you will be affirming the proposition that by Scots and English law alike a manufacturer of products, which he sells in such a form as to show that he intends them to reach the ultimate consumer in the form in which they left him with no reasonable possibility of intermediate examination, and with the knowledge that the absence of reasonable care in the preparation or putting up of the products will result in an injury to the consumer's life or property, owes a duty to the consumer to take that reasonable care.

It is a proposition which I venture to say no one in Scotland or England who was not a lawyer would for one moment doubt. It will be an advantage to make it clear that the law in this matter, as in most others, is in accordance with sound common sense. I think that this appeal should be allowed.

LORD TOMLIN. I think that if the appellant is to succeed it must be upon the proposition that every manufacturer or repairer of any article is under a duty to everyone who may thereafter legitimately use the article to exercise due care in the manufacture or repair. It is logically impossible to stop short of this point. Moreover, the fact that an article of food is sent out in a sealed container can have no relevancy on the question of duty; it is only a factor which may render it easier to bring negligence home to the manufacturer.

The alarming consequences of accepting the validity of this proposition were pointed out by the defendant's counsel, who said: "For example, every one of the sufferers by such an accident as that which recently happened on the Versailles Railway might have his action against the manufacturer of the defective axle."

LORD THANKERTON. It is clear, in my opinion, that neither the law of Scotland nor the law of England will hold that the manufacturer has any duty towards the consumer to exercise diligence. In such a case the remedy of the consumer, if any, will lie against the intervening party from whom he has purchased the article. I am aware that the American courts have taken a view more favorable to the consumer.

The appellant argues that there are special circumstances in the present case: the respondent, in placing his ginger-beer upon the market, has intentionally so excluded interference with, or examination of, the article by any intermediate handler of the goods between himself and the consumer that he has, of his own accord, brought himself into direct relationship with the consumer, with the result that the consumer is entitled to rely upon the exercise of diligence by the manufacturer to secure that the article shall not be harmful to the consumer.

The case of *Mullen v. Barr & Co., Ltd.*, 1929 S.C. 461 [a lower-court decision], related to facts similar in every respect except that the foreign matter was a decomposed mouse. In these cases the court (Lord Hunter dissenting) held that the manufacturer owed no duty to the consumer. The view of the majority was that the English authorities excluded the existence of such a duty.[41]

LORD MACMILLAN. The only difference in fact between the Mullen Case and the present case is that it was a mouse and not a snail that was found in the ginger-beer. The reason given by their Lordships in the Mullen Case for assoilizing the defendants was that negligence had not been proved. However, as Lord Esher said in *Emmens v. Pottle*, 16 Q.B.D. 354, 357-58 (1885), "any proposition the result of which would be to show that the common law of England is wholly unreasonable and unjust, cannot be part of the common law of England."

The appellant in the present instance asks that her case be approached as a case of delict [tort], not as a case of breach of contract. The fact that there is a contractual relationship between the parties which may give rise to an action for breach of contract, does not exclude the co-existence of a right of action founded on negligence as between the same parties, independently of the contract, though arising out of the relationship in fact brought about by the contract.

The law takes no cognizance of carelessness in the abstract. It concerns itself with carelessness only where there is a duty to take care and where failure in that duty has caused damage. In such circumstances carelessness assumes the legal quality of negligence. What, then, are the circumstances which give rise to this duty to take care? In the daily contacts of social and business life human beings are thrown into, or place themselves in, an infinite variety of relations with their fellows; and the law can refer only to the standards of the reasonable man in order to determine whether any particular relation gives rise to a duty to take care as between those who stand in that relation to each other. The grounds of action may be as various and manifold as human errancy; and the conception of legal responsibility may develop in adaptation to altering social conditions and standards. The criterion of judgment must adjust and adapt itself to the changing circumstances of life. The categories of negligence are never closed. The cardinal principle of liability is that the party complained of should owe to the party complaining a duty to take care, and that the party complaining should be able to prove that he has suffered damage in consequence of a breach of that duty. Where there is room for diversity of view, it is in determining what circumstances will establish such a relationship between the parties as to give rise, on the one side, to a duty to take care, and on the other side to a right to have care taken.

To descend from these generalities to the circumstances of the present case, I do not think that any reasonable man or any twelve reasonable men would hesitate to hold that, if the appellant establishes her allegations, the respondent has exhibited carelessness in the conduct of his business. For a manufacturer of aerated water to store his empty bottles in a place where snails can get access to them, and to fill his bottles without taking any adequate precautions by inspection or otherwise to ensure that they contain no deleterious foreign matter, may reasonably be characterized as carelessness without applying too exacting a standard.

To whom does he owe a duty to take care? That duty, in my opinion, he owes to those whom he intends to consume his products.

I can readily conceive that where a manufacturer has parted with his product and it has passed into other hands it may well be exposed to vicissitudes which may render it defective or noxious, for which the manufacturer could not in any view be held to be to blame. It may be a good general rule to regard responsibility as ceasing when control ceases. So, also, where between the manufacturer and the user there is interposed a party who has the means and opportunity of examining the manufacturer's product before he re-issues it to the actual user. But where, as in the present case, the article of consumption is so prepared as to be intended

---

[41] *Editor's Note*: The Mullen Case was overruled in consequence of the decision in *Donoghue v. Stevenson*.

to reach the consumer in the condition in which it leaves the manufacturer, and the manufacturer takes steps to ensure this by sealing or otherwise closing the container so that the contents cannot be tampered with, I regard his control as remaining effective until the article reaches the consumer and the container is opened by him.

The burden of proof must always be upon the injured party to establish that the defect which caused the injury was present in the article when it left the hands of the party whom he sues, that the defect was occasioned by the carelessness of that party, and that the circumstances are such as to cast upon the defender a duty to take care not to injure the pursuer. There is no presumption of negligence in such a case as the present, nor is there any justification for applying the maxim, *res ipsa loquitur*. Negligence must be both averred and proved. The appellant accepts this burden of proof, and in my opinion she is entitled to have an opportunity of discharging it if she can. I am accordingly of opinion that this appeal should be allowed, the judgment of the Second Division of the Court of Session reversed, and the judgment of the Lord Ordinary restored.

8. Julius Stone: The Indeterminacy of Holdings[42]

There are two principal theories of finding the holding in a case, the modern theory and the classical theory.[43] The modern theory asserts that the holding is controlled by the relation between the "material facts" of a case and the decision on those facts. Here the holding consists of the reasoning necessary to explain the decision on the material facts. The classical theory, on the other hand, says that the holding is the principle explicitly propounded by the court itself as "necessary for," or "as a basis of," its decision. Whatever the other differences between

them, both these theories seem to share two assumptions. One is that there is normally one and only one holding of a case; the other is that such a holding can be delimited from an examination of the particular case itself.

The assumption that the "material facts" will yield only one holding would imply, if true, that there is only one set of such "material facts" which is to be related to the holding. And this immediately confronts the theory with a main difficulty. This is that, apart from any explicit or implicit assertion of materiality by the court, there will always be more than one, and indeed many, competing versions of "the material facts"; and there will therefore not be merely one but many holdings, any of which will explain the decision on those facts, and no one of which therefore is strictly necessary to explain it. For apart from any selection by the court, all the logical possibilities remain open; and in the logician's sense it is possible to draw as many general propositions from a given decision (each of which will "explain" it) as there are possible combinations of distinguishable facts in it. It is in these terms that the question—What single principle does a particular case establish?—is strictly nonsensical, that is, inherently incapable of being answered.

If the holding of a case is deemed to turn on the facts in relation to the decision, and the following nine fact-elements are to be found in the report, there (so far as logical possibilities are concerned) be as many rival holdings as there are possible combinations of distinguishable facts in it. What is more, each of the following fact-elements is usually itself capable of being stated at various levels of generality, all of which embrace "the fact" in question in the decision, but each of which may yield a different result in the different fact-situation of a later case. The range of "material" fact-elements of *Donoghue v. Stevenson*, standing alone, might be over-simplified into a list somewhat as follows, each material fact being itself stated at alternative levels of generality:

(a) *Material Fact as to the Agent of Harm.* Dead snails, *or* any snails, *or* any noxious physical foreign body, *or* any noxious foreign element, physical or not, *or* any noxious element.

(b) *Material Fact as to Vehicle of Harm.* An opaque bottle of ginger-beer, *or* an opaque bottle of beverage, *or* any bottle of

[42] Excerpted from Julius Stone, Legal System and Lawyers' Reasonings 268-74(1964).
[43] *Editor's Note:* Again I have altered the terminology of the text in order to ensure clarity. Professor Stone refers to the *"ratio decidendi"* of a case; I substitute the term "holding." He uses "holding" as synonymous with "decision"; I have substituted the term "decision."

beverage, *or* any container of commodities for human consumption, *or* any container of any chattels for human use, *or* any chattel whatsoever, *or* any thing (including land or buildings).

(c) *Material Fact as to Defendant's Identity*. A manufacturer of goods nationally distributed through dispersed retailers, *or* any manufacturer, *or* any person working on the object for reward, *or* any person working on the object, *or* anyone dealing with the object.

(d) *Material Fact as to Potential Danger from Vehicle of Harm*. Object likely to become dangerous by negligence, *or* whether or not so.

(e) *Material Fact as to Injury to Plaintiff*. Physical personal injury, *or* nervous or physical personal injury, *or* any injury.

(f) *Material Fact as to Plaintiff's Identity*. A Scots widow, *or* a Scotswoman, *or* a woman, *or* any adult, *or* any human being, *or* any legal person.

(g) *Material Fact as to Plaintiff's Relation to Vehicle of Harm*. Donee of purchaser from retailer who bought directly from the defendant, *or* the purchaser from such retailer, *or* the purchaser from anyone, *or* any person related to such purchaser or donee, *or* other person, *or* any person into whose hands the object rightfully comes, *or* any person into whose hands it comes at all.

(h) *Material Fact as to Discoverability of Agent of Harm*. The noxious element being not discoverable by inspection of any intermediate party, *or* not so discoverable without destroying the saleability of the commodity, *or* not so discoverable by any such party who had a duty to inspect, *or* not so discoverable by any such party who could reasonably be expected *by the defendant* to inspect, or not discoverable by any such party who could reasonably be expected *by the court or a jury* to inspect.

(i) *Material Fact as to Time of Litigation*. The facts complained of were litigated in 1932, *or* any time before 1932, *or* at any time.

We are considering the question of "materiality" apart from any view on that matter expressed by the court itself. As to none of the foregoing facts (a) through (i), and as to none of the several alternative levels of generality of each of them, could it be said, taking the facts and decision of *Donoghue v. Stevenson* alone, that it was on its face not "material" in the logical sense to the decision in that case. Even as to the time of litigation, as to which we are most tempted to say that this at least must be "immaterial" on the face of it, we cannot assert with dogmatism that *Donoghue v. Stevenson* should have been, and would in fact have been, so decided in 1800. (It is of course not time *as such* which makes the difference but the fact that the human and physical factors surrounding the question have undergone continual change in the *interim*.)

It follows that logically, *i.e.* apart from any special indication that should be drawn from the court's own attitude, that the holding of *Donoghue v. Stevenson* did not compel later courts to impose liability in any case where only some of the above possible "material" facts, and some levels of statement of them, were found. Another way of saying this is that (apart still from such special indication by the court) a holding drawn from a case by the "material facts" method can only be prescriptive or binding for a later case whose facts are "on all fours" *in every respect*. And since the italicized words must be taken seriously, this reduces the range of the holding to the vanishing point. Outside this range, the question always is whether in the later court's view the presence in the instant case of *some* of the fact elements (a) through (i), at some of their alternative levels of generalization, is more relevant to its decision than is the absence of *the rest of them*. And this is not a question of the "materiality" of the facts to the decision in the precedent case imposing itself on the later court. It is rather a question of the analogical relevance of the prior holding to the later case, requiring the later court to choose between possibilities presented by the precedent case.

At this point, then, *before* we begin searching for the precedent court's own assertion as to which facts and levels of statement of them are "material"—that is, before taking up the "classical" theory—it is correct to say that the questions: What single principle does a particular case establish? What is the holding of this case as at the time of its decision? are strictly nonsensical. For they can only be answered by saying that there is no such single principle or holding that can in terms of the "material facts" test be binding in a later case.

With respect to the "classical theory," we must look at either the "explicit" or "implicit" view of the court itself as to which is the "material" level of statement of each "material" fact. Are we to say that merely because the House of Lords in *Donoghue v. Stevenson* might have stated the material facts as to the agent and vehicle of harm in terms of snails and bottles of beverage, this concludes one way or another a later case as to defects in cartons of butter or the wheels of automobiles? Is it reasonable to assume that courts using language appropriate to the case before them do, or could, address themselves in their choice of language to all the levels of generality at which each "material" fact (a) through (i) of the concrete case is capable of statement, not to speak of the possible combinations and variations of these facts, and the implications of all these for as yet unforeseen future cases? Yet unless it is reasonable it would reduce judgment in later cases to a kind of lottery (turning on the chance of words used) to say that the later decision is controlled by that level of generalized statement of the assumed "material fact" which is explicit in the precedent court's judgment. And to admit also that level which might be "implicit" in the precedent court's judgment would in most cases be merely to impute to the precedent court a choice of levels of generalized statement (and therefore of the reach of the holding in that case) which must in reality be made by the later court.

Once it is granted that a "material fact" of the precedent case can be stated at various levels of generality, each of which is correct for that case, any of these levels of statement is potentially a "material fact." Insofar as the holding is determined by each "material fact," then what the precedent case yields must be a number of potential holdings competing with each other to govern future cases of which the facts may fall within one level of generality but not within another. An automobile in bad repair can be a noxious physical object, but no one can call it an opaque bottle containing a reputed snail.

9. Frederick Schauer: Generalizations[44]

Even if there is in the precedent case no

explicit statement of the category of which the precedent case is a member, it is likely that the precedent court will indicate its reasons for deciding in one way rather than another. Given that a reason is a reason only because it is logically prior to and broader than the decision that it is a reason for, a reason can be seen as itself a generalization. Consequently a subsequent court can use the reasoning in the precedent case to construct the generalization which in turn will comprise the factual predicate of a potentially constraining rule.

At times, however, there will be no authoritative characterization, whether direct or through the mediation of a rationale, in the precedent case. This can happen as a consequence of indeterminacy in the language of a judicial opinion, or because there may (both in law and without) be no written opinion at all. Yet even in the absence in the precedent case of an authoritative characterization supplying an authoritative generalization, the constraints of precedent may not be quite as illusory as is often supposed. Even if no two events are exactly alike, and even if nothing in the precedent case mandates the appropriate generalizing category, it is a mistake to assume that the decisionmaker in the instant case is largely unconstrained in determining what events are assimilable with what other events.

D. Justification

1. Karl Llewellyn: Justification and Wisdom[45]

It is a fact in our legal system that judges are by no means free to be *arbitrary,* and our vital need that they shall not be free to be *arbitrary* has been caught into rationales or doctrines about "laws and not men," and about "rules determining cases." But it is also a fact that our legal system does adjust to the individual case *and* to changes in our

[44] FREDERICK SCHAUER, PLAYING BY THE RULES: A PHILOSOPHICAL EXAMINATION OF RULE-BASED DECI-

SION-MAKING IN LAW AND IN LIFE 181-86 (1991). Copyright 1991 by Frederick Schauer. Reprinted by permission.

[45] KARL N. LLEWELLYN, JURISPRUDENCE 134-36 (1962). Copyright 1962 by the University of Chicago. Used with permission.

conditions and institutions; and that fact means that judges and other officials are free to some real degree to be *just* and *wise*, and that we have a vital need that judges and other officials shall continue to be to some real degree free to be *wise and just*. That fact happens, however, *not* to have been caught into an equally familiar, equally sharp, or equally precious rationale or doctrine. Yet it needs to be; it is no less a vital part of our legal system and of our judges' duty. There is the law, which we know as impersonal, and think of as clear; there is the right outcome, which we feel as also impersonal, and think of as hard to find, but capable of being found, and the office of the judge is to fulfill the demands of *both*, together.

The tradition of the judge's craft stabilizes the work of our judges and guides it, and the ideals of that craft also stabilize and guide. Is the judge's craft something that is wholly ineffable or spiritual or personal, so much so as to yield nothing at all to careful study, so much so as to lay no foundation for more effective doctrine which can get closer to really doing what the doctrine we have is supposed to be doing? One studies the art and craft of the judge's office by studying particular officers at work in their office, and seeking for the similarities in their attitudes and behavior. This has been misconceived [by critics of legal realism] as being a delving into the vagaries of individuals; what it is, instead, is a search for predictabilities and proper lines of work in the judge's office which transcend individuality.

2. Neil MacCormick: Justification of Decisions[46]

At least since Richard Wasserstrom made the point in his *The Judicial Decision* (1961), it has been widely—perhaps universally—acknowledged that legal reasoning in the judicial setting is concerned with the *justification* of decisions. Judicial opinions are set out by way of justification of decisions. Decisions themselves as "acts of will" are not, of course, logical conclusions that follow necessarily from justificatory statements of judicial opinion. But if it can be shown by sound reasoning that a decision pronounced by a judge is one that gives proper effect to the rights and/or liabilities of the parties affected, the decision so pronounced is a justified one. Decisions so justified, albeit "acts of will," are not mere arbitrary volitions; they are decisions grounded in good reasons. Processes of reasoning that relate to decision making by way of establishing whether there are good reasons for (or against) such decisions are in an obvious sense processes of practical reasoning. They issue in conclusions about what ought, or ought not, to be decided and indeed to be done.

3. David Lyons: Legalistic Justification[47]

Justification can only be built upon a non-arbitrary foundation. It can appeal to prevailing values or preferences only if they are regarded as sound or if on other grounds it is fair to use them as a basis for settling disputes. For this reason, we cannot be satisfied with the suggestion, sometimes made, that a judge must decide hard cases by appealing to her own personal values, her own sense of right and justice. If we believe that judicial decisions can be justified in any cases, then we are committed to the more general proposition that genuine justification is sometimes possible. This is presupposed by the doctrine of legalistic justification, which assumes that there are good and sufficient reasons for applying and enforcing the established rules of law—reasons that must be capable of justifying what we do to people in the process. The considerations that may be capable of justifying such a prac-

[46] Neil MacCormick, *Legal Reasoning and Practical Reason*, in PETER A. FRENCH, THEODORE E. UEHLING, JR., & HOWARD K. WETTSTEIN (EDS.), MIDWEST STUDIES IN POLITICAL PHILOSOPHY VOL. VII: SOCIAL AND POLITICAL PHILOSOPHY 271, 273 (1982). Copyright 1982 Univ. of Minnesota Press. Reprinted by permission.

[47] David Lyons, *Justification and Judicial Responsibility*, 72 CALIFORNIA LAW REVIEW 178, 185 (1984). Copyright 1984 California Law Review. Reprinted by permission.

tice cannot amount to the merely personal values of a judge.

We should settle for no less in hard cases. A court must appeal to principles or policies that are capable of determining how such cases should be decided. These principles or policies must be regarded as more than merely the personal values of the judge. Of course, a judge is obliged to reach a conclusion about what those principles or policies are so that she can apply them. But she would not be appealing to them merely as her own personal values. She would be making a judgment concerning the principles or policies that are capable of justifying decisions.

E. Reasoning by Analogy

1. Lon Fuller: The Analogical Development of the Common Law[46]

It will be useful at this point to consider a kind of paradigm instance of a case-by-case growth of legal doctrine. The cases are of course schematic and hypothetical. They are given in the order of their assumed chronology. The parties in each case are different persons, but to facilitate comparisons the symbols used to designate the parties will be the same throughout and will indicate the role played by the particular party; thus in all five cases O will designate the original owner of the horse which came by theft or fraud into the hands of T.

Case No. 1. T steals O's horse and sells it to G, who pays full value for it and has no reason to know it had been stolen from O. O brings suit against G to recover the horse. *Held*, for O. One of the deterrents to thievery is the difficulty of disposing of stolen goods. If a purchaser like G were able to take goods free of the claim of the true owner, a market for stolen goods would be created and thus an incentive to theft. In any event, it was impossible for T, a thief who had no rightful title to the horse, to pass any title to G; he who has nothing can give nothing.

Case No. 2. T buys a horse from O giving as payment a forged note purporting to be that of X. T knew that the note was forged. After delivering the horse to T, O discovers that he has been defrauded. He brings suit against T to recover the horse. It is argued on behalf of T that O delivered the horse to him with the intent to confer title; the horse is now T's and O's only remedy is to sue for the price. *Held*, for O. The passage of title was vitiated by the fraud of T; title throughout remained in O.

Case No. 3. The case is similar to Case No. 2, except that after receiving possession of the horse, T sold it to G, who knew T had bought it from O but had no reason to know that T had worked any fraud on O. O brings suit against G to recover the horse. It is argued on behalf of O that title remained in him in accordance with the principle laid down in Case No. 2. Since T had no title, he could pass none to G. *Held*, for G. It would be an intolerable burden on commerce if purchasers of property were compelled to scrutinize the details of a transaction by which the former owner voluntarily delivered it into the hands of the person now offering it for sale. Fraud takes many and subtle forms; if the victim could not recognize it, it is unreasonable to ask of a stranger to the transaction that he ascertain whether it was present. With respect to Case No. 2, all that was said there was with reference to the legal relations between the owner and the defrauder; the court's mind was not directed toward the possibility that a subsequent purchaser, like G, might intervene. The principle we are here applying is that if the horse is in the hands of T or of someone who knew of his fraud, it may be recovered by O. In the hands of an innocent purchaser, like G, the horse may not be recovered by O, for reasons we have already indicated.

Case No. 4. The case is like Case No. 3, except that after buying the horse from T, G sold it to K, who, before he bought the horse from G, had been informed of the fraud worked by T on O. O sues K to recover the horse. It is argued on behalf of O that K was not an innocent purchaser, since he knew of T's fraud when he bought the horse. In accordance with the principle laid down in Case No. 3, O became entitled to the horse when it came into the hands of K. *Held*, for K. If the argument made by O were accepted,

[46] Lon L. Fuller, *The Forms and Limits of Adjudication*, 92 HARV. L. REV. 375-77 (1978).

it would be possible for a person in the position of *O* to destroy the value of the title acquired by *G* simply by giving general publicity to the fact that *T* had induced the sale by fraud. Thus the objective of protecting the bona fide purchaser *G* would be defeated, for his property would become unsalable. When the court in Case No. 3 said that *O* could recover the horse from anyone who knew of the fraud of *T*, it did not have in mind the possibility that the horse might have passed previously through the hands of a bona fide purchaser like *G*. When the horse was bought from *T* by *G*, title to it was perfected and was no longer vulnerable to attack by *O*. *G* was then free to sell it to anyone he saw fit.

Case No. 5. This case is like Case No. 4, except that *K* not only knew of *T*'s fraud but had participated in it by forging *X*'s name on the note used by *T* to pay *O* for the horse. *O* sues *K* to recover the horse. *K* rests his defense on the reasoning of Case No. 4; *G* had title to the horse and was free to sell it to anyone he saw fit. If *K* was guilty of any misconduct, that is a question for the criminal law; it ought not affect his property rights. *Held*? . . . perhaps it would be well to suspend the series at this point and leave to the reader the burden of decision and the more onerous burden of explanation.

Although the development here traced is considerably neater than anything likely to be encountered in legal history, I assume that lawyers would generally agree that this sort of thing does occur. I assume also it will be agreed that, despite the zigzag pattern which the decisions seem to present, the process illustrated is a "rational" one, falling within the limits of meaningful adjudication. What is the source of this "rational" quality? It seems clear that it derives from the fact that the courts engaged in this development are drawing out the necessary, or at least the reasonable, implications of a regime of private property and exchange.

2. Oliver Wendell Holmes: The Growth of the Law[49]

The growth of the law is very apt to take place in this way. Two widely different cases suggest a general distinction, which is a clear one when stated broadly. But as new cases cluster around the opposite poles, and begin to approach each other, the distinction becomes more difficult to trace; the determinations are made one way or the other on a very slight preponderance of feeling, rather than of articulate reason; and at last a mathematical line is arrived at by the contact of contrary decisions, which is so far arbitrary that it might equally well have been drawn a little farther to one side or to the other, but which must have been drawn somewhere in the neighborhood of where it falls.

F. Hohfeldian Analytic Jurisprudence

1. Wesley Newcomb Hohfeld: Analytic Jurisprudence[50]

The main purpose of the writer is to emphasize certain oft-neglected matters that may aid in the understanding and in the solution of practical, everyday problems of the law. With this end in view, the present article will discuss, as of chief concern, the basic conceptions of the law—the legal elements that enter into all types of jural interests.

One of the greatest hindrances to the clear understanding, the incisive statement, and the true solution of legal problems frequently arises from the express or tacit assumption that all legal relations may be reduced to "rights" and "duties," and that these latter categories are therefore adequate for the purpose of analyzing even the most complex legal interests, such as trusts, options, escrows, "future" interests, corporate interests, etc. Even if the difficulty related merely to inadequacy and ambiguity of terminology, its seriousness would nevertheless be worthy of definite recognition and persistent effort toward improvement; for in any closely reasoned problem, whether legal or non-le-

---

[49] OLIVER WENDELL HOLMES, JR., THE COMMON LAW 101 (Howe ed. 1963).

[50] Wesley Newcomb Hohfeld, *Some Fundamental Legal Conceptions as Applied in Judicial Reasoning*, 23 YALE L.J. 16 (1913-14).

gal, chameleon-hued words are a peril both to clear thought and to lucid expression. As a matter of fact, however, the above mentioned inadequacy and ambiguity of terms unfortunately reflect, all too often, corresponding paucity and confusion as regards actual legal conceptions. That this is so may appear in some measure from the discussion to follow.

The strictly fundamental legal relations are, after all, *sui generis*; and thus it is that attempts at formal definition are always unsatisfactory, if not altogether useless. Accordingly, the most promising line of procedure seems to consist in exhibiting all of the various relations in a scheme of "opposites" and "correlatives," and then proceeding to exemplify their individual scope and application in concrete cases. An effort will be made to pursue this method:

Jural *Opposites*	rights no-rights	privilege duty	power disability	immunity liability
Jural *Correlatives*	right duty	privilege no-right	power liability	immunity disability

Rights and Duties. As already intimated, the term "rights" tends to be used indiscriminately to cover what in a given case may be a privilege, a power, or an immunity, rather than a right in the strictest sense.

If X has a right against Y that Y shall stay off X's land, the correlative (and equivalent) is that Y is under a duty toward X to stay off the place. If, as seems desirable, we should seek a synonym for the term "right" in this limited and proper meaning, perhaps the word "claim" would prove the best. The latter has the advantage of being a monosyllable.

Privileges and "No-Rights." As indicated in the above scheme of jural relations, a privilege is the opposite of a duty, and the correlative of a "no-right." In the example last put, whereas X has a *right* or *claim* that Y, the other man, should stay off the land, himself has the *privilege* of entering on the land; or, in equivalent words, X does not have a duty to stay off. The privilege of entering is the negation of a duty to stay off. As indicated by this case, some caution is necessary at this point, for, always, when it is said that a given privilege is the mere negation of a *duty*, what is meant, of course, is a *duty* having a content or tenor precisely *opposite* to

that of the privilege in question. Thus, if, for some special reason, X has contracted with Y to go on X's own land, it is obvious that X has, as regards Y, both the privilege of entering and the *duty of entering*. The privilege is perfectly consistent with this sort of duty—for the latter is of the same content or tenor as the privilege; but it still holds good that, as regards Y, X's privilege of entering is the precise negation of a duty *to stay off*. Similarly, if A has not contracted with B to perform certain work for the latter, A's privilege of *not* doing so is the very negation of a duty of *doing* so. Here again the duty contrasted is of a content or tenor exactly opposite to that of the privilege.

Passing now to the question of "correlatives," it will be remembered, of course, that a duty is the invariable correlative of that legal relation which is most properly called a right or claim. That being so, if further evidence be needed as to the fundamental and important difference between a right (or claim) and a privilege, surely it is found in the fact that the correlative of the latter relation is a "no-right," there being no single term available to express the latter conception. Thus, the correlative of X's right that Y shall not enter on the land is Y's duty not to enter; but the correlative of X's privilege of entering himself is manifestly Y's "no-right" that X shall not enter.

Powers and Liabilities. As indicated in the preliminary scheme of jural relations, a legal power (as distinguished, of course, from a mental or physical power) is the opposite of legal disability, and the correlative of legal liability. But what is the intrinsic nature of a legal power as such? Is it possible to analyze the conception represented by this constantly employed and very important term of legal discourse? Too close an analysis might seem metaphysical rather than useful; so that what is here presented is intended only as an approximate explanation sufficient for all practical purposes.

A change in a given legal relation may result (1) from some superadded fact or group of facts not under the volitional control of a human being (or human beings); or (2) from some superadded fact or group of facts which are under the volitional control of one or more human beings. As regards the second class of cases, the person (or persons) whose volitional control is paramount may be said to have the (legal) power to effect the particular change of legal relations that is involved in the problem.

Many examples of legal powers may readily be given. Thus, *X*, the owner of ordinary personal property "in a tangible object" has the power to extinguish his own legal interest (rights, powers, immunities, etc.) through that totality of operative facts known as abandonment; and—simultaneously and correlatively—to create in other persons privileges and powers relating to the abandoned object, *e.g.*, the power to acquire title by appropriating it. *Similarly*, *X* has the power to transfer his interest to *Y*—that is, to extinguish his own interest and concomitantly create in *Y* a new and corresponding interest. So also *X* has the power to create contractual obligations of various kinds.

As regards all the "legal powers" thus far considered, possibly some caution is necessary. If, for example, we consider the ordinary property owner's power of alienation, it is necessary to distinguish carefully between the *legal* power, the *physical* power to do the things necessary for the "exercise" of the legal power, and, finally, the privilege of doing these things—that is, if such privilege does really exist. It may or may not. Thus if *X*, a landowner, has contracted with *Y* that *X* will not alienate to *Z*, the acts of *X* necessary to exercise the power of alienating to *Z* are privileged as between *X* and every party other than *Y*; but, obviously, as between *X* and *Y*, the former has no privilege of doing the necessary acts; or conversely, he is under a duty to *Y* not to do what is necessary to exercise the power.

Immunities and Disabilities. As already brought out, immunity is the correlative of disability ("no power"), and the opposite, or negation, of liability. Perhaps it will also be plain that a power bears the same general contrast to an immunity that a right does to a privilege. A right is one's affirmative claim against another, and a privilege is one's freedom from the right or claim of another. Similarly, a power is one's affirmative "control" over a given legal relation as against another; whereas an immunity is one's freedom from the legal power or "control" of another as regards some legal relation.

2. Joseph William Singer: Hohfeld's Analytic Jurisprudence[51]

In 1913, Wesley Newcomb Hohfeld published his famous article in the Yale Law Journal on fundamental distinctions among types of legal rights. To the modern reader, Hohfeld's analysis appears at once pathbreaking and naive. At the time of its publication the article generated similarly contradictory reactions. His analysis was regarded by some as a brilliant innovation and by others as a perpetuation of the old conceptualist nonsense.

Hohfeld's article is significant because it represents the complete rejection of the meta-theory of self-regarding acts as a means to describe or justify the legal system. His analysis is also an important element of the legal realist assault on conceptualism. Hohfeld not only re-exposed the fundamental contradiction in liberal political theory, but offered a method of critique that could be used to attack future efforts to resolve the contradiction by revival of the classical sophistry.

3. Jack M. Balkin: The Hohfeldian Approach to Law[52]

Hohfeld offers us a theory of the arbitrary nature of a right, or more generally, of any legally protected interest. The nature and extent of a person's rights are dependent upon the correlative duties of others. A right does not owe its existence to its connection to an individual, or a piece of property. Rather, a right is simply a legal guarantee that one has the privilege to engage in certain actions and invoke the power of the state to prevent other persons from engaging in certain other actions. Thus, my right of

---

[51] Joseph William Singer, *The Legal Rights Debate in Analytical Jurisprudence from Bentham to Hohfeld*, 1982 WISCONSIN LAW REVIEW 975. Reprinted by permission.

[52] Jack M. Balkin, *The Hohfeldian Approach to Law and Semiotics*, 44 UNIVERSITY OF MIAMI LAW REVIEW 1119 (1990). Copyright 1990 J.M. Balkin. Reprinted by permission.

freedom of speech is defined by my right to inflict emotional injury on you when I say things that you do not like, as well as your nonright to prevent me from doing so and the government's duty to protect me in my infliction of injury on you. Indeed, not only do rights become mutually self-defining, but so do legally cognizable injuries, for a legally cognizable injury is simply the flip side of a legally protected interest. A property right, then, is not an attribute or thing that inheres in the property itself, or in its owner. Rather, it is the state's legal sanction to perform or refrain from performing certain types of actions. I have a right to the use of my property to the extent that I cannot be punished or penalized for my use of it. Conversely, my property rights are unlawfully abridged to the extent that the state will penalize those persons who interfere with them.

It follows from Hohfeld's work that what constitutes a legally protected interest is arbitrary, and is not defined by the nature of things. Rather, the "nature of things" in a legal sense is defined by the mutually self-defined relations of legal ideas. Just as reality is shaped and created by language, so too legal and political reality is shaped and created by mutually defined legal and political rights, powers, and duties. The state's allocation of legally sanctioned violence is established by mutually self-defining relations, and is not derivable from the concept of right itself, just as the concepts involved in our understanding of reality are mutually self-defining—their particular contours are not necessitated by things in themselves. Put another way, concepts like private property, consent, and liberty do not simply represent previously existing things in the world. Rather, they result from the system of differences between legal and moral concepts, and in so doing constitute the political world that we live in.

As this last statement demonstrates, Hohfeld's insight had quite radical implications, although it was at first misunderstood as simply a retreat into conceptualism and formalism. In fact, however, it led to a devastating critique of these forms of legal thought, a critique from which we have never quite recovered. Indeed, one can say without too much exaggeration that Hohfeld's analysis of rights discourse made much of the later work of the legal realists possible.

Consider the argument that protection of the private speech of pornographers establishes a system of private power that silences women and contributes to their subordination. In Hohfeldian terms, to the extent that the state protects the rights of pornographers, it allows women to be injured by the deleterious effects of pornography. Moreover, some feminists argue that protection of pornography actually reduces the real (as opposed to formal) freedom of women to speak. This is analogous to the realists' analysis of contract rights—the realists argued that one does not have freedom of contract if the economic system created by the state's laws puts one in a situation of vastly unequal bargaining power. Similarly, the feminist critique of traditional first amendment jurisprudence argues that one does not really have free speech if one is not taken seriously or is unable or even afraid to speak because of one's subordinated role in society. The state enforced freedom of the pornographer to speak results in the silencing of women harmed by pornography, even though the formal right to speak is guaranteed. From the feminist critique we can see that "free speech," like contract or property, is an arbitrary signifier whose meaning is constituted by the system of differences between it and other legal and political concepts, and simultaneously constitutes relations of power in our society.

I would now like to offer an example of how the Hohfeldian analysis of legal concepts works in practice. Suppose that the failure of General Motors (GM) to equip its vehicles with airbags costs the American public some $300 thousand a year in accident costs, including pain, suffering, and medical expenses. Suppose also that it would cost GM only $200 thousand a year to install airbags in its automobiles. Now assume that a series of lawsuits is brought against GM by plaintiffs who were driving GM cars and got into accidents; the plaintiffs sue GM for the additional injuries caused by GM's failure to install airbags in the cars they were driving. Should we make GM pay for their injuries? If we adopt a negligence standard for unintentionally caused injuries, we would conclude that yes, of course GM should pay, because $200 thousand a year is less than $300 thousand a year. That is to say, the burden of taking safety precautions is less than the expected loss from the failure to take those precautions. GM is therefore at fault and should have to pay.

Note that this is a fault based argument for a standard of negligence—if you cause injury by not taking precautions that are cost-benefit justified from the standpoint of society as a whole, you have done something morally wrong and therefore should pay damages. Moreover, this argument is based upon common sense notions of fault, causation, and harm. A person or corporation that fails to take such cost-benefit justified precautions is at fault, and because the failure to take those precautions causes harm to others, they should have to pay money damages. But each of these concepts—fault, causation, and harm—is a legal concept that does not simply stand for an independently existing entity in the real world. Rather, the concepts of fault, causation, and harm obtain their meaning from their relation to other legal concepts—for example, property and contract rights.

Thus, imagine that counsel for GM argues as follows: Why is it just to make GM pay $200 thousand to save $300 thousand in accident costs to perfect strangers? Allowing a cause of action in negligence here will force GM either to install airbags in all of its cars at a cost of $200 thousand a year or continue to pay money damages at a rate of $300 thousand a year, as injured plaintiffs line up at the judicial trough to collect huge sums of income without a day's work. Thus, GM is being forced to divert at least $200 thousand of its hard earned profits for expenditures it had no desire to undertake. Put more bluntly, the use of a negligence standard in this case amounts to outright theft of GM's property and a redistribution to others, either in the form of direct subsidies, or in a forced investment of capital and labor in airbag technology.

Perhaps you will object to this argument on the grounds that GM's property rights are limited by its moral and legal responsibilities to others. Perhaps you will say that GM's property rights end where its responsibilities to others begin, so that GM may use its property in any way it wants as long as it does not injure the rights of others. Thus, because GM's wrongful use of its property caused injury to others, it has no right to prevent the government from taking its property.

Yet at this point it should become clear that the concepts of property and fault are mutually defined. One cannot know whether GM's property is really being taken unless one knows whether GM is at fault. Indeed, once we assume that GM is at fault, it is GM who is taking the property of others—in the form of lost wages, medical expenses, and pain and suffering—by its callous disregard of human safety and welfare. Allowing GM to save money by refusing to install airbags is effectively a wealth transfer from the victims of its negligence to GM. Put another way, not allowing plaintiffs to sue GM for negligence allows GM to fatten its profit margins through human carnage and the suffering of others.

This example should make clear that notions of property rights are parasitic upon notions of fault. But that is only half the story. Notions of fault are also parasitic on notions of property rights and contract rights. Let us return to the argument of the counsel for GM. Perhaps she might concede that if GM were at fault, there would be no question of compensation. She might agree with our assessment that the person who is at fault should bear the risk of loss, and that one should never be allowed wrongfully to use one's property so as to injure the rights of others. However, why is it clear that GM is at fault for not installing airbags? GM has the right to make cars and place them before the public, and if the public wishes to purchase those cars and drive them, that is their choice. There is absolutely no fault involved in GM's placing its product in the hands of a willing buyer. GM is merely exercising its rights to free contract.

Any plaintiffs injured in GM cars rode in them out of their own free will. If they had wanted airbags in their cars, they could have demanded that the airbags be installed and paid GM for the extra cost of this option. Alternatively, they could have installed the airbags themselves or hired a third party to do it, and absorbed the cost in that fashion. If anyone is at fault for the extra costs incurred by the plaintiffs, it is the plaintiffs themselves for failing to ask for safety equipment they now insist should have been in their cars all along. The person at fault should bear the risk of loss, and should not be able to shift the loss to persons who make an innocent and lawful use of their own property.

Indeed, what the plaintiffs really want is to have it both ways. They are at fault for not asking for airbags that they themselves admit were necessary, and then, when they get themselves involved in accidents that were not GM's fault, they want GM to subsidize the cost of the extra safety precautions that they were not willing to pay for in the first place. There is no problem with the general proposition that GM may use its property in any way it likes as long as it does not invade the rights of others. But in this case, GM did not harm the interests of the plaintiffs or invade the plaintiffs' rights. The plaintiffs caused their own injury by failing to spend a little extra money for safety precautions. If anything, holding GM liable allows the plaintiffs to use their contract and property rights to interfere with GM's property rights because they are now perfectly free to get into accidents and tax GM for their own failure to invest in safety precautions.

To know what the lawful property and contract rights of GM and the plaintiffs are, we need to know who is at fault for not having airbags installed in GM cars. However, in order to know who is at fault, it appears we must first determine what is a lawful use of one's property or a lawful exercise of the right to contract. With respect to GM, this involves the nature of products that it can sell to willing buyers without incurring liability for damages, and conversely, with respect to the plaintiffs, the boundaries of the concept of assumption of risk. The concepts of property, contract, and fault are thus mutually defined. Just as Saussure taught us that in linguistics there are no positive terms, legal terms also have a mutually self-defining quality. In the more modern language of deconstruction, we would say that property, contract, and fault exist in a relation of difference, of mutual dependence and differentiation, in which each concept bears the traces of the others.

Perhaps you may sense that there is something wrong with the arguments of GM's counsel. Although the concept of fault seems difficult to pin down at first, we can give it determinate content by invoking the concept of causation. We know that GM is at fault because it was GM's failure to install the airbags that caused the harm to the plaintiffs. Thus, the notion of fault depends on the more basic idea of causal responsibil-ity. Yet the notion of causal responsibility is parasitic on other concepts, including fault. Is not the cause of the plaintiffs' harm (1) the plaintiffs' involvement in an accident, which is either the plaintiffs' fault or that of third parties, but certainly not GM's and (2) the plaintiffs' failure to demand that airbags be installed, coupled with (3) plaintiffs' voluntary action in driving or riding in a car without airbags? In order to know who really caused the accident and thus who is at fault, we must have more than a notion of but-for causation, for in this case both the plaintiffs' and GM's actions are but-for causes of the injury. Yet it will be difficult for us to arrive at such a notion without invoking other legal concepts, such as fault. To understand this point better, suppose that a plaintiff drove a GM car while drunk and then sued GM for not installing a device that made it impossible for a person to start the ignition without passing a breathalyser test. Would we say that GM caused this accident by failing to install such a device, even if the cost of this device were minimal in comparison to the number of lives that might be saved by it? Or would we say that the cause of the accident was the plaintiff's drunken driving? Perhaps we would distinguish the breathalyser case on the grounds that a person who drives drunk causes the accident because he is at fault. Note, however, that at this point causation has become parasitic on notions of fault, instead of the other way around. Yet the same is true of the airbags case. In order to know whether GM or the plaintiffs caused the harm, we might have to decide whether GM was at fault for placing a product on the market that could have been safer, or whether the plaintiffs were at fault for choosing to purchase and misuse the product. Fault, causation, contract, and property rights have all become intertwined.

These conclusions are related to Hohfeld's basic idea that a legal right is a privilege to inflict harm that is either not legally cognizable or is otherwise without legal remedy. The concept of legal fault depends upon whether one is acting within one's rights, but of course one's rights depend upon the corresponding rights of others to protection from harm, while those harms that the law will remedy depend upon what one's rights are, and so on. Thus, legal fault and legally remediable harm become two sides of the same coin, while legal rights and legally non-remediable harm are also two sides of the same coin. Indeed, we can understand all of our rights of contract and property, or our rights to freedom of action and protection of our security, as allocations of power by the state. Put another way, these are privileges granted by the state to private actors to inflict nonremediable harms upon each other. My right to freedom of contract involves my right to injure my competitors by underselling them, to injure my employees by fixing their wages and working conditions, or to injure my customers by refusing to deal with them or by raising my prices. My property rights involve my right to use my property in a way others do not like, as well as my right to invoke the aid of the state if someone attempts to take my property from me or put it to a contrary use. Private property is a state sanctioned monopoly in the use and disposition of things, enforced by the state's monopoly over the use and license of legally sanctioned violence.

4. Guido Calabresi & A. Douglas Melamed: Entitlements[53]

The first issue which must be faced by any legal system is one we call the problem of "entitlement." Whenever a state is presented with the conflicting interests of two or more people, or two or more groups of people, it must decide which side to favor. Absent such a decision, access to goods, services, and life itself will be decided on the basis of "might makes right"—whoever is stronger or shrewder will win. Hence the fundamental thing that law does is to decide which of the conflicting parties will be entitled to prevail. The entitlement to make noise versus the entitlement to have silence, the entitlement to pollute versus the entitlement to breathe clean air, the entitlement to have children versus the en-

titlement to forbid them—these are the first order of legal decisions. Having made its initial choice, society must enforce that choice. Simply setting the entitlements does not avoid the problem of "might makes right"; a minimum of state intervention is always necessary. Our conventional notions make this easy to comprehend with respect to private property. If Taney owns a cabbage patch and Marshall, who is bigger, wants a cabbage, he will get it unless the state intervenes. But it is not so obvious that the state must also intervene if it chooses the opposite entitlement, communal property. If large Marshall has grown some communal cabbages and chooses to deny them to small Taney, it will take state action to enforce Taney's entitlement to the communal cabbages. The same symmetry applies with respect to bodily integrity. Consider the plight of the unwilling ninety-eight pound weakling in a state which nominally entitles him to bodily integrity but will not intervene to enforce the entitlement against a lustful Juno. Consider then the plight—absent state intervention—of the ninety-eight pounder who desires an unwilling Juno in a state which nominally entitles everyone to use everyone else's body. The need for intervention applies in a slightly more complicated way to injuries. When a loss is left where it falls in an auto accident, it is not because God so ordained it. Rather it is because the state has granted the injurer an entitlement to be free of liability and will intervene to prevent the victim's friends, if they are stronger, from taking compensation from the injurer. The loss is shifted in other cases because the state has granted an entitlement to compensation and will intervene to prevent the stronger injurer from rebuffing the victim's requests for compensation.

The state not only has to decide whom to entitle, but it must also simultaneously make a series of equally difficult second order decisions. These decisions go to the manner in which entitlements are protected and to whether an individual is allowed to sell or trade the entitlement. In any given dispute, for example, the state must decide not only which side wins but also the kind of protection to grant. It is with the latter decisions, decisions which shape the subsequent relationship between the winner and

[53] Guido Calabresi & A. Douglas Melamed, *Property Rules, Liability Rules, and Inalienability: One View of the Cathedral*, 85 HARVARD LAW REVIEW 1089 (1972). Copyright 1972 by the Harvard Law Review Association and reprinted by permission.

the loser, that this article is primarily concerned. We shall consider three types of entitlements—entitlements protected by property rules, entitlements protected by liability rules, and inalienable entitlements. The categories are not, of course, absolutely distinct; but the categorization is useful since it reveals some of the reasons which lead us to protect certain entitlements in certain ways.

[1] An entitlement is protected by a property rule to the extent that someone who wishes to remove the entitlement form its holder must buy it from him in a voluntary transaction in which the value of the entitlement is agreed upon by the seller. It is the form of entitlement which gives rise to the least amount of state intervention: once the original entitlement is decided upon, the state does not try to decide its value. It lets each of the parties say how much the entitlement is worth to him, and gives the seller a veto if the buyer does not offer enough. Property rules involve a collective decision as to who is to be given an initial entitlement but not as to the value of the entitlement.

[2] Whenever someone may destroy the initial entitlement if he is willing to pay an objectively determined value for it, an entitlement is protected by a liability rule. This value may be what it is thought the original holder of the entitlement would have sold it for. But the holder's complaint that he would have demanded more will not avail him once the objectively determined value is set. Obviously, liability rules involve an additional stage of state intervention: not only are entitlements protected, but their transfer or destruction is allowed on the basis of a value determined by some organ of the state rather than by the parties themselves.

[3] An entitlement is inalienable to the extent that its transfer is not permitted between a willing buyer and a willing seller. The state intervenes not only to determine who is initially entitled and to determine the compensation that must be paid if the entitlement is taken or destroyed, but also to forbid its sale under some or all circumstances. Inalienability rules are thus quite different from property and liability rules. Unlike those rules, rules of inalienability not only "protect" the entitlement; they may also be viewed as limiting or regulating the grant of the entitlement itself.

It should be clear that most entitlements to most goods are mixed. Taney's house may be protected by a property rule in situations where Marshall wishes to purchase it, but a liability rule where the government decides to take it by eminent domain, and by a rule of inalienability in situations where Taney is drunk or incompetent.

Examples: Liability rules are used in cases of accidents. If we were to give victims a property entitlement not to be accidentally injured we would have to require all who engage in activities that may injure individuals to negotiate with them before an accident, and to buy the right to knock off an arm or a leg. Such pre-accident negotiations would be extremely expensive, often prohibitively so. To require them would thus preclude many activities that might, in fact, be worth having. And, after an accident, the loser of the arm or leg can always very plausibly deny that he would have sold it at the price the buyer would have offered. Indeed, where negotiations after an accident do occur—for instance pretrial settlements—it is largely because the alternative is the collective valuation of the damages.

Inalienability rules are used where external costs are nonmonetizable. If Taney is allowed to sell himself into slavery, or to take undue risks of becoming penniless, or to sell a kidney, Marshall may be harmed, simply because Marshall is a sensitive man who is made unhappy by seeing slaves, paupers, or persons who die because they have sold a kidney.

Marshall could pay Taney not to sell his freedom to Chase the slaveowner; but because Marshall is not one but many individuals, freeloader and information costs could make such transactions practically impossible. The state could intervene by objectively valuing the external cost to Marshall and requiring Chase to pay that cost. But since the external cost to Marshall does not lend itself to an acceptable objective measurement, such liability rules are not appropriate. The state must, therefore, either ignore the external costs to Marshall, or if it judges them great enough, forbid the transaction that gave rise to them by making Taney's freedom inalienable.

Nuisance or pollution s one of the most interesting areas where the question of who will be given an entitlement, and how it will be protected, is in frequent issue. Traditionally the nuisance-pollution problem is viewed in terms of three rules. First, Taney may not pollute unless his neighbor (his only neighbor let us assume), Marshall, allows it (Marshall may enjoin Taney's nuisance). Second, Taney may pollute but must compensate Marshall for damages caused (nuisance is found but the remedy is limited to damages). Third, Taney may pollute at will and can only be stopped by Marshall if Marshall pays him off (Taney's pollution is not held to be a nuisance to Marshall). In our terminology rules one and two (nuisance with injunction, and with damages only) are entitlements to Marshall. The first is an entitlement to be free from pollution and is protected by a property rule; the second is also an entitlement to be free from pollution but is protected only by a liability rule. Rule three (no nuisance) is instead an entitlement to Taney protected by a property rule, for only by buying Taney out at Taney's price can Marshall end the pollution.

The very statement of these rules in the context of our framework suggests that something is missing. Missing is a fourth rule representing an entitlement in Taney to pollute, but an entitlement which is protected only by a liability rule. The fourth rule, really a kind of partial eminent domain coupled with a benefits tax, can be stated as follows: Marshall may stop Taney from polluting, but if he does he must compensate Taney.

5. Arthur Jacobson: Critique of Hohfeld[54]

Suppose I sue you for not showing up at my house for dinner, when you accepted the invitation and I purchased the food, cooked it, and did not invite someone else. Hohfeld believes that (1) plaintiff has "no-right" to compel defendant to come to dinner, and (2) defendant has a "privilege" not to come. Since each statement is correlative with the other, the court need not make both statements for a legally complete description of

the relations between you and me over the dinner. Just because courts choose not to talk about defendant's privilege not to come to dinner does not mean defendant does not have one by virtue of the court's judgment. By leaving the defendant's decision not to come to dinner unregulated, Hohfeld would argue, courts are nevertheless making a legal statement about the decision. The defendant's legal status is to have a privilege. The arguing point is that through the conception of "privilege" law regulates even those actions which it seems not to regulate. Hohfeld's legal universe has no legally empty corners. Corners we might regard as legally empty Hohfeld fills with privilege.

Hohfeld's completion of the legal universe in this manner has a basic flaw. Judgments (at least at common law) never state that defendant has a privilege, only that plaintiff has not suggested a right for the violation of which the court imposes a liability. Judgments never say, in other words, that plaintiff has "no-right," only that plaintiff has not successfully suggested a right.

Although plaintiff may not have successfully suggested a right on the basis of which a court is prepared to render judgment against defendant, defendant does not have assurance that he can perform any range of actions. "Privilege" means little to one planning action if we confine it to rights a possible plaintiff happens to articulate. "Privilege" in the sense Hohfeld must mean it is trivial.

Plaintiff's "no-right" thus does not reflexively lead to defendant's "privilege." The two states are not correlative, since defendant's inquiry supposes a perfect plaintiff articulating all possible rights, whereas plaintiff's inquiry supposes only that he articulate a single right leading to liability.

6. Madeline Morris: The Structure of Entitlements[55]

Individuals have a variety of interests. A society must decide which of those interests to give legal force. Beth, for instance, has

---

[54] Excerpted from Arthur J. Jacobson, *Hegel's Legal Plenum*, 10 CARDOZO L. REV. 877, 881-83 (1989).

[55] Madeline Morris, *Structure of Entitlements*, 78 CORNELL LAW REVIEW 822 (1993). Copyright 1993 Cornell Law Review. Reprinted by permission.

interests in maintaining bodily integrity, discriminating against blacks, and running a cattle farm on her land. The society in which Beth lives might give some legal force to Beth's interests in maintaining bodily integrity and in cattle farming, but none to her interest in discriminating. By giving legal force to an interest, society transforms it from a mere private interest into a legal entitlement.

The allocation and construction of legal entitlements is, however, more problematic than that. The various interests to which we wish to give legal force may come into conflict. Beth's interest in cattle farming on her land may conflict with Robert's interest in freedom from noxious odors on his adjoining land, another interest to which we would like to give legal force. Because any interest to which we would like to give legal force is liable to come into conflict with other interests to which we would also like to give legal force, entitlements must be complex objects. Entitlements must be constructed so that they do more than simply "give legal force" to certain interests. They must also specify the extent and type of legal force that a given interest has in any particular context and in relation to any other particular entitlement.

An important starting point for an analysis of the structure of entitlements is to ask: Why would we want to have various forms of entitlement? The brief answer is that no single entitlement form will function beneficially in every legal context. The form of an entitlement shapes the incentives of the affected parties and also determines the distribution of advantages and disadvantages (of wealth, broadly) between parties. No single entitlement form creates optimal incentives and distributions for every kind of social interaction. Rather, in different contexts, different entitlement forms because of their distinct incentive structures and consequent behavioral effects, and because of their distributive results promote social goals.

Guido Calabresi and A. Douglas Melamed, recognizing that different entitlement forms are beneficial in different contexts, identified three forms of entitlement: property, liability, and inalienability rules. They then analyzed the efficiency and distributive implications of each, and gave examples of contexts in which each entitlement form would be valuable. The recognition that the

form of an entitlement can foster or impede goals of efficiency and of distributive justice immediately gives rise to two questions: First, what are all the possible entitlement forms? And second, what are the efficiency and distributive characteristics of each form?

Writing early this century, W.N. Hohfeld attempted to identify entitlements' fundamental components. Working in a tradition of analytic jurisprudence whose inception is associated with the work of Jeremy Bentham, Hohfeld offered a typology of "jural relations." This typology consists of an identification of the rights, privileges, powers, and immunities that, alone or in combination, constitute legal entitlements. Hohfeld thus attempted to identify entitlements' fundamental components. He did not, however, go on to combine those components to identify the set of possible entitlement forms nor to analyze the efficiency and distributive implications of different forms of entitlement.

In a sense, Hohfeld and, later, Calabresi and Melamed, were approaching the same problem analyzing the structure of entitlements from opposite directions. Hohfeld asked what building blocks entitlements are made of, but did not then attempt to put those blocks together to identify the universe of entitlement forms, nor to analyze each form's efficiency and distributive characteristics. Calabresi and Melamed analyzed the characteristics of the three particular entitlement forms they identified (property, liability, and inalienability rules), but did not attempt to determine what other forms of entitlement there might be nor to ascertain what components entitlements are composed of.

Employment discrimination law, for instance, may benefit from a consideration of the full range of entitlement forms. Entitlements against employment discrimination have traditionally been viewed exclusively as fully inalienable. One may not sell nor give away one's equal employment entitlements. That sole focus on full inalienability in equal employment law is most appropriate where the discriminatory acts in question are motivated by stereotyping or animus. But what of "rational discrimination" differential treatment motivated not, directly or indirectly, by animus, but instead by, say, a profit motive? In such circumstances, where equal employment goals conflict with other legitimate goals, consideration of entitlement forms other than full inalienability may prove most valuable.

Consideration of entitlement forms other than full inalienability raises new options for handling complex employment discrimination issues such as fetal protection. Fetal protection recently arose as an equal employment issue when some employers sought to exclude all fertile women from jobs involving exposure to substances harmful to fetuses.[56] Such occupational exposure, the employers contended, is unavoidable given currently available technology.

In *International Union, UAW v. Johnson Controls, Inc.*,[57] the Supreme Court held that Title VII of the Civil Rights Act of 1964 prohibits female-exclusionary fetal protection policies. But, as mentioned earlier, the Johnson Controls decision has not fully satisfied any camp. Many feminists have criticized the decision, objecting that, while the decision is more favorable to women than a holding for the defendants would have been, Johnson Controls still leaves women with the burden of fetal protection; it is still women who must either self-exclude from fetal-hazardous jobs, or constrain their reproductive lives in accordance with job conditions, or else risk fetal harm and resulting congenital disabilities in their children.

The fetal protection debate has consisted, essentially, of two polar positions: first, that female-exclusionary fetal protection policies violate women's equal employment entitlements and therefore must be enjoined, and second, that such policies do not violate women's equal employment entitlements and so must be permitted. The bipolar nature of the debate has reflected an underlying assumption that equal employment entitlements must necessarily be constructed as fully inalienable, that is, that women may not transfer their equal employment entitlements.

But a consideration of the available entitlement forms yields alternative approaches to the fetal protection problem. The possibility of constructing women's equal employment entitlements in the fetal protection context as entitlement forms other than full inalienability offers potential efficiency and distributive benefits. For example, if women's equal employment entitlements in the fetal protection context were constructed as Property-rule entitlements, then employers might purchase agreements from female employees to forbear from reproduction during a designated period. Such purchases would be voluntary transactions at negotiated prices. Under such an arrangement, female workers could agree in exchange for compensation not to give birth during some specified period. This sort of a scheme would address the problems of fetal risk without leaving the full burden of fetal protection on women. At the same time, requiring employers to bear the costs of workplace fetal protection would provide incentives for technological and other development to provide for future workplaces free from fetal hazards.

Of course, using a Property rule in this context might give rise to transaction-cost problems. If employers were permitted to employ only women who charged attractive prices for the in-kind components of their equal employment entitlements (*i.e.*, their entitlements to submit to no greater reproductive limitations than male employees), then competition for employment might drive down the price of women's in-kind components to zero (an outcome that some would favor as efficient and others would object to on efficiency and/or distributive grounds). If, on the other hand, employers were prohibited from firing (or not hiring) women who "charge too much" for the in-kind components of their equal employment entitlements, then women could "hold up" employers for sums exceeding the actual value to the women of their in-kind components.

If such transaction-cost problems rendered use of Property rules undesirable in the fetal protection context, then Liability, Reverse Liability, and Combined Liability and Reverse Liability rules could be considered. Such rules would allow employers (un-

---

[56] Because fetal harm could result from substance exposures occurring before a woman knows she is pregnant, excluding only pregnant workers from the jobs at issue would not provide adequate fetal protection, the employers have argued. Hence, the employers have instituted policies excluding all fertile women.

[57] 499 U.S. 187, L. Ed. 2d 158, 111 S. Ct. 1196 (1991).

der a Liability rule) or women (under a Reverse Liability rule) or both (under a Combined rule) to force transfer of the in-kind component at a collectively set price. Under a Liability rule, female workers would be required to transfer the in-kind components of their equal-reproductive-freedom-in-employment entitlements to employers as a condition of employment. Such use of a Liability rule would preclude "hold ups" of the employer by pre-determining the sale price (but would also, of course, reduce women workers' autonomy, since effectuating a compensated transfer of equal reproductive freedom would be a condition of employment). Under a Reverse Liability rule, employers would be required to purchase in-kind entitlements to equal reproductive freedom in employment at the pre-set price from women electing to force a transfer. Use of a Reverse Liability rule would help to avoid a bidding down of the price of the in-kind components. A Combined Liability and Reverse Liability rule would render the benefits afforded by both the Liability and the Reverse Liability rules (but would, like the Liability rule, also limit women's autonomy).

Any of the entitlement forms here considered could be modified by a no-gift/minimum-price constraint if it were feared that underpricing of the in-kind component might result from allowing price negotiations to occur in the shadow of the collectively-set price. It should also be noted that successful use of any of the rules here considered would require that employers be prohibited (in practice as well as in theory) from refusing to employ women because of fetal protection costs.

Thus, efficiency and distributive goals might be better achieved in the fetal protection context by considering a range of possible entitlement forms rather than limiting our thinking to allow only for Full Inalienability rules in equal employment law. This is not to say that these alternative entitlement forms offer a fetal-protection panacea. Indeed, application of any of the rules here considered would give rise to a panoply of practical and theoretical complexities.

What the consideration of a range of entitlement forms does offer in the fetal protection context is options: previously unseen and unconsidered approaches to the problem of fetal protection are revealed once a range of entitlement forms is considered.

In these equal employment areas, considering a broad range of entitlement forms, rather than being limited to the traditional conception of equal employment entitlements as exclusively fully inalienable, holds the promise of leading to more desirable and more just results. Such a broadened exploration offers potential benefits in areas in which innovative ideas are very much needed.

QUESTIONS AND COMMENTS FOR YOUR CONSIDERATION

1. Hohfeld had six jural concepts (right, duty, privilege, power, liability, and immunity) or perhaps seven (if you want to count "disability"). Calebresi-Melamed had three jural concepts (property, liability, inalienability), or perhaps four (if you add "partial eminent domain coupled with a benefits tax"). Morris has over a dozen, mostly permutations from Hohfeld and Calabresi-Melamed. Does this disparity in number and name indicate that jural concepts are indeterminate? Or do you sense that they are simply undergoing evolution and will someday settle down into a handful (or several handfuls) of generally accepted concepts?

2. How helpful are Professor Morris' own jural concepts to her discussion of the fetal protection problem? Do they confuse or clarify? Did you find them to be of heuristic value?

3. Did you find heuristic value in Professor Balkin's use of jural concepts in his GM hypothetical?

5

Realism

A. The Prediction Theory of Law

1. Oliver Wendell Holmes: The Bad Man Theory[1]

If you want to know the law and nothing else, you must look at it as a bad man, who cares only for the material consequences which such knowledge enables him to predict, not as a good one, who finds his reasons for conduct, whether inside the law or outside of it, in the vaguer sanctions of conscience. The theoretical importance of the distinction is no less, if you would reason on your subject aright. The law is full of phraseology drawn from morals, and by the mere force of language continually invites us to pass from one domain to the other without perceiving it, as we are sure to do unless we have the boundary constantly before our minds. The law talks about rights, and duties, and malice, and intent, and negligence, and so forth, and nothing is easier, or, I may say, more common in legal reasoning, than to take these words in their moral sense, at some stage of the argument, and so to drop into fallacy.

No doubt simple and extreme cases can be put of imaginable laws which the statute-making power would not dare to enact, even in the absence of written constitutional prohibitions, because the community would rise in rebellion and fight; and this gives some plausibility to the proposition that the law, if not a part of morality, is limited by it. But this limit of power is not coextensive with any system of morals.

Take the fundamental question, What constitutes the law? You will find some text writers telling you that it is something dif-ferent from what is decided by the courts of Massachusetts or England, that it is a system of reason, that it is a deduction from principles of ethics or admitted axioms or what not, which may or may not coincide with the decisions. But if we take the view of our friend the bad man we shall find that he does not care two straws for the axioms or deductions, but that he does want to know what the Massachusetts or English courts are likely to do in fact. I am much of his mind. The prophecies of what the courts will do in fact, and nothing more pretentious, are what I mean by the law.

I trust that no one will understand me to be speaking with disrespect of the law because I criticize it so freely. I venerate the law, and especially our system of law, as one of the vastest products of the human mind. No one knows better than I do the countless number of great intellects that have spent themselves in making some addition or improvement, the greatest of which is trifling when compared with the mighty whole. It has the final title to respect that it exists, that it is not a Hegelian dream, but a part of the lives of men. But one may criticize even what one reveres. Law is the business to which my life is devoted and I should show less than devotion if I did not do what in me lies to improve it, and, when I perceive what seems to me the ideal of its future, if I hesitated to point it out and to press toward it with all my heart.

I have been speaking about the study of the law, and I have said next to nothing of what commonly is talked about in that connection—textbooks and the case system, and all the machinery with which a student comes most immediately in contact. Nor shall I say anything about them. Theory is my subject, not practical details. The modes of teaching have been improved since my time, no doubt, but ability and industry will master the raw material with any mode.

---

[1] Oliver Wendell Holmes, *The Path of the Law*, 10 HARV. L. REV. 61 (1897).

Theory is the most important part of the dogma of the law, as the architect is the most important man who takes part in the building of a house. The most important improvements of the last twenty-five years are improvements in theory. It is not to be feared as impractical, for, to be competent, it simply means going to the bottom of the subject.

I heard a story, the other day, of a man who had a valet to whom he paid high wages, subject to deduction for faults. One of his deductions was, "For lack of imagination, five dollars." The lack is not confined to valets. The object of ambition, power, generally presents nowadays in the form of money alone. Money is the most immediate form, and is a proper object of desire. But, as Hegel says, "It is in the end not the appetite, but the opinion, which has to be satisfied." To an imagination of any scope the most far-reaching form of power is not money, it is the command of ideas. If you want great examples read Mr. Leslie Stephen's "History of English Thought in the Eighteenth Century," and see how a hundred years after his death the abstract speculations of Descartes had become a practical force controlling the conduct of men. Read the works of the great German jurists, and see how much more the world is governed today by Kant than by Bonaparte. We cannot all be Descartes or Kant, but we all want happiness. And happiness, I am sure from having known many successful men, cannot be won simply by being counsel for great corporations and having an income of fifty thousand dollars. An intellect great enough to win the prize needs other food besides success. The remoter and more general aspects of the law are those which give it universal interest. It is through them that you not only become a great master in your calling, but connect your subject with the universe and catch an echo of the infinite, a glimpse of its unfathomable process, a hint of the universal law.

2. Karl Llewellyn: The Bramble Bush[2]

Rules are important so far as they help

you to predict what judges will do. That is all their importance except as pretty playthings.

3. Fred Rodell: Is Law an Exact Science?[3]

Is law an exact science? No pretense was ever more absurd.

None of The Law's answers to problems is preordained, precise, or inevitable; and that it is indeed the lawyers, with their dreary double-talk, and not The Law, that mass of ambiguous abstractions, that run the show. Even if The Law will be considered a big machine that gives automatic answers to legally-worded questions, it is the lawyers and the lawyer-judges who phrase the questions and decide which buttons to push.

4. Lon Fuller: Critique of Realism[4]

A suggestion first made by Holmes in 1897, and developed systematically by Bingham in 1912,[5] has today [1940] been taken up by a sufficient number of writers so that we may properly speak of a "realist" school. This view has sought its criterion of positivism not in what judges *say* but in what they *do*. According to this view, a rule of law is a generalization about the way judges act; or, as it has been phrased, the law consists in patterns of judicial behavior. These patterns of behavior are the object of the lawyer's study, just as the behavior of atoms constitutes a field of research for the physicist.

We must recall what legal positivism sets out to do. Its object is to develop a criterion which will enable us to distinguish between those ideas or meanings which are only try-

---

[2] KARL LLEWELLYN, THE BRAMBLE BUSH 9 (1960).

[3] FRED RODELL, WOE UNTO YOU, LAWYERS 157-59 (1939).

[4] Excerpted from LON L. FULLER, THE LAW IN QUEST OF ITSELF 52-56 (1940). Copyright by Northwestern University; used by permission.

[5] Bingham, *What is the Law?* 11 Mich. L. Rev. 1, 109 (1912).

ing to become law and those which have suc-ceeded—to set up a kind of finishing line, as it were. With Austin the test was, roughly, "Those ideas and meanings have become law which have been approved as such by the sovereign." This test is rejected by the real-ists because Austin's sovereign is a purely imaginary creature. Gray tried to tie the law down to the expressed meanings of the indi-vidual judge. Obviously, however, the notion that the law lies in the meanings of particu-lar individuals in particular situations can offer no definite criterion of positivism, and no assurance against a relativistic-subjectiv-ism in which the distinction between what is and what ought to be is lost.

QUESTIONS AND COMMENTS FOR YOUR CONSIDERATION

1. Recall Kelsen's positivistic description of an individual "out in the cold"—trying to guess what not to do so as to avoid the wrath of the officials of the state. The best bet for such an individual is to try to *predict* what state officials will do. In turn, that prediction can only be made if state officials act with a certain degree of *regularity* and *consistency*. Does Kelsen's positivism lead inevitably to legal realism?

2. If Holmes is right—that the law consists of predicting what courts will do in fact—then the question for the attorney is: what materials shall we look at in order to make our predictions as accurate as possible?

3. Would a realist, at the outset, restrict her choice of materials to *legal* materi-als—*i.e.*, the kinds of writings that are found in libraries and on computer retrieval systems?

4. What if psychological attitudes are more important in predicting judicial behavior than rules written down in statutes? Wouldn't a lawyer's *job* then be to look into these psychological determinants of judicial behavior?

5. Legal realism has helped us open our minds to considerations that go beyond cases, rules and statutes. Recall how open Justice Handy was to all kinds of considerations that were "off the books" in reaching his decision that the speluncean explorers's conviction should be reversed. Thus, as a twentieth-cen-tury phenomenon in American legal thought, legal realism is a liberating phenome-non. Its present-day offshoot, critical legal studies, is also a liberating phenome-non. But does the fact that something may be a liberating phenomenon necessarily mean that it is right, useful, efficacious, or worthy of pursuit?

5. Jerome Frank: Law and the Modern Mind[6]

Only a limited degree of legal certainty can be attained. The current demand [1930] for exactness and predictability in law is in-capable of satisfaction because a greater de-gree of legal finality is sought than is procur-able, desirable or necessary. The widespread notion that law either is or can be made approximately stationary and certain is irra-tional and should be classed as an illusion or myth.

Why do men seek unrealizable certainty in law? Because they have not yet relin-quished the childish need for an authorita-tive father and unconsciously have tried to find in the law a substitute for those attri-butes of firmness, sureness, certainty and infallibility ascribed in childhood to the fa-ther.

Most of us are unwilling—and for the most part unable—to concede to what an extent we are controlled by deep rooted bi-

---

[6]Excerpts from JEROME FRANK, LAW AND THE MODERN MIND 11-12, 21, 101 ff, 126 ff, 137-38, 143-47 (1930).

ases. We cherish the notion that we are grown-up and rational, that we know why we think and act as we do, that our thoughts and deeds have an objective reference, that our beliefs are not biases but are the result of direct observation of objective data. We are able thus to delude ourselves by giving "reasons" for our attitudes. When challenged by ourselves or others to justify our positions or our conduct, we manufacture ex post facto a host of "principles" which we induce ourselves to believe are conclusions reasoned out by logical processes from actual facts in the actual world. So we persuade ourselves that our lives are governed by Reason.

This practice of making ourselves appear, to ourselves and others, more rational than we are, has been termed "rationalization."

The practice of law is one of the major arts of rationalization. We can now understand the better why the young lawyer is baffled by the huge gap between what he has learned in school and what he observes in the office and the courtroom. It is clear, too, why older lawyers, regardless of their spoken creeds, often are more daring and creative than recent graduates. Experience has schooled the older men to deal flexibly with changing realities and yet, without hypocrisy, use locutions which enable them to pay tribute to an unconscious childish insistence on the achievement of impossible legal certainty (an insistence often more intense among the laity than among lawyers).

In theory the judge begins with some rule or principle of law as his premiss, applies this premiss to the facts, and thus arrives at his decision. Now, since the judge is a human being and since no human being in his normal thinking processes arrives at decisions (except in dealing with a limited number of simple situations) by the route of any such syllogistic reasoning, it is fair to assume that the judge, merely by putting on the judicial ermine, will not acquire so artificial a method of reasoning. Judicial judgments, like other judgments, doubtless, in most cases, are worked out backward from conclusions tentatively formulated.

Professor Tulin has made an illustrative study.[7] While driving at a reckless rate of speed, a man runs over another, causing severe injuries. The driver of the car is drunk at the time. He is indicted for the statutory crime of "assault with intent to kill." The question arises whether his act constitutes that crime or merely the lesser statutory crime of "reckless driving." The courts of several states have held one way, and the courts of several other states have held the other.

The first group maintain that a conviction for assault with intent to kill cannot be sustained in the absence of proof of an actual purpose to inflict death. In the second group of states the courts have said that it was sufficient to constitute such a crime if there was a reckless disregard of the lives of others, such recklessness being said to be the equivalent of actual intent.

With what, then, appears to be the same facts before them, these two groups of courts seem to have sharply divided in their reasoning and in the conclusions at which they have arrived. But upon closer examination it has been revealed by Tulin that, in actual effect, the results arrived at in all these states have been more or less the same. In Georgia, which may be taken as representative of the second group of states, the penalty provided by the statute for reckless driving is far less than that provided, for instance, in Iowa, which is in the first group of states. If, then, a man is indicted in Georgia for reckless driving while drunk, the courts can impose on him only a mild penalty; whereas in Iowa the judge, under an identically worded indictment, can give a stiff sentence. In order to make it possible for the George courts to give a reckless driver virtually the same punishment for the same offense as can be given by an Iowa judge, it is necessary in Georgia to construe the statutory crime of assault with intent to kill so that it will include reckless driving while drunk; if, and only if, the Georgia court so construes the statute, can it impose the same penalty under the same facts as could the Iowa courts under their reckless driving statute. On the other hand, if the Iowa court were to construe the Iowa statute as the Georgia court construes the Georgia statute, the punishment of the reckless driver in Iowa would be too severe.

In other words, the courts in these cases began with the results they desired to accomplish; they wanted to give what they consid-

[7] Tulin, *The Role of Penalties in Criminal Law*, 27 Yale L.J. 1048.

ered to be adequate punishment to drunken drivers; their conclusions determined their reasoning.

But the conception that judges work back from conclusions to principles is so heretical that it seldom finds expression. Daily, judges, in connection with their decisions, deliver so-called opinions in which they purport to set forth the bases of their conclusions. Yet you will study these opinions in vain to discover anything remotely resembling a statement of the actual judging process. They are written in conformity with the time-honored theory. They picture the judge applying rules and principles to the facts, that is, taking some rule or principle (usually derived from opinions in earlier cases) as his major premiss, employing the facts of the case as the minor premiss, and then coming to his judgment by processes of pure reasoning.

Now and again some judge, more clear-witted and outspoken than his fellows, describes (when off the bench) his methods in more homely terms. Recently Judge Hutcheson essayed such an honest report of the judicial process. He tells us that after canvassing all the available material at his command and duly cogitating on it, he gives his imagination play,

> and brooding over the cause, waits for the feeling, the hunch—that intuitive flash of understanding that makes the jump-spark connection between question and decision and at the point where the path is darkest for the judicial feet, sets its light along the way. In feeling or "hunching" out his decisions, the judge acts not differently from but precisely as the lawyers do in working on their cases, with only this exception, that the lawyer, in having a predetermined destination in view—to win the lawsuit for his client—looks for an regards only those hunches which keep him in the path that he has chosen, while the judge, being merely on his way with a roving commission to find the just solution, will follow his hunch wherever it leads him. The vital motivating impulse for the decision is an intuitive sense of what is right or wrong in the particular case; and the astute judge, having so decided, enlists his every faculty and belabors his lag-

gard mind, not only to justify that intuition to himself, but to make it pass muster with his critics. Accordingly, he passes in review all of the rules, principles, legal categories, and concepts which he may find useful, directly or by an analogy, so as to select from them those which in his opinion will justify his desired result.[8]

If the law consists of the decisions of the judges and if those decisions are based on the judge's hunches, then the way in which the judge gets his hunches is the key to the judicial process. Whatever produces the judge's hunches makes the law.

What, then, are the hunch-producers? What are the stimuli which make a judge feel that he should try to justify one conclusion rather than another?

The rules and principles of law are one class of such stimuli. But there are many others, concealed or unrevealed, not frequently considered in discussions of the character or nature of law. To the infrequent extent that these other stimuli have been considered at all, they have been usually referred to as the political, economic and moral prejudices of the judge. The undisclosed attitudes of judges have been said to be a function of their "education," "race," and "class," their views of "public policy" or "social advantage," their "economic and social philosophies," or their "notions of fair play."

But are not those categories—political, economic, and moral biases—too gross, too crude, too wide? A man's political or economic prejudices are frequently cut across by his affection for or animosity to some particular individual or group, due to some unique experience he has had; or a racial antagonism which he entertains may be deflected in a particular case by a desire to be admired by some one who is devoid of such antagonisms. Moreover, in learning the facts with reference to which one forms an opinion, and often long before the time when a hunch arises with reference to the situation as a whole, these more minute and distinctly personal biases are operating constantly. So

---

[8] Hutcheson, *The Judgment Intuitive: The Function of the 'Hunch' in Judicial Decisions*, 14 CORNELL L. REV. 274.

the judge's sympathies and antipathies are likely to be active with respect to the persons of the witness, the attorneys and the parties to the suit. His own past may have created plus or minus reactions to women, or blonde men, or plumbers, or ministers, or college graduates, or Democrats. A certain twang or cough or gesture may start up memories pleasant or painful to the man. Those memories of the judge, while he is listening to a witness with such a twang or cough or gesture, may affect the judge's initial hearing of, or subsequent recollection of, what the witness said, or the weight or credibility which the judge will attach to the witness's testimony.

Judges are called on not to make rules, but to decide which side of some immediate controversy is to win. The rules are incidental, the decisions are the thing.

Whenever a judge decides a case he is making law: the law of that case, not the law of future cases not yet before him. What the judge does and what he says may somewhat influence what other judges will do or say in other cases. But what the other judges decide in those other cases, as a result of whatever influences, will be the law in those cases. The law of any case is what the judge decides.

Judges, or some third person viewing their handiwork, may choose to generalize from their decisions, may claim to find common elements in their decisions. But those descriptions of alleged common elements are, at best, some aid to lawyers in guessing or bring about future judicial conduct or some help to judges in settling other disputes. The rules will not directly decide any other cases in any given way, nor authoritatively compel the judges to decide those other cases in any given way; nor make it possible for lawyers to bring it about that the judges will decide any other cases in any given way, nor infallibly to predict how the judges will decide any other cases. Rules, whether stated by judges or others, whether in statutes, opinions or textbooks by learned authors, are not the Law, but are only among some many of the sources to which judges go in making the law of the cases tried before them. There is no rule by which you can force a judge to follow an old rule or by which you can predict when he will verbalize his

conclusions in the form of a new rule, or by which he can determine when to consider a case as an exception to an old rule, or by which he can make up his mind whether to select one or another old rule to explain or guide his judgment. His decision is primary, the rules he may happen to refer to are incidental.

The law, therefore, consists of decisions, not of rules. If so, then whenever a judge decides a case he is making law. The most conservative or timid judge, deny it though he may, is constantly engaged in law-making; if he were to see himself objectively he would doubtless feel like Moliere's M. Jourdain who was astonished to learn that all his life he had been talking prose.

What then is the part played by legal rules and principles? We have seen that one of their chief uses is to enable the judges to give formal justifications—rationalizations —of the conclusions at which they otherwise arrive. From that point of view these formulas are devices for concealing rather than disclosing what the law is. At their worst they hamper the clear thinking of the judges, compelling them to shove their thoughts into traditional forms, thus impeding spontaneity and the quick running of ideas; they often tempt the lazy judge away from the proper task of creative thinking to the easier work of finding platitudes that will serve in the place of robust cerebration.

At their best, when properly employed, they have undeniable value. The conscientious judge, having tentatively arrived at a conclusion, can check up to see whether such a conclusion, without unfair distortion of the facts, can be linked with the generalized points of view theretofore acceptable. If none such are discoverable, he is forced to consider more acutely whether his tentative conclusion is wise, both with respect to the case before him and with respect to possible implications for future cases.

But it is surely mistaken to deem law merely the equivalent of rules and principles. The lawyer who is not moderately alive to the fact of the limited part that rules play is of little service to his clients. The judge who does not learn how to manipulate those abstractions will become like that physician, described by Mill, "who preferred that patients should die by rule rather than live contrary to it." The number of cases which should be disposed of by routine application of rules is limited. to apply rules mechanically usually signifies laziness, or callousness to the peculiar factors presented by the controversy.

Viewed from any angle, the rules and principles do not constitute law. They may be aids to the judge in tentatively testing or formulating conclusions; they may be positive factors in bending his mind towards wise or unwise solutions of the problem before him. They may be the formal clothes in which he dresses up his thoughts. But they do not and cannot completely control his mental operations and is therefore unfortunate that either he or the lawyers interested in his decision should accept them as the full equivalent of that decision. If the judge so believes, his thinking will be the less effective. If the lawyers so believe, their opinions on questions of law (their guesses as to future decisions) will be unnecessarily inaccurate.

It is sometimes asserted that to deny that law consists of rules is to deny the existence of rules. That is specious reasoning. To deny that a cow consists of grass is not to deny the reality of grass or that the cow eats it.

All judges exercise discretion, individualize abstract rules, make law. Shall the process be concealed or disclosed? The fact is, and every lawyer knows it, that those judges who are the most lawless, or most swayed by the perverting influences of their emotional natures, or most dishonest, are often the very judges who use most meticulously the language of compelling mechanical logic, who elaborately wrap about themselves the pretense of merely discovering and carrying out existing rules, who sedulously avoid any indications that they individualize cases. If every judicial opinion contained a clear exposition of all the actual grounds of the decision, the tyrants, the bigots and the dishonest men on the bench would lose their disguises and become known for what they are.

The pretense that judges are without the power to exercise an immense amount of discretion and to individualize controversies, does not relieve us of those evils which result from the abuse of that judicial power. On the contrary, it increases the evils. The honest, well-trained judge with the completest possible knowledge of the character of his powers and of his own prejudices and weaknesses is the best guaranty of justice. Efforts to eliminate the personality of the judge are doomed to failure. The correct course is to recognize the necessary existence of this personal element and to act accordingly.

With few exceptions, our discussions of law posit an "ideal," super-human, passionless, judge. In an occasional aside we admit that a judge may be affected by "weakness" when he allows his feelings to enter into his reasoning. But the manner of referring to these "weaknesses" indicates a belief that they are exceptional and pathological. Now even if the humanness of judges were pathological, it would deserve explicit attention as part of a liberal understanding or science of the law. But calm observation discloses that such "frailties" are normal, not diseased; recurrent, not exceptional. And a study of law which shoves the consideration of the normal and usual into a footnote and labels it "unusual and morbid" cannot lead to anything like an adequate understanding of our subject.

Ideals and counsels of perfection which are not remotely realizable lead to vicious betrayals of those who come under their influence. If law students are taught law in terms of the conduct of ideal or nonexistent judges, then when later those students become practitioners or judges, they are unlikely to be at their best in coping with the ways of the actual judging process.

We need to see that biases and prejudices and conditions of attention affect the judge's reasoning as they do the reasoning of ordinary men. Our law schools must become, in part, schools of psychology applied to law in all its phases. In law schools, in law offices and law courts there must be explicit recognition of the meaning of the phrase "human nature in law." Indeed the dishonesty of judges and other governmental officials is proper subject-matter for study by lawyers. That a certain judge is corrupt is highly important to the honest lawyer and his client. It may be imperative to avoid trying a case before a judge suspected of being dominated by a political boss interested in the case.

Judges should be well trained not only in rules of law but also in the best available methods of psychology. And among the most important objects which would be subject to his scrutiny as a psychologist would be his own personality so that he might become keenly aware of his own prejudices, biases, antipathies, and the like, not only in connection with attitudes political, economic and moral but with respect to more minute and less easily discoverable preferences and disinclinations.

6. Karl Llewellyn: Real Rules[9]

Whether "rules of law" be pure paper rules, or are the accepted patter of the law officials, they remain present, and their presence remains an actuality. First of all they appear as what they are: rules of authoritative ought, addressed to officials, telling officials what the officials ought to do. To which the officials either pay no heed at all (the pure paper rule; the dead-letter statute; the obsolete case) or listen partly (the rule "construed" out of recognition; the rule to which lip-service only is paid, while practice runs another course) or listen with all care (the rule with which the official practice pretty accurately coincides). I think that every such official precept-on-the-books (statute, doctrine laid down in the decision of a court, administrative regulation) tacitly contains an element of pseudo-description along with its statement of what officials ought to do; a tacit statement that officials do act according to the tenor of the rule; a tacit prediction that officials will act according to its tenor. Neither statement nor prediction is often true *in toto*. And the first point of the approach here made is skepticism as to the truth of either in the case in hand. Yet it is an accepted convention to act and talk as if this statement and prediction were most solemn truth; a tradition marked peculiarly among the legal profession when engaged officially. It is indeed of first importance to remember that such a tradition contains a tendency to verify itself. But no more so than to remember that such a tendency

is no more powerful than its opposite: that other tendency to move quietly into falsifying the prediction in fact, while laying on an ointment of conventional words to soothe such as wish to believe the prediction has worked out.

Thus the problem of official formulations of rules and rights becomes complex. First, as to formulation already present, already existent; the accepted doctrine. There, I repeat, one lifts an eye canny and skeptical as to whether judicial behavior is in fact what the paper rule purports (implicitly) to state. One seeks the real practice on the subject, by study of how the cases do in fact eventuate. One seeks to determine how far the paper rule is real, how far *merely* paper. One seeks an understanding of *actual* judicial behavior, in the comparison of rule with practice; one follows also the use made of the paper rule in argument by judges and by counsel, and the apparent influence of its official presence on decisions. One seeks to determine when it is stated, but ignored; when it is stated and followed; when and why it is *expressly* narrowed or extended or modified so that a new paper rule is created. One observes the level of *silent* application or modification or escape, in the "interpretation" of the facts of a case, in contrast to that other and quite distinct level of express wrestling with the language of the paper rule. One observes how strongly ingrained is the tradition of requiring a good paper justification, in terms of officially accepted paper rules, before any decision, however appealing on the facts, can be regarded as likely of acceptance. And by the same token, one observes the importance of the official formulae as tools of argument and persuasion; one observes both the stimuli to be derived form, and the limitations set by, their language. Very rapidly, too, one perceives that neither are all official formulae alike in these regards, nor are all courts, nor are all times and circumstances for the same formula in the same court. The *handling* of the official formulae to influence court behavior then comes to appear as an art, capable only to a limited extent of routinization or (to date) of accurate and satisfying description. And the discrepancy, great or small, between the official formula and what actually results, obtains the limelight attention it deserves.

[9]Excerpted from Karl Llewellyn, *A Realistic Jurisprudence—The Next Step*, 30 COLUM. L. REV. 431, 449-51 (1930).

QUESTIONS AND COMMENTS FOR YOUR CONSIDERATION

1. How does Llewellyn's notion of rules differ from Frank's?
2. Is Llewellyn more inclined than Frank to give credence to rules as having a potential to constrain judicial decision-making?

7. Rabelais: Gargantua and Pantagruel[10]

TRINQUAMELLE: How is it that you decide these cases?

JUDGE BRIDLEGOOSE: I very briefly shall answer you, according to the doctrine and instructions of *Leg. ampliorem § in refutatoriis, c. de appel*, which conforms to what is said in *Gloss. 1. 1. ff. quod met. causa Gaudent breviate moderni*. My practice is therein as the custom of the judicatory requires, unto which our law commandeth us to have regard, and by the rule thereof still to direct and regulate our actions and procedures; *ut not. extra. de consuet. in c. ex. litertis et ibi innoc.* For having well and exactly seen, surveyed, overlooked, reviewed, recognized, read, and read over again, turned and tossed over, seriously perused and examined the bills of complaint, accusations, impeachments, indictments, warnings, citations, summonings, comparitions, appearances, mandates, commissions, delegations, instructions, informations, inquests, prepartoires, productions, evidences, proofs, allegations, depositions, cross speeches, contradictions, supplications, requests, petitions, inquiries, instruments of the deposition of witnesses, rejoinders, replies, confirmations of former assertions, duplicates, triplicates, answers to rejoinders, writings, deeds, reproaches, disabling of witnesses, confronting of them together, declarations, denunciations, libels, certificates, royal missives, letters of appeal, letters of attorney, instruments of compulsion, delineatories, anticipatories, evocations, messages, dimissions, issues, exceptions, dilatory pleas, demurs, compositions, injunctions, reliefs, reports, returns, confessions, acknowledgments, exploits, executions, and other such-like confects and spiceries, both at the one and the other side, as a good judge ought to do, in conformity to what hath been noted thereupon—*Spec. de ordination, Para. 3 et Tit. de Offi. omn. jud. para. fin. et de rescriptis praesentat para. 1.* —I posit on the end of a table in my closet all the pokes and bags of the defendant, and then allow unto him the first hazard of the dice. And it is mentioned, 1. *favorabiliores. ff. de reg. jur. et in cap. cum sunt eod. tit. lib. 6*, which saith, *Quum sunt partium jura obscura, reo potius favendum est quam actori.* That being done, I thereafter lay down upon the end of the same table the bags and satchels of the plaintiff, *visum visu*, just over against one another; for *Opposita juxta se posita clarius elucescunt: ut not. in lib. I para. Videamus. ff. de his qui sunt sui vel alieni juris, et in 1 munerum. § mixta. ff. de mun. et hon.* Then do I likewise and sembably throw the dice for him, and forthwith livre him his chance.

TRINQUAMELLE: Yea but, my friend, seeing it is by the lot, chance, and throw of the dice that you award your judgments and decisions, why do you not livre up these fair throws and chances at the very same day and hour, without any further procrastination or delay, that the parties appear before you? To what use can those writings serve you, those papers and other procedures contained in the bags and pokes of the lawyers?

JUDGE BRIDLEGOOSE: They serve my turn in three things very exquisite, requisite, and authentical. First, for formality sake, the omission whereof, that it maketh all, whatever is done, to be of no force or value, is excellently proved, by *Spec. I, tit. de instr. edit. et eit. de rescript. praesent.*

Secondly, they are useful and steadable to me in lieu of some other honest and healthful exercise. The late Master Othoman Vadet, a prime physician, hath frequently told me that the lack and default of bodily exercise is the chief, if not the sole and only cause of the little health and short lives of all the offices of justice. Now, *resolutorie loquendo*, I should say that there is no exercise, sport,

---

[10] From FRANÇOIS RABELAIS, GARGANTUA ET PANTAGRUEL (1533; Urquhart tr. 1653).

game, play, no recreation in all this palatine, palatial, or parliamentary world, more aromatizing and fragrant than to empty and void bags and purses, turn over papers and writings, quote margins and backs of scrolls and rolls, fill panniers, and take inspection of causes, *Ex. Bart et. Joan de Pra. in 1 false. de condit. ed deomonst. ff.*

Thirdly, I consider that time ripeneth and bringeth all things to maturity, that by time everything cometh to be made manifest and patent, and that time is the father of truth and virtue. *Gloss in 1. I. cod. de servit. authent. de restit. et ea quae pa. et spec. tit. de requisit. cons.* Therefore is it that I defer, protract, delay, prolong, intermit, surcease, pause, linger, suspend, prorogate, drive out,wire-draw, and shift off the time of giving a definitive sentence, to the end that the suit or process, being well fanned and winnowed, tossed, and canvassed to and fro, narrowly, precisely, and nearly garbled, sifted, searched, and examined, and on all hands exactly argued, disputed, and debated, may, by succession of time, come at last to its full ripeness and maturity. By means whereof, when the fatal hazard of the dice ensueth thereupon, the parties cast or condemned by the said aleatory chance will with much greater patience, and more mildly and gently, endure and bear up the disastrous load of their misfortune, than if they had been adjudicated at their first arrival unto the court, as *not. gl. ff. de excus. tut. 1 tria. onera.*

8. Richard Posner: Why Judges Write as They Do[11]

Most judicial opinions even in the toughest cases depict the process of reasoning as a logical deduction (syllogistic or enthymematic) from previous decisions or from statutes viewed as transparent sources of rules, and, consistent with the logical form, imply that even the very toughest case has a right and a wrong answer and only a fool

would doubt that the author of the opinion had hit on the right one. This is also the style of much law review commentary. Such a style of writing may seem obviously inconsistent with a skeptical jurisprudence—but is it really? Here is an area where skepticism about skepticism may prevent us from jumping to conclusions prematurely. Maybe the dogmatic style, pretense of humility, and ostentatious abnegation of will that characterizes judicial opinions serve a social purpose. By concealing from the judges themselves the degree to which they exercise discretion, the formalist mode may make them more restrained: virtue begins in hypocrisy (maybe). By pulling the wool over the public's eyes, the pretense of certitude and neutrality may strengthen the political position of the courts in our society, and maybe that is a good thing—or maybe not. The psychology of judging may make it impossible for most judges to take a detached view of their decisions. Maybe law clerks, who today write most judicial opinions, just cannot write any other way. Only one things is clear: We should not be so naive as to infer the nature of the judicial process from the rhetoric of judicial opinions.

9. Lon Fuller: The Bad Man Revisited[12]

Realism starts with an undoubted fact, that it is often possible to formulate rules which more adequately express the motives on which judges act than do the rules "laid down" by the judges themselves.[13] The realists pass over from this undoubted fact to the conclusion that there must exist a sharp line between the rules that judges act on and those they talk about; that there must exist a field which is pure judicial behavior and nothing else. The error is equivalent to supposing that because one can definitely assert that *Point A* is north of *Point B* it must follow

---

[11] Richard A. Posner, *The Jurisprudence of Skepticism*, 86 MICHIGAN LAW REVIEW 827, 865 (1988). Copyright 1988 by The Michigan Law Review Association. Reprinted by permission.

[12] Excerpted from LON L. FULLER, THE LAW IN QUEST OF ITSELF 58-63, 92-95 (1940). Copyright by Northwestern University; used by permission.

[13] Ihering's discussion of this phenomenon of "latent rules," written in 1852, remains, I believe, unsurpassed. 1 GEIST DES ROMISCHEN RECHTS § 3 (7th ed. 1924).

that there exists some dividing line beyond which everything is North and below which everything is South. There is no such thing as a field which consists simply of judicial behavior; it is in fact a greater phantom than Austin's sovereign, which at least had the merit of corresponding to something in the ordinary man's thinking about law.

My basic criticism of legal realism is directed against its positivistic spirit. I do not care how realism defines words, but I am concerned with the way it directs the application of human energies in the law. If we look at the movement in that light, I think we can say that its program has been largely shaped by two, and possibly three, assumptions. First, the realists have assumed that a rigorous separation of *is* and *ought* is possible, and that one may study the law in isolation from its ethical context. Secondly, they have assumed that this separation of *is* and *ought* is something so obviously desirable that it is not necessary to justify the expenditure of human energy needed to achieve it. Thirdly—and here we must depend to a greater degree on inference—they have apparently assumed that nothing worthwhile can be said about the *ought* until after the *is* has been scientifically and exhaustively charted. These assumptions are, in my opinion, false, and to the extent that they have been taken seriously their effects on American legal thinking have been injurious.

Fortunately, they have not always been taken seriously, even by the leaders of the movement. Professor Llewellyn, in particular, has given repeated demonstration of a lively and uninhibited interest in "the ethical side of the law," and one gains the impression that a "rigorous severance of *is* and *ought*" is, even as a theory, becoming every year less evident in his writings. But we must judge a movement not simply in terms of the practices of its ablest exponents, but also in terms of its effects on the main body of those whose activities it touches. Viewed in this aspect, the realist movement seems to me to have continued, and even to have reinforced, the positivistic bent which has restrained legal thinking in this country now for nearly a century. However seriously the realist definition of law may be taken, it has in military parlance created a diversion behind which the positivistic attitude has been able to gain an extension of life. By giving legal positivism an appearance of modernity

and sophistication, the realist movement has made continued adherence to that position intellectually respectable, and has encouraged the natural sloth which clings to positivism as the only way of escaping what the practical lawyer horrendously describes as "philosophy."

Even in the case of its most discerning adherents, it is by no means clear that the realist view has always been lacking in an inhibitive effect. One may cite here the example of the most illustrious realist of them all, Justice Oliver Wendell Holmes. Certainly it cannot be said that the positivism of his early essays was ever completely sloughed off during his career as a judge. One who surveys his contributions to the American common law and compares them with those, let us say, of Cardozo, cannot escape a sense of disappointment. Even his most ardent admirers will have to admit, I believe, that his influence as a judge—at least in the field of private law—fell far short of being commensurate with his general intellectual stature. For him the notion that the law is something severable from one's notions of what it ought to be seems to have had a real and inhibitive meaning. One may admire his fidelity to a faith. But was it for the ultimate good of our law? I think there is reason to doubt it.

For the purpose of drawing a line between law and morality, Holmes suggested that we place ourselves in the position of the bad man, who cares nothing for good and evil or for the praise or blame of his fellows, and who is deterred only by the threat of tangible penalties. By viewing the law through his eyes, we may see it as it really is, washed with cynical acid, and divorced from ethical values. It is a very convincing figure which he offers us, and it makes a working kind of positivism seem quite plausible. Yet it is apparent that this bad man of Holmes is himself an abstraction, in two senses.

In the first place, it will be noted that it is a peculiar sort of bad man who is worried about judicial decrees and is indifferent to extralegal penalties, who is concerned about a fine of two dollars but apparently not about the possible loss of friends and customers. To define the law in terms of the viewpoint of one with this attitude is to some extent a begging of the question, and amounts almost to saying that the law is that which concerns one who is concerned only with the law.

In the second place, Holmes assumes that his bad man has already reached a conclusion concerning the legal risks of a particular line of conduct, and he neglects to inquire into the process by which this man would actually arrive at such a conclusion. Let us see for ourselves how this bad man, faced with a specific problem of conduct, would have to reason. He wants to know what it is likely to cost him to attain a particular objective. Because of the peculiarly juristic orientation of his fears, he will be deterred only by judicial penalties. He must ask himself, then, "What are the chances that my conduct may lead to a detrimental interference in my affairs by the courts?" To answer that, he must ask, "How will my conduct be viewed by judges?" This question he cannot answer merely by consulting the letter of the law, for he will still not know in what direction the letter will strained in cases of doubt. Nor will it be enough for him "to know his judge." Even if the judge who will decide his case has pronounced and recognizable biases, a bias is, after all, only one factor in a complex equation, and to calculate its effects one must analyze the ethical forces with which it will come in conflict. In the end, our bad man cannot escape having to decide a question of morality. He will have to ask, "How would I myself view my conduct if I were not interested in it? How would it be viewed by a disinterested third party? Would it seem to him to be good or evil?" Only when he has answered this question will he have rounded out the equation on the basis of which he can calculate accurately the chances of judicial intervention in his affairs.

In short, our bad man, if he is effectively to look after his own interests, will have to learn to look at the law through the eyes of a good man. To be a good positivist, he will have to become a natural-law lawyer.

10. Karl Llewellyn: The Prediction Theory Works Only for Lawyers[14]

For a counselor at work on counseling,

what the courts *do* is thus the most important part of the law . . . But *judges* (trial judges and appellate) cannot see law that way.

11. H.L.A. Hart: The Prediction Theory Cannot Work for a Judge[15]

If we look closely at the activity of the judge or official who punishes deviations from legal rules, we see that rules are involved in this activity in a way which the predictive account leaves quite unexplained. For the judge, in punishing, takes the rule as his *guide* and the breach of the rule as his *reason* and *justification* for punishing the offender. He does not look upon the rule as a statement that he and others are likely to punish deviations, though a spectator might look upon the rule in just this way. The predictive aspect of the rule (though real enough) is irrelevant to his purposes, whereas its status as a guide and justification is essential. The same is true of informal reproofs administered for the breach of non-legal rules. We say that we reprove or punish a man *because* he has broken the rule; and not merely that it was probable that we would reprove or punish him.

12. Anthony D'Amato: The Prediction Theory Can Work for a Judge[16]

Most people seeking legal advice want the attorney's prediction of what a court (or other official) will do if the client undertakes such-and-such a course of action. The best that the lawyer can do is to state her prediction in percentage terms: "If you do thus-and-so, there's an 80% chance that you'll be sued and you'll lose; however, if you modify your plan in the way that I'll suggest, then your chances of prevailing in any subsequent lawsuit will be close to 90%."

---

[14] Llewellyn, *On Reading and Using the Newer Jurisprudence*, in LLEWELLYN, JURISPRUDENCE: REALISM IN THEORY AND PRACTICE 142 (1962).

[15] H.L.A. HART, THE CONCEPT OF LAW 10-11 (1961).

[16] Based on Anthony D'Amato, *The Limits of Legal Realism*, 87 YALE L.J. 468 (1978).

People make the same predictions for themselves in the absence of lawyers. A driver says, "Assuming there's a police car around that I can't see but is tracking my speed by radar, if I exceed the speed limit by 5 miles per hour, I'm 95% sure they won't arrest me for speeding; if I go 10 miles over the limit, there's probably a 50-50 chance of getting stopped; and if I go 20 miles over the limit, I'm probably taking a 95% chance of getting a ticket."

Predictions of what courts and other officials will do form a pervasive part of every person's everyday life. There are hundreds of actions we refrain from doing each day because we can confidently predict that doing those things will probably lead to our arrest and conviction. Society functions in terms of constant mental predictions of what the probable official reaction will be to various choices that people make all the time.

Judges and other officials know that society functions this way. So long as official behavior is *predictable*, then we will have an ordered and smoothly functioning society. If suddenly official behavior became unpredictable and random, then social chaos and anarchy would rapidly ensue. (There would be no incentive to refrain from shoplifting— for example—if official behavior were so random that you are just as likely to be punished for shoplifting as you would be for *not* shoplifting.) Judges and other officials want a smooth and well functioning society for two reasons. First, they are citizens within the society, so they stand personally to benefit from a system where all official behavior (not just their own) is predictable. Second, a predictable legal system maximizes their own power. For if society were anarchic and chaotic, officials by definition would have no control over it. To be sure, they might still punish individual persons, but if the punishments are random, then no one else's conduct is going to be influenced by the officials' decisions.[17]

A link can thus be established between the officials' decisions and the previous predictions of those decision. To maximize their power, officials will strive to fulfill, as much as possible, the prior expectations of the parties.

Since judges are aware of the role played by attorneys in predicting judicial behavior to clients, then if my preceding arguments are accepted, it follows that a judge will attempt to reinforce the attorney's prediction of the judge's own decision. The judge can reconstruct the attorney's advice by putting himself in the attorney's position at the time the attorney met with her client, and simply saying to himself, "What prediction would I have made at that time as attorney to this client? I assume that all I would know would be what any attorney might know at that time—the client's plan of action, the state of the common law and statutory law at that time, and how judges in general—because I don't know what particular judge might wind up handling their case—might view the client's action in light of the then existing case and statutory law."[18]

What if the attorney in fact made a legal blunder—for example, she forgot to shepardize one of her main authorities, and if she had done so she would have found that the case she was relying upon had been reversed on appeal? Should the judge put himself in the position of *that* attorney, and say, in effect, that he must fulfill her prediction of what courts would decide even though her prediction was quite erroneous? Clearly not. If the attorney's prediction was wrong because the attorney made a legal blunder, then even if the client acted in good faith on that advice, the court should not reinforce the blunder by building it in to the court's own decision. The reason, within legal realism, is quite obvious. The judge is entitled to assume that most attorneys, advising most

---

[17] In short, it is not in the judge's self-interest to behave in the self-defeating ways that Rex—Lon Fuller's fictional lawmaker—behaved. Rex simply failed to control the behavior of his own subjects by acting in eight different ways that frustrated his subjects' ability to predict how he (and his fellow officials) would judge their actions. [Fuller's discussion was presented in Chapter 3, *supra*.]

[18] I am not claiming that judges go through this reasoning process consciously. Indeed, many judges may do it instinctively, without being aware of it. But whether they do it consciously, or instinctively, or not at all, my claim is that the reasoning process I am advocating is a coherent one, that it removes Hart's apparent paradox of the self-fulfillment of predictions of judicial behavior.

clients, will properly do their homework, which includes shepardizing cases. So *most* social interactions will proceed on the basis of attorneys' predictions that are correctly built upon case-law expectations. The fact that this particular attorney failed to shepardize the case she was relying upon is simply an aberration. It is not the judge's job, after all, to fulfill the particular expectations of the particular parties to a case; rather, it is the judge's job to maximize social order by fulfilling the expectable past predictions of most attorneys giving advice to most clients.

An extension of this reasoning—from attorneys to judges themselves—will demonstrate the inapplicability of Professor Hart's paradox of the judge who does not (and presumably cannot) predict his own decisions. Professor Hart's paradox works, if at all, only in the following limited situation. Suppose Judge Bridlegoose is the only judge in his jurisdiction; he gets every case that comes up, and there is no appellate court (and no Supreme Court). Lawyers in that jurisdiction will make predictions to clients about how Judge Bridlegoose would probably decide their cases. Then, when some of those cases reach Judge Bridlegoose, he is faced with Hart's paradox: how can he decide the case by predicting what he himself would decide? Wouldn't such a prediction involve an infinite regress (he must predict how he would predict if he were predicting how he would predict, etc.)?

Let us take a brief detour from the unusual case of Judge Bridlegoose and consider the normal situation where there are several (or many) judges in a jurisdiction and their case load is assigned randomly. Attorneys who give advice to clients will then be faced with the job of predicting how any judge—chosen at random—might decide a particular case or fact situation. The attorney's mental picture of the judge who will decide a given case becomes a composite picture. This composite picture is made up of what the attorney generally knows about judges in her jurisdiction. And what she generally knows about them is their typical way of deciding cases in her jurisdiction—knowledge that can be obtained by reading their opinions, reading statutes and guessing how judges will respond to the application of

those statutes to the client's fact situation, and so on. In other words, the attorney is doing the law job that is typical of her profession. Her prediction of how "a judge" will behave is based on a lifetime of experience in estimating how a fact situation will "play out" if it is litigated.

Thus, when a case comes before a judge in that jurisdiction, the judge will know that the attorneys used a composite picture in making their predictions about how any judge would decide the case. The judge then uses that composite picture (of which he himself is only a small and indistinguishable element) in retrospectively engaging in the same prediction that the attorney made— *i.e.*, on those facts at the time they occurred, what would an attorney have estimated were the chances of winning the case given the legal materials (statutes, cases, etc.) that were in existence at that time? There is no paradox of self-prediction involved here, because the judge will make the retrospective prediction using as a model the composite picture of a judge. In short, the judge decides the case the way *a judge*—any judge within the jurisdiction assigned at random to the case—would decide the case.

Now we can return to Judge Bridlegoose. He does not have available a composite picture of judges, because he is the only judge in the jurisdiction. So, when he looks at the picture of "a judge" in his jurisdiction, he is looking at a picture of himself. Yet I contend there are two ways of resolving Hart's paradox of self-prediction. The first is for Judge Bridlegoose to picture an "average judge," and not to picture himself. This means, of course, that Judge Bridlegoose, in his decisions, will have to decide cases the way an average judge would decide them, omitting his personal idiosyncrasies and prejudices. This may be hard to do, but to the extent that Judge Bridlegoose succeeds in removing his own personal proclivities from his decisional processes, the more his picture of an "average judge" will become the picture that attorneys in his jurisdiction use to predict how he will decide cases. In short, the more that Judge Bridlegoose behaves like an average (faceless) judge, the more that lawyers will base their predictions on the expected behavior of "a judge."

But let us now suppose that Judge Bridlegoose insists on using his own portrait; he does not want to picture the "average judge" but rather wants to picture himself. After all, he says, echoing Gilbert and Sullivan, "I am the true embodiment of the law." Nevertheless, Hart's paradox can be resolved if Judge Bridlegoose chooses the right *time* that his picture was taken. He should regard his picture as having been taken at the time the events occurred that gave rise to the litigation in the case before him. Let's say that those events occurred a year ago. A year ago, the attorney, attempting to predict what Judge Bridlegoose would decide, constructed her mental picture of the judge on the basis of all the public facts that were known about the judge at that time, including everything he had said in his judicial opinions. If Judge Bridlegoose wants to maximize public order and his own power as a judge (which I argued above are the reasons why judges want to be predictable in their decision-making), he has to use as his retrospective picture of the judge the portrait of himself that could have been fashioned by a good attorney out of publicly available materials a year ago. To the extent that Judge Bridlegoose chooses *not* to do this—for example, by injecting into the case certain personal prejudices that he now has that he didn't have a year ago, or injecting into the case prejudices that he may have had a year ago but were secret at that time and known only to himself—then to that extent Judge Bridlegoose has injected a random and unpredictable element into his lawmaking. Since this would be self-defeating,[19] it would not be in Judge Bridlegoose's interest to inject these publicly unknowable elements into

this decision. In brief, if he insists on using his own picture (instead of the picture of an "average judge"), then it should be a picture that could have been taken of him based on public materials that were available to the attorney a year ago when the facts of her case arose.

Let me suggest a minor and a major conclusion to this exercise. The minor conclusion is that Hart's paradox of the self-predicting judge is not an impediment to Holmes' observation[20] that law means "the prophecies of what courts will do in fact."[21] The major conclusion—stimulated by Professor Hart's challenge—is a critique of those legal realists who say that *any* influence on a judge, and *any* personal idiosyncrasies and biases of a judge, are a realistic part of what goes into a lawyer's prediction of how a judge will behave. Under their view, what a judge had for breakfast—or other secret and personal biases and prejudices—may be relevant to predicting how he will decide a case. What I am suggesting here, especially as we analyze the legal realists' easiest case (a single judge in a jurisdiction), is that judges have an interest in consciously departing from personal idiosyncrasies as they attempt to fulfill the public's predictions of judicial behavior. In retrospectively reconstructing those predictions, the judges use a composite picture of a judge or a picture of an "average" judge instead of pictures of themselves, or their own picture as the public saw it at the time the cause of action arose.

---

[19] As Fuller has in general pointed out; *see* footnote 17.

[20] Holmes' observation was not original with Holmes; he derived it from several nineteenth century German jurists whose works for the most part had not been translated into English at the time (1897) that Holmes wrote THE PATH OF THE LAW.

[21] *See* the opening excerpt in this Chapter.

QUESTIONS AND COMMENTS FOR YOUR CONSIDERATION

1. In addition to Hart's paradox, another apparent paradox stemming from the prediction theory of law was one that I suggested in 1978.[22] It is that "the law" that applies to any person at any point in time can be different depending on which attorney the person consults. Suppose something happens to you and you want to sue the person who is responsible. Or suppose that did something (or failed to do something) and someone threatens to sue you. You go to Attorney A, explain the facts of the case, and ask, "What are my chances of winning if this is litigated?" Attorney A responds "Sixty percent." Assume this is an absolutely accurate statement, representing Attorney A's precise degree of confidence in what will happen.[23]

Now you go to Attorney B and she says, "Seventy-five percent." You have every reason to believe that she, too, has given you a precisely accurate statement of her degree of confidence in what will happen if the case is litigated.

Has "the law" changed? Isn't it true that the only thing that has changed is your choice of attorney? Law students, in particular, seem to want to believe that the law itself is not changed, that as between Attorney A and Attorney B one is "right" and one is "wrong" in stating the odds of whether you will win if the case goes to litigation. What do you think?

2. Let us look further into Question 1. How can both attorneys be precisely right? Suppose Attorney A has some familiarity, but not too much, with cases of your type. Suppose Attorney B is an expert in the area of law involved in your case. Assuming that both are being totally honest with you, isn't it possible that if you put the case in Attorney A's hands he will in fact have a 60% chance of winning, given his degree of familiarity with your kind of case? Moreover, isn't it possible that Attorney B would in fact have a 75% chance of winning because this case is within her expertise and therefore she in fact has a better chance of winning for you?

If you admit these possibilities, then what is the point of insisting on an objective reality for law? How would we ever know what that objective reality is? All we know about law is how it is *perceived* by people who study it and work within it, people like lawyers. Different lawyers will see it in different ways, not necessarily because some have clear vision and some don't, but often because they have equal clarity of vision and an equal ability to factor in their own differential advocacy into their prediction of what the result of a particular case will be.

Consider the famous Rorschach ink-blot test. Two patients are shown the same ink-blot; Patient A sees a Medusa figure, Patient B sees a scorpion. We ask the psychiatrist what it "really" is, and she says, "nothing but an ink blot." Who is "right"?

Law in one sense is a lot of marks of ink on lots of pieces of paper. What people

---

[22] Anthony D'Amato, *The Limits of Legal Realism*, 87 YALE L.J. 468 (1978).

[23] The term for a person's probability assessment of a one-time (unique) occurrence obviously cannot be based on long-run probabilistic calculations. Instead, it is a measure of the person's *degree of confidence* in the prediction. The technical term for degree of confidence is "subjective probability," as explained in the article just cited.

"see" in these marks may depend on many factors, but we can be fairly sure that no two people see exactly the same thing. Recall how many vehemous dissents you read in appellate court opinions. If the "law" meant the same thing to everyone, how could two judges sitting on the same bench and hearing the same presentation come out with diametrically opposite conclusions as to the law?

Should we conclude that law is, after all, relative to the observer? This is a hard conclusion to reach for students of the law (not just law students but many professors who write about the law). But doesn't the public reach that conclusion all the time? How often have you heard street-talk to the effect, "if you get in trouble with the law, hire the best lawyer you can afford"? Why not hire the cheapest lawyer? Is there a pervasive public perception that the law that you get is, to some extent, the law you're willing to pay for? Or is this conclusion absolutely intolerable to students of the law?

3. What are the implications of the preceding two questions for the practicing lawyer? Might lawyers try to attract more clients by jacking up the percentage of their predictions? If so, should the Bar Association Ethics Committee monitor these conversations between lawyers and clients? Or should the matter be left to the marketplace? Is it surprising that the better the attorney, the more likely the attorney will be absolutely candid in presenting the odds of winning if a case goes to litigation? Is it surprising that "hustler" attorneys who may charge "bargain basement rates" seem to be less candid? How often do the latter tell clients, "No problem! Leave it to me and your worries are over. Just make out the retainer check."[24] If these questions are *not* surprising, what market forces are in play that account for this disparity in attorney behavior?

4. What are the implications of the prediction theory for the assignment of judges to cases? Is it critically important for achieving justice and predictability that, within all jurisdictions, the assignment of judges to handle particular cases should be conducted randomly?

5. A *New Yorker* cartoon showed two judges walking down the courthouse steps. One says to the other: "Some days when I'm feeling rotten I give 'em ten years. Other days when I'm feeling good I give 'em six months for the exact same crime. I figure, it all averages out."

What implications for legal relativity? For legal realism?

6. Critics of legal realism have attempted to characterize it by the following epithet: "The state of a judge's digestion is just as important as the state of the law." Important to whom?

7. What is your assessment of the following (fanciful) attorney's argument made in court:

"Your honor, the waitress in the coffee shop where you have your breakfast each morning has kindly provided us with the records of your orders over the past three years. We have correlated them with the sentences you have handed down during the same period of time. Our statisticians tell us that, within a 95% confidence level, whenever you've had a side order of ham your sentences that

---

[24] A cartoon depicts a lawyer phoning the client the court's decision. "I've got bad news and good news. The bad news is that you got twenty years. The good news is that I'm going to lunch."

day average six months, but when you've had a side order of sausage your sentences that day average ten years. We are happy to remind your honor that this morning you had ham with your breakfast. Our client has pleaded guilty, and we ask your honor to impose a sentence of not more than six months."

Does this (fanciful) argument constitute a refutation of legal realism in whole or in part?

8. Before you draw too many fixed conclusions from Question 7, consider the following variation. It is invented on the basis of a remark made to the editor by a Chicago attorney, who said that in a certain town in downstate Illinois, the judges invariably decide against litigants who are represented by "those high-falutin' attorneys from Chicago."

Suppose you are a Chicago attorney and your client is facing a misdemeanor charge in that downstate town. You advise your client to get a local attorney, telling him that Chicago attorneys always lose in that town. He says, "No, I want you to represent me. Those people down there, attorneys and judges, are against me anyway, and I have confidence in you, so go down there and I know you'll do your best and I won't hold it against you if you lose."

What can you do? Consider the following (fanciful) argument:

"Your honor, my client is from Chicago and was arrested down here for something he didn't do, and I'd like to defend him. I practice law in Chicago. Now, before going into the evidence in this case, I'd like to point out something relevant. I have done a survey of all the cases decided in this town in the past three years, and out of that list I have noted all the cases in which one side was represented by an attorney from Chicago and the other side was represented by a local attorney. In some of these cases the Chicago attorney represented the plaintiff, in others the Chicago attorney represented the defendant. The total is 217. In each and every one of these 217 cases, the decision was awarded to the party who was represented by a local attorney. I have asked an expert in statistics to determine the odds that in 217 cases the most legally meritorious side would correlate exactly with the home base of that side's attorney. The statistician tells me—and I have a copy of her report that I will place on the public record of this case—that the odds against this happening fairly are over one hundred trillion to one. In other words, your honor, the pattern here amounts to an unconstitutional denial of justice to at least some meritorious persons who are represented by Chicago attorneys.

"In proceeding with this case, I ask you to take this pattern of decision-making into consideration. I have every confidence that now that this pattern has been brought to your attention, my client's evidence will be heard fairly and impartially according to the dictates of justice."

Does this (fanciful) argument constitute a vindication of legal realism in whole or in part?

9. What are the relevant jurisprudential differences between the situations suggested in Question 7 and Question 8?

B. Easy Cases

1. Frederick Schauer: Easy Cases Are Unlitigated Cases[25]

There are no easy cases in the Supreme Court. If the case were that easy, *certiorari* would have been denied, the appeal would have been dismissed for want of a substantial federal question, or a clearly erroneous result below would have been overturned summarily. In most cases, therefore, the very presence of a full Supreme Court opinion indicates that the case was considered at least slightly difficult for some reason. From this vantage point, it appears that the Supreme Court, far from being the first place to look for easy cases, ought to be the last place.

If one looks at the federal and state appellate courts instead of looking at the Supreme Court, the situation appears rather different. In these courts, at least with respect to appeals of right, no screening mechanism ensures that the time and energy of the judiciary is not wasted on restating the obvious. In appeals as of right, therefore, there are many cases that would be perceived by the court involved, the academic world, other external observers—indeed by everyone except the appellant—as easy. In these instances, claims are either upheld or denied on the basis of little more than mechanical application of existing rules with little anguish on the part of the court.

The previous paragraph presupposes that there *is* such a thing as an easy case in an appellate court. It assumes that there are at least some cases in which the result flows almost inexorably from a relatively straightforward application of plainly applicable and identifiable legal rules contained in easily located preexisting legal materials. The claim, however, is exactly what the Realists deny. In its more extreme versions, Realism would maintain that sufficient precedents, some conflicting and many intersecting at various angles, exist so that an appellate judge can rationalize from precedent or written law a result conceived prior to consulta-

tion of that precedent or law. Under this view, a judge's own moral, political, psychological, Oedipal, or intestinal predilections determine the result. The judge only constructs a *post hoc* legal justification for the nonlegally derived result in order not to affront the accepted myths of society, including the myth of the rule of law.

As will shortly become apparent, I believe this view to be an accurate description of *some* judicial decisions, and maybe even *many* judicial decisions. To take this view as an accurate generalization of *all* or of even *most* judicial decisions, however, seems at least erroneous and at times preposterous. But at this particular point I do not want to get bogged down in my differences with the Realists. For the time being, therefore, I am willing to concede that the Realists are correct. I will concede that there are few, if any, easy cases in any appellate court.

Are there, then, easy cases in the trial courts? In terms of cases that reach trial and decision, there are probably very few. Indeed, easy cases are most likely less prevalent in trial courts than in appellate courts.[26]

---

[26] *Editor's Note*: Does this statement of Professor Schauer's strike you as incoherent? Consider a case which at the trial level is an "easy case" (according to whatever definition you want to apply to the word "easy"). If these easy cases are appealed, they should remain "easy" on appeal. And if more of these easy cases are appealed than the "hard" cases at the trial level, then there might very well be a preponderance of "easy" cases at the appellate level than at the trial level. But this is a very strange assumption—that the easy cases will be successfully appealed, while the hard cases will not. The idea conflicts with common sense. We might well expect more of the "hard" cases to be appealed that the "easy" cases. If that is so, how can Professor Schauer say that the easy cases are most likely more prevalent at the appellate level?

Note Professor Schauer's next two sentences. He seems to be saying that once a "hard" case at the trial level is stripped down of its many indeterminate issues, and then appealed, it may appear to the appellate court to be "easy." This indeed seems to be a straightforward proposition. But note what appears to have happened. If the case of *Jones v. Smith* at the trial level is a "hard" case, but on appeal (because its issues have been stripped down) it seems "easy," then Professor Schauer is suggesting that the "case" is "easy" at the appellate level. But this only makes sense if he has split the case of *Jones v. Smith* into two cases—a trial case and an appellate case. Yet why

---

[25] Excerpted from Frederick Schauer, *Easy Cases*, 58 SOUTHERN CALIFORNIA LAW REVIEW 399, 409-14 (1985). Copyright 1985 by the University of Southern California. Reprinted by permission.

The appellate process narrows the issues, but, since trials take place prior to this narrowing, they raise a substantially larger number of factual and legal issues. And as the number of issues increases, the potential justifications for making a decision one way or another also increase, thus making it more difficult to designate as "easy" any final trial court decision.

Despite this potential to claim that there are fewer "easy" cases at the trial court level, there is reason to believe this hypothesis is suspect. Few cases that are filed reach final decision after a full evidentiary hearing. Many are settled, and many others are decided by the various devices designed to sort out the hard cases from the easy ones, particularly summary judgment and dismissals on the pleadings. Nevertheless, one can hew to the Realist line with respect to pretrial determinations. To Jerome Frank,[27] for example, the injection of contested factual issues at any point in the trial process was sufficient to make uncertain the results in almost every case that in some way wound up in court.

Again, I do not want my argument to turn at this point on my disagreements with Realism. So let me make another concession, one that is rather broader than the previous one: I will concede that there are few if any easy cases anywhere in the litigation process, and that any case filed in a court is capable of being decided one way or another relatively unconstrained by precedent or written law.

---

would anyone want to split the same case into two cases? If we insist that *Jones v. Smith* is the same case, whether at the trial level or on appeal—and this is a most reasonable insistence—then it doesn't magically become transformed from a hard case at trial to an easy case on appeal. Rather, we ought to conclude that the stripping-down process (that made the case appear easy to the appellate judges) was itself a distortion of the real rights of the parties. If *Jones v. Smith* is a hard case to begin with, no number of appellate courts can transform it into an easy case. It remains "hard." The only thing that has changed, apparently, is that the appellate courts erroneously think that the stripped down case is "easy."

[27] I am referring here primarily to Frank's "fact-skepticism." *See* JEROME FRANK, COURTS ON TRIAL (1949).

Despite this broad concession, I still believe that there are many easy cases, but we can see this only by removing the blinkers of much of traditional legal theory. To many, the analysis of easy cases ends with the litigation process, ignoring the huge number of "cases" that never leave the lawyer's office. In a strict sense these matters are not "cases" if a "case" is restricted to mean a matter that is filed in a court. These are, however, matters in which someone has found it desirable to take legal advice, and thus it seems as if the law is at least presumptively relevant. Some of such matters will ripen into real "cases," and we can assume, arguendo, that most will be in some sense hard cases. Nevertheless, there are many circumstances that may involve an actual or potential dispute, and may therefore occasion a visit to the lawyer, but may never reach the courthouse. Every time some claimed grievance stays in the lawyer's office because litigation seems futile, we have an easy case.

In addition to matters involving actual or potential disputes, there are also instances in which a transaction is arranged, a course of action planned, or a recommendation given on the basis of what the law requires or prohibits, in the absence of a dispute or grievance. Sometimes the law governing such matters is unclear, and thus the advice may resemble the decision of a hard case. In many other cases, however, a lawyer's advice is likely to be a product of legal mandates that are largely unequivocal.

It is not always the case that the law, however clear, will be followed in those instances in which planning rather than resolution of preexisting grievances or disputes is involved. For example, a transaction may be so important that one or more of the participants is willing to assume the risk of inconsistency with the law. Here the transaction is likely to be designed with one eye on litigation strategy, or on minimizing the chances of apprehension by the authorities. More commonly, however, transactions can be designed more flexibly. The aim is frequently to avoid any legal difficulties—to create, in a sense, the easy case.

Although there are many instances in which uncertainty about a proposed course of conduct prompts a person to follow legal advice, the quantity of such instances, however large, is dwarfed by the number of times that the law guides behavior without any intervention whatsoever by lawyers, judges, or police officers. Every time I stop at a "STOP" sign, pay my taxes on or before April 15, file a conflict of interest disclosure form with my state employer, or refrain from watering my lawn because of drought control regulations, I am, solely because of legal mandate, doing something I would not otherwise have done. In each of these instances, the divergence between the behavior that would have occurred but for the law and the behavior that occurred because of the law can be called a "legal event," although hardly as visible or famous as a hard case that reaches an appellate court. There is, nevertheless, no reason to consider following the law less important than breaking the law, or less important than playing close to the line. All are very much part of the law. It is only because of the frequency with which the law is followed that the significance of this commonplace phenomenon is ignored. Following the law is a legal event, and the vast majority of *these* legal events are easy cases.

Once we expand our notion of a "case" to include all legal events, it becomes clear that there *are* easy cases in constitutional law— lots of them. The parties know, without litigating and without consulting lawyers . . . that a twenty-nine year old is not going to be President of the United States.

The conventional response to the foregoing argument is what I call "the argument from weird cases." This response provides an unclear application of any example of linguistic clarity, and is a standard, if confused, weapon in the lawyer's argumentative arsenal. For example, in response to any number of provisions relating to years and dates, it is possible to imagine an intervening change in the calendar. Ever since Macbeth mistakenly relied on the linguistic precision of the witches' prophesy, people have been able to construct weird and fanciful instances in which even the clearest language breaks down.

The easy answer to the argument from weird cases is the observation that the weird hypothetical cases are wildly counterfactual. The calendar is unlikely to be changed, and people who are born while crossing the International Date Line, or on February 29, are unlikely to ascend to offices for which the inauguration day is the disputed day in the year of their minimum eligibility.[28]

The easy answer would be quite appealing but for the fact that real life is often every bit as counterfactual as the wildest imaginings of the most creative, imaginative, or demented law professor. Although it is surely fund to make up weird cases, such an exercise is hardly necessary to demonstrate that no constitutional provision can be presumed to be so unequivocal as to preclude any possibility of a disputed application.

2. Anthony D'Amato: Unlitigated Cases May Not Be Easy[29]

No responsible attorney would ever advise her client that if the client chooses to file a lawsuit there is a 100% chance of winning. For there is always some uncertainty in any prediction about a decision that a human being will make. No matter how clear the "law" on the client's side of the case appears to be, a judge might be persuaded to make an exception in favor of the defendant. Or the judge may find that the law is not as clear as the plaintiff thinks.

By the same token, any lawyer will agree that some cases are easier to win than other cases. There is surely a discernible difference between an "easier" and a "harder" case.[30] But no case is so "easy" that its result

---

[28] *Editor's Note: See* the discussion in Chapter 6 on the Constitutional provision that a person must have attained the age of 35 to be eligible for the office of President.

[29] Based on Anthony D'Amato, *Aspects of Deconstruction: Refuting Indeterminacy With One Bold Thought*, 85 Nw. U. L. Rev. 113 (1990); Anthony D'Amato, *Aspects of Deconstruction: The Failure of the Word 'Bird,'* 84 Nw. U. L. Rev. 536 (1990); Anthony D'Amato, *Aspects of Deconstruction: The 'Easy Case' of the Under-aged President*, 84 Nw. U. L. Rev. 250 (1990); *and* Anthony D'Amato, *Pragmatic Indeterminacy*, 85 Nw. U. L. Rev. 148 (1990).

[30] Thus Steven Burton rightly uses the terms "easier cases" and "harder cases" instead of the more problematic terms "easy case" and "hard case." Steven J. Burton, An Introduction to Law and Legal Reasoning 125 (1985).

can be predicted with certainty.[31]

Frederick Schauer draws a distinction between a legal case and a legal event. When rules are introduced in cases (which include all litigation, whether at the trial or appellate levels), Professor Schauer concedes the force of the Realist position that one can never be 100% certain how a judge (or jury) will apply (or not apply) the rule. But when rules are not the subject of litigation, yet guide our conduct, Professor Schauer calls them "legal events." Thus, when I stop my car at a red light, I am engaging in the legal event of applying a rule ("stop at the red signal") to my own behavior. As to legal events, Professor Schauer argues that for most of them there is no doubt whatsoever about the applicability of the rule.

As I read Professor Schauer, he appears to be saying that if in the course of an everyday legal event I apply Rule X, I can be certain about its clear application. But if I choose to litigate, then uncertainty appears. Yet why should uncertainty suddenly appear simply because I have chosen to litigate? After all, the facts remain the same. And the rule (Rule X) remains the same. I fail to see any logical reason why Rule X clearly applies to event E so long as it is not litigated, but does not clearly apply to event E when someone wishes to litigate its applicability.

Suppose event E is: a police officer stops me for speeding and gives me a ticket. If I decide to pay my fine and plead guilty, does that mean that the speeding rule clearly applies to my driving, whereas if I decide to contest the case in court the speeding rule suddenly does not clearly apply to my driving? Surely my mental decision whether or not to litigate cannot change the ontological status of the event and the rule.

The problem with Professor Schauer's thesis goes even deeper than that. How does he *know* that uncontested legal events are examples of clear application of rules? These are, after all, unrecorded legal events. It's

---

[31] The term "easy case" in jurisprudence appears to have been invented by H.L.A. HART. THE CONCEPT OF LAW 119-50 (1961). (Of course, the expression "easy case" was in common usage long before Hart employed it in a jurisprudential context.)

like saying "the most beautiful music in the world has never been composed," or "if Shakespeare had lived five more years he would have written his best play."

People can simply be *wrong* in "applying" legal rules to everyday legal events. Professor Schauer says that every time he stops at a STOP sign he is responding to a legal rule. Every time? Suppose you are driving down a narrow street and an ambulance drives up behind you, its siren blaring. You come to the corner and there is a STOP sign. Do you stop or do you drive through and get out of the way of the ambulance?

We cannot *prove* that an "easy legal event" exists. We may think along with Professor Schauer that many such easy events exist, but what criteria of proof do we have? We might be *wrong* about the legal rule; we may think we're following the rule, but unbeknownst to us, the rule was repealed yesterday or the case that announced the rule was overruled or the rule is an inaccurate statement of our legal obligation or the rule never existed but "folk wisdom" said it existed, and so forth. Moreover, we might be wrong about believing that our own conduct is in conformity with the rule. Thus "legal events" in Professor Schauer's definition are instances of (purported) rule-following that are never *verified* by submission to a court. So even if we think that we are unproblematically following a rule, neither we nor anyone else can ever prove that we are indeed following that rule. Yet, as soon as we try to *verify* a legal event in court, the problematics of the trial process set in and Professor Schauer concedes that the case is not easy.

The lesson that we should draw is *not* that all rules are indeterminate, that rules of law do not matter, that "anything goes," that nihilism shall from now on reign supreme in the world of American jurisprudence. Charges of this type, which have indeed been seriously proposed in various law review articles, seriously misconstrue the purpose of those writers who, like myself, believe in the possibility of deconstruction of written formulas. Our position is not nihilistic but rather it is rather modest. We think that the idea of language that "locks on" to reality should be abandoned—it presents a very false sense of security. Neither the world of language or the microscopic world of atomic physics is capable of certainty. To say that the law *is* a certain rule or principle is to sional procedure, an institutional process, which takes into account various rules and principles—indeed, which tries to give them the greatest possible weight in the determination of results—but it is not a procedure which is exempt from human or mechanical error, misperception, misjudgment, or unanticipated changes in context.

C. The Judge's Perspective

1. Richard Posner: The Judicial Reasoning Process[32]

The first step in deciding a tough antitrust case, a case not controlled by precedent, is to extract (not—it goes without saying—by a deductive process), from the relevant legislative texts and history, from the institutional characteristics of courts and legislatures, and, lacking definitive guidance from these sources, from a social vision as well, an overall concept of antitrust law to guide decision. A popular candidate for such a concept today is the economic concept of wealth maximization, but it is, needless to say, a contestable choice. Having made this choice (the current Supreme Court has almost, but not quite, made the choice for

him), the judge will then want to canvass the relevant precedents, and other sources, for information that might help in deciding the case at hand. This is step two. Step three is a policy judgment (in some cases it might approximate a logical deduction) resolving the case in accordance with the principles of wealth maximization. Step four returns to the precedents, but now viewed as authorities rather than merely as data; the judge will want to make sure that the policy judgment made in step three is not ruled out by authoritative precedent. Actually this is the third rather than the second time that the judge will have consulted precedents, since they must be consulted at the outset to determine whether the case is indeed in the open areas; if not, the four-step analysis that I have described is pretermitted.

The suggested approach describes, I believe, the actual (though often implicit) reasoning process that good judges use in the tough cases. It also recasts legal analysis in those cases as a form of policy analysis, with legal materials being used only for help in setting an initial orientation and in providing specific data, and later as a source of possible constraints. Such analysis is not arbitrary, but often it merely forecloses certain outcomes rather than generating a unique one.

QUESTIONS AND COMMENTS FOR YOUR CONSIDERATION

1. American legal realism, which seemed to have run its course as a movement by 1960, got its second wind with the advent of the movement that called itself "critical legal studies" in the 1980s. The crits made assertions like "legal argumentation disguises its own inherent indeterminacy,"[33] "rules are the opiate of the masses,"[34] "interpretation is transformation,"[35] and "legal discourse paints an idealized fantasy of order."[36] Are these assertions tantamount to pouring old (legal realist) wine in new bottles with fancy new labels?

2. With one possible exception, the crits do not seem to have made new discoveries in analytic jurisprudence. The exception is the crits' emphasis on

---

[32] Richard A. Posner, *The Jurisprudence of Skepticism*, 86 MICHIGAN LAW REVIEW 827, 863 (1988). Copyright 1988 by The Michigan Law Review Association. Reprinted by permission.

[33] Clare Dalton, *An Essay in the Deconstruction of Contract Doctrine*, 94 YALE L.J. 997, 1007 (1985).

[34] MARK KELMAN, A GUIDE TO CRITICAL LEGAL STUDIES 63 (1987).

[35] Drucilla Cornell, *From the Lighthouse: The Promise of Redemption and the Possibility of Legal Interpretation*, 11 CARDOZO L. REV. 1687 (1990).

[36] Robert Gordon, *Unfreezing Legal Reality: Critical Approaches to Law*, 15 FLA. ST. U.L. REV. 195, 198 (1987).

politics. Although the legal realists had talked about "officials" in their view of law as a prediction of what officials do, for the most part the legal realists focused on just one class of officials—judges. The crits have emphasized that studying the entire legal hierarchy of the state—not just the judiciary—is critical to the work of a lawyer.[37] The crits have reminded law professors that the larger picture—the state in its entire political-legal hierarchy—has to be part of the very conception of "law" that law students should study in law school. Do you agree?

3. Ironically, one of the lasting contributions made by a critical legal scholar deals not with the political hierarchy, but rather focuses on judicial decision-making. It is the following contribution by Duncan Kennedy, a leading crit. He says, "I think of this exercise as an extension of the legal realist project."[38]

2. Duncan Kennedy: Imagining a Judge's Reasoning Process[39]

This paper attempts to describe the process of legal reasoning as I imagine I might do it if I were a judge assigned a case that initially seemed to present a conflict between "the law" and "how-I-want-to-come-out." The judge is a federal district court judge in Boston. Suppose there is a strike of union bus drivers going on in Boston. The company hires nonunion drivers and sets out to resume service. On the first day union members lie down in the street outside the bus station to prevent the buses from passing. They do not disturb the general flow of traffic, and they are nonviolent. The local police arrest them and cart them off, but this takes hours. They are charged with disturbing the peace and obstructing a public way (misdemeanors) and released on light bail. The next day other union members obstruct, with similar results. The buses run, but only late and amid a chaotic jumble. The company goes into federal court for an injunction against the union tactic.

When I first think about this case, not being a labor law expert, but having some general knowledge, I think, "There is no way they will be able to get away with this. The rule of law is going to be that workers cannot prevent the employer from making use of the buses during the strike. The company will get its injunction."

I disagree with this imagined rule. I don't think management should be allowed to operate the means of production [m.o.p.] with substitute labor during a strike. I think there should be a rule that until the dispute has been resolved, neither side can operate the m.o.p. without the permission of the other (barring various kinds of extraordinary circumstances). This view is part of a general preference for transforming the current modes of American economic life in a direction of greater worker self-activity, worker control and management of enterprise, in a decentralized setting that blurs the lines between "owner" and "worker," and "public" and "private" enterprise.

My feeling that the law is against me in this case is a quick intuition about the way things have to be. I haven't actually read any cases or articles that describe what the employer can and can't do with the m.o.p. during a strike.

If there is a rule that the employer can do what he wants with the m.o.p., I think it will probably turn out to be true that there is relief in federal court (under the rubric of unfair labor practices?). If relief is available, I have a strong feeling that the workers threaten irreparable injury to the employer, so that he can show the various things usually required to justify an injunction. But I also vaguely remember that federal courts

---

[37] Lawyers, of course, have always recognized this factor. A good lawyer does not simply advise a client about what judges might do; rather, she gives additional advice about other avenues of relief, such as appealing to various administrative agencies or asking for special legislative relief.

[38] Duncan Kennedy, *Freedom and Constraint in Adjudication: A Critical Phenomenology*, 36 J. LEG. EDUC. 518 n. 1 (1986).

[39] Duncan Kennedy, "Freedom and Constraint in Adjudication: A Critical Phenomenology," 36 Journal of Legal Education 518-62 (1986). Excerpts reprinted by permission.

aren't supposed to issue injunctions in labor disputes.

There is lots of uncertainty here. I am not sure that a federal district court has jurisdiction under the labor law statutes to intervene on the employer's behalf when the local authorities are already enforcing the local general law about obstructing public ways. I am not sure that if there is a basis for federal intervention, an injunction is appropriate. I will have to look into all these things before I'm at all sure how this case will or should come out.

On the other hand, I am quite sure the employer can use the m.o.p. as he pleases. And I am quite, quite sure that if there is such a rule, then the workers have violated it here. I am sure that what I mean by the rule is that the employer has both a privilege to act and a right to protection against interference, and that what the workers did here *was* interference.

Since the supposed rule of law that I don't like won't get applied so as to lead to an injunction unless all the uncertainties are resolved against the workers, I do not yet confront a direct conflict between the law and how-I-want-to-come-out. But I already have the feeling of "the law" as a constraint on me. It's time to ask what that means.

The initial apparent objectivity of the objectionable rule. I use the word objectivity here to indicate that from my point of view the *application of the rule to this case* feels like a nondiscretionary, necessary, compulsory procedure. I can no more deny that, if there is such a rule, the workers have violated it, than I can deny that I am at this minute in Cambridge, Massachusetts, sitting on a chair, using a machine called a typewriter. The rule just applies itself. What I *meant* by interfering with the owner's use of the m.o.p. was workers lying down in the street when the employer tries to drive the buses out to resume service during the strike. I'm sure from the description that the workers actually intended to do exactly what the rule says they have no right to do.

Note that this sense of objectivity is internal—it's what happens in my head. But the minute I begin to think about the potential conflict between the law and how-I-want-to-come-out a quite different question will arise. How will other people see this case,

supposing that the preliminary hurdles are overcome?

Sometimes it will seem to me that everyone (within the relevant universe) will react to this case as one to which the rule applies. I imagine them going through the same process I did, and it is instantly obvious that they too will see the workers as having violated the rule. If this happens, the rule application acquires a double objectivity. The reaction of other people is an anticipated fact like my anticipation that the sun will rise tomorrow or that this glass will break if I drop it on the floor.

It is important not to mush these forms of objectivity together. It is possible for me to see the case as "not clearly governed by the rule" when I do my interior rule application, but to anticipate that the relevant others will see it as "open and shut." And it is possible for me to see it as clear but to anticipate that others will see it as complex and confusing.

The next thing that happens is that I set to work on the problem of this case. I already have, as part of my life as I've lived it up to this moment, a set of intentions, a life-project as a judge, that will orient me among the many possible attitudes I could take to this work.

It so happens that I see myself as a political activist, someone with the "vocation of social transformation," as Roberto Unger put it. I see the set of rules in force as chosen by the people who had the power to make the choices in accord with their views on morality and justice and their own self-interest. And I see the rules as remaining in force because victimized groups have not had the political vision and energy and raw power to change them. I see myself as a focus of political energy for change in an egalitarian, communitarian, decentralized, democratic socialist direction (which doesn't mean these slogans are any help in figuring out what the hell to do in any particular situation).

Given my general orientation, the work I am going to do in this case will have two objectives, which may or may not conflict. I want these specific workers to get away with obstructing the buses, and I want to move the law as much as possible in the direction of allowing workers a measure of legally legitimated control over the disposition of the m.o.p. during a strike.

If my only objective were to avoid an injunction against lying down in front of the buses during this strike, I would be tempted toward a strategy that would allow me to avoid altogether the apparent legal rule forbidding worker interference. I could just delay, in the hope that the workers will win the strike before I'm forced to rule. I could focus on developing a new version of the facts, and hope to deny the injunction on that basis, or I could look for a "technicality" having no apparent substantive relevance (e.g., the statute of frauds, a mistake in the caption of a pleading).

On a more substantive level, I could put my energy into researching the issues of federal jurisdiction and the appropriateness of an injunction. Here, if the effort paid off, I might be able to move the law in a way favorable to workers in general, even though the move wouldn't formally address worker control over the m.o.p. during a strike.

But the strategy I want to discuss here is that of frontal assault on the application of the rule that the workers can't obstruct the company's use of the m.o.p. If this strategy succeeds, the result will be both to get the workers off in this case *and* to accomplish my law reform objective. There will be a small reduction in employers' power to invoke the state apparatus, a change that will be practically useful in future legal disputes over strikes. And the mantle of legal legitimacy will shift a little, from all out endorsement of management prerogatives to a posture that legitimates, to some degree, workers' claims to rights over the m.o.p.

What I see as interesting about the situation as I have portrayed it up to this point is that we are not dealing with a "case governed by a rule," but rather with a perception that a rule probably governs, and that applying the rule will very likely produce a particular (pro-employer) result. The judge is neither free nor bound. I don't see it that way from inside the situation. From inside the situation, the question is, Where am I going to deploy the resources I have available for this case? The issue is how should I direct my *work* to bring about an outcome that accords with my sense of justice. My situation as a judge (initial perceived conflict between "the law" and how-I-want-to-come-out) is thus quite like that of a lawyer who is brought a case by a client and on first run-

through is afraid the client will lose. The question is, Will this first impression hold up as I set to work to develop the best possible case on the other side?

Having to work to achieve an outcome is in my view fundamental to the situation of the judge. It is neither a matter of being bound nor a matter of being free. Or, you could say that the judge is both free *and* bound—free to deploy work in any direction but limited by the pseudo-objectivity of the rule-as-applied, which he may or may not be able to overcome.

Isn't what I am doing illegitimate, from the standpoint of legality, right from the start? One could argue that since I think the law favors the company I have no business trying to develop the best possible case for the union. But this misunderstands the rules of the game of legality. All members of the community know that one's initial impression that a particular rule governs and that when applied to the facts it yields X result is *often* wrong. That's what makes law such a trip. What at first looked open and shut is ajar, and what looked vague and altogether indeterminate abruptly reveals itself to be quite firmly settled under the circumstances.

So it is an important part of the role of judges and lawyers to test whatever conclusions they have reached about "the correct legal outcome" by trying to develop the best possible argument on the other side. In my role as an activist judge I am simply doing what I'm supposed to when I test my first impression against the best pro-union argument I can develop.

If I manage to develop a legal argument against the injunction, the ideal of impartiality requires me to test that argument in turn against a newly worked-out best counterargument in favor of the company. Eventually, my time will run out, and I'll just have to decide.

What would betray legality would be to adopt the wrong attitude at the *end* of the reasoning process, when I've reached a conclusion about "what the law requires" and found it still conflicts with how-I-want-to-come-out.

For the moment, I'm free to play around.

The euphoric moment in which I conceive legal reasoning as "playing around with the rule" doesn't last long. What follows is panic as I rack my brain for *any* way around the overwhelming sense that if the rule is "workers can't interfere with the owner's use of the m.o.p. during a strike," then I cannot do anything for the union. I am ashamed of this panic. It's not just that I'm not coming up with anything; I also feel that I *should* be coming up with something. It's a disgrace—it shows I lack legal reasoning ability.

As my panic deepens, I begin to consider alternatives. If I can't mount an attack on the rule-as-applied, maybe I will have to research the earlier contract between the union and the bus company. I have a strong feeling that contracts are manipulable if one applies concepts like good faith, implication of terms, and the public interest, all relevant here. Maybe I'll have to try to "read something in." But this approach is clearly less good than going right for the rule itself.

Then I start thinking about the federal injunction aspect of the case, as opposed to the labor tort aspect. I'm sure that the combination of the 1930s anti-injunction statute with federal court injunctive enforcement of at least some terms in collective bargaining agreements must have made a total hash of the question of when federal courts will grant injunctions. If only I could worry just about *that*, I bet I could easily come up with a good pro-worker argument. But that move is also less good than going for the rule.

Then there are the really third-rate solutions based on the hope that the facts will turn out to be at least arguably different than they seemed to be when I first heard about the case, and that the company's lawyers will make a stupid technical mistake.

All the while I'm desperately racking my brains. I think I have good maxims for legal reasoning, but what are they? The rule represents a compromise between two conflicting policies, so there must be a gray area where the terms of the compromise are not clear. But this case seems clear. There are *always* exceptions to the rule. But I can't think of any here.

When an idea starts to come, it just comes, little by little getting clearer, as I work to tease it out, flesh it out, add analogies. Here it is:

Of course (oh, how I love to feel that reassuring "of course" tripping off my tongue at the beginning of an argument), it is not *literally* true that the workers are forbidden from "interfering with the owners' use of the m.o.p. during a strike." They can picket and use all kinds of publicity measures to dissuade people from riding the company's buses.

Here I begin to lose my grip again. Lying down in the roadway is a far cry from picketing, which doesn't interfere at all *physically* with the company's use of the buses and is after all justified as an exercise of First Amendment rights. This exception won't do me any good.

After more false leads and panic I come back to my exception. The workers did lie down in the street to block the buses, but they did not intend to and did not in fact use force to prevent them from rolling. After all, they submitted peacefully to arrest. And the press was everywhere. Obviously the worker on the ground *could not have* physically prevented the bus from rolling, because it could have rolled right over him.

Still, on those two days of lie-ins the company failed to resume service in the fashion it had planned. The workers did physically obstruct the owner's use of the m.o.p. and were delighted to do so. The disruption wasn't just a side effect.

On the other hand, maybe I can argue that the demonstration was a symbolic protest, an attempt to (a) exert moral suasion on the company by impressing it with the extreme feeling of the workers and their willingness to take risks, their sense that the company is theirs as much as management's, and (b) a gesture toward the public through the media.

I will emphasize the non-violent civil disobedience aspects: a physical tactic that *could not in fact* have prevented the use of the m.o.p. by the company, and submission to arrest.

I could hold that because of these factors there should be no federal labor law injunctive remedy beyond what is accorded under state law (narrow version). Or that this demonstration is the exercise of First Amendment rights, so that injunction of a nonviolent civil disobedient protest would be an unconstitutional restriction of expression, even though it is of course perfectly permissible for the state to arrest the demonstrators and subject them to its normal criminal process (broad version).

By this time, I'm getting high. I have no idea whether this line of argument will work. I have even lost track of exactly how this argument can be brought to bear in the employer's federal court action for an injunction. (This is probably because I've gotten into an argument on the merits before clarifying in my own mind what the basis of federal jurisdiction may be, and before getting into the anti-injunction Wagner Act issue.) But I am nonetheless delighted. My heart lifts because it seems that the work of legal reasoning within my pro-worker project is paying off.

What I've tried to do here is to turn this into a First Amendment prior restraint (or at least a "free speech policy") case. I relied on the idea that there had to be some limit to the employer's freedom from interference, came up with picketing by trying to imagine what the workers certainly *could* do to him, and then looked for an extension of the picketing idea to embrace the particular facts of this case.

Another way to put it is that I stopped imagining the rule of "no interference" as the only thing out there—as dominating an empty field and therefore grabbing up and incorporating any new fact-situation that had anything at all "sort of like interference" .n it. I tried to find the other rules that set the limits of this one, so I could tuck my case under their wing. Once I identified those other affirmative rules (protecting picketing and other First-Amendment-based attacks on the employer's use of the m.o.p.), I restated the facts of the lie-in to emphasize those aspects that fit (nonviolence, submission to arrest, one prone body can't stop a Sceni cruiser bus unless the Sceni cruiser wants to be stopped).

The minute I get rolling, new wrinkles occur to me. Maybe we should see the lie-in as an appeal by union workers to the nonunion replacement bus drivers. It is they, not the union members, who actually stop the buses on the street and fail thereby to carry out the company's plan to resume service. It would be all right to try to persuade the nonunion replacements with flyers, to picket them, to threaten them with anger and nonassociation, to guilt trip them and swear at them. The lie-in is just a small extension of those tactics. It is a physical statement to them. Will this fly? I have no idea. It

is part of the brainstorming process, rather than a deduction of the rule that covers the case. It is part of the work of producing lots of alternative ways at the problem, hoping that one of them will break through. I am already wondering whether it's even worth the time to pursue this approach further.

My model of constraint is that people (me as a judge) want to back up their statement of a preference for an outcome (the workers should not be enjoined) with an argument to the effect that to enjoin the workers would "violate the law." We can't understand how this desire to legalize my position constrains me without saying something about why I want to do it.

First, I see myself as having promised some diffuse public that I will "decide according to law," and it is clear to me that a minimum meaning of this pledge is that I won't do things for which I don't have a good legal argument. (This statement says nothing about just how tightly this promise constrains me as to the merits).

Second, various people in my community will sanction me severely if I do not offer a good legal argument for my action. It is not just that I may be reversed and will have broken my promise. It is also that both friends and enemies will see me as having violated a role constraint that they approve of (for the most part), and they will make me feel their disapproval.

Third, I want my position to stick. Although I am free to decide the case any way I want in the sense that no one will physically prevent me from entering a decree for either side, I am bound by the appellate court's reaction. By developing a strong legal argument I make it dramatically less likely that my outcome will be reversed.

Fourth, by engaging in legal argument I can shape the outcomes of future cases and influence popular consciousness about what kinds of action are legitimate—as here, for example, I can marginally influence what people think about worker interference with the m.o.p. during a strike.

Fifth, every case is part of my life-project of being a liberal activist judge. What I do in this case will affect my ability to do things in other cases, enhancing or diminishing my legal and political credibility as well as my technical reputation with the various constituencies that will notice.

Sixth, since I see legal argument as a branch of ethical argument, I would like to know for my own purposes how my position looks translated into this particular ethical medium.

I might be able to achieve some of these objectives at least some of the time without engaging in direct challenges to my initial intuition that the law is adverse. I don't want to be absolute about it, since I can conceive situations in which I think I would go quite unhesitatingly for a "nonlegal" approach. But there will be many, many situations in which it appears that, if I wish to achieve my goals, the only way or the obviously best way is to try legal argument.

Note that I would have to do *something* even if I wanted to grant. the injunction. When I say that my first impression of the law is that it favors the employer's case, I mean that I don't anticipate any difficulty in working up a good argument for the injunction. I see that project as easy, as not much work.

By contrast, deciding *not* to enjoin involves not just the work of pushing pencil across paper to get down thoughts already well worked out before I even begin, but the work of creating something out of nothing. This is a cost of deciding for the workers, and it has at least two aspects. First, the work of creating a good legal argument is hard, scary, and time-consuming. I have limited resources in my life as a judge, and the workers are asking me to allocate them here, when I could put them into some other hard case or just spend all my time on easy cases. My limited store of time and energy for the hard work of creating legal arguments that go against my first impression of what the law is constrains me from doing all kinds of things I could do as judge if I weren't constrained.

I don't want this point to sound minor, because it isn't. There are lots and lots and lots of rules I would like to change or at least reform. If I could do it by fiat, perhaps I would do a lot of it, do it quite fast, and in a way that might be called holistic. But if I have to generate a legal argument for every change, there is no way I can do a lot, do it fast, or do it holistically.

The second way in which I experience the law as a constraint in my hypothetical is that it is one of the determinants of what we might call the "legitimacy cost" of deciding for the workers. Just as there are competitors for my time and creativity as a legal arguer, there are also competitors claiming shares of the *mana* or *charisma* or whatever that attends my position as a judge. In our case, assume that *everyone* has the same initial impression that the law favors the employer. If I decide for the employer, people who know that this decision goes against my personal views may grant my decision some increased legitimacy. They may see me as more able to indicate what the correct legal result is in the next case, because they believe I perceived and followed the law in this one, even when I didn't like it.

This factor aside, no one will be able to say much about "what kind of judge he is" from my decision to go along with the collective initial impression. Going along would be costless in terms of legitimacy. My legitimating power is depleted or augmented only when I try to do something out of the ordinary.

I imagine this effect to be a function of two aspects of the situation. The first is the degree of "stretch" from our initial impression of the law to the result I decree. The second is the impact on this distance—we might call it the obviousness gap—of my opinion defending my out-of-the-ordinary result.

The greater the initial perception of stretch, the more of my stock of legitimacy is at stake. Of course, the very notion of legitimating power is that I can reduce the perceived distance between what the law requires and what I decree just by decreeing it. That is the nature of my institutional *mana* or *charisma*. But nothing guarantees that my legitimating power will cause people to see this result as the one that was right all along. That outcome depends on how great the stretch was, and in my own case it is likely that the stretch will be much greater than I can overcome just because the president of the United States has put some black robes on me.

If my automatic legitimating power falls short of fully normalizing the outcome, I will lose legitimating power for the next case—my stock will be depleted—*unless* I devise an opinion (cast as a legal argument) that makes up the deficit, or even increases the stock. In order to make up the deficit I have to write an opinion that will convince the good faith observer struggling to understand what the law is that in fact my result was not out of the ordinary at all. Rather it was a correct perception, albeit a minority perception, of what the law really required all along.

In other words, I can build up my legitimating power through instances of persuading people through legal argument. If they have had the experience of my "being right" before, experiences of my changing their view of the law, then they will be susceptible in the future to believe what I tell them the law is, quite independently of the argument I can muster.

The greater the initial distance between my proposed result and what one would expect, the greater the positive value of persuading the observer through legal argument. You will attribute power to me just in the measure that you find yourself saying, "I never thought he could persuade me of *that*!" Even if I don't persuade you, I gain power if you say, "He didn't convince me, but I never thought he could get me to take the proposition seriously, and here I am arguing hard against it!" On the other hand, if the distance was small to begin with, persuading you that I was right in my initial impression will do no more than very marginally increase my store of legitimating power.

I also increase my power to the extent that my persuasive efforts spill over from this particular case and cause you to reassess other outcomes you had thought preeminently legally correct. This is my ability to make my case a "leading case" that will be cited over and over in increasingly distant reaches of law-space as the years go by. My name on that opinion is a help the next time I have an unconventional view on the merits, because it has increased my legitimating power even if in the next case I don't have much in the way of an argument.

Suppose we have an earlier labor case in which the question was whether there was a First Amendment right to mass picketing, and the courts ruled that there was not, and that the activity should be enjoined as an unfair labor practice or as a tortious interference with the employer's right to use the m.o.p. during a strike. That case is "on the boundary" if it is the "furthest" the employer's right has been extended and the furthest

the workers' right of expression has been cut back. If a mass picketing case were followed by a case holding that individual picketing is also tortious, then that case would be the one on the boundary, if I perceived individual picketing as at the same time less of an interference with the employer's property rights, and more plausibly a protected speech activity.

I imagine the facts of the case (I learned them from the opinion or from somewhere else, such as a classroom or a newspaper) as defining *the position of the case in the field of law*. We may grasp that position as close to a boundary line, or on it, or as so far within the boundary that these facts seem "easy" and the general rule just "applies itself" to them. Legal argument with the facts of the case means restating them so that the case appears in a different part of the field than it did initially.

Remember that my objective is to make my lie-in look like a case plausibly covered by the rule permitting speech-type interferences with the m.o.p., rather than like a case clearly governed by the rule of no interferences with the m.o.p. Suppose that a mass picketing case has already gone against the workers. My first impression is that the lie-in is "even worse" from an interference point of view, and simultaneously "weaker" as a speech case. I will try to restate the facts of the mass picketing case to make it reappear in the field as more of an interference than the lie-in, and as less plausibly a case of protected speech.

I will do this by emphasizing that, in the mass picketing case, the court found that the workers were trying to physically prevent substitute workers from entering the plant, and that the situation was always on the verge of violence. I will de-emphasize the opinion's references to the signs and shouted slogans of the mass picket. By contrast, I will argue that the workers in the lie-in submitted peacefully to arrest, and could never have physically prevented passage of the buses by lying in front of them.

My hope is that you will eventually perceive the two cases as located in just the opposite position from that you saw them in initially, so that I can draw the boundary between rather than around them. Mass picketing will then fall on the side of interference, the lie-in on the side of speech.

Policies as forces in the field. Policy arguments are reasons for adopting a particular holding or mini-rule. They are aimed more specifically than philosophical or social theoretical justifications of whole systems and more abstractly than appeals to the raw equities immanent in "the facts." Policy argument is "second order" in relation to rule application or argument from precedent. The arguer can pick and choose from a truly enormous repertoire of typical policy arguments and modify what he finds to fit the case at hand. The arguments come in matched contrary pairs, like certainty vs. flexibility, security vs. freedom of action, property as incentive to labor vs. property as incipient monopoly, no liability without fault vs. as between two innocents he who caused the damage should pay, the supremacy clause vs. local initiative, and so on.

A policy is not invalidated just because I ignore it in a case where it arguably applies. Our rough notion is that the two sides of the matched pair "differ in strength" from case to case. We might see the property-as-incentive-to-labor argument as very strong if the issue is whether there should be any private rights at all in mechanisms of interstate commerce, but as quite weak if the question is whether there should be a right to prevent peaceful individual picketing of an interstate bus company involved in a labor dispute.

In a typical legal argument, policies are elaborated and strongly asserted without regard to their matched pairs. When I argue for state law criminal penalties, I don't have to explain, either as judge or as advocate, the rational basis of my endorsement of "nip it in the bud" here, and my contrary endorsement of "repression breeds violence" when we get to the injunction. In a sense, then, the practice of legal arguers (lawyers, judges, treatise writers) is endlessly contradictory. I assert my policy as "valid" and as "requiring" an outcome, and then blithely reject it and in the next case, endorse its exactly matching opposite without giving any meta-level explanation of what keys me into one side or the other.

From the inside, however, I know from the beginning that this is just "the way we do" legal argument. I don't take the surface claim that the policy is "valid" and "requires" the outcome seriously at all. I work with a model of the opposing policies as forces or vectors, each of which has some "pull" on any given fact-situation. They *seem* logically contradictory (how can I believe, at the same time, that "there should be no liability without fault," and that "as between two innocents he who caused the damage should pay") or so indeterminate that they can serve only as after-the-fact rationalizations of decisions reached on other grounds (who knows whether the injunction will "nip violence in the bud" or "just drive it underground and make it worse"?). But there is a sense in which both policies are valid at the same time, in every case. The question is which one turns out to be "stronger," or to weigh more in a "balancing test" applied to these particular facts, rather than which is correct in the abstract.

We can represent the process of arranging cases in a field, and the process of fixing a boundary between permitted and forbidden acts, in terms of this imagery of vectors and balancing. For example, the imaginary mass picketing and individual picketing cases discussed earlier had fact situations and holdings, but they also "involved" or "implicated" various policies. The mass picketing case implicated the general social policy in favor of political association and the general social policy against the use of force to resolve disputes. (Each case implicates as many policies as I can plausibly think up. Those mentioned here are illustrative, not exhaustive.)

Suppose we see the lie-in, in relation to mass picketing, as a "better" First Amendment case, and as a less serious interference with the employer's use of the m.o.p. during a strike. The "second order" interpretation of this intuitive ordering is that pro-speech policies apply more strongly, and pro-property policies less strongly, than in the mass picketing case. As we move from fact-situation to fact-situation across the field, the speech policy gets weaker, and the property policy stronger, until at the boundary they are in equilibrium. At this point a very small change in the relative forces of the policies produces a dramatic change in result. We "draw the line" and treat cases beyond the line repressively.

What this means is that we have to add to our model of the field of law the notion that, at every point in the field, contradictory policies exert different levels of force.

Boundary lines in the field represent points of equilibrium of opposing forces. At points not on boundaries, one or another set of policies predominates. The policies are to be understood as gradients; they are strongest in the "core," where a given general rule seems utterly obvious in its application and also utterly "appropriate as a matter of social policy." The argument set supporting the general rule diminishes in force as we move from the core outward toward the periphery, and ultimately to a boundary with another general rule.

[My policy argument can be the following:]

First, I develop a potential holding for my lie-in case, such as that there shall be no federal injunction of nonviolent civil disobedient protests in labor disputes. Then I develop some policy arguments as to why this rule is preferable to an alternative (usually a straw man) or to the rule proposed by the employer. For example, I argue that if the workers feel strongly enough to undergo arrest and criminal charges, they almost certainly feel strongly enough to do something violent if they are not permitted their symbolic protest. It follows that, far from "nipping violence in the bud," an injunction will likely lead to unorganized individual acts of violence, such as shooting out bus tires on the open highway.

But this argument is unlikely to be enough. Once I have taken the step into the "second order," forsaking the strategy of mere rule application, I evoke in the mind of my audience the whole force field of this area of law. I will now have to take steps to preserve the coherence of the overall policy "picture." This means restating policy arguments in other decided cases. For example, suppose that in the mass picketing case the court justified a prohibitory rule on the ground that unless you nip violence in the bud it develops until it is unstoppable.

My problem is that in the lie-in case I am arguing that worker anger makes it important to tolerate civil disobedience, and this position seems inconsistent with a "nipping in the bud" strategy against mass picketing. In order to restore order to the field, I will "distinguish" the mass picketing case as follows. Mass picketing is essentially uncontrollable and naturally tends to escalate toward violence. In the civil disobedience case, by contrast, the police exercise detailed and intense control. Though the initial emotion may be greater in the lie-in, the setting allows the release of emotion without escalation. Since the situation is already under control but still serving to release emotion, an injunction is likely to be counterproductive overkill.

(Let me remind the patient reader that I have no idea whether the preceding policy arguments and distinctions are "any good," that is, whether they would be persuasive to a person a little knowledgeable in the field. One begins the work of legal argument enveloped in ignorance of what the law "is" and with little sense of what may be the conventional wisdom about how the law works in practice. I will find out about these matters by doing research and by asking people. In consequence, I'll flatly abandon some arguments while I develop others. What I am trying to do here is describe what the work process in its initial stages feels like from the inside.)

Overruling. When I first began thinking about this subject, the possibility of overruling seemed a dramatically important aspect of the judicial activist's situation. Indeed, it seemed to mean that there is no such thing as a conflict between "the law" and how-I-want-to-come-out, since I can change the law by overruling to make it correspond to my heart's desire. On further reflection, this has come to seem a shallow view.

First, overruling is subject to the calculus of legitimacy I have been describing. I can't overrule with impunity any more than I can disturb the field with impunity in any other way. The set of maxims by which the overruling decision will be judged are pretty vague, but if the decision isn't convincing, I will find myself less able to persuade the next time around and feeling guilty about violating role constraints.

Second, my power to overrule, seen as a kind of ultimate power to reorder the field, is counterbalanced by the notion of legislative supremacy. I can't "overrule" a statute. *But* the statute may be trumped by the state and federal constitutions, of which I am interpreter here. *But* though I can use the constitutions to overrule the statute, I have no power to overrule the constitutions themselves. *But* even this is not the end of the story, since the constitutions don't seem, *a priori*, to be any more conceivably self-applying than any other set of legal norms. Many great cases branch down from the sacred texts, and these I *can* overrule.

The upshot of these twists and turns is that I decide about overruling enmeshed in the field of law, subject to its typical constraint that I argue persuasively across some perceived obviousness gap, or forfeit my charismatic power and get reversed on appeal into the bargain.

In my role as a liberal activist judge, I have long-term goals with respect to the configuration of the various fields I work in. For example, suppose that I can decide the lie-in case for the workers if I emphasize one aspect of the facts but in the process will reenforce a boundary in the field that I see as congealed injustice. My goal of law reform may be to collapse that boundary—say by establishing that there is no *a priori* distinction between worker rights in the m.o.p. and ownership rights—so that the concept of ownership cannot define a core of employer prerogative that must remain immune from worker meddling during a strike.

I may be willing to sacrifice something in the way of total convincingness in this particular lie-in case in order to disorder the field. Maybe I will emphasize the extent to which the holding of my lie-in case conflicts with holdings in the long string of picketing cases, so as to create a consciousness of discontinuity that will induce workers and their lawyers to expand the lie-in into a deep salient extending toward the core of the employer's property rights.

I have been developing through the preceding discussion a particular strategy for arguing against an injunction of the lie-in. Some elements of the strategy are: the choice of a First Amendment general defense of the action; the choice not to attack state law civil and criminal penalties short of injunction; the choice to distinguish mass picketing cases as coercive rather than as "not speech," and so on. It seems obvious to me that there must be other possible strategies, though for the moment the only one that comes to mind is that of using the Wagner Anti-injunction Act.

One of the effects of adopting a strategy is a kind of tunnel vision: one is inside the strategy, sensitive to its internal economy, its history of trade-offs, attuned to developing it further but at least temporarily unable to imagine any other way to go.

But a **strategy** is also a *practical commitment*. Because it hangs together, the strategy imposes multiple constraints on how I respond to any new aspect of the case. It's not just a matter of logical consistency: the strategy has a tone and a style. For example, hard-nosed nip-it-in-the-bud rhetoric about mass picketing will be in tension with repression-just-makes-it-worse rhetoric in the lie-in, even though there is no logical problem. Moreover, a strategy is an investment of time. Once I've put in the work of developing its many interlocking parts, it will cost me plenty if I respond to a new question with an answer that would force revision of everything that's gone before.

In legal argument as in other production processes, practitioners have an intuitive idea of efficiency in the deployment of the available materials. Anyone who has done legal argument knows what it means to do it "neatly" or "elegantly," meaning at a minimum expenditure of . . . something. A part of this complex notion is that if you are mainly interested in who wins the particular case, you should persuade us that the lie-in is non-enjoinable with the least possible restatement of the facts and holdings of other cases, the least possible rearrangement of policy vectors, and the least possible movement of the boundary between free speech and interference with property. If, by contrast, you want to "make some law," you should do that, too, so as to accomplish the greatest possible movement of the boundary with the least possible disturbance of the other elements of the field.

A kind of quotient notion emerges. Success at the skill of legal argument can be measured by how little you disturb the field in order to persuasively achieve a given restructuring, whether it's a big restructuring through law making or a small one by making sure the good guys win this case. It's the ratio rather than the absolute amount of movement or of disturbance that counts.

My uncertainty about whether I will succeed in making a convincing argument. Up to now I have presented the activity of argument as a kind of work, undertaken in a medium, with a purpose. The purpose was to convince the audience that, contrary to our initial impression, a decision denying an injunction in the lie-in is in accord with the law. I undertake this argumentative labor with a number of ulterior motives, such as avoiding reversal on appeal, fulfilling my obligation to the public, and so forth. I hope that by developing a convincing argument against the injunction I will avoid a loss of credibility as a judge (indeed, I hope to increase my credibility through a strong opinion).

There is an ideal scenario in which I am able to represent the legal field so that the law corresponds exactly to how-I-want-to-come-out. What was initially an impacted field with the lie-in unequivocally prohibited (an easy case) becomes, to the surprise of my public, an impacted field in which the lie-in is a case that is clearly permitted (or at least not enjoinable). I close a large obviousness gap by a field manipulation that is notably elegant—a dramatic change in outcome with surprisingly little disturbance of the elements of the field.

When my reasoning turns out this way, I feel euphoria, indeed a moment of dangerous omnipotence, delight at the plasticity of the natural/social field-medium, and narcissistic ecstasy at the favorable reaction of my public (not to speak of sober joy at all the good I will be able to do with my increased credibility). But before you put me down as an egotist, I want to add that some element of this pleasure is quite legitimate. I had an intuition about the justice of the situation—how-I-wanted-to-come-out in this case was in accord with an intuition that the law as I initially apprehend it was unfair to a particular group. If I have succeeded in making the law fairer to that group, my pleasure will be in part an altruistic emotion that seems to me no cause for shame: I will have helped out. Too bad it doesn't always turn out that way.

The normative power of the field. Throughout the discussion to this point, I have spoken as a judge who knows how he wants to come out and is vigorously trying to bring the law into accord. Sometimes I apprehend the law as plastic and cooperative, sometimes as resistant or even adamant, but me and my favored outcome are always the same. It is now time to critique the how-I-want-to-come-out pole of our duality. First, however, let's reify it with an acronym: HIWTCO.

HIWTCO is not a datum given externally, something that comes into the picture from outside. HIWTCO is *relative to the field.* This is true in the weak sense that I have decided HIWTCO in response to a question posed in terms of the existing social universe that includes law. I don't want these particular workers, living in our particular society under a particular set of legal rules to be enjoined from lying-in. I can't even formulate HIWTCO without referring to this legal context to give that result a meaning.

But HIWTCO is relative to the law field in a much more interesting and important way. I've been treating the law field as though it were a physical medium, clay or bricks, when what it is in fact is a set of declarations by other people (possibly including an earlier me) about how ethically serious people ought to respond to situations of conflict. As I manipulate the field, I am reading and rereading these declarations, apparently addressed to me, and trying to absorb their messages about what I ought to do. Indeed, before I ever heard of this case, I was already knowledgeable about hundreds of opinions by judges and lawyers and legislators about how to handle conflicts roughly analogous to this one.

As a preliminary matter this means that we are *not* dealing with a confrontation between "my gut feeling about the case" and the law, unless we understand my "gut" as an organ deeply conditioned by existence in our legalized universe. I simply don't have intuitions about social justice that are independent of my knowledge of what judges and legislators have done in the past about situations like the one before me. Other actors in the legal system have influenced, persuaded, outraged, puzzled, and instructed me, until I can never be sure in what sense an opinion I strongly hold is "really" mine rather than theirs. I don't even think such a question has an answer.

But the more important point is that my initial impression of conflict between the law and HIWTCO may disappear because HIWTCO changes, as well as because I manage to change the law. Further, the very resistance of the law to change in the direction of HIWTCO may impel HIWTCO to change in the direction of the law. I may find myself persuaded by my study of the materials that my initial apprehension of HIWTCO was wrong. I may find that I now want to come out the way I initially perceived the law coming out. This is what I mean by the normative power of the field.

I try to move the law in the direction of HIWTCO, and to the extent the law is resistant, I find HIWTCO under pressure to move toward the law. But neither HIWTCO nor the law field are physical objects. If I experience "pressure" as I read through the legal materials, if the very fact of my initial apprehension that the law favors the employer exerts pressure, it is because the field is a message rather than a thing. It is a message of a kind I'm familiar with, a message of a kind I've dealt with before. Indeed, I am one of the authors of the message.

Precedents come to me as stories called fact situations that judges resolved in particular ways. What they did interests me in the way an earlier painter's work might interest a later painter. But interest is too weak a word. Especially when they are put together in patterns, precedents reveal possibilities that it would have taken me a long time to come up with, or that I might never have come up with at all. I look at six outcomes, and I say to myself, "Oh, they devised a strategy of banning all picketing, but allowing just about any kind of secondary boycott. Hmm. I wonder why. Oh, I get it, they had a rough distinction between physically confrontive and nonconfrontive tactics. Or maybe they were concerned with workers' freedom not to contract in the boycott cases, and worried about the implications for business combinations if they banned labor combinations."

It is no good telling me that my reverence for the messages of these ancients is "irrational." It's not a question of rationality. When I read their words, it is as though I myself were talking. (Of course, when I'm reading my own earlier opinions, it is me in an earlier incarnation who's talking.) I am not able to treat their ethical pronouncements about how to decide cases like this one as though they were a set of randomly generated possible answers to a math problem. In that case, I test each answer "coldly," so to speak, without any investment at all in its correctness or incorrectness. But as I sit reading the messages of the ancients about cases like this one (or even, I may sometimes feel with horror, about this very case neatly antici-

pated), I can't remain neutral. I want them to agree with me. And I want to agree with them. I feel I *ought* to agree with them.

In this state of mind, I may find myself adopting the voice of the ancients, knowing what they are talking about when they extol the sacredness of owner's rights and feeling that what they are saying accurately expresses something that I think too. I set out to manipulate the field so that the law would favor the lie-in, but in order to do that I have to enter into the discourse of law. In the process, I have to undergo its intimate prestige. I discover that I know what they were talking about because I myself am capable of thinking just what they thought. At that point, the normative force of the field is just one side in an interior discussion between my divided selves about who really should win this case anyway.

The message I apprehend as "the law" is at several removes from a conviction of my own about what I want to do. It is a message I have to decode, rather than a thought immediately accessible to me inside my own mind. There will always be an element of mystery as to whose message it is, whether I have properly understood it, whether it is "applicable" here at all. Until I "make it my own" and begin to argue the side of the law against HIWTCO, the message hovers between the life I can give it and the status of dead formula. The message is from the past, from people who put it together in the past (including my past self, if I was involved). Even if I can understand it and enter into it, it is yesterday's newspaper, queer-looking because so much has happened that it doesn't and couldn't take into account. The message that is the field was not developed by a clairvoyant as a message to the future; it is the product of judges deciding cases and writing opinions to deal with their problems, though with an eye toward the shape of the field for future cases. The way we constructed the field dates it and thereby deprives it of the normative bite it would have if it spoke in the voice of someone looking over my shoulder as I study the facts of the lie-in.

The architects of the law of labor relations applicable here were turn-of-the-century conservative state court judges and New Deal reformers. I have mixed feelings about both groups and about the legal structures of which these by-ways of labor law form a part. At least, my own evaluation of the message and its senders seems to have a great effect on how and how strongly I feel it.

The costs of conversion. I don't want to be converted to the view that I should enjoin the lie-in. My initial opinion that there should be no injunction is in character: as soon as it occurs to me I hold it dear as an emanation of my true self. Like a collection of knick-knacks, my opinions, along with my past, my work, my family, are a store of treasures I don't want to give up.

My social identity, moreover, is bound up with the ritual of agreeing, publicly, with others about issues like this. Other people see me as a person who holds particular kinds of views, and they like me or dislike me partly on that basis (however lamentable such superficiality on their part may be). I'm dependent on their good opinion. If I change my views, some will regard me as a turncoat, as weak-willed or stupid, a fluff-head or an opportunist.

Those who tend to favor management aren't likely to form favorable opinions that will make up for what I lose by conversion, since they won't know whether to trust me. Still worse, perhaps, is my sense that those who hold the view I might convert to—that the injunction should issue—are a bunch I'd hate, as of now, to join. When I think of myself as one of them, I shrink from my imagined turncoat self.

Legal argument, in which I take up and work with the message of the field, and maybe end up espousing it against my current correct and virtuous position, looks like working in a nuclear plant at the risk of radiation sickness. It looks like fooling around with heroin: you think you have it under control, and one morning you wake up already addicted. You've gone from one (good) state to another (bad) state without ever having a moment of choice about it.

I think this fear of being converted without choice, somehow forced from one's own view into another, is deep in almost everyone involved with law. It leads progressive-minded people to ask things like, "Will law school warp my mind?" Or to assert that they think something is legally right but totally morally wrong. Or that law is made-up noise that reinforces things as they are, so it's not worth the trouble to argue within its (even though it's manipulable) when the facts cry out for direct moral response.

Even if in contemplation I admit that the conversion might be to a "better view," I still don't want it to happen. Just because it's a better view doesn't mean that moving to it is painless. I don't want to be converted, but I do believe in the possibility of progress in my own views. I believe things now that I used to think were stupid, and I think I'm better off for having been through the process of enlightenment, however painful. So my fear of conversion is qualified by my longing for truth and for change and interesting conflict.

I may still be deeply influenced against the normative power of the law field by the fear of *false conversion.* Maybe what looks like a very compelling legal, moral, utilitarian, political argument against HIWTCO has a flaw a mile wide. Maybe the company's lawyers even know it does, and maybe I'll be suckered into believing it because I lack constructive as well as critical argumentative ability. (I might be great most of the time but have screwed up here, despite my previous record.) If this happens, I will experience a momentary pleasure of conversion (with attendant mild pains), followed by a subsequent devastating awakening to my own mistake, then humiliation if I change my mind back, and shame if I find myself unable to admit my error and forced to persist in pretending my new wrong position is right.

What to do in case of conflict between the law and HIWTCO. My answer to this question is unhelpful: it depends on the circumstances.

1. Go along with the law. In spite of my conviction that social justice requires me to deny the injunction, I issue it, along with an opinion denouncing the law and urging reform. I make the very convincing legal argument for an injunction that comes to mind in an impacted field such as this one. A crucial question is how I explain my obedience, that is, my willingness to act as the instrument of injustice.

2. Withdraw from the case. I neither issue the injunction nor deny it. I withdraw, explaining that I think the law is unjust and that my feelings against it make it inappropriate for me to preside and repugnant to me to be involved in administering this regime. A crucial question is how I justify begging off while insisting that someone else do the dirty work, if I intend to stick around for the more attractive assignments.

3. *Decide against the injunction on the basis of what the law should be*. I deny the injunction, honestly explaining my inability to come up with a plausible legal argument against it. Though I may be reversed on appeal (and quickly at that), I exercise what power I have to further HIWTCO. This may be decisive if the litigants are evenly matched out in the world. Accept what consequences my bureaucratic superiors and my colleagues and peers decide to inflict (highly indeterminate). I appeal to them to accept my outcome as the correct one in this and future cases, thereby changing the law. A crucial question is who authorized me to take the law into my own hands.

4. *Decide against the injunction on the basis of an implausible legal argument*. Maybe it will look good to others, even though I think it stinks; I can never be sure in advance. Maybe it will turn out in my own hindsight to be a better argument than I thought. But what about the dishonesty of bad faith argument?

5. *Decide against the injunction on the basis of fact findings I know to be false*. As the trial judge, I decide to pretend to believe an account of the facts of the lie-in that I know to be false, and deny the injunction on that basis. This is obviously an extreme measure.

The rule of law. I can imagine hypothetical situations in which each of these courses of action in the face of conflict would be appropriate. I don't think any of them can be either endorsed or excluded *a priori*. From within the perspective of my imagined judge, the story is over when she reaches the moment of decision. Whether she should always follow the law in cases of conflict is a question that we answer as best we can through reflection and argument about our political system, about the actual laws in force within that system, and about particular cases.

QUESTIONS AND COMMENTS FOR YOUR CONSIDERATION

1. Is a reader's willingness to go along with Professor Kennedy's train of thought a function of whether the reader is pro-management or pro-union?

2. If *you* are a lawyer for management, and the judge assigned to your case is a judge like Professor Kennedy, how *helpful* (if it is helpful at all) is it to you to know that "your" judge thinks the way that Professor Kennedy reveals? Would you change the way you write your brief if you knew that your judge is like Professor Kennedy? Why? How?

3. The obvious candor of Professor Kennedy's self-analysis is of course tempered by our knowledge of the fact that he is not himself a judge and is only imagining what it might be like to decide a case. Ideally the legal literature would benefit greatly from a totally candid account by a real judge about how that judge decided a real case. Yet despite the fact that thousands of literate judges have served on benches in the United States alone, your editor knows of no such account! (If you know of one, let me know and it will be included in the second edition of this Anthology!)

4. *Why* does no such "real" judicial introspective account exist? Are judges *incapable* of that degree of candor? Or, are they capable but under no circumstances willing to reveal to the public what really goes on? Or, is Professor Kennedy's account simply erroneous from top to bottom?

5. Judge Hutcheson came close to a Kennedy-like candor in the excerpt quoted at the beginning of this chapter in the section by Jerome Frank. Judge Richard Posner was candid about judicial opinion-making in the section directly preceding

Professor Kennedy's piece. Yet neither of these accounts describe exactly what went on in a single *real* case.

6. The judge's ability to "restate the facts" appears relatively benign in Professor Kennedy's account. Is it possible for a judge to restate the facts in such a way as to be *unfair* to one of the parties—*i.e.*, by omitting a critically important fact or subsuming it under an apparently harmless circumlocution (such as, "the plaintiff has stressed other aspects of this case, but the court finds those additional considerations irrelevant to the issues involved herein.")? In the most egregious situation, might a judge actually *invent* "facts" that did not occur, or misstate "facts" that did occur, in order to support the judge's desired outcome? For a case in which several prominent judges resorted to just this kind of judicial "creativity" in order to avoid having to admit that a provably innocent man was prison, *see* Anthony D'Amato, *The Ultimate Injustice: When a Court Misstates the Facts*, 11 Cardozo Law Review 1313 (1990).

6

Pragmatism

In Chapter 4, we saw that Formalists would like words to have exact meanings, to hitch precisely on to the world. In Chapter 5, we saw the Realists' attack on Formalism: that relying on words is a dangerous business if you're a lawyer, because you may be surprised to see what judges and other officials can do to those words. Realism is a frontal attack upon Formalism.

But perhaps the attack was carried too far. Even if we agree with the Realists that legal rules do not conclusively constrain officials, we know that most of the time legal rules affect their behavior. Consider a mother saying to a four-year-old child, "Always look both ways before you cross a street!" The parent is laying down a "rule" that is expected to exercise a form of constraint upon the child's behavior. True, the child may forget the rule or disregard it, but that does not mean that the mother is wasting her breath. She knows that her words will probably have *some* effect upon the child in *most* cases and *decisive* effect upon the child in *some* cases.

Because Realists have focused on judicial motivations other than words, they have failed to provide us with an adequate theory about words. As we shall see in the present Chapter, Pragmatism takes a middle position between Formalism's insistence that words have plain meanings and Realism's position that words may count for next to nothing.

It's hard to define Pragmatism, and well it might be, because Pragmatists dislike definitions. Definitions are themselves formal, suggesting logic and exactitude. Pragmatism—in the philosophy of John Dewey and Charles Sanders Pierce, and currently championed by Richard Rorty—rebels against this notion of exactitude. A definition, to a Pragmatist, is just a rule of thumb.

Thus, rather than attempt to define Pragmatism, let us look at some examples that illustrate the difference between Formalism and Pragmatism. We might start with a case that has attracted considerable attention in recent legal literature: how to interpret the qualifications of office of the President of the United States under Article II Section 1 of the Constitution:

> No person except a natural born citizen, or a citizen of the United States, at the time of the adoption of this constitution, shall be eligible to the office of president; neither shall any person be eligible to that office who shall not have attained to the age of thirty-five years, and been fourteen years a resident within the United States.

Among the several Constitutional qualifications is the 35-year minimum age. Focusing on this qualification, the Formalist would say it clearly means that absolutely no one under any circumstances can be eligible for the presidency without having attained the age of 35. The Pragmatist would reply that the clause means that just about any person at any time has to be 35 before being eligible for the presidency. Why does the Pragmatist insist on some degree of fuzziness as compared to the Formalist?

In abstract terms, the Pragmatist could explain that the world itself is somewhat fuzzy, that life is somewhat fuzzy. We can all "get along" in society most of the time by respecting our institutions and our fellow citizens. Language and legal rules, including the rules in the Constitution, are part of our institutional and cultural heritage. These are good guidelines, good rules of thumb, but there is no point pretending that they are absolute prescriptions that disallow any possible deviation no matter what the circumstances.

The Formalist could respond by making two points. First, *unless* we regard legal rules as absolutes, we open up an unconstrained process of chipping away at the rules for self-serving reasons until they lose all force and effect. Second, if you don't want to follow what the Constitution provides, amend it. The Framers were aware that in the future there might be rules in the Constitution that would become too onerous, and so they provided for an amendment process. (Note the similarity of this second point to the concept of "legislative flagellation" we considered in discussing Positivism.)

The Pragmatist may respond to these two points by demonstrating that there can be an occasion or occasions when everyone (everyone except, perhaps, the die-hard Formalist) will agree that a person who has not attained the age of 35 should be eligible for the presidency under the Constitution, and at those times it might not be feasible or timely to amend the Constitution. Consider the materials that follow.

A. Indeterminacy

1. Anthony D'Amato: The Case of the Under-aged President[1]

When a Pragmatist says that *all* cases are to some degree problematic, the Formalist gleefully pulls out a favorite crystal-clear case and asserts "not this one!" The most popular of these "easy cases," judging from the amount of law-review commentary on it, was mooted by Frank Easterbrook in 1983:

When the Constitution says that the President must be thirty-five years old, we cannot be certain whether it means thirty-five as the number of revolutions of the world around the sun, as a percentage of average life expectancy (so that the Constitution now has age fifty as a minimum), or as a minimum number of years after puberty (so the minimum now is thirty or so).[2]

Despite the fact that Judge Easterbrook cited the provision as an example of uncertainty, when Frederick Schauer peered into it he saw nothing but a crystal-clear "easy case":

The parties concerned know, without litigating and without consulting lawyers, that a twenty-nine year-old is not going to be President of the United States. In response to any number of provisions relating to years and dates, it is possible

---

[1] Anthony D'Amato, *Aspects of Deconstruction: The 'Easy Case' of the Under-aged President*, 84 Nw. U. L. Rev. 250 (1989). Copyright 1990 by Anthony D'Amato. Reprinted with the permission of the Northwestern University Law Review. The term "deconstructionist" has been changed to "Pragmatist" for present purposes. Although in general "deconstruction" only partially overlaps with "pragmatism," as far as the excerpts herein are concerned, the overlap between the two terms makes them congruent for present purposes.

---

[2] Frank Easterbrook, *Statutes' Domains*, 50 U. Chi. L. Rev. 533, 536 (1983).

to imagine an intervening change in the calendar. Ever since Macbeth mistakenly relied on the linguistic precision of the witches' prophesy, people have been able to construct weird and fanciful instances in which even the clearest language breaks down. The easy answer to the argument from weird cases is the observation that the weird hypothetical cases are wildly counterfactual.[3]

Replying for the Pragmatists, Gary Peller argued that a court could interpret the constitutional provision as "*signifying* to the Framers a certain level of maturity rather than some intrinsically significant number of years."[4] Girardeau Spann spelled it out: a 34-year-old runs for President claiming "The purpose behind the rule is to ensure the President possesses a minimum degree of maturity and experience, and I, at thirty-four, am more experienced and mature than most at forty."[5]

Formalist Kenney Hegland conceded that Professor Spann may have shown indeterminacy in a case one year below the constitutional line, but says that at best it is a close case. Instead, Professor Hegland asks us to consider an "easy case," where "the candidate is eighteen years old and is, by admission, quite immature." Professor Hegland obviously feels that this new case clinches the argument for Formalism:

> The constitutional provision dictates against the candidacy. A judge, assuming good faith, could not avoid the provision, even if a judge wanted to do so. Resources and imagination can always create arguments; they cannot always create *good* arguments and therefore cannot always produce doctrinal uncertainty.[6]

Professor Hegland's argument is a loaded one; he says that anyone who disagrees with him cannot be using a good argument. It is a heads-I-win-tails-you-lose kind of offer. In short, if a critic of his position fails to articulate a rationale for allowing the 18-year old to run for President, then Hegland wins; if a critic does come up with a rationale, the rationale itself must be bad or outrageous and hence the critic loses.[7]

Key to this debate is the emotional impact upon the reader suggested by the term "outrageous." What seems "outrageous" depends upon context. Thus we have to look at the underlying contextual assumptions we have in our minds in considering the arguments of Professors Schauer, Peller, Spann, and Hegland. These contextual assumptions turn out to be quite conservative; they are based on a feeling that society will go on pretty much the same way it has gone on in the past. But surprises can occur—not just abrupt shifts but also surprises within our normal context.

Consider an example in recent history which came close to challenging the constitutional requirements about the President. George Romney was a serious contender for the Republican Party nomination for President in 1968. But he was not a "natural born citizen"—a requirement also appearing in Article II Section 1. This fact presented a "legal problem" for Romney, as the media referred to it at the time. But the "legal problem" was not viewed as disabling; rather, it was seen as just a "negative" in the Romney "picture." Every candidate has negatives; this one was a Romney negative. It probably would not have been enough to derail the Romney nomination (an entirely different factor led to his ultimate downfall as a candidate.[8])

How did Romney handle his "Constitutional" problem? One tactic was what he told *The New York Times* when he announced his candidacy:

> Mr. Romney said his birth in a Mor-

---

[3] Frederick Schauer, *Easy Cases*, 58 S. Cal. L. Rev. 399, 414, 420 (1985).

[4] Gary Peller, *The Metaphysics of American Law*, 73 Cal. L. Rev. 1151, 1174 (1985).

[5] Girardeau Spann, *Deconstructing the Legislative Veto*, 68 Minn. L. Rev. 473, 532-33 (1984).

[6] Kenney Hegland, *Goodbye to Deconstruction*, 58 S. Cal. L. Rev. 1203, 1207-08 (1985).

---

[7] In fact, every writer who poses an outrageously "easy" case uses this ploy.

[8] Romney made the mistake in the early days of his campaign of referring to his experience as an American prisoner of war. He said that his enemy captors "brainwashed" him. Obviously, Romney was simply referring to the kind of psychological process that was used. However, the American public took the word literally; they were afraid of entrusting the government to a President whose brain was washed out.

mon colony in Chihuahua, Mexico, would be no barrier to his election. The Constitution requires that the President be a "natural born citizen of the United States." He said the question had been studied by several law firms and that since both his parents were American he was a "natural born" American.

"There can be no question on this point," he said.[9]

A Formalist would certainly have a question on this point. "Natural born" does not mean born of American parents; it has always meant being born within territorial United States. But clearly Romney's strategy was to defuse the issue, get nominated by the Republican Party, and leave the matter to scholars to discuss later on.

What *would* have happened had Romney been elected President? Formalists might have agitated for a constitutional amendment—which would have to be retroactive to help Romney—taking out the "natural born citizen" qualification. If the Republicans endorsed that idea and their candidate won the election, it might be difficult, post-election, to obtain the large majorities needed to pass a constitutional amendment. The strategy that most likely would be adopted by the Republicans would be to wait and defend the Romney presidency in the courts.

Suppose someone brought a legal action against Romney to declare that he could not serve as President. One immediate defense the Romney team would use would be to challenge the standing of the plaintiff. Under *Frothingham v. Mellon*,[10] the plaintiff's standing would be indistinguishable from that of any citizen in the United States, and hence there is arguably no standing at all.

If the lack-of-standing argument won, then we might effectively conclude that the qualifications for President listed in Article II Section 1, are unenforceable and hence only of political value. This political value is not the same as no value; after all, during the election campaign one of the charges hurled against Romney was that he was not a natu-

ral born citizen and hence would be an "unconstitutional" President. But it would at least mean that this is no "easy case."

Suppose, to take Professor Spann's example, a 34-year-old were elected President. By the time a lawsuit was filed—and assuming that the "standing" issue could be surmounted—a court would probably hold the case moot on the ground that the President, by now, was over 35. Although the Constitution says "eligible for office," it does not say *when* the eligibility must occur. One might argue that if the President will attain the age of 35 at some point while he or she is in office, the Constitutional requirement is met. A court might even stretch this reasoning—if a majority of the justices felt that it was vital to the security of the United States that this particular candidate assume the Presidency—to include a projected second term. With this bit of bootstrap even Professor Schauer's 29-year-old could make it to the Oval Office.

I said above that the Romney example was only a help to understanding the relativity of contexts in construing texts. Professors Schauer and Hegland can surely argue that my lack-of-standing conjecture is not what they had in mind when they were positing a clear case of the under-aged President, for I have simply avoided making a legal argument on the merits. They claim that there is no *good* nor *reasonable* argument—*i.e.*, no non-outrageous argument—that could be made on the merits that would defeat the 35-year-old qualification.

I think there is a good constitutional argument that can be made on the merits, one that does not seem "tricky" as the previous suggestions may have struck the reader. But simply to announce the argument would be to fall into the contextual trap that impliedly assumes the present context to be the one that applies. It is indeed hard to imagine in the context of the present day a major party putting forth an 18-year-old person as presidential nominee. Hence my reply to Professors Schauer and Hegland would be, "your so-called easy case of the 18-year-old candidate is itself outrageous—it will not come up." I suggest that this is a more realistic reply to Professor Schauer's hypothetical than proceeding to argue the merits and then encountering *his* reply that *my* argument is outrageous!

---

[9] *Romney Declares He's in '68 Race; Predicts Victory*, THE NEW YORK TIMES, p. 1, col. 1, at p. 62, col. 1 (Nov. 19, 1989).

[10] 262 U.S. 447 (1923).

But debating points aside, we must address the 18-year-old case on its merits. To do so we must imagine a suitable context; we must imagine why it might someday be likely, and seem reasonable, that an underaged candidate would be put forth by a major party in a serious way as a nominee for President. Only by imagining a plausible context *in which the posited case arises* can we evaluate supporting arguments as to their legal reasonableness.[11]

However, if we are willing to supply a suitable context in which we can imagine that an 18-year-old will be seriously put forth as a presidential nominee by a major party and have a serious chance of winning the election, then the legal argument I will be making will appear quite reasonable. We can easily speculate as to future contexts. Perhaps a student-led revolution in the United States may lead to demands for new leadership and a compromise is reached where the students put forth their leader (the 18-year-old) against the incumbent President. Or, as in science-fiction, what if at some future date an unstoppable virus causes the death of all persons over twenty-years old; the 18-year-old candidate may be one of the oldest available! In such a drastic situation, no Supreme Court would invalidate the election and leave the nation without a President; rather, a lawsuit challenging the 18-year-old would be thrown out of court as frivolous.

Given any context in which it is *reasonable* to imagine an 18-year-old Presidential nominee, my constitutional argument would be the following. The qualifications for President are listed in Article II, which is in the body of the Constitution. Every provision in the body of the Constitution is subject to amendment, and must be assumed to have been superseded or qualified by any relevant amendment. Here the relevant amendments are the Fifth and Fourteenth Amendments. The 35-year provision is a nullity because it

sets up an unconstitutional discrimination against younger persons based on an irrational age limit. Age discrimination—in a matter that would *restrict* the right of the people to elect a President of their own choosing—is clearly a violation of the Due Process Clause of the Fifth Amendment, and the Due Process and Equal Protection Clauses of the Fourteenth Amendment.[12]

My constitutional argument is not itself *dependent* upon the change of context which I have assumed. But the contextual change *is* important in overcoming the "outrageousness" test which, after all, is the last refuge of Formalists. If I flatly claim that the 35-year-old qualification amounts to age discrimination in violation of the Fifth and Fourteenth Amendments, a formalist might well characterize my argument as "outrageous." But it will appear far less outrageous—in fact, it will appear quite normal and ordinary!—if we actually have a serious case of a Presidential nominee who fails to meet one of the Article II qualifications. To some extent, the Romney case was a case in point.

Hence, once we get over the "outrageousness" (or "weird" or "non-standard") hurdle, we can find that even in the present context a legal argument exists (here, age discrimination) that could suddenly make the case appear not "easy" at all.

"Outrageousness" always depends upon the context in which the argument is made. If no context is specified, the present context is assumed—but that is a *real* context. The relativity of contexts assures, for the Pragmatist, the relativity of texts.

2. John Dewey: General Propositions[13]

Justice Oliver Wendell Holmes said in one of his Supreme Court opinions, "General principles do not decide concrete cases."

[11] *Cf.* Professor Tushnet: "The cases are weird until someone finds it worthwhile to pursue them. Then we see that what we thought of as constraints built into the language were only constraints built into our accepted ways of doing things." Mark Tushnet, *A Note on the Revival of Textualism in Constitutional Theory,* 58 S. CAL. L. REV. 683, 688 n.24 (1985).

[12] My argument is not even dependent upon the existence of the Fifth and Fourteenth Amendments. In their absence, a court could nevertheless find nondiscrimination in matters pertaining to age to be "implicit in the concept of ordered liberty."

[13] John Dewey, *Logical Method and Law,* 10 CORNELL L.Q. 17, 22 (1924).

No concrete proposition, that is to say one with material dated in time and placed in space, follows from any general statements or from any connection between them.

3. Ludwig Wittgenstein: Extending Rules to Hypothetical Situations[14]

If you imagine certain facts otherwise, describe them otherwise, than the way they are, then you can no longer imagine the application of certain concepts, because the rules for their application have no analogue in the new circumstances.

So what I am saying comes to *this*: A law is given for human beings and a jurisprudent may well be capable of drawing consequences for any case that ordinarily comes his way; thus the law evidently has its use, makes sense. Nevertheless its validity presupposes all sorts of things, and if the being that he is to judge is quite deviant from ordinary human beings, then *e.g.* the decision whether he has done a deed with evil intent will become not difficult but (simply) impossible.

QUESTIONS AND COMMENTS FOR YOUR CONSIDERATION

1. Lawrence Solum writes: "It is not difficult to imagine easy cases where a particular action clearly does not violate *any* legal rule. If a homeowner eats ice cream in the privacy of her home, it will not give rise to any legal action.[15]

Can you imagine a context that would give rise to liability for the homeowner? Consider this question before reading one possible solution given in the following insert.

> If you give me a temporary license to be gruesome: the homeowner's child is starving, and indeed starves to death, while the homeowner eats the ice cream. In this case, the homeowner's action (or inaction) gives rise to a criminal case; the state will (or at least should) bring charges of negligent manslaughter.[16]

2. Frederick Schauer writes: "If someone points a finger at a living, breathing, flying pelican and says 'That is not a bird,' she simply does not know what the word 'bird' means."[17]

Although this example is not part of a legal rule, it is a formalist assertion that a word can be invariable across all contexts, an assertion that a pragmatist would dispute. Can you supply a context that would refute the "pelican" example? Note that Professor Schauer has ruled out toy pelicans or a pelican on a movie screen. Consider this for a moment before reading one possible solution given in the following insert.

> She could have been referring to her *finger* and not to the pelican that was seen flying by. She then bends her finger and says, "That is not a bird; it's a unicorn." Then she makes a loose fist and says, "This is a bird." Her use is pictographic, not directive. It is similar to making shadow pictures of animals by hand and fingers in the path of a light that is projected on a wall in a dark room.

---

[14] Ludwig Wittgenstein, Zettel § 350 (1970). The passage was called to my attention by Brian Bix, *H.L.A. Hart and the Open Texture of Language*, 10 Law & Phil. 51, 61 (1991). For further discussions of Wittgenstein, *see* Brian Bix, Law, Language, and Legal Determinacy (1993).

[15] Lawrence Solum, *On the Indeterminacy Crisis: Critiquing Legal Dogma*, 54 U. Chi. L. Rev. 462, 472 (1987).

[16] Anthony D'Amato, *Aspects of Deconstruction: The 'Easy Case' of the Under-aged President*, 84 Nw. U. L. Rev. 250, 256 (1990).

[17] Frederick Schauer, *Formalism*, 97 Yale L.J. 509, 512 (1988).

3. Fala, President Franklin D. Roosevelt's famous Scottie, had a tendency to climb on both furniture and visitors in Roosevelt's Hyde Park home. One visitor whom Fala obviously distressed and who thought dogs should not be given such freedom was Secretary of State Cordell Hull. Calling upon his diplomatic skills, he said to the President, "A dog exists very well out in a yard." FDR replied smoothly, "Ah, my dear Hull, that is just the point. Fala is not a dog."[18]

Can you think of a linguistic argument to support the President? This is not a situation where one has to imagine a different context. Consider the example for a moment before looking at a possible solution given in the following insert.

> President Roosevelt was communicating to Secretary Hull the proposition that, for purposes of playing around in the living room, Fala was more a family member than a dog. Since FDR knew that Hull was operating under a definition of "dog" that included a *connotation* of an unruly animal not fit for indoor living, the President proceeded to attack *that* connotation. From FDR's point of view, the term "dog" was doing too much work—it was prejudging the issue, blocking Hull's mind from reconceptualizing the situation.[19]

4. Some Formalists are likely to get exasperated by the foregoing questions and examples. They rule out weird or outrageous contexts because they fear that unless words are taken to mean precisely what they say, the door will have been opened to nihilism. They accept the fact that the legal structure of our society is a structure based on words, and therefore they regard Pragmatists or Deconstructionists who challenge the meanings of words as enemies of law and order. Do you agree?

The Pragmatist, in turn, has a different kind of fear—a fear that literalness can lead to gross injustice in some cases. People whose claims are perfectly sensible and reasonable can nevertheless run afoul of a literalist-minded judge who "applies" a legal rule against them even though the result violates common sense and justice. Weren't Judge Truepenny and Judge Keen guilty of this kind of literalness in the Case of the Speluncean Explorers?

4. Oliver Wendell Holmes: Logic and Law[20]

The actual life of the law has not been logic: it has been experience. The felt necessities of the times, the prevalent moral and political theories, intuitions of public policy, avowed or unconscious, even the prejudices which judges share with their fellow men, have had a good deal more to do than the syllogism in determining the rules by which men should be governed.

The language of judicial decision is mainly the language of logic. And the logical method and form flatter that longing for certainty and for repose which is in every human mind. But certainty generally is an illusion.

5. Saul Kripke: Wittgenstein on Rules[21]

Wittgenstein replaces the question "What must be the case for this sentence to be true?" by two others: first, "Under what conditions

[18] F. SCHULER & R. MOORE, THE PEARL HARBOR COVER-UP 90-91 (1976).

[19] Anthony D'Amato, *Aspects of Deconstruction: The Failure of the Word "Bird,"* 84 Nw. U. L. REV. 536, 540 (1990).

[20] OLIVER WENDELL HOLMES, THE COMMON LAW 1; OLIVER WENDELL HOLMES, COLLECTED LEGAL PAPERS 50.

[21] SAUL KRIPKE, WITTGENSTEIN ON RULES AND PRIVATE LANGUAGE 73, 77-78 (1982). Copyright 1982 Harvard University Press. Excerpted by permission.

may this form of words be appropriately asserted (or denied)?"; second, given an answer to the first question, "What is the role, and the utility, in our lives of our practice of asserting (or denying) the form of words under these conditions?"

All that is needed to legitimize assertions that someone means something is that there be roughly specifiable circumstances under which they are legitimately assertable, and that the game of asserting them under such conditions has a role in our lives. No supposition that "facts correspond" to these assertions is needed.

B. Plain Meaning

1. Anthony D'Amato: Plain Meaning[22]

One of the most currently popular ideas in jurisprudence is that legal rules should be interpreted according to their plain or ordinary meaning. Justice Antonin Scalia has championed this position in his decisions and addresses.[23] The plain meaning approach fits hand-in-glove with legal formalism, defined by Frederick Schauer as characterizing a decisionmaker who "reaches the result indicated by some legal rule, independent of that decisionmaker's own best judgment and independent of the result that might be reached by direct application of the justification lying behind the rule."[24] I like to think of plain meaning as analogous to the curved spikes that one often sees at the entrance to a parking lot or parking garage—you can drive your car forward over the spikes, but if you try to back up, the spikes will puncture all your tires. In most cases the curved spikes work fairly well, but

sometimes situations can arise where the curved spikes are a disaster—*e.g.*, there is a fire in the parking garage, or you have a heart tremor and you want to back out of the lot and drive to the hospital. The rigidity and lack of human reasonableness of the curved spikes means that their cheap cost is spread out over many cases, most of which are easily accommodated, but a few of which can be expensively counterproductive. Similarly, if we take a rigid approach to legal rules, although our approach may work or seem to work well in the run-of-the-mill cases, sometimes situations arise where rigidity produces grave injustice. Can a rule *ever* have a "plain meaning" that works the way the curved spikes work? Take the ordinary red traffic signal outside your window and observe that thousands and thousands of cars duly stop at that signal every day and then proceed on the green signal. Isn't it plain that "red" means "stop your car"? Surely these thousands and thousands of cases, you may well claim, are not *problematic* or *indeterminate*! They seem to stand for a rule that has a clear meaning to all reasonably situated observers.

As an advocate of Pragmatic Indeterminacy, my position regarding the "red light" situation is two-fold. The first problem is one of knowledge. Do we really know that each and every one of those thousands of cases is not problematic? Is it possible that some driver stopped at the red light when she should not have stopped, and that in stopping she endangered the life of a child passenger who had to be rushed to a hospital? The second question is one of language. Suppose the traffic signal is bright orange and not "red," or the vehicle we are driving is a motorized wheelchair, or that it is unclear *when* we should stop (*i.e.*, we have reached the halfway point in the intersection of the streets when the light turns red). If this apparently nonproblematic rule contains hidden ambiguities or difficulties of application, is every rule inherently ambiguous, vague, or indeterminate?

I begin with the argument that a word does not "have" a meaning. A word is only a puff of vibrating air, or ink marks on paper. Words *represent*—that is, they call to our minds—a cluster of contextually induced meanings, a cluster that is slightly different for every user of the language. Sometimes

[22] Excerpted from Anthony D'Amato, *Counterintuitive Consequences of 'Plain Meaning,'* 33 Ariz. L. Rev. 529 (1991).

[23] *See, e.g.*, Burnham v. Superior Court of Cal., 110 S.Ct. 2105, 2117-19 (1990) (plurality opinion of Scalia, J.); Employment Div., Dep't of Human Resources v. Smith, 110 S.Ct. 1595 (1990); Scalia, *The Rule of Law as a Law of Rules*, 56 U. Chi. L. Rev. 1175 (1989).

[24] Schauer, *Rules and the Rule of Law*, 14 Harv. J.L. & Pub. Pol. 645, 664 (1991).

these slight differences are enough to block or frustrate communication; often they do not matter too much. All the Pragmatist can be sure of is that we can never be absolutely sure whether the different meanings attributed to the same words by speaker and listener will amount to enough of a difference to lead to disputes between them and, in some cases, lawsuits.

Calling attention to the inherent indeterminacy of language leads many legal scholars to cling to a hope that there is a plain meaning, out of fear that otherwise they will plunge into a nihilistic nightmare. Justice Scalia seems to prefer "plain meaning" as a way to keep lower courts under control (but of course he must *assume* that insisting on plain meaning can do this kind of job). I do not deny, as a practical matter, that in ordinary circumstances when nothing too much turns on it, indeterminate words can be used *as if* they are determinate. In this connection I like Margaret Jane Radin's notion of the "trivial case":

> [J]udges will not look deeply into cases that are apparently trivial, such as cases involving only a small fine, unless a sore thumb catches the judge's attention and makes her think that something "extremely wrong" may lurk beneath the surface. [On the other hand] . . . the very fact that the case involves the death penalty may preclude the psychological shortcut for the judge.[25]

The important point to note here is that a case is trivial or not depending on the consequences to the parties of an adverse decision. Whether an automobile went through a stop sign can be trivial if what is at stake is a potential fine of $25, or non-trivial if what is at stake is a tort case involving $250,000 in damages that turns on the possible "violation of statute" as supplying the negligence component.

Thus, to take an actual example, suppose a stake worth millions of dollars turns on the meaning of the short and simple phrase "prior to December 31." Consider what hap-

pened in the case of *United States v. Locke*. . . .

2. United States v. Locke

United States v. Locke
471 U.S. 84 (1985)

FACTS. Section 314 of the Federal Land Policy and Management Act of 1976 (FLPMA) establishes a federal recording system that is designed to rid federal lands of stale mining claims and to provide federal land managers with up-to-date information that allows them to make informed land management decisions. Section 314(b) requires that mining claims located prior to FLPMA's enactment be initially recorded with the Bureau of Land Management (BLM) within three years of the enactment, and §314(a) requires that the claimant, in the year of initial recording and "prior to December 31" of every year after that, file with state officials and the BLM a notice of intention to hold a claim, an affidavit of assessment work performed on the claim, or a detailed reporting form. Section 314(c) provides that failure to comply with either of these requirements "shall be deemed conclusively to constitute an abandonment" of the claim.

The relevant text of FLPMA (43 U.S.C. §1744) provides:

> The owner of an unpatented lode or placer mining claim located prior to October 21, 1976, shall, within the three-year period following October 21, 1976 and prior to December 31 of each year thereafter, file the instruments required by paragraphs (1) and (2) of this subsection. . . .

Appellees (the Lockes) are owners of 10 unpatented mining claims on federal land in Nevada. Appellees' predecessors located these claims in 1952 and 1954, and appellees have, since they purchased the claims in 1960, earned their livelihood by producing gravel and other building materials from them. From 1960 to the present, they have produced approximately $4 million worth of materials. During the 1979-1980 assessment year alone, they produced gravel and

---

[25] *See* Radin, *Presumptive Positivism and Trivial Cases,* 14 HARV. J.L. & PUB. POL. 823, 833 (1991).

other materials worth more than $1 million.

The Lockes fully complied with FLPMA's initial recordation requirement by properly filing a notice of location on October 19, 1979. In order to ascertain how to comply with the subsequent yearly recordation requirements, the Lockes sent their daughter, who worked in their business office, to the Ely, Nevada, office of the BLM. There she inquired into how and when they should file the assessment notice and was told, among other things, that the documents should be filed at the Reno office "on or before December 31, 1980." Following this advice, the Lockes hand-delivered their documents at the Reno office on that date. On April 4, 1981, they received notice from the BLM that their mining claims were "abandoned and void" because they had filed on, rather than prior to, December 31. It is this 1-day difference in the interpretation of the statutory deadline that gives rise to the present controversy.

JUSTICE MARSHALL delivered the opinion of the Court.

At the end of 1980, appellees failed to meet on time their first annual obligation to file with the Federal Government. After allegedly receiving misleading information from a BLM employee, appellees waited until December 31 to submit to BLM the annual notice of intent to hold or proof of assessment work performed required under the FLPMA. Before the District Court, appellees asserted that the FLPMA requirement of a filing "prior to December 31 of each year" should be construed to require a filing "on or before December 31." Thus, appellees argued, their December 31 filing had in fact complied with the statute, and the BLM had acted *ultra vires* in voiding their claims.

Although the District Court did not address this argument, the argument raises a question sufficiently legal in nature that we choose to address it even in the absence of lower court analysis. It is clear to us that the plain language of the statute simply cannot sustain the gloss appellees would put on it. As even counsel for appellees conceded at oral argument, FLPMA's section 1744 "is a statement that Congress wanted it filed by December 30th. I think that is a clear statement. . . ." Tr. of Oral Arg. 27; *see also id.*, at 37 ("A literal reading of the statute would require a December 30th filing . . ."). While we will not allow a literal reading of a statute to produce a result "demonstrably at odds with the intentions of its drafters," *Griffin v. Oceanic Contractors, Inc.*, 458 U.S. 564, 571 (1982), with respect to filing deadlines a literal reading of Congress' words is generally the only proper reading of those words. To attempt to decide whether some date other than the one set out in the statute is the date actually "intended" by Congress is to set sail on an aimless journey, for the purpose of a filing deadline would be just as well served by nearly any date a court might choose as by the date Congress has in fact set out in the statute. Actual purpose is sometimes unknown, and such is the case with filing deadlines; as might be expected, nothing in the legislative history suggests why Congress chose December 30 over December 31 as the last day on which the required filings could be made. But "[deadlines] are inherently arbitrary," while fixed dates "are often essential to accomplish necessary results." *United States v. Boyle*, 469 U.S. 241, 249 (1984). Faced with the inherent arbitrariness of filing deadlines, we must, at least in a civil case, apply by its terms the date fixed by the statute.

In so saying, we are not insensitive to the problems posed by congressional reliance on the words "prior to December 31." But the fact that Congress might have acted with greater clarity or foresight does not give courts a *carte blanche* to redraft statutes in an effort to achieve that which Congress is perceived to have failed to do. "There is a basic difference between filling a gap left by Congress' silence and rewriting rules that Congress has affirmatively and specifically enacted." *Mobil Oil Corp. v. Higginbotham*, 436 U.S. 618, 625 (1978). Nor is the Judiciary licensed to attempt to soften the clear import of Congress' chosen words whenever a court believes those words lead to a harsh result. On the contrary, deference to the supremacy of the Legislature, as well as recognition that Congressmen typically vote on the language of a bill, generally requires us to assume that "the legislative purpose is expressed by the ordinary meaning of the words used." *Richards v. United States*, 369 U.S. 1, 9 (1962). "Going behind the plain language of a statute in search of a possibly contrary congressional intent is 'a step to be taken cautiously' even under the best of circumstances." *Amer-*

ican Tobacco Co. v. Patterson, 456 U.S. 63, 75 (1982). When even after taking this step nothing in the legislative history remotely suggests a congressional intent contrary to Congress' chosen words, and neither appellees nor the dissenters have pointed to anything that so suggests, any further steps take the courts out of the realm of interpretation and place them in the domain of legislation. The phrase "prior to" may be clumsy, but its meaning is clear. Under these circumstances, we are obligated to apply the "prior to December 31" language by its terms.

We cannot press statutory construction "to the point of disingenuous evasion" even to avoid a constitutional question. We therefore hold that BLM did not act *ultra vires* in concluding that appellees' filing was untimely.

A final statutory question must be resolved. The District Court held that, even if the statute required a filing on or before December 30, appellees had "substantially complied" by filing on December 31. We cannot accept this view of the statute.

The notion that a filing deadline can be complied with by filing sometime after the deadline falls due is, to say the least, a surprising notion, and it is a notion without limiting principle. If 1-day late filings are acceptable, 10-day late filings might be equally acceptable, and so on in a cascade of exceptions that would engulf the rule erected by the filing deadline; yet regardless of where the cutoff line is set, some individuals will always fall just on the other side of it. Filing deadlines, like statutes of limitations, necessarily operate harshly and arbitrarily with respect to individuals who fall just on the other side of them, but if the concept of a filing deadline is to have any content, the deadline must be enforced. A filing deadline cannot be complied with, substantially or otherwise, by filing late—even by one day.[26]

---

[26] Since 1982, BLM regulations have provided that filings due on or before December 30 will be considered timely if postmarked on or before December 30 and received by BLM by the close of business on the following January 19. Appellees and the dissenters attempt to transform this regulation into a blank check generally authorizing "substantial compliance" with the filing requirements. We disagree for two reasons. First, the regulation was not in effect when appellees filed in 1980; it therefore cannot now be relied on to

Given the advice of the BLM agent, [the appellees could argue] that the United States was equitably estopped from forfeiting appellees' claims. We leave any further treatment of this issue, including fuller development of the record, to the District Court on remand.

JUSTICE O'CONNOR, concurring.

If the facts are as alleged by appellees, allowing the Bureau of Land Management (BLM) to extinguish active mining claims that appellees have owned and worked for more than 20 years would seem both unfair and inconsistent with the purposes underlying FLPMA.

The Government has not disputed that appellees sought in good faith to comply with the statutory deadline. Appellees contend that in order to meet the requirements of the FLPMA, they contacted the BLM and were informed by agency personnel that they could file the required materials on December 31, 1980. Appellees apparently relied on this advice and hand-delivered the appropriate documents to the local BLM office on that date. The BLM accepted the documents for filing, but some three months later sent appellees a notice stating that their mining claims were "abandoned and void" because the filing was made on, rather than prior to, December 31, 1980. Although BLM regulations clarify the filing deadlines contained in §314, the existence of those regulations does not imply that appellees were unjustified in their confusion concerning the deadlines or in their reliance on the advice provided by BLM's local office. The BLM itself in 1978 issued an explanatory pamphlet stating that the annual filings were to be made "on or before December 31" of each year. Moreover, the BLM evidently has come to understand the need to clarify the nature

---

validate a purported "substantial compliance" in 1980. Second, that an agency has decided to take account of holiday mail delays by treating as timely filed a document postmarked on the statutory filing date does not require the agency to accept all documents hand-delivered any time before January 19. The agency rationally could decide that either of the options in this sort of situation—requiring mailings to be received by the same date that hand-deliveries must be made or requiring mailings to be postmarked by that date—is a sound way of administering the statute.

of the annual filing requirement, because it now sends reminder notices every year to holders of recorded mining claims warning them that the deadline is approaching and that filings must be made on or before December 30.

The unusual facts alleged by appellees suggest that the BLM's actions might estop the Government from relying on the FLPMA to obliterate a property interest that has provided a family's livelihood for decades. The Court properly notes that the estoppel issue was not addressed by the District Court and will be open on remand.

JUSTICE STEVENS, with whom JUSTICE BRENNAN joins, dissenting.

The Court's opinion is contrary to the intent of Congress, engages in unnecessary constitutional adjudication, and unjustly creates a trap for unwary property owners. First, the choice of the language "prior to December 31" is, at least, ambiguous, and, at best, "the consequence of a legislative accident, perhaps caused by nothing more than the unfortunate fact that Congress is too busy to do all of its work as carefully as it should."[27] In my view, Congress actually intended to authorize an annual filing at any time prior to the close of business on December 31st, that is, prior to the end of the calendar year to which the filing pertains. Second, even if Congress irrationally intended that the applicable deadline for a calendar year should end one day before the end of the calendar year that has been recognized since the amendment of the Julian Calendar in 8 B.C., it is clear that appellees have substantially complied with the requirements of the statute.

A careful reading of FLPMA discloses at least three respects in which its text cannot possibly reflect the actual intent of Congress. First, the description of what must be filed in the initial filing and subsequent annual filings is quite obviously garbled. Read literally, §314(a)(2) of the FLPMA seems to require that a notice of intent to hold the claim and an affidavit of assessment work performed on the claim must be filed "on a detailed report provided by §28-1 of Title 30."

One must substitute the word "or" for the word "on" to make any sense at all out of this provision. This error should cause us to pause before concluding that Congress commanded blind allegiance to the remainder of the literal text of the FLPMA.

Second, the express language of the statute is unambiguous in describing the place where the second annual filing shall be made. If the statute is read inflexibly, the owner must "file in the office of the Bureau" the required documents. Yet the regulations that the Bureau itself has drafted, quite reasonably, construe the statute to allow filing in a mailbox, provided that the document is actually received by the Bureau prior to the close of business on January 19th of the year following the year in which the statute requires the filing to be made. A notice mailed on December 30, 1982, and received by the Bureau on January 19, 1983, was filed "in the office of the Bureau" during 1982 within the meaning of the statute, but one that is hand-delivered to the office on December 31, 1982, cannot be accepted as a 1982 "filing."

The Court finds comfort in the fact that the implementing regulations have eliminated the risk of injustice. But if one must rely on those regulations, it should be apparent that the meaning of the statute itself is not all that obvious. The regulations do not use the language "prior to December 31"; instead, they use "on or before December 30 of each year."[28] The Bureau's drafting of the regulations using this latter phrase indicates that the meaning of the statute itself

---

[27] Delaware Tribal Business Committee v. Weeks, 430 US 73, 97 (1977) (Stevens, J., dissenting) (emphasis added).

[28] 43 CFR § 3833.2-1(b)(1) (1984). It is undisputed that the regulations did not come to the attention of the appellees. To justify the forfeiture in this case on the ground that appellees are chargeable with constructive notice of the contents of the Federal Register is no more acceptable to me today than it would have been to Justice Jackson in 1947. "To my mind, it is an absurdity to hold that every farmer who insures his crops knows what the Federal Register contains or even knows that there is such a publication. If he were to peruse this voluminous and dull publication as it is issued from time to time in order to make sure whether anything has been promulgated that affects his rights, he would never need crop insurance, for he would never get time to plant any crops." Federal Crop Insurance Corporation v. Merrill, 332 U.S. 380, 387 (1947) (Jackson, J., dissenting).

is not quite as "plain" as the Court assumes; if the language were plain, it is doubtful that the Bureau would have found it necessary to change the language at all.

In light of the foregoing, I cannot believe that Congress intended the words "prior to December 31 of each year" to be given the literal reading the Court adopts today. The statutory scheme requires periodic filings on a calendar-year basis. The end of the calendar year is, of course, correctly described either as "prior to the close of business on December 31," or "on or before December 31," but it is surely understandable that the author of FLPMA might inadvertently use the words "prior to December 31" when he meant to refer to the end of the calendar year. As the facts of this case demonstrate, the scrivener's error is one that can be made in good faith. The risk of such an error is, of course, the greatest when the reference is to the end of the calendar year. That it was in fact an error seems rather clear to me because no one has suggested any rational basis for omitting just one day from the period in which an annual filing may be made, and I would not presume that Congress deliberately created a trap for the unwary by such an omission.

It would be fully consistent with the intent of Congress to treat any filing received during the 1980 calendar year as a timely filing for that year. Such an interpretation certainly does not interfere with Congress' intent to establish a federal recording system designed to cope with the problem of stale mining claims on federal lands. The system is established, and apparently, functioning.[29] Moreover, the claims here were ac-

tive; the Bureau was well aware that the appellees intended to hold and to operate their claims.

Additionally, a sensible construction of the statute does not interfere with Congress' intention to provide "an easy way of discovering which Federal lands are subject to either valid or invalid mining claim locations."[30] The Bureau in this case was well aware of the existence and production of appellees' mining claims; only by blinking reality could the Bureau reach the decision that it did. It is undisputed that the appellees made the first 1980 filing on August 29, 1980, and made the second required filing on December 31, 1980; the Bureau did not declare the mining claims "abandoned and void" until April 4, 1981. Thus, appellees lost their entire livelihood for no practical reason, contrary to the intent of Congress, and because of the hypertechnical construction of a poorly drafted statute, which an agency interprets to allow "filings" far beyond December 30 in some circumstances, but then interprets inflexibly in others. I have no doubt that Congress would have chosen to adopt a construction of the statute that filing take place by the end of the calendar year if its attention had been focused on this precise issue.

In sum, this case presents an ambiguous statute, which, if strictly construed, will destroy valuable rights of appellees, property owners who have complied with all local and federal statutory filing requirements apart from a 1-day "late" filing caused by the Bu-

---

[29] Several amici have filed materials listing numerous cases in which it is asserted that the Bureau is using every technical construction of the statute to suck up active mining claims much as a vacuum cleaner, if not watched closely, will suck up jewelry or loose money. *See* Brief for Mountain States Legal Foundation, claiming that an "overwhelming number of mining claims have been lost to the pitfalls of section 314" and claiming that from 1977 to 1984 "unpatented mining claimants lost almost 20,000 active locations due to the technical rigors and conclusive presumption of section 314"; Brief for Alaska Miners Association, stating that well over 1,400 claims were invalidated from 1979-1983 because § 1744(a)(1) filings were made on December 31; Letter from Bureau's Billings, Montana Office stating that 198 claims were invalidated from 1979-1983 because § 1744(a)(1) fil-

ings were made on December 31); Letter from Bureau's Wyoming State Office stating that 11 claims were invalidated in 1980-1982 because § 1744(a)(2) filings were made on December 31); Letter from Bureau's Arizona State Office stating that "approximately 500 claims have been invalidated due to filing an affidavit one day late"); Brief for Mobil Oil Corporation, claiming to be in a situation similar to the appellees'. According to the Bureau's own calculations, thousands of active mining claims have been terminated because filings made on December 31 were considered untimely. These representations confirm the picture painted by amici of a federal bureaucracy virtually running amok, and surely operating contrary to the intent of Congress, by terminating the valuable property rights of hardworking, productive citizens of our country.

[30] S. Rep. No. 94-583, p. 65 (1975).

reau's own failure to mail a reminder notice necessary because of the statute's ambiguity and caused by the Bureau's information to appellees that the date on which the filing occurred would be acceptable. Further, long before the Bureau declared a technical "abandonment," it was in complete possession of all information necessary to assess the activity, locations, and ownership of appellees' mining claims and it possessed all information needed to carry out its statutory functions. Finally, the Bureau has not claimed that the filing is contrary to the congressional purposes behind the statute, that the filing affected the Bureau's land-use planning functions in any manner, or that it interfered "in any measurable way" with the Bureau's need to obtain information. A showing of substantial compliance necessitates a significant burden of proof; appellees, whose active mining claims will be destroyed contrary to Congress' intent, have convinced me that they have substantially complied with the statute.

QUESTIONS AND COMMENTS FOR YOUR CONSIDERATION

1. Arguing the case for the United States in the Supreme Court was Carolyn F. Corwin. With her on the briefs were Solicitor General Lee, Assistant Attorney General Habicht, Deputy Solicitor General Claiborne, David C. Shilton, and Arthur E. Gowran. Harold A. Swafford argued the cause for appellees. With him on the brief was John W. Hoffman.

If the Lockes' claim was to stand or fall upon the interpretation of the phrase "prior to December 31," why did Mr. Stafford concede during oral argument that FLPMA's section 1744 "is a statement that Congress wanted it filed by December 30th. I think that is a clear statement"? Did he not concede away the entire case?

Is it possible that Mr. Stafford himself was a believer in "plain meaning" to the extent that he could not imagine any alternative to his own interpretation of the phrase "prior to December 31"? Or was he engaging in the strategy of trying to appear "reasonable" to the nine Justices of the Supreme Court by conceding that the statutory words meant "December 30" and then hoping, by his "reasonableness," to win on his argument that the Locke's "substantially complied" with the statute by filing on the 31st?

2. Why was the majority of the Court so determined to insist on the "plain meaning" of the FLPMA even though, as Justice Marshall said, deadlines are "inherently arbitrary"? Isn't the majority's motive obvious? Doesn't it want to *control lower courts* by removing their latitude to engage in loose interpretation of Congressional statutes? (Surely the Supreme Court is not worried about its *own* latitude in interpreting statutes; after all, it is the highest court. But since it does not have the time to review all lower court determinations—indeed, the Court only reviews a tiny fraction of lower-court cases—it desires some other mechanism of keeping the reins taut on lower-court judges. That mechanism, it appears from the majority's opinion, is an insistence on plain meaning.)

3. Does "plain meaning" work to constrain judges? Formalists would like to think so. Most Positivists would agree. Would you expect lower-court judges to follow the Supreme Court's lead in insisting on "plain meaning" even when the meaning leads to arbitrariness or injustice? At some point, isn't a judge likely to say, "Why am I a judge, if all I'm supposed to do is apply the dictionary meanings of words in statutes? Why should I be oblivious to the effect—sometimes the ridiculous and arbitrary effect—that applying dictionary meanings will have on

the parties? What kind of a life does the Supreme Court think I should have?"

4. As we saw at the beginning of this Chapter, the 35-year requirement for the age of persons eligible to be President could be reconstrued if the context cried out for reconstruction. Would a similar argument from context apply to the filing of mining claims under the FLPMA?

5. Can you think of *any* context where even the Supreme Court would allow the filing on December 31st? Surely there is at least one: the Lockes arrive at the business office of the BLM in the early afternoon of December 30th, but they are barred entry into the office. The employees inside keep the doors locked; they eat their lunch and dinner inside the office and then sleep on cots until one minute after midnight. Then they open the door and invite the Lockes to come in and register. Of course, now it is too late for the Lockes—the date is December 31st, so they lose their mining claims.

6. However, in the usual context, mining claims will be lost unless filed on or before December 30th. So says the Supreme Court, and who can argue with the Supreme Court once it has decided a case? Yet Attorney Swafford had a chance to argue to the Supreme Court before it had made its decision. What argument could he have made that the phrase "prior to December 31" really means "on or before December 31"? Remember: Mr. Swafford could not think of any conceivable way to make such an argument.

7. Couldn't Mr. Swafford had argued that Congress meant, by "prior to December 31," *prior to the close of business on December 31*?

8. But suppose for the moment that Congress meant, by the phrase "prior to," something that only occurs before something else starts. Let us engage in a legislative drafting thought experiment. Suppose that Congress wanted to give mining claimants the chance to file their annual updates before the end of the calendar year. How could Congress, *using the phrase "prior to"*, signify that claimants had until the close of business on December 31st to file their reports? To do so, Congress would have had to provide: "prior to January 1." By using the latter phrase, Congress would have made it clear that the mining report could be filed all the way up to the close of business on December 31.

Let us continue this thought experiment. Recall that the relevant section of the FLPMA at present provides:

> The owner of an unpatented lode or placer mining claim located prior to October 21, 1976, shall, within the three-year period following October 21, 1976 and prior to December 31 of each year thereafter, file the instruments required by paragraphs (1) and (2) of this subsection.
> . . .

Now, suppose that we insert "prior to January 1." The statute would then read:

> The owner of an unpatented lode or placer mining claim located prior to October 21, 1976, shall, within the three-year period following October 21, 1976 and prior to January 1 of each year thereafter, file the instruments required by paragraphs (1) and (2) of this subsection. .
> . .

But now look at the grotesque ambiguity that has been created. Does "January 1 of each year thereafter" mean the current year or the following year? If you have a mining claim and you've filed on October 20, 1976, does that mean that you have to again file prior to January 1, 1977? Or does it mean that, after filing on October 20, 1976, you have the entire calendar year 1977 to file your claim? A literal or "plain meaning" reading of the statute would suggest that you have to file again within a two month and eleven day period after October 20, 1976, yet this literal reading would be absurd because your filing has been so recent. Or consider a second literal or "plain meaning" reading of the statute as we have revised it. Does "prior to January 1 of each year thereafter" mean that you have to file the claim *on* January 1 prior to the close of business on January 1? For example, within calendar year 1985, do you have to file your claim prior to the close of business on January 1, 1985 because, as the statute says, 1985 is a "year thereafter" and therefore you need to file on January 1st of that year? This reading would mean that everyone would have to file the claim during one day each year, on January 1st (a day that is normally a federal holiday!)

Therefore may we not conclude, on the basis of this thought experiment, that *if* Congress meant by the words "prior to" the meaning that the Supreme Court (and Attorney Swafford) gave to them—that is, "prior to" means "the day before"—then *if* Congress wanted to give claimants up through December 31 to file their claims (a not unreasonable presumption because December 31 is within the calendar year for the annual renewal of claims), Congress would have been forced to adopt the phrase "prior to January 1"? Yet since the latter phrase would have raised far more questions that it would solve, we should go back and check our original postulate—that "prior to" means "the day before" and not "prior to the close of business on." Indeed, we should conclude that the only reasonable way that Congress *could have* provided for a December 31st deadline while *retaining* the phrase "prior to" would be to do what Congress actually did, namely, to say "prior to December 31."

Isn't December 31, after all, the "plain meaning" of the phrase that Congress actually used?

9. As a result of the *Locke* case, isn't the Supreme Court instructing lower courts to use the "strange plain meaning" of statutory language instead of the "reasonable plain meaning"? If so, how could that strategy result in controlling the decision-making of lower courts?

10. Isn't the Supreme Court of the United States, in short, engaging in a jurisprudentially naive insistence on literal meaning in an attempt to control lower court decision-making? And isn't that strategy doomed to fail? Isn't the *Locke* case an excellent *negative* example to cite in favor of Pragmatism?

C. Anti-Formalism

In Chapter 4 we read Dworkin's famous effort to show that a correct answer theoretically exists in the law even for the hardest case. His right-answer thesis is designed to throw cold water on the Realist claim that a judge might invent *new* law to adjudicate rights. The rights thesis stands for the proposition that no matter which judge hears a case, existing law—and it is important to emphasize that by "existing law" we mean the law at the time that the dispute arose—would govern the rights of the parties. Litigants would have an important psychological assurance that their dispute was governed by existing rules at the time it arose, an assurance similar to the fundamental understanding of any person who plays any game or sport that the rules of the game will not be changed after the game begins.

Formalists and Realists thus debate whether it is possible or impossible for the law "in place" at the moment a dispute arises to control and govern the dispute. Is there any way that their debate can be settled logically and decisively? Consider the following argument.

1. Kenneth Kress: Is Strict Formalism Impossible?[31]

Dworkin's [Formalist] theory of legal reasoning is built on the proposition that litigants are entitled to the enforcement of preexisting legal rights. One way in which the rights thesis expresses this major claim is by presupposing that litigants have a right to have decisions in civil cases determined by settled law. In Dworkin's theory, settled law (together with moral theory) determines litigants' rights and litigants' rights determine the proper outcome. Thus, decisions are a function of, among other things, the settled law.

The argument I call the "ripple effect" relies upon these features of the rights thesis. In particular, the ripple effect argument depends upon legal rights being a function of settled law and upon the temporal gap between events being litigated and their eventual adjudication.

Judicial decisions change the settled law. Often, if not always, the settled law will be changed between the occurrence of events being litigated and their eventual adjudication. In consequence, a litigant's rights will sometimes also be changed. If changes in the settled law change the dispositive legal right, a litigant who would have prevailed given the legal rights existing at the time of the occurrence will lose because he no longer has that right at the time of adjudication. The opposite is true of the opposing litigant.

This is retroactive application of law. The

ripple effect argument suggests that the rights thesis sometimes enforces the wrong preexisting right. The rights thesis does not enforce the right that the prevailing party had when the events being litigated occurred, but rather the possibly different right existing at the time of adjudication.

Dworkin's theory tells us that in a hard case, when a judge is called upon to decide a legal question Q that is not a logical (or theoretical) consequence of the principles P, he must do so by determining whether Q or not-Q coheres better with the soundest theory of law STL. Consider a case where Q coheres better with STL than not-Q does and the judge so holds. By virtue of that judicial decision Q is no longer part of the true but unsettled law UC. It is now part of the settled law. This disturbs the theory STL and, as one would expect in a coherence theory, has ripple effects on the rest of the system. More precisely, settled law now contains one more proposition, namely Q. Call the new settled law SL'. The new soundest theory of law STL' will, in general, differ from STL since it must explain and justify the additional data Q. (Since Q was part of the unsettled law, neither Q nor not-Q followed logically or theoretically from P.) While STL' need not necessarily cohere with a different set of propositions than STL, in most cases STL' will so differ. With at most rare exceptions, STL' will cohere with a different set of propositions than STL did. That is, for some proposition X of the set of nonconsequences N, X cohered better with STL than not-X did, and was hence true and a member of UC with respect to STL before the decision. After the decision, not-X coheres better with STL'. X was true but became false as a ripple effect of Q being settled by explicit judicial decision. Thus, while the judge discovered and did not create the truth of Q, the question at issue, he nonetheless created as an unintended consequence the truth of

³¹ Kenneth Kress, *Legal Reasoning and Coherence Theories: Dworkin's Rights Thesis, Retroactivity, and the Linear Order of Decisions*, 72 CALIFORNIA LAW REVIEW 369, 380-83 (1984). Copyright California Law Review 1984. Reprinted by permission.

not-X. In a sense this should have been obvious: judicial decisions change the law.

Once it is admitted that judicial decisions can change the truth value of propositions of unsettled law by the ripple effect, it is easy to see how retroactive application of law can arise. Suppose that a lawsuit is pending in which X is dispositive. In the above example, if Q is settled after the events that gave rise to the lawsuit but before it comes to judgment, the law will change from X to *not-X* and a litigant will be subject to retroactive application of law.[32]

Note that the judge has inadvertently caused retroactive application of law, without exercising discretion. Q was the right answer, required by Dworkin's theory of adjudication, since Q cohered better with *STL* than *not-Q* did. Thus, we see that Dworkin's rights thesis requires that, without exercising discretion, judges sometimes retroactively apply law. Dworkin claims that the rights thesis is preferable to positivism because by avoiding judicial discretion it avoids retroactive application of law. That claim goes awry because it equates judicial

discretion with judicial creation of law. In fact, it is the creation of new law, and not judicial discretion, that leads to the possibility of retroactivity. Once the concepts of law creation and judicial discretion are distinguished, it is possible to see how, without exercising discretion, applying law created (perhaps by other judges) after the events being litigated occurred can result in retroactive application of law. The acts of "law creation" by prior judges that result in the current judge's nondiscretionary yet retroactive application of law were themselves performed without exercising judicial discretion, according to Dworkin's own theory.

A simplified example will illustrate the basic thrust of the ripple effect argument. Consider a hypothetical jurisdiction which is just developing the law of privity of contract. Suppose that in this jurisdiction, a case holds that direct contractual relations give rise to liability. For example, one may sue those from whom one purchases defective merchandise; liability exists at one step removed. However, another case holds that there is no liability six steps down the line. If consumer A buys from retailer B who bought from local distributor C, who bought from regional distributor D . . . who bought from manufacturer G, A may not recover from G even if the product is defective. Assume for the sake of illustration what is undoubtedly false, that each step in the chain of privity is of equal moral and legal "distance" in the relevant respects.[33]

The geometric model of the doctrine of precedent tells one, in a hard case, to split the legally relevant distance between the closest cases on point. If a novel privity case were to come up in our jurisdiction at this point in time, the judge should find liability if the plaintiff is two or three steps removed since, by our assumption, two and three are closer to one than to six, and four and five are closer to six than to one. However, suppose that the next case decided is four steps

---

[32] The argument is quite general. It requires only that legal truths sometimes change when settled law is enlarged by new decisions and that sometimes such changes occur in legal propositions that are dispositive of cases where the events occurred prior to the change and the adjudication occurs after the change.

The generality of the argument can be seen even more clearly in light of a set-theoretic characterization of coherence. Conceive of coherence as a mathematical function from sets of accepted data (or truths) to sets consisting of all true propositions including those true by virtue of coherence with accepted data. In Dworkin's theory, for example, the coherence function will take as argument (or input) institutional histories (or settled law) and will produce as value (or output) the complete set of legal truths given that institutional history. All that is required for ripple effects is that sometimes different inputs result in different outputs from the coherence function C. Put set theoretically, all that is required is that the coherence function C be nonconstant. In other words, a restriction of the image of C is a function.

Given that minimal condition, ripple effects will occur. As noted above, retroactive application of law will occur if any such ripple effects change dispositive propositions of cases whose events occurred prior to the ripple effect and whose adjudication occurs after.

---

[33] I have deliberately chosen an example where it is wildly implausible to suppose that the steps in question are of equal morally or legally relevant distance in order to focus on the general point. A more plausible example would draw attention to the details of the example, and whether the example's steps were of equal distance, thereby losing sight of the general point.

removed and the judge correctly finds no liability. If a case three steps removed comes up at this point, the plaintiff will lose because three is closer to four, the closest no-liability case, than to one, the closest liability case. Although our imaginary plaintiff would have won had his case preceded the four-step case, he now loses. This situation creates a race to the courthouse that appears contrary to our notions of justice. If the three-and four-step cases are going up the appellate ladder simultaneously, an unfortunate situation results. If the four-step case reaches the top first, the defendants in the three-and four-step cases win; if the three-step case reaches the top first, both plaintiffs win.

Of course, this is only a fanciful example. It assumes that precedent or argument by analogy is the whole of legal reasoning, while in any sophisticated legal system it will only play a part. Nonetheless, to the extent that precedent plays a part, the ripple effect will occur, bringing in its wake retroactive applications of law.

2. Anthony D'Amato: An Appreciation of Kress's Result[34]

An important contribution to the break-

---

[34] Excerpted from Anthony D'Amato, *Pragmatic Indeterminacy*, 85 Nw. U. L. Rev. 148, 176-79 (1990).

down of Formalism was made by Ken Kress in 1984. He showed that the time between when the facts of a case arise and when the case is adjudicated in a court will necessarily affect the state of the law applied to the case. For during the gap between facts and adjudication, *intervening* decisions in other cases will be handed down, and these will have some impact on the content of the law that will be applied to the instant case. It follows from Professor Kress's significant thought experiment that the law can *never* be determinate at the moment that people act; or, in other words, that no one can know precisely what the law is when one needs to know it in order to act legally.

For all cases are connected to all other cases through the mental process of analogy. The legal system is in effect a "closed system"; any new decision has a potential impact on all subsequent decisions. Because of this potential impact that arises *after* the facts in the instant case, Professor Kress has proved that all cases are to some extent indeterminate. Or, in other words, a judge can never decide a case precisely according to rules that were in place at the time the events in the case arose. By extension, no person can say at any point in time that all the legal rules applicable to her planned course of action are in principle knowable. For it is and must remain possible, as Professor Kress has demonstrated, that new decisional rules that arise *after* she has taken her action—decisional rules that she cannot possibly know—could be retroactively applied to decide her own fact situation.

QUESTIONS AND COMMENTS FOR YOUR CONSIDERATION

1. Would it be practical for a court to announce, in deciding a case, that *only* precedential decisions will be taken into account that were handed down prior to the time that the facts arose that gave rise to the dispute in the present case?

2. Suppose the facts in the present case, case *Q*, arose in 1993. Suppose the trial occurs in 1996. Suppose that a different case, case *N*, was decided in 1995. Suppose that the decision in *N* would have a decisive impact upon the decision in *Q* if the judge in *Q* were willing to take the decision in *N* into account. Now suppose that the plaintiff in *Q* (who would be adversely affected by acknowledging the decision in *N*) objects on the ground that, when the facts of *Q* arose in 1993, there was at that time no decision in *N* and therefore it would be unfair to acknowledge the result in *N* in deciding case *Q*. What argument can the other party to the litigation make? Suppose the facts in *N* arose in 1992? Then could

the defendant in *Q* argue that, since the facts in *N* arose in 1992, a year prior to when the facts of case *Q* arose, the decision in the case *N* should be applicable to case *Q*? What counter-argument would the plaintiff in *P* make? Who would have the better argument, plaintiff or defendant? Could the defendant in *P* argue that the judge in *N* after all simply applied the law as it was at the time of the facts, namely 1992, and therefore the court's opinion in *N* was not a new statement of the law but rather simply an explication of what the law was in 1992? Thus, since the facts in case *Q* arose a year later, the law in 1992 (as laid down by the decision in *N* in 1995) should be applied.

3. Is Professor Kress's thesis helped or hurt by the theory that judges find the law rather than make it?

4. Is it unrealistic to assume that all cases are affected by the decisions in all other cases, no matter how "on point" those other cases are? Yet, as we saw in the argument of Julius Stone in Chapter 4, the principle of *stare decisis* is in principle unbounded. At some level of generality, any case can be said to have a precedential impact upon any other case.

5. But suppose case *N*, decided yesterday, is quite different from case *Q* which is to be decided today. Also, suppose that case *N* was handed down in a different jurisdiction. Can we say that case *N* has absolutely no impact upon the decision in *Q*? Suppose the judge in *Q* happens to read about the decision in *N* in the morning newspaper; suppose it sets the judge thinking about case *Q* in a different way, and that afternoon the judge hands down a decision in *Q* that is different from the one that would have been handed down had the judge not seen the newspaper report of the decision in *N*. This may be far-fetched, but can we say with assurance that it can never happen?

D. Pragmatism

1. Richard Rorty: Pragmatism[35]

The pragmatist simply asks himself the same question about a text which the engineer or the physicist asks himself about a puzzling physical object: how shall I describe this in order to get it to do what I want? Occasionally a great physicist or a great critic comes along and gives us a new vocabulary which enables us to do a lot of new and marvelous things. Then we may exclaim that we have now found out the true nature of matter, or poetry, or whatever. But Hegel's ghost, embodied in Kuhn's romantic philosophy of science or Bloom's philosophy of romantic poetry, reminds us that vocabularies

are as mortal as men. The pragmatist reminds us that a new and useful vocabulary is just that, not a sudden unmediated vision of things or texts as they are.

2. Richard Posner: A Pragmatist Manifesto[36]

Beginning in the 1960s with the waning of logical positivism, pragmatism came charging back in the person of Richard Rorty, followed in the 1970s by critical legal studies—the radical child of legal realism—and in the 1980s by a school of legal neopragmatists, including some feminists.

[35] RICHARD RORTY, CONSEQUENCES OF PRAGMATISM 153 (1982). Copyright 1982 University of Minnesota. Reprinted by permission.

[36] Excerpted from RICHARD POSNER, THE PROBLEMS OF JURISPRUDENCE 460-69 (1990). Copyright 1990 by the President and Fellows of Harvard College. Reprinted by permission.

In this account pragmatism stands for a progressively more emphatic rejection of Enlightenment dualisms such as subject and object, mind and body, perception and reality, form and substance, those dualisms being regarded as the props of a conservative social, political, and legal order.

"Truth" is a problematic concept for a pragmatist. Its essential meaning, after all, is observer independence, which is just what the pragmatist is inclined to deny. It is no surprise, therefore, that the pragmatists' stabs at defining truth—truth is what is fated to be believed in in the long run (Charles Sanders Pierce), truth is what is good to believe (William James), or truth is what survives in the competition among ideas (Oliver Wendell Holmes)—are riven by paradox. The pragmatist's real interest is not in truth at all but in belief justified by social need.

Pragmatism in the sense that I find congenial means looking at problems concretely, experimentally, without illusions, with a full awareness of the limitations of human reason, with a sense of the "localness" of human knowledge, the difficulty of translations between cultures, the unattainability of "truth," the consequent importance of keeping diverse paths of inquiry open, the dependence of inquiry on culture and social institutions, and above all the insistence that social thought and action be evaluated as instruments to valued human goals rather than as ends in themselves. These dispositions, which are more characteristic of scientists than of lawyers (and in an important sense pragmatism is the ethics of scientific inquiry), have no political valence. They can, I believe, point the way to a clearer understanding of law. Law as currently conceived in the academy and the judiciary has too theocratic a cast. There is too much emphasis on authority, certitude, rhetoric, and tradition, too little on consequences and on social-scientific techniques for measuring consequences. There is too much confidence, too little curiosity, and insufficient regard for the contributions of other disciplines. Jurisprudence itself is much too solemn and self-important. Its votaries write too marmoreal, hieratic, and censorious a prose. Law and religion were long intertwined, and many parallels and overlaps remain. Law, too, has its high priests, its sacred texts and sacred cows, its hermeneutic mysteries, its robes and temples, rituals and ceremonies.

Law needs more of the scientific spirit than it has—the spirit of inquiry, challenge, fallibilism, open-mindedness, respect for fact, and acceptance of change. I use "spirit" advisedly. I am not referring to the particulars of scientific discourse, although economics and other social sciences have a large role to play in any modern system of law.

I find pragmatism bracing; others may find it paralyzing. Pragmatist skepticism about "truth" might, for example, be thought to undermine the nation's commitment to free speech. If there is no truth "out there," how can free speech be defended by reference to its efficacy in bringing us nearer to truth? Actually, that is not such a difficult question. If there is no truth out there, this should make us particularly wary of people who claim to have found the truth and who argue that further inquiry would be futile or subversive and therefore should be forbidden. If there is no objective truth, moreover, this makes it all the more important to maintain the conditions necessary for the unforced inquiry required to challenge and defeat all those false claims to have found the truth at last.

2. John Dewey: Law, Logic and Pragmatism[37]

Men do not begin thinking with premises. They begin with some complicated and confused case, apparently admitting of alternative modes of treatment and solution. Premises only gradually emerge from analysis of the total situation. The problem is not to draw a conclusion from given premises; that can best be done by a piece of inanimate machinery by fingering a keyboard. The problem is to *find* statements of general principle and of particular fact which are worthy to serve as premises.

We generally begin with some vague anticipation of a conclusion (or at least of alternative conclusions), and then we look around for principles and data which will substanti-

---

[37] John Dewey, *Logical Method and Law*, 10 CORNELL L.Q. 17, 23-27 (1924).

ate it or which will enable us to choose intelligently between rival conclusions. No lawyer ever thought out the case of a client in terms of a logical syllogism. He begins with a conclusion which he intends to reach, favorable to his client of course, and then analyzes the facts of the situation to find material out of which to construct a favorable statement of facts, to *form* a minor premise. At the same time he goes over recorded cases to find rules of law employed in cases which can be presented as similar, rules which will substantiate a certain way of looking at and interpreting the facts. And as his acquaintance with rules of law judged applicable widens, he probably alters perspective and emphasis in selection of the facts which are to form his eventual data. And as he learns more of the facts of the case he may modify his selection of rules of law upon which he bases his case.

I do not for a moment set up this procedure as a model of scientific method; it is too precommitted to the establishment of a particular and partisan conclusion to serve as such a model. But it does illustrate, in spite of this deficiency, the particular point which is being made here: namely, that thinking actually sets out from a more or less confused situation, which is vague and ambiguous with respect to the conclusion it indicates, and that the formation of both major premise and minor proceed tentatively and correlatively in the course of analysis of this situation and of prior rules. In strict logic, the conclusion does not follow from the premises; conclusions and premises are two ways of stating the same thing. Thinking may be defined either as a development of premises or development of a conclusion; as far as it is one operation it is the other. Courts not only reach decisions; they expound them, and the exposition must state justifying reasons. The mental operations therein involved are somewhat different from those involved in arriving at a conclusion. The logic of exposition is different from that of search and inquiry. In the latter, the situation as it exists is more or less doubtful, indeterminate, and problematic with respect to what it signifies. It unfolds itself gradually and is susceptible of dramatic surprise.

Exposition implies that a definitive solution is reached, that the situation is now determinate with respect to its legal implica-

tion. Its purpose is to set forth grounds for the decision reached so that it will not appear as an arbitrary dictum, and so that it will indicate a rule for dealing with similar cases in the future. It is highly probable that the need of justifying to others conclusions reached and decisions made has been the chief cause of the origin and development of logical operations in the precise sense; of abstraction, generalization, regard for consistency of implications. It is quite conceivable that if no one had ever had to account to others for his decisions, logical operations would never have developed, but men would use exclusively methods of inarticulate intuition and impression, feeling; so that only after considerable experience in accounting for their decisions to others who demanded a reason, or exculpation, and were not satisfied till they got it, did men begin to give an account to themselves of the process of reaching a conclusion in a justified way. However this may be, it is certain that in judicial decisions the only alternative to arbitrary dicta, accepted by the parties to a controversy only because of the authority or prestige of the judge, is a rational statement which formulates grounds and exposes connecting or logical links.

It is at this point that the chief stimulus and temptation to mechanical logic and abstract use of formal concepts come in. Just because the personal element cannot be wholly excluded, while at the same time the decision must assume as nearly as possible an impersonal, objective, rational form, the temptation is to surrender the vital logic which has actually yielded the conclusion and to substitute for it forms of speech which are rigorous in appearance and which give an illusion of certitude.

Another moving force is the undoubted need for the maximum possible of stability and regularity of expectation in determining courses of conduct. Men need to know the legal consequences which society through the courts will attach to their specific transactions, the liabilities they are assuming, the fruits they may count upon in entering upon a given course of action.

This is a legitimate requirement from the standpoint of the interests of the community and of particular individuals. Enormous confusion has resulted, however, from confusion of *theoretical* certainty and practical certainty. There is a wide gap separating the reasonable proposition that judicial decisions should possess the maximum possible regularity in order to enable persons in planning their conduct to foresee the legal import of their acts, and the absurd because impossible proposition that every decision should flow with formal logical necessity from antecedently known premises. To attain the former result there are required general principles of interpreting cases—rules of law—and procedures of pleading and trying cases which do not alter arbitrarily. But principles of interpretation do not signify rules so right that they can be stated once for all and then be literally and mechanically adhered to. For the situations to which they are to be applied do not literally repeat one another in all details, and questions of degree of this factor or that have the chief weight in determining which general rule will be employed to judge the situation in question. A large part of what has been asserted concerning the necessity of absolutely uniform and immutable antecedent rules of law is in effect an attempt to evade the really important issue of finding and employing rules of law, substantive and procedural, which will actually secure to the members of the community a reasonable measure of practical certainty of expectation in framing their courses of conduct. The mechanical ease of the court in disposing of cases and not the actual security of agents is the real cause, for example, of making rules of pleading hard and fast.[38] The result introduces an unnecessary element of gamble into the behavior of those seeking settlement of disputes, while it affords to the judges only that factitious ease and simplicity which is supplied by any routine habit of action.[39] It sub-stitutes a mechanical procedure for the need of analytic thought.

There is of course every reason why rules of law should be as regular and as definite as possible. But the amount and kind of antecedent assurance which is actually attainable is a matter of fact, not of form. It is large wherever social conditions are pretty uniform, and when industry, commerce, transportation, etc., move in the channels of old customs. It is much less whenever invention is active and when new devices in business and communication bring about new forms of human relationship. Thus the use of power machinery radically modifies the old terms of association of master and servant and fellow servants; rapid transportation brings into general use commercial bills of lading; mass production engenders organization of laborers and collective bargaining; industrial conditions favor concentration of capital. In part legislation endeavors to reshape old rules of law to make them applicable to new conditions. But statutes have never kept up with the variety and subtlety of social change. They cannot at the very best avoid some ambiguity, which is due not only to carelessness but also to the intrinsic impossibility of foreseeing all possible circumstances, since without such foresight definitions must be vague and classifications indeterminate. Hence to claim that old forms are ready at hand that cover every case and that may be applied by formal syllogizing is to pretend to a certainty and regularity which cannot exist in fact. The effect of the pretension is to increase practical uncertainty and social instability. Just because circumstances are really novel and not covered by old rules, it is a gamble which old rule will be declared regulative of a particular case, so that shrewd and enterprising men are encouraged to sail close to the wind and trust to ingenious lawyers to find some rule under which they can get off scot free. Here is where the great practical evil of the doctrine of immutable and necessary antecedent rules[40] comes in. It sanctifies the old; adherence to it in practice constantly widens the gap between current social conditions and the principles used by the courts. The

---

[38] *Editor's Note:* Dewey wrote this in 1924, well before the liberalization introduced in the Federal Rules of Civil Procedure which have abolished the old hard-and-fast rules of pleading in favor of a more liberal construction as well as liberal rules of amendment.

[39] *Editor's Note:* Dewey might have added—although it is implicit in his word "factitious ease"—that rigid rules have hidden costs: they make the stakes of conformity higher for the parties, giving the parties an incentive to pass the costs back to the judge in the form of excessive argumentation about the draconian consequences of adhering to the formal rules of pleading.

---

[40] *Editor's Note:* In other words, Formalism strictly defined.

effect is to breed irritation, disrespect for law, together with virtual alliances between the judiciary and entrenched interests.

Newer rules may be needed and useful at a certain juncture, and yet they may also become harmful and socially obstructive if they are hardened into absolute and fixed antecedent premises. But if they are conceived as tools to be adapted to the conditions in which they are employed rather than as absolute and intrinsic "principles," attention will go to the facts of social life, and the rules will not be allowed to engross attention and become absolute truths to be maintained intact at all costs. Otherwise we shall in the end merely have substituted one set of formally absolute and immutable syllogistic premises for another set.

I should indeed not hesitate to assert that the sanctification of ready-made antecedent universal principles as methods of thinking is the chief obstacle to the kind of thinking which is the indispensable prerequisite of steady, secure and intelligent social reforms in general and social advance by means of law in particular. If this be so, infiltration into law of a more experimental and flexible logic is a social as well as an intellectual need.

QUESTIONS AND COMMENTS FOR YOUR CONSIDERATION

1. Imagine that you are a pragmatic judge considering the interpretation of statutes. Instead of looking for a specific theory of interpretation or a specific set of instructions (such as, apply the "plain meaning" of the statute), should you ask yourself: "what is the legislature's job, and how can I help the legislature?"

2. Suppose you start with the hypothesis that the legislature wishes to tell everyone exactly what to do. If this were the legislature's "job," how could the legislature accomplish it? The legislature might enact, for example, highly specific legislation, such as, "Editors of anthologies on analytic jurisprudence are hereby required to pay a surtax of $5,000 to the Internal Revenue Service." Such a statute would have admirable specificity and raise few questions of interpretation. But there are at least two grave faults with it. First, the courts might invalidate it as an unconstitutional bill of attainder.[41] Second, if Congress wanted to use such a statute as a legislative model, it would immediately get swamped in specifics. If Congress wanted to enact one tax statute for every citizen in the United States, it would have to pass 250,000,000 bills; if it wanted then to enact 10 non-tax statutes affecting each person in the United States (e.g., a Medicare statute, a criminal statute, a drivers' licensing statute, etc.), it would have to enact 10 X 250,000,000 bills. But even if such fine-tuning by the legislature could be accomplished (i.e., with high-powered computers), the statutes would constantly have to be revised as people's situations changed.

3. Can a legislature achieve exact control over each subject's life by passing non-individualized statutes? Clearly any non-individualized statute would have to be interpreted and applied by the courts. Suppose Congress enacts the following: "All teachers of jurisprudence are hereby required to pay a surtax of $5,000 to

---

[41] In the United States, the statute would probably be held unconstitutional as a prohibited bill of attainder or a bill of pains and penalties. In other countries, courts might very well reach the same conclusion even if their constitutions did not prohibit bills of attainder. A court could reach such a conclusion simply by noting that the legislature is given "legislative" powers, and yet a statute naming an individual and providing a penalty cannot be an act of "legislation"—it is instead an act of adjudication, and hence is outside the legislative power.

the Internal Revenue Service." This tax might be invalidated by the courts as an unconstitutional restriction upon free expression as guaranteed by the First Amendment. But suppose the statute withstands constitutional challenge. Nevertheless there is considerable vagueness as to the term "teachers of jurisprudence." Is someone who writes a book or anthology about jurisprudence a "teacher" of that subject to any future reader of the book? Is a college professor of philosophy who assigns Hobbes' *The Leviathan* in a course in political theory a "teacher of jurisprudence"? And what about all the real-world shifting that will occur as a result of the enactment of such a statute—the names of courses being changed from "Jurisprudence" to "Legal Philosophy," the banning of textbooks with the word "jurisprudence" in the title and the substitution of similar books that do not use that word, and other moves designed to reduce taxes? To be sure, Congress may be *content* with these shifts and dodges if its primary purpose was not to raise revenue but to discourage the enterprise known as "jurisprudence." The statute would clearly succeed in discouraging (but perhaps never eliminating) the study of jurisprudence, although we might find that subject smuggled back in under new names. Even so, this kind of legislation seems a long way from the initial premise of achieving exact control over the lives of citizens.

4. Additionally, are not many statutes ambiguous by design? The final wording of a statute in the United States is usually the result of a bill enacted by the House of Representatives, a similar but not identical bill enacted by the Senate, and a draft prepared by the Joint Committee to reconcile the two versions. There is often intense lobbying over the final language of the bill. Some interest groups, if they feel adversely impacted by the Senate or House's version of a bill, achieve a "softening" of the language in its later legislative states, so that they are not directly impacted by the final provisions of the bill. More importantly, the very ability of a draft bill to achieve a majority vote in both houses of Congress, and avoid a veto by the President, is often a direct consequence of its studied ambiguity. Different congresspersons can "read into" a statute different things if the statute is sufficiently vague or ambiguous. Sometimes both the proponents and the opponents of legislation can report a "victory" to their constituents back home when they read contrary things into their interpretations of the final piece of legislation. In short, a pragmatic judge might not wish to assume as a blanket rule that the legislature as a whole really wanted to control any given activity with maximum specificity. Rather, a statute might serve the political interests of congresspersons if the statute meant "all things to all people" or at least many things to many different people.

5. You may wish at this point to re-read Professor Fuller's cautionary tale about Rex's eight failures to enact legislation in Chapter 2, Section A, *supra*. What Rex (as the supreme legislator) failed to appreciate was that he was just a player in a context. It was the legal context as a whole—judges, administrators, other legislators, the public—that Rex was embedded in. Rex could push the context this way or that, but he could not totally control it. Thus, if you are a pragmatic judge deciding how best you can help the legislature do its job, isn't it part of the definition of the legislature's "job" the legislature's own place in the context—*i.e.*, the legal system? Isn't part of the legislature's function to take *you* into account in enacting *its* statutes? If the legislature ignores *you*, the law-applier,

then won't it find its job harder to accomplish? Conversely, when you are presented with a statute, should you not read it sympathetically from the point of view of a legislature that desires to communicate with you (and with the citizenry as a whole)?

6. Recall Dworkin's essay in Chapter 4, *supra*, that there exists in each case a single "right answer," even if it requires a judge who has all the time in the world to read all the legal materials in the world to find it. How would a Pragmatist answer Professor Dworkin? Would a Pragmatist dispute Dworkin's demonstration that a Judge Hercules is theoretically conceivable? Or would a Pragmatist simply say that Dworkin's "solution" to the "right answer" thesis is utterly impractical in the workaday world, and hence only of "academic" interest?

4. Anthony D'Amato: The Entropy of Rules[42]

Positivists have attempted to combat legal uncertainty by adding more and more statutes and regulations to the body of law while accepting a permissive attitude toward the jurisdiction of courts. Positivists view legislation as a continuous process of plugging the gaps between previous statutes, and courts as "discretionary" legislatures inventing new rules and applying them retroactively to parties. Even so, real-world variety outstrips the ability of legislatures to catch up to the ingenuity of persons who, disadvantaged by the law on the books, modify and adjust their conduct so that if falls in the cracks between existing rules or comes more ambiguously within any given rule, thus casting cast doubt upon any attempt on the part of potential claimants to bring them to legal account.

The evidence that the law is becoming more uncertain is all around us; the question is how to interpret it. For example, one might look at the increasing growth in reported judicial decisions, statutes, and regulations as an increasingly successful attempt to impose precision upon human activities. One might see in the verbosity of the multi-volume set of the Code of Federal Regulations rules of sophistication, detail, and clarity. But I would regard those same volumes as a futile and sometimes mad attempt to encapsulate real-world

transactions in elusive and ambiguous legal prose. Indeed, I would contend that the increasing volume of litigation and rulemaking results in internal contradictions, a multiplication of ambiguities, and normative specifications that invite persons to avoid rules of law by planning their activities around them.

The inexorable growth of uncertainty in law is analogous to the concept of entropy in physical chemistry. "Entropy" may be defined as disorder, so that increasing the entropy of a substance increases its physical disorder: "when you melt a crystal, since you thereby destroy the neat and permanent arrangement of the atoms or molecules and turn the crystal lattice into a continually changing random distribution," you are increasing the crystal's entropy.[43] One might analogize a legal rule to driving a new car—it is easier to scratch or dent the finish of the new car than it is to prevent all scratches and dents. Rules of law seem to be delicate structures, easily made, increasingly ambiguous and uncertain with each new application, and only with great difficulty preserved in their original form, meaning, intent, and purpose.

5. Peter H. Schuck: Legal Complexity[44]

Some scholars, like Jason Johnston and

---

[42] Anthony D'Amato, *Uncertainty*, 71 CALIFORNIA LAW REVIEW 1, 39-40 (1983). Copyright 1983 Anthony D'Amato.

[43] ERWIN SCHRÖDINGER, WHAT IS LIFE? 78 (1944).
[44] Peter H. Schuck, *Legal Complexity: Some Causes, Consequences, and Cures*, 42 DUKE L.J. 1, 18-19, 32-33 (1992). Copyright 1992 by The Duke Law Journal. Reprinted by permission.

Carol Rose, argue that incentives endogenous to the litigation process generate a pattern of perpetual oscillation between bright-line and open-ended rule forms.[45] Others, however, discern an inexorable trend toward indeterminacy. Priest and Klein, for example, show that disputes turning on determinate rules will be settled rather than litigated (regardless of their content), which assures that the rules litigants bring to court are at the indeterminate end of the spectrum.[46] Making a related point, Anthony D'Amato argues that because a rule is easier to challenge than to defend, and a rule that disadvantages tends to invite challenge, the resulting litigation systematically favors the evolution of more indeterminate rules.[47] Henderson and Eisenberg also claim that indeterminate rules tend to favor plaintiffs, but for different reasons. They emphasize that such rules, by creating jury questions, enhance the settlement value of plaintiffs' claims, and that this trend is a one-way ratchet: courts, having adopted indeterminate rules, find it hard to go back to more precise ones.[48] Richard Epstein likewise sees a firm trend toward indeterminacy, but ascribes it to the incentives of lawyers, who seek to maximize demand for their services by promoting more complex rules that invite expert interpretation and manipulation.[49] Michelle White argues that tax lawyers, like tax accountants and the Internal Revenue Service, have vested interests in a complex tax law, although each group favors a different level of complexity.[50] Boris Bittker sug-

gests that since tax experts' analytical and critical skills account for much of the law's complexity, they cannot be expected to make it simpler and more enforceable.[51]

Should we view legal complexity as a problem? If we suppose that legal rules are largely epiphenomenal, reflecting the underlying social conditions to which they relate, then we might want law's complexity to keep pace with society's. Social complexity is growing remorselessly.

Interdependencies increase. Cultures and markets fragment. Values and technologies change. Bureaucracies expand. Under these conditions, a denser, more intricate legal system may be both inevitable and desirable.

This is true, I believe, but only up to a point. A more complex law entails many significant transaction costs which must be accounted for. Such law tends to be more costly and cumbersome to administer, more difficult for lawmakers to formulate and agree upon, and more difficult to reform once established. Administrators and subjects of such law must invest more in order to learn what it means, when and how it applies, and whether the costs of complying with it are worth incurring. Other costs of administering a complex legal system include those related to bargaining about and around the system's rules and litigating over them.

Thus, legal complexity magnifies transaction costs by generating uncertainty. Complexity-induced costs can be both inefficient and unfair. In fields as diverse as agency regulation, trusts and estates, and torts, complexity can inhibit beneficial transactions, impose deadweight losses, create frustrating delays, consume the energies of talented individuals, breed new and difficult-to-resolve disputes, and discourage compliance. Promoting passivity and entrenching the status quo, legal complexity can stultify a society that often depends on vigorous action in solving problems. Complexity's costs, moreover, impose disproportionate burdens on the poor by raising prices and necessitating the services of lawyers and other professionals trained in the management of complexity.

---

[45] Jason S. Johnston, *Uncertainty, Chaos, and the Torts Process: An Economic Analysis of Legal Form*, 76 CORNELL L. REV. 341, 371 (1991); Carol M. Rose, *Crystals and Mud in Property Law*, 40 STAN. L. REV. 577, 603-04 (1988).

[46] George L. Priest & Benjamin Klein, *The Selection of Disputes for Litigation*, 13 J. LEGAL STUD. 1 (1984).

[47] Anthony D'Amato, *Legal Uncertainty*, 71 CAL. L. REV. 1, 23-24 (1983).

[48] James A. Henderson, Jr. & Theodore Eisenberg, *The Quiet Revolution in Products Liability: An Empirical Study of Legal Change*, 37 UCLA L. REV. 479, 515 (1990).

[49] Richard A. Epstein, *The Political Economy of Product Liability Reform*, 78 AM. ECON. REV. pt. 2, at 311, 313 (1988).

[50] Michelle J. White, *Why Are Taxes So Complex and Who Benefits?*, 47 TAX NOTES 341 (1990).

---

[51] Boris L. Bittker, *Tax Reform and Tax Simplification*, 29 U. MIAMI L. REV. 1, 10-11 (1974).

6. Anthony D'Amato: Pragmatic Indeterminacy[52]

A theory we can call Pragmatic Indeterminacy would at the outset reject H.L.A. Hart's proposition that every word has a determinate, non-disputable core meaning. The Pragmatic Indeterminist does not necessarily have to assert that words *lack* determinate core meanings—for that in itself would be an absolute claim. Rather, it is sufficient for a Pragmatic Indeterminist to assert that there can be no determinate evidence that one person's "core meaning" for a given word is the same as another person's, or that one person's "core meaning" in a given context does not vary from that same person's "core meaning" in a different context. Whether real-world conduct "falls within" a "core meaning" of some word or phrase is a matter of human judgment, and different judges may judge differently. The conduct in question can never be *bounded by words*, because it physically connects to the background, to the rest of the universe. A word or sentence only *highlights* a facet of the conduct, but does not *encapsulate* it. Hence it is inevitably a matter of interpretation whether real-world conduct "falls within" the meaning of any word or phrase, because the decision-maker must arbitrarily exclude physical extensions of that conduct that she considers irrelevant.[53] Nor is the formalist saved by the notion of "irrelevancy," because *that* notion—pervasive in every area of the law—begs its own question.

Many formalists are surprised if they study the way words are used in the course of a trial. Opposing parties often seem to attribute totally different meanings and understandings to rather ordinary contractual words that are in dispute. Meanings can also change dramatically depending on the tone and tenor of the spoken word. Trial transcripts are notoriously defective in their inability to capture the emphasis that witnesses put on the words they utter.

Central to the notion of legal pragmatism is the acknowledgment that the law is a predictable phenomenon. In our everyday behavior, we predict what a court (or the police, or other persons) would do if we acted differently. Lawyers are better than laypersons at predicting what officials will do. If lawyers had no ability to predict judicial behavior at all, there would be no law, only chaos. This general predictability is expectable in any system that is fairly characterized as legal.

Experienced lawyers can make educated guesses about how judges will probably decide many cases and controversies. A client walks in the door with a legal problem, and within a few minutes, an attorney can start giving probabilistic legal advice that the client can use to good advantage in planning further behavior. Of course, because each fact situation is unique, we can never know as a matter of "objective probability" that the lawyer's advice is accurate. But "subjective probability" works quite well in these cases.[54]

If the results of courts were *not* fairly predictable, then lawyers could not give probabilistic legal advice and pretty soon no one would pay lawyers for their advice. For Pragmatic Indeterminacy, some nontrivial degree of judicial regularity and predictability is required. So long as we have a non-chaotic society, we can be fairly confident that "law" *works* in that society.

What is our evidence that law works? The evidence, I submit, cannot be found in legal materials. All the reported cases in the world cannot give us any assurance as to what courts will actually decide. This apparently startling proposition can be readily tested by a thought experiment. Suppose you come across fifty volumes of the reported cases of a particular jurisdiction. You read all the cases and note an amazing consistency: there are no overrulings, each case cites precedents, and when you look up the

---

[52] Excerpted from Anthony D'Amato, *Pragmatic Indeterminacy*, 85 NORTHWESTERN UNIVERSITY LAW REVIEW 148 (1990). Copyright 1990 Anthony D'Amato. Reprinted by courtesy of the author and Northwestern University Law Review.

[53] Compare the significant philosophical demonstration by C.I. LEWIS, AN ANALYSIS OF KNOWLEDGE AND VALUATION 50-55 (1946). Lewis undermined the common notion that a word "corresponds" to something in the real world by showing that locating or even pointing to any object presupposes a frame of reference.

[54] *See* ANTHONY D'AMATO, JURISPRUDENCE: A DESCRIPTIVE AND NORMATIVE ANALYSIS OF LAW 21-34 (1984) (discussion of subjective probability).

precedents, you find that they are "on all fours" even by your own standards, no matter how rigorous your standards are. None of this means that real people have in fact been treated predictably or consistently. For all you know, the statements of facts in the reported cases may be misstatements of what really occurred. The "law-facts" (such as "the plaintiff was also negligent") can be wildly at variance with the real-world facts. You might even find, on further investigation, that all the reported cases in this jurisdiction were *plagiarized* from case reports of another jurisdiction. The judges in "our" jurisdiction simply copied the opinions of other judges and tacked them on to their own cases in an attempt to "look legal." I am not saying that this strange state of affairs is likely, only that it is conceivable.[55] The thought experiment simply shows that we cannot use court reports as *evidence* of what is happening in the real world.

Our evidence that law works must instead come from lawyers and the public. If most people, including lawyers, believe that litigated cases are not decided randomly but can be predicted at a confidence level ranging, say, from fifty-five to ninety percent depending on the case, then they are probably right because they are talking from experience with decisions the courts have made in their own jurisdictions. Societies that view their court systems as generally issuing unsurprising rulings are in effect accurately understanding that their courts are behaving within predictable limits. Our evidence for popular belief in judicial predictability is the care people take to structure their transactions by taking into account the risk of having them upset by challenges in court. If the risk were wholly unspecifiable, people would not be able to make plans in light of what courts might decide.

Yet we must acknowledge the possibility that differently situated observers may draw different distinctions between similar cases. The result is that law-words, absolute

though they may appear when printed on paper, can only point to likely or probable results in particular cases (all of which is another way of saying that there are no easy cases). Pragmatic Indeterminacy would therefore consider it to be a category mistake to use notions of "legally right" or "legally correct" in criticizing a given decision. For "legally right" and "legally correct" are logical notions, referring to the consistency of formal deductive systems. These terms have a place in the abstract construction of tautological legal systems, such as the blackletter rules of the various Restatements. But they cannot be used in the empirical criticism of cases without smuggling in a normative element. Hence, although we often use the words "correct" or "incorrect" in criticizing judicial decisions, the fact that any decision is a matter of probability combined with the fact that no case is "easy" means that either side can *legitimately* win any individual case. I maintain not only that our real world is one of probabilities and not certainties, as quantum theory has amply demonstrated,[56] but also that our legal world is

---

[55] Comparative law scholars familiar with European decisions may recognize an element of truth in this scenario. Sometimes the judicial rationales explicating "the law" appear to be free-floating boilerplate opinions unrelated to the facts of the case at hand (except for an occasional "fill-in-the-blanks" kind of reference to the instant case).

[56] *See* P. SUPPES, PROBABILISTIC METAPHYSICS 85-99 (1984); 1 L. KRUGER, L.J. DATSO, M. HEIDELBERGER, THE PROBABILISTIC REVOLUTION 237-60, 295-304 (1987); 2 L. KRUGER, L.J. DATSO, M. HEIDELBERGER, THE PROBABILISTIC REVOLUTION 373-435 (1987). The mistake that many newcomers to quantum theory make is to assume that it predicts the probability that electrons (or other quanta) can be found at a particular place. This is quite wrong; in fact, the electron itself is a probabilistic phenomenon and not an "entity." As Max Born put it, there are "waves of matter." M. BORN, THE RESTLESS UNIVERSE 151-54 (1951). The Fermi-Einstein statistics suggest "not merely that elementary particles are unlike bodies [but] that there are no such denizens of space-time at all ..." V.W. QUINE, PURSUIT OF TRUTH 35 (1990). In short, the real world we see—the world of matter and space is itself—in a way that no one can fathom except through the mathematical language of quantum theory—probabilistic and not solidly certain. I think that exactly the same point can be made about law. I am not saying that law is like quantum mechanics, but only that if the universe we live in is a probabilistic and not a determinate one, it is not so strange to argue that law is also just a matter of probabilities. Thus, when we predict how a case will come out, we are not predicting what the law "is" at a certain level of confidence the way the meteorologist predicts tomorrow's weather. Rather, our prediction *constitutes* the law.

made up only of probabilities and not certainties.

The realization that law only tells you what might happen to you and not what will necessarily happen is perhaps a "soft" view of law. I think it is more humanistic than the dictatorial view of legal positivism which regards laws as a set of determinate commands. The soft view of law considers human deciders (judges) as being part of, rather than apart from, the law.[57]

To put matters bluntly, I believe that all the law on the books—statutes, legislative history, regulations, precedents—simply serves a retrieval function. It helps a judge retrieve (locate) similar cases, similar situations, similar pictures of what the legislature had in mind when it enacted a statute, mental images of relevant contexts, and even hypothetical cases. Although Formalism errs in saying that law-words constrain judicial decisions, law-words do play an important heuristic role in initially identifying previous decisions so that they may be compared with present situations.

My contention that the language of law at best serves a retrieval function is concededly a deflationary view of law.[58] Many people, accustomed to nobler sentiments where law is concerned, may regard the retrieval thesis as a step backward. I suggest that it is a gain. If we have been fooling ourselves that law words constrain judges in individual cases, then we can dispense with a considerable amount of time-consuming theorizing about law and about whether specific decisions were correctly decided under the law. We will then have time to turn our attention to things that matter, such as justice. In my view, the legal profession has nothing to do with serving law and everything to do with serving justice. To say that a lawyer is bound by "law" is in effect to enlist lawyers in implementing the state's policies, irrespective of whether those policies are enlightened or brutal. It is to a dictator's advantage to say that lawyers should be guided by "law." But "law" is simply not worth being guided by, except to the extent that it reflects justice in society. If we don't say that a plumber serves his tools, we should not say that a lawyer serves the law. To the extent that we lawyers are professionals, our allegiance is not to law but to achieving justice in society.[59]

If we wish to achieve justice, our primary focus should be upon the particular facts of cases. "Legal" conceptions can sometimes blind us to the pivotal facts of a case, such as the considerations that led one party to attempt to take unfair advantage of the other party. Often "legal" conceptions rule out those considerations as being "irrelevant." But if we understand the notion of "irrelevancy" as tautological within the legal system (as I have argued above), then we should ask the further question: "irrelevant as to what?" If the "what" is "justice," then, I would contend, it is not irrelevant at all.[60]

---

[57] Ultimately, the subjects of law (you and I) are also as much a part of the law as are judges—an insight of Hegel's. See Jacobson, *Hegel's Legal Plenum*, 10 CARDOZO L. REV. 877 (1989).

[58] It is in the spirit of pragmatism put forth in Richard Rorty's deflationary view of philosophy. See RICHARD RORTY, CONSEQUENCES OF PRAGMATISM (1982); RICHARD RORTY, CONTINGENCY, IRONY, AND SOLIDARITY (1989).

[59] *Editor's Note:* "Justice" is the theme of the next Chapter in this Anthology.

[60] The tendency of recent casebooks to truncate the statement of facts of cases and instead pile on legal rhetoric is a move in precisely the wrong direction. There should be far greater attention paid in law school teaching to the facts of cases, including even facts that the court omitted in its "statement of facts." I have made this suggestion previously in Anthony D'Amato, *The Decline and Fall of Law Teaching in the Age of Student Consumerism*, 37 J. LEG. EDUC. 461 (1987).

7

Justice

Anyone may criticize a given statute or judicial decision as unjust. This would be an "external" commentary upon the law. No matter what you mean by "justice," you may make such a criticism at any time. In doing so, you don't affect the content of the law; you simply take the content as given, and criticize it.

Radically different is the claim that justice is part of the law, that a judge must take justice into account in deciding a given case. This final Chapter is devoted mainly to the latter "internal" notion of justice. The internal version has practical, everyday implications for lawyers in their practice and judges in their decision-making. It goes to the heart of the legal enterprise because it could help shape and determine the content of law.

A. Morality and Justice

1. Hans Kelsen: The Pure Theory of Law[1]

The Pure Theory of Law attempts to answer the question what and how the law *is*, not how it ought to be. It is a science of law (jurisprudence), not legal politics.

It is called a "pure" theory of law, because it only describes the law and attempts to eliminate from the object of this description everything that is not strictly law. Its aim is to free the science of law from alien elements.

The Pure Theory of Law insists upon a clear separation of the concept of law from that of justice, and renounces any justification of positive law by a kind of superlaw, leaving that problematical task to religion or social metaphysics.

2. Lon L. Fuller: Recognizing Injustice[2]

I believe that there are imperfectly rationalized elements in the law which we are intellectually and morally bound to recognize. The most important of these relates to the concept of justice itself. It seems impossible to give an adequate definition of justice; the quest for justice is in this sense an "irrational" one. Yet this does not prevent the lawyer from recognizing clear cases of injustice. The lawyer is in this respect in no different position than is the physician, who can recognize plain cases of disease and yet cannot define health itself except in terms which are formal and tautological. The lawyer who in name of a narrow "rationalism" asserts that his profession has nothing to do with justice presents a spectacle no less sorry than that of a physician who might decide to give up healing the sick because he found he could not reduce the concept of health, the ulti-

---

[1] Excerpted from: (a) Hans Kelsen, The Pure Theory of Law 1 (M. Knight, tr. 1967); (b) Hans Kelsen, What is Justice? 301-02 (1957).

[2] Excerpted from Lon L. Fuller, *My Philosophy of Law*, in Julius Rosenthal Foundation, My Philosophy of Law 111, 121 (1941).

mate objective of his activities, to Euclidean exactness.

3. Hans Kelsen: The Subjectivity of Justice[3]

There is not, and cannot be, an objective criterion of justice because the statement "something is just or unjust" is a judgment of value referring to an ultimate end, and these value judgments are by their very nature subjective in character, because based on emotional elements of our mind, on our feelings and wishes. They cannot be verified by fact, as can statements about reality.

This is the reason why in spite of the attempts made by the most illustrious thinkers of mankind to solve the problem of justice, there is not only no agreement but the most passionate antagonism in answering the question of what is just.

4. Anthony D'Amato: the Objectivity of Justice[4]

Of course, no one is likely to have the identical sense of justice as someone else. But if everyone's sense of justice were plotted out as circles on a plane, we would find that most people's circles overlapped with most other people's. The amount of shared similar experiences about justice that we have probably far exceeds the number of disparate experiences. Consider, as one example, the "justice" we learned in the schoolyard. A large "bully" snatches the warm mittens of a smaller child; some children tease and "make fun of" a child who has a stutter disability; the boys exclude a girl from one of their games even though she can play it as well as any of them. Even at that early age, our sense of justice was developed enough so that we were appalled by those behaviors. (If we participated in them, we later felt quite ashamed of ourselves.) I have some confidence that I am talking here about *universal* reactions to the same events. I would be quite surprised if anyone reading this article would disagree with any of these three examples and assert sincerely that the bully was acting properly or that the children who teased the stutterer were behaving justly.

Many of the examples we learned about justice in the schoolyard were (unfortunately) negative examples. We learned about justice even from these negative examples, because we (or others whom we respected and trusted) *criticized* the unjust behavior. Yet our childhoods were filled for the most part with thousands of positive examples of justice. The way our parents treated us, the way we "got along" with friends in the neighborhood, the stories we heard at Sunday School or read in the comics and graphic novels, the movies we saw, the anecdotes we heard—we can't remember them now, and we couldn't even remember all of them then. But we did learn a "lesson" from them, and that was that the right way to behave was to behave fairly toward other people. Those who behaved unjustly in the stories were punished in the end (sometimes only by God, if it was a Biblical story). And we learned not simply the fact that they were punished, but that they deserved to be punished for what they did. When we ourselves were punished by our mother or father for a bad thing that we did, we learned that what we did was bad and that the punishment was appropriate. Of course, not everyone learned these lessons and not everyone's parents were fair. (But even the child of unfair parents soon learned, from talking with playmates, that her parents were unfair; and she, perhaps, grew up to be a much fairer person than everyone else because she was reacting negatively to the bad example set by her parents.)

We had thousands of experiences, we heard thousands of stories, and we gradually learned (among many other things, of course) what constituted justice and fairness. We probably were never given a *definition* of justice. We were rarely if ever told, by our parents or teachers, what in general we had to do to be just, although we may have been told what we had to do to be just in specific situations. As we grew older, we continued to hear stories and we refined our

[3] Excerpted from HANS KELSEN, WHAT IS JUSTICE? 295-96 (1957). Reprinted by permission.

[4] Excerpted from Anthony D'Amato, *On the Connection Between Law and Justice*, 26 U.C. DAVIS L. REV. 527, 559-62 (1993).

notions of justice and fairness. In law school (or at least, when I went to law school) we read thousands of cases. These cases are all little morality plays, where we read about what people did and how they were judged. They, too, honed our sense of justice.

The only way I could communicate my sense of justice to you would be to recount for you the hundreds of thousands of experiences and stories that through my life have made up for me my sense of justice. If I could recap these for you—if my mind were a video recorder—I would simply run the tape for you and trust that you would draw the same lesson from these stories that I drew. But that can't be done, and even if it could, the video show would take a few years and would omit the emotions that I felt on each occasion when, for example, I felt outraged or sorry when someone acted unjustly. Yet if you ask me what I *mean* by justice, the only way I could tell you would be to run that imaginary video recorder for you. I can't put justice in words, because I never learned it "in words" in the first place. I learned it through personal experiences, including the vicarious experiences of hearing stories.

But even if we had the time and technology, and I played the mental videotape for you, I suspect that you would quickly become bored. You would say something like, "except for a change of characters and locale, the fact is that I've heard and experienced all these stories before. I heard some of your stories just the way you heard them—stories from the Bible, stories from history, stories of heroic deeds, etc. There's practically nothing new in these stories for me. There's practically nothing you can teach me about justice that I don't already know."

Some writers have suggested that we have a better sense of injustice than we have of justice. They point out that when we see something that is unjust, or hear about something that is unjust, most everyone's reaction is the same as ours. We can all agree on what is unjust, whereas we find it hard to say what justice is.

If you believe that it's easier to spot an injustice than to say what justice is, I would have no objection to that description. Perhaps many judges on the bench listen to the testimony and arguments until something strikes them as unjust. Their "sense of injustice" may tell them that one of the parties tried to take unfair advantage of the other side. Analytically, however, I contend that if you know what injustice is you also must know what justice is. The real reason why there is attractiveness in the notion of one's sense of injustice is that it always comes into play when a story is told that strikes the listener as unjust. On the other hand, it seems difficult to *say* what constitutes justice in the absence of a collection of stories. But this is, in effect, the point I've been making all along. Our notion of what "justice" is—as well as our notion of what "injustice" is—comes from the conclusions we have drawn about thousands of stories and experiences. Naturally we find it hard to specify what *justice* is, because we are writing a definition on a blank slate, so to speak, in the absence of a collection of stories. Yet when we hear a single story, we can readily tell whether the outcome is just or unjust—or, at least, we know what additional information to request in order that we have enough facts to reach a verdict about justice or injustice.

The very confidence that people have, who speak about our "sense of injustice"—that everyone has the same, or practically the same, sense of injustice—is another way of demonstrating my contention that our notion of justice is far more likely to be largely shared with other people in our community than it is to be different from the notions of other people. These other people include judges. That is why, when as a lawyer we listen to a client's story and make an initial determination whether the client is likely to prevail if the story is tested at a trial, we test the story against *our own* sense of justice. For we are quite confident that *our* sense of justice is rather likely to be shared by whatever judge is assigned to our case.

5. H.L.A. Hart: Justice and Equality[5]

The general principle of the idea of justice is that individuals are entitled in respect of each other to a certain relative position of

---

[5] H.L.A. HART, THE CONCEPT OF LAW 159, 165 (2d ed. 1994). Copyright Oxford University Press, 1961. Reprinted by permission of the publisher.

equality or inequality. This is something to be respected in the vicissitudes of social life when burdens or benefits fall to be distributed; it is also something to be restored when it is disturbed. Hence justice is traditionally thought of as maintaining or restoring a *balance* or *proportion*, and its leading precept is often formulated as "Treat like cases alike"; though we need to add to the latter "and treat different cases differently."

It is conceivable that there might be a moral outlook which did not put individuals on a footing of reciprocal equality in these matters. The moral code might forbid Barbarians to assault Greeks but allow Greeks to assault Barbarians. In such cases a Barbarian may be thought morally bound to compensate a Greek for injuries done though entitled to no such compensation himself. The moral order here would be one of inequality in which victim and wrongdoer were treated differently. For such an outlook, repellent though it may be to us, the law would be just only if it reflected this difference and treated different cases differently.

QUESTIONS AND COMMENTS FOR YOUR CONSIDERATION

1. Professor Hart's example of the Greeks and Barbarians is worthy of deep analysis. If it seems remote to you, substitute "husband" for "Greek" and "wife" for "Barbarian," change the time to the present, and shift the locale to a fundamentalist Islamic country. Under both the civil and religious laws of some of these countries, a husband is entitled to "discipline" his wife—that is, he may beat her. It is illegal for a wife to strike her husband. Suppose you see a videotape of an Islamic husband beating his wife. Would you say to yourself, "Yes, that's justice"? Isn't that precisely what Professor Hart is claiming that you are compelled to say?

2. Suppose that the videotape then goes on to show an interview of the husband and wife. The husband says, "I disciplined my wife because that is my right as a religious and God-fearing Muslim." The wife says, "I must have failed to please my husband. That is why he beat me. It was my fault; I must learn to be a better wife." Isn't this a precise illustration of Professor Hart's premise that the *moral code* is one of inequality? And aren't the responses by the husband and wife evidence of that very moral code? Are you not required, by the dictates of logic as explained by Professor Hart, to conclude (even though it is repellant for you to so conclude) that the *law* of the Islamic country where the videotape was taken is in fact a just law?

3. If you are uncomfortable with the conclusions of Questions 1 and 2, can you say, "Well, the husband and wife depicted in the videotape regard their system as just, but I regard it as unjust"? Of course, you *can* say this, but if you do, aren't you using two different definitions of justice in the same sentence?

4. If you want to use the same definition of justice each time you use it, then aren't you compelled to say that either the husband and wife, or you, are *incorrectly* using the term? (For example, by saying, "they incorrectly regard their system as just.")

5. If you employ the statement suggested in Question 4, suppose the husband and wife hear of your remark and send you an e-mail message saying, "No, it's *you* who are incorrect in criticizing our conduct as unjust.") Would you conclude (a) "it's a stand-off, and therefore justice itself is relative to the observer and indeterminate," or (b) "one of us is right and it's me?"

6. Suppose now that *you* live in that Islamic country, having moved there two

years ago, and the husband and wife live in the apartment next to you. You have also studied the Koran intensively and have taken crash courses in Islam. There is no doubt in your mind that, under the moral code of the community and the state in which you now reside, wives are forbidden to assault their husbands while husbands are allowed to assault their wives. Would you now conclude that when your neighbor beats his wife, justice is being served? Isn't Professor Hart saying that you are forced to reach that conclusion?

7. If you wish to repudiate these various forced conclusions, what, precisely, is wrong with Professor Hart's argument?

8. Is there something about Positivism—or Hart's own version of Positivism—that logically compels Hart to make the argument he in fact made about Greeks and Barbarians?[*]

9. If something is wrong with Hart's argument, is that same thing wrong with Positivism?

10. Would you regard the content of "justice" as being dependent upon the concept of absolute morality that was suggested in the discussion of substantive natural law in Chapter 3?

B. The Tension Between Law and Justice

One can hardly imagine a more unjust institution in the history of the human race than the institution of slavery. A human being was treated as a chattel, as the property of the slaveowner. Slaves had a characteristic that the slaveowners found most inconvenient—when they could, they ran away. Thus when the United States Constitution was being drafted, the Framers had to do something about the runaway slave problem. The Southern slave states said they would not join the new nation unless slaves that ran away to the Northern free states were returned to the slaveowners. Some Framers regarded slavery as immoral and were hesitant to enter into a "compact with the Devil" in order to appease the slaveowning interests in the Southern states. What was to be called the "Great Compromise" was the object of intense debate and drafting. Adopted as Article 4, Section 2, Clause 3 of the Constitution, the "Fugitive Slave Clause" read as follows:

> No person held to service or labour in one state, under the laws thereof, escaping into another, shall, in consequence of any law or Regulation therein, be discharged from such service or labour, but shall be delivered up on claim of the party to whom such service or labour may be due.

Note that the clause did not use the word "slave," and did not refer to race; obviously the final language was adopted to assuage the sensibilities of persons morally opposed to slavery. At the same time, the clause in substance appeared to do what the slaveholding states wanted—(a) to prevent Northern states from adopting legislation that would abolish slavery and free from bondage any es-

---

[*]*A hint by the editor:* Does Hart's "moral code" strike you as something similar to legislation?

caped slaves, and (b) to set up an imperative that the slaveowners may retrieve the runaway slaves.

It is not my purpose here to recount the history of constitutional interpretation of the Fugitive Slave Clause, the statutes enacted by Congress to enforce it, or the various ways that Northern abolitionist states attempted to delay or obstruct slaveowners from reclaiming escaped slaves. This history has been recounted in many books, notably Robert M. Cover's *Justice Accused: Antislavery and the Judicial Process* (1975). Rather, I want to focus on one case: *Thomas Sims' Case* decided in 1851 in Massachusetts. By that year, the abolitionist sentiment in Boston and other cities was very strong. Thomas Sims was a fugitive slave, caught in Boston and temporarily imprisoned by a federal marshal while a writ of *habeas corpus* was argued on his behalf. Would Lemuel Shaw, Chief Judge of the Supreme Judicial Court of Massachusetts, issue or deny the writ? If justice to Mr. Sims would be served by issuing the writ, what about the Fugitive Slave Clause (which by 1851 had been held to be constitutional by the United States Supreme Court)? Was this to be a clash between the strongest possible dictates of justice on the one hand, and "law" on the other?

1. Leonard W. Levy: the Sims Affair[7]

It was notorious that no fugitive slave had ever been returned from Boston. Webster Whigs were dismayed that the whole state of Massachusetts was known as the cradle of "mad Abolitionism." It had become a matter of pride, not alone in the South, that a fugitive should be seized in Boston and taken back to slavery. Then, on Thursday evening, April 3, 1851, the city government of Boston was presented with an opportunity to make good on its promises of loyally enforcing the Fugitive Slave Act: Thomas Sims was taken into custody as a fugitive slave belonging to Mr. James Potter, a rice planter of Chatham County, Georgia.

Sims spent that night, and the rest of his nights in Boston, confined to the jury room of the Court House which was reserved for use in federal cases. He was thus technically imprisoned in a federal jail. This expedient was resorted to because there was no United States prison in Massachusetts, and because state law prohibited the use of its prisons for detaining any person accused of being a fugitive slave. In the courtroom prison, Sims was kept under close guard by the men of Charles Devens, the United States Marshal.

On the next morning, Boston awoke to witness one of the most extraordinary spectacles in its existence. During the night, the Court House had been barricaded. Under the direction of City Marshal Francis Tukey, iron chains had been girded entirely around the building. Its approaches were cleared by a belt of ropes and chains along the sidewalks, and heavy links stretched across its doorways. The Court House was in fetters, "bound to the Georgia cotton presses." Here was a visible answer, thought Bronson Alcott, to the question, "What has the North to do with slavery?" Tukey had concentrated his men on the scene. The entire regular police force, reinforced by great numbers of special police, patrolled the area and were stationed around and within the building. Wendell Phillips estimated the total number of police at no less than five hundred! Only authorized persons could get within ten feet of the Court House and pass the armed cordon. In effect, this meant that the city government of Boston had temporarily suspended the right of an ordinary citizen in a free Commonwealth to attend public sessions of its courts.

News of the arrest and of the exceptional

[7] Excerpted from LEONARD W. LEVY, THE LAW OF THE COMMONWEALTH AND CHIEF JUSTICE SHAW 91-3 (1957). Copyright 1957 by Leonard W. Levy. Reprinted by permission.

scenes at the Court House hurried about the city. Several hundred people, infected with curiosity, clogged Court Square from early morning till ten at night. There was no organized attempt at disturbance, although the police were jeered at and scolded by women; on the other hand, repeated cheers were given for the Union. Not till midnight was the square emptied of the crowds for that day. Word of the whole affair reached Henry Wadsworth Longfellow, who recorded in his journal:

> April 4, 1851. There is much excitement in Boston about the capture of an alleged fugitive slave. O city without soul! When and where will this end? Shame that the great Republic, the "refuge of the oppressed," should stoop so low as to become the Hunter of Slaves.

Low indeed was the stooping, for the chains across the door of the temple of justice were neither low enough to step over nor high enough to walk under. Those who entered the Court House on special business, lawyers, city officers, members of the press (who could enter if their views on the slavery question were safe enough), commissioners, and judges—even the judges—all had to bow their backs and creep beneath the chains. Tukey, the satrap in charge, had ordered it so. Chief Justice Lemuel Shaw of the Supreme Judicial Court, the great Shaw, venerated for his wisdom and for his advanced age, was among the first that morning to stoop beneath the chains. Decades before, Shaw himself had commented that one of the many evils in legally sanctioning slavery was that it degraded ministers of the law and profaned the sanctuary of justice.

2. Thomas Sims's Case[a]

SHAW, C.J. This is a petition for a writ of *habeas corpus* to bring the petitioner before this court, with a view to his discharge from imprisonment.

Fugitive slaves [are] designated in the constitution as persons held to service or labor in one state under the laws thereof, escaping into another.

[When the Revolutionary War ended,] the condition of the independent communities was that of sovereign states, varying greatly in regard to extent of territory, numbers and strength, with the usual powers incident to sovereign states, of declaring war and peace, making treaties, and exercising an exclusive control and jurisdiction over all persons and subjects within their respective territories. These would have been their rights and powers, had no union been formed.

In some of the states, large numbers of slaves were held; in others a few only; but some, it is believed, in all, except Massachusetts, in which slavery was considered as abolished by the Declaration of Rights, adopted as part of the constitution of 1780. Had no union been formed, the state would have been left to assert and defend their rights against each other by war only. If two states bordered on each other, one a slave state and the other a free state, there would of course be a constant effort of slaves to escape into the free state, and a constant temptation to slave owners to follow and recapture them, which must be done by force, unless sanctioned by treaty. Such acts on both sides must be regarded by each as violations of the exclusive territorial rights of the other, and a justifiable cause of war. There would naturally be a constant border war, leading either to interminable hostility, or to the subjugation of one by the other. This state of things could only be avoided by a treaty, by which one party should stipulate not to permit its own territory to be used as an asylum for fugitive slaves escaping from the other, and the other party should engage to restrain its own subjects from making hostile incursions into the territory of the other. It would be in vain for the government of the free state to insist that they would enter into no such compact, because slavery is wrong and unjust; each sovereign power has a right, by the recognized law of nations, to decide for itself, upon its own internal condition and regulations, within its own territory.

The evils existing immediately before the adoption of the constitution, and the greater and more appalling evils in prospect, indi-

---

[a]61 Mass. (7 Cush.) 285 (1851).

cated the absolute necessity of forming a more perfect union, in order to secure the peace and prosperity of all the states. This could only be done by the several states renouncing and relinquishing a portion of their powers of sovereignty. The [Fugitive Slave] clause seems to have been, in character, a treaty. It was a solemn compact, entered into by the delegates of states then sovereign and independent, and free to remain so, on great deliberation, and on the highest considerations of justice and policy, and reciprocal benefit, and in order to secure the peace and prosperity of all the states.

We are to look at the [Fugitive Slave] clause, to ascertain its true meaning and effect. We think it was intended to guaranty to the owner of a slave, living within the territory of a state in which slavery is permitted, the rights conferred upon such owner, by the laws of such state; and that no state should make its own territory an asylum and sanctuary for fugitive slaves, by any law or regulation, by which a slave, who had escaped from a state where he owed labor or service into such state or territory, should avoid being reclaimed.

The fugitive must not only owe service or labor in another state, but he must have *escaped* from it. This is the extent of the right of the master. It is founded in the compact, and limited by the compact. It has therefore been held, that if a slave is brought into this state by his master, or comes here in the course of his occupation or employment without having *escaped*, he is not within the case provided for by the constitution. *Commonwealth v. Aves*, 18 Pick. 193. This results not so much from the voluntary act of the master in bringing or permitting the slave to be brought within the limits of a free state, as because the law by which the person is held to slavery in his own state is local, and has no extraterritorial operation, and because he is not within the provision of the constitution, under which he may be lawfully removed, not having escaped.

Considering, therefore, the nature of the subject, the urgent necessity for a speedy and prompt decision, we have not thought it expedient to delay the judgment. I have, therefore, to state, in behalf of the court, under the weighty responsibility which rests upon us, and as the unanimous opinion of the court, that the writ of *habeas corpus* prayed for cannot be granted. *Writ refused.*

QUESTIONS AND COMMENTS FOR YOUR CONSIDERATION

1. Nowhere in his opinion does Chief Justice Shaw mention the name of Thomas Sims. Do you find this omission revealing?

2. Nowhere in his opinion does Shaw mention the consequences for Mr. Sims of being returned to Georgia. It was common knowledge that when a fugitive slave was brought back, he was publicly flogged. Rarely were slaves killed by their owners because, after all, they were "property," and property owners do not normally destroy their own property. But whipping could "teach the runaway a lesson" as well as teach a lesson to other potential runaways.

3. Does Shaw's approach remind you of Hart's view of justice between The Greeks and Barbarians?

3. Robert M. Cover: The Antislavery Judge[9]

The antislavery judge confronting doctrinal divergence and an intense dialectical environment provides a classic instance of cognitive dissonance. In one sense there was a general, pervasive disparity between the individual's image of himself as a moral human being, opposed to human slavery as part of his moral code, and his image of himself as a faithful judge, applying legal rules impersonally—which rules required in many instances recognition, facilitation, or legitimization of slavery. That general, latent inconsistency was ordinarily not a very difficult one to handle. For commonly accepted and supported notions of professional responsibility either isolated such inconsistency from scrutiny or justified, by ipse dixit, the choice of role fidelity. However, in the abolitionist states these notions began to break down. The judge was confronted with the claim that the divergent character of the doctrinal pattern justified reexamination of the role assumptions. And this claim for reexamination was no abstraction. The ideological advocate and resister made and reiterated the demand in dramatic and personal circumstances. The normal appeal to a professional role would no longer be sufficient, for it was just that role that had been put at issue.

Each slave case potentially generated a more particular dissonance between antipathy to a result that would condemn a man, fundamentally innocent, to underserved

slavery and the knowledge or belief that such an action was required by fidelity to role expectations and rules. Whatever a judge had decided in accord with the role expectations, the knowledge of his having sent a man back to slavery or having refused to emancipate a man, was dissonant with his image of himself as someone morally opposed to slavery. If a judge were to decide in favor of the Negro in violation of the role strictures, however, his decision would be dissonant with his image of himself as a man faithful to his judicial obligations. There would be a disturbing inconsistency whenever expectations arising from one or the other of those self-images was violated in the course of the decision. The antislavery bar and movement could be expected to dramatize and publicize such dilemmas of conscience, thus making the problem all the more painful and all the more personal.

Shaw's antislavery reputation was as widespread and secure as that of any judicial figure before 1850. He believed in fugitive rendition as a necessary evil. His conception of policy as well as of duty pointed to compliance. But this in no sense may be taken as a retreat from the recognition of the injustice or cruelty done the victim of rendition, nor does it signal a lesser opposition to slavery *per se*. I would tender a guess that Shaw's singular act that so captured the imagination of the abolitionists—the bowing beneath the federally imposed chains surrounding the courthouse for the Sims case— was also an act fraught with symbolic import for Shaw himself. The chains were not of his making. He would have preferred that they not be necessary, but they were there, and his only choice was between accepting the yoke of office or resigning it. The sense of overwhelming and external compulsion, the subjugation of deep personal instinct to social necessity was symbolized by the Justice's acceptance of the chains.

[9] Excerpted from Robert M. Cover, Justice Accused: Antislavery and the Judicial Process 228-29, 250 (1975). Copyright 1975 by Yale University. Reprinted by permission.

QUESTIONS AND COMMENTS FOR YOUR CONSIDERATION

1. Is Professor Cover's picture of Chief Justice Shaw's painful dilemma convincing to you? In reading Shaw's opinion, do you get an image of a judge in a profound moral crisis? Do you accept Professor Cover's statement that "in no sense" may Shaw's devotion to the duty of sending Sims back "be taken as a retreat from the recognition of the injustice or cruelty" done to Sims? How does Cover *know* this? By his study of psychology?

2. Some additional facts about Lemuel Shaw may throw light on the previous Question 5. After studying law as an apprentice, he married Eliza Knapp, the daughter of a wealthy Boston merchant. In 1813 he became a director of the New England Bank. He amassed considerable wealth, holding a fairly large amount of insurance company and bank stock. He also held several thousand acres of land in Kentucky, a slave state.[10] His last years of practice before accepting the Chief Justiceship brought him $15,000 to $20,000 annually, which was a phenomenal sum at that time. In his law practice he represented, in addition to banks and insurance companies, the major New England mills. These mills derived their profits from processing southern cotton that was picked by slaves.

Is it possible that Justice Shaw's professed abolitionist sentiments were a cover for his real interests? Was this a cover that Professor Cover missed seeing?

3. A Formalist would say that Justice Shaw had no choice: the Fugitive Slave Clause was crystal clear, it had been interpreted by Congress and the courts to apply to situations of fugitive slaves, and Thomas Sims was a clear example of a fugitive slave. But wouldn't a Realist say that a judge always has a choice?

4. Could Shaw have gotten around the Fugitive Slave Clause if he had really wanted to? Do any of the following possibilities appeal to you?

(a) THESIS: The Fugitive Slave Clause was in the body of the Constitution. The body of the Constitution was amended by the first Ten Amendments. Hence, the Due Process Clause of the Fifth Amendment modifies the Fugitive Slave Clause. Mr. Sims' right to due process of law was violated by any judicial proceeding in Massachusetts the result of which would be to remit Mr. Sims without due process to flogging and a life of enslavement.

ANTITHESIS: Under Georgia law, Thomas Sims is not a person, and hence is not entitled to Due Process protection.

THESIS: Georgia law does not apply extraterritorially in Massachusetts, as the opinion in the Sims Case says. Under Massachusetts law, Thomas Sims is a person who is entitled to Due Process protection.

(b) THESIS: The Fugitive Slave Clause only applies to persons "held" to service or labor in a state; once having escaped from that state, the person is no longer "held" to service in that state.

ANTITHESIS: Everyone knows that "held" means "in bondage," and clearly Thomas Sims was in bondage in Georgia.

THESIS: Georgia law does not apply extraterritorially in Massachusetts, so the word "held" must be construed according to Massachusetts law and not Georgia law.

(c) THESIS: The Fugitive Slave Clause requires a delivering up to the party to whom service or labor "may be due." But Mr. Sims' service or labor is not "due" to anyone, because under Georgia law only persons can owe their service or labor to someone else, and since Mr. Sims is only "property" under Georgia law and not a "person," he can have no obligations in Georgia.

ANTITHESIS: Thomas Sims' service or labor is "due" to his owner, James Potter, by operation of Georgia law. Georgia law only *designates* Sims as owing his labor to Potter; it is irrelevant whether Sims himself owes anything.

THESIS: Georgia law does not apply extraterritorially in Massachusetts, and hence a designation under Georgia law has no effect in Massachusetts.

---

[10] Although I have expended considerable time and effort researching the matter, I have not been able to determine whether there were slaves on the Kentucky lands owned by Lemuel Shaw. There is no mention of the point either way in the extensive microfilm archives of Shaw's papers, nothing in all the biographies about Shaw, and eminent historians of slavery were unable to answer my question.

5. Do the foregoing possibilities strike you as doing violence to the language of the Fugitive Slave Clause? Shouldn't the Clause be interpreted in light of its purpose—which was to effect a "Great Compromise" among the states and allow the new union to be formed?

6. How can we be sure that words like "held" and "due" in the Fugitive Slave Clause of the Constitution should be interpreted according to the *theory* of the Great Compromise and hence be given the meaning that Justice Shaw favors? Isn't it possible that *some* of the Framers of the Constitution *agreed* to the draft language that became Article 4, Section 2, Clause 3, because (a) they *disagreed* with the idea of any Great Compromise, (b) they wanted to see slavery frustrated and eventually abolished, (c) they thought that the language would slip by the Southern states who were all too anxious to interpret it to apply to fugitive slaves, (d) they believed that some future abolitionist court could seize upon the words "held" and "due" and find that those words meant one thing in the slave state and a different thing in the free state, and (e) they hoped that when a future judge in a free state had to construe the clause, that judge—if he really believed that slavery was unjust—would construe the words "held" and "due" so as not to require the court to send back the fugitive?

7. Since *all* legislation and *all* judicial opinions are texts that have been agreed upon by legislators and judges, isn't it always open to a future court—if faced with an apparent dissonance between justice and language—to "read in" to the text of the statute or judicial opinion an intent that corresponds to the interpretive stance that the court itself wants to take? Isn't that what *interpretation* is all about?

8. If the kind of open-ended interpretation suggested in Questions 6 and 7 does not appeal to you, would you acknowledge that it could appeal to a judge? If the judge were particularly adept at language, wouldn't it be possible for the judge to arrive at an interpretation like that in Questions 6 and 7 even if you yourself would not do so? Indeed, isn't it possible that Chief Justice Lemuel Shaw was sufficiently adept at interpreting legal language that he *could have* found a way around the Fugitive Slave Clause like one or more of the possibilities suggested in Question 6? But if this is true, then what about Professor Cover's view that Shaw was torn between his hatred of slavery and his fidelity to law? Is Professor Cover's view tenable?

9. Is it ever tenable to posit a "cognitive dissonance" between a matter of justice in the real world and a matter of words on a piece of paper?

10. When a judge admits (or implies) that a decision is unjust but is nevertheless compelled by the law, should we believe that judge? Didn't Justice Keen admit almost this much in the Speluncean Explorers Case?

11. The psychology of "multiple personality" has been the subject of recent study. People who evidence having several personalities usually have one "alter" who is responsible and another "alter" who is irresponsible. Which of these is the true person? Where is the "soul" located? Isn't the creation of an irresponsible alter a cop-out? Consider the double personality of Justice Keen in the Case of the Speluncean Explorers. In his "personal capacity" he would free the defendants, but in his "judicial capacity" he voted to convict them. Should we absolve Justice Keen of responsibility by saying that his is a double personality? What about Justice Lemuel Shaw? In his abolitionist role he would free Mr. Sims, but in his

judicial role he sends Mr. Sims to Georgia to be flogged and enslaved. Was Shaw asking for public absolution by donning his judicial robes and claiming that he could not do otherwise? What did Shaw really think? Where was his soul really located?

C. Lawyers and Justice

1. Arthur J. Jacobson: The Role of The Lawyer in D'Amato's Jurisprudence[11]

D'Amato's method is to locate the source of law in those whose job it is to predict for ordinary citizens what law would be were authoritative legal institutions to create norms and apply them to particular actions projected by those citizens. The Archimedes point of D'Amato's jurisprudence is neither the abstract creation of norms through legislation (as for Bentham) nor the concrete application of norms in adjudication (as for Dworkin or John Chipman Gray), but rather the counseling (or self-counseling) of citizens as to the probable creation and application of norms by authoritative legal institutions (or other citizens) in specific instances of projected action.

The hero of D'Amato's jurisprudence is the lawyer, who succeeds in two tasks crucial to method. (The ordinary citizen also performs these tasks acting as his own lawyer.) First, by predicting what law would be were authoritative legal institutions to create norms and apply them to particular projected actions, the lawyer induces clients to obey legal norms. His inducement works for two reasons. Clients first learn of norms from a representative of the legal system friendly to their interests; and the lawyer's account of norms, which seeks to enhance those interests, is the first and arguably most important step in the process of norm creation and application that constitutes law for clients. Law appears to clients not only as the imposition of social constraints, but also as an instrument of power. Second, by

providing the authoritative legal institutions with citizens prepared to obey his predictions, the lawyer encourages the institutions to conform their creation and application of norms to the predictions. Authoritative legal institutions, like commanders scrambling to lead a willful column of soldiers, are persuaded to adopt a lawyer's account of norms in order to protect the institutions' power.

Law in D'Amato's jurisprudence constitutes a conspiracy between citizens and authoritative legal institutions—each acting within their sphere to maximize their power. The broker of the conspiracy at the center of the legal system is the lawyer. American jurisprudence—from Madison to Llewellyn—has traditionally regarded power as the destroyer of law. D'Amato has found a way to turn power into law's chief creative element.

2. Anthony D'Amato: Elmer's Rule[12]

A young man named Elmer E. Palmer living in New York State in 1882 decided to murder his grandfather. Elmer believed that by doing so he would inherit under his grandfather's will. Perhaps he calculated that a long prison term plus eventual parole was "worth" the money, or maybe he had his own heirs to whom he wanted to pass the estate. In any event, there was no law on the New York books that said that a murderer could not inherit under the terms of a will if he kills the testator. However, when Elmer's case for inheriting the money reached the New York's highest court, in the case of *Riggs v. Palmer*,[13] the New York

---

[11] Excerpted from Arthur J. Jacobson, *Foreword* to JURISPRUDENCE: A DESCRIPTIVE AND NORMATIVE ANALYSIS OF LAW. Copyright 1984 Martinus Nijhoff Publishers. Reprinted by permission.

[12] Excerpted from Anthony D'Amato, *Elmer's Rule: A Jurisprudential Dialogue*, 60 IOWA LAW REVIEW 1129 (1975). Copyright 1975 by the University of Iowa. Reprinted by permission.

[13] 115 N.Y. 506, 22 N.E. 188 (1889).

Court of Appeals held that Elmer, who had by then been convicted of second-degree murder, could not then inherit the estate under the terms of his grandfather's will.[14]

Justice Cardozo wrote of this case that two analytical paths pointed in different directions and the judges selected the path that seemed better to lead to "justice."[15] Ronald Dworkin has claimed that the case demonstrates the triumph of certain "principles" over what are called "rules of law."[16] More recently, Richard Taylor has argued that there was no "law" at all about murderers inheriting from testators before the actual decision in Riggs, and that consequently the decision itself was the only "law" that affected Elmer.[17]

All of these approaches, but especially Taylor's, suggest that the decision in Riggs was largely unpredictable and therefore must have come as something of a surprise to Elmer and his attorney. Of course, looking at this case today, we are not especially concerned with the particular fact whether Elmer was surprised by the result. But the notions of surprise and unpredictability raise a more basic issue: what business does a court have in surprising anyone? Shouldn't a court fulfill people's expectations of the law? Shouldn't a court behave as predictably as it possibly can? More basic even than these questions is the question of just what we mean when we refer to "law." Of course, that question is as enormous as it is basic, but I would suggest that we do have at least a minimal conception of law that most people would not challenge. Minimally, law is a means for affecting the behavior (modifying it, channeling it, or changing it) of the people to whom the law is addressed. If law did not at least fulfill such a function, we would hardly call it "law" or be interested in it.

But if law means something that affects behavior, can we say that the law prior to the decision in Riggs could have affected Elmer's behavior? If we can in fact so conclude, then to some extent the law either did not or should not have come as a surprise to Elmer: in dealing with his case, the courts were simply ratifying in a reasonably predictable manner a norm (or a "rule or "principle") that existed in some sense before Elmer put the poison in his grandfather's food. To the same extent, we would not be as troubled by the apparent discretion or "legislative function" attributed to the New York court by various writers of jurisprudence. And we would also reinforce our own conception about the proper rule of a court—that in adjudicating past behavior, a court should apply norms that were in existence at the time of that past behavior. For if a court does not do this, it would be acting prospectively—as a legislator—in making rules. But the prospective action would apply retrospectively—to the losing party in the case. This would strike against our notions of fairness and undermine our belief in the viability of the definition of "law" suggested above. If a court is to be "fair" and to proceed according to "justice," it should not invent rules and then apply them retroactively to litigants.

Instead of analyzing Elmer's case conventionally, I shall invent a dialogue between Elmer and his attorney. The dialogue will attempt to indicate what notice, if any, Elmer might have received had he discussed with his attorney the question of the "law" prior to his decision to murder his grandfather. Of course, the dialogue is constructed with all the benefits of hindsight, including especially the ultimate decision by the New York courts. The lawyer, like the dialogue itself, is purely fictitious. Through dramatic license I hope to present in the clearest way I can what Elmer and a reasonably perceptive attorney might have concluded had they seriously examined the *Riggs v. Palmer* issue before the New York courts decided the case. Any final judgment as to the plausibility of the minidrama is left to the reader.

ACT ONE: office of an Attorney in Upstate New York, February, 1882

ATTORNEY: Have a seat, Elmer. What's on your mind these days? Miss Fetch says you have a question to ask me.

ELMER: That's right, I do. I want to know whether an heir under a will

---

[14] *Id.* at 514-15, 22 N.E. at 191.

[15] Benjamin Cardozo, The Nature of the Judicial Process 41 (1921).

[16] *Editor's Note*: Relevant portions of the essay by Professor Dworkin are reprinted in Chapter 2 of this Anthology, at page 65.

[17] Taylor, *Law and Morality*, 43 N.Y.U. L. Rev. 611, 626 (1968).

would still get the property even if he killed the testator.

ATTORNEY: I didn't know you knew all those legal terms, like "testator" and "heir." Have you been reading Blackstone or Kent?

ELMER: As a matter of fact, I did take out the Blackstone book from the library. But it wasn't any help on this issue.

ATTORNEY: Well, I'm glad you're so interested in the law. But I'm a bit surprised about the question you asked. What made you think of it?

ELMER: Well—

ATTORNEY: I can imagine you would come up with lots of questions after reading some of Blackstone. But a question that doesn't even exist in Blackstone is another matter. Was there actually something in Blackstone's book that made you come up with this particular question?

ELMER: No. I read about it in a dime novel the other day.

ATTORNEY: And you rushed out to look up the law?

ELMER: That's right.

ATTORNEY: Are you sure you don't know anyone who's planning to murder his rich old uncle?

ELMER: Oh, no sir.

ATTORNEY: Do you know anyone who has any notions of murder in mind?

ELMER: No, I don't.

ATTORNEY: Now don't get me wrong in my asking this, Elmer, but just out of curiosity, your grandfather has quite a bit of money, and you'd be the only logical beneficiary.

ELMER: I don't see what that has to do with it.

ATTORNEY: Nothing, my boy, nothing at all. You just set my mind thinking. Would you know, by the way, whether you are the beneficiary under your grandfather's will?

ELMER: Isn't that something you would know?

ATTORNEY: No, as a matter of fact. Your grandfather used another lawyer in town. But I know he has a will, all right.

ELMER: Well, I think I'm mentioned in his will. But I can't be sure. Anyway, my question has nothing to do with me.

ATTORNEY: I know that, Elmer, and I'm glad of it. I suppose it would be natural for a beneficiary under a will sometimes to wonder when the testator is going to die, or whether he might change the will before he dies. But I'm sure that those thoughts are not at all what prompts your question.

ELMER: Not at all. But I would like to know the law on the point.

ATTORNEY: I can't give you an answer off hand. But I'll do some research on it, just out of curiosity. Here are a couple of books you might look into, too. You can come back in about a week and we'll discuss it at that time.

ELMER: Thanks. I'll see what the books say. Maybe there's a rule in one of them that covers the point.

ATTORNEY: I tend to doubt it, since there was no rule in Blackstone. But we'll see. Meanwhile, I want you to know one thing.

ELMER: Yes?

ATTORNEY: Murder, as you know, is the most heinous crime of all. Anyone who murders anyone else deserves to be hanged. I wouldn't hesitate to turn over any information I have about any murder to the police, even if it's information about someone who is a client of mine.

ELMER: A client?

ATTORNEY: A client who I know committed a murder—so long as I didn't get the information in confidence from the client himself after the fact as part of my job in representing him. Even then, I wouldn't know whether to represent him, but I don't suppose I could turn him over to the police. But if someone is my client and I find out that he committed a murder, the fact that he is my client won't stop me from calling the police.

ELMER: I think I understand. But why are you telling me this?

ATTORNEY: I just want you to know, Elmer, about how I view my responsibility as a lawyer. You came in here and asked me a question about murderers and testators. Just suppose, Elmer, that your grandfather dies an unnatural death. In such a situation, the fact that you asked me the question about a murderer inheriting under a will would tend to throw a tiny bit of suspicion your way—

ELMER: But—

ATTORNEY: —even if you were perfectly innocent! You see, now that you've asked me the question in a connection that has absolutely nothing to do with any action that you yourself are contemplating, I would not regard it as confidential information under an attorney-client privilege if subsequently there is an investigation of any possible unnatural death of your grandfather.

ELMER: I see.

ATTORNEY: All right, then. Come in next week and we'll discuss your interesting question.

ELMER: [in an old-fashioned "aside" to the audience] Drat! I shouldn't have asked him. I should have done the research by myself. But how? I don't know how to do the research. I had to ask an attorney. Oh, well, now that I've asked him, I might as well go through with the investigation. Whatever damage has been done can't be undone. I'll see him next week and get his opinion.

Commentary. In one sense, nothing has happened so far. Elmer has simply asked a question of his attorney. But in another sense something important has been suggested about the meaning of "law". We have seen that the attorney himself is part of the legal system in more than just the technical sense that he is an "officer of the court. The attorney represents Elmer's first contact with the legal process that is beginning to take shape around Elmer's question. As Elmer himself has discovered by failing to find the question even mentioned in Blackstone or Kent, the two most consulted works of the time, "Can a beneficiary inherit if he murders the testator?" is not an inquiry to which the legal system provided an easy answer. But the legal system, through the attorney himself, has started to respond. Even though the attorney has only said so far that he doesn't know the answer to the question, in fact he has begun to reveal that answer by the very attitude that he has taken toward Elmer's question. His attitude, Elmer has discovered, is markedly negative. The attorney will research it as an "interesting" question, but he has made it clear that he would be repelled if this question had any practical significance to Elmer. Thus, if Elmer were a very discerning chap, he might have said to himself that the lawyer's negative attitude is a good indication that the legal system as a whole will also have a negative attitude toward such a question, for the lawyer is part of the legal system. But Elmer does not understand the institutional role of a lawyer. Instead, Elmer's view of the lawyer seems to be that he is a highly paid research assistant.

ACT TWO: The same, a week later.

ATTORNEY: Come in, Elmer. I've had a chance to research that question of yours now. I've turned up some interesting information.

ELMER: Is there any law on the subject?

ATTORNEY: Well, that's a large question. Let's break it down. What do you mean by "law"?

ELMER: A statute?

ATTORNEY: Fine, we'll start with that. I've done the research and the fact is that there is no New York statute that deals with the subject of a beneficiary taking if he murdered the testator. There are lots of statutes, of course, that deal with taking under wills, but there is none on the particular question you raise. In addition, there are no relevant federal statutes.

ELMER: How about other states? Or don't they count?

ATTORNEY: In fact, I've not been able to come up with any legislation of any other state on this matter, and I suspect that if I looked at the legislation of other countries I wouldn't find anything either. Of course, statutes in other states or countries would not be binding in New York, but it is interesting that your question never seems to have occurred to any legislative body in all recorded history.

ELMER: How about cases?

ATTORNEY: There is no case in the books involving the murder of a testator by the beneficiary.

ELMER: None at all?

ATTORNEY: That's right, to be precise about the matter. But you see, Elmer, an attorney's job can't end by just looking up the question of whether there was exactly the same case ever decided previously. There may be what we call an analogous case.

ELMER: I don't know what that might be.

ATTORNEY: Well, I found a case that was decided in North Carolina that involved a wife's right to dower.[18] She had been convicted of being an accessory before the fact to the murder of her husband. In other words, she was involved in the murder of her husband, and yet she was claiming a share of his estate.

ELMER: That sounds pretty close to the question I asked you.

ATTORNEY: I thought so too.

ELMER: What was the ruling?

ATTORNEY: The court held that the wife was entitled to dower.

ELMER: And that's the only case on the books?

ATTORNEY: Right. The only case tends to suggest that a murderer can inherit anyway.

ELMER: That just about answers my question, then.

ATTORNEY: Not so fast. There are several things we have to consider. In the first place, as I told you, it was a North Carolina case, not a New York case.

ELMER: Does that mean it has no effect in New York State?

ATTORNEY: No, not exactly. As a matter of fact, I suspect that the New York courts would want to follow the only precedent in point even if it is a decision in another state. Judges, you might know, have some feeling that the law should be consistent, and so that would feel a pressure to reach the same result as North Carolina. But they are not bound to do so.

ELMER: Not bound, you mean, like they would be if it were a New York decision?

ATTORNEY: Exactly. And even if it were a New York case, a later court could overrule the precedent. But such instances of overruling a precedent are very rare.

ELMER: So what you're saying is that a New York court probably would follow North Carolina case?

ATTORNEY: Yes. At least, judges in this state would take the North Carolina case into account as an important factor. But now let's look at a second issue. Just how close is a case of dowry to a case involving a will?

ELMER: It's exactly the same thing.

ATTORNEY: But a will isn't a dowry.

ELMER: I mean, the principle is the same.

ATTORNEY: You're right that we have to look to the principle. But what is the principle?

ELMER: The principle is inheriting an estate from someone you've killed.

ATTORNEY: Well, Elmer, that's one principle. But let's analyze it a different way. Suppose we have a testator who announces to the beneficiary that he is going to change his will, and the beneficiary fears that the change may be quite adverse to the beneficiary.[19]

---

[18] Gwens v. Owens, 100 N.C. 240, 6 S.E. 794 (1888). I have taken a slight dramatic license. Owens in fact arose after Elmer poisoned his grandfather, but before the decision in Riggs v. Palmer, which discussed and rejected "the doctrine of that case." 115 N.Y. at 514, 22 N.E. at 190-91.

[19] Such a situation is the main ingredient in a superb detective novel by Agatha Christie. See AGATHA CHRISTIE, HERCULE POIROT'S CHRISTMAS (1938).

If the beneficiary hurries up and murders the testator before the testator can change the will, then he will have profited enormously by the murder. But look at the dowry situation. There the husband can't change the way the estate will devolve even if he wanted to.

ELMER: But the wife gets the estate sooner by murdering her husband.

ATTORNEY: Very true. But that's true for the will situation as well. Indeed, the murderer in both cases gets the property sooner than he would have if the owner died a natural death. So that is a point of similarity. But I've been talking about a point of difference.

ELMER: So the cases are different?

ATTORNEY: Yes. Or at least I should say, a judge could find a difference between a will case and a dowry case if he wanted to.

ELMER: Why would he want to?

ATTORNEY: Do you think a judge will want to reward a murderer for his crime by allowing him to inherit the estate?

ELMER: I don't know. But isn't it something outside the law to say whether someone gets rewarded or not? I mean, shouldn't the judges just apply the law, and not look at the effects of their decisions?

ATTORNEY: That certainly is an approach, and a thoughtful one. But I think judges won't ignore the effects of what they do. Why should they? Justice isn't "blind" in that sense. A judge is part of the real world.

ELMER: Yes, but a judge is also someone who applies the law.

ATTORNEY: Elmer, "the law" isn't just the statutes and the cases, as I'm trying to point out to you. Certainly the law is partly that, in fact mainly that. But it can be a bit more, too. It can involve the reasons behind the law. It can involve deep-seated principles that we all share. It can involve looking at the effects of decisions. It can involve "justice." All these things are the things a judge should "apply."

ELMER: But all that looks pretty vague to me.

ATTORNEY: Well, the question you ask hasn't come up yet, so what do you expect? Surely you don't expect the law to provide answers in the books to questions that haven't come up! So we have to proceed in what you call a vague fashion, since there isn't a better alternative. But let's get down to brass tacks. There is a second reply you might give to my question about a murderer rewarded for what he has done.

ELMER: I can't think of it.

ATTORNEY: It's simply this. The United States Constitution and the Constitution of the State of New York provide certain procedures and safeguards for a person accused of a crime. A person may be declared guilty only after he has been given the right to a jury trial, the right to confront witnesses, and after the case has been proved against him beyond a reasonable doubt. When all that happens and a person is declared guilty, he cannot be punished beyond the punishment prescribed by the law. A person convicted of a felony for which the maximum penalty is 10 years in prison cannot be sentenced by a judge to 20 years in prison, for example.

ELMER: What does this have to do with my question?

ATTORNEY: Simply this. We assume that you have a convicted murderer. Whatever his punishment is, it is that which has been prescribed by the criminal law. Now the murderer can argue that no other court or official should add to that punishment by taking away the property he has inherited. Any additional punishment would be something that exceeds the punishment prescribed by the criminal law.

ELMER: So it would be illegal for a court to deny the murderer his inheritance?

ATTORNEY: I didn't say that. I'm only giving you an argument, one that may have been in the minds of the judges in North Carolina in the dowry case.

ELMER: But surely a court can't act contrary to the Constitution.

ATTORNEY: That's right. But remember, a court interprets the Constitution. If it doesn't think it is acting contrary to the Constitution, nothing I can tell you in this office is going to change that fact. Besides, a court might get around the problem of additional punishment.

ELMER: How?

ATTORNEY: By saying that the murderer isn't being deprived of his property, because the property hasn't been "vested" in him. If the property isn't vested in him, the court isn't taking it away.

ELMER: That sounds fishy.

ATTORNEY: It is, in a way. What the court would be saying is that the property isn't the murderer's until the court itself has construed the will. If part of the court's construction of the will is to read in an exception for murderers, then the exception has been read in before the property got to the murderer. So the court would be taking nothing away from him.

ELMER: That's not only fishy. Surely the court would be taking away from the murderer something that would otherwise be his.

ATTORNEY: Not quite. It would be "his" if he weren't a murderer! But, I agree, this line of argument is pretty suspicious. I only want to point out to you that a court would be capable of coming up with it just in order to refute the "additional penalty" argument that I gave you. So we have to conclude that the additional penalty point is only an argument, not a conclusive thing by any means.

ELMER: Well, can I ask if there are any more reasons in favor of allowing the murderer to take under the will?

ATTORNEY: I've thought of a third one, though it's not likely that a court would pay much attention to it if it comes up in argument. But let me give you a possible situation. Suppose the testator has an estate worth a million and five dollars. He draws up a will dividing his estate into two parts abso-lute: a million dollars goes to his son, and the remainder to a tiny organization called Citizens for the Restoration of British Sovereignty in America. Then his son murders him. Suppose the court were to decide that the son cannot inherit the million dollars because he murdered the testator. Should the million then be paid over to the CRBSA? You see, the estate has to go somewhere. It can't revert back to the state because any such rule would encourage the judiciary, which is part of the state, to find such reversions. There are laws that require that the estate go to the beneficiaries. So who would the court be benefiting by disinheriting the murderer?

ELMER: You mean, in any will at all there will be a question of who gets the money if the murderer doesn't get it?

ATTORNEY: Exactly. Giving the money to the other persons in the will might be worse than giving it to the murderer. Of course, it's not really a question of worse or better, but of the intent of the testator. Suppose a court says that it cannot imagine that the testator, if he was aware of the problem, would have intended to give the money to a murderer? All right, but then what would have been his intent? To make my preceding example stronger, suppose his son has several children, but the father instead of providing directly for the grandchildren in the will gave the estate outright to the son. Then the son murders the father. The son is convicted of murder and on his way to the gallows. If the court takes the money away from the son and instead gives it to the CRBSA, the court in fact will be depriving the grandchildren of the estate. Surely the testator would not have wanted such a result. We can suppose that even if he knew about the murder, he would still have wanted his grandchildren to inherit the estate and not be left penniless after their father is hanged.

ELMER: As long as these speculations seem to have something to do with the law, I might as well mention a couple of ideas I've had since our last conversation.

ATTORNEY: Such as?

ELMER: Suppose the testator wants the beneficiary to murder him? Suppose he's told the beneficiary that he's looking for some way to die but doesn't believe in suicide or is afraid to commit suicide. Or, he might be in great pain and ask the beneficiary to put him out of his pain.

ATTORNEY: Very good. Elmer, you've been doing a powerful lot of thinking about all this. But you've never taken any interest in the law before. Why this great interest on your part?

ELMER: Nothing in particular. It's just that your ideas have led me to think about it.

ATTORNEY: Well, although it seems far-fetched, a testator might want to be murdered. Of course, that would still be murder, but I take it your real point is that if the testator wanted to be murdered he would still have intended that the murderer take under the will.

ELMER: Yes.

ATTORNEY: So what do you think?

ELMER: Well, as I said at the beginning, I think the case is more solid than ever. There's no statute or case saying a murderer should be read out of his victim's will. And there seem to be several strong reasons which support allowing a murderer to collect under the will. I agree that you have shown that each of the reasons is not itself conclusive on the court—it can wriggle out of any one of them by some idea or other like the one you call "vesting." But taken together they should be conclusive. Don't you agree?

ATTORNEY: No.

ELMER: Why?

ATTORNEY: Let's look at the effect of a decision allowing a murderer to take under a will. The public will be put on notice that one way to get an estate would be to murder the testator. Lots of crazy people might be encouraged to do so.

ELMER: But isn't that a policy decision for the legislature to make?

ATTORNEY: I agree. It would be bet-ter if a legislature made it. But a legislature might not get around to doing it, and meanwhile a court is faced with an actual case. The court shouldn't reach a "bad" result simply by thinking that the legislature will come along later and correct it. A court is under some pressure to come up with good results irrespective of what the legislature will do.

ELMER: And yet you still think that a court is not going to allow the murderer to inherit under the will. Why?

ATTORNEY: Well, Elmer, after all this thinking and research, it comes down in my mind to a kind of intuitive feeling. I predict, on the basis of what I know about courts and judges and the legal system, that a court simply will not want to be party to a murderer's scheme to collect under a will. It's as simple as that. The judiciary will not want to be involved in that kind of enterprise. A court faced with the question would probably hold that the murderer cannot inherit. The court will perceive its decision to be in accordance with "justice." That might not mean precisely that the right party will receive the funds (recall my CRBSA example), but I think a court simply will not want to think of itself as any sort of an instrument enabling a murderer to profit from his crime.

ELMER: So you think the court would probably act contrary to the law?

ATTORNEY: Not at all, Elmer. It might be acting contrary to some rules, and it might not be able to cite a statutory rule in its favor. But the law is something more than those rules. As I've tried to suggest to you, law is really a prediction of what courts will decide. I'll give you my prediction right here and now. I predict that there's a better than 50-50 chance that the court will not allow the murderer to inherit the property.

ELMER: That's your intuition?

ATTORNEY: Yes, in a way. It's the same intuition I had when you first came into the office. All the research we've done in between hasn't really changed my opinion.

ELMER: Well, thank you very much for your opinion. I can't see how you could reach that result in the light of all the statutes and cases and other considerations that we talked about. Your idea of law is too vague for me. I guess I just don't think of law that way.

ATTORNEY: You're entitled to your opinion. I just hope that in your lifetime and mine no court will ever be faced with this particular question. As much as I'd like to know whether my idea of the law is right or not, I hope your question is never answered by any court.

—The End—

Postscript. After the curtain comes down on the law office scene, Elmer commits the murder off-stage. A subsequent drama, entitled *People v. Elmer Palmer*, ends in a conviction of second-degree murder. After that there is a third drama that takes place in Probate Court entitled *Riggs v. Palmer*, in which Elmer is stripped of his rights under the will and the estate is awarded instead to the next closest relatives, Elmer's aunts.

Conclusion. Of course, even if Elmer had in fact talked with a lawyer, we know that he was not deterred from killing his grandfather. But something like the foregoing dialogue might have occurred to deter other nameless would-be murderers before 1889; the idea of killing a testator in order to take under a will was at least conceivable for centuries before the time that Elmer did it. There is no way we will ever know whether any such deterrent was operative, but if the lawyer's intuitive reactions are any persuasive indication, what occurred in the lawyer's office was real law.

D. Compromise as Exact Justice

1. John E. Coons: The Common Law Should Provide for Compromise Verdicts[20]

So long as a judge is required to choose

winner and loser on an all-or-nothing basis, common law doctrine does not provide him the variety of alternatives necessary to achieve perfect adjustment in hard cases. Under a system of winner-take-all the one-sided result reached upon principle in the close case must continue to trouble the conscience of the law. Only the power to adjust quantatively the rights and responsibilities of the parties could provide the court with sufficient alternatives to face this problem directly.

Judicial activism in chambers is matched only by judicial paralysis on the bench. The "fair" decision promoted in private is one unattainable by law. That which the judge thinks just he cannot order. That which in chambers he calls "unjust" he orders and defends with thirty pages of rhetoric.

Cases theoretically amenable to imposed compromise are exceedingly numerous. Any dispute involving injuries or rights that can be evaluated in money is a potential subject of apportionment. Broadly speaking, most civil cases in which a remedy at law exists could be handled under rules creating proportional rights if this were inoffensive on policy grounds. Indeed, it is often suggested that apportionment is now being achieved on a grand scale by a variety of sub rosa techniques and in a multiplicity of situations. Averaging by juries, the ignoring of contributory negligence except as mitigation, and—where multiple claims are involved—a distribution of the prizes between plaintiff and defendant all make possible a rough quantitative calculus of justice. Aunt Emma gets the house, but the court finds that the testator surely meant Uncle Charlie to have the farm.

Imposition of compromise is conceivable in a variety of cases. Consider the following examples:

1. A and B are unsecured creditors of X whose assets are insufficient to satisfy both A and B.

2. An Act of God destroys part of the grain stored in Jones' grain elevator by A, B, C, and Jones.

3. The good ship Marylyn survives a tempest by throwing overboard cargo belonging to A. Cargo of B and C is thereby saved.

4. A and B collide at an intersection with resulting damage and injuries. Both were negligent, but B was more negligent.

---

[20] Excerpted from John E. Coons, *Approaches to Court Imposed Compromise—The Uses of Doubt and Reason*, 58 Nw. U. L. Rev. 750, 751-57 (1964). Reprinted by permission.

5. A check, of which *A* is the holder, bears what is apparently *B*'s signature. *B* denies signing such a check. Handwriting experts disagree with each other. There is no other evidence.

6. *A* swears he is the owner of an un-branded cow in *B*'s possession. *B* swears the cow is his. There is no other evidence.

7. *A* purchases a hi-fi set at a reputable store. The set was sold to the store by *X* who had borrowed it from *B*. *B* demands its return. The store is insolvent. *X* is gone.

8. *T* leaves an ambiguous will. It is impossible to tell whether he intended *X* or *Y* as his devisee of Blackacre.

Example 4 is a case which would involve judicially imposed compromise only in a comparative negligence state. In other state an all-or-nothing result would be inevitable, limited only by the possibility of "improper" jury averaging.

In Examples 5 and 6 the result will be all-or-nothing under any existing view, even if the finder of fact considers the probabilities exactly equal.

In Example 7 the owner generally prevails under common law. In Example 9 the court will probably award the lot to either *X* or *Y* after a more or less convincing application of "rules of construction", thus potentially defeating *T*'s intention by 100%. It may also declare the devise unenforceable thereby insuring that same result.

In Example 6, *A* as plaintiff would receive short shrift in a replevin action for the cow unless he is an extraordinarily convincing witness. Given substantially equal credibility, *A* fails on two grounds—that he has failed to overcome the presumption of ownership arising from *B*'s possession of the cow, and (what amounts to the same thing) that he has failed to overcome what Wigmore first styled the "risk of non-persuasion." In other words, the plaintiff has failed to sustain his burden of proving ownership by something called a "preponderance of the evidence."

It may be said that the imposition of the burden of persuasion has at least the beneficial function of getting the case decided, of taking it off the hands of the court, and of fixing the rights of the parties so that life may resume a stable pattern. This is surely true but begs the question. Any judgment by the court describing coherently the respective rights of the parties has that same consequence. Important as it is, the mere termination of litigation is not self-justifying, even in opaque factual situations. Justification must wait upon a showing that there is no better alternative.

It also may be said that winner-take-all is an aspect of a healthy judicial conservatism which stands in balanced inertia until impelled by sufficient proof to move to the aid of the litigant seeking its intervention. It is a preference, in other words, for doing nothing. Now the virtues of doing nothing are legion. They cannot be invoked, however, to justify a universal judicial inertia, for there are simply too many cases in which justice must move in order to stand still. Is it an expression of conservatism to refuse to act between two parties in a dispute over a valuable right? Or may the refusal itself often constitute the most decisive kind of judicial action simply by preserving a *status quo*? Some higher convenience than a mere verbal conservatism must be pleaded to justify an all-or-nothing result formally based on an equality of proof. Again the question is whether any superior alternative can be suggested.

My thesis is: Where a judgment for one party in a civil case at law can be based upon no greater probability of factual accuracy than its opposite, and where no reason of policy intervenes, the court should divide between the parties in equal quantitative parts the rights and/or duties at issue. What happens then to the disputed cow? Simply this: If the trier of fact finds the truth of the matter indeterminate in the sense of an equivalence of probabilities, the court may order the beast sold and the proceeds divided or may award her to either party upon payment of half the value to the adversary.

If my thesis is applied to Example 8 (thus awarding half of Blackacre to *X* and half to *Y*), an objection can be made that the testator's intention is violated by 50 per cent. The alternative of being 100 per cent correct half the time might be preferred, since it can easily be disguised under rules of construction.

QUESTIONS AND COMMENTS FOR YOUR CONSIDERATION

1. In Professor Coons' Example 1, would a rule that treated *A* and *B* equally tend to erode the policy of encouraging debtors to secure or register their claims?

2. In Professor Coons' Example 3, would you need to know more information about the placement, weight, and ostensible value of the various cargoes? Would that information itself, at trial, be undervalued if there were an apportionment rule in effect?

3. With respect to the remainder of Professor Coons' examples, and in particular with respect to negligence cases and Professor Coons' Example 4, do you agree or disagree with the following argument by Professor Arthur Jacobson?

2. Arthur J. Jacobson: The Common Law Should Not Provide For Compromise Verdicts[21]

Look closely at an accident in which both persons who were injured were negligent. We can set up one of three rules. Either both persons recover for the injuries caused by the other's negligence, or neither recovers (the rule of contributory negligence), or each recovers in proportion to the quantum of negligence the other contributed to the accident (the rule of comparative negligence). The first choice is inconsistent with the requirement that the negligent act cause the victim's injury. It is impossible to say which person's negligence caused one person's injury where both were negligent. To choose the first leads to punishing persons for "negligence in the air," that is, negligence that does not cause injury (since we cannot possibly know whose negligence "caused" which injuries). The third choice also offends causation, but softens the offense by instituting a version of compromise verdict.

Common Law forbids compromise verdicts, because persons who face such verdicts cannot use them to deal with each other after the verdicts. In the case of two negligent parties to an accident, a compromise verdict gives the following message: you must be careful only to persons who are also careful.

If you are lucky enough to have an accident with a person who is also not being careful, then you are released of a portion of your obligation to be careful. Since you cannot tell in advance with whom you will have an accident, you may adjust your behavior to a standard of care which is appropriate to facing persons who have an average level of carelessness, not to persons who are always careful. This lesser level of care in turn communicates a lesser obligation to be careful on the part of those other persons, and so on. Comparative negligence eliminates the spirit of reciprocal care which Common Law strives to inculcate.

E. Justice as Part of the Content of Law

1. Gerry Spence: How Cases Are Decided[22]

You decide on emotions. Justice is an emotion.

2. Oliver Wendell Holmes: Justice vs. Law[23]

I have said to my brethren many times

---

[21] Excerpted from Arthur J. Jacobson, *Hegel's Legal Plenum*, 10 CARDOZO LAW REVIEW 877, 903-04 (1989). Copyright 1989 by Arthur J. Jacobson. Reprinted by permission.

[22] Gerry Spence, Remarks on "Larry King Live," CNN television broadcast of Sept. 26, 1995 (regarding the closing arguments in the O.J. Simpson case).

[23] Justice Oliver Wendell Holmes, quoted in MAX LERNER, THE MIND AND FAITH OF JUSTICE HOLMES 435 (1943).

that I hate justice, which means that if a man begins to talk about that, for one reason or another he is shirking thinking in legal terms.

3. Karl Llewellyn: The Newer Jurisprudence[24]

The job of a lawyer is to show how the goal of "justice" in his case can be attained within the framework of the law. The fact is that in a huge number of cases *there is enough leeway and give within the framework of our law* to allow what is felt as justice being attained in the case without departing from that framework.

I wish I had the skill to make this clear. For it is simple fact that when men think consciously about a problem in its general aspects, they think especially about the *parts* of that problem which are intellectually hard and intellectually articulate, about the parts which call for research and for which they must resort to books and to the definite, printed word. The rest of what goes into the problem they mostly forget or else assume; in any event they do not talk or write about it. So that the very lawyer who is most careful about the "atmosphere" of his very case, and who most deftly works each time to make the court feel justice on his side of it, to make the court want to accept his good and solid line of legal argument and reject his adversary's line of legal argument (which really, just as *legal* argument, is about as good and solid as his own)—that same lawyer will be telling you the next day that it was the rules which decided that case; he "simply" got the court to "see" "the true" rule and its bearing.

4. Anthony D'Amato: On the Connection Between Law and Justice[25]

This essay argues that justice is an inher-

ent component of the law, not separate or distinct from it. Given the history of the topic, I start with a disclaimer. The issues involved here are as vast as they are fundamental. I do not pretend to have a definitive solution. I do, however, attempt a suggestive solution, based on an extended hypothetical case. If you, the reader, are not persuaded by it, I hope at least that it may have heuristic value for you.

The argumentative use of hypothetical cases not only characterizes good classroom teaching in law schools, but it is found in questions judges ask from the bench during oral argument and in many other areas of law study and practice. My intention here is to use a single, extended hypothetical case to demonstrate that justice is an integral part of law. Surely this is a heavy load to dump on one hypothetical example. If I can pull it off, the hypothetical case will have to be well selected.

The most important selection criterion is that the hypothetical case must not be idiosyncratic. Thus it should be set in any jurisdiction, and not a particular jurisdiction (such as the United States). In addition, it should be an ordinary, even humdrum, example, to avoid charges that I have reached for something unusual and hence inapplicable to ordinary circumstances.

I will choose a motor vehicle regulation that, so far as I know, is standard in many countries: the parallel (double) white lines down the center of a road. I will focus on the parallel lines and not the statutory regulation behind it, because once we look at a particular statute, we might have an interpretive problem that could vary from country to country or from language to language. The parallel lines therefore offer a purely semantic and generalizable legal rule, meaning, in effect, "don't cross me." The driver of a car understands the parallel lines as a legal prohibition, barring vehicles from driving over and hence crossing the parallel lines. It is this *meaning* that I will focus upon, rather than any particular set of statutory words that purports to express the meaning. Nevertheless, in order to make the example realistic, I will invent a back-up example of a regulation that gives legal effect to the white lines.

Since this example will involve justice, I must make the justice element in the hypo-

[24] KARL L. LLEWELLYN, JURISPRUDENCE: REVISION IN THEORY AND PRACTICE 137 (1962). Copyright by the University of Chicago. Reprinted by permission.

[25] Excerpted from Anthony D'Amato, *On the Connection Between Law and Justice*, 26 UNIVERSITY OF CALIFORNIA AT DAVIS LAW REVIEW 527, 564-81 (1993). Copyright 1993 Anthony D'Amato.

thetical case as uncontroversial as possible. No purpose would be served by getting into an extended discussion of whether an act related to this example is itself just or unjust, which would then require having to *assume* its injustice in order to get on with the project. Hence, the act I choose that is uncontrovertibly unjust is running over and killing an innocent child. The child is an "innocent child" in the sense that it has not committed a crime such that execution of the child would be an appropriate penalty. But in my hypothetical case it is a "darting child"—one who runs out in front of a moving automobile at the last minute. If the driver of the car wants to avoid killing the child, the driver's only option (as I construct this hypothetical case) would be to drive across the parallel lines.

Before I sketch in the details of this imagined case, let me comment on the phrase that I have placed in quotation marks: "innocent child." A person could argue that a child who darts out into the street at the last minute in front of a moving car is hardly "innocent." The child is at least guilty of an error in judgment, and perhaps guilty of disobeying its parents' instructions. Nevertheless, I can hardly imagine anyone seriously arguing that killing the child is an appropriate penalty for the child's error in judgment or its disobedience of its parents. To be sure, we might imagine a society—H.G. Wells imagined one in his famous short story, *The Time Machine*—where killing pedestrians is a routine aspect of driving a car. (In Wells' future society, there is a severe overpopulation problem, so no one objects to the bizarre practice of running over pedestrians.) But I don't think that any reasonable person would maintain, in today's world, that justice is served by killing the darting child.

Let us now sketch in a few details. The darting child runs out into the street from behind a car parked at the curb. No driver of an oncoming car could have seen the child getting ready to leap into the street, because the child was small in size and completely hidden by the parked car; only when the child darted out into the street was the child visible. Hence we completely rule out any possible negligence on the part of the driver of the car. Moreover, we must stipulate that it is physically possible, without risk of personal injury, for the driver to avoid hitting the child by crossing the parallel white lines. At that moment there is no car coming in the opposite direction in the other lane that would hit the driver's car head-on if the driver crossed the lines, so driving to the left and crossing the double parallel lines would be safe for the driver. Moreover, we stipulate that the driver cannot steer to the right, because there are parked cars along the curb and he would hit those cars—and even possibly glance off them and run over the child in any event. Hence, what we have is a road with two lanes, one going in each direction, with parallel white lines down the middle, a driver proceeding in one of those lanes, a child who darts in front of the driver at the last minute, and the opportunity for the driver to avoid hitting the child by crossing the parallel lines and driving (temporarily) in the other lane. There is no car or other vehicle in the other lane at the moment when this event occurs.

Now let us split this hypothetical case into two similar cases. (A) In the first case, driver A sees the child at the last minute, drives across the parallel lines, avoiding the child, and then drives back into the proper lane after the child is passed. (B) In the second case, driver B sees the child at the last minute, refrains from crossing the parallel lines (though physically able to do so),[26] and runs over and kills the child. In both cases, a police officer is present at the scene, observing everything that occurred. In neither case is there any factual dispute or conflicting testimony. I will mostly discuss the first case of driver A (Alice); the second case of driver B (Bruce) will serve primarily as a contrasting background.

The Arrest. In case (A), right after Alice has swerved successfully to avoid hitting the darting child, the police officer on the scene flags her down and gives her a ticket:

---

[26] Philosophers will recognize this as a "counterfactual." *See* 2 DAVID LEWIS, PHILOSOPHICAL PAPERS 3-31 (1986). Whatever the difficulties of modal logic in asserting the possibility of doing something other than that which the actor did, law has always proceeded on the assumption that a defendant is "blameworthy" in the sense that he or she could have acted differently. (If the defendant was insane, or was physically coerced, and hence unable to act differently, all legal systems recognize an excuse.)

ALICE: Why are you giving me a ticket? I avoided killing that child.

OFFICER: I know. I'm glad you did. But you still committed a traffic violation.

ALICE: Are you saying that I should have stayed in my lane and run over the child?

OFFICER: You have to realize that by saving the child's life you violated the law. I'm sure you felt it was the right thing to do.

ALICE: Yes, I did. And didn't you?

OFFICER: Yes. It was the right thing to do. I'm sure the judge in traffic court will agree, and say that the violation was only a technical one.

ALICE: Then why give me a ticket?

OFFICER: Well, it was a violation. Technical or not, you violated the law. My job is to arrest anyone who violates the law. It's not my job to make a judgment on why you did what you did, even though, as I said, I think you did the right thing in this case.

ALICE: But this means I have to show up in traffic court. And already your stopping me has delayed me from meeting my business appointment.

OFFICER: I'm sorry. The judge will be sympathetic, take my word for it.

In Traffic Court. The next scene is in traffic court, where the judge listens patiently to the Police Officer and to Alice. There is no conflicting testimony.

JUDGE: I find the defendant guilty of crossing the parallel lines. Please pay the clerk $50. This will be entered on your driving record as a moving traffic infraction. A third conviction for such an offense within a two-year period means suspension of your driver's license.

ALICE: Wait a minute. Are you saying I should have run over the child?

JUDGE: This court will not give legal advice. The duty of this court is to pass judgment on past events, not to advise you about what you should have done or what you should do in the future. But having said this, let me add a personal observation. I am frankly surprised at your behavior here this morning. You are taking the attitude that the law should somehow grant you a personal exception for crossing the parallel lines, something which the law does not do for any other driver. We are all subject to the law, you, myself, and everyone else.

ALICE: But judge, I did the right thing. I avoided killing an innocent child.

JUDGE: Do you really believe that you did the morally right thing?

ALICE: Yes, I do.

JUDGE: Then why are you complaining about paying the fine? Surely $50 is a trivial price to pay for saving the life of an innocent child! If you are as morally secure in your convictions as you say you are, then you should pay the fine cheerfully, and go home with the feeling that you saved a life and did the right thing. Next case!

ALICE: Well, I want to appeal your decision.

JUDGE: That's your privilege. You have thirty days to file an appeal. But you have to pay the fine on your way out this morning.

Alice's Appeal. Alice's friends try to dissuade her from proceeding with the appeal. They point out that she has already lost valuable time in traffic court, plus $50, plus the time when she was arrested in the first place. They tell her that an appeal will be expensive, far more expensive than the $50 she might get back if she wins. But they don't know Adamant Alice. She has no intention of accepting the status of lawbreaker when she felt she did nothing wrong, even though it was only a relatively minor infraction of a traffic regulation.

She looks up the jurisdiction's traffic regulations. Since this is a "generic" hypothetical, let us assume that she finds the following in the state's traffic code:

§205. Streets shall be clearly marked for the purpose of traffic regulation.

(a) If a roadway is marked by a broken white line which traverses its length, motorists may cross the broken white line if it is safe to do so and only after first signaling their intention to do so.

(b) If a roadway is marked by a solid white line which traverses its length, motorists may not cross the line except in an emergency, and then only if safe to do so.

(c) If a roadway is marked by a double white line (parallel lines) which traverses its length, motorists may not cross the line.

§206. The penalty for violating any provision of §205 shall be $50. The violator shall be charged with a moving vehicle traffic violation.

In her Brief before the Intermediate Appellate Court, Alice argues that the parallel line rule, while reasonable in the vast majority of cases, worked an injustice in her case. The court should carve out an exception for "darting-child cases" in the name of justice.

Here are some excerpts from the appellate court's majority opinion:

Normally we would affirm without opinion an apparently minor case such as this one. However, because of the philosophical issues involved, we have decided to append a brief written opinion to our judgment of affirmance.

The appellant argues that §205, as applied, works an injustice. It is unjust to penalize her, she argues, for temporarily and technically violating the parallel-line rule when her purpose was to save the life of an innocent child.

The law, however, is plain and admits of no exceptions. There is nothing in §205 that can fairly be read as providing an exception in cases where, in the driver's personal judgment, there is an important need to violate the rule.

Our interpretation of §205 is based on the section as a whole, not simply on (c) (the parallel line paragraph). The statutory scheme is comprehensive and admits of no exceptions. In particular, if the legislature had wanted to allow the appellant to cross a dividing line under the facts of her particular case, it would have provided for a *single* white line under paragraph (g). But in fact the traffic department, on the roadway the appellant used, painted parallel lines as provided in (c). This may be taken as a deliberate legislative

decision to bar the crossing of the dividing lines even in the event of an emergency.

We are not unmindful of the appellant's courageous decision to violate the law in order to save a child's life. But the fact is that she violated the law. The law's penalty is, as the trial judge said, a small price to pay for saving the life of a child.

This court does not have the power to change the law. That power is reserved to the legislature. A court has a far more limited role: to apply the law as written. Even if we were persuaded that if a court were ever to depart from the plain meaning of a statute, and further that the instant case is the most justifiable case for such a departure, nevertheless there is a vast hidden cost involved if a court were to take such a step. We would be eroding the public's confidence in the plain meaning of statutes. Further, we would undermine the legislature's confidence in the judiciary. We would be setting up the courts as the ultimate, unelected, undemocratic arbiter of the law.

Courts must respect the plain meaning of statutes. As the Supreme Court of the United States said in *United States v. Locke*,[27] even if the legislative rule is *arbitrary*, it must be accorded its plain meaning. If that was true in *Locke*, it is *a fortiori* true in the present case. For the parallel-line rule is far from being arbitrary. It is the rule deliberately chosen by the legislature. If on occasion its application appears to work an injustice, a court may not invoke the concept of injustice to overrule the law itself. We have no constitutional mandate to invalidate laws, or write exceptions into laws when their plain language admits of no exceptions, all in the name of that vague and subjective term "justice." Instead, in a democracy, it is the legislature—reflecting the will of the people—which decides questions of justice by creating

---

[27] 471 U.S. 84 (1985). *Editor's Note*: The Locke Case was excerpted and discussed in Chapter 6 of this Anthology.

laws and on occasion creating exceptions to laws. If a court were to take on a legislative role, the court would eventually imperil its own existence. The ensuing uncertainty would far outweigh the occasional injustice felt by some persons such as the appellant when a law is applied exactly according to its terms.

The appellant in her brief virtually concedes that the parallel-line rule was correctly applied in her case. She asks this court to create an "exception" to the rule. But our job is simply to apply the law as written. We would suggest that the appellant expend her energies in petitioning the legislature to amend the parallel-line rule, instead of asking this court to act as if it were a legislature.

If the preceding opinion strikes you as eminently reasonable and persuasive, it is because I have deliberately used concepts and phrases that are hallowed in judicial history. These concepts are familiar to all lawyers. They "resonate" in some of our deepest conceptions of the limited role of the judiciary. But although I have made the argument as persuasive as I can, I want to show that it is really constructed on a bed of sand, that it is ultimately unconvincing, that it is unsound as a matter of law.

To begin the process of chipping away at the majority's opinion, here is an invented excerpt from the Intermediate Appellate Court's *dissent* in Alice's case:

Assume for a moment that the parallel divider lines had no legal significance. Suppose they were simply painted on the roadway as a guide for motorists. Indeed, in the early days of automobile travel, road signs were placed simply to help traffic flow more easily. The early traffic signal light was invented simply to reduce the confusion at intersections when drivers at right angles to each other misinterpreted each other's signals as to who should proceed first. It was only after traffic signals were installed and working that some state legislatures began enacting statutes that made the signals legally compulsory.

Under our temporary assumption that the parallel lines in the present case are without legal significance, no one would seriously maintain that the appellant should run over a child when she had the clear alternative of running over the white lines. In fact, if the appellant did kill the child instead of observing the (legally insignificant) parallel lines, she could be prosecuted for manslaughter or even murder. There is hardly a clearer case of injustice than one in which a temporary and safe deviation from a given route is not taken when the cost of not taking it is the life of an innocent child.

The only difference between our assumed case and the actual instant case is that the parallel lines are backed by legislation. But why should that make a difference where a child's life is concerned? For in the present case, the appellant made a temporary and safe deviation from a *prescribed* route in order to save a child's life. It would have been morally monstrous of her to run over the child in such circumstances.

Yet the majority is penalizing her for *not* killing the child. I'm afraid that Charles Dickens' observation in *Oliver Twist* will be applied by commentators to the holding in the present case: "The law's a ass, a idiot." When the law itself is the only difference between saving or not saving the life of a child, how can my colleagues vote to penalize the appellant for what she did?

The appellant's obligation in driving her car was not to drive blindly. Our obligation is not to apply the law blindly. The decision below should have been reversed.

The dissenting judge has made an emotional appeal. But the judge has not been articulate as to exactly how the appellant's conduct comes within the law. The connection between justice and the law, in other words, is not explicit in the dissenting judge's opinion. So, our story continues.

The Television Special. While Alice's case is on appeal, let us assume case (B) occurs. Bruce runs over the darting child. The officer on the scene assisted in calling the ambulance (useless, the child was dead), but otherwise did not give Bruce a ticket. Shortly thereafter, there is a TV Special on the darting child. Alice and Bruce are interviewed. Here are some excerpts from Bruce's interview:

BRUCE: It was horrible. Tragic. I saw the child dart out in front of my car.

TV REPORTER: Did you think of crossing the double white lines so as to avoid hitting the child?

BRUCE: I don't know. I did and I didn't. I'm just not a person who breaks the law. I've never been arrested. Even for a traffic violation. I've tried and tried to think about that moment, the poor child, but some voice was telling me not to cross the double lines. I mean, I've never crossed the double lines. Even if I was going to be injured myself, like running my car into a hole in the road, I still wouldn't have crossed the lines.

TV REPORTER: Knowing what you know now, if you had it to do over again, would you cross the white lines to avoid hitting the child?

BRUCE: Well, sure. But it's easy to say that now. If you're a law abiding citizen, and you've ever been in that kind of situation, your instinct is to obey the law. I can't be sure that I would have acted differently, knowing what I know now. Although I hope I can act differently if, God forbid, it should ever happen again.

The parents of the dead child are interviewed, followed by an interview with a member of the state legislature:

TV REPORTER: Do you think that the driver, Bruce, did the right thing?

MOTHER: Of course not. He's a monster. I can't believe he would deliberately run over my child. He should be prosecuted for murder.

FATHER: It's more the law's fault than Bruce's fault. You've interviewed Alice on this program. She did the right thing. She avoided hitting a darting child. But some dumb judges found her guilty of violating the traffic regulation!

TV REPORTER: So the really guilty parties are the judges?

FATHER: Right. How can they penalize Alice for saving a child, and do nothing about Bruce, who ran over our own daughter?

MOTHER: For shame.

VOICEOVER: But traffic rules say you can't cross a white line. Aren't the legislators who passed the law in the first place the real murderers here?

LEGISLATOR: My committee is going to hold hearings on this white-line business.

TV REPORTER: Did you ever intend that the white-line law should stop people from crossing it even to save the life of a child?

LEGISLATOR: We never thought of that contingency. But speaking for myself, the answer to your question is no. Certainly, if someone had asked us whether the law prohibited a driver from crossing the white lines to avoid hitting a child, every legislator, myself included, would say that saving the child's life comes first.

TV REPORTER: Would you have ever expected that a court would fine Alice for crossing the white lines to save a child?

LEGISLATOR: Of course not. Those judges were out to lunch.

TV REPORTER: But you passed a statute with no exceptions.

LEGISLATOR: True. But we passed the statute in the expectation that human beings, people who are called judges, would apply the statute in a sensible way. The so-called judges in Alice's case acted like robots, like computers. Maybe we should put computers on the bench and save a lot of money. But the legislature pays high judicial salaries so as to have judges who can apply the law in light of the requirements of justice.

TV REPORTER: And a computer can't do that?

LEGISLATOR: Right. The one thing we can't program into a computer is a sense of justice. So that's why we pay judges their high salaries, and give them lifetime tenure. We legislators expect the judges to act like sensible human beings. And here they do dumb things, like fining Alice for saving a child's life.

TV REPORTER: So you think it was unfair for the court to fine Alice $50?

LEGISLATOR: It's not the $50 that bothers me. I don't think it's the $50 that bothers Alice, judging from what she said on this program.

TV REPORTER: Well, then what does bother you?

LEGISLATOR: The precedent of it. The outcome in Alice's case sends a message to the public. To people like Bruce. It says, "it's always illegal to cross the parallel white lines, no matter what." And some people out there—a minority will absorb that message, people like Bruce. They will decide that if a court tells them something is illegal, then they won't do it. Period. It builds up an instinctive reaction in people: never cross the double lines. And so we can expect from time to time continued loss of life. Even the life of one child is too high a price to pay. That's what I find so troublesome about what the court did in Alice's case.

The Legislative Hearings. The TV program generated intense public disapproval of the Intermediate Appellate Court's holding in Alice's case. Alice asked the state's Supreme Court to review her case. Before the Supreme Court could hear Alice's case, the legislature decided to hold public hearings on revision of the traffic code.

It was soon apparent to any impartial observer of the legislative hearings that reforming the traffic code was an enormously complex problem. Testimony was first heard from people who sympathized with Alice, who asked the legislative committee to add a final clause to §205(c) so that the provision would read in full as follows:

(c) If a roadway is marked by a double white line (parallel line) which traverses its length, motorists may not cross the line except if it is safe to do so and if it is absolutely necessary to save the life of a darting child.

But later witnesses pointed out that the phrase "absolutely necessary" replicates all the previous problems, because drivers like Bruce will be wondering whether it really is "absolutely necessary" and their hesitation might be fatal for the darting child. Others pointed out that the phrase "darting child" is underinclusive; what if a child who is simply standing in the road is suddenly seen by the driver? A legislator suggested omitting the phrases "absolutely necessary" and "darting." But another legislator said that then the phrase "save the life of a child" might apply to a child *inside* the driver's car, as would be the case if the driver were hurrying to get the child to the emergency room of a nearby hospital. Others pointed out that "save life" was underinclusive; a driver should not be required to hit the child, instead of crossing the white lines, if the driver reasonably believes that the child will only be seriously injured by the collision but not actually killed.

Then came the senior citizens lobby. Why "child" at all? Why not just "person"? After all, a senior citizen might wander out into the middle of the street at the wrong time. What if someone fell out of the trunk of a car, or the back of a truck, in front of the driver? Suppose that person has jumped out of a car of kidnapers. The person would, though no personal fault, suddenly be sitting, standing, or lying directly in front of the motorist. Therefore the statute should specifically exclude all persons who, for whatever reason, find themselves in the street in front of an oncoming car whose driver has a clear the choice of averting them by crossing the dividing lines.

As a result of this onslaught of citizen testimony, some legislators suggested that the word "child" be changed to "person." But then the animal-rights lobbyists showed up. Why shouldn't it be right to cross the double white lines to save the life of a darting squirrel? Or cat? A legislator replied that it was more important to run over the squirrel than to allow drivers to cross the double white lines, because crossing the double white lines created a significant risk of accident to human life; after all, that's why the double white lines are there in the first place. But the lobbyist replied that the language "if safe to do so" solves this problem; it means that a motorist certainly cannot cross the double lines if it is unsafe to do so, even if the purpose is to save the life of a dog or cat or other innocent animal.

After several days, a legislator proposed cutting through the morass simply by using the general term "emergency." A double-white line could be crossed, if safe to do so, in any emergency.

For a few moments it seemed as if this was the most reasonable way out of the difficulty.

But then one legislator pointed out that the new change would render the double-white divider lines the exact equivalent of the single white divider lines. In other words, §205(c) would read the same as §205(b). Someone pointed out that this was the simplest and most elegant solution; by simplifying the traffic code instead of adding to it, it would solve everyone's problems. But another legislator suggested that there must have been a legislative reason in the first place to have double white lines, and we shouldn't do away with them before considering what that reason was.

Legislative research revealed that, in the beginning, there were only single white divider lines on roadways. It was permissible to cross those lines when safe to do so in the event of an emergency. But in practice motorists began to get into the habit of crossing the single white line too often. The concept of "emergency" became attenuated in the minds of motorists. When stopped by police officers, the motorists would argue vehemently that there was indeed an emergency. "Emergencies" included: a need to get to the airport in time to catch a plane, a need to get to an important business meeting on time, a need to avoid hitting a darting squirrel, a need to "save a marriage" by getting home for dinner in time, and so forth. So the legislature, in its wisdom, decided to use double white lines to eliminate all these "excuses" that motorists were concocting.

Thus it seemed to the committee that the double-white lines served a useful function.

Nevertheless, Alice's case was troubling. How could an exception be written in to solve Alice's case and yet not be so broad as the term "emergency," which would open the door to all the problems formerly connected with the single white line?

No matter how much they struggled with the statute, the legislators could not come up with a form of words that would solve Alice's problem (and related problems, such as darting persons who are not children), and yet keep the double-lines "tight" so that motorists would not, over time, disregard them by concocting excuses.

An expert in psychological linguistics was called to the legislative hearings. She told the committee that words, symbols, and signs, such as double white lines down a highway, only make sense to the human mind in the context in which they occur and with the history that they have in the mind of the observer. For example, a "Stop" sign on a street corner would be unintelligible to a visitor from outer space. Assuming the ET visitor could read English, what is it that should stop? Should the visitor stop breathing? Stop every internal organ from functioning? How long should they stay stopped? By observing traffic patterns, the visitor would conclude that "stop" means "stop for a brief period of time," and appears to apply only to motor-driven vehicles and not bicycles, and so forth. In other words, the ET visitor would begin to fill in the context and begin to make sense out of the "Stop" sign.

Any law is necessarily general, she continued. Even if the law contains an exception, the exception itself is a generalization. Laws, like words and signals and signs, can only have a general signification. But real people working in the real world can only use these generalizations as guides to their behavior in the context in which they (necessarily) interpret the generalizations.[28] For example, Alice interpreted the double white lines as a general prohibition on her driving behavior. She wouldn't cross the double white lines just because she felt like doing so. But she regarded that general prohibition as trumped in the unforeseen case of a darting child. Why did she "interpret" the double white lines as not constraining her to run over the child? Simply because, in the split second in which the situation came up, it struck her as absurd that a traffic regulation should require her to deliberately kill a child.[29] And therefore, she interpreted that

---

[28] *Editor's Note*: In other words, the psychological linguist here is expressing the jurisprudential position we considered in the previous Chapter.

[29] *Editor's Note*: Is the fundamental error of the *Locke* case (discussed in Chapter 6 of this Anthology) the reaffirmation by the Supreme Court that deadlines are inherently arbitrary, and that therefore, in cognate cases, courts should literally apply *arbitrary* legislative proscriptions?

traffic regulation as being trumped by the emergency of a darting child.

We use general words, signs, and symbols, and enact general rules, because they are the most efficient ways of communicating to people in general about situations in general. But general efficiency should not equal general compulsion. The double white lines, the expert summed up, are efficient just the way they are in conveying a message to drivers. That message may amount to: "don't cross the dividing lines unless there is an objectively compelling reason rooted in justice that overrides the lines." But the important point, she concluded, "is that you don't want to put into the statute what I've just said, because if you did, you would simply erode and undermine the very message that the dividing lines are meant to convey. You will open the door to self-serving excuses from drivers about what constitute objectively compelling reasons. My opinion is that the dividing lines already contain this very message if they are reasonably interpreted by reasonable drivers and reasonable judges."

Alice's Case in the Supreme Court. Alice's petition for *certiorari* is accepted by the Supreme Court in the jurisdiction in which she resides. The justices of the court are aware of the developments and arguments as I have recounted them above, but of course refer only obliquely to them. (Courts want the public to think that their judgments are based on existing law, and not on the twists and turns of political arguments, linguistics experts, and media coverage.)

The Supreme Court unanimously decides to overrule the Intermediate Appellate Court and enter a judgment in Alice's favor. (How do I know this? Because I'm making it all up.) Let us assume that the Court in its opinion restates and revisits all the arguments that we have examined so far, so there is no need to repeat them. I will only present those parts of the Court's opinion that make either new arguments or present the old ones in a new light:

Difficulties arise in statutory interpretation when a statute is viewed as a computer program. A computer lacks human reason, human judgment, and human sensitivity. It will literally do what the programmer wants it to do.

(Parenthetically, it is interesting to note that in this age of computerization, we can see more clearly than ever the difference between people and machines. In the nineteenth century's age of industrialization, a machine was regarded as the height of efficiency and rationality. Perhaps the leading legal positivists of that era were attracted to a mechanical jurisprudence because of the general fascination with machines. Today, because computers can do so much, we see their limitations more clearly than ever.)

The police officer who arrested Alice acted in the manner of a computer. He found that Alice had crossed the double white lines and he concluded that the traffic regulations prohibited such crossing. There was no thought involved; the actions could have been handled by a computerized robot wearing a police uniform.

The traffic court similarly acted in computerized fashion in finding Alice guilty of a traffic infraction. To be sure, the presiding judge indicated by his remarks that he realized the moral ramifications of the situation. But since these moral considerations were dicta—indeed, he explicitly disavowed any bearing that they might have on his decision—he acted, for all intents and purposes, as a computer.

What is worse, both the arresting officer and the traffic court judge treated Alice as if she were also a computerized robot. Alice-the-robot committed a programming malfunction in failing to remain on her side of the double-line highway divider. Even if the car were to run over ten schoolchildren crossing the street, the Alice-the-robot would make a computer error if she crossed the divider.

Is there any requirement that we extend these errors further and regard the legislature itself as robotic? The legislature is made up of real persons. We cannot imagine that they wanted darting children to be killed when they enacted §205(c) of the Motor Vehicle Act. Since they are representatives of the people, we must give them the interpretive courtesy of regarding their statutes as addressed to human beings and not computers. And we must attribute to them their own interpretive expectation that their statutes will be enforced by human police officers and human judges who have human feelings, and not by emotionless entities like computers.

But we do not rest our opinion on any such assumption of the need to extend interpretive courtesy to the legislature. Let us consider what the legislature would have enacted if the legislators had thought of the possibility of a case such as the darting child. The legislature could have taken two paths. First, it might have written an exception for the darting-child case right into the statute. Second, it might have written an exception for the darting-child case *out* of the statute, that is, by deliberately excluding such an exception. These are the only two possibilities (short of doing nothing). Let us consider each of them.

First, let us assume that the legislature wrote into the double white-lines provision an exception for avoiding darting children. [Here, the Supreme Court recounts the arguments given above in the discussion of the legislative hearings. The Court concludes by agreeing with the expert in psycholinguistics that the very expression of such an exception in the statute tends to erode the intent of the statute and broaden the scope of the exception.]

For these reasons, we conclude that the best "exception" provision the legislature could have written into the law would have been an exception "if justice so requires." But the problem is that if the exception were written exactly like that, drivers would self-construe it too broadly. Yet we believe that the "justice" exception is implicit in the statute (and in every statute). Since such an expression, if explicit, would be subject to abuse, we must ourselves construe its scope on a case-by-case basis in interpreting the true meaning of the statute. In this respect, the traffic regulation in the present case is no different from any statute in any case.

The only reasonable way for a court to interpret a statute is to interpret it in light of the context of justice in which it is designed to play a part. In particular, we hold that courts should not interpret statutes literally if literal interpretation would do violence to the dictates of justice. For it is only a humane concession to the public interest to assume that rational adults are entitled to interpret statutes as if they are written against a societal background of justice, and not as if they are disengaged from all social and human considerations (like an emotionless computer program).

The justice considerations we have just mentioned will of course vary depending upon the situation and context to which the statute applies. This is not a weakness, but a strength. Courts must interpret statutes not mechanically, but the way people faced with new situations (many of which the legislature never contemplated) will reasonably interpret them.

In the particular case of a traffic regulation, the broad context is that of traffic safety and efficiency. Traffic regulations are designed to allow drivers of motor vehicles to proceed efficiently to their destinations with due regard to their own safety, the safety of other drivers, and the safety of pedestrians. Each regulation is a legislative attempt to balance these considerations. Thus, for example, the double-white divider lines are intended to keep drivers in their own lanes and prohibit them, in general, from crossing the lines. Crossing the lines might endanger their lives and the lives of drivers of oncoming vehicles. But the "safety" aspect of the double white lines is contradicted if they are interpreted in such a way as to endanger pedestrians. To interpret the double-white lines as requiring a motorist to run over a darting child, when the motorist safely could have crossed the lines, is to do violence to the broad purpose of the legislature in enacting traffic regulations. If the "plain meaning" doctrine as enunciated by the appellate court below is given unbridled priority, then such a contradiction would indeed be expected to occur. The "plain meaning" rule as the court below interpreted it would mean that, in the name of safety, innocent children should be run over. The inconsistency with the purpose of promoting safety on our highways and roadways is manifest. No so-called rule of interpretation, whether "plain meaning" or any other, should hinder a court from interpreting a statute according to the fundamental dictates of justice that underlie the legislature's broad purpose.

Second, let us take the opposite assumption: that the darting-child exception is explicitly excluded from the statute. For example, §205 might read:

> (c) If a roadway is marked by a double white line (parallel line) which traverses its length, motorists may not cross the line, even to save the life of a darting child.

This latter clause, as we have imagined it, seems unlike any bill that any conceivable legislature would ever enact. And yet it constitutes the exact interpretation that the police officer and the traffic court have given to the existing §205(c)! For both the police officer and the traffic court judge found the petitioner to have violated §205(c) by crossing the line, even though it was an uncontroverted fact that the petitioner crossed the line to save the life of a darting child.

The fact that the clause we have imagined is outrageous, is just another way of concluding that it is outrageous for any court to assume that the legislature intended that §205(c) be interpreted as if such a clause were actually contained in the statute.

The analysis can be extended further. Suppose that a legislature in a fit of absent-mindedness *did* enact the clause we have just imagined. Surely there would be a public outcry—indeed, the same kind of public outcry, of we take judicial notice, that occurred in recent weeks in connection with such "darting child" cases. The public surely would have found it outrageous

for a legislature to contemplate the death of innocent children in a statute regulating traffic. Indeed, any legislator who is at all attuned to public concerns would reasonably expect such an public outcry to attend any attempt to pass a bill containing the clause we have just imagined. And therefore, such a clause simply would not have been proposed by any legislator who wished to get re-elected. And if by some fluke it was proposed, we find inconceivable the possibility that it would be enacted into law.

If such a clause would neither have been proposed nor enacted, then a subsequent court, interpreting the actual provision that *was* enacted, should not infer that it has such a clause. To do so would unconscionably distort the meaning of the provision that was in fact enacted.

But finally, we assume the outrageous. Let us consider what would happen if a legislature actually enacted §205(c) containing a clause that motorists may not cross the lines even to save the life of a darting child. If there were such a statute, would a traffic court be entitled to find the petitioner guilty of a traffic offense?

We think not—even in that clearest of all possible "plain meaning" cases. A court should instead hold such a statutory provision invalid as contrary to the elementary considerations of justice that underlie the legal system as a whole.[30] When the state sentences someone to death, the accused person is entitled to a fair and public trial. The accused person must be found guilty beyond a reasonable doubt of a capital offense. These hallowed procedural safeguards are required in all cases where the legal system enforces the ul-

---

[30] I am purposefully keeping this language in abstract terms. If the court is a court in the United States, then the Due Process Clause can be invoked as a specific constitutional provision invalidating such a statute. In addition, the Bill of Attainder Clause might be invoked, as well as Justice Frankfurter's generalized notion of "ordered liberty."

timate penalty of death against any individual. Accordingly, any traffic regulation that in advance condemns to death an innocent child, when the child's death could have been safely averted by the driver, violates these societal considerations of elementary justice. A court simply will not give effect to a statute, even a lowly statute such as a traffic regulation, if it contains a provision that requires a motorist to run over a child or other person. The pedestrian cannot constitutionally be sentenced to death by traffic regulation.

For all these reasons, therefore, we conclude that it makes no sense to interpret §205 the way it was interpreted by the courts below. The real meaning of §205—the meaning as exactly enacted by the legislature—is not contained in the words of §205 abstracted from the societal context in which those words were intended to apply. Rather, the real meaning is contained in the way the legal system as a whole impacts upon the social system, namely, to assist in delivering justice to that social system. Thus, if we were to omit considerations of fairness and justice in interpreting statutes, we would fail to do justice to the reason for the existence of statutes.

The decision below is overruled.

Conclusion. If the preceding hypothetical case strikes you as a generic one—applicable, with modifications, to any real-life situation where a statute impacts upon human behavior—then I hope I have proved that it is legally impermissible to omit "justice" considerations from the interpretation and application of statutes. For the "justice" considerations are built in to the very enterprise of affecting human behavior through law.

I have said little about the common law. If I have proven that justice is an inherent part of what statutes mean, then in the absence of statutes—when a court is simply engaging in common-law adjudication—justice considerations are just as compelling if not more compelling. If a court must interpret statutes in light of a justice context, then surely they must interpret their own previous decisions in the same light.

The most important factor in the entire legal equation is that of a court made up of human (not robotic) judges. These judges are called upon to decide cases and controversies, to apply "the law" to human conflicts. The point of my essay has been to show that "the law" *includes* considerations of justice. Put more precisely, the legal system is a system of the application of justice to human conflicts. As I hope to have shown, a court cannot simply apply "justice" without law, because the law—the full panoply of rules, statutes, and precedents—help us interpret the facts of the parties' situation. No decision can be based on justice if relevant facts are unknown to the decision-maker. Since the facts in Alice's case include the parallel divider lines and the reason the legislature put those lines there, no court can legitimately interpret those facts without including in its interpretation the "justice background" that is an essential part of the context of those facts.

F. Justice and Adjudication

1. Lon Fuller: The Adversary System[31]

The expression "the adversary system" can be used in a narrow sense. When we speak of "the adversary system" in its narrow sense we are referring to a certain philosophy of adjudication, a conception of the way the trial of cases in courts of law should be conducted, a view of the roles that should be played by advocates and by judge and jury in the decision of a controversy.

The philosophy of adjudication that is expressed in "the adversary system" is, speaking generally, a philosophy that insists on keeping distinct the function of the advocate, on the one hand, from that of the judge, or of the judge from that of jury, on the other. The decision of the case is for the judge, or for the judge and jury. That decision must be as objective and as free from bias as it possibly can. The Constitution of Massachu-

---

[31] Lon L. Fuller, *The Adversary System*, TALKS ON AMERICAN LAW 30-43 (Harold J. Berman, ed. 1961). Copyright 1961 Random House. Reprinted by permission.

setts provides—in language that in its idiom calls at once to mind the spirit of a great age, the Age of the Enlightenment and of the American and French Revolutions—that "It is the right of every citizen to be tried by judges as free, impartial and independent as the lot of humanity will admit." If the judge is to perform that high function—a function which the Constitution recognizes may put human nature to a severe test—then the rules of procedure that govern a trial must be such that they do not compel or invite him to depart from the difficult role in which he is cast. It is not his place to take sides. He must withhold judgment until all the evidence has been examined and all the arguments have been heard.

The judge and jury must, then, be excluded from any partisan role. At the same time, a fair trial requires that each side of the controversy be carefully considered and be given its full weight and value. But before a judge can gauge the full force of an argument, it must be presented to him with partisan zeal by one not subject to the restraints of judicial office. The judge cannot know how strong an argument is until he has heard it from the lips of one who has dedicated all the powers of his mind to its formulation.

This is the function of the advocate. His task is not to decide but to persuade. He is not expected to present the case in a colorless and detached manner, but in such a way that it will appear in that aspect most favorable to his client. He is not like a jeweler who slowly turns a diamond in the light so that each of its facets may in turn be fully revealed. Instead the advocate holds the jewel steadily, as it were, so as to throw into bold relief a single aspect of it. It is the task of the advocate to help the judge and jury to see the case as it appears to interested eyes, in the aspect it assumes when viewed from that corner of life into which fate has cast his client.

This is in general what we mean by the adversary system when we apply that phrase to the trial of controversies before courts. As I have indicated, there is a broader use of the phrase which extends it—by way of analogy and with many qualifications—to decisions not rendered by judges and juries but in the great society that lies outside the courtroom. There is a kind of adversary system that may be said to under-lie the conduct of a legislative chamber, an industrial enterprise, or a university. I shall touch briefly on some aspects of this broader conception toward the end of my talk. For the time being I should like to examine more closely the adversary system which underlies the trial of cases in courts of law.

Let me begin with that aspect of the adversary philosophy which is most puzzling—not to say, most offensive—to the layman. The ethical standards of the legal profession make it perfectly proper for a lawyer to undertake in a criminal case the defense of a man whom he knows to be guilty.

It should be carefully noted that in the United States a lawyer is not bound to defend a guilty man. Unless he has been appointed by the court to act as a public defender, the lawyer may decline to defend a man with whom he does not wish to be associated, whether that man be guilty or innocent. The rule I am discussing is one which says that without impropriety a lawyer may, if he sees fit, defend a man he knows to be guilty. Not only that, but the lawyer may render this service for a fee; he may, without qualms of conscience, accept compensation for appearing in court to plead the cause of a man whom he knows to be guilty.

At this point the layman is apt to lose his patience with the legal profession and its curious moral views. "Surely," he says, "something must be wrong when, on the one hand, we have courts that are supposed to find out whether a man is actually guilty and when, on the other, we allow a skilled lawyer to come into court to help a guilty man with his persuasive skill. Since the whole object of the machinery of justice is to separate the guilty from the innocent, the lawyer ought to advance that object by coming forward and informing the court that his client is guilty." So the layman is likely to view the matter.

Nor is the layman often convinced by the arguments generally advanced to justify the lawyer in defending a man he knows to be guilty. What are those arguments? Well, it is said that a man charged with crime should not have his guilt determined in the privacy of a lawyer's office but in open court by due process of law. If every lawyer whom the accused approaches declines to take the case because he appears to be guilty, then the accused is, in effect, condemned out of court and denied the formal trial to which the law entitles him. It is further said that appearances are often deceiving; many a man has appeared to be plainly guilty until the patiently turning wheels of justice disclosed his innocence. Even confessions are not always to be trusted. Cases are not uncommon where a woman, let us say, confesses to a crime in order to save her guilty husband. Or again, a person under great mental stress and moved by some obscure desire for self-punishment may confess to a crime he never committed so that he may expiate imaginary ones. Because all these things can happen and inferences of guilt are so often mistakes, it is argued that the lawyer has no right to judge the guilt or innocence of his client before the case is tried. If he refuses to defend a client because he thinks he is guilty, the lawyer is wrongfully usurping the office of judge and jury.

How convincing to the layman is this attempt to justify the rule? I do not think it is likely to remove his doubts. The argument is apt to seem to him a little too clever, a little too pat. What then do I as a lawyer think of the argument? I think it has some validity. I reach this conclusion on the basis of the testimony of some of my brothers of the bar. A lawyer who has a wide experience in criminal cases can sometimes give a dramatic instance where he represented a client he firmly believed to be guilty only to have some unexpected turn in the evidence prove that his client was innocent.

Yet even this sort of experience is not wholly decisive of the issue. It may be answered that all human judgments are subject to error. One must calculate probabilities. We may concede that there is some chance that an experienced lawyer, with a knowledge of human nature and access to the most intimate facts, may erroneously conclude that his client is guilty when in fact he is innocent. But the chance is so slight that it may be argued it should be neglected in the actual conduct of affairs.

We may attempt to answer this argument in turn by saying that where the guilt of innocence of a human being is an issue, a calculation of mere probabilities is out of place. But the true answer goes deeper. The reason lies in considerations of an order different from those I have so far been discussing. The purpose of the rule is not merely to protect the innocent person against the possibility of an unjust conviction, precious as that objective is. The purpose of the rule is to preserve the integrity of society itself. It aims to keeping sound and wholesome the procedures by which society visits its condemnation on an erring member.

Why have courts and trials at all? Why bother with judges and juries, with pleas and counterpleas? When disputes arise or accusations are made, why should not the state simply appoint honest and intelligent men to make investigations? Why not let these men, after they have sifted the evidence and resolved apparent contradictions, make their findings without the aid of advocates and without the fanfare and publicity of a trial?

Arrangements tending in this direction are not unknown historically. One of them has at various times and in various forms been familiar on the European continent. This is the institution of the investigating magistrate, *le juge d'instruction, der Untersuchungsrichter*. In important criminal cases this official makes his own investigations and reaches his own conclusions on the basis of the evidence. To be sure, he has never been given the power to make a final determination of guilt. Yet his findings tend to influence the trial that follows; the form he has given to his inquiry tends to shape the proceeding in court and often tips the balance in cases of doubt.

No such office or institution exists in the countries of the common law, including the United States. Why do we reject an arrangement that seems so reasonable in its quiet efficiency? In answer I might simply draw on the European experience and quote a French observer who remarked that in cases where the *juge d'instruction* reaches the conclusion that no prosecution should be brought, it is usually with a tinge of regret that he signs the necessary documents. European experience also suggests that political interests are often involved in charges of crime and that it is desirable in order to prevent abuse that every fact bearing on guilt be tried in courts open to the public.

But publicity is not of itself a guarantee against the abuse of legal procedures. The public trials of alleged traitors that nearly always follow violent revolutions are a sufficlient testimonial to this fact. What is essential is that the accused have at his side throughout a skilled lawyer, pledged to see that his rights are protected. When the matter comes for final trial in court, the only participation accorded to the accused in that trial lies in the opportunity to present proofs and reasoned arguments on his behalf. This opportunity cannot be meaningful unless the accused is represented by a professional advocate. If he is denied this representation the processes of public trial become suspect and tainted. It is for this reason that I say that the integrity of society itself demands that the accused be represented by counsel. If he is plainly guilty this representation may become in a sense symbolic. But the symbolism is of vital importance. It marks society's determination to keep unsoiled and beyond suspicion the procedures by which men are condemned for a violation of its laws.

The lawyer appearing on behalf of an accused person is not present in court merely to represent his client. He represents a vital interest of society itself, he plays an essential role in one of the fundamental processes of an ordered community. The rules that govern his conduct make this clear.

It is a fundamental principle of the lawyer's canons of ethics that he may not state to the judge or jury that he personally believes in the innocence of his client. He may say, for example, "I submit that the evidence fails to establish the guilt of my client." But he may not say, "I personally know my client to be innocent," just as he may not be asked by the judge or jury whether he believes his client to be guilty.

These rules concerning the lawyer's conduct in court are not only important in themselves, but also for the spirit that lies back of them. They make it clear that the lawyer is present, not as an individual with all of his likes and dislikes, beliefs and disbeliefs, but as one who plays an important role in the process of social decision. At no time is the lawyer a mere agent of his client. If he disapproves of his client's conduct during the trial, he may—though this is often a painfully difficult decision—withdraw from the case. Obviously, he may not participate in the fabrication of testimony, just as he may not, to free his client, cast suspicion on innocent persons.

So important is the defense lawyer's role that where the accused cannot find a lawyer who will represent him, or cannot afford to pay for a lawyer, it is the practice for the court to appoint a lawyer to represent him. Under our constitutional system a failure of the court to do this may render a conviction against the accused invalid. Notwithstanding these formal guarantees, our American practice at present leaves much room for improvement. The public service of defending a man, who would otherwise be without a lawyer, is usually poorly paid, and busy and able lawyers are often loath to take on the burdens of such an assignment. There is, however, an active movement now to improve this situation and to provide adequately paid and competent counsel for every person accused of serious crime.

I have so far emphasized chiefly the role of the lawyer in the defense of criminal cases. But the need for an adversary presentation, with both sides vigorously upheld, is also present in civil suits. For one thing, there is an element of social condemnation in almost all adverse legal judgments, so that the considerations that apply to criminal cases are also relevant to civil controversies. To be found guilty of negligent driving or of breaking a contract does not carry the stigma of a criminal conviction, but in these cases, too, society must be concerned that even the qualified condemnation implied in an adverse civil judgement should not be visited on one who has not had a chance to present his case fully.

More important in complicated controversies is the contribution that an adversary presentation makes to a properly grounded decision, a decision that takes account of all the facts and relevant rules. In a statement issued recently by a committee of the American Bar Association, it was pointed out how, in the absence of an adversary presentation, there is a strong tendency by any deciding official to reach a conclusion at an early stage and to adhere to that conclusion in the face of conflicting considerations later developed. In the language of the committee:

"What generally occurs in practice is that at some early point a familiar pattern will seem to emerge from the evidence; an accustomed label is waiting for the case and, without waiting for further proofs, this label is promptly assigned to it. It is a mistake to suppose that this premature cataloguing must necessarily result from impatience, prejudice or mental sloth. Often it proceeds from a very understandable desire to bring the hearing into some order and coherence, for without some tentative theory of the case there is no standard of relevance by which testimony may be measured. But what starts as a preliminary diagnosis designed to direct the inquiry tends, quickly and imperceptibly, to become a fixed conclusion, as all that confirms the diagnosis makes a strong imprint on the mind, while all that runs counter to it is received with diverted attention.

"An adversary presentation seems the only effective means for combating this natural human tendency to judge too swiftly in terms of the familiar that which is not yet fully known. The arguments of counsel hold the case, as it were, in suspension between two opposing interpretations of it. While the proper classification of the case is thus kept unresolved, there is time to explore all of its peculiarities and nuances." This phrasing of the matter makes it clear, I believe, why an adversary presentation of a controversy is perhaps the most effective means we have of combating the evils of bureaucracy. Bureaucracy exists, of course, in all countries, and it is a force for good as well as evil. But is it not true that whenever we use the term "bureaucrat" in a critical sense, we mean an official who, in the language I have quoted, tends "to judge too swiftly in terms of the familiar that which is not yet fully known," an official who concludes, before I have had a chance to explain my case to him, that it is just like that of the man who was ahead of me in the line? And is not the only sure cure for this evil an adversary presentation that will "hold the case. . .in suspension between. . .opposing interpretations," until the deciding official can "explore all its peculiarities and nuances"?

I do not have time to explore all the implications of the adversary system, nor to compare the different ways in which that system and its underlying philosophy find expression in the laws of different countries. I should like, however, to record my discontent with the implications sometimes drawn from the adversary system in my own country. One of these lies in the notion that a judge should throughout the trial remain passive; somewhat like a well-behaved child, he speaks only when spoken to. His role is thought of as being that of an umpire who is stirred to action only when he must resolve a dispute that arises between the contending lawyers. This notion is, I believe, based on a profound mistake. The essence of the adversary system is that each side is accorded a participation in the decision that is reached, a participation that takes the form of presenting proofs and arguments. If that participation is to be meaningful it must take place within an orderly frame, and it is the duty of the judge to see to it that the trial does not degenerate into a disorderly contest in which the essential issues are lost from view. Furthermore, when the party is given through his attorney an opportunity to present arguments, this opportunity loses its value if argument has to be directed into a vacuum. To argue his case effectively, the lawyer must have some idea of what is going on inside the judge's mind. A more active participation by the judge—assuming it stops short of a prejudgment of the case itself—can therefore enhance the meaning and effectiveness of an adversary presentation.

I have only a few minutes to touch on an expanded sense of the adversary system that applies its philosophy to decisions reached by less formal procedures, let us say, decisions reached in the course of operating an industrial or educational enterprise. In the conduct of any human enterprise, collective decisions must always involve a compromise of interests that are at least partially divergent. For example, in the operation of a factory one may distinguish among the following groups: (1) those whose primary objective is to produce a maximum of goods, (2) those whose primary interest is in developing a satisfied work force, working under conditions of complete dignity and impartial justice, and (3) those whose main urge is to improve the product, even at the cost of some present inefficiency. Each of these interests is a legitimate and proper one, yet each must be qualified by a recognition of the legitimate demands of the others.

An effective consensus cannot be reached unless each party understands fully the position of the others. This understanding cannot be obtained unless each party is permitted to state fully what its own interest is and to urge with partisan zeal the vital importance of that interest to the enterprise as a whole. At the same time, since an effective consensus requires an understanding and willing cooperation of all concerned, no party should so abandon himself in advocacy that he loses the power to comprehend sympathetically the views of those with different interests. What is required here is a spirit that can be called that of tolerant partisanship. This implies not only tolerance for opposing viewpoints, but tolerance for a partisan presentation of those viewpoints, since without that presentation they may easily be lost from sight.

A passage from John Stuart Mill is eloquent on this point: "We need not suppose that when power resides in an exclusive class, that class will knowingly and deliberately sacrifice the other classes to themselves: it suffices that, in the absence of its natural defenders, the interest of the excluded is always in danger of being overlooked; and, when looked at, is seen with very different eyes from those of the persons whom it directly concerns."

In the end, the justification for the adversary system lies in the fact that it is a means by which the capacities of the individual may be lifted to the point where he gains the power to view reality through eyes other than his own, where he is able to become as impartial, and as free from prejudice, as "the lot of humanity will admit."

2. Anthony D'Amato: Advocacy and Justice[32]

Justice is what law is for; justice is what judges should render; justice is what lawyers should achieve. Law without justice is nothing but a set of tools, incapable of solving human problems. Like any tool, law may facilitate the solution of a given problem—although misconceived laws may create

more problems than they solve. If legal education did nothing more than train students in how to find and use the tools of the trade, then that education would hardly be ennobling, would hardly bestow upon lawyering the label of "profession," would hardly account for students' decisions to become lawyers. Nor can we lawyers fall back on the position that our only duty is to serve our clients, because some things that clients want done should not be done (such as planning a crime). It is our professional responsibility to stop clients from doing such things. If serving a client is a lawyer's highest aspiration, than that lawyer is just a hired gun. To the contrary, the reason law is properly called a profession is because our job is to help achieve justice—justice for our clients, to be sure, but justice nevertheless. By achieving justice for our clients we add a measure of justice to society. The more that justice is meted out to individuals, the more society will become a just society. Louis Brandeis once said that a lawyer's duty is not to his client, but to his client's situation. That has always seemed to me to be a profound observation, yet I venture to suggest that it could be modified: a lawyer's duty is to the justice within a client's situation.

3. Lon Fuller: Adjudication and Justice[33]

Adjudication is a process that is resorted to in many different contexts. We have adjudication by courts and administrative tribunals clothed with governmental authority and power. We have it in the home when father hears the case of *Mary v. John* for the replevin of one rubber ball. We have it as a voluntary measure in labor relations, and as a means of settling disputes among nations.

In all of these contexts adjudication retains certain constant features. To take an obvious example, it cannot be successful unless there is a chance for both sides to be

---

[32] Excerpted with modifications from Anthony D'Amato, *On the Connection Between Law and Justice*, 26 UNIVERSITY OF CALIFORNIA AT DAVIS LAW REVIEW 527, 528-29 (1993). Copyright 1993 Anthony D'Amato.

[33] Excerpted from Lon L. Fuller, *Adjudication as an Object of Inquiry for Legal Philosophy*, in LON L. FULLER, THE PRINCIPLES OF SOCIAL ORDER 260-63 (Kenneth Winston, ed. 1981).

heard; this is just as true in the home when father decides between Mary and John as it is in the Supreme Court. An even more obvious proposition is that adjudication cannot achieve its purpose if the adjudicator is bribed by one party. That in some countries judges habitually receive bribes no more disproves this proposition than the fact that some savages use wooden shovels shows that in their peculiar culture there exists a value judgment that wooden shovels are better than steel shovels. There are good and bad ways of conducting adjudication that are independent of cultural influences, just as there are good and bad shovels that are similarly independent. The optimum conditions for the operation of adjudication are never fully achieved, and in borderline cases there may be difficulty in stating just what those conditions are. But this does not mean that adjudication does not contain a solid core of purpose that defines in general how it should and should not be conducted.

What I am suggesting is that legal philosophy can take adjudication in its various contexts and ask questions like the following: What kinds of human relations are best organized and regulated by adjudication, and what kinds are better left to other organizational procedures, such as negotiation and voluntary settlement, majority vote, or expert managerial authority? What are the consequences where adjudication is given problems inappropriate to its capacities, and how can the damage done be minimized? What are the procedural limitations which adjudication must respect if it is to be effective, not only in the sense of teaching an apt and intelligent decision, but also in retaining the respect of the losing party?

I believe that adjudication, as a means for organizing human relations, can be discussed intelligently, even though we are unable to define with precision its assumed end, namely, justice. I suggest that we can arrive at a better understanding of the aim we call justice if we discuss critically the various means by which it is imperfectly realized. Such a program at least allows us to get under way. It does not tell us we must hold up our exploration until we already know the things we seek to learn through exploration.

EDITOR'S EPILOGUE

A few years ago I was invited to give a paper at Whittier College of Law in Los Angeles. I got there early and wandered through the corridors of the school. Posted on the office door of Professor Michael Bazyler was a quotation that caught my eye. I read it with interest and a dawning sense of recognition. The name at the bottom of the quotation was mine! After getting over the surprise, I read it again with a critical eye (if that's possible with one's own work), and hey, it didn't seem half bad. While I never would have thought to single it out from all the stuff I've written, once somebody else did, it seemed like a fairly good summation of my philosophy of law. With your kind indulgence, I repeat it here:

> The Moment of Truth for a practicing attorney occurs whenever a prospective client tells a story that seems morally compelling but legally hopeless. That is where the attorney's legal research should begin, not where it should end. Too much injustice persists in the world because tired legal thinking has accepted unjust patterns as inevitable.